ALL GLORY TO ŚRĪ GURU AND GAURĀṄGA

ŚRĪMAD BHĀGAVATAM

of

KṚṢṆA-DVAIPĀYANA VYĀSA

यच्च व्रजन्त्यनिमिषामृषभानुवृत्त्या
दूरेयमा ह्युपरि नः स्पृहणीयशीलाः ।
भर्तुर्मिथः सुयशसः कथनानुराग-
वैक्लव्यबाष्पकलया पुलकीकृताङ्गाः ॥२५॥

yac ca vrajanty animiṣām ṛṣabhānuvṛttyā
dūre yamā hy upari naḥ spṛhaṇīya-śīlāḥ
bhartur mithaḥ suyaśasaḥ kathanānurāga-
vaiklavya-bāṣpa-kalayā pulakī-kṛtāṅgāḥ

(p. 664)

BOOKS by
His Divine Grace
A. C. Bhaktivedanta Swami Prabhupāda

Bhagavad-gītā As It Is
Śrīmad-Bhāgavatam, cantos 1–10 (12 vols.)
Śrī Caitanya-caritāmṛta (17 vols.)
Teachings of Lord Caitanya
The Nectar of Devotion
The Nectar of Instruction
Śrī Īśopaniṣad
Easy Journey to Other Planets
Kṛṣṇa Consciousness: The Topmost Yoga System
Kṛṣṇa, The Supreme Personality of Godhead (3 vols.)
Perfect Questions, Perfect Answers
Teachings of Lord Kapila, the Son of Devahūti
Transcendental Teachings of Prahlāda Mahārāja
Dialectic Spiritualism—A Vedic View of Western Philosophy
Teachings of Queen Kuntī
Kṛṣṇa, the Reservoir of Pleasure
The Science of Self-Realization
The Path of Perfection
Search for Liberation
Life Comes from Life
The Perfection of Yoga
Beyond Birth and Death
On the Way to Kṛṣṇa
Geetār-gan (Bengali)
Vairāgya-vidyā (Bengali)
Buddhi-yoga (Bengali)
Bhakti-ratna-bolī (Bengali)
Rāja-vidyā: The King of Knowledge
Elevation to Kṛṣṇa Consciousness
Kṛṣṇa Consciousness: The Matchless Gift
Back to Godhead magazine (founder)

A complete catalog is available upon request.

Bhaktivedanta Book Trust
3764 Watseka Avenue
Los Angeles, California 90034

Bhaktivedanta Book Trust
P.O. Box 262
Botany
N. S. W. 2019, Australia

ŚRĪMAD BHĀGAVATAM

Third Canto
"The Status Quo"

(Part One—Chapters 1-16)

With the Original Sanskrit Text,
Its Roman Transliteration, Synonyms,
Translation and Elaborate Purports

by

His Divine Grace
A. C. Bhaktivedanta Swami Prabhupāda
Founder-*Ācārya* of the International Society for Krishna Consciousness

THE BHAKTIVEDANTA BOOK TRUST
Los Angeles • London • Paris • Bombay • Sydney • Hong Kong

Readers interested in the subject matter of this book
are invited by the International Society for Krishna Consciousness
to correspond with its Secretary at either of the following addresses:

International Society for Krishna Consciousness
P. O. Box 262
Botany
N. S. W. 2019
Australia

International Society for Krishna Consciousness
3764 Watseka Avenue
Los Angeles, California 90034

First Printing, 1987: 5,000 copies

Printed in Singapore

Library of Congress Cataloging in Publication Data (Revised)

Purāṇas. Bhāgavatapurāṇa. English and Sanskrit.
Śrīmad-Bhāgavatam: with the original Sanskrit text, its roman transliteration, synonyms, translation and elaborate purports.

In English and Sanskrit.
Translation of: Bhāgavatapurāṇa
Includes index.
Contents: 1st canto. Creation—2nd canto. The cosmic manifestation—3rd canto. The status quo (2 v)—4th canto. The creation of the fourth order (2 v)—5th canto. The creative impetus—6th canto. Prescribed duties for mankind—7th canto. The science of God—8th canto. Withdrawal of the cosmic creations—9th canto. Liberation—10th canto. The summum bonum (4 v)—11th canto. General history (2 v)—12th canto. The age of deterioration.
Cantos 10 (v 2-4), 11 and 12 by Hridayananda dāsa Goswami, completing the great work of His Divine Grace A. C. Bhaktivedanta Swami Prabhupāda; Sanskrit editing by Gopīparāṇadhana dāsa Adhikārī.
1. Purāṇas. Bhāgavatapurāṇa—Criticism, interpretation, etc.
I. Bhaktivedanta Swami, A. C., 1896-1977. II. Title.
BL1140.4.B432E5 1987 294.5'925 87-25585
ISBN 0-89213-252-3 (v. 3)

Table of Contents

CHAPTER FIVE

Vidura's Talks With Maitreya

CHAPTER SIX

CHAPTER SEVEN

CHAPTER EIGHT

Manifestation of Brahmā From Garbhodakaśāyī Viṣṇu   **341**

CHAPTER NINE

Brahmā's Prayers for Creative Energy   **373**

CHAPTER THIRTEEN
The Appearance of Lord Varāha

CHAPTER FOURTEEN
Pregnancy of Diti in the Evening

Appendixes

Preface

We must know the present need of human society. And what is that need? Human society is no longer bounded by geographical limits to particular countries or communities. Human society is broader than in the Middle Ages, and the world tendency is toward one state or one human society. The ideals of spiritual communism, according to *Śrīmad-Bhāgavatam*, are based more or less on the oneness of the entire human society, nay, of the entire energy of living beings. The need is felt by great thinkers to make this a successful ideology. *Śrīmad-Bhāgavatam* will fill this need in human society. It begins, therefore, with an aphorism of Vedānta philosophy, *janmādy asya yataḥ*, to establish the ideal of a common cause.

Human society, at the present moment, is not in the darkness of oblivion. It has made rapid progress in the field of material comforts, education and economic development throughout the entire world. But there is a pinprick somewhere in the social body at large, and therefore there are large-scale quarrels, even over less important issues. There is need of a clue as to how humanity can become one in peace, friendship and prosperity with a common cause. *Śrīmad-Bhāgavatam* will fill this need, for it is a cultural presentation for the respiritualization of the entire human society.

Śrīmad-Bhāgavatam should be introduced also in the schools and

Mahārāja in order to change the demoniac face of society.

kaumāra ācaret prājño
dharmān bhāgavatān iha
durlabhaṁ mānuṣaṁ janma
tad apy adhruvam arthadam
(*Bhāg.* 7.6.1)

Disparity in human society is due to lack of principles in a godless civilization. There is God, or the Almighty One, from whom everything emanates, by whom everything is maintained and in whom everything

Preface

We must know the present need of human society. And what is that need? Human society is no longer bounded by geographical limits to particular countries or communities. Human society is broader than in the Middle Ages, and the world tendency is toward one state or one human society. The ideals of spiritual communism, according to *Śrīmad-Bhāgavatam,* are based more or less on the oneness of the entire human society, nay, of the entire energy of living beings. The need is felt by great thinkers to make this a successful ideology. *Śrīmad-Bhāgavatam* will fill this need in human society. It begins, therefore, with an aphorism of Vedānta philosophy, *janmādy asya yataḥ,* to establish the ideal of a common cause.

Human society, at the present moment, is not in the darkness of oblivion. It has made rapid progress in the fields of material comforts, education and economic development throughout the entire world. But there is a pinprick somewhere in the social body at large, and therefore there are large-scale quarrels, even over less important issues. There is need of a clue as to how humanity can become one in peace, friendship and prosperity with a common cause. *Śrīmad-Bhāgavatam* will fill this need, for it is a cultural presentation for the respiritualization of the entire human society.

Śrīmad-Bhāgavatam should be introduced also in the schools and colleges, for it is recommended by the great student-devotee Prahlāda Mahārāja in order to change the demoniac face of society.

kaumāra ācaret prājño
dharmān bhāgavatān iha
durlabhaṁ mānuṣaṁ janma
tad apy adhruvam artha-dam
(*Bhāg.* 7.6.1)

Disparity in human society is due to lack of principles in a godless civilization. There is God, or the Almighty One, from whom everything emanates, by whom everything is maintained and in whom everything is merged to rest. Material science has tried to find the ultimate source of creation very insufficiently, but it is a fact that there is one ultimate source of everything that be. This ultimate source is explained rationally and authoritatively in the beautiful *Bhāgavatam*, or *Śrīmad-Bhāgavatam.*

Śrīmad-Bhāgavatam is the transcendental science not only for knowing the ultimate source of everything but also for knowing our relation with Him and our duty toward perfection of the human society on the basis of this perfect knowledge. It is powerful reading matter in the Sanskrit language, and it is now rendered into English elaborately so that simply by a careful reading one will know God perfectly well, so much so that the reader will be sufficiently educated to defend himself from the onslaught of atheists. Over and above this, the reader will be able to convert others to accepting God as a concrete principle.

Śrīmad-Bhāgavatam begins with the definition of the ultimate source. It is a bona fide commentary on the *Vedānta-sūtra* by the same author, Śrīla Vyāsadeva, and gradually it develops into nine cantos up to the highest state of God realization. The only qualification one needs to study this great book of transcendental knowledge is to proceed step by step cautiously and not jump forward haphazardly as with an ordinary book. It should be gone through chapter by chapter, one after another. The reading matter is so arranged with the original Sanskrit text, its English transliteration, synonyms, translation and purports so that one is sure to become a God-realized soul at the end of finishing the first nine cantos.

The Tenth Canto is distinct from the first nine cantos because it deals directly with the transcendental activities of the Personality of Godhead, Śrī Kṛṣṇa. One will be unable to capture the effects of the Tenth Canto without going through the first nine cantos. The book is complete in twelve cantos, each independent, but it is good for all to read them in small installments one after another.

I must admit my frailties in presenting *Śrīmad-Bhāgavatam,* but still I am hopeful of its good reception by the thinkers and leaders of society on the strength of the following statement of *Śrīmad-Bhāgavatam* (1.5.11):

tad-vāg-visargo janatāgha-viplavo
yasmin prati-ślokam abaddhavaty api

nāmāny anantasya yaśo 'ṅkitāni yac
chṛṇvanti gāyanti gṛṇanti sādhavaḥ

"On the other hand, that literature which is full of descriptions of the transcendental glories of the name, fame, form and pastimes of the unlimited Supreme Lord is a transcendental creation meant for bringing about a revolution in the impious life of a misdirected civilization. Such transcendental literature, even though irregularly composed, is heard, sung and accepted by purified men who are thoroughly honest."

Oṁ tat sat

A. C. Bhaktivedanta Swami

Introduction

"This *Bhāgavata Purāṇa* is as brilliant as the sun, and it has arisen just after the departure of Lord Kṛṣṇa to His own abode, accompanied by religion, knowledge, etc. Persons who have lost their vision due to the dense darkness of ignorance in the age of Kali shall get light from this *Purāṇa*." (*Śrīmad-Bhāgavatam* 1.3.43)

The timeless wisdom of India is expressed in the *Vedas,* ancient Sanskrit texts that touch upon all fields of human knowledge. Originally preserved through oral tradition, the *Vedas* were first put into writing five thousand years ago by Śrīla Vyāsadeva, the "literary incarnation of God." After compiling the *Vedas,* Vyāsadeva set forth their essence in the aphorisms known as *Vedānta-sūtras. Śrīmad-Bhāgavatam* (*Bhāgavata Purāṇa*) is Vyāsadeva's commentary on his own *Vedānta-sūtras.* It was written in the maturity of his spiritual life under the direction of Nārada Muni, his spiritual master. Referred to as "the ripened fruit of the tree of Vedic literature," *Śrīmad-Bhāgavatam* is the most complete and authoritative exposition of Vedic knowledge.

After compiling the *Bhāgavatam,* Vyāsa imparted the synopsis of it to his son, the sage Śukadeva Gosvāmī. Śukadeva Gosvāmī subsequently recited the entire *Bhāgavatam* to Mahārāja Parīkṣit in an assembly of learned saints on the bank of the Ganges at Hastināpura (now Delhi). Mahārāja Parīkṣit was the emperor of the world and was a great *rājarṣi* (saintly king). Having received a warning that he would die within a week, he renounced his entire kingdom and retired to the bank of the Ganges to fast until death and receive spiritual enlightenment. The *Bhāgavatam* begins with Emperor Parīkṣit's sober inquiry to Śukadeva Gosvāmī: "You are the spiritual master of great saints and devotees. I am therefore begging you to show the way of perfection for all persons, and especially for one who is about to die. Please let me know what a man should hear, chant, remember and worship, and also what he should not do. Please explain all this to me."

Śukadeva Gosvāmī's answer to this question, and numerous other questions posed by Mahārāja Parīkṣit, concerning everything from the nature of the self to the origin of the universe, held the assembled sages in rapt attention continuously for the seven days leading up to the

Introduction

"This *Bhāgavata Purāṇa* is as brilliant as the sun, and it has arisen just after the departure of Lord Kṛṣṇa to His own abode, accompanied by religion, knowledge, etc. Persons who have lost their vision due to the dense darkness of ignorance in the age of Kali shall get light from this *Purāṇa.*" (*Śrīmad-Bhāgavatam* 1.3.43)

The timeless wisdom of India is expressed in the *Vedas,* ancient Sanskrit texts that touch upon all fields of human knowledge. Originally preserved through oral tradition, the *Vedas* were first put into writing five thousand years ago by Śrīla Vyāsadeva, the "literary incarnation of God." After compiling the *Vedas,* Vyāsadeva set forth their essence in the aphorisms known as *Vedānta-sūtras. Śrīmad-Bhāgavatam* (*Bhāgavata Purāṇa*) is Vyāsadeva's commentary on his own *Vedānta-sūtras.* It was written in the maturity of his spiritual life under the direction of Nārada Muni, his spiritual master. Referred to as "the ripened fruit of the tree of Vedic literature," *Śrīmad-Bhāgavatam* is the most complete and authoritative exposition of Vedic knowledge.

After compiling the *Bhāgavatam,* Vyāsa imparted the synopsis of it to his son, the sage Śukadeva Gosvāmī. Śukadeva Gosvāmī subsequently recited the entire *Bhāgavatam* to Mahārāja Parīkṣit in an assembly of learned saints on the bank of the Ganges at Hastināpura (now Delhi). Mahārāja Parīkṣit was the emperor of the world and was a great *rājarṣi* (saintly king). Having received a warning that he would die within a week, he renounced his entire kingdom and retired to the bank of the Ganges to fast until death and receive spiritual enlightenment. The *Bhāgavatam* begins with Emperor Parīkṣit's sober inquiry to Śukadeva Gosvāmī: "You are the spiritual master of great saints and devotees. I am therefore begging you to show the way of perfection for all persons, and especially for one who is about to die. Please let me know what a man should hear, chant, remember and worship, and also what he should not do. Please explain all this to me."

Śukadeva Gosvāmī's answer to this question, and numerous other questions posed by Mahārāja Parīkṣit, concerning everything from the nature of the self to the origin of the universe, held the assembled sages in rapt attention continuously for the seven days leading up to the king's death. The sage Sūta Gosvāmī, who was present in that assembly when Śukadeva Gosvāmī first recited *Śrīmad-Bhāgavatam,* later repeated the *Bhāgavatam* before a gathering of sages in the forest of Naimiṣāraṇya. Those sages, concerned about the spiritual welfare of the people in general, had gathered to perform a long, continuous chain of sacrifices to counteract the degrading influence of the incipient age of Kali. In response to the sages' request that he speak the essence of Vedic wisdom, Sūta Gosvāmī repeated from memory the entire eighteen thousand verses of *Śrīmad-Bhāgavatam,* as spoken by Śukadeva Gosvāmī to Mahārāja Parīkṣit.

The reader of *Śrīmad-Bhāgavatam* hears Sūta Gosvāmī relate the questions of Mahārāja Parīkṣit and the answers of Śukadeva Gosvāmī. Also, Sūta Gosvāmī sometimes responds directly to questions put by Śaunaka Ṛṣi, the spokesman for the sages gathered at Naimiṣāraṇya. One therefore simultaneously hears two dialogues: one between Mahārāja Parīkṣit and Śukadeva Gosvāmī on the bank of the Ganges, and another at Naimiṣāraṇya between Sūta Gosvāmī and the sages at Naimiṣāraṇya forest, headed by Śaunaka Ṛṣi. Furthermore, while instructing King Parīkṣit, Śukadeva Gosvāmī often relates historical episodes and gives accounts of lengthy philosophical discussions between such great souls as Nārada Muni and Vasudeva. With this understanding of the history of the *Bhāgavatam,* the reader will easily be able to follow its intermingling of dialogues and events from various sources. Since philosophical wisdom, not chronological order, is most important in the text, one need only be attentive to the subject matter of *Śrīmad-Bhāgavatam* to appreciate fully its profound message.

The translators of this edition compare the *Bhāgavatam* to sugar candy—wherever you taste it, you will find it equally sweet and relishable. Therefore, to taste the sweetness of the *Bhāgavatam,* one may begin by reading any of its volumes. After such an introductory taste, however, the serious reader is best advised to go back to the First Canto and then proceed through the *Bhāgavatam,* canto after canto, in its natural order.

This edition of the *Bhāgavatam* is the first complete English translation of this important text with an elaborate commentary, and it is the first widely available to the English-speaking public. The first twelve volumes (Canto One through Canto Ten, Part One) are the product of the scholarly and devotional effort of His Divine Grace A. C. Bhaktivedanta Swami Prabhupāda, the founder-*ācārya* of the International

Society for Krishna Consciousness and the world's most distinguished teacher of Indian religious and philosophical thought. His consummate Sanskrit scholarship and intimate familiarity with Vedic culture and thought as well as the modern way of life combine to reveal to the West a magnificent exposition of this important classic. After the departure of Śrīla Prabhupāda from this world in 1977, his monumental work of translating and annotating *Śrīmad-Bhāgavatam* has been continued by his disciples Hridayananda dāsa Goswami and Gopīparāṇadhana dāsa.

Readers will find this work of value for many reasons. For those interested in the classical roots of Indian civilization, it serves as a vast reservoir of detailed information on virtually every one of its aspects. For students of comparative philosophy and religion, the *Bhāgavatam* offers a penetrating view into the meaning of India's profound spiritual heritage. To sociologists and anthropologists, the *Bhāgavatam* reveals the practical workings of a peaceful and scientifically organized Vedic culture, whose institutions were integrated on the basis of a highly developed spiritual world view. Students of literature will discover the *Bhāgavatam* to be a masterpiece of majestic poetry. For students of psychology, the text provides important perspectives on the nature of consciousness, human behavior and the philosophical study of identity. Finally, to those seeking spiritual insight, the *Bhāgavatam* offers simple and practical guidance for attainment of the highest self-knowledge and realization of the Absolute Truth. The entire multivolume text, presented by the Bhaktivedanta Book Trust, promises to occupy a significant place in the intellectual, cultural and spiritual life of modern man for a long time to come.

—The Publishers

CHAPTER ONE

Questions by Vidura

TEXT 1

श्रीशुक उवाच
एवमेतत्पुरा पृष्टो मैत्रेयो भगवान् किल ।
क्षत्त्रा वनं प्रविष्टेन त्यक्त्वा स्वगृहमृद्धिमत् ॥ १ ॥

śrī-śuka uvāca
evam etat purā pṛṣṭo
maitreyo bhagavān kila
kṣattrā vanaṁ praviṣṭena
tyaktvā sva-gṛham ṛddhimat

śrī-śukaḥ uvāca—Śrī Śukadeva Gosvāmī said; *evam*—thus; *etat*—this; *purā*—formerly; *pṛṣṭaḥ*—being asked; *maitreyaḥ*—the great sage Maitreya; *bhagavān*—His Grace; *kila*—certainly; *kṣattrā*—by Vidura; *vanam*—forest; *praviṣṭena*—entering; *tyaktvā*—renouncing; *sva-gṛham*—own house; *ṛddhimat*—prosperous.

TRANSLATION

Śukadeva Gosvāmī said: After renouncing his prosperous home and entering the forest, King Vidura, the great devotee, asked this question of His Grace Maitreya Ṛṣi.

TEXT 2

यद्वा अयं मन्त्रकृद्वो भगवानखिलेश्वरः ।
पौरवेन्द्रगृहं हित्वा प्रविवेशात्मसात्कृतम् ॥ २ ॥

yad vā ayaṁ mantra-kṛd vo
bhagavān akhileśvaraḥ

pauravendra-gṛhaṁ hitvā
praviveśātmasāt kṛtam

yat—the house; *vai*—what else is there to say; *ayam*—Śrī Kṛṣṇa; *mantra-kṛt*—minister; *vaḥ*—you people; *bhagavān*—the Personality of Godhead; *akhila-īśvaraḥ*—the Lord of everything; *pauravendra*—Duryodhana; *gṛham*—house; *hitvā*—giving up; *praviveśa*—entered; *ātmasāt*—identify with oneself; *kṛtam*—so accepted.

TRANSLATION

What else is there to say about the residential house of the Pāṇḍavas? Śrī Kṛṣṇa, the Lord of everything, acted as your minister. He used to enter that house as if it were His own, and He did not take any care of Duryodhana's house.

PURPORT

According to the Gauḍīya *acintya-bhedābheda-tattva* philosophy, anything which satisfies the senses of the Supreme Lord, Śrī Kṛṣṇa, is also Śrī Kṛṣṇa. For example, Śrī Vṛndāvana-dhāma is nondifferent from Śrī Kṛṣṇa (*tad-dhāma vṛndāvanam*) because at Vṛndāvana the Lord enjoys the transcendental bliss of His internal potency. Similarly, the house of the Pāṇḍavas was also the source of transcendental bliss for the Lord. It is mentioned here that the Lord identified the house with His own Self. Thus the house of the Pāṇḍavas was as good as Vṛndāvana, and Vidura should not have given up that place of transcendental bliss. Therefore the reason for his quitting the house was not exactly family misunderstanding; rather, Vidura took the opportunity to meet Ṛṣi Maitreya and discuss transcendental knowledge. For a saintly person like Vidura, any disturbance due to worldly affairs is insignificant. Such disturbances, however, are sometimes favorable for higher realization, and therefore Vidura took advantage of a family misunderstanding in order to meet Maitreya Ṛṣi.

TEXT 3

राजोवाच
कुत्र क्षत्तुर्भगवता मैत्रेयेणास सङ्गमः ।
कदा वा सह संवाद एतद्वर्णय नः प्रभो ॥ ३ ॥

rājovāca
kutra kṣattur bhagavatā
maitreyeṇāsa saṅgamaḥ
kadā vā saha-saṁvāda
etad varṇaya naḥ prabho

rājā uvāca—the King said; *kutra*—wherein; *kṣattuḥ*—with Vidura; *bhagavatā*—and with His Grace; *maitreyeṇa*—with Maitreya; *āsa*—there was; *saṅgamaḥ*—meeting; *kadā*—when; *vā*—also; *saha*—with; *saṁvādaḥ*—discussion; *etat*—this; *varṇaya*—describe; *naḥ*—unto me; *prabho*—O my lord.

TRANSLATION

The King asked Śukadeva Gosvāmī: Where and when did the meeting and discussion take place between Saint Vidura and His Grace Maitreya Muni? Kindly oblige, my lord, and describe this to us.

PURPORT

Exactly as Śaunaka Ṛṣi inquired of Sūta Gosvāmī and Sūta Gosvāmī replied, so Śrīla Śukadeva Gosvāmī replied to King Parīkṣit's inquiries. The King was very anxious to understand the meaningful discussion that took place between the two great souls.

TEXT 4

न ह्यल्पार्थोदयस्तस्य विदुरस्यामलात्मनः ।
तस्मिन् वरीयसि प्रश्नः साधुवादोपबृंहितः ॥ ४ ॥

na hy alpārthodayas tasya
vidurasyāmalātmanaḥ
tasmin varīyasi praśnaḥ
sādhu-vādopabṛṁhitaḥ

na—never; *hi*—certainly; *alpa-artha*—small (unimportant) purpose; *udayaḥ*—raised; *tasya*—his; *vidurasya*—of Vidura; *amala-ātmanaḥ*—of the saintly man; *tasmin*—in that; *varīyasi*—highly purposeful; *praśnaḥ*—question; *sādhu-vāda*—things approved by saints and sages; *upabṛṁhitaḥ*—full with.

TRANSLATION

Saint Vidura was a great and pure devotee of the Lord, and therefore his questions to His Grace Ṛṣi Maitreya must have been very purposeful, on the highest level, and approved by learned circles.

PURPORT

Questions and answers among different classes of men have different value. Inquiries by mercantile men in a business exchange cannot be expected to be highly purposeful in spiritual values. Questions and answers by different classes of men can be guessed by the caliber of the persons concerned. In *Bhagavad-gītā,* the discussion was between Lord Śrī Kṛṣṇa and Arjuna, the Supreme Person and the supreme devotee respectively. The Lord admitted Arjuna to be His devotee and friend (Bg. 4.3), and therefore any sane man can guess that the discussion was on the topic of the *bhakti-yoga* system. Actually the whole *Bhagavad-gītā* is based on the principle of *bhakti-yoga.* There is a difference between *karma* and *karma-yoga. Karma* is regulated action for the enjoyment of the fruit by the performer, but *karma-yoga* is action performed by the devotee for the satisfaction of the Lord. *Karma-yoga* is based on *bhakti,* or pleasing the Lord, whereas *karma* is based on pleasing the senses of the performer himself. According to *Śrīmad-Bhāgavatam,* one is advised to approach a bona fide spiritual master when one is actually inclined to question from an elevated level of spiritual understanding. A common man who has no interest in spiritual values has no need to approach a spiritual master just as a matter of following fashion.

As a student, Mahārāja Parīkṣit was serious about learning the science of God, and Śukadeva Gosvāmī was a bona fide spiritual master in the transcendental science. Both of them knew that the topics discussed by Vidura and Ṛṣi Maitreya were elevated, and thus Mahārāja Parīkṣit was very interested in learning from the bona fide spiritual master.

TEXT 5

सूत उवाच

स एवमृषिवर्योऽयं पृष्टो राज्ञा परीक्षिता ।
प्रत्याह तं सुबहुवित्प्रीतात्मा श्रूयतामिति ॥ ५ ॥

sūta uvāca
sa evam ṛṣi-varyo 'yaṁ
pṛṣṭo rājñā parīkṣitā
praty āha taṁ subahu-vit
prītātmā śrūyatām iti

sūtaḥ uvāca—Śrī Sūta Gosvāmī said; *saḥ*—he; *evam*—thus; *ṛṣi-varyaḥ*—the great *ṛṣi; ayam*—Śukadeva Gosvāmī; *pṛṣṭaḥ*—being questioned; *rājñā*—by the King; *parīkṣitā*—Mahārāja Parīkṣit; *prati*—to; *āha*—replied; *tam*—unto the King; *su-bahu-vit*—highly experienced; *prīta-ātmā*—fully satisfied; *śrūyatām*—please hear me; *iti*—thus.

TRANSLATION

Śrī Suta Gosvāmī said: The great sage Śukadeva Gosvāmī was highly experienced and was pleased with the King. Thus being questioned by the King, he said to him, "Please hear the topics attentively."

TEXT 6

श्रीशुक उवाच
यदा तु राजा स्वसुतानसाधून्
पुष्णन्नधर्मेण विनष्टदृष्टिः ।
भ्रातुर्यविष्ठस्य सुतान् विबन्धून्
प्रवेश्य लाक्षाभवने ददाह ॥ ६ ॥

śrī-śuka uvāca
yadā tu rājā sva-sutān asādhūn
puṣṇan na dharmeṇa vinaṣṭa-dṛṣṭiḥ
bhrātur yaviṣṭhasya sutān vibandhūn
praveśya lākṣā-bhavane dadāha

śrī-śukaḥ uvāca—Śrī Śukadeva Gosvāmī said; *yadā*—when; *tu*—but; *rājā*—King Dhṛtarāṣṭra; *sva-sutān*—his own sons; *asādhūn*—dishonest; *puṣṇan*—nourishing; *na*—never; *dharmeṇa*—on the right path; *vinaṣṭa-dṛṣṭiḥ*—one who has lost his insight; *bhrātuḥ*—of his brother; *yaviṣṭhasya*—younger; *sutān*—sons; *vibandhūn*—having no guardian (father); *praveśya*—made to enter; *lākṣā*—lacquer; *bhavane*—in the house; *dadāha*—set on fire.

TRANSLATION

Śrī Śukadeva Gosvāmī said: King Dhṛtarāṣṭra became blind under the influence of impious desires to nourish his dishonest sons, and thus he set fire to the lacquer house to burn his fatherless nephews, the Pāṇḍavas.

PURPORT

Dhṛtarāṣṭra was blind from birth, but his blindness in committing impious activities to support his dishonest sons was a greater blindness than his physical lack of eyesight. The physical lack of sight does not bar one from spiritual progress. But when one is blind spiritually, even though physically fit, that blindness is dangerously detrimental to the progressive path of human life.

TEXT 7

यदा सभायां कुरुदेवदेव्याः
केशाभिमर्शं सुतकर्म गर्ह्यम् ।
न वारयामास नृपः स्नुषायाः
स्वास्रैर्हरन्त्याः कुचकुङ्कुमानि ॥ ७ ॥

yadā sabhāyām kuru-deva-devyāḥ
keśābhimarśaṁ suta-karma garhyam
na vārayām āsa nṛpaḥ snuṣāyāḥ
svāsrair harantyāḥ kuca-kuṅkumāni

yadā—when; *sabhāyām*—the assembly; *kuru-deva-devyāḥ*—of Draupadī, the wife of godly Yudhiṣṭhira; *keśa-abhimarśam*—insult by grabbing her hair; *suta-karma*—action taken by his son; *garhyam*—which was abominable; *na*—did not; *vārayām āsa*—forbid; *nṛpaḥ*—the King; *snuṣāyāḥ*—of his daughter-in-law; *svāsraiḥ*—by her tears; *harantyāḥ*—of she who was washing; *kuca-kuṅkumāni*—red dust on her breast.

TRANSLATION

The King did not forbid his son Duḥśāsana's abominable action of grabbing the hair of Draupadī, the wife of the godly King Yudhiṣṭhira, even though her tears washed the red dust on her breast.

TEXT 8

द्यूते त्वधर्मेण जितस्य साधोः
सत्यावलम्बस्य वनं गतस्य ।
न याचतोऽदात्समयेन दायं
तमोजुषाणो यदजातशत्रोः ॥ ८ ॥

dyūte tv adharmeṇa jitasya sādhoḥ
satyāvalambasya vanaṁ gatasya
na yācato 'dāt samayena dāyaṁ
tamo-juṣāṇo yad ajāta-śatroḥ

dyūte—by means of gambling; *tu*—but; *adharmeṇa*—by unfair tricks; *jitasya*—of the vanquished; *sādhoḥ*—a saintly person; *satya-avalambasya*—one who embraced truth as shelter; *vanam*—forest; *gatasya*—of the goer; *na*—never; *yācataḥ*—when asked for; *adāt*—delivered; *samayena*—in due course; *dāyam*—right share; *tamaḥ-juṣāṇaḥ*—overwhelmed by illusion; *yat*—as much as; *ajāta-śatroḥ*—of one who had no enemy.

TRANSLATION

Yudhiṣṭhira, who was born without any enemy, was unfairly defeated in gambling. But because he had taken the vow of truthfulness, he went off to the forest. When he came back in due course and begged the return of his rightful share of the kingdom, he was refused by Dhṛtarāṣṭra, who was overwhelmed by illusion.

PURPORT

Mahārāja Yudhiṣṭhira was the rightful heir to his father's kingdom. But just to favor his own sons, headed by Duryodhana, Dhṛtarāṣṭra,

Mahārāja Yudhiṣṭhira's uncle, adopted various unfair means to cheat his nephews of their rightful share of the kingdom. At last the Pāṇḍavas demanded only five villages, one for each of the five brothers, but that was also refused by the usurpers. This incident led to the War of Kurukṣetra. The Battle of Kurukṣetra, therefore, was induced by the Kurus, and not the Pāṇḍavas.

As *kṣatriyas*, the proper livelihood of the Pāṇḍavas was only to rule, and not to accept any other occupation. A *brāhmaṇa*, *kṣatriya* or *vaiśya* will not accept employment for his livelihood under any circumstances.

TEXT 9

यदा च पार्थप्रहितः सभायां
जगद्गुरुर्यानि जगाद कृष्णः ।
न तानि पुंसाममृतायनानि
राजोरु मेने क्षतपुण्यलेशः ॥ ९ ॥

yadā ca pārtha-prahitaḥ sabhāyāṁ
jagad-gurur yāni jagāda kṛṣṇaḥ
na tāni puṁsām amṛtāyanāni
rājoru mene kṣata-puṇya-leśaḥ

yadā—when; *ca*—also; *pārtha-prahitaḥ*—being advised by Arjuna; *sabhāyām*—in the assembly; *jagat-guruḥ*—of the teacher of the world; *yāni*—those; *jagāda*—went; *kṛṣṇaḥ*—Lord Kṛṣṇa; *na*—never; *tāni*—such words; *puṁsām*—of all men of sense; *amṛta-ayanāni*—as good as nectar; *rājā*—the King (Dhṛtarāṣṭra or Duryodhana); *uru*—very important; *mene*—did consider; *kṣata*—dwindling; *puṇya-leśaḥ*—fragment of pious acts.

TRANSLATION

Lord Kṛṣṇa was sent by Arjuna into the assembly as the spiritual master of the whole world, and although His words were heard by some [like Bhīṣma] as pure nectar, it was not so for the others, who were completely bereft of the last farthing of past pious works. The King [Dhṛtarāṣṭra or Duryodhana] did not take the words of Lord Kṛṣṇa very seriously.

PURPORT

Lord Kṛṣṇa, who is the spiritual master of the entire universe, accepted the duty of a messenger, and, deputed by Arjuna, went to the assembly of King Dhṛtarāṣṭra on a peace mission. Kṛṣṇa is everyone's Lord, yet because He was the transcendental friend of Arjuna, He gladly accepted the role of messenger, exactly like an ordinary friend. That is the beauty of the Lord's behavior with His pure devotees. He reached the assembly and spoke about peace, and the message was relished by Bhīṣma and other great leaders because it was spoken by the Lord Himself. But due to the exhaustion of the pious results of their past deeds, Duryodhana, or his father, Dhṛtarāṣṭra, did not take the message very seriously. That is the way of persons who have no credit of pious deeds. By past pious deeds, one may become the king of a country, but because the results of the pious acts of Duryodhana and company were dwindling, it became evident from their actions that they were sure to lose the kingdom to the Pāṇḍavas. The message of Godhead is always like nectar to the devotees, but it is just the opposite to the nondevotees. Sugar candy is always sweet to a healthy man, but it tastes very bitter to persons suffering from jaundice.

TEXT 10

यदोपहूतो भवनं प्रविष्टो
मन्त्राय पृष्टः किल पूर्वजेन ।
अथाह तन्मन्त्रदृशां वरीयान्
यन्मन्त्रिणो वैदुरिकं वदन्ति ॥१०॥

yadopahūto bhavanaṁ praviṣṭo
mantrāya pṛṣṭaḥ kila pūrvajena
athāha tan mantra-dṛśāṁ varīyān
yan mantriṇo vaidurikaṁ vadanti

yadā—when; *upahūtaḥ*—was called by; *bhavanam*—the palace; *praviṣṭaḥ*—entered; *mantrāya*—for consultation; *pṛṣṭaḥ*—asked by; *kila*—of course; *pūrvajena*—by the elder brother; *atha*—thus; *āha*—said; *tat*—that; *mantra*—advice; *dṛśām*—just suitable; *varīyān*—

excellent; *yat*—that which; *mantriṇaḥ*—the ministers of state, or expert politicians; *vaidurikam*—instructions by Vidura; *vadanti*—do they say.

TRANSLATION

When Vidura was invited by his elder brother [Dhṛtarāṣṭra] for consultation, he entered the house and gave instructions which were exactly to the point. His advice is well known, and instructions by Vidura are approved by expert ministers of state.

PURPORT

Political suggestions by Vidura are known as expert, just as, in modern times, Paṇḍita Cāṇakya is considered the authority in good counsel in both political and moral instructions.

TEXT 11

अजातशत्रोः प्रतियच्छ दायं
तितिक्षतो दुर्विषहं तवागः ।
सहानुजो यत्र वृकोदराहिः
श्वसन् रुषा यत्त्वमलं बिभेषि ॥११॥

ajāta-śatroḥ pratiyaccha dāyaṁ
titikṣato durviṣahaṁ tavāgaḥ
sahānujo yatra vṛkodarāhiḥ
śvasan ruṣā yat tvam alaṁ bibheṣi

ajāta-śatroḥ—of Yudhiṣṭhira, who has no enemy; *pratiyaccha*—return; *dāyam*—legitimate share; *titikṣataḥ*—of he who is so forbearing; *durviṣaham*—unbearable; *tava*—your; *āgaḥ*—offense; *saha*—along with; *anujaḥ*—younger brothers; *yatra*—wherein; *vṛkodara*—Bhīma; *ahiḥ*—revenging snake; *śvasan*—breathing heavily; *ruṣā*—in anger; *yat*—whom; *tvam*—you; *alam*—verily; *bibheṣi*—do fear.

TRANSLATION

[Vidura said:] You must now return the legitimate share to Yudhiṣṭhira, who has no enemies and who has been forbearing

His Divine Grace
A. C. Bhaktivedanta Swami Prabhupāda
Founder-Ācārya of the International Society for Krishna Consciousness

PLATE ONE: Vidura, his ears pained by the arrows of Duryodhana's sharp words, felt afflicted to the core of his heart. Placing his bow at the door, he quit his brother's palace. (*p. 16*)

PLATE TWO: With one hand, Balarāma and Kṛṣṇa caught hold of the hind legs of the ass demons, wheeled them around and threw them into the tops of the palm trees. (*p. 98*)

PLATE THREE: Lord Kṛṣṇa came out of the besieged city in Hi
four-armed form (holding a disc, club, lotus and conch) and passe
right through the assembly of soldiers without looking at the untouch
able king, Kālayavana. Kālayavana got down from his chariot and ra

after Kṛṣṇa, but the Lord stayed just out of reach. Engraged, Kāla-yavana addressed Him: "O Kṛṣṇa! I have heard You are a great hero, but I see You are running away from battle like a coward!" (*p. 113*)

PLATE FOUR: In an autumn night brightened by moonshine, the Lord enjoyed the *rāsa* dance as the central beauty of the assembly of His young girl friends, attracting them with His pleasing songs. Lord Kṛṣṇa expanded Himself, entering between each pair of *gopīs*, and as He placed His arms around their necks, each girl thought He was

standing next to her alone. The demigods and their wives were overwhelmed with eagerness to witness the *rāsa* dance, and they crowded the sky with hundreds of celestial airplanes. The *rāsa* dance is the highest stage of the exchange of feelings between the Lord and the living entities. (*pp. 102, 413*)

PLATE FIVE: Foreseeing the end of His family (the Yadu dynasty) and desiring to conclude His earthly pastimes, Lord Kṛṣṇa went to a secluded spot on the bank of the river Sarasvatī and sat down beneath a young banyan tree. There Uddhava and Maitreya joined Him. (*pp. 137-42*)

PLATE SIX: At Hardwar, the source of the celestial Ganges River, Vidura met Maitreya Muni and inquired from him as follows: "O great sage, please instruct me on how one should live for real happiness." (*pp. 179-81*)

PLATE SEVEN: After sitting in meditation on a lotus for more than three hundred trillion years, Lord Brahmā developed the pure intelligence with which to see the Supreme Lord within his heart. (*p. 362*)

PLATE EIGHT: At the end of Brahmā's day a great fire emanates from the numerous mouths of Saṅkarṣaṇa, the Lord's serpent bed, and the three worlds are devastated. (*pp. 480-81*)

PLATE NINE: Lord Brahmā's anger came out from between his eyebrows as a child of mixed blue and red color. This child was Rudra (Śiva), the incarnation of anger. (*pp. 499-504*)

PLATE TEN: The qualities of nescience; the great sages; the Vedic hymns; the arts and sciences—these and many other elements of the cosmos were generated from the body and mind of Lord Brahmā. (*pp. 494–534*)

PLATE ELEVEN: The four Kumāras, great sages appearing like children, directly saw the Supreme Personality of Godhead in the spiritual world, the kingdom of God. The Lord was accompanied by His asso-

ciates, who were worshiping Him with a fan, an umbrella and other paraphernalia. The sages had been impersonalists, but upon seeing the Lord they became His devotees. (*pp. 686-692*)

PLATE TWELVE: While the sage Kaśyapa was meditating in trance, his wife, Diti, afflicted by sex desire, begged him for sexual intercourse. (*pp. 597-98*)

through untold sufferings due to your offenses. He is waiting with his younger brothers, among whom is the revengeful Bhīma, breathing heavily like a snake. Surely you are afraid of him.

TEXT 12

पार्थांस्तु देवो भगवान्मुकुन्दो
गृहीतवान् सक्षितिदेवदेवः ।
आस्ते स्वपुर्यां यदुदेवदेवो
विनिर्जिताशेषनृदेवदेवः ॥१२॥

pārthāṁs tu devo bhagavān mukundo
gṛhītavān sakṣiti-deva-devaḥ
āste sva-puryāṁ yadu-deva-devo
vinirjitāśeṣa-nṛdeva-devaḥ

pārthān—the sons of Pṛthā (Kuntī); *tu*—but; *devaḥ*—the Lord; *bhagavān*—the Personality of Godhead; *mukundaḥ*—Śrī Kṛṣṇa, who awards liberation; *gṛhītavān*—has taken up; *sa*—with; *kṣiti-deva-devaḥ*—the *brāhmaṇas* and the demigods; *āste*—is present; *sva-puryām*—along with His family; *yadu-deva-devaḥ*—worshiped by the royal order of the Yadu dynasty; *vinirjita*—who have been conquered; *aśeṣa*—unlimited; *nṛdeva*—kings; *devaḥ*—Lord.

TRANSLATION

Lord Kṛṣṇa, the Personality of Godhead, has accepted the sons of Pṛthā as His kinsmen, and all the kings of the world are with Lord Śrī Kṛṣṇa. He is present in His home with all His family members, the kings and princes of the Yadu dynasty, who have conquered an unlimited number of rulers, and He is their Lord.

PURPORT

Vidura gave Dhṛtarāṣṭra very good counsel regarding political alliance with the sons of Pṛthā, the Pāṇḍavas. The first thing he said was that Lord Kṛṣṇa was intimately related with them as their cousin. Because Lord Kṛṣṇa is the Supreme Personality of Godhead, He is worshipable by all *brāhmaṇas* and demigods, who are the controllers of the universal affairs. Besides that, Lord Kṛṣṇa and His family members, the royal order of the Yadu dynasty, were the conquerors of all kings of the world.

The *kṣatriyas* used to fight the kings of various dominions and kidnap their beautiful princess-daughters, after conquering their relatives. This system was laudable because the *kṣatriyas* and the princesses would be married only on the basis of the chivalry of the conquering *kṣatriya.* All the young princes of the Yadu dynasty married the daughters of other kings in this way, by chivalrous force, and thus they were conquerors of all the kings of the world. Vidura wanted to impress upon his elder brother that fighting with the Pāṇḍavas was fraught with many dangers because they were supported by Lord Kṛṣṇa, who had conquered, even in His childhood, demons like Kaṁsa and Jarāsandha and demigods like Brahmā and Indra. Therefore all universal power was behind the Pāṇḍavas.

TEXT 13

स एष दोषः पुरुषद्विडास्ते
गृहान् प्रविष्टो यमपत्यमत्या ।
पुष्णासि कृष्णाद्विमुखो गतश्री-
स्त्यजाश्वशैवं कुलकौशलाय ॥१३॥

sa eṣa doṣaḥ puruṣa-dviḍ āste
gṛhān praviṣṭo yam apatya-matyā
puṣṇāsi kṛṣṇād vimukho gata-śrīs
tyajāśv aśaivaṁ kula-kauśalāya

saḥ—he; *eṣaḥ*—this; *doṣaḥ*—offense personified; *puruṣa-dviṭ*—envious of Lord Kṛṣṇa; *āste*—exists; *gṛhān*—household; *praviṣṭaḥ*—entered; *yam*—whom; *apatya-matyā*—thinking to be your son; *puṣṇāsi*—maintaining; *kṛṣṇāt*—from Kṛṣṇa; *vimukhaḥ*—in opposition; *gata-śrīḥ*—devoid of everything auspicious; *tyaja*—give up; *āśu*—as soon as possible; *aśaivam*—inauspicious; *kula*—family; *kauśalāya*—for the sake of.

TRANSLATION

You are maintaining offense personified, Duryodhana, as your infallible son, but he is envious of Lord Kṛṣṇa. And because you

are thus maintaining a nondevotee of Kṛṣṇa, you are devoid of all auspicious qualities. Relieve yourself of this ill fortune as soon as possible and do good to the whole family!

PURPORT

A good son is called *apatya,* one who does not allow his father to fall down. The son can protect the father's soul when the father is dead by offering sacrifices to please the Supreme Lord, Viṣṇu. This system is still prevalent in India. After the death of his father, a son goes to offer sacrifices at the lotus feet of Viṣṇu at Gayā and thus delivers the father's soul if the father is fallen. But if the son is already an enemy of Viṣṇu, how, in such an inimical mood, can he offer sacrifice unto Lord Viṣṇu's lotus feet? Lord Kṛṣṇa is directly the Personality of Godhead, Viṣṇu, and Duryodhana was inimical to Him. He would therefore be unable to protect his father, Dhṛtarāṣṭra, after his death. He himself was to fall down because of his faithlessness towards Viṣṇu. How, then, could he protect his father? Vidura advised Dhṛtarāṣṭra to get rid of such an unworthy son as Duryodhana as soon as possible if he was at all anxious to see to the good of his family.

According to the moral instructions of Cāṇakya Paṇḍita, "What is the use of a son who is neither a learned man nor a devotee of the Lord?" If a son is not a devotee of the Supreme Lord, he is just like blind eyes—a source of trouble. A physician may sometimes advise the extrication of such useless eyes from their sockets so that one can be relieved of the constant trouble. Duryodhana was exactly like blind, troubling eyes; he would be a source of great trouble to the family of Dhṛtarāṣṭra, as foreseen by Vidura. Vidura therefore rightly advised his eldest brother to get rid of this source of trouble. Dhṛtarāṣṭra was wrongly maintaining such personified offense under the mistaken impression that Duryodhana was a good son, able to liberate his father.

TEXT 14

इत्यूचिवांस्तत्र सुयोधनेन
प्रवृद्धकोपस्फुरिताधरेण ।
असत्कृतः सत्स्पृहणीयशीलः
क्षत्ता सकर्णानुजसौबलेन ॥१४॥

ity ūcivāṁs tatra suyodhanena
pravṛddha-kopa-sphuritādhareṇa
asat-kṛtaḥ sat-spṛhaṇīya-śīlaḥ
kṣattā sakarṇānuja-saubalena

iti—thus; *ūcivān*—while speaking; *tatra*—there; *suyodhanena*—by Duryodhana; *pravṛddha*—swollen with; *kopa*—anger; *sphurita*—flapping; *adhareṇa*—lips; *asat-kṛtaḥ*—insulted; *sat*—respectable; *spṛhaṇīya-śīlaḥ*—desirable qualities; *kṣattā*—Vidura; *sa*—with; *karṇa*—Karṇa; *anuja*—younger brothers; *saubalena*—with Śakuni.

TRANSLATION

While speaking thus, Vidura, whose personal character was esteemed by respectable persons, was insulted by Duryodhana, who was swollen with anger and whose lips were trembling. Duryodhana was in company with Karṇa, his younger brothers and his maternal uncle Śakuni.

PURPORT

It is said that giving good counsel to a foolish person causes the fool to become angry, just as feeding milk to a snake only increases its venomous poison. Saint Vidura was so honorable that his character was looked up to by all respectable persons. But Duryodhana was so foolish that he dared to insult Vidura. This was due to his bad association with Śakuni, his maternal uncle, as well as with his friend Karṇa, who always encouraged Duryodhana in his nefarious acts.

TEXT 15

क एनमत्रोपजुहाव जिह्मं
दास्याः सुतं यद्बलिनैव पुष्टः ।
तस्मिन् प्रतीपः परकृत्य आस्ते
निर्वास्यतामाशु पुराच्छ्वसानः ॥१५॥

ka enam atropajuhāva jihmaṁ
dāsyāḥ sutaṁ yad-balinaiva puṣṭaḥ

tasmin pratīpaḥ parakṛtya āste
nirvāsyatām āśu purāc chvasānaḥ

kaḥ—who; *enam*—this; *atra*—here; *upajuhāva*—called for; *jihmam*—crooked; *dāsyāḥ*—of a kept mistress; *sutam*—son; *yat*—whose; *balinā*—by whose subsistence; *eva*—certainly; *puṣṭaḥ*—grown up; *tasmin*—unto him; *pratīpaḥ*—enmity; *parakṛtya*—enemy's interest; *āste*—situated; *nirvāsyatām*—get him out; *āśu*—immediately; *purāt*—from the palace; *śvasānaḥ*—let him breathe only.

TRANSLATION

Who asked him to come here, this son of a kept mistress? He is so crooked that he spies in the interest of the enemy against those on whose support he has grown up. Toss him out of the palace immediately and leave him with only his breath.

PURPORT

When getting married, the *kṣatriya* kings would take on several other youthful girls along with the married princess. These girl attendants of the king were known as *dāsīs*, or attendant mistresses. By intimate association with the king, the *dāsīs* would get sons. Such sons were called *dāsī-putras*. They had no claim to a royal position, but they would get maintenance and other facilities just like princes. Vidura was the son of such a *dāsī*, and he was thus not counted amongst the *kṣatriyas*. King Dhṛtarāṣṭra was very affectionate toward his younger *dāsī-putra* brother, Vidura, and Vidura was a great friend and philosophical advisor to Dhṛtarāṣṭra. Duryodhana knew very well that Vidura was a great soul and well-wisher, but unfortunately he used strong words to hurt his innocent uncle. Duryodhana not only attacked Vidura's birth, but also called him an infidel because he seemed to support the cause of Yudhiṣṭhira, whom Duryodhana considered his enemy. He desired that Vidura be immediately put out of the palace and deprived of all his possessions. If possible, he would have liked him caned until he was left with nothing but his breath. He charged that Vidura was a spy of the Pāṇḍavas because he advised King Dhṛtarāṣṭra in their favor. Such is the situation of palace life and the intricacies of diplomacy that even a faultless person like Vidura could be charged with something abominable and punished. Vidura was struck with wonder at such unexpected behavior from his nephew Duryodhana, and before anything actually happened, he decided to leave the palace for good.

TEXT 16

स्वयं धनुर्द्वारि निधाय मायां
भ्रातुः पुरो मर्मसु ताडितोऽपि ।
स इत्थमत्युल्बणकर्णबाणै-
र्गतव्यथोऽयादुरु मानयानः ॥१६॥

svayaṁ dhanur dvāri nidhāya māyāṁ
bhrātuḥ puro marmasu tāḍito 'pi
sa ittham atyulbaṇa-karṇa-bāṇair
gata-vyatho 'yād uru mānayānaḥ

svayam—he himself; *dhanuḥ dvāri*—bow on the door; *nidhāya*—keeping; *māyām*—the external nature; *bhrātuḥ*—brother's; *puraḥ*—from the palace; *marmasu*—in the core of the heart; *tāḍitaḥ*—being afflicted; *api*—in spite of; *saḥ*—he (Vidura); *ittham*—like this; *ati-ulbaṇa*—severely; *karṇa*—ear; *bāṇaiḥ*—by the arrows; *gata-vyathaḥ*—without being sorry; *ayāt*—excited; *uru*—great; *mānayānaḥ*—so thinking.

TRANSLATION

Thus being pierced by arrows through his ears and afflicted to the core of his heart, Vidura placed his bow on the door and quit his brother's palace. He was not sorry, for he considered the acts of the external energy to be supreme.

PURPORT

A pure devotee of the Lord is never perturbed by an awkward position created by the external energy of the Lord. In *Bhagavad-gītā* (3.27) it is stated:

prakṛteḥ kriyamāṇāni
guṇaiḥ karmāṇi sarvaśaḥ
ahaṅkāra-vimūḍhātmā
kartāham iti manyate

A conditioned soul is absorbed in material existence under the influence of different modes of external energy. Absorbed in the false ego, he thinks that he is doing everything by himself. The external energy of the Lord, the material nature, is fully under the control of the Supreme Lord, and the conditioned soul is fully under the grip of the external energy. Therefore, the conditioned soul is fully under the control of the law of the Lord. But, due to illusion only, he thinks himself independent in his activities. Duryodhana was acting under such influence of the external nature, by which he would be vanquished at the ultimate end. He could not accept the sound advice of Vidura, but on the contrary he insulted that great soul, who was the well-wisher of his whole family. Vidura could understand this because he was a pure devotee of the Lord. In spite of being very strongly insulted by Duryodhana's words, Vidura could see that Duryodhana, under the influence of *māyā*, the external energy, was making progress on the path toward his own ruination. He therefore considered the acts of the external energy to be supreme, yet he also saw how the internal energy of the Lord helped him in that particular situation. A devotee is always in a renounced temperament because the worldly attractions can never satisfy him. Vidura was never attracted by the royal palace of his brother. He was always ready to leave the place and devote himself completely to the transcendental loving service of the Lord. Now he got the opportunity by the grace of Duryodhana, and instead of being sorry at the strong words of insult, he thanked him from within because it gave him the chance to live alone in a holy place and fully engage in the devotional service of the Lord. The word *gata-vyathaḥ* (without being sorry) is significant here because Vidura was relieved from the tribulations which trouble every man entangled in material activities. He therefore thought that there was no need to defend his brother with his bow because his brother was meant for ruination. Thus he left the palace before Duryodhana could act. *Māyā*, the supreme energy of the Lord, acted here both internally and externally.

TEXT 17

स निर्गतः कौरवपुण्यलब्धो
गजाह्वयात्तीर्थपदः पदानि ।
अन्वाक्रमत्पुण्यचिकीर्षयोर्व्यां
अधिष्ठितो यानि सहस्रमूर्तिः ॥१७॥

sa nirgataḥ kaurava-puṇya-labdho
gajāhvayāt tīrtha-padaḥ padāni
anvākramat puṇya-cikīrṣayorvyāṁ
adhiṣṭhito yāni sahasra-mūrtiḥ

saḥ—he (Vidura); *nirgataḥ*—after having quit; *kaurava*—the Kuru dynasty; *puṇya*—piety; *labdhaḥ*—so achieved; *gaja-āhvayāt*—from Hastināpura; *tīrtha-padaḥ*—of the Supreme Lord; *padāni*—pilgrimages; *anvākramat*—took shelter; *puṇya*—piety; *cikīrṣayā*—desiring so; *urvyām*—of high grade; *adhiṣṭhitaḥ*—situated; *yāni*—all those; *sahasra*—thousands; *mūrtiḥ*—forms.

TRANSLATION

By his piety, Vidura achieved the advantages of the pious Kauravas. After leaving Hastināpura, he took shelter of many places of pilgrimages, which are the Lord's lotus feet. With a desire to gain a high order of pious life, he traveled to holy places where thousands of transcendental forms of the Lord are situated.

PURPORT

Vidura was undoubtedly a highly elevated and pious soul, otherwise he would not have taken his birth in the Kaurava family. To have high parentage, to possess wealth, to be highly learned and to have great personal beauty are all due to past pious acts. But such pious possessions are not sufficient for obtaining the grace of the Lord and being engaged in His transcendental loving service. Vidura considered himself less pious, and therefore he decided to travel to all the great places of pilgrimage in the world in order to achieve greater piety and advance nearer to the Lord. At that time, Lord Kṛṣṇa was personally present in the world, and Vidura could have at once approached Him directly, but he did not do so because he was not sufficiently freed from sin. One cannot be one hundred percent devoted to the Lord unless and until he is completely free from all effects of sin. Vidura was conscious that by the association of the diplomatic Dhṛtarāṣṭra and Duryodhana he had lost his piety and was therefore not fit to associate at once with the Lord. In *Bhagavad-gītā* (7.28) this is confirmed in the following verse:

yeṣāṁ tv anta-gataṁ pāpaṁ
janānāṁ puṇya-karmaṇām
te dvandva-moha-nirmuktā
bhajante māṁ dṛḍha-vratāḥ

Persons who are sinful *asuras* like Kaṁsa and Jarāsandha cannot think of Lord Kṛṣṇa as the Supreme Personality of Godhead, the Absolute Truth. Only those who are pure devotees, those who follow the regulative principles of religious life as prescribed in the scriptures, are able to engage themselves in *karma-yoga* and then *jñāna-yoga* and thereafter, by pure meditation, can understand pure consciousness. When God consciousness is developed, one can take advantage of the association of pure devotees. *Syān mahat-sevayā viprāḥ puṇya-tīrtha-niṣevaṇāt:* one is able to associate with the Lord even during the existence of this life.

Places of pilgrimages are meant for eradicating the sins of the pilgrims, and they are distributed all over the universe just to give facility to all concerned for attaining pure existence and God realization. One should not be satisfied, however, merely by visiting the places of pilgrimage and performing one's prescribed duties; he should be eager to meet the great souls who are already there, engaged in the service of the Lord. In each and every place of pilgrimage, the Lord is present in His various transcendental forms.

These forms are called *arcā-mūrtis*, or forms of the Lord which can be easily appreciated by the common man. The Lord is transcendental to our mundane senses. He cannot be seen with our present eyes, nor can He be heard with our present ears. To the degree that we have entered into the service of the Lord or to the proportion to which our lives are freed from sins, we can perceive the Lord. But even though we are not free from sins, the Lord is kind enough to allow us the facility of seeing Him in His *arcā-mūrtis* in the temple. The Lord is all-powerful, and therefore He is able to accept our service by presentation of His *arcā* form. No one, therefore, should foolishly think the *arcā* in the temple to be an idol. Such an *arcā-mūrti* is not an idol but the Lord Himself, and to the proportion to which one is free from sins, he is able to know the significance of the *arcā-mūrti.* The guidance of a pure devotee is therefore always required.

In the land of Bhāratavarṣa there are many hundreds and thousands of places of pilgrimage distributed all over the country, and by traditional practice the common man visits such holy places during all seasons of the year. Some of the *arcā* representations of the Lord situated in different places of pilgrimage are mentioned herewith. The Lord is present at Mathurā (the birthplace of Lord Kṛṣṇa) as Ādi-keśava; the Lord is present at Purī (Orissa) as Lord Jagannātha (also known as Puruṣottama); He is present at Allahabad (Prayāga) as Bindu-mādhava; at Mandara Hill He is present as Madhusūdana. In the Ānandāraṇya, He is known as Vāsudeva, Padmanābha and Janārdana; at Viṣṇukāñcī, He is known as Viṣṇu; and at Māyāpura, He is known as Hari. There are millions and billions of such *arcā* forms of the Lord distributed all over the universe. All these *arcā-mūrtis* are summarized in the *Caitanya-caritāmṛta* in the following words:

sarvatra prakāśa tāṅra—bhakte sukha dite
jagatera adharma nāśi' dharma sthāpite

"The Lord has so distributed Himself all over the universe just to give pleasure to the devotees, to give the common man facility to eradicate his sins, and to establish religious principles in the world."

TEXT 18

पुरेषु पुण्योपवनाद्रिकुञ्जे-
ष्वपङ्कतोयेषु सरित्सरःसु ।
अनन्तलिङ्गैः समलङ्कृतेषु
चचार तीर्थायतनेष्वनन्यः ॥१८॥

pureṣu puṇyopavanādri-kuñjeṣv
apaṅka-toyeṣu sarit-saraḥsu
ananta-liṅgaiḥ samalaṅkṛteṣu
cacāra tīrthāyataneṣv ananyaḥ

pureṣu—holy places like Ayodhyā, Dvārakā and Mathurā; *puṇya*—piety; *upavana*—the air; *adri*—hill; *kuñjeṣu*—in the orchards; *apaṅka*—without sin; *toyeṣu*—in the water; *sarit*—river; *saraḥsu*—lakes; *ananta-liṅgaiḥ*—the forms of the Unlimited; *samalaṅkṛteṣu*—being so decorated; *cacāra*—executed; *tīrtha*—places of pilgrimage; *āyataneṣu*—holy lands; *ananyaḥ*—alone or seeing Kṛṣṇa alone.

TRANSLATION

He began to travel alone, thinking only of Kṛṣṇa, through various holy places like Ayodhyā, Dvārakā and Mathurā. He traveled where the air, hill, orchard, river and lake are all pure and sinless and where the forms of the Unlimited decorate the temples. Thus he performed the pilgrim's progress.

PURPORT

These *arcā* forms of the Lord may be considered idols by the atheists, but that does not matter for persons like Vidura or His many other servants. The forms of the Lord are mentioned here as *ananta-liṅga.* Such forms of the Lord have unlimited potency, the same as that of the Lord Himself. There is no difference between the potencies of the *arcā* and those of the personal forms of the Lord. The example of the postbox and post office may be applied here. The little postboxes distributed all over the city have the same potency as the postal system in general. The duty of the post office is to carry letters from one place to another. If one puts letters in postboxes authorized by the general post office, the function of carrying letters is performed without a doubt. Similarly, the *arcā-mūrti* can also deliver the same unlimited potency of the Lord as when He is personally present. Vidura, therefore, could see nothing but Kṛṣṇa in the different *arcā* forms, and ultimately he was able to realize Kṛṣṇa alone and nothing else.

TEXT 19

गां पर्यटन्मेध्यविविक्तवृत्तिः
सदाप्लुतोऽधःशयनोऽवधूतः ।
अलक्षितः स्वैरवधूतवेषो
व्रतानि चेरे हरितोषणानि ॥१९॥

gāṁ paryaṭan medhya-vivikta-vṛttiḥ
sadāpluto 'dhaḥ śayano 'vadhūtaḥ
alakṣitaḥ svair avadhūta-veṣo
vratāni cere hari-toṣaṇāni

gām—earth; *paryaṭan*—traversing; *medhya*—pure; *vivikta-vṛttiḥ*—independent occupation for living; *sadā*—always; *āplutaḥ*—sanctified; *adhaḥ*—on the earth; *śayanaḥ*—lying; *avadhūtaḥ*—without dressing (of the hair, etc.); *alakṣitaḥ*—without being seen; *svaiḥ*—alone; *avadhūta-veṣaḥ*—dressed like a mendicant; *vratāni*—vows; *cere*—performed; *hari-toṣaṇāni*—that pleased the Lord.

TRANSLATION

While so traversing the earth, he simply performed duties to please the Supreme Lord Hari. His occupation was pure and independent. He was constantly sanctified by taking his bath in holy places, although he was in the dress of a mendicant and had no hair dressing nor a bed on which to lie. Thus he was always unseen by his various relatives.

PURPORT

The first and foremost duty of a pilgrim is to satisfy the Supreme Lord Hari. While traveling as a pilgrim, one should not be worried about pleasing society. There is no need to depend on social formalities or occupation or dress. One should remain always absorbed in the function of pleasing the Lord. Thus sanctified by thought and action, one is able to realize the Supreme Lord by the process of a pilgrim's journey.

TEXT 20

इत्थं व्रजन् भारतमेव वर्षं
कालेन यावद्गतवान् प्रभासम् ।
तावच्छशास क्षितिमेकचक्रा-
मेकातपत्रामजितेन पार्थः ॥२०॥

itthaṁ vrajan bhāratam eva varṣaṁ
kālena yāvad gatavān prabhāsam
tāvac chaśāsa kṣitim eka-cakrām
ekātapatrām ajitena pārthaḥ

ittham—like this; *vrajan*—while traveling; *bhāratam*—India; *eva*—only; *varṣam*—the tract of land; *kālena*—in due course of time; *yāvat*—when; *gatavān*—visited; *prabhāsam*—the Prabhāsa pilgrimage site; *tāvat*—at that time; *śaśāsa*—ruled; *kṣitim*—the world; *eka-cakrām*—by one military force; *eka*—one; *ātapatrām*—flag; *ajitena*—by the mercy of the unconquerable Kṛṣṇa; *pārthaḥ*—Mahārāja Yudhiṣṭhira.

TRANSLATION

Thus, when he was in the land of Bhāratavarṣa traveling to all the places of pilgrimage, he visited Prabhāsakṣetra. At that time Mahārāja Yudhiṣṭhira was the emperor and held the world under one military strength and one flag.

PURPORT

More than five thousand years ago, while Saint Vidura was traveling the earth as a pilgrim, India was known as Bhāratavarṣa, as it is known even today. The history of the world cannot give any systematic account for more than three thousand years into the past, but before that the whole world was under the flag and military strength of Mahārāja Yudhiṣṭhira, who was the emperor of the world. At present there are hundreds and thousands of flags flapping in the United Nations, but during the time of Vidura there was, by the grace of Ajita, Lord Kṛṣṇa, only one flag. The nations of the world are very eager to again have one state under one flag, but for this they must seek the favor of Lord Kṛṣṇa, who alone can help us become one worldwide nation.

TEXT 21

तत्राथ शुश्राव सुहृद्विनष्टिं
वनं यथा वेणुजवह्निसंश्रयम् ।
संस्पर्धया दग्धमथानुशोचन्
सरस्वतीं प्रत्यगियाय तूष्णीम् ॥२१॥

tatrātha śuśrāva suhṛd-vinaṣṭiṁ
vanaṁ yathā veṇuja-vahni-saṁśrayam
saṁspardhayā dagdham athānuśocan
sarasvatīṁ pratyag iyāya tūṣṇīm

tatra—there; *atha*—thereafter; *śuśrāva*—heard; *suhṛt*—kinsmen; *vinaṣṭim*—all dead; *vanam*—forest; *yathā*—as much as; *veṇu-ja-vahni*—fire due to the bamboos; *saṁśrayam*—friction with one another; *saṁspardhayā*—by violent passion; *dagdham*—burnt; *atha*—thus; *anuśocan*—thinking; *sarasvatīm*—the River Sarasvatī; *pratyak*—westward; *iyāya*—went; *tūṣṇīm*—silently.

TRANSLATION

At the place of pilgrimage at Prabhāsa, it came to his knowledge that all his relatives had died due to violent passion, just as an entire forest burns due to fire produced by the friction of bamboos. After this he proceeded west, where the River Sarasvatī flows.

PURPORT

Both the Kauravas and the Yādavas were relatives of Vidura, and Vidura heard of their extinction due to fratricidal war. The comparison of the friction of forest bamboos to that of passionate human societies is appropriate. The whole world is compared to a forest. At any moment there may be a flare-up of fire in the forest due to friction. No one goes to the forest to set it on fire, but due only to friction between bamboos, fire takes place and burns an entire forest. Similarly, in the greater forest of worldly transaction, the fire of war takes place because of the violent passion of the conditioned souls illusioned by the external energy. Such a worldly fire can be extinguished only by the water of the mercy cloud of saints, just as a forest fire can be extinguished only by rains falling from a cloud.

TEXT 22

तस्यां त्रितस्योशनसो मनोश्च
पृथोरथाग्नेरसितस्य वायोः ।
तीर्थं सुदासस्य गवां गुहस्य
यच्छ्राद्धदेवस्य स आसिषेवे ॥२२॥

tasyāṁ tritasyośanaso manoś ca
pṛthor athāgner asitasya vāyoḥ
tīrthaṁ sudāsasya gavāṁ guhasya
yac chrāddhadevasya sa āsiṣeve

tasyām—on the bank of the River Sarasvatī; *tritasya*—the pilgrimage site named Trita; *uśanasaḥ*—the pilgrimage site named Uśanā; *manoḥ ca*—as also of the pilgrimage site named Manu; *pṛthoḥ*—that of Pṛthu; *atha*—thereafter; *agneḥ*—that of Agni; *asitasya*—that of Asita; *vāyoḥ*—that of Vāyu; *tīrtham*—places of pilgrimages; *sudāsasya*—of the name Sudāsa; *gavām*—that of Go; *guhasya*—that of Guha; *yat*—thereupon; *śrāddhadevasya*—of the name Śrāddhadeva; *saḥ*—Vidura; *āsiṣeve*—duly visited and performed the rituals.

TRANSLATION

On the bank of the River Sarasvatī there were eleven places of pilgrimage, namely, (1) Trita, (2) Uśanā, (3) Manu, (4) Pṛthu, (5) Agni, (6) Asita, (7) Vāyu, (8) Sudāsa, (9) Go, (10) Guha and (11) Śrāddhadeva. Vidura visited all of them and duly performed rituals.

TEXT 23

अन्यानि चेह द्विजदेवदेवैः
कृतानि नानायतनानि विष्णोः ।
प्रत्यङ्गमुख्याङ्कितमन्दिराणि
यद्दर्शनात्कृष्णमनुस्मरन्ति ॥२३॥

anyāni ceha dvija-deva-devaiḥ
kṛtāni nānāyatanāni viṣṇoḥ
pratyaṅga-mukhyāṅkita-mandirāṇi
yad-darśanāt kṛṣṇam anusmaranti

anyāni—others; *ca*—also; *iha*—here; *dvija-deva*—by the great sages; *devaiḥ*—and the demigods; *kṛtāni*—established by; *nānā*—various; *āyatanāni*—various forms; *viṣṇoḥ*—of the Supreme Personality of Godhead; *prati*—each and every; *aṅga*—part; *mukhya*—the chief; *aṅkita*—marked; *mandirāṇi*—temples; *yat*—which; *darśanāt*—by seeing from a distance; *kṛṣṇam*—the original Personality of Godhead; *anusmaranti*—constantly remembers.

TRANSLATION

There were also many other temples of various forms of the Supreme Personality of Godhead Viṣṇu, established by great sages and demigods. These temples were marked with the chief emblems of the Lord, and they reminded one always of the original Personality of Godhead, Lord Kṛṣṇa.

PURPORT

Human society is divided into four social orders of life and four spiritual divisions, applying to each and every individual person. This system is called *varṇāśrama-dharma* and has already been discussed in many places in this great literature. The sages, or persons who completely devoted themselves to the spiritual upliftment of the entire human society, were known as *dvija-deva*, the best amongst the twice-born. The denizens of superior planets, from the moon planet and upwards, were known as *devas.* Both the *dvija-devas* and the *devas* always establish temples of Lord Viṣṇu in His various forms, such as Govinda, Madhusūdana, Nṛsiṁha, Mādhava, Keśava, Nārāyaṇa, Padmanābha, Pārthasārathi and many others. The Lord expands Himself in innumerable forms, but all of them are nondifferent from one another. Lord Viṣṇu has four hands, and each hand holds a particular item—either a conchshell, wheel, club or lotus flower. Of these four emblems, the *cakra,* or wheel, is the chief. Lord Kṛṣṇa, being the original Viṣṇu form, has only one emblem, namely the wheel, and therefore He is sometimes called the Cakrī. The Lord's *cakra* is the symbol of the power by which the Lord controls the whole manifestation. The tops of Viṣṇu temples are marked with the symbol of the wheel so that people may have the chance to see the symbol from a very long distance and at once remember Lord Kṛṣṇa. The purpose of building very high temples is to give people a chance to see them from a distant place. This system is carried on in India whenever a new temple is constructed, and it appears that it is coming down from a time before recorded history. The foolish propaganda by atheists that temples were contructed only in later days is refuted here because Vidura visited these temples at least five thousand years ago, and the temples of Viṣṇu were in existence long, long before Vidura visited them. The great sages and demigods never established statues of men or demigods, but they established temples of Viṣṇu for the benefit of common men, to raise them to the platform of God consciousness.

TEXT 24

ततस्त्वतिव्रज्य सुराष्ट्रमृद्धं
सौवीरमत्स्यान् कुरुजाङ्गलांश्च ।
कालेन तावद्यमुनामुपेत्य
तत्रोद्धवं भागवतं ददर्श ॥२४॥

tatas tv ativrajya surāṣṭram ṛddhaṁ
sauvīra-matsyān kurujāṅgalāṁś ca
kālena tāvad yamunām upetya
tatroddhavaṁ bhāgavataṁ dadarśa

tataḥ—from there; *tu*—but; *ativrajya*—by passing over; *surāṣṭram*—the kingdom of Surat; *ṛddham*—very wealthy; *sauvīra*—the kingdom of Sauvīra; *matsyān*—the kingdom of Matsya; *kurujāṅgalān*—the kingdom of western India up to the Delhi province; *ca*—also; *kālena*—in course of time; *tāvat*—as soon as; *yamunām*—bank of the River Yamunā; *upetya*—reaching; *tatra*—there; *uddhavam*—Uddhava, one of the prominent Yadus; *bhāgavatam*—the great devotee of Lord Kṛṣṇa; *dadarśa*—happened to see.

TRANSLATION

Thereafter he passed through very wealthy provinces like Surat, Sauvīra and Matsya and through western India, known as Kurujāṅgala. At last he reached the bank of the Yamunā, where he happened to meet Uddhava, the great devotee of Lord Kṛṣṇa.

PURPORT

The tract of land comprising about one hundred square miles from modern Delhi to the Mathurā district in Uttar Pradesh, including a portion of the Gurgaon district in Punjab (East India), is considered to be the topmost place of pilgrimage in all of India. This land is sacred because Lord Kṛṣṇa traveled through it many times. From the very beginning of His appearance, He was at Mathurā in the house of His maternal uncle Kaṁsa, and He was reared by His foster father Mahārāja Nanda at Vṛndāvana. There are still many devotees of the Lord lingering there in ecstasy in search of Kṛṣṇa and His childhood associates, the *gopīs.* It is not that such devotees meet Kṛṣṇa face to face in that tract of land, but a devotee's eagerly searching after Kṛṣṇa is as good as his seeing Him personally. How this is so cannot be explained, but it is factually realized by those who are pure devotees of the Lord. Philosophically, one can understand that Lord Kṛṣṇa and His remembrance are on the absolute plane and that the very idea of searching for Him at Vṛndāvana in pure God consciousness gives more pleasure to the devotee than seeing Him face to face. Such devotees of the Lord see Him face to face at every moment, as confirmed in the *Brahma-saṁhitā* (5.38):

premāñjana-cchurita-bhakti-vilocanena
santaḥ sadaiva hṛdayeṣu vilokayanti
yaṁ śyāmasundaram acintya-guṇa-svarūpaṁ
govindam ādi-puruṣaṁ tam ahaṁ bhajāmi

"Those who are in ecstasy of love with the Supreme Personality of Godhead, Lord Śyāmasundara [Kṛṣṇa], see Him always in their hearts due to love and devotional service rendered to the Lord." Both Vidura and Uddhava were such elevated devotees, and therefore they both came to the bank of the Yamunā and met each other.

TEXT 25

स वासुदेवानुचरं प्रशान्तं
बृहस्पतेः प्राक् तनयं प्रतीतम् ।
आलिङ्ग्य गाढं प्रणयेन भद्रं
स्वानामपृच्छद्भगवत्प्रजानाम् ॥२५॥

sa vāsudevānucaraṁ praśāntaṁ
bṛhaspateḥ prāk tanayaṁ pratītam
āliṅgya gāḍhaṁ praṇayena bhadraṁ
svānām apṛcchad bhagavat-prajānām

saḥ—he, Vidura; *vāsudeva*—Lord Kṛṣṇa; *anucaram*—constant companion; *praśāntam*—very sober and gentle; *bṛhaspateḥ*—of Bṛhaspati, the learned spiritual master of the demigods; *prāk*—formerly; *tanayam*—son or disciple; *pratītam*—acknowledged; *āliṅgya*—embracing; *gāḍham*—very feelingly; *praṇayena*—in love; *bhadram*—auspicious; *svānām*—his own; *apṛcchat*—asked; *bhagavat*—of the Personality of Godhead; *prajānām*—family.

TRANSLATION

Then, due to his great love and feeling, Vidura embraced him [Uddhava], who was a constant companion of Lord Kṛṣṇa and formerly a great student of Bṛhaspati's. Vidura then asked him for news of the family of Lord Kṛṣṇa, the Personality of Godhead.

PURPORT

Vidura was older than Uddhava, like a father, and therefore when the two met, Uddhava bowed down before Vidura, and Vidura embraced him because Uddhava was younger, like a son. Vidura's brother Pāṇḍu was Lord Kṛṣṇa's uncle, and Uddhava was a cousin to Lord Kṛṣṇa. According to social custom, therefore, Vidura was to be respected by Uddhava on the level of his father. Uddhava was a great scholar in logic, and he was known to be a son or disciple of Bṛhaspati, the greatly learned priest and spiritual master of the demigods. Vidura asked Uddhava about the welfare of his relatives, although he already knew that they were no longer in the world. This inquiry appears to be very queer, but Śrīla Jīva Gosvāmī states that the news was shocking to Vidura, who therefore inquired again due to great curiosity. Thus his inquiry was psychological and not practical.

TEXT 26

कच्चित्पुराणौ पुरुषौ स्वनाभ्य-
पाद्मानुवृत्त्येह किलावतीर्णौ ।
आसात उर्व्याः कुशलं विधाय
कृतक्षणौ कुशलं शूरगेहे ॥२६॥

kaccit purāṇau puruṣau svanābhya-
pādmānuvṛttyeha kilāvatīrṇau
āsāta urvyāḥ kuśalaṁ vidhāya
kṛta-kṣaṇau kuśalaṁ śūra-gehe

kaccit—whether; *purāṇau*—the original; *puruṣau*—Personalities of Godhead (Kṛṣṇa and Balarāma); *svanābhya*—Brahmā; *pādma-anuvṛttyā*—by the request of the one who is born from the lotus; *iha*—here; *kila*—certainly; *avatīrṇau*—incarnated; *āsāte*—are; *urvyāḥ*—in the world; *kuśalam*—well-being; *vidhāya*—for doing so; *kṛta-kṣaṇau*—the elevators of everyone's prosperity; *kuśalam*—all well; *śūra-gehe*—in the house of Śūrasena.

TRANSLATION

[Please tell me] whether the original Personalities of Godhead, who incarnated Themselves at the request of Brahmā [who is born

out of the lotus flower from the Lord] and who have increased the prosperity of the world by elevating everyone, are doing well in the house of Śūrasena.

PURPORT

Lord Kṛṣṇa and Balarāma are not two different Personalities of Godhead. God is one without a second, but He expands Himself in many forms without their being separate from one another. They are all plenary expansions. The immediate expansion of Lord Kṛṣṇa is Baladeva, and Brahmā, born from the lotus flower from Garbhodakaśāyī Viṣṇu, is an expansion of Baladeva. This indicates that Kṛṣṇa and Baladeva are not subjected to the regulations of the universe; on the contrary, the whole universe is under Their subjugation. They appeared at the request of Brahmā to liberate the burden of the world, and They relieved the world by many superhuman activities so that everyone became happy and prosperous. Without the grace of the Lord, no one can become happy and prosperous. Because the happiness of the family of the Lord's devotees depends on the happiness of the Lord, Vidura first of all inquired about the well-being of the Lord.

TEXT 27

कच्चित्कुरूणां परमः सुहृन्नो
भामः स आस्ते सुखमङ्ग शौरिः ।
यो वै स्वसॄणां पितृवद्ददाति
वरान् वदान्यो वरतर्पणेन ॥२७॥

kaccit kurūṇāṁ paramaḥ suhṛn no
bhāmaḥ sa āste sukham aṅga śauriḥ
yo vai svasṝṇāṁ pitṛvad dadāti
varān vadānyo vara-tarpaṇena

kaccit—whether; *kurūṇām*—of the Kurus; *paramaḥ*—greatest; *suhṛt*—well-wisher; *naḥ*—our; *bhāmaḥ*—brother-in-law; *saḥ*—he; *āste*—is; *sukham*—happy; *aṅga*—O Uddhava; *śauriḥ*—Vasudeva; *yaḥ*—one who; *vai*—certainly; *svasṝṇām*—of the sisters; *pitṛ-vat*—like a father; *dadāti*—gives; *varān*—everything desirable; *vadānyaḥ*—munificent; *vara*—wife; *tarpaṇena*—by pleasing.

TRANSLATION

[Please tell me] whether the best friend of the Kurus, our brother-in-law Vasudeva, is doing well. He is very munificent. He is like a father to his sisters, and he is always pleasing to his wives.

PURPORT

Lord Kṛṣṇa's father, Vasudeva, had sixteen wives, and one of them, named Pauravī or Rohiṇī, the mother of Baladeva, was the sister of Vidura. Vasudeva, therefore, was the husband of Vidura's sister, and thus they were brothers-in-law. Vasudeva's sister Kuntī was the wife of Pāṇḍu, Vidura's elder brother, and in that sense also, Vasudeva was brother-in-law to Vidura. Kuntī was younger than Vasudeva, and it was the duty of the elder brother to treat younger sisters as daughters. Whenever anything was needed by Kuntī, it was munificently delivered by Vasudeva, due to his great love for his younger sister. Vasudeva never dissatisfied his wives, and at the same time he supplied the objects desired by his sister. He had special attention for Kuntī because she became a widow at an early age. While inquiring about Vasudeva's welfare, Vidura remembered all about him and the family relationship.

TEXT 28

कच्चिद्वरूथाधिपतिर्यदूनां
प्रद्युम्न आस्ते सुखमङ्ग वीरः ।
यं रुक्मिणी भगवतोऽभिलेभे
आराध्य विप्रान् स्मरमादिसर्गे ॥२८॥

kaccid varūthādhipatir yadūnāṁ
pradyumna āste sukham aṅga vīraḥ
yaṁ rukmiṇī bhagavato 'bhilebhe
ārādhya viprān smaram ādi-sarge

kaccit—whether; *varūtha*—of the military; *adhipatiḥ*—commander-in-chief; *yadūnām*—of the Yadus; *pradyumnaḥ*—the son of Kṛṣṇa named Pradyumna; *āste*—is; *sukham*—happy; *aṅga*—O Uddhava; *vīraḥ*—the great warrior; *yam*—whom; *rukmiṇī*—the wife of Kṛṣṇa named Rukmiṇī; *bhagavataḥ*—from the Personality of Godhead; *abhilebhe*—got as a prize; *ārādhya*—pleasing; *viprān*—*brāhmaṇas;* *smaram*—Cupid (Kāmadeva); *ādi-sarge*—in his previous life.

TRANSLATION

O Uddhava, please tell me how is Pradyumna, the commander-in-chief of the Yadus, who was Cupid in a former life? Rukmiṇī bore him as her son from Lord Kṛṣṇa, by the grace of brāhmaṇas whom she pleased.

PURPORT

According to Śrīla Jīva Gosvāmī, Smara (Cupid, or Kāmadeva) is one of the eternal associates of Lord Kṛṣṇa. Jīva Gosvāmī has explained this very elaborately in his treatise *Kṛṣṇa-sandarbha.*

TEXT 29

कच्चित्सुखं सात्वतवृष्णिभोज-
दाशार्हकाणामधिपः स आस्ते ।
यमभ्यषिञ्चच्छतपत्रनेत्रो
नृपासनाशां परिहृत्य दूरात् ॥२९॥

kaccit sukhaṁ sātvata-vṛṣṇi-bhoja-
dāśārhakāṇām adhipaḥ sa āste
yam abhyaṣiñcac chata-patra-netro
nṛpāsanāśāṁ parihṛtya dūrāt

kaccit—whether; *sukham*—is all well; *sātvata*—the Sātvata race; *vṛṣṇi*—the Vṛṣṇi dynasty; *bhoja*—the Bhoja dynasty; *dāśārhakāṇām*—the Dāśārha race; *adhipaḥ*—King Ugrasena; *saḥ*—he; *āste*—does exist; *yam*—whom; *abhyaṣiñcat*—installed; *śata-patra-netraḥ*—Lord Śrī

Kṛṣṇa; *nṛpa-āsana-āśām*—hope of the royal throne; *parihṛtya*—giving up; *dūrāt*—at a distant place.

TRANSLATION

O my friend, [tell me] whether Ugrasena, the King of the Sātvatas, Vṛṣṇis, Bhojas and Dāśārhas, is now doing well. He went far away from his kingdom, leaving aside all hopes of his royal throne, but Lord Kṛṣṇa again installed him.

TEXT 30

कच्चिद्धरेः सौम्य सुतः सदृक्ष
आस्तेऽग्रणी रथिनां साधु साम्बः ।
असूत यं जाम्बवती व्रताढ्या
देवं गुहं योऽम्बिकया धृतोऽग्रे ॥३०॥

kaccid dhareḥ saumya sutaḥ sadṛkṣa
āste 'graṇī rathināṁ sādhu sāmbaḥ
asūta yaṁ jāmbavatī vratāḍhyā
devaṁ guhaṁ yo 'mbikayā dhṛto 'gre

kaccit—whether; *hareḥ*—of the Personality of Godhead; *saumya*—O grave one; *sutaḥ*—son; *sadṛkṣaḥ*—similar; *āste*—fares well; *agraṇīḥ*—foremost; *rathinām*—of the warriors; *sādhu*—well behaved; *sāmbaḥ*—Sāmba; *asūta*—gave birth; *yam*—whom; *jāmbavatī*—Jāmbavatī, a queen of Lord Kṛṣṇa's; *vratāḍhyā*—enriched by vows; *devam*—the demigod; *guham*—of the name Kārttikeya; *yaḥ*—whom; *ambikayā*—unto the wife of Śiva; *dhṛtaḥ*—born; *agre*—in the previous birth.

TRANSLATION

O gentle one, does Sāmba fare well? He exactly resembles the son of the Personality of Godhead. In a previous birth he was born as Kārttikeya in the womb of the wife of Lord Śiva, and now he has been born in the womb of Jāmbavatī, the most enriched wife of Kṛṣṇa.

PURPORT

Lord Śiva, one of the three qualitative incarnations of the Personality of Godhead, is the plenary expansion of the Lord. Kārttikeya, born of him, is on the level of Pradyumna, another son of Lord Kṛṣṇa. When Lord Śrī Kṛṣṇa descends into the material world, all His plenary portions also appear with Him to exhibit different functions of the Lord. But for the pastimes at Vṛndāvana, all functions are performed by the Lord's different plenary expansions. Vāsudeva is a plenary expansion of Nārāyaṇa. When the Lord appeared as Vāsudeva before Devakī and Vasudeva, He appeared in His capacity as Nārāyaṇa. Similarly, all the demigods of the heavenly kingdom appeared as associates of the Lord in the forms of Pradyumna, Sāmba, Uddhava, etc. It is learned here that Kāmadeva appeared as Pradyumna, Kārttikeya as Sāmba, and one of the Vasus as Uddhava. All of them served in their different capacities in order to enrich the pastimes of Kṛṣṇa.

TEXT 31

क्षेमं स कच्चिद्युयुधान आस्ते
यः फाल्गुनाल्लब्धधनूरहस्यः ।
लेभेऽञ्जसाधोक्षजसेवयैव
गतिं तदीयां यतिभिर्दुरापाम् ॥३१॥

kṣemaṁ sa kaccid yuyudhāna āste
yaḥ phālgunāl labdha-dhanū-rahasyaḥ
lebhe 'ñjasādhokṣaja-sevayaiva
gatiṁ tadīyāṁ yatibhir durāpām

kṣemam—all good; *saḥ*—he; *kaccit*—whether; *yuyudhānaḥ*—Sātyaki; *āste*—is there; *yaḥ*—one who; *phālgunāt*—from Arjuna; *labdha*—has achieved; *dhanuḥ-rahasyaḥ*—one who understands the intricacies of military art; *lebhe*—also achieved; *añjasā*—summarily; *adhokṣaja*—of the Transcendence; *sevayā*—by service; *eva*—certainly; *gatim*—destination; *tadīyām*—transcendental; *yatibhiḥ*—by great renouncers; *durāpām*—very difficult to achieve.

TRANSLATION

O Uddhava, does Yuyudhāna fare well? He learned the intricacies of the military art from Arjuna and attained the transcendental destination which is very difficult to reach even for great renouncers.

PURPORT

The destination of transcendence is to become the personal associate of the Personality of Godhead, who is known as *adhokṣaja*, He who is beyond the reach of the senses. The renouncers of the world, the *sannyāsīs*, give up all worldly connections, namely, family, wife, children, friends, home, wealth—everything—to attain the transcendental bliss of Brahman happiness. But *adhokṣaja* happiness is beyond Brahman happiness. The empiric philosophers enjoy a transcendental quality of bliss by philosophical speculation on the Supreme Truth, but beyond that pleasure is the pleasure enjoyed by Brahman in His eternal form of the Personality of Godhead. Brahman bliss is enjoyed by living entities after liberation from material bondage. But Parabrahman, the Personality of Godhead, enjoys eternally a bliss of His own potency, which is called the *hlādinī* potency. The empiric philosopher who studies Brahman by negation of the external features has not yet learned the quality of the *hlādinī* potency of Brahman. Out of many potencies of the Omnipotent, there are three features of His internal potency—namely *saṁvit*, *sandhinī* and *hlādinī*. And in spite of their strict adherence to the principles of *yama*, *niyama*, *āsana*, *dhyāna*, *dhāraṇā* and *prāṇāyāma*, the great *yogīs* and *jñānīs* are unable to enter into the internal potency of the Lord. This internal potency is, however, easily realized by the devotees of the Lord by dint of devotional service. Yuyudhāna achieved this stage of life, just as he achieved expert knowledge in military science from Arjuna. Thus his life was successful to the fullest extent from both the material and spiritual angles of vision. That is the way of devotional service to the Lord.

TEXT 32

कच्चिद् बुधः स्वस्त्यनमीव आस्ते
श्वफल्कपुत्रो भगवत्प्रपन्नः ।

यः कृष्णपादाङ्कितमार्गपांसु-
ष्वचेष्टत प्रेमविभिन्नधैर्यः ॥३२॥

kaccid budhaḥ svasty anamīva āste
śvaphalka-putro bhagavat-prapannaḥ
yaḥ kṛṣṇa-pādāṅkita-mārga-pāṁsuṣv
aceṣṭata prema-vibhinna-dhairyaḥ

kaccit—whether; *budhaḥ*—very learned; *svasti*—well; *anamīvaḥ*—faultless; *āste*—does exist; *śvaphalka-putraḥ*—the son of Śvaphalka, Akrūra; *bhagavat*—regarding the Personality of Godhead; *prapannaḥ*—surrendered; *yaḥ*—one who; *kṛṣṇa*—the Lord; *pāda-aṅkita*—marked with footprints; *mārga*—path; *pāṁsuṣu*—in the dust; *aceṣṭata*—exhibited; *prema-vibhinna*—lost in transcendental love; *dhairyaḥ*—mental equilibrium.

TRANSLATION

Please tell me whether Akrūra, the son of Śvaphalka, is doing well. He is a faultless soul surrendered unto the Personality of Godhead. He once lost his mental equilibrium due to his ecstasy of transcendental love and fell down on the dust of a road which was marked with the footprints of Lord Kṛṣṇa.

PURPORT

When Akrūra came to Vṛndāvana in search of Kṛṣṇa, he saw the footprints of the Lord on the dust of Nanda-grāma and at once fell on them in ecstasy of transcendental love. This ecstasy is possible for a devotee who is fully absorbed in incessant thoughts of Kṛṣṇa. Such a pure devotee of the Lord is naturally faultless because he is always associated with the supremely pure Personality of Godhead. Constant thought of the Lord is the antiseptic method for keeping oneself free from the infectious contamination of the material qualities. The pure devotee of the Lord is always in company with the Lord by thinking of Him. Yet, in the particular context of time and place, the transcendental emotions take a different turn, and this breaks the mental equilibrium of the devotee. Lord Caitanya displayed the typical example of transcendental ecstasy, as we can understand from the life of this incarnation of God.

TEXT 33

कच्चिच्छिवं देवकभोजपुत्र्या
विष्णुप्रजाया इव देवमातुः ।
या वै स्वगर्भेण दधार देवं
त्रयी यथा यज्ञवितानमर्थम् ॥३३॥

kaccic chivaṁ devaka-bhoja-putryā
viṣṇu-prajāyā iva deva-mātuḥ
yā vai sva-garbheṇa dadhāra devaṁ
trayī yathā yajña-vitānam artham

kaccit—whether; *śivam*—everything well; *devaka-bhoja-putryāḥ*—of the daughter of King Devaka-bhoja; *viṣṇu-prajāyāḥ*—of she who gave birth to the Personality of Godhead; *iva*—like that of; *deva-mātuḥ*—of the mother of the demigods (Aditi); *yā*—one who; *vai*—indeed; *sva-garbheṇa*—by her own womb; *dadhāra*—conceived; *devam*—the Supreme Lord; *trayī*—the *Vedas; yathā*—as much as; *yajña-vitānam*—of spreading the sacrifice; *artham*—purpose.

TRANSLATION

As the Vedas are the reservoir of sacrificial purposes, so the daughter of King Devaka-bhoja conceived the Supreme Personality of Godhead in her womb, as did the mother of the demigods. Is she [Devakī] doing well?

PURPORT

The *Vedas* are full of transcendental knowledge and spiritual values, and thus Devakī, the mother of Lord Kṛṣṇa, conceived the Lord in her womb as the personified meaning of the *Vedas.* There is no difference between the *Vedas* and the Lord. The *Vedas* aim at the understanding of the Lord, and the Lord is the *Vedas* personified. Devakī is compared to the meaningful *Vedas* and the Lord to their purpose personified.

TEXT 34

अपिस्विदास्ते भगवान् सुखं वो
यः सात्वतां कामदुघोऽनिरुद्धः ।
यमामनन्ति स्म हि शब्दयोनिं
मनोमयं सत्त्वतुरीयतत्त्वम् ॥३४॥

apisvid āste bhagavān sukhaṁ vo
yaḥ sātvatāṁ kāma-dugho 'niruddhaḥ
yam āmananti sma hi śabda-yoniṁ
mano-mayaṁ sattva-turīya-tattvam

api—as also; *svit*—whether; *āste*—does He; *bhagavān*—the Personality of Godhead; *sukham*—all happiness; *vaḥ*—of you; *yaḥ*—one who; *sātvatām*—of the devotees; *kāma-dughaḥ*—source of all desires; *aniruddhaḥ*—the plenary expansion Aniruddha; *yam*—whom; *āmananti*—they accept; *sma*—from yore; *hi*—certainly; *śabda-yonim*—the cause of the Ṛg *Veda; manaḥ-mayam*—creator of the mind; *sattva*—transcendental; *turīya*—the fourth expansion; *tattvam*—principle.

TRANSLATION

May I inquire whether Aniruddha is doing well? He is the fulfiller of all the desires of the pure devotees and has been considered from yore to be the cause of the Ṛg Veda, the creator of the mind and the fourth plenary expansion of Viṣṇu.

PURPORT

Ādi-caturbhuja, the original expansions from Baladeva, are Vāsudeva, Saṅkarṣaṇa, Pradyumna and Aniruddha. All of Them are *viṣṇu-tattvas*, or nondifferent Personalities of Godhead. In the incarnation of Śrī Rāma, all these different expansions appeared for particular pastimes. Lord Rāma is the original Vāsudeva, and His brothers were Saṅkarṣaṇa,

Pradyumna and Aniruddha. Aniruddha is also the cause of Mahā-Viṣṇu, from whose breathing the *Ṛg Veda* appeared. All this is nicely explained in the *Mārkaṇḍeya Purāṇa.* In the incarnation of Lord Kṛṣṇa, Aniruddha appeared as the son of the Lord. Lord Kṛṣṇa in Dvārakā is the Vāsudeva expansion of the original group. The original Lord Kṛṣṇa never leaves Goloka Vṛndāvana. All the plenary expansions are one and the same *viṣṇu-tattva,* and there is no difference in Their potency.

TEXT 35

अपिस्विदन्ये च निजात्मदैव-
मनन्यवृत्त्या समनुव्रता ये ।
हृदीकसत्यात्मजचारुदेष्ण-
गदादयः स्वस्ति चरन्ति सौम्य ॥३५॥

apisvid anye ca nijātma-daivam
ananya-vṛttyā samanuvratā ye
hṛdīka-satyātmaja-cārudeṣṇa-
gadādayaḥ svasti caranti saumya

api—as also; *svit*—whether; *anye*—others; *ca*—and; *nija-ātma*—of one's own self; *daivam*—Śrī Kṛṣṇa; *ananya*—absolutely; *vṛttyā*—faith; *samanuvratāḥ*—followers; *ye*—all those who; *hṛdīka*—Hṛdīka; *satya-ātmaja*—the son of Satyabhāmā; *cārudeṣṇa*—Cārudeṣṇa; *gada*—Gada; *ādayaḥ*—and others; *svasti*—all well; *caranti*—pass time; *saumya*—O sober one.

TRANSLATION

O sober one, others, such as Hṛdīka, Cārudeṣṇa, Gada and the son of Satyabhāmā, who accept Lord Śrī Kṛṣṇa as the soul of the self and thus follow His path without deviation—are they well?

TEXT 36

अपि स्वदोर्भ्यां विजयाच्युताभ्यां
धर्मेण धर्मः परिपाति सेतुम् ।

दुर्योधनोऽतप्यत यत्सभायां
साम्राज्यलक्ष्म्या विजयानुवृत्त्या ॥३६॥

api sva-dorbhyāṁ vijayācyutābhyāṁ
dharmeṇa dharmaḥ paripāti setum
duryodhano 'tapyata yat-sabhāyāṁ
sāmrājya-lakṣmyā vijayānuvṛttyā

api—as also; *sva-dorbhyām*—own arms; *vijaya*—Arjuna; *acyutābhyām*—along with Śrī Kṛṣṇa; *dharmeṇa*—on religious principles; *dharmaḥ*—King Yudhiṣṭhira; *paripāti*—maintains; *setum*—the respect of religion; *duryodhanaḥ*—Duryodhana; *atapyata*—envied; *yat*—whose; *sabhāyām*—royal assembly; *sāmrājya*—imperial; *lakṣmyā*—opulence; *vijaya-anuvṛttyā*—by the service of Arjuna.

TRANSLATION

Also let me inquire whether Mahārāja Yudhiṣṭhira is now maintaining the kingdom according to religious principles and with respect for the path of religion. Formerly Duryodhana was burning with envy because Yudhiṣṭhira was being protected by the arms of Kṛṣṇa and Arjuna as if they were his own arms.

PURPORT

Mahārāja Yudhiṣṭhira was the emblem of religion. When he was ruling his kingdom with the help of Lord Kṛṣṇa and Arjuna, the opulence of his kingdom surpassed all imaginations of the opulence of the kingdom of heaven. His actual arms were Lord Kṛṣṇa and Arjuna, and thus he surpassed everyone's opulence. Duryodhana, being envious of this opulence, planned so many schemes to put Yudhiṣṭhira into difficulty, and at last the Battle of Kurukṣetra was brought about. After the Battle of Kurukṣetra, Mahārāja Yudhiṣṭhira was again able to rule his legitimate kingdom, and he reinstated the principles of honor and respect for religion. That is the beauty of a kingdom ruled by a pious king like Mahārāja Yudhiṣṭhira.

TEXT 37

किं वा कृताघेष्वघमत्यमर्षी
भीमोऽहिवद्दीर्घतमं व्यमुञ्चत् ।
यस्याङ्घ्रिपातं रणभूर्न सेहे
मार्गं गदायाश्चरतो विचित्रम् ॥३७॥

kiṁ vā kṛtāgheṣv agham atyamarṣī
bhīmo 'hivad dīrghatamaṁ vyamuñcat
yasyāṅghri-pātaṁ raṇa-bhūr na sehe
mārgaṁ gadāyāś carato vicitram

kim—whether; *vā*—either; *kṛta*—performed; *agheṣu*—unto the sinners; *agham*—angry; *ati-amarṣī*—unconquerable; *bhīmaḥ*—Bhīma; *ahi-vat*—like a cobra; *dīrgha-tamam*—long-cherished; *vyamuñcat*—has released; *yasya*—whose; *aṅghri-pātam*—putting on the steps; *raṇa-bhūḥ*—the field of battle; *na*—could not; *sehe*—tolerate; *mārgam*—the path; *gadāyāḥ*—by the clubs; *carataḥ*—playing; *vicitram*—wonderful.

TRANSLATION

[Please tell me] whether the unconquerable Bhīma, who is like a cobra, has released his long-cherished anger upon the sinners? The field of battle could not tolerate even the wonderful playing of his club when he stepped on the path.

PURPORT

Vidura knew the strength of Bhīma. Whenever Bhīma was on the battlefield, his steps on the path and the wonderful playing of his club were unbearable for the enemy. Powerful Bhīma did not take steps against the sons of Dhṛtarāṣṭra for a long time. Vidura's inquiry was whether he had yet released his anger, which was like that of a suffering cobra. When a cobra releases its venom after long-cherished anger, its victim cannot survive.

TEXT 38

कच्चिद्यशोधा रथयूथपानां
गाण्डीवधन्वोपरतारिरास्ते ।

अलक्षितो यच्छरकूटगूढो
मायाकिरातो गिरिशस्तुतोष ॥३८॥

kaccid yaśodhā ratha-yūthapānāṁ
gāṇḍīva-dhanvoparatārir āste
alakṣito yac-chara-kūṭa-gūḍho
māyā-kirāto giriśas tutoṣa

kaccit—whether; *yaśaḥ-dhā*—famous; *ratha-yūthapānām*—amongst the great chariot warriors; *gāṇḍīva*—Gāṇḍīva; *dhanva*—bow; *uparata-ariḥ*—one who has vanquished the enemies; *āste*—doing well; *alakṣitaḥ*—without being identified; *yat*—whose; *śara-kūṭa-gūḍhaḥ*—being covered by arrows; *māyā-kirātaḥ*—false hunter; *giriśaḥ*—Lord Śiva; *tutoṣa*—was satisfied.

TRANSLATION

[Please tell me] whether Arjuna, whose bow bears the name Gāṇḍīva and who is always famous amongst the chariot warriors for vanquishing his enemies, is doing well. He once satisfied Lord Śiva by covering him with arrows when Śiva came as an unidentified false hunter.

PURPORT

Lord Śiva tested Arjuna's strength by picking a quarrel with him over a hunted boar. He confronted Arjuna in the false dress of a hunter, and Arjuna covered him with arrows until Lord Śiva was satisfied with Arjuna's fighting. He offered Arjuna the Pāśupati weapon and blessed him. Here Vidura inquired about the great warrior's well-being.

TEXT 39

यमावुतस्वित्तनयौ पृथायाः
पार्थैर्वृतौ पक्ष्मभिरक्षिणीव ।
रेमात उद्दाय मृधे स्वरिक्थं
परात्सुपर्णाविव वज्रिवक्त्रात् ॥३९॥

yamāv utasvit tanayau pṛthāyāḥ
pārthair vṛtau pakṣmabhir akṣiṇīva
remāta uddāya mṛdhe sva-rikthaṁ
parāt suparṇāv iva vajri-vaktrāt

yamau—twins (Nakula and Sahadeva); *utasvit*—whether; *tanayau*—sons; *pṛthāyāḥ*—of Pṛthā; *pārthaiḥ*—by the sons of Pṛthā; *vṛtau*—protected; *pakṣmabhiḥ*—by shields; *akṣiṇī*—of the eyes; *iva*—like; *remāte*—playing carelessly; *uddāya*—snatching; *mṛdhe*—in the fight; *sva-riktham*—own property; *parāt*—from the enemy Duryodhana; *suparṇau*—Garuḍa, the carrier of Lord Viṣṇu; *iva*—like; *vajri-vaktrāt*—from the mouth of Indra.

TRANSLATION

Are the twin brothers who are protected by their brothers doing well? Just as the eye is always protected by the eyelid, they are protected by the sons of Pṛthā, who snatched back their rightful kingdom from the hands of their enemy Duryodhana, just as Garuḍa snatched nectar from the mouth of Indra, the thunderbolt carrier.

PURPORT

Indra, the King of heaven, carries a thunderbolt in his hand and is very strong, yet Garuḍa, the carrier of Lord Viṣṇu, was able to snatch nectar from his mouth. Similarly, Duryodhana was as strong as the King of heaven, and still the sons of Pṛthā, the Pāṇḍavas, were able to snatch away their kingdom from Duryodhana. Both Garuḍa and the Pārthas are pet devotees of the Lord, and thus it was possible for them to face such strong enemies.

Vidura's inquiry was about the youngest brothers of the Pāṇḍavas, namely Nakula and Sahadeva. These twin brothers were sons of Mādrī, the stepmother of the other Pāṇḍavas. But although they were stepbrothers, because Kuntī took charge of them after the departure of Mādrī with her husband Mahārāja Pāṇḍu, Nakula and Sahadeva were as good as the other three Pāṇḍavas, Yudhiṣṭhira, Bhīma and Arjuna. The five brothers are known in the world as regular brothers. The three elder

Pāṇḍavas took care of the younger brothers, just as the eyelid takes care of the eye. Vidura was anxious to know whether, after winning back their own kingdom from the hands of Duryodhana, the younger brothers were still living happily under the care of the elder brothers.

TEXT 40

अहो पृथापि ध्रियतेऽर्भकार्थे
राजर्षिवर्येण विनापि तेन ।
यस्त्वेकवीरोऽधिरथो विजिग्ये
धनुर्द्वितीयः ककुभश्चतस्रः ॥४०॥

aho pṛthāpi dhriyate 'rbhakārthe
rājarṣi-varyeṇa vināpi tena
yas tv eka-vīro 'dhiratho vijigye
dhanur dvitīyaḥ kakubhaś catasraḥ

aho—O my lord; *pṛthā*—Kuntī; *api*—also; *dhriyate*—bears her life; *arbhaka-arthe*—for the sake of fatherless children; *rājarṣi*—King Pāṇḍu; *varyeṇa*—the best; *vinā api*—without him; *tena*—him; *yaḥ*—one who; *tu*—but; *eka*—alone; *vīraḥ*—the warrior; *adhirathaḥ*—commander; *vijigye*—could conquer; *dhanuḥ*—the bow; *dvitīyaḥ*—the second; *kakubhaḥ*—directions; *catasraḥ*—four.

TRANSLATION

O my lord, is Pṛthā still living? She lived only for the sake of her fatherless children; otherwise it was impossible for her to live without King Pāṇḍu, who was the greatest commander and who alone conquered the four directions simply with the help of a second bow.

PURPORT

A faithful wife cannot live without her lord, the husband, and therefore all widows used to voluntarily embrace the burning fire which consumed the dead husband. This system was very common in India because all the wives were chaste and faithful to their husbands. Later on, with the advent of the age of Kali, the wives gradually began to be less adherent to their husbands, and the voluntary embrace of the fire by the widows became a thing of the past. Very recently the system was abolished, since the voluntary system had become a forcible social custom.

When Mahārāja Pāṇḍu died, both his wives, namely Kuntī and Mādrī, were prepared to embrace the fire, but Mādrī requested Kuntī to live for the sake of the younger children, the five Pāṇḍavas. This was agreed upon by Kuntī at the added request of Vyāsadeva. In spite of her great bereavement, Kuntī decided to live, not to enjoy life in the absence of her husband, but only to give protection to the children. This incident is referred to here by Vidura because he knew all the facts about his sister-in-law Kuntīdevī. It is understood that Mahārāja Pāṇḍu was a great warrior and that he alone, with the help of bow and arrow, could conquer the world's four directions. In the absence of such a husband, it was almost impossible for Kuntī to live on even as a widow, but she had to do it for the sake of the five children.

TEXT 41

सौम्यानुशोचे तमधःपतन्तं
भ्रात्रे परेताय विदुद्रुहे यः ।
निर्यापितो येन सुहृत्स्वपुर्या
अहं स्वपुत्रान् समनुव्रतेन ॥४१॥

saumyānuśoce tam adhaḥ-patantaṁ
bhrātre paretāya vidudruhe yaḥ
niryāpito yena suhṛt sva-puryā
ahaṁ sva-putrān samanuvratena

saumya—O gentle one; *anuśoce*—just lamenting; *tam*—him; *adhaḥ-patantam*—gliding down; *bhrātre*—on his brother's; *paretāya*—death; *vidudruhe*—revolted against; *yaḥ*—one who; *niryāpitaḥ*—driven out; *yena*—by whom; *suhṛt*—well-wisher; *sva-puryāḥ*—from his own house; *aham*—myself; *sva-putrān*—with his own sons; *samanu-vratena*—accepting the same line of action.

TRANSLATION

O gentle one, I simply lament for he [Dhṛtarāṣṭra] who rebelled against his brother after death. By him I was driven out of my own house, although I am his sincere well-wisher, because he accepted the line of action adopted by his own sons.

PURPORT

Vidura did not ask about the welfare of his elder brother because there was no chance of his well-being, only news of his gliding down to hell. Vidura was a sincere well-wisher for Dhṛtarāṣṭra, and he had a thought about him in the corner of his heart. He lamented that Dhṛtarāṣṭra could rebel against the sons of his dead brother Pāṇḍu and that he could drive him (Vidura) out of his own house on the dictation of his crooked sons. In spite of these actions, Vidura never became an enemy of Dhṛtarāṣṭra but continued to be his well-wisher, and at the last stage of Dhṛtarāṣṭra's life, it was Vidura only who proved to be his real friend. Such is the behavior of a Vaiṣṇava like Vidura: he desires all good, even for his enemies.

TEXT 42

सोऽहं हरेर्मर्त्यविडम्बनेन
दृशो नृणां चालयतो विधातुः ।
नान्योपलक्ष्यः पदवीं प्रसादा-
च्चरामि पश्यन् गतविस्मयोऽत्र ॥४२॥

so 'ham harer martya-viḍambanena
dṛśo nṛṇāṁ cālayato vidhātuḥ
nānyopalakṣyaḥ padavīṁ prasādāc
carāmi paśyan gata-vismayo 'tra

saḥ aham—therefore, I; *hareḥ*—of the Personality of Godhead; *martya*—in this mortal world; *viḍambanena*—without being recognized; *dṛśaḥ*—on sight; *nṛṇām*—of the people in general; *cālayataḥ*—bewildering; *vidhātuḥ*—in order to do it; *na*—not; *anya*—other; *upalakṣyaḥ*—seen by others; *padavīm*—glories; *prasādāt*—by the grace of; *carāmi*—do travel; *paśyan*—by seeing; *gata-vismayaḥ*—without doubt; *atra*—in this matter.

TRANSLATION

I am not astonished at this, having traveled over the world without being seen by others. The activities of the Personality of Godhead, which are like those of a man in this mortal world, are bewildering to others, but I know of His greatness by His grace, and thus I am happy in all respects.

PURPORT

Although he was the brother of Dhṛtarāṣṭra, Vidura was completely different. By the grace of Lord Kṛṣṇa, he was not foolish like his brother, and thus his brother's association could not influence him. Dhṛtarāṣṭra and his materialistic sons wanted to falsely lord it over the world by dint of their own strength. The Lord encouraged them in this, and thus they became more and more bewildered. But Vidura wanted to achieve sincere devotional service of the Lord and therefore became a soul absolutely surrendered to the Absolute Personality of Godhead. He could realize this in the progress of his pilgrim's journey, and thus he was freed from all doubts. He was not at all sorry to be bereft of his hearth and home because he now had experience that dependence on the mercy of the Lord is a greater freedom than so-called freedom at home. A person should not be in the renounced order of life unless he is firmly convinced of being protected by the Lord. This stage of life is explained in *Bhagavad-gītā* as *abhayaṁ sattva-saṁśuddhiḥ:* every living entity is factually completely dependent on the mercy of the Lord, but unless one is in the pure state of existence, he cannot be established in this position. This stage of dependence is called *sattva-saṁśuddhiḥ,* or purification of one's existence. The result of such purification is exhibited in fearlessness. A devotee of the Lord, who is called *nārāyaṇa-para,* is never afraid of anything because he is always aware of the fact that the Lord protects him in all circumstances. With this conviction, Vidura traveled alone, and he was not seen or recognized by any friend or foe. Thus he enjoyed freedom of life without obligation to the many duties of the world.

When Lord Śrī Kṛṣṇa was personally present in the mortal world in His eternal, blissful form of Śyāmasundara, those who were not pure devotees of the Lord could not recognize Him or know His glories. *Avajānānti māṁ mūḍhā mānuṣīṁ tanum āśritam* (Bg. 9.11): He is always bewildering to the nondevotees, but He is always seen by the devotees by dint of their pure devotional service to Him.

TEXT 43

नूनं नृपाणां त्रिमदोत्पथानां
महीं मुहुश्चालयतां चमूभिः ।
वधात्प्रपन्नार्तिजिहीर्षयेशो-
ऽप्युपैक्षताघं भगवान् कुरूणाम् ॥४३॥

nūnaṁ nṛpāṇāṁ tri-madotpathānāṁ
mahīṁ muhuś cālayatāṁ camūbhiḥ
vadhāt prapannārti-jihīrṣayeśo
'py upaikṣatāghaṁ bhagavān kurūṇām

nūnam—of course; *nṛpāṇām*—of the kings; *tri*—three; *mada-utpathānām*—going astray out of false pride; *mahīm*—earth; *muhuḥ*—constantly; *cālayatām*—agitating; *camūbhiḥ*—by movement of soldiers; *vadhāt*—from the act of killing; *prapanna*—surrendered; *ārti-jihīrṣaya*—willing to relieve the distress of the sufferers; *īśaḥ*—the Lord; *api*—in spite of; *upaikṣata*—waited; *agham*—offenses; *bhagavān*—the Supreme Lord; *kurūṇām*—of the Kurus.

TRANSLATION

Despite His being the Lord and being always willing to relieve the distress of sufferers, He [Kṛṣṇa] refrained from killing the Kurus, although they committed all sorts of sins and although He saw other kings constantly agitating the earth by their strong military movements carried out under the dictation of three kinds of false pride.

PURPORT

As declared in *Bhagavad-gītā*, the Lord appears in the mortal world to execute His much-needed mission of killing the miscreants and giving protection to the suffering faithful. In spite of that mission, Lord Kṛṣṇa tolerated the insult to Draupadī by the Kurus and the injustices perpetrated against the Pāṇḍavas, as well as insults to Himself. The question may be raised, "Why did He tolerate such injustices and insults in His presence? Why did He not chastise the Kurus immediately?" When Draupadī was insulted in the assembly by the Kurus by their attempt to see her naked in the presence of all, the Lord protected Draupadī by supplying an unlimited length of clothing. But He did not chastise the insulting party immediately. This silence of the Lord did not mean, however, that He excused the offenses of the Kurus. There were many other kings on earth who had become very proud of three kinds of possessions—wealth, education and followers—and they were constantly agitating the earth by movements of military strength. The Lord was just waiting to get them together on the Battlefield of Kurukṣetra and kill them all at one time, just to make a short-cut in His killing mission. Godless kings or heads of state, when puffed up by advancement of material wealth, education and increase of population, always make a show of military strength and give trouble to the innocent. When Lord Kṛṣṇa was personally present, there were many such kings all over the world, and He thus arranged for the Battle of Kurukṣetra. In His manifestation of *viśva-rūpa*, the Lord expressed His mission of killing as follows: "I have willingly descended on the earth in My capacity of inexorable Time in order to decrease the unwanted population. I shall finish all those who have assembled here except you, the Pāṇḍavas. This killing does not wait for you to take part in it. It is already arranged: all will be killed by Me. If you want to become famous as the hero of the battlefield and thus enjoy the booty of war, then, O Savyasācī, just become the immediate cause of this killing and thus take the credit. I have already killed all the great warriors—Bhīṣma, Droṇa, Jayadratha, Karṇa and many other great generals. Do not worry. Fight the battle and be famous as a great hero." (Bg. 11.32–34)

The Lord always wants to see His devotee as the hero of some episode which He Himself performs. He wanted to see His devotee and friend

Arjuna as the hero of the Battle of Kurukṣetra, and thus He waited for all the miscreants of the world to assemble. That, and nothing else, is the explanation of His waiting.

TEXT 44

अजस्य जन्मोत्पथनाशनाय
कर्माण्यकर्तुर्ग्रहणाय पुंसाम् ।
नन्वन्यथा कोऽर्हति देहयोगं
परो गुणानामुत कर्मतन्त्रम् ॥४४॥

ajasya janmotpatha-nāśanāya
karmāṇy akartur grahaṇāya puṁsām
nanv anyathā ko 'rhati deha-yogaṁ
paro guṇānām uta karma-tantram

ajasya—of the unborn; *janma*—appearance; *utpatha-nāśanāya*—for the sake of annihilating the upstarts; *karmāṇi*—works; *akartuḥ*—of one who has nothing to do; *grahaṇāya*—to take up; *puṁsām*—of all persons; *nanu anyathā*—otherwise; *kaḥ*—who; *arhati*—may deserve; *deha-yogam*—contact of the body; *paraḥ*—transcendental; *guṇānām*—of the three modes of nature; *uta*—what to speak of; *karma-tantram*—the law of action and reaction.

TRANSLATION

The appearance of the Lord is manifested for the annihilation of the upstarts. His activities are transcendental and are enacted for the understanding of all persons. Otherwise, since the Lord is transcendental to all material modes, what purpose could He serve by coming to earth?

PURPORT

Īśvaraḥ paramaḥ kṛṣṇaḥ sac-cid-ānanda-vigrahaḥ (*Brahma-saṁhitā* 5.1): the form of the Lord is eternal, blissful and all-knowing. His so-called birth is therefore an appearance only, like the birth of the sun on the horizon. His birth does not, like that of the living entities, take place under the influence of material nature and the bondage of the reactions of past deeds. His works and activities are independent pastimes and are not subject to the reactions of material nature. In *Bhagavad-gītā* (4.14) it is said:

na māṁ karmāṇi limpanti
na me karma-phale spṛhā
iti māṁ yo 'bhijānāti
karmabhir na sa badhyate

The law of *karma* enacted by the Supreme Lord for the living entities cannot be applicable to Him, nor has the Lord any desire to improve Himself by activities like those of ordinary living beings. Ordinary living beings work for the improvement of their conditional lives. But the Lord is already full of all opulence, all strength, all fame, all beauty, all knowledge and all renunciation. Why should He desire improvement? No one can excel Him in any opulence, and therefore the desire for improvement is absolutely useless for Him. One should always discriminate between the activities of the Lord and those of ordinary living beings. Thus one may come to the right conclusion regarding the Lord's transcendental position. One who can come to the conclusion of the Lord's transcendence can become a devotee of the Lord and can at once be free from all reactions of past deeds. It is said, *karmāṇi nirdahati kintu ca bhakti-bhājām:* the Lord minimizes or nullifies the reactionary influence of the devotee's past deeds. (*Brahma-saṁhitā* 5.54)

The activities of the Lord are to be accepted and relished by all living entities. His activities are to attract the ordinary man towards the Lord. The Lord always acts in favor of the devotees, and therefore ordinary men who are fruitive actors or seekers of salvation may be attracted to the Lord when He acts as protector of the devotees. The fruitive actors can attain their goals by devotional service, and the salvationists can also attain their goal in life by devotional service to the Lord. The devotees do not want the fruitive results of their work, nor do they want any kind of salvation. They relish the glorious superhuman activities of the Lord, such as His lifting Govardhana Hill and His killing the demon Pūtanā in infancy. His activities are enacted to attract all kinds of men—*karmīs*, *jñānīs* and *bhaktas*. Because He is transcendental to all laws of *karma*, there is no possibility of His accepting a form of *māyā* as is forced on the ordinary living entities who are bound by the actions and reactions of their own deeds.

The secondary purpose of His appearance is to annihilate the upstart *asuras* and to stop the nonsense of atheistic propaganda by less intelligent persons. By the Lord's causeless mercy, the *asuras* who are killed personally by the Personality of Godhead get salvation. The meaningful appearance of the Lord is always distinct from ordinary birth. Even the pure devotees have no connection with the material body, and certainly the Lord, who appears as He is, in His *sac-cid-ānanda* form, is not limited by a material form.

TEXT 45

तस्य प्रपन्नाखिललोकपाना-
मवस्थितानामनुशासने स्वे ।
अर्थाय जातस्य यदुष्वजस्य
वार्तां सखे कीर्तय तीर्थकीर्तेः ॥४५॥

tasya prapannākhila-lokapānām
avasthitānām anuśāsane sve
arthāya jātasya yaduṣv ajasya
vārtāṁ sakhe kīrtaya tīrtha-kīrteḥ

tasya—His; *prapanna*—surrendered; *akhila-loka-pānām*—all rulers of the entire universe; *avasthitānām*—situated in; *anuśāsane*—under the control of; *sve*—own self; *arthāya*—for the interest of; *jātasya*—of the born; *yaduṣu*—in the family of the Yadus; *ajasya*—of the unborn; *vārtām*—topics; *sakhe*—O my friend; *kīrtaya*—please narrate; *tīrtha-kīrteḥ*—of the Lord, whose glories are chanted in the places of pilgrimage.

TRANSLATION

O my friend, please, therefore, chant the glories of the Lord, who is meant to be glorified in the places of pilgrimage. He is unborn, and yet He appears by His causeless mercy upon the

surrendered rulers of all parts of the universe. Only for their interest did He appear in the family of His unalloyed devotees the Yadus.

PURPORT

There are innumerable rulers all over the universe in different varieties of planets: the sun-god in the sun planet, the moon-god in the moon planet, Indra in the heavenly planet, Vāyu, Varuṇa, and those in the Brahmaloka planet, where Lord Brahmā is living. All are obedient servants of the Lord. Whenever there is any trouble in the administration of the innumerable planets in different universes, the rulers pray for an appearance, and the Lord appears. The *Bhāgavatam* (1.3.28) has already confirmed this in the following verse:

ete cāṁśa-kalāḥ puṁsaḥ
kṛṣṇas tu bhagavān svayam
indrāri-vyākulaṁ lokaṁ
mṛḍayanti yuge yuge

In every millennium, whenever there is any trouble for the obedient rulers, the Lord appears. He also appears for the sake of His pure unalloyed devotees. The surrendered rulers and the pure devotees are always strictly under the control of the Lord, and they are never disobedient to the desires of the Lord. The Lord is therefore always attentive to them.

The purpose of pilgrimages is to remember the Lord constantly, and therefore the Lord is known as *tīrtha-kīrti.* The purpose of going to a place of pilgrimage is to get the chance to glorify the Lord. Even today, although times have changed, there are still pilgrimage sites in India. For example, in Mathurā and Vṛndāvana, where we had a chance to stay, people are awake from early in the morning at 4 A.M. up until nighttime and are constantly engaged, some way or other, in chanting the holy glories of the Lord. The beauty of such a pilgrimage site is that automatically one remembers the holy glories of the Lord. His name, fame, quality, form, pastimes and entourage are all identical to the Lord, and therefore chanting the glories of the Lord invokes the personal presence of the Lord. Anytime or anywhere pure devotees meet and chant the glories of the Lord, the Lord is present without any doubt. It is said by the Lord Himself that He always stays where His pure devotees chant His glories.

Thus end the Bhaktivedanta purports of the Third Canto, First Chapter, of the Śrīmad-Bhāgavatam, *entitled "Questions by Vidura."*

CHAPTER TWO

Remembrance of Lord Kṛṣṇa

TEXT 1

श्रीशुक उवाच

इति भागवतः पृष्टः क्षत्त्रा वार्तां प्रियाश्रयाम् ।
प्रतिवक्तुं न चोत्सेह औत्कण्ठ्यात्स्मारितेश्वरः ॥ १ ॥

śrī-śuka uvāca
iti bhāgavataḥ pṛṣṭaḥ
kṣattrā vārtāṁ priyāśrayām
prativaktuṁ na cotseha
autkaṇṭhyāt smāriteśvaraḥ

śrī-śukaḥ uvāca—Śrī Śukadeva said; *iti*—thus; *bhāgavataḥ*—the great devotee; *pṛṣṭaḥ*—being asked; *kṣattrā*—by Vidura; *vārtām*—message; *priya-āśrayām*—regarding the dearest; *prativaktum*—to reply; *na*—not; *ca*—also; *utsehe*—became eager; *autkaṇṭhyāt*—by excessive anxiety; *smārita*—remembrance; *īśvaraḥ*—the Lord.

TRANSLATION

Śrī Śukadeva Gosvāmī said: When the great devotee Uddhava was asked by Vidura to speak on the messages of the dearest [Lord Kṛṣṇa], Uddhava was unable to answer immediately due to excessive anxiety at the remembrance of the Lord.

TEXT 2

यः पञ्चहायनो मात्रा प्रातराशाय याचितः ।
तन्नैच्छद्रचयन् यस्य सपर्यां बाललीलया ॥ २ ॥

yaḥ pañca-hāyano mātrā
prātar-āśāya yācitaḥ
tan naicchad racayan yasya
saparyāṁ bāla-līlayā

yaḥ—one who; *pañca*—five; *hāyanaḥ*—years old; *mātrā*—by his mother; *prātaḥ-āśāya*—for breakfast; *yācitaḥ*—called for; *tat*—that; *na*—not; *aicchat*—liked; *racayan*—playing; *yasya*—whose; *saparyām*—service; *bāla-līlayā*—childhood.

TRANSLATION

He was one who even in his childhood, at the age of five years, was so absorbed in the service of Lord Kṛṣṇa that when he was called by his mother for morning breakfast, he did not wish to have it.

PURPORT

From his very birth, Uddhava was a natural devotee of Lord Kṛṣṇa, or a *nitya-siddha*, a liberated soul. From natural instinct he used to serve Lord Kṛṣṇa, even in his childhood. He used to play with dolls in the form of Kṛṣṇa, he would serve the dolls by dressing, feeding and worshiping them, and thus he was constantly absorbed in the play of transcendental realization. These are the signs of an eternally liberated soul. An eternally liberated soul is a devotee of the Lord who never forgets Him. Human life is meant for reviving one's eternal relation with the Lord, and all religious injunctions are meant for awakening this dormant instinct of the living entity. The sooner this awakening is brought about, the quicker the mission of human life is fulfilled. In a good family of devotees, the child gets the opportunity to serve the Lord in many ways. A soul who is already advanced in devotional service has the opportunity to take birth in such an enlightened family. This is confirmed in the *Bhagavad-gītā* (6.41). *Śucīnāṁ śrīmatāṁ gehe yoga-bhraṣṭo 'bhijāyate:* even the fallen devotee gets the opportunity to take his birth in the family of a well-situated *brāhmaṇa* or in a rich, well-to-do mercantile family. In both these families there is a good opportunity to revive one's sense of God consciousness automatically because particularly in these families the worship of Lord Kṛṣṇa is regularly performed and the child gets the opportunity to imitate the process of worship called *arcanā.*

The *pāñcarātrikī* formula for training persons in devotional service is temple worship, whereby the neophytes get the opportunity to learn devotional service to the Lord. Mahārāja Parīkṣit also used to play with Kṛṣṇa dolls in his childhood. In India the children in good families are still given dolls of the Lord like Rāma and Kṛṣṇa, or sometimes the demigods, so that they may develop the aptitude of service to the Lord. By the grace of the Lord we were given the same opportunity by our parents, and the beginning of our life was based on this principle.

TEXT 3

स कथं सेवया तस्य कालेन जरसं गतः ।
पृष्टो वार्तां प्रतिब्रूयाद्भर्तुः पादावनुस्मरन् ॥ ३ ॥

sa kathaṁ sevayā tasya
kālena jarasaṁ gataḥ
pṛṣṭo vārtāṁ pratibrūyād
bhartuḥ pādāv anusmaran

saḥ—Uddhava; *katham*—how; *sevayā*—by such service; *tasya*—his; *kālena*—in course of time; *jarasam*—invalidity; *gataḥ*—undergone; *pṛṣṭaḥ*—asked for; *vārtām*—message; *pratibrūyāt*—just to reply; *bhartuḥ*—of the Lord; *pādau*—His lotus feet; *anusmaran*—remembering.

TRANSLATION

Uddhava thus served the Lord continually from childhood, and in his old age that attitude of service never slackened. As soon as he was asked about the message of the Lord, he at once remembered all about Him.

PURPORT

Transcendental service to the Lord is not mundane. The service attitude of the devotee gradually increases and never becomes slackened.

Generally, in old age a person is allowed retirement from mundane service. But in the transcendental service of the Lord there is no retirement at all; on the contrary, the service attitude increases more and more with the progress of age. In the transcendental service there is no satiation, and therefore there is no retirement. Materially, when a man becomes tired by rendering service in his physical body, he is allowed retirement, but in the transcendental service there is no feeling of fatigue because it is spiritual service and is not on the bodily plane. Service on the bodily plane dwindles as the body grows older, but the spirit is never old, and therefore on the spiritual plane the service is never tiresome.

Uddhava undoubtedly became old, but that does not mean that his spirit became old. His service attitude matured on the transcendental plane, and therefore as soon as he was questioned by Vidura about Lord Kṛṣṇa, he at once remembered his Lord by reference to the context and forgot himself on the physical plane. That is the sign of pure devotional service to the Lord, as will be explained later on (*lakṣaṇaṁ bhakti-yogasya*, etc.) in Lord Kapila's instructions to His mother, Devahūti.

TEXT 4

स मुहूर्तमभूत्तूष्णीं कृष्णाङ्घ्रिसुधया भृशम् ।
तीव्रेण भक्तियोगेन निमग्नः साधु निर्वृतः ॥ ४ ॥

sa muhūrtam abhūt tūṣṇīṁ
kṛṣṇāṅghri-sudhayā bhṛśam
tīvreṇa bhakti-yogena
nimagnaḥ sādhu nirvṛtaḥ

saḥ—Uddhava; *muhūrtam*—for a moment; *abhūt*—became; *tūṣṇīm*—dead silent; *kṛṣṇa-aṅghri*—the lotus feet of the Lord; *sudhayā*—by the nectar; *bhṛśam*—well matured; *tīvreṇa*—by very strong; *bhakti-yogena*—devotional service; *nimagnaḥ*—absorbed in; *sādhu*—good; *nirvṛtaḥ*—fully in love.

TRANSLATION

For a moment he remained dead silent, and his body did not move. He became absorbed in the nectar of remembering the

Lord's lotus feet in devotional ecstasy, and he appeared to be going increasingly deeper into that ecstasy.

PURPORT

On the inquiry by Vidura about Kṛṣṇa, Uddhava appeared to be awakened from slumber. He appeared to regret that he had forgotten the lotus feet of the Lord. Thus he again remembered the lotus feet of the Lord and remembered all his transcendental loving service unto Him, and by so doing he felt the same ecstasy that he used to feel in the presence of the Lord. Because the Lord is absolute, there is no difference between His remembrance and His personal presence. Thus Uddhava remained completely silent for a moment, but then he appeared to be going deeper and deeper into ecstasy. Feelings of ecstasy are displayed by highly advanced devotees of the Lord. There are eight kinds of transcendental changes in the body—tears, shivering of the body, perspiration, restlessness, throbbing, choking of the throat, etc.—and all were manifested by Uddhava in the presence of Vidura.

TEXT 5

पुलकोद्भिन्नसर्वाङ्गो मुञ्चन्मीलद्दृशा शुचः ।
पूर्णार्थो लक्षितस्तेन स्नेहप्रसरसंप्लुतः ॥ ५ ॥

pulakodbhinna-sarvāṅgo
muñcan mīlad-dṛśā śucaḥ
pūrṇārtho lakṣitas tena
sneha-prasara-samplutaḥ

pulaka-udbhinna—bodily changes of transcendental ecstasy; *sarva-aṅgaḥ*—every part of the body; *muñcan*—smearing; *mīlat*—opening; *dṛśā*—by the eyes; *śucaḥ*—tears of grief; *pūrṇa-arthaḥ*—complete achievement; *lakṣitaḥ*—thus observed; *tena*—by Vidura; *sneha-prasara*—extensive love; *samplutaḥ*—thoroughly assimilated.

TRANSLATION

It was so observed by Vidura that Uddhava had all the transcendental bodily changes due to total ecstasy, and he was trying to

wipe away tears of separation from his eyes. Thus Vidura could understand that Uddhava had completely assimilated extensive love for the Lord.

PURPORT

The symptoms of the highest order of devotional life were observed by Vidura, an experienced devotee of the Lord, and he confirmed Uddhava's perfectional stage of love of Godhead. Ecstatic bodily changes are manifested from the spiritual plane and are not artificial expressions developed by practice. There are three different stages of development in devotional service. The first stage is that of following the regulative principles prescribed in the codes of devotional service, the second stage is that of assimilation and realization of the steady condition of devotional service, and the last stage is that of ecstasy symptomized by transcendental bodily expression. The nine different modes of devotional service, such as hearing, chanting and remembering, are the beginning of the process. By regular hearing of the glories and pastimes of the Lord, the impurities in the student's heart begin to be washed off. The more one is cleansed of impurities, the more one becomes fixed in devotional service. Gradually the activities take the forms of steadiness, firm faith, taste, realization and assimilation, one after another. These different stages of gradual development increase love of God to the highest stage, and in the highest stage there are still more symptoms, such as affection, anger and attachment, gradually rising in exceptional cases to the *mahā-bhāva* stage, which is generally not possible for the living entities. All these were manifested by Lord Śrī Caitanya Mahāprabhu, the personification of love of God.

In the *Bhakti-rasāmṛta-sindhu* by Śrīla Rūpa Gosvāmī, the chief disciple of Lord Śrī Caitanya Mahāprabhu, these transcendental symptoms displayed by pure devotees like Uddhava are systematically described. We have written a summary study of *Bhakti-rasāmṛta-sindhu* entitled *The Nectar of Devotion*, and one may consult this book for more detailed information on the science of devotional service.

TEXT 6

शनकैर्भगवल्लोकान्नृलोकं पुनरागतः ।
विमृज्य नेत्रे विदुरं प्रीत्याहोद्धव उत्स्मयन् ॥ ६ ॥

śanakair bhagaval-lokān
nṛlokaṁ punar āgataḥ
vimṛjya netre viduraṁ
prītyāhoddhava utsmayan

śanakaiḥ—gradually; *bhagavat*—the Lord; *lokāt*—from the abode; *nṛlokam*—the planet of the human beings; *punaḥ āgataḥ*—coming again; *vimṛjya*—wiping; *netre*—eyes; *viduram*—unto Vidura; *prītyā*—in affection; *āha*—said; *uddhavaḥ*—Uddhava; *utsmayan*—by all those remembrances.

TRANSLATION

The great devotee Uddhava soon came back from the abode of the Lord to the human plane, and wiping his eyes, he awakened his reminiscence of the past and spoke to Vidura in a pleasing mood.

PURPORT

When Uddhava was fully absorbed in the transcendental ecstasy of love of God, he actually forgot all about the external world. The pure devotee lives constantly in the abode of the Supreme Lord, even in the present body, which apparently belongs to this world. The pure devotee is not exactly on the bodily plane, since he is absorbed in the transcendental thought of the Supreme. When Uddhava wanted to speak to Vidura, he came down from the abode of the Lord, Dvārakā, to the material plane of human beings. Even though a pure devotee is present on this mortal planet, he is here in relation to the Lord for engagement in transcendental loving service, and not for any material cause. A living entity can live either on the material plane or in the transcendental abode of the Lord, in accordance with his existential condition. The conditional changes of the living entity are explained in the *Caitanya-caritāmṛta* in the instructions given to Śrīla Rūpa Gosvāmī by Lord Śrī Caitanya: "The living entities all over the universes are enjoying the effects of the respective fruitive results of their own work, life after life. Out of all of them, some may be influenced by the association of pure devotees and thus get the chance to execute devotional service by attainment of taste. This taste is the seed of devotional service, and one who is fortunate enough to have received such a seed is advised to sow it in the core of his heart. As one cultivates a seed by pouring water to fructify it, the seed of devotional service sown in the heart of the devotee may be cultured by pouring water in the form of hearing and chanting of the holy name and pastimes of the Lord. The creeper of devotional service, so nourished, gradually grows, and the devotee, acting as a gardener, goes on pouring the water of constant hearing and chanting. The creeper of devotional service gradually grows so high that it passes through the entire material universe and enters into the spiritual sky, growing still higher and higher until it reaches the planet Goloka Vṛndāvana. The devotee-gardener is in touch with the abode of the Lord even from the material plane by dint of performing devotional service to the Lord simply by hearing and chanting. As a creeper takes shelter of another, stronger tree, similarly the creeper of devotional service, nourished by the devotee, takes shelter of the lotus feet of the Lord and thus becomes fixed. When the creeper is fixed, then the fruit of the creeper comes into existence, and the gardener who nourished it is able to enjoy this fruit of love, and his life becomes successful." That Uddhava attained this stage is evident from his dealings. He could simultaneously reach the supreme planet and still appear in this world.

TEXT 7

उद्धव उवाच

कृष्णद्युमणिनिम्लोचे गीर्णेष्वजगरेण ह ।
किं नु नः कुशलं ब्रूयां गतश्रीषु गृहेष्वहम् ॥ ७ ॥

uddhava uvāca
kṛṣṇa-dyumaṇi nimloce
gīrṇeṣv ajagareṇa ha
kiṁ nu naḥ kuśalaṁ brūyāṁ
gata-śrīṣu gṛheṣv aham

uddhavaḥ uvāca—Śrī Uddhava said; *kṛṣṇa-dyumaṇi*—the Kṛṣṇa sun; *nimloce*—having set; *gīrṇeṣu*—being swallowed; *ajagareṇa*—by the great snake; *ha*—in the past; *kim*—what; *nu*—else; *naḥ*—our; *kuśalam*—welfare; *brūyām*—may I say; *gata*—gone away; *śrīṣu gṛheṣu*—in the house; *aham*—I.

TRANSLATION

Śrī Uddhava said: My dear Vidura, the sun of the world, Lord Kṛṣṇa, has set, and our house has now been swallowed by the great snake of time. What can I say to you about our welfare?

PURPORT

The disappearance of the Kṛṣṇa sun may be explained as follows, according to the commentary of Śrīla Viśvanātha Cakravartī Ṭhākura. Vidura was struck with great sorrow when he got the hint of the annihilation of the great Yadu dynasty as well as of his own family, the Kuru dynasty. Uddhava could understand the grief of Vidura, and therefore he first of all wanted to sympathize with him by saying that after the sunset everyone is in darkness. Since the entire world was merged in the darkness of grief, neither Vidura nor Uddhava nor anyone else could be happy. Uddhava was as much aggrieved as Vidura, and there was nothing further to be said about their welfare.

The comparison of Kṛṣṇa to the sun is very appropriate. As soon as the sun sets, darkness automatically appears. But the darkness experienced by the common man does not affect the sun itself either at the time of sunrise or of sunset. Lord Kṛṣṇa's appearance and disappearance are exactly like that of the sun. He appears and disappears in innumerable universes, and as long as He is present in a particular universe there is all transcendental light in that universe, but the universe from which He passes away is put into darkness. His pastimes, however, are everlasting. The Lord is always present in some universe, just as the sun is present in either the eastern or the western hemisphere. The sun is always present either in India or in America, but when the sun is present in India, the American land is in darkness, and when the sun is present in America, the Indian hemisphere is in darkness.

As the sun appears in the morning and gradually rises to the meridian and then again sets in one hemisphere while simultaneously rising in the other, so Lord Kṛṣṇa's disappearance in one universe and the beginning of His different pastimes in another take place simultaneously. As soon as one pastime is finished here, it is manifested in another universe. And thus His *nitya-līlā*, or eternal pastimes, are going on without ending. As the sunrise takes place once in twenty-four hours, similarly the pastimes of Lord Kṛṣṇa take place in a universe once in a daytime of Brahmā, the account of which is given in the *Bhagavad-gītā* as 4,300,000,000 solar years. But wherever the Lord is present, all His different pastimes as described in the revealed scriptures take place at regular intervals.

As at sunset the snakes become powerful, thieves are encouraged, ghosts become active, the lotus becomes disfigured and the *cakravākī* laments, so with the disappearance of Lord Kṛṣṇa, the atheists feel enlivened, and the devotees become sorry.

TEXT 8

दुर्भगो बत लोकोऽयं यदवो नितरामपि ।
ये संवसन्तो न विदुर्हरिं मीना इवोडुपम् ॥ ८ ॥

durbhago bata loko 'yaṁ
yadavo nitarām api
ye saṁvasanto na vidur
hariṁ mīnā ivoḍupam

durbhagaḥ—unfortunate; *bata*—certainly; *lokaḥ*—universe; *ayam*—this; *yadavaḥ*—the Yadu dynasty; *nitarām*—more specifically; *api*—also; *ye*—those; *saṁvasantaḥ*—living together; *na*—did not; *viduḥ*—understand; *harim*—the Personality of Godhead; *mīnāḥ*—the fishes; *iva uḍupam*—like the moon.

TRANSLATION

This universe with all its planets is most unfortunate. And even more unfortunate are the members of the Yadu dynasty because they could not identify Lord Hari as the Personality of Godhead, any more than the fish could identify the moon.

PURPORT

Uddhava lamented for the unfortunate persons of the world who could not recognize Lord Śrī Kṛṣṇa in spite of seeing all His transcendental godly qualities. From the very beginning of His appearance within the prison bars of King Kaṁsa up to His *mausala-līlā*, although He exhibited His potencies as the Personality of Godhead in the six opulences of wealth, strength, fame, beauty, knowledge and renunciation, the foolish persons of the world could not understand that He was the Supreme Lord. Foolish persons might have thought Him an extraordinary historic figure because they had no intimate touch with the Lord, but more unfortunate were the family members of the Lord, the members of the Yadu dynasty, who were always in company with the Lord but were unable to recognize Him as the Supreme Personality of Godhead. Uddhava lamented his own fortune also because although he knew Kṛṣṇa to be the Supreme Personality of Godhead, he could not properly use the opportunity to render devotional service to the Lord. He regretted everyone's misfortune, including his own. The pure devotee of the Lord thinks himself most unfortunate. That is due to excessive love for the Lord and is one of the transcendental perceptions of *viraha*, the suffering of separation.

It is learned from the revealed scriptures that the moon was born from the milk ocean. There is a milk ocean in the upper planets, and there Lord Viṣṇu, who controls the heart of every living being as Paramātmā (the Supersoul), resides as the Kṣīrodakaśāyī Viṣṇu. Those who do not believe in the existence of the ocean of milk because they have experience only of the salty water in the ocean should know that the world is also called the *go*, which means the cow. The urine of a cow is salty, and according to Āyur-vedic medicine the cow's urine is very effective in treating patients suffering from liver trouble. Such patients may not have any experience of the cow's milk because milk is never given to liver patients. But the liver patient may know that the cow has milk also, although he has never tasted it. Similarly, men who have experience only of this tiny planet where the saltwater ocean exists may take information from the revealed scriptures that there is also an ocean of milk, although we have never seen it. From this ocean of milk the moon was born, but the fish in the milk ocean could not recognize that the moon was not another fish and was different from them. The fish took the moon to be one of them or maybe something illuminating, but nothing more. The unfortunate persons who do not recognize Lord Kṛṣṇa are like such fish. They take Him to be one of them, although a little extraordinary in opulence, strength, etc. The *Bhagavad-gītā* (9.11) confirms such foolish persons to be most unfortunate: *avajānanti māṁ mūḍhā mānuṣīṁ tanum āśritam.*

TEXT 9

इङ्गितज्ञाः पुरुप्रौढा एकारामाश्च सात्वताः ।
सात्वतामृषभं सर्वे भूतावासममंसत ॥ ९ ॥

iṅgita-jñāḥ puru-prauḍhā
ekārāmāś ca sātvatāḥ
sātvatām ṛṣabhaṁ sarve
bhūtāvāsam amaṁsata

iṅgita-jñāḥ—expert in psychic study; *puru-prauḍhāḥ*—highly experienced; *eka*—one; *ārāmāḥ*—relaxation; *ca*—also; *sātvatāḥ*—devotees, or own men; *sātvatām ṛṣabham*—head of the family; *sarve*—all; *bhūta-āvāsam*—all-pervading; *amaṁsata*—could think.

TRANSLATION

The Yadus were all experienced devotees, learned and expert in psychic study. Over and above this, they were always with the Lord in all kinds of relaxations, and still they were only able to know Him as the one Supreme who dwells everywhere.

PURPORT

In the *Vedas* it is said that the Supreme Lord or the Paramātmā cannot be understood simply by the strength of one's erudition or power of mental speculation: *nāyam ātmā pravacanena labhyo na medhayā na bahunā śrutena* (*Kaṭha Upaniṣad* 1.2.23). He can be known only by one who has the mercy of the Lord. The Yādavas were all exceptionally learned and experienced, but in spite of their knowing the Lord as the one who lives in everyone's heart, they could not understand that He is the original Personality of Godhead. This lack of knowledge was not due to their insufficient erudition; it was due to their misfortune. In Vṛndāvana, however, the Lord was not even known as the Paramātmā because the residents of Vṛndāvana were pure unconventional devotees of the Lord and could think of Him only as their object of love. They did not know that He is the Personality of Godhead. The Yadus, or the residents of Dvārakā, however, could know Lord Kṛṣṇa as Vāsudeva, or the Supersoul living everywhere, but not as the Supreme Lord. As scholars of the *Vedas*, they verified the Vedic hymns: *eko devaḥ . . . sarva-bhūtādhivāsaḥ . . . antaryāmī . . .* and *vṛṣṇīnāṁ para-devatā. . . .* The Yadus, therefore, accepted Lord Kṛṣṇa as the Supersoul incarnated in their family, and not more than that.

TEXT 10

देवस्य मायया स्पृष्टा ये चान्यदसदाश्रिताः ।
भ्राम्यते धीर्न तद्वाक्यैरात्मन्युप्तात्मनो हरौ ॥१०॥

devasya māyayā spṛṣṭā
ye cānyad asad-āśritāḥ
bhrāmyate dhīr na tad-vākyair
ātmany uptātmano harau

devasya—of the Personality of Godhead; *māyayā*—by the influence of external energy; *spṛṣṭāḥ*—infected; *ye*—all those; *ca*—and; *anyat*—others; *asat*—illusory; *āśritāḥ*—being taken to; *bhrāmyate*—bewilder; *dhīḥ*—intelligence; *na*—not; *tat*—of them; *vākyaiḥ*—by those words; *ātmani*—in the Supreme Self; *upta-ātmanaḥ*—surrendered souls; *harau*—unto the Lord.

TRANSLATION

Under no circumstances can the words of persons bewildered by the illusory energy of the Lord deviate the intelligence of those who are completely surrendered souls.

PURPORT

Lord Śrī Kṛṣṇa is the Supreme Personality of Godhead according to all the evidences of the *Vedas*. He is accepted by all *ācāryas*, including Śrīpāda Śaṅkarācārya. But when He was present in the world, different classes of men accepted Him differently, and therefore their calculations of the Lord were also different. Generally, persons who had faith in the revealed scriptures accepted the Lord as He is, and all of them merged into great bereavement when the Lord disappeared from the world. In the First Canto we have already discussed the lamentation of Arjuna and Yudhiṣṭhira, to whom the disappearance of Lord Kṛṣṇa was almost intolerable up to the end of their lives.

The Yādavas were only partially cognizant of the Lord, but they are also glorious because they had the opportunity to associate with the Lord, who acted as the head of their family, and they also rendered the Lord intimate service. The Yādavas and other devotees of the Lord are different from those who wrongly calculated Him to be an ordinary human personality. Such persons are certainly bewildered by the illusory energy. They are hellish and are envious of the Supreme Lord. The illusory energy acts very powerfully on them because in spite of their elevated mundane education, such persons are faithless and are infected by the mentality of atheism. They are always very eager to establish that Lord Kṛṣṇa was an ordinary man who was killed by a hunter due to His many impious acts in plotting to kill the sons of Dhṛtarāṣṭra and Jarāsandha, the demoniac kings of the earth. Such persons have no faith in the statement of the *Bhagavad-gītā* that the Lord is unaffected by the reactions of work: *na māṁ karmāṇi limpanti.* According to the atheistic point of view, Lord Kṛṣṇa's family, the Yadu dynasty, was vanquished due to being cursed by the *brāhmaṇas* for the sins committed by Kṛṣṇa in killing the sons of Dhṛtarāṣṭra, etc. All these blasphemies do not touch the heart of the devotees of the Lord because they know perfectly well what is what. Their intelligence regarding the Lord is never disturbed. But those who are disturbed by the statements of the *asuras* are also condemned. That is what Uddhava meant in this verse.

TEXT 11

प्रदर्श्यातप्ततपसामवितृप्तदृशां नृणाम् ।
आदायान्तरधाद्यस्तु स्वबिम्बं लोकलोचनम् ॥११॥

pradarśyātapta-tapasām
avitṛpta-dṛśāṁ nṛṇām
ādāyāntar adhād yas tu
sva-bimbaṁ loka-locanam

pradarśya—by exhibiting; *atapta*—without undergoing; *tapasām*—penances; *avitṛpta-dṛśām*—without fulfillment of vision; *nṛṇām*—of persons; *ādāya*—taking; *antaḥ*—disappearance; *adhāt*—performed;

yaḥ—He who; *tu*—but; *sva-bimbam*—His own form; *loka-locanam*—public vision.

TRANSLATION

Lord Śrī Kṛṣṇa, who manifested His eternal form before the vision of all on the earth, performed His disappearance by removing His form from the sight of those who were unable to see Him [as He is] due to not executing required penance.

PURPORT

In this verse the word *avitṛpta-dṛśām* is most significant. The conditioned souls in the material world are all trying to satisfy their senses in various ways, but they have failed to do so because it is impossible to be satisfied by such efforts. The example of the fish on land is very appropriate. If one takes a fish from the water and puts in on the land, it cannot be made happy by any amount of offered pleasure. The spirit soul can be happy only in the association of the supreme living being, the Personality of Godhead, and nowhere else. The Lord, by His unlimited causeless mercy, has innumerable Vaikuṇṭha planets in the *brahmajyoti* sphere of the spiritual world, and in that transcendental world there is an unlimited arrangement for the unlimited pleasure of the living entities.

The Lord Himself comes to display His transcendental pastimes, typically represented at Vṛndāvana, Mathurā and Dvārakā. He appears just to attract the conditioned souls back to Godhead, back home to the eternal world. But for want of sufficient piety, the onlookers are not attracted by such pastimes of the Lord. In *Bhagavad-gītā* it is said that only those who have completely surpassed the way of sinful reaction can engage themselves in the transcendental loving service of the Lord. The entire Vedic way of ritualistic performances is to put every conditioned soul on the path of piety. By strict adherence to the prescribed principles for all orders of social life, one can attain the qualities of truthfulness, control of the mind, control of the senses, forbearance, etc., and can be elevated to the plane of rendering pure devotional service to the Lord. Only by such a transcendental vision are one's material hankerings fully satisfied.

When the Lord was present, persons who were able to satisfy their material hankerings by seeing Him in true perspective were thus able to go back with Him to His kingdom. But those persons who were unable to see the Lord as He is remained attached to material hankerings and were not able to go back home, back to Godhead. When the Lord passed beyond the vision of all, He did so in His original eternal form, as stated in this verse. The Lord left in His own body; He did not leave His body as is generally misunderstood by the conditioned souls. This statement defeats the false propaganda of the faithless nondevotees that the Lord passed away like an ordinary conditioned soul. The Lord appeared in order to release the world from the undue burden of the nonbelieving *asuras*, and after doing this, He disappeared from the world's eyes.

TEXT 12

यन्मर्त्यलीलौपयिकं स्वयोग-
मायाबलं दर्शयता गृहीतम् ।
विस्मापनं स्वस्य च सौभगर्द्धेः
परं पदं भूषणभूषणाङ्गम् ॥१२॥

yan martya-līlaupayikaṁ sva-yoga-
māyā-balaṁ darśayatā gṛhītam
vismāpanaṁ svasya ca saubhagarddheḥ
paraṁ padaṁ bhūṣaṇa-bhūṣaṇāṅgam

yat—His eternal form which; *martya*—mortal world; *līlā-upayikam*—just suitable for the pastimes; *sva-yoga-māyā-balam*—potency of the internal energy; *darśayatā*—for manifestation; *gṛhītam*—discovered; *vismāpanam*—wonderful; *svasya*—of His own; *ca*—and; *saubhaga-ṛddheḥ*—of the opulent; *param*—supreme; *padam*—ultimate stand; *bhūṣaṇa*—ornament; *bhūṣaṇa-aṅgam*—of the ornaments.

TRANSLATION

The Lord appeared in the mortal world by His internal potency, yoga-māyā. He came in His eternal form, which is just suitable for His pastimes. These pastimes were wonderful for everyone, even for those proud of their own opulence, including the Lord Him-

self in His form as the Lord of Vaikuṇṭha. Thus His [Śrī Kṛṣṇa's] transcendental body is the ornament of all ornaments.

PURPORT

In conformity with the Vedic hymns (*nityo nityānāṁ cetanaś cetanānām*), the Personality of Godhead is more excellent than all other living beings within all the universes in the material world. He is the chief of all living entities; no one can surpass Him or be equal to Him in wealth, strength, fame, beauty, knowledge or renunciation. When Lord Kṛṣṇa was within this universe, He seemed to be a human being because He appeared in a manner just suitable for His pastimes in the mortal world. He did not appear in human society in His Vaikuṇṭha feature with four hands because that would not have been suitable for His pastimes. But in spite of His appearing as a human being, no one was or is equal to Him in any respect in any of the six different opulences. Everyone is more or less proud of his opulence in this world, but when Lord Kṛṣṇa was in human society, He excelled all His contemporaries within the universe.

When the Lord's pastimes are visible to the human eye, they are called *prakaṭa*, and when they are not visible they are called *aprakaṭa*. In fact, the Lord's pastimes never stop, just as the sun never leaves the sky. The sun is always in its right orbit in the sky, but it is sometimes visible and sometimes invisible to our limited vision. Similarly, the pastimes of the Lord are always current in one universe or another, and when Lord Kṛṣṇa disappeared from the transcendental abode of Dvārakā, it was simply a disappearance from the eyes of the people there. It should not be misunderstood that His transcendental body, which is just suitable for the pastimes in the mortal world, is in any way inferior to His different expansions in the Vaikuṇṭhalokas. His body manifested in the material world is transcendental par excellence in the sense that His pastimes in the mortal world excel His mercy displayed in the Vaikuṇṭhalokas. In the Vaikuṇṭhalokas the Lord is merciful toward the liberated or *nitya-mukta* living entities, but in His pastimes in the mortal world He is merciful even to the fallen souls who are *nitya-baddha*, or conditioned forever. The six excellent opulences which He displayed in the mortal world by the agency of His internal potency, *yoga-māyā*, are rare even in the

Vaikuṇṭhalokas. All His pastimes were manifested not by the material energy but by His spiritual energy. The excellence of His *rāsa-līlā* at Vṛndāvana and His householder life with sixteen thousand wives is wonderful even for Nārāyaṇa in Vaikuṇṭha and is certainly so for other living entities within this mortal world. His pastimes are wonderful even for other incarnations of the Lord, such as Śrī Rāma, Nṛsiṁha and Varāha. His opulence was so superexcellent that His pastimes were adored even by the Lord of Vaikuṇṭha, who is not different from Lord Kṛṣṇa Himself.

TEXT 13

यद्धर्मसूनोर्बत राजसूये
निरीक्ष्य दृक्स्वस्त्ययनं त्रिलोकः ।
कार्त्स्न्येन चाद्येह गतं विधातु-
रर्वाक्सृतौ कौशलमित्यमन्यत ॥१३॥

yad dharma-sūnor bata rājasūye
nirīkṣya dṛk-svastyayanaṁ tri-lokaḥ
kārtsnyena cādyeha gataṁ vidhātur
arvāk-sṛtau kauśalam ity amanyata

yat—the form which; *dharma-sūnoḥ*—of Mahārāja Yudhiṣṭhira; *bata*—certainly; *rājasūye*—in the arena of the *rājasūya* sacrifice; *nirīkṣya*—by observing; *dṛk*—sight; *svastyayanam*—pleasing; *tri-lokaḥ*—the three worlds; *kārtsnyena*—in sum total; *ca*—thus; *adya*—today; *iha*—within the universe; *gatam*—surpassed; *vidhātuḥ*—of the creator (Brahmā); *arvāk*—recent mankind; *sṛtau*—in the material world; *kauśalam*—dexterity; *iti*—thus; *amanyata*—contemplated.

TRANSLATION

All the demigods from the upper, lower and middle universal planetary systems assembled at the altar of the rājasūya sacrifice performed by Mahārāja Yudhiṣṭhira. After seeing the beautiful bodily features of Lord Kṛṣṇa, they all contemplated that He was the ultimate dexterous creation of Brahmā, the creator of human beings.

PURPORT

There was nothing comparable to the bodily features of Lord Kṛṣṇa when He was present in this world. The most beautiful object in the material world may be compared to the blue lotus flower or the full moon in the sky, but even the lotus flower and the moon were defeated by the beauty of the bodily features of Lord Kṛṣṇa, and this was certified by the demigods, the most beautiful living creatures in the universe. The demigods thought that Lord Kṛṣṇa, like themselves, was also created by Lord Brahmā, but in fact Brahmā was created by Lord Kṛṣṇa. It was not within the power of Brahmā to create the transcendental beauty of the Supreme Lord. No one is the creator of Kṛṣṇa; rather, He is the creator of everyone. As He says in *Bhagavad-gītā* (10.8), *ahaṁ sarvasya prabhavo mattaḥ sarvaṁ pravartate.*

TEXT 14

यस्यानुरागप्लुतहासरास-
लीलावलोकप्रतिलब्धमानाः ।
व्रजस्त्रियो दृग्भिरनुप्रवृत्त-
धियोऽवतस्थुः किल कृत्यशेषाः ॥१४॥

yasyānurāga-pluta-hāsa-rāsa-
līlāvaloka-pratilabdha-mānāḥ
vraja-striyo dṛgbhir anupravṛtta-
dhiyo 'vatasthuḥ kila kṛtya-śeṣāḥ

yasya—whose; *anurāga*—attachment; *pluta*—enhanced by; *hāsa*—laughter; *rāsa*—humors; *līlā*—pastimes; *avaloka*—glancing; *pratilabdha*—obtained thereof; *mānāḥ*—anguished; *vraja-striyaḥ*—damsels of Vraja; *dṛgbhiḥ*—with the eyes; *anupravṛtta*—following; *dhiyaḥ*—by intelligence; *avatasthuḥ*—sat silently; *kila*—indeed; *kṛtya-śeṣāḥ*—without finishing household duties.

TRANSLATION

The damsels of Vraja, after pastimes of laughter, humor and exchanges of glances, were anguished when Kṛṣṇa left them. They

used to follow Him with their eyes, and thus they sat down with stunned intelligence and could not finish their household duties.

PURPORT

In His boyhood at Vṛndāvana, Lord Kṛṣṇa was notorious as a teasing friend in transcendental love to all the girls His age. His love for them was so intense that there is no comparison to that ecstasy, and the damsels of Vraja were so much attached to Him that their affection excelled that of the great demigods like Brahmā and Śiva. Lord Kṛṣṇa finally admitted His defeat before the transcendental affection of the *gopīs* and declared that He was unable to repay them for their unalloyed affection. Although the *gopīs* were seemingly anguished by the Lord's teasing behavior, when Kṛṣṇa would leave them they could not tolerate the separation and used to follow Him with their eyes and minds. They were so stunned by the situation that they could not finish their household duties. No one could excel Him even in the dealing of love exchanged between boys and girls. It is said in the revealed scriptures that Lord Kṛṣṇa personally never goes beyond the boundary of Vṛndāvana. He remains there eternally because of the transcendental love of the inhabitants. Thus even though He is not visible at present, He is not away from Vṛndāvana for a moment.

TEXT 15

स्वशान्तरूपेष्वितरैः स्वरूपै-
रभ्यर्द्यमानेष्वनुकम्पितात्मा ।
परावरेशो महदंशयुक्तो
ह्यजोऽपि जातो भगवान् यथाग्निः ॥१५॥

sva-śānta-rūpeṣv itaraiḥ sva-rūpair
abhyardyamāneṣv anukampitātmā
parāvareśo mahad-aṁśa-yukto
hy ajo 'pi jāto bhagavān yathāgniḥ

sva-śānta-rūpeṣu—unto the peaceful devotees of the Lord; *itaraiḥ*—others, nondevotees; *sva-rūpaiḥ*—according to their own modes of nature; *abhyardyamāneṣu*—being harassed by; *anukampita-ātmā*—the all-compassionate Lord; *para-avara*—spiritual and material; *īśaḥ*—controller; *mahat-aṁśa-yuktaḥ*—accompanied by the plenary portion of *mahat-tattva; hi*—certainly; *ajaḥ*—the unborn; *api*—although; *jātaḥ*—is born; *bhagavān*—the Personality of Godhead; *yathā*—as if; *agniḥ*—the fire.

TRANSLATION

The Personality of Godhead, the all-compassionate controller of both the spiritual and material creations, is unborn, but when there is friction between His peaceful devotees and persons who are in the material modes of nature, He takes birth just like fire, accompanied by the mahat-tattva.

PURPORT

The devotees of the Lord are by nature peaceful because they have no material hankering. A liberated soul has no hankering, and therefore he has no lamentation. One who wants to possess also laments when he loses his possession. Devotees have no hankerings for material possessions and no hankerings for spiritual salvation. They are situated in the transcendental loving service of the Lord as a matter of duty, and they do not mind where they are or how they have to act. *Karmīs, jñānīs* and *yogīs* all hanker to possess some material or spiritual assets. *Karmīs* want material possessions, *jñānīs* and *yogīs* want spiritual possessions, but devotees do not want any material or spiritual assets. They want only to serve the Lord anywhere in the material or spiritual worlds that the Lord desires, and the Lord is always specifically compassionate towards such devotees.

The *karmīs, jñānīs* and *yogīs* have their particular mentalities in the modes of nature, and therefore they are called *itara* or nondevotees. These *itaras*, including even the *yogīs*, sometimes harass the devotees of the Lord. Durvāsā Muni, a great *yogī*, harassed Mahārāja Ambarīṣa because the latter was a great devotee of the Lord. And the great *karmī* and *jñānī* Hiraṇyakaśipu even harassed his own Vaiṣṇava son, Prahlāda Mahārāja. There are many instances of such harassment of the peaceful devotees of the Lord by the *itaras*. When such friction takes place, the Lord, out of His great compassion towards His pure devotees, appears in person, accompanied by His plenary portions controlling the *mahat-tattva.*

The Lord is everywhere, in both the material and spiritual domains, and He appears for the sake of His devotees when there is friction between His devotee and the nondevotee. As electricity is generated by friction of matter anywhere and everywhere, the Lord, being all-pervading, appears because of the friction of devotees and nondevotees. When Lord Kṛṣṇa appears on a mission, all His plenary portions accompany Him. When He appeared as the son of Vasudeva, there were differences of opinion about His incarnation. Some said, "He is the Supreme Personality of Godhead." Some said, "He is an incarnation of Nārāyaṇa," and others said, "He is the incarnation of Kṣīrodakaśāyī Viṣṇu." But actually He is the original Supreme Personality of Godhead—*kṛṣṇas tu bhagavān svayam*—and Nārāyaṇa, the *puruṣas* and all other incarnations accompany Him to function as different parts of His pastimes. *Mahad-aṁśa-yuktaḥ* indicates that He is accompanied by the *puruṣas,* who create the *mahat-tattva.* It is confirmed in the Vedic hymns, *mahāntaṁ vibhum ātmānam.*

Lord Kṛṣṇa appeared, just like electricity, when there was friction between Kaṁsa and Vasudeva and Ugrasena. Vasudeva and Ugrasena were the Lord's devotees, and Kaṁsa, a representative of the *karmīs* and *jñānīs,* was a nondevotee. Kṛṣṇa, as He is, is compared to the sun. He first appeared from the ocean of the womb of Devakī, and gradually He satisfied the inhabitants of the places surrounding Mathurā, just as the sun enlivens the lotus flower in the morning. After gradually rising to the meridian of Dvārakā, the Lord set like the sun, placing everything in darkness, as described by Uddhava.

TEXT 16

मां खेदयत्येतदजस्य जन्म-
विडम्बनं यद्वसुदेवगेहे ।
व्रजे च वासोऽरिभयादिव स्वयं
पुराद् व्यवात्सीद्यदनन्तवीर्यः ॥१६॥

māṁ khedayaty etad ajasya janma-
viḍambanaṁ yad vasudeva-gehe

vraje ca vāso 'ri-bhayād iva svayaṁ
purād vyavātsīd yad-ananta-vīryaḥ

mām—to me; *khedayati*—gives me distress; *etat*—this; *ajasya*—of the unborn; *janma*—birth; *viḍambanam*—bewildering; *yat*—that; *vasudeva-gehe*—in the home of Vasudeva; *vraje*—in Vṛndāvana; *ca*—also; *vāsaḥ*—inhabitation; *ari*—enemy; *bhayāt*—because of fear; *iva*—as if; *svayam*—Himself; *purāt*—from Mathurā Purī; *vyavātsīt*—fled; *yat*—one who is; *ananta-vīryaḥ*—unlimitedly powerful.

TRANSLATION

When I think of Lord Kṛṣṇa—how He was born in the prison house of Vasudeva although He is unborn, how He went away from His father's protection to Vraja and lived there incognito out of fear of the enemy, and how, although unlimitedly powerful, He fled from Mathurā in fear—all these bewildering incidents give me distress.

PURPORT

Because Lord Śrī Kṛṣṇa is the original person from whom everything and everyone has emanated—*ahaṁ sarvasya prabhavaḥ* (Bg. 10.8), *janmādy asya yataḥ* (Vs. 1.1.2)—nothing can be equal to or greater than Him. The Lord is supremely perfect, and whenever He enacts His transcendental pastimes as a son, a rival or an object of enmity, He plays the part so perfectly that even pure devotees like Uddhava are bewildered. For example, Uddhava knew perfectly well that Lord Śrī Kṛṣṇa is eternally existent and can neither die nor disappear for good, yet he lamented for Lord Kṛṣṇa. All these events are perfect arrangements to give perfection to His supreme glories. It is for enjoyment's sake. When a father plays with his little son and the father lies down on the floor as if defeated by the son, it is just to give the little son pleasure, and nothing more. Because the Lord is all-powerful, it is possible for Him to adjust opposites such as birth and no birth, power and defeat, fear and fearlessness. A pure devotee knows very well how it is possible for the Lord to adjust opposite things, but he laments for the nondevotees who, not knowing the supreme glories of the Lord, think of Him as imaginary simply because there are so many apparently contradictory statements in the scriptures. Factually there is nothing contradictory; everything is possible when we understand the Lord as the Lord and not as one of us, with all our imperfection.

TEXT 17

दुनोति चेतः स्मरतो ममैतद्
यदाह पादावभिवन्द्य पित्रोः ।
ताताम्ब कंसादुरुशङ्कितानां
प्रसीदतं नोऽकृतनिष्कृतीनाम् ॥१७॥

dunoti cetaḥ smarato mamaitad
yad āha pādāv abhivandya pitroḥ
tātāmba kaṁsād uru-śaṅkitānāṁ
prasīdataṁ no 'kṛta-niṣkṛtīnām

dunoti—it gives me pain; *cetaḥ*—heart; *smarataḥ*—while thinking of; *mama*—my; *etat*—this; *yat*—as much as; *āha*—said; *pādau*—feet; *abhivandya*—worshiping; *pitroḥ*—of the parents; *tāta*—My dear father; *amba*—My dear mother; *kaṁsāt*—out of Kaṁsa's; *uru*—great; *śaṅkitānām*—of those who are afraid; *prasīdatam*—be pleased with; *naḥ*—Our; *akṛta*—not executed; *niṣkṛtīnām*—duties to serve you.

TRANSLATION

Lord Kṛṣṇa begged pardon from His parents for Their [Kṛṣṇa's and Balarāma's] inability to serve their feet, due to being away from home because of great fear of Kaṁsa. He said, "O mother, O father, please excuse Us for this inability." All this behavior of the Lord gives me pain at heart.

PURPORT

It appears that Lord Kṛṣṇa and Baladeva were both very greatly afraid of Kaṁsa, and therefore They had to hide Themselves. But if Lord Kṛṣṇa and Baladeva are the Supreme Personality of Godhead, how was it possible that They were afraid of Kaṁsa? Is there any contradiction in such statements? Vasudeva, due to his great appreciation for Kṛṣṇa, wanted to give Him protection. He never thought that Kṛṣṇa was the Supreme Lord and could protect Himself; he thought of Kṛṣṇa as his son. Because Vasudeva was a great devotee of the Lord, he did not like to think that Kṛṣṇa might be killed like his other children. Morally, Vasudeva was bound to deliver Kṛṣṇa to the hands of Kaṁsa because he had promised to turn over all his children. But out of his great love for Kṛṣṇa he broke his promise, and the Lord was very pleased with Vasudeva for his transcendental mentality. He did not want to disturb the intense affection of Vasudeva, and thus He agreed to be carried by His father to the house of Nanda and Yaśodā. And just to test the intense love of Vasudeva, Lord Kṛṣṇa fell down in the waters of the Yamunā while His father was crossing the river. Vasudeva became mad after his child as he tried to recover Him in the midst of the rising river.

These are all glorified pastimes of the Lord, and there is no contradiction in such manifestations. Since Kṛṣṇa is the Supreme Lord, He was never afraid of Kaṁsa, but to please His father He agreed to be so. And the most brilliant part of His supreme character was that He begged pardon from His parents for being unable to serve their feet while absent from home because of fear of Kaṁsa. The Lord, whose lotus feet are worshiped by demigods like Brahmā and Śiva, wanted to worship the feet of Vasudeva. Such instruction by the Lord to the world is quite appropriate. Even if one is the Supreme Lord, one must serve his parents. A son is indebted to his parents in so many ways, and it is the duty of the son to serve his parents, however great the son may be. Indirectly, Kṛṣṇa wanted to teach the atheists who do not accept the supreme fatherhood of God, and they may learn from this action how much the Supreme Father has to be respected. Uddhava was simply struck with wonder by such glorious behavior of the Lord, and he was very sorry that he was unable to go with Him.

TEXT 18

को वा अमुष्याङ्घ्रिसरोजरेणुं
विस्मर्तुमीशीत पुमान् विजिघ्रन् ।
यो विस्फुरद्भ्रूविटपेन भूमे-
र्भारं कृतान्तेन तिरश्चकार ॥१८॥

ko vā amuṣyāṅghri-saroja-reṇuṁ
vismartum īśīta pumān vijighran
yo visphurad-bhrū-viṭapena bhūmer
bhāraṁ kṛtāntena tiraścakāra

kaḥ—who else; *vā*—either; *amuṣya*—the Lord's; *aṅghri*—feet; *saroja-reṇum*—dust of the lotus; *vismartum*—to forget; *īśīta*—may be able; *pumān*—person; *vijighran*—smelling; *yaḥ*—one who; *visphurat*—expanding; *bhrū-viṭapena*—by the leaves of the eyebrows; *bhūmeḥ*—of the earth; *bhāram*—burden; *kṛta-antena*—by deathblows; *tiraścakāra*—executed.

TRANSLATION

Who, after smelling the dust of His lotus feet even once, could ever forget it? Simply by expanding the leaves of His eyebrows, Kṛṣṇa has given the deathblow to those who were burdening the earth.

PURPORT

Lord Kṛṣṇa cannot be accepted as one of the human beings, even though He played the role of an obedient son. His actions were so extraordinary that by the simple raising of His eyebrows He could deliver deathblows to those who were burdening the earth.

TEXT 19

दृष्टा भवद्भिर्ननु राजसूये
चैद्यस्य कृष्णं द्विषतोऽपि सिद्धिः ।
यां योगिनः संस्पृहयन्ति सम्यग्
योगेन कस्तद्विरहं सहेत ॥१९॥

dṛṣṭā bhavadbhir nanu rājasūye
caidyasya kṛṣṇaṁ dviṣato 'pi siddhiḥ
yāṁ yoginaḥ saṁspṛhayanti samyag
yogena kas tad-virahaṁ saheta

dṛṣṭā—it has been seen; *bhavadbhiḥ*—by your good self; *nanu*—of course; *rājasūye*—in the assembly of the *rājasūya* sacrifice performed by Mahārāja Yudhiṣṭhira; *caidyasya*—of the King of Cedi (Śiśupāla); *kṛṣṇam*—unto Kṛṣṇa; *dviṣataḥ*—envying; *api*—in spite of; *siddhiḥ*—success; *yām*—which; *yoginaḥ*—the *yogīs; saṁspṛhayanti*—verily desire; *samyak*—fully; *yogena*—by performance of *yoga; kaḥ*—who; *tat*—His; *viraham*—separation; *saheta*—can tolerate.

TRANSLATION

You have personally seen how the King of Cedi [Śiśupāla] achieved success in yoga practice, although he hated Lord Kṛṣṇa. Even the actual yogīs aspire after such success with great interest by performance of their various practices. Who can tolerate separation from Him?

PURPORT

Lord Kṛṣṇa's causeless mercy was exhibited in the great assembly of Mahārāja Yudhiṣṭhira. He was merciful even to His enemy the King of Cedi, who always tried to be an envious rival of the Lord. Because it is not possible to be a bona fide rival of the Lord, the King of Cedi was extremely malicious toward Lord Kṛṣṇa. In this he was like many other *asuras*, such as Kaṁsa and Jarāsandha. In the open assembly of the *rājasūya* sacrifice performed by Mahārāja Yudhiṣṭhira, Śiśupāla insulted Lord Kṛṣṇa, and he was finally killed by the Lord. But it was seen by everyone in the assembly that a light flashed out of the body of the King of Cedi and merged into the body of Lord Kṛṣṇa. This means that Cedirāja achieved the salvation of attaining oneness with the Supreme, which is a perfection most desired by the *jñānīs* and *yogīs* and for which they execute their different types of transcendental activities.

It is a fact that persons who are trying to understand the Supreme Truth by their personal endeavors of mental speculation or mystic powers of *yoga* achieve the same goal as others who are personally killed by the Lord. Both achieve the salvation of merging in the *brahmajyoti* rays of the transcendental body of the Lord. The Lord was merciful even to His enemy, and the success of the King of Cedi was observed by everyone who was present in the assembly. Vidura was also present there, and therefore Uddhava referred the incident to his memory.

TEXT 20

तथैव चान्ये नरलोकवीरा
य आहवे कृष्णमुखारविन्दम् ।
नेत्रैः पिबन्तो नयनाभिरामं
पार्थास्त्रपूतः पदमापुरस्य ॥२०॥

tathaiva cānye nara-loka-vīrā
ya āhave kṛṣṇa-mukhāravindam
netraiḥ pibanto nayanābhirāmaṁ
pārthāstra-pūtaḥ padam āpur asya

tathā—as also; *eva ca*—and certainly; *anye*—others; *nara-loka*—human society; *vīrāḥ*—fighters; *ye*—those; *āhave*—on the battlefield (of Kurukṣetra); *kṛṣṇa*—Lord Kṛṣṇa's; *mukha-aravindam*—face like a lotus flower; *netraiḥ*—with the eyes; *pibantaḥ*—while seeing; *nayana-abhirāmam*—very pleasing to the eyes; *pārtha*—Arjuna; *astra-pūtaḥ*—purified by arrows; *padam*—abode; *āpuḥ*—achieved; *asya*—of Him.

TRANSLATION

Certainly others who were fighters on the Battlefield of Kurukṣetra were purified by the onslaught of Arjuna's arrows, and while seeing the lotuslike face of Kṛṣṇa, so pleasing to the eyes, they achieved the abode of the Lord.

PURPORT

The Supreme Personality of Godhead, Lord Śrī Kṛṣṇa, appears in this world for two missionary purposes: to deliver the faithful and to annihilate the miscreants. But because the Lord is absolute, His two different kinds of actions, although apparently different, are ultimately one and the same. His annihilation of a person like Śiśupāla is as auspicious as His actions for the protection of the faithful. All the warriors who fought against Arjuna but who were able to see the lotuslike face of the Lord on the battlefront achieved the abode of the Lord, exactly as the devotees of the Lord do. The words "pleasing to the eyes of the seer" are very significant. When the warriors from the other side of the battlefield saw

Lord Kṛṣṇa at the front, they appreciated His beauty, and their dormant instinct of love of God was awakened. Śiśupāla saw the Lord also, but he saw Him as his enemy, and his love was not awakened. Therefore Śiśupāla achieved oneness with the Lord by merging in the impersonal glare of His body, called the *brahmajyoti*. Others, who were in the marginal position, being neither friends nor enemies but slightly in love of Godhead by appreciating the beauty of His face, were at once promoted to the spiritual planets, the Vaikuṇṭhas. The Lord's personal abode is called Goloka Vṛndāvana, and the abodes where His plenary expansions reside are called the Vaikuṇṭhas, where the Lord is present as Nārāyaṇa. Love of Godhead is dormant in every living entity, and the entire process of devotional service unto the Lord is meant for awakening this dormant, eternal love of Godhead. But there are degrees of such transcendental awakening. Those whose love of God is awakened to the fullest extent go back to the Goloka Vṛndāvana planet in the spiritual sky, whereas persons who have just awakened to love of Godhead by accident or association are transferred to the Vaikuṇṭha planets. Essentially there is no material difference between Goloka and Vaikuṇṭha, but in the Vaikuṇṭhas the Lord is served in unlimited opulence, whereas in Goloka the Lord is served in natural affection.

This love of God is awakened by the association of pure devotees of the Lord. Here the word *pārthāstra-pūtaḥ* is significant. Those who saw the beautiful face of the Lord on the Battlefield of Kurukṣetra were purified first by Arjuna when he made his onslaught with arrows. The Lord appeared for the mission of diminishing the burden of the world, and Arjuna was assisting the Lord by fighting on His behalf. Arjuna personally declined to fight, and the whole instruction of the *Bhagavad-gītā* was given to Arjuna to engage him in the fight. As a pure devotee of the Lord, Arjuna agreed to fight in preference to his own decision, and thus Arjuna fought to assist the Lord in His mission of diminishing the burden of the world. All the activities of a pure devotee are executed on behalf of the Lord because a pure devotee of the Lord has nothing to do for his personal interest. Arjuna's killing was as good as killing by the Lord Himself. As soon as Arjuna shot an arrow at an enemy, that enemy became purified of all material contaminations and became eligible to be transferred to the spiritual sky. Those warriors who appreciated the lotus feet of the Lord and saw His face at the front had their dormant love of

God awakened, and thus they were transferred at once to Vaikuṇṭhaloka, not to the impersonal state of *brahmajyoti* as was Śiśupāla. Śiśupāla died without appreciating the Lord, while others died with appreciation of the Lord. Both were transferred to the spiritual sky, but those who awakened to love of God were transferred to the planets of the transcendental sky.

Uddhava seemingly lamented that his own position was less than that of the warriors on the Battlefield of Kurukṣetra because they had attained to Vaikuṇṭha whereas he remained to lament the disappearance of the Lord.

TEXT 21

स्वयं त्वसाम्यातिशयस्त्र्यधीशः
स्वाराज्यलक्ष्म्याप्तसमस्तकामः ।
बलिं हरद्भिश्चिरलोकपालैः
किरीटकोट्येडितपादपीठः ॥२१॥

svayaṁ tv asāmyātiśayas tryadhīśaḥ
svārājya-lakṣmy-āpta-samasta-kāmaḥ
baliṁ haradbhiś cira-loka-pālaiḥ
kirīṭa-koṭy-eḍita-pāda-pīṭhaḥ

svayam—Himself; *tu*—but; *asāmya*—unique; *atiśayaḥ*—greater; *tri-adhīśaḥ*—Lord of the three; *svārājya*—independent supremacy; *lakṣmī*—fortune; *āpta*—achieved; *samasta-kāmaḥ*—all desires; *balim*—worshiping paraphernalia; *haradbhiḥ*—offered by; *cira-loka-pālaiḥ*—by the eternal maintainers of the order of creation; *kirīṭa-koṭi*—millions of helmets; *eḍita-pāda-pīṭhaḥ*—feet honored by prayers.

TRANSLATION

Lord Śrī Kṛṣṇa is the Lord of all kinds of threes and is independently supreme by achievement of all kinds of fortune. He is worshiped by the eternal maintainers of the creation, who offer Him the paraphernalia of worship by touching their millions of helmets to His feet.

PURPORT

Lord Śrī Kṛṣṇa is so mild and merciful, as described in the above verses, and yet He is the Lord of all kinds of threes. He is the Supreme Lord of the three worlds, the three qualities of material nature and the three *puruṣas* (Kāraṇodakaśāyī, Garbhodakaśāyī and Kṣīrodakaśāyī Viṣṇu). There are innumerable universes, and in each and every universe there are different manifestations of Brahmā, Viṣṇu and Rudra. Besides that, there is the Śeṣa-mūrti who bears all the universes on His hoods. And Lord Kṛṣṇa is the Lord of all of them. As the incarnation of Manu, He is the original source of all Manus in innumerable universes. Each universe has manifestations of 504,000 Manus. He is the Lord of the three principal potencies, namely *cit-śakti*, *māyā-śakti* and *taṭastha-śakti*, and He is the complete master of six kinds of fortune—wealth, strength, fame, beauty, knowledge and renunciation. There is none who can excel Him in any matter of enjoyment, and certainly there is no one greater than Him. No one is equal to or greater than Him. It is the duty of everyone, whoever and wherever one may be, to surrender completely unto Him. It is not wonderful, therefore, that all the transcendental controllers surrender to Him and make all offerings of worship.

TEXT 22

तत्तस्य कैङ्कर्यमलं भृतान्नो
विग्लापयत्यङ्ग यदुग्रसेनम् ।
तिष्ठन्निषण्णं परमेष्ठिधिष्ण्ये
न्यबोधयद्देव निधारयेति ॥२२॥

tat tasya kaiṅkaryam alaṁ bhṛtān no
viglāpayaty aṅga yad ugrasenam
tiṣṭhan niṣaṇṇaṁ parameṣṭhi-dhiṣṇye
nyabodhayad deva nidhārayeti

tat—therefore; *tasya*—His; *kaiṅkaryam*—service; *alam*—of course; *bhṛtān*—the servitors; *naḥ*—us; *viglāpayati*—gives pain; *aṅga*—O Vidura; *yat*—as much as; *ugrasenam*—unto King Ugrasena; *tiṣṭhan*—being seated; *niṣaṇṇam*—waiting upon Him; *parameṣṭhi-dhiṣṇye*—on the royal throne; *nyabodhayat*—submitted; *deva*—addressing my Lord; *nidhāraya*—please know it; *iti*—thus.

TRANSLATION

Therefore, O Vidura, does it not pain us, His servitors, when we remember that He [Lord Kṛṣṇa] used to stand before King Ugrasena, who was sitting on the royal throne, and used to submit explanations before him, saying, "O My lord, please let it be known to you"?

PURPORT

Lord Kṛṣṇa's gentle behavior before His so-called superiors such as His father, grandfather and elder brother, His amiable behavior with His so-called wives, friends and contemporaries, His behavior as a child before His mother Yaśodā, and His naughty dealings with His young girl friends cannot bewilder a pure devotee like Uddhava. Others, who are not devotees, are bewildered by such behavior of the Lord, who acted just like a human being. This bewilderment is explained by the Lord Himself in the *Bhagavad-gītā* (9.11) as follows:

avajānanti māṁ mūḍhā
mānuṣīṁ tanum āśritam
paraṁ bhāvam ajānanto
mama bhūta-maheśvaram

Persons with a poor fund of knowledge belittle the Personality of Godhead, Lord Kṛṣṇa, not knowing His exalted position as the Lord of everything. In *Bhagavad-gītā* the Lord has explained His position clearly, but the demoniac atheistic student squeezes out an interpretation to suit his own purpose and misleads unfortunate followers into the same mentality. Such unfortunate persons merely pick up some ṣlogans from the great book of knowledge, but are unable to estimate the Lord as the Supreme Personality of Godhead. Pure devotees like Uddhava, however, are never misled by such atheistic opportunists.

TEXT 23

अहो बकी यं स्तनकालकूटं
जिघांसयापाययदप्यसाध्वी ।

लेभे गतिं धात्र्युचितां ततोऽन्यं
कं वा दयालुं शरणं व्रजेम ॥२३॥

aho bakī yaṁ stana-kāla-kūṭaṁ
jighāṁsayāpāyayad apy asādhvī
lebhe gatiṁ dhātry-ucitāṁ tato 'nyaṁ
kaṁ vā dayāluṁ śaraṇaṁ vrajema

aho—alas; *bakī*—the she-demon (Pūtanā); *yam*—whom; *stana*—of her breast; *kāla*—deadly; *kūṭam*—poison; *jighāṁsayā*—out of envy; *apāyayat*—nourished; *api*—although; *asādhvī*—unfaithful; *lebhe*—achieved; *gatim*—destination; *dhātrī-ucitām*—just suitable for the nurse; *tataḥ*—beyond whom; *anyam*—other; *kam*—who else; *vā*—certainly; *dayālum*—merciful; *śaraṇam*—shelter; *vrajema*—shall I take.

TRANSLATION

Alas, how shall I take shelter of one more merciful than He who granted the position of mother to a she-demon [Pūtanā] although she was unfaithful and she prepared deadly poison to be sucked from her breast?

PURPORT

Here is an example of the extreme mercy of the Lord, even to His enemy. It is said that a noble man accepts the good qualities of a person of doubtful character, just as one accepts nectar from a stock of poison. In His babyhood, He was administered deadly poison by Pūtanā, a she-demon who tried to kill the wonderful baby. And because she was a demon, it was impossible for her to know that the Supreme Lord, even though playing the part of a baby, was no one less than the same Supreme Personality of Godhead. His value as the Supreme Lord did not diminish upon His becoming a baby to please His devotee Yaśodā. The Lord may assume the form of a baby or a shape other than that of a human being, but it doesn't make the slightest difference; He is always the same Supreme. A living creature, however powerful he may become by dint of severe penance, can never become equal to the Supreme Lord.

Lord Kṛṣṇa accepted the motherhood of Pūtanā because she pretended to be an affectionate mother, allowing Kṛṣṇa to suck her breast. The Lord accepts the least qualification of the living entity and awards him the highest reward. That is the standard of His character. Therefore, who but the Lord can be the ultimate shelter?

TEXT 24

मन्येऽसुरान् भागवतांस्त्र्यधीशे
संरम्भमार्गाभिनिविष्टचित्तान् ।
ये संयुगेऽचक्षत तार्क्ष्यपुत्र-
मंसे सुनाभायुधमापतन्तम् ॥२४॥

manye 'surān bhāgavatāṁs tryadhīśe
saṁrambha-mārgābhiniviṣṭa-cittān
ye saṁyuge 'cakṣata tārkṣya-putram
aṁse sunābhāyudham āpatantam

manye—I think; *asurān*—the demons; *bhāgavatān*—great devotees; *tri-adhīśe*—unto the Lord of the threes; *saṁrambha*—enmity; *mārga*—by the way of; *abhiniviṣṭa-cittān*—absorbed in thought; *ye*—those; *saṁyuge*—in the fight; *acakṣata*—could see; *tārkṣya-putram*—Garuḍa, the carrier of the Lord; *aṁse*—on the shoulder; *sunābha*—the wheel; *āyudham*—one who carries the weapon; *āpatantam*—coming forward.

TRANSLATION

I consider the demons, who are inimical toward the Lord, to be more than the devotees because while fighting with the Lord, absorbed in thoughts of enmity, they are able to see the Lord carried on the shoulder of Garuḍa, the son of Tārkṣya [Kaśyapa], and carrying the wheel weapon in His hand.

PURPORT

The *asuras* who fought against the Lord face to face got salvation due to their being killed by the Lord. This salvation of the demons is not due to their being devotees of the Lord; it is because of the Lord's causeless mercy. Anyone who is slightly in touch with the Lord, somehow or other, is greatly benefited, even to the point of salvation, due to the excellence of the Lord. He is so kind that He awards salvation even to His enemies because they come into contact with Him and are indirectly absorbed in Him by their inimical thoughts. Actually, the demons can never be equal to the pure devotees, but Uddhava was thinking in that way because of his feelings of separation. He was thinking that at the last stage of his life he might not be able to see the Lord face to face as did the demons. The fact is that the devotees who are always engaged in the devotional service of the Lord in transcendental love are rewarded many hundreds and thousands of times more than the demons by being elevated to the spiritual planets, where they remain with the Lord in eternal, blissful existence. The demons and impersonalists are awarded the facility of merging in the *brahmajyoti* effulgence of the Lord, whereas the devotees are admitted into the spiritual planets. For comparison, one can just imagine the difference between floating in space and residing in one of the planets in the sky. The pleasure of the living entities on the planets is greater than that of those who have no body and who merge with the molecules of the sun's rays. The impersonalists, therefore, are no more favored than the enemies of the Lord; rather, they are both on the same level of spiritual salvation.

TEXT 25

वसुदेवस्य देवक्यां जातो भोजेन्द्रबन्धने ।
चिकीर्षुर्भगवानस्याः शमजेनाभियाचितः ॥२५॥

vasudevasya devakyāṁ
jāto bhojendra-bandhane
cikīrṣur bhagavān asyāḥ
śam ajenābhiyācitaḥ

vasudevasya—of the wife of Vasudeva; *devakyām*—in the womb of Devakī; *jātaḥ*—born of; *bhoja-indra*—of the King of the Bhojas; *bandhane*—in the prison house; *cikīrṣuḥ*—for doing; *bhagavān*—the Personality of Godhead; *asyāḥ*—of the earth; *śam*—welfare; *ajena*—by Brahmā; *abhiyācitaḥ*—being prayed for.

TRANSLATION

The Personality of Godhead, Lord Śrī Kṛṣṇa, being prayed to by Brahmā to bring welfare to the earth, was begotten by Vasudeva in the womb of his wife Devakī in the prison of the King of Bhoja.

PURPORT

Although there is no difference between the Lord's pastimes of appearance and disappearance, the devotees of the Lord do not generally discuss the subject matter of His disappearance. Vidura inquired indirectly from Uddhava about the incident of the Lord's disappearance by asking him to relate *kṛṣṇa-kathā*, or topics on the history of Lord Kṛṣṇa. Thus Uddhava began the topics from the very beginning of His appearance as the son of Vasudeva and Devakī in the prison of Kaṁsa, the King of the Bhojas, at Mathurā. The Lord has no business in this world, but when He is so requested by devotees like Brahmā, He descends on the earth for the welfare of the entire universe. This is stated in *Bhagavad-gītā* (4.8): *paritrāṇāya sādhūnāṁ vināśāya ca duṣkṛtām/ dharma-saṁsthāpanārthāya sambhavāmi yuge yuge.*

TEXT 26

ततो नन्दव्रजमितः पित्रा कंसाद्विबिभ्यता ।
एकादश समास्तत्र गूढार्चिः सबलोऽवसत् ॥२६॥

tato nanda-vrajam itaḥ
pitrā kaṁsād vibibhyatā
ekādaśa samās tatra
gūḍhārciḥ sa-balo 'vasat

tataḥ—thereafter; *nanda-vrajam*—cow pastures of Nanda Mahārāja; *itaḥ*—being brought up; *pitrā*—by His father; *kaṁsāt*—from Kaṁsa; *vibibhyatā*—being afraid of; *ekādaśa*—eleven; *samāḥ*—years; *tatra*—therein; *gūḍha-arciḥ*—covered fire; *sa-balaḥ*—with Baladeva; *avasat*—resided.

TRANSLATION

Thereafter, His father, being afraid of Kaṁsa, brought Him to the cow pastures of Mahārāja Nanda, and there He lived for eleven years like a covered flame with His elder brother, Baladeva.

PURPORT

There was no necessity of the Lord's being dispatched to the house of Nanda Mahārāja out of fear of Kaṁsa's determination to kill Him as soon as He appeared. It is the business of the *asuras* to try to kill the Supreme Personality of Godhead or to prove by all means that there is no God or that Kṛṣṇa is an ordinary human being and not God. Lord Kṛṣṇa is not affected by such determination of men of Kaṁsa's class, but in order to play the role of a child He agreed to be carried by His father to the cow pastures of Nanda Mahārāja because Vasudeva was afraid of Kaṁsa. Nanda Mahārāja was due to receive Him as his child, and Yaśodāmayī was also to enjoy the childhood pastimes of the Lord, and therefore to fulfill everyone's desire, He was carried from Mathurā to Vṛndāvana just after His appearance in the prison house of Kaṁsa. He lived there for eleven years and completed all His fascinating pastimes of childhood, boyhood and adolescence with His elder brother, Lord Baladeva, His first expansion. Vasudeva's thought of protecting Kṛṣṇa from the wrath of Kaṁsa is part of a transcendental relationship. The Lord enjoys more when someone takes Him as his subordinate son who needs the protection of a father than He does when someone accepts Him as the Supreme Lord. He is the father of everyone, and He protects everyone, but when His devotee takes it for granted that the Lord is to be protected by the devotee's care, it is a transcendental joy for the Lord. Thus when Vasudeva, out of fear of Kaṁsa, carried Him to Vṛndāvana, the Lord enjoyed it; otherwise, He had no fear from Kaṁsa or anyone else.

TEXT 27

परीतो वत्सपैर्वत्सांश्चारयन् व्यहरद्विभुः ।
यमुनोपवने कूजद्द्विजसंकुलिताङ्घ्रिपे ॥२७॥

parīto vatsapair vatsāṁś
cārayan vyaharad vibhuḥ
yamunopavane kūjad-
dvija-saṅkulitāṅghripe

parītaḥ—surrounded by; *vatsapaiḥ*—cowherd boys; *vatsān*—calves; *cārayan*—herding, tending; *vyaharat*—enjoyed by traveling; *vibhuḥ*—

the Almighty; *yamunā*—the Yamunā River; *upavane*—gardens on the shore; *kūjat*—vibrated by the voice; *dvija*—the twice-born birds; *saṅkulita*—densely situated; *aṅghripe*—in the trees.

TRANSLATION

In His childhood, the Almighty Lord was surrounded by cowherd boys and calves, and thus He traveled on the shore of the Yamunā River, through gardens densely covered with trees and filled with vibrations of chirping birds.

PURPORT

Nanda Mahārāja was a landholder for King Kaṁsa, but because by caste he was a *vaiśya*, a member of the mercantile and agricultural community, he maintained thousands of cows. It is the duty of the *vaiśyas* to give protection to the cows, just as the *kṣatriyas* are to give protection to the human beings. Because the Lord was a child, He was put in charge of the calves with His cowherd boy friends. These cowherd boys were great *ṛṣis* and *yogīs* in their previous births, and after many such pious births, they gained the association of the Lord and could play with Him on equal terms. Such cowherd boys never cared to know who Kṛṣṇa was, but they played with Him as a most intimate and lovable friend. They were so fond of the Lord that at night they would only think of the next morning when they would be able to meet the Lord and go together to the forests for cowherding.

The forests on the shore of the Yamunā are all beautiful gardens full of trees of mango, jackfruit, apples, guava, oranges, grapes, berries, palmfruit and so many other plants and fragrant flowers. And because the forest was on the bank of the Yamunā, naturally there were ducks, cranes and peacocks on the branches of the trees. All these trees and birds and beasts were pious living entities born in the transcendental abode of Vṛndāvana just to give pleasure to the Lord and His eternal associates, the cowherd boys.

While playing like a small child with His associates, the Lord killed many demons, including Aghāsura, Bakāsura, Pralambāsura and Gardabhāsura. Although He appeared at Vṛndāvana just as a boy, He was actually like the covered flames of a fire. As a small particle of fire can kindle a great fire with fuel, so the Lord killed all these great demons, beginning from His babyhood in the house of Nanda Mahārāja. The land of Vṛndāvana, the Lord's childhood playground, still remains today, and anyone who visits these places enjoys the same transcendental bliss, although the Lord is not physically visible to our imperfect eyes. Lord Caitanya recommended this land of the Lord as identical with the Lord and therefore worshipable by the devotees. This instruction is taken up especially by the followers of Lord Caitanya known as the Gauḍīya Vaiṣṇavas. And because the land is identical with the Lord, devotees like Uddhava and Vidura visited these places five thousand years ago in order to have direct contact with the Lord, visible or not visible. Thousands of devotees of the Lord are still wandering in these sacred places of Vṛndāvana, and all of them are preparing themselves to go back home, back to Godhead.

TEXT 28

कौमारीं दर्शयंश्चेष्टां प्रेक्षणीयां व्रजौकसाम् ।
रुदन्निव हसन्मुग्धबालसिंहावलोकनः ॥२८॥

kaumārīṁ darśayaṁś ceṣṭāṁ
prekṣaṇīyāṁ vrajaukasām
rudann iva hasan mugdha-
bāla-siṁhāvalokanaḥ

kaumārīm—just suitable to childhood; *darśayan*—while showing; *ceṣṭām*—activities; *prekṣaṇīyām*—worthy to be seen; *vraja-okasām*—by the inhabitants of the land of Vṛndāvana; *rudan*—crying; *iva*—just like; *hasan*—laughing; *mugdha*—struck with wonder; *bāla-siṁha*—lion cub; *avalokanaḥ*—looking like that.

TRANSLATION

When the Lord displayed His activities just suitable for childhood, He was visible only to the residents of Vṛndāvana. Sometimes He would cry and sometimes laugh, just like a child, and while so doing He would appear like a lion cub.

PURPORT

If anyone wants to enjoy the childhood pastimes of the Lord, then he has to follow in the footsteps of the residents of Vraja like Nanda, Upananda and other parental inhabitants. A child may insist on having something and cry like anything to get it, disturbing the whole neighborhood, and then immediately after achieving the desired thing, he laughs. Such crying and laughing is enjoyable to the parents and elderly members of the family, so the Lord would simultaneously cry and laugh in this way and merge His devotee-parents in the humor of transcendental pleasure. These incidents are enjoyable only by the residents of Vraja like Nanda Mahārāja, and not by the impersonalist worshipers of Brahman or Paramātmā. Sometimes when attacked in the forest by demons, Kṛṣṇa would appear struck with wonder, but He looked on them like the cub of a lion and killed them. His childhood companions would also be struck with wonder, and when they came back home they would narrate the story to their parents, and everyone would appreciate the qualities of their Kṛṣṇa. Child Kṛṣṇa did not belong only to His parents, Nanda and Yaśodā; He was the son of all the elderly inhabitants of Vṛndāvana and the friend of all contemporary boys and girls. Everyone loved Kṛṣṇa. He was the life and soul of everyone, including the animals, the cows and the calves.

TEXT 29

स एव गोधनं लक्ष्म्या निकेतं सितगोवृषम् ।
चारयन्ननुगान् गोपान् रणद्वेणुररीरमत् ॥२९॥

sa eva go-dhanaṁ lakṣmyā
niketaṁ sita-go-vṛṣam
cārayann anugān gopān
raṇad-veṇur arīramat

saḥ—He (Lord Kṛṣṇa); *eva*—certainly; *go-dhanam*—the treasure of cows; *lakṣmyāḥ*—by opulence; *niketam*—reservoir; *sita-go-vṛṣam*—beautiful cows and bulls; *cārayan*—herding; *anugān*—the followers; *gopān*—cowherd boys; *raṇat*—blowing; *veṇuḥ*—flute; *arīramat*—enlivened.

TRANSLATION

While herding the very beautiful bulls, the Lord, who was the reservoir of all opulence and fortune, used to blow His flute, and thus He enlivened His faithful followers, the cowherd boys.

PURPORT

As He grew to six and seven years old, the Lord was given charge of looking after the cows and bulls in the grazing grounds. He was the son of a well-to-do landholder who owned hundreds and thousands of cows, and according to Vedic economics, one is considered to be a rich man by the strength of his store of grains and cows. With only these two things, cows and grain, humanity can solve its eating problem. Human society needs only sufficient grain and sufficient cows to solve its economic problems. All other things but these two are artificial necessities created by man to kill his valuable life at the human level and waste his time in things which are not needed. Lord Kṛṣṇa, as the teacher of human society, personally showed by His acts that the mercantile community, or the *vaiśyas,* should herd cows and bulls and thus give protection to the valuable animals. According to *smṛti* regulation, the cow is the mother and the bull the father of the human being. The cow is the mother because just as one sucks the breast of one's mother, human society takes cow's milk. Similarly, the bull is the father of human society because the father earns for the children just as the bull tills the ground to produce food grains. Human society will kill its spirit of life by killing the father and the mother. It is mentioned herein that the beautiful cows and bulls were of various checkered colors—red, black, green, yellow, ash, etc. And because of their colors and healthy smiling features, the atmosphere was enlivening.

Over and above all, the Lord used to play His celebrated flute. The sound vibrated by His flute would give His friends such transcendental pleasure that they would forget all the talks of the *brahmānanda* which is so praised by the impersonalists. These cowherd boys, as will be explained by Śukadeva Gosvāmī, were living entities who had accumulated heaps of pious acts and thus were enjoying with the Lord in person and were hearing His transcendental flute. The *Brahma-saṁhitā* (5.30) confirms the Lord's blowing His transcendental flute.

veṇuṁ kvaṇantam aravinda-dalāyatākṣaṁ
barhāvataṁsam asitāmbuda-sundarāṅgam
kandarpa-koṭi-kamanīya-viśeṣa-śobhaṁ
govindam ādi-puruṣaṁ tam ahaṁ bhajāmi

Brahmājī said, "I worship Govinda, the primeval Lord, who plays on His transcendental flute. His eyes are like lotus flowers, He is decorated with peacock plumes, and His bodily color resembles a fresh black cloud although His bodily features are more beautiful than millions of cupids." These are the special features of the Lord.

TEXT 30

प्रयुक्तान् भोजराजेन मायिनः कामरूपिणः ।
लीलया व्यनुदत्तांस्तान् बालः क्रीडनकानिव ॥३०॥

prayuktān bhoja-rājena
māyinaḥ kāma-rūpiṇaḥ
līlayā vyanudat tāṁs tān
bālaḥ krīḍanakān iva

prayuktān—engaged; *bhoja-rājena*—by King Kaṁsa; *māyinaḥ*—great wizards; *kāma-rūpiṇaḥ*—who could assume any form they liked; *līlayā*—in the course of the pastimes; *vyanudat*—killed; *tān*—them; *tān*—as they came there; *bālaḥ*—the child; *krīḍanakān*—dolls; *iva*—like that.

TRANSLATION

The great wizards who were able to assume any form were engaged by the King of Bhoja, Kaṁsa, to kill Kṛṣṇa, but in the course of His pastimes the Lord killed them as easily as a child breaks dolls.

PURPORT

The atheist Kaṁsa wanted to kill Kṛṣṇa just after His birth. He failed to do so, but later on he got information that Kṛṣṇa was living in Vṛndāvana at the house of Nanda Mahārāja. He therefore engaged many wizards who could perform wonderful acts and assume any form they liked. All of them appeared before the child-Lord in various forms, like Agha, Baka, Pūtanā, Śakaṭa, Tṛṇāvarta, Dhenuka and Gardabha, and they tried to kill the Lord at every opportunity. But one after another, all of them were killed by the Lord as if He were only playing with dolls. Children play with toy lions, elephants, boars and many similar dolls, which are broken by the children in the course of their playing with them. Before the Almighty Lord, any powerful living being is just like a toy lion in the hands of a playing child. No one can excel God in any capacity, and therefore no one can be equal to or greater than Him, nor can anyone attain the stage of equality with God by any kind of endeavor. *Jñāna*, *yoga* and *bhakti* are three recognized processes of spiritual realization. The perfection of such processes can lead one to the desired goal of life in spiritual value, but that does not mean that one can attain a perfection equal to the Lord's by such endeavors. The Lord is the Lord at every stage. When He was playing just like a child on the lap of His mother Yaśodāmayī or just like a cowherd boy with His transcendental friends, He continued to remain God, without the slightest diminution of His six opulences. Thus He is always unrivaled.

TEXT 31

विपन्नान् विषपानेन निगृह्य भुजगाधिपम् ।
उत्थाप्यापाययद्गावस्तत्तोयं प्रकृतिस्थितम् ॥३१॥

vipannān viṣa-pānena
nigṛhya bhujagādhipam
utthāpyāpāyayad gāvas
tat toyaṁ prakṛti-sthitam

vipannān—perplexed in great difficulties; *viṣa-pānena*—by drinking poison; *nigṛhya*—subduing; *bhujaga-adhipam*—the chief of the reptiles; *utthāpya*—after coming out; *apāyayat*—caused to drink; *gāvaḥ*—the cows; *tat*—that; *toyam*—water; *prakṛti*—natural; *sthitam*—situated.

TRANSLATION

The inhabitants of Vṛndāvana were perplexed by great difficulties because a certain portion of the Yamunā was poisoned by

the chief of the reptiles [Kāliya]. The Lord chastised the snake-king within the water and drove him away, and after coming out of the river, He caused the cows to drink the water and proved that the water was again in its natural state.

TEXT 32

अयाजयद्गोसवेन गोपराजं द्विजोत्तमैः ।
वित्तस्य चोरुभारस्य चिकीर्षन् सद्व्ययं विभुः ॥३२॥

ayājayad go-savena
gopa-rājaṁ dvijottamaiḥ
vittasya coru-bhārasya
cikīrṣan sad-vyayaṁ vibhuḥ

ayājayat—made to perform; *go-savena*—by worship of the cows; *gopa-rājam*—the king of the cowherds; *dvija-uttamaiḥ*—by the learned *brāhmaṇas; vittasya*—of the wealth; *ca*—also; *uru-bhārasya*—great opulence; *cikīrṣan*—desiring to act; *sat-vyayam*—proper utilization; *vibhuḥ*—the great.

TRANSLATION

The Supreme Lord, Kṛṣṇa, desired to utilize the opulent financial strength of Mahārāja Nanda for worship of the cows, and also He wanted to give a lesson to Indra, the King of heaven. Thus He advised His father to perform worship of go, or the pasturing land and the cows, with the help of learned brāhmaṇas.

PURPORT

Since He is the teacher of everyone, the Lord also taught His father, Nanda Mahārāja. Nanda Mahārāja was a well-to-do landholder and owner of many cows, and, as was the custom, he used to perform yearly worship of Indra, the King of heaven, with great opulence. This worship of demigods by the general populace is also advised in the Vedic literature just so people can accept the superior power of the Lord. The demigods are servants of the Lord deputed to look after the management of various activities of universal affairs. Therefore it is advised in the Vedic scriptures that one should perform *yajñas* to appease the demigods. But one who is devoted to the Supreme Lord has no need to appease the demigods. Worship of the demigods by common people is an arrangement for acknowledging the supremacy of the Supreme Lord, but it is not necessary. Such appeasement is generally recommended for material gains only. As we have already discussed in the Second Canto of this literature, one who admits the supremacy of the Supreme Personality of Godhead does not need to worship the secondary demigods. Sometimes, being worshiped and adored by less intelligent living beings, the demigods become puffed up with power and forget the supremacy of the Lord. This happened when Lord Kṛṣṇa was present in the universe, and thus the Lord wanted to give a lesson to the King of heaven, Indra. He therefore asked Mahārāja Nanda to stop the sacrifice offered to Indra and to use the money properly by performing a ceremony worshiping the cows and the pasturing ground on the hill of Govardhana. By this act Lord Kṛṣṇa taught human society, as He has instructed in the *Bhagavad-gītā* also, that one should worship the Supreme Lord by all acts and by all their results. That will bring about the desired success. The *vaiśyas* are specifically advised to give protection to the cows and their pasturing ground or agricultural land instead of squandering their hard-earned money. That will satisfy the Lord. The perfection of one's occupational duty, whether in the sphere of duty to oneself, one's community or one's nation, is judged by the degree to which the Lord is satisfied.

TEXT 33

वर्षतीन्द्रे व्रजः कोपाद्भग्नमानेऽतिविह्वलः ।
गोत्रलीलातपत्रेण त्रातो भद्रानुगृह्णता ॥३३॥

varṣatīndre vrajaḥ kopād
bhagnamāne 'tivihvalaḥ
gotra-līlātapatreṇa
trāto bhadrānugṛhṇatā

varṣati—in pouring water; *indre*—by the King of heaven, Indra; *vrajaḥ*—the land of cows (Vṛndāvana); *kopāt bhagnamāne*—having been in anger on being insulted; *ati*—highly; *vihvalaḥ*—perturbed; *gotra*—the hill for the cows; *līlā-ātapatreṇa*—by the pastime umbrella;

trātaḥ—were protected; *bhadra*—O sober one; *anugṛhṇatā*—by the merciful Lord.

TRANSLATION

O sober Vidura, King Indra, his honor having been insulted, poured water incessantly on Vṛndāvana, and thus the inhabitants of Vraja, the land of cows, were greatly distressed. But the compassionate Lord Kṛṣṇa saved them from danger with His pastime umbrella, the Govardhana Hill.

TEXT 34

शरच्छशिकरैर्मृष्टं मानयन् रजनीमुखम् ।
गायन् कलपदं रेमे स्त्रीणां मण्डलमण्डनः ॥३४॥

śarac-chaśi-karair mṛṣṭaṁ
mānayan rajanī-mukham
gāyan kala-padaṁ reme
strīṇāṁ maṇḍala-maṇḍanaḥ

śarat—autumn; *śaśi*—of the moon; *karaiḥ*—by the shining; *mṛṣṭam*—brightened; *mānayan*—thinking so; *rajanī-mukham*—the face of the night; *gāyan*—singing; *kala-padam*—pleasing songs; *reme*—enjoyed; *strīṇām*—of the women; *maṇḍala-maṇḍanaḥ*—as the central beauty of the assembly of women.

TRANSLATION

In the third season of the year, the Lord enjoyed as the central beauty of the assembly of women by attracting them with His pleasing songs in an autumn night brightened by moonshine.

PURPORT

Before leaving the land of cows, Vṛndāvana, the Lord pleased His young girl friends, the transcendental *gopīs*, in His *rāsa-līlā* pastimes. Here Uddhava stopped his description of the Lord's activities.

Thus end the Bhaktivedanta purports of the Third Canto, Second Chapter, of the Śrīmad-Bhāgavatam, *entitled "Remembrance of Lord Kṛṣṇa."*

CHAPTER THREE

The Lord's Pastimes Out of Vṛndāvana

TEXT 1

उद्धव उवाच
ततः स आगत्य पुरं स्वपित्रो-
श्चिकीर्षया शं बलदेवसंयुतः ।
निपात्य तुङ्गाद्रिपुयूथनाथं
हतं व्यकर्षद् व्यसुमोजसोर्व्याम् ॥ १ ॥

uddhava uvāca
tataḥ sa āgatya puraṁ sva-pitroś
cikīrṣayā śaṁ baladeva-saṁyutaḥ
nipātya tuṅgād ripu-yūtha-nāthaṁ
hataṁ vyakarṣad vyasum ojasorvyām

uddhavaḥ uvāca—Śrī Uddhava said; *tataḥ*—thereafter; *saḥ*—the Lord; *āgatya*—coming; *puram*—to the city of Mathurā; *sva-pitroḥ*—own parents; *cikīrṣayā*—wishing well; *śam*—well-being; *baladeva-saṁyutaḥ*—with Lord Baladeva; *nipātya*—dragging down; *tuṅgāt*—from the throne; *ripu-yūtha-nātham*—leader of public enemies; *hatam*—killed; *vyakarṣat*—pulled; *vyasum*—dead; *ojasā*—by strength; *urvyām*—on the ground.

TRANSLATION

Śrī Uddhava said: Thereafter Lord Kṛṣṇa went to Mathurā City with Śrī Baladeva, and to please Their parents They dragged Kaṁsa, the leader of public enemies, down from his throne and killed him, pulling him along the ground with great strength.

PURPORT

King Kaṁsa's death is only briefly described here because such pastimes are vividly and elaborately described in the Tenth Canto. The Lord proved to be a worthy son of His parents even at the age of sixteen years. Both brothers, Lord Kṛṣṇa and Lord Baladeva, went to Mathurā from Vṛndāvana and killed Their maternal uncle, who had given so much trouble to Their parents, Vasudeva and Devakī. Kaṁsa was a great giant, and Vasudeva and Devakī never thought that Kṛṣṇa and Balarāma (Baladeva) would be able to kill such a great and strong enemy. When the two brothers attacked Kaṁsa on the throne, Their parents feared that now Kaṁsa would finally get the opportunity to kill their sons, whom they had hidden for so long in the house of Nanda Mahārāja. The parents of the Lord, due to parental affection, felt extreme danger, and they almost fainted. Just to convince them that They had actually killed Kaṁsa, Kṛṣṇa and Baladeva pulled Kaṁsa's dead body along the ground to encourage them.

TEXT 2

सान्दीपनेः सकृत्प्रोक्तं ब्रह्माधीत्य सविस्तरम् ।
तस्मै प्रादाद्वरं पुत्रं मृतं पञ्चजनोदरात् ॥ २ ॥

sāndīpaneḥ sakṛt proktaṁ
brahmādhītya sa-vistaram
tasmai prādād varaṁ putraṁ
mṛtaṁ pañca-janodarāt

sāndīpaneḥ—of Sāndīpani Muni; *sakṛt*—once only; *proktam*—instructed; *brahma*—all the *Vedas* with their different branches of knowledge; *adhītya*—after studying; *sa-vistaram*—in all details; *tasmai*—unto him; *prādāt*—rewarded; *varam*—a benediction; *putram*—his son; *mṛtam*—who was already dead; *pañca-jana*—the region of the departed souls; *udarāt*—from within.

TRANSLATION

The Lord learned all the Vedas with their different branches simply by hearing them once from His teacher, Sāndīpani Muni,

whom He rewarded by bringing back his dead son from the region of Yamaloka.

PURPORT

No one but the Supreme Lord can become well versed in all the branches of Vedic wisdom simply by hearing once from his teacher. Nor can anyone bring a dead body back to life after the soul has already gone to the region of Yamarāja. But Lord Kṛṣṇa ventured to the planet of Yamaloka and found the dead son of His teacher and brought him back to his father as a reward for the instructions received. The Lord is constitutionally well versed in all the *Vedas*, and yet to teach by example that everyone must go to learn the *Vedas* from an authorized teacher and must satisfy the teacher by service and reward, He Himself adopted this system. The Lord offered His services to His teacher, Sāndīpani Muni, and the *muni*, knowing the power of the Lord, asked something which was impossible to be done by anyone else. The teacher asked that his beloved son, who had died, be brought back to him, and the Lord fulfilled the request. The Lord is not, therefore, an ingrate to anyone who renders Him some sort of service. The devotees of the Lord who always engage in His loving service are never to be disappointed in the progressive march of devotional service.

TEXT 3

समाहुता भीष्मककन्यया ये
श्रियः सवर्णेन बुभूषयैषाम् ।
गान्धर्ववृत्त्या मिषतां स्वभागं
जह्रे पदं मूर्ध्नि दधत्सुपर्णः ॥ ३ ॥

samāhutā bhīṣmaka-kanyayā ye
śriyaḥ savarṇena bubhūṣayaiṣām
gāndharva-vṛttyā miṣatāṁ sva-bhāgaṁ
jahre padaṁ mūrdhni dadhat suparṇaḥ

samāhutāḥ—invited; *bhīṣmaka*—of King Bhīṣmaka; *kanyayā*—by the daughter; *ye*—all those; *śryaḥ*—fortune; *sa-varṇena*—by a similar sequence; *bubhūṣayā*—expecting to be so; *eṣām*—of them; *gāndharva*—in marrying; *vṛttyā*—by such a custom; *miṣatām*—carrying so; *sva-bhāgam*—own share; *jahre*—took away; *padam*—feet; *mūrdhni*—on the head; *dadhat*—placed; *suparṇaḥ*—Garuḍa.

TRANSLATION

Attracted by the beauty and fortune of Rukmiṇī, the daughter of King Bhīṣmaka, many great princes and kings assembled to marry her. But Lord Kṛṣṇa, stepping over the other hopeful candidates, carried her away as His own share, as Garuḍa carried away nectar.

PURPORT

Princess Rukmiṇī, the daughter of King Bhīṣmaka, was actually as attractive as fortune itself because she was as valuable as gold both in color and in value. Since the goddess of fortune, Lakṣmī, is the property of the Supreme Lord, Rukmiṇī was actually meant for Lord Kṛṣṇa. But Śiśupāla was selected as her bridegroom by Rukmiṇī's elder brother, although King Bhīṣmaka wanted his daughter to be married to Kṛṣṇa. Rukmiṇī invited Kṛṣṇa to take her away from the clutches of Śiśupāla, so when the bridegroom, Śiśupāla, came there with his party with the desire to marry Rukmiṇī, Kṛṣṇa all of a sudden swept her from the scene, stepping over the heads of all the princes there, just as Garuḍa carried away nectar from the hands of the demons. This incident will be clearly explained in the Tenth Canto.

TEXT 4

ककुद्मिनोऽविद्धनसो दमित्वा
स्वयंवरे नाग्नजितीमुवाह ।
तद्भग्नमानानपि गृध्यतोऽज्ञा-
ञ्जघ्नेऽक्षतः शस्त्रभृतः स्वशस्त्रैः ॥ ४ ॥

kakudmino 'viddha-naso damitvā
svayaṁvare nāgnajitīm uvāha
tad-bhagnamānān api gṛdhyato 'jñāñ
jaghne 'kṣataḥ śastra-bhṛtaḥ sva-śastraiḥ

kakudminaḥ—bulls whose noses were not pierced; *aviddha-nasaḥ*—pierced by the nose; *damitvā*—subduing; *svayaṁvare*—in the open competition to select the bridegroom; *nāgnijitīm*—Princess Nāgnijitī; *uvāha*—married; *tat-bhagnamānān*—in that way all who were disappointed; *api*—even though; *gṛdhyataḥ*—wanted; *ajñān*—the fools; *jaghne*—killed and wounded; *akṣataḥ*—without being wounded; *śastra-bhṛtaḥ*—equipped with all weapons; *sva-śastraiḥ*—by His own weapons.

TRANSLATION

By subduing seven bulls whose noses were not pierced, the Lord achieved the hand of Princess Nāgnajitī in the open competition to select her bridegroom. Although the Lord was victorious, His competitors asked the hand of the princess, and thus there was a fight. Well equipped with weapons, the Lord killed or wounded all of them, but He was not hurt Himself.

TEXT 5

प्रियं प्रभुर्ग्राम्य इव प्रियाया
विधित्सुरार्च्छद् द्युतरुं यदर्थे ।
वज्र्याद्रवत्तं सगणो रुषान्धः
क्रीडामृगो नूनमयं वधूनाम् ॥ ५ ॥

priyaṁ prabhur grāmya iva priyāyā
vidhitsur ārcchad dyutaruṁ yad-arthe
vajry ādravat taṁ sa-gaṇo ruṣāndhaḥ
krīḍā-mṛgo nūnam ayaṁ vadhūnām

priyam—of the dear wife; *prabhuḥ*—the Lord; *grāmyaḥ*—ordinary living being; *iva*—in the manner of; *priyāyāḥ*—just to please; *vidhitsuḥ*—wishing; *ārcchat*—brought about; *dyutarum*—the *pārijāta* flower tree; *yat*—for which; *arthe*—in the matter of; *vajrī*—Indra, the King of heaven; *ādravat tam*—went forward to fight with Him; *sa-gaṇaḥ*—with full strength; *ruṣā*—in anger; *andhaḥ*—blind; *krīḍā-mṛgaḥ*—henpecked; *nūnam*—of course; *ayam*—this; *vadhūnām*—of the wives.

TRANSLATION

Just to please His dear wife, the Lord brought back the pārijāta tree from heaven, just as an ordinary husband would do. But Indra, the King of heaven, induced by his wives (henpecked as he was), ran after the Lord with full force to fight Him.

PURPORT

The Lord once went to the heavenly planet to present an earring to Aditi, the mother of the demigods, and His wife Satyabhāmā also went with Him. There is a special flowering tree called the *pārijāta*, which grows only in the heavenly planets, and Satyabhāmā wanted this tree. Just to please His wife, like an ordinary husband, the Lord brought back the tree, and this enraged Vajrī, or the controller of the thunderbolt. Indra's wives inspired him to run after the Lord to fight, and Indra, because he was a henpecked husband and also a fool, listened to them and dared to fight with Kṛṣṇa. He was a fool on this occasion because he forgot that everything belongs to the Lord.

There was no fault on the part of the Lord, even though He took away the tree from the heavenly kingdom, but because Indra was henpecked, dominated by his beautiful wives like Śacī, he became a fool, just as all persons who are dominated by their wives are generally foolish. Indra thought that Kṛṣṇa was a henpecked husband who only by the will of His wife Satyabhāmā took away the property of heaven, and therefore he thought that Kṛṣṇa could be punished. He forgot that the Lord is the proprietor of everything and cannot be henpecked. The Lord is fully independent, and by His will only He can have hundreds and thousands of wives like Satyabhāmā. He was not, therefore, attached to Satyabhāmā because she was a beautiful wife, but He was pleased with her devotional service and thus wanted to reciprocate the unalloyed devotion of His devotee.

TEXT 6

सुतं मृधे खं वपुषा ग्रसन्तं
दृष्ट्वा सुनाभोन्मथितं धरित्र्या ।
आमन्त्रितस्तत्तनयाय शेषं
दत्त्वा तदन्तःपुरमाविवेश ॥ ६ ॥

sutaṁ mṛdhe khaṁ vapuṣā grasantaṁ
dṛṣṭvā sunābhonmathitaṁ dharitryā
āmantritas tat-tanayāya śeṣaṁ
dattvā tad-antaḥ-puram āviveśa

sutam—son; *mṛdhe*—in the fight; *kham*—the sky; *vapuṣā*—by his body; *grasantam*—while devouring; *dṛṣṭvā*—seeing; *sunābha*—by the Sudarśana wheel; *unmathitam*—killed; *dharitryā*—by the earth; *āmantritaḥ*—being prayed for; *tat-tanayāya*—to the son of Narakāsura; *śeṣam*—that which was taken from; *dattvā*—returning it; *tat*—his; *antaḥ-puram*—inside the house; *āviveśa*—entered.

TRANSLATION

Narakāsura, the son of Dharitrī, the earth, tried to grasp the whole sky, and for this he was killed by the Lord in a fight. His mother then prayed to the Lord. This led to the return of the kingdom to the son of Narakāsura, and thus the Lord entered the house of the demon.

PURPORT

It is said in other *Purāṇas* that Narakāsura was the son of Dharitrī, the earth, by the Lord Himself. But he became a demon due to the bad association of Bāṇa, another demon. An atheist is called a demon, and it is a fact that even a person born of good parents can turn into a demon by bad association. Birth is not always the criterion of goodness; unless and until one is trained in the culture of good association, one cannot become good.

TEXT 7

तत्राहृतास्ता नरदेवकन्याः
कुजेन दृष्ट्वा हरिमार्तबन्धुम् ।
उत्थाय सद्यो जगृहुः प्रहर्ष-
व्रीडानुरागप्रहितावलोकैः ॥ ७ ॥

tatrāhṛtās tā nara-deva-kanyāḥ
kujena dṛṣṭvā harim ārta-bandhum

utthāya sadyo jagṛhuḥ praharṣa-
vrīḍānurāga-prahitāvalokaiḥ

tatra—inside the house of Narakāsura; *āhṛtāḥ*—kidnapped; *tāḥ*—all those; *nara-deva-kanyāḥ*—daughters of many kings; *kujena*—by the demon; *dṛṣṭvā*—by seeing; *harim*—the Lord; *ārta-bandhum*—the friend of the distressed; *utthāya*—at once got up; *sadyaḥ*—then and there; *jagṛhuḥ*—accepted; *praharṣa*—joyfully; *vrīḍa*—shyness; *anurāga*—attachment; *prahita-avalokaiḥ*—by eager glances.

TRANSLATION

There in the house of the demon, all the princesses kidnapped by Narakāsura at once became alert upon seeing the Lord, the friend of the distressed. They looked upon Him with eagerness, joy and shyness and offered to be His wives.

PURPORT

Narakāsura kidnapped many daughters of great kings and kept them imprisoned in his palace. But when he was killed by the Lord and the Lord entered the house of the demon, all the princesses were enlivened with joy and offered to become His wives because the Lord is the only friend of the distressed. Unless the Lord accepted them, there would be no chance of their being married because the demon kidnapped them from their fathers' custody and therefore no one would agree to marry them. According to Vedic society, girls are transferred from the custody of the father to the custody of the husband. Since these princesses had already been taken away from the custody of their fathers, it would have been difficult for them to have any husband other than the Lord Himself.

TEXT 8

आसां मुहूर्त एकस्मिन्नानागारेषु योषिताम् ।
सविधं जगृहे पाणीननुरूपः स्वमायया ॥ ८ ॥

āsāṁ muhūrta ekasmin
nānāgāreṣu yoṣitām

sa-vidhaṁ jagṛhe pāṇīn
anurūpaḥ sva-māyayā

āsām—all those; *muhūrte*—at one time; *ekasmin*—simultaneously; *nānā-āgāreṣu*—in different compartments; *yoṣitām*—of the women; *sa-vidham*—with perfect rituals; *jagṛhe*—accepted; *pāṇīn*—hands; *anu-rūpaḥ*—exactly to match; *sva-māyayā*—by His internal potency.

TRANSLATION

All those princesses were lodged in different apartments, and the Lord simultaneously assumed different bodily expansions exactly matching each and every princess. He accepted their hands in perfect rituals by His internal potency.

PURPORT

In the *Brahma-saṁhitā* (5.33) the Lord is described as follows in regard to His innumerable plenary expansions:

advaitam acyutam anādim ananta-rūpam
ādyaṁ purāṇa-puruṣaṁ nava-yauvanaṁ ca
vedeṣu durlabham adurlabham ātma-bhaktau
govindam ādi-puruṣaṁ tam ahaṁ bhajāmi

"The Lord, Govinda, whom I worship, is the original Personality of Godhead. He is nondifferent from His innumerable plenary expansions, who are all infallible, original and unlimited and who have eternal forms. Although He is primeval, the oldest personality, He is always fresh and young." By His internal potency the Lord can expand Himself into various personalities of *svayaṁ-prakāśa* and again into *prābhava* and *vaibhava* forms, and all of them are nondifferent from one another. The forms into which the Lord expanded to marry the princesses in different apartments were all slightly different just to match each and every one of them. They are called *vaibhava-vilāsa* forms of the Lord and are effected by His internal potency, *yoga-māyā*.

TEXT 9

तास्वपत्यान्यजनयदात्मतुल्यानि सर्वतः ।
एकैकस्यां दश दश प्रकृतेर्विबुभूषया ॥ ९ ॥

tāsv apatyāny ajanayad
ātma-tulyāni sarvataḥ
ekaikasyāṁ daśa daśa
prakṛter vibubhūṣayā

tāsu—unto them; *apatyāni*—offspring; *ajanayat*—begot; *ātma-tulyāni*—all like Himself; *sarvataḥ*—in all respects; *eka-ekasyām*—in each and every one of them; *daśa*—ten; *daśa*—ten; *prakṛteḥ*—for expanding Himself; *vibubhūṣayā*—so desiring.

TRANSLATION

Just to expand Himself according to His transcendental features, the Lord begot in each and every one of them ten offspring with exactly His own qualities.

TEXT 10

कालमागधशाल्वादीननीकै रुन्धतः पुरम् ।
अजीघनत्स्वयं दिव्यं स्वपुंसां तेज आदिशत् ॥१०॥

kāla-māgadha-śālvādīn
anīkai rundhataḥ puram
ajīghanat svayaṁ divyaṁ
sva-puṁsāṁ teja ādiśat

kāla—Kālayavana; *māgadha*—the King of Magadha (Jarāsandha); *śālva*—King Śālva; *ādīn*—and others; *anīkaiḥ*—by the soldiers; *rundhataḥ*—being encircled; *puram*—the city of Mathurā; *ajīghanat*—killed; *svayam*—personally; *divyam*—transcendental; *sva-puṁsām*—of His own men; *tejaḥ*—prowess; *ādiśat*—exhibited.

TRANSLATION

Kālayavana, the King of Magadha and Śālva attacked the city of Mathurā, but when the city was encircled by their soldiers, the Lord refrained from killing them personally, just to show the power of His own men.

PURPORT

After the death of Kaṁsa, when Mathurā was encircled by the soldiers of Kālayavana, Jarāsandha and Śālva, the Lord seemingly fled from the city, and thus He is known as Ranchor, or one who fled from fighting. Actually, the fact was that the Lord wanted to kill them through the agency of His own men, devotees like Mucukunda and Bhīma. Kālayavana and the King of Magadha were killed by Mucukunda and Bhīma respectively, who acted as agents of the Lord. By such acts the Lord wanted to exhibit the prowess of His devotees, as if He were personally unable to fight but His devotees could kill them. The relationship of the Lord with His devotees is a very happy one. Actually, the Lord descended at the request of Brahmā in order to kill all the undesirables of the world, but to divide the share of glory He sometimes engaged His devotees to take the credit. The Battle of Kurukṣetra was designed by the Lord Himself, but just to give credit to His devotee Arjuna (*nimitta-mātraṁ bhava savyasācin*), He played the part of the charioteer, while Arjuna was given the chance to play the fighter and thus become the hero of the Battle of Kurukṣetra. What He wants to do Himself by His transcendental plans, He executes through His confidential devotees. That is the way of the Lord's mercy towards His pure unalloyed devotees.

TEXT 11

शम्बरं द्विविदं बाणं मुरं बल्वलमेव च ।
अन्यांश्च दन्तवक्रादीनवधीत्कांश्च घातयत् ॥११॥

śambaraṁ dvividaṁ bāṇaṁ
muraṁ balvalam eva ca
anyāṁś ca dantavakrādīn
avadhīt kāṁś ca ghātayat

śambaram—Śambara; *dvividam*—Dvivida; *bāṇam*—Bāṇa; *muram*—Mura; *balvalam*—Balvala; *eva ca*—as also; *anyān*—others; *ca*—also; *dantavakra-ādīn*—like Dantavakra and others; *avadhīt*—killed; *kān ca*—and many others; *ghātayat*—caused to be killed.

TRANSLATION

Of kings like Śambara, Dvivida, Bāṇa, Mura, Balvala and many other demons, such as Dantavakra, some He killed Himself, and some He caused to be killed by others [Śrī Baladeva, etc.].

TEXT 12

अथ ते भ्रातृपुत्राणां पक्षयोः पतितान्नृपान् ।
चचाल भूः कुरुक्षेत्रं येषामापततां बलैः ॥१२॥

atha te bhrātṛ-putrāṇāṁ
pakṣayoḥ patitān nṛpān
cacāla bhūḥ kurukṣetraṁ
yeṣām āpatatāṁ balaiḥ

atha—thereafter; *te*—your; *bhrātṛ-putrāṇām*—of the nephews; *pakṣayoḥ*—of both sides; *patitān*—killed; *nṛpān*—kings; *cacāla*—shook; *bhūḥ*—the earth; *kurukṣetram*—the Battle of Kurukṣetra; *yeṣām*—of whom; *āpatatām*—traversing; *balaiḥ*—by strength.

TRANSLATION

Then, O Vidura, the Lord caused all the kings, both the enemies and those on the side of your fighting nephews, to be killed in the Battle of Kurukṣetra. All those kings were so great and strong that the earth seemed to shake as they traversed the warfield.

TEXT 13

सकर्णदुःशासनसौबलानां
कुमन्त्रपाकेन हतश्रियायुषम् ।

सुयोधनं सानुचरं शयानं
भग्नोरुमूर्व्यां न ननन्द पश्यन् ॥१३॥

sa karṇa-duḥśāsana-saubalānāṁ
kumantra-pākena hata-śriyāyuṣam
suyodhanaṁ sānucaraṁ śayānaṁ
bhagnorum ūrvyāṁ na nananda paśyan

saḥ—He (the Lord); *karṇa*—Karṇa; *duḥśāsana*—Duḥśāsana; *saubalānām*—Saubala; *kumantra-pākena*—by the intricacy of ill advice; *hata-śriya*—bereft of fortune; *āyuṣam*—duration of life; *suyodhanam*—Duryodhana; *sa-anucaram*—with followers; *śayānam*—lying down; *bhagna*—broken; *ūrum*—thighs; *ūrvyām*—very powerful; *na*—did not; *nananda*—take pleasure; *paśyan*—seeing like that.

TRANSLATION

Duryodhana was bereft of his fortune and duration of life because of the intricacy of ill advice given by Karṇa, Duḥśāsana and Saubala. When he lay on the ground with his followers, his thighs broken although he was powerful, the Lord was not happy to see the scene.

PURPORT

The fall of Duryodhana, the leading son of Dhṛtarāṣṭra, was not pleasing to the Lord, although He was on the side of Arjuna and it was He who advised Bhīma how to break the thighs of Duryodhana while the fight was going on. The Lord is constrained to award punishment upon the wrongdoer, but He is not happy to award such punishments because the living entities are originally His parts and parcels. He is harder than the thunderbolt for the wrongdoer and softer than the rose for the faithful. The wrongdoer is misled by bad associates and by ill advice, which is against the established principles of the Lord's order, and thus he becomes subject to punishment. The surest path to happiness is to live by the principles laid down by the Lord and not disobey His established laws, which are enacted in the *Vedas* and the *Purāṇas* for the forgetful living entities.

TEXT 14

कियान् भुवोऽयं क्षपितोरुभारो
यद्द्रोणभीष्मार्जुनभीममूलैः ।
अष्टादशाक्षौहिणिको मदंशै-
रास्ते बलं दुर्विषहं यदूनाम् ॥१४॥

kiyān bhuvo 'yaṁ kṣapitoru-bhāro
yad droṇa-bhīṣmārjuna-bhīma-mūlaiḥ
aṣṭādaśākṣauhiṇiko mad-aṁśair
āste balaṁ durviṣahaṁ yadūnām

kiyān—what is this; *bhuvaḥ*—of the earth; *ayam*—this; *kṣapita*—abated; *uru*—very great; *bhāraḥ*—burden; *yat*—which; *droṇa*—Droṇa; *bhīṣma*—Bhīṣma; *arjuna*—Arjuna; *bhīma*—Bhīma; *mūlaiḥ*—with the help; *aṣṭādaśa*—eighteen; *akṣauhiṇikaḥ*—phalanxes of military strength (*vide Bhāg.* 1.16.34); *mat-aṁśaiḥ*—with My descendants; *āste*—are still there; *balam*—great strength; *durviṣaham*—unbearable; *yadūnām*—of the Yadu dynasty.

TRANSLATION

[After the end of the Battle of Kurukṣetra, the Lord said:] The abatement of the earth's great burden, eighteen akṣauhiṇīs, has now been effected with the help of Droṇa, Bhīṣma, Arjuna and Bhīma. But what is this? There is still the great strength of the Yadu dynasty, born of Myself, which may be a more unbearable burden.

PURPORT

It is a wrong theory that due to an increase in population the world becomes overburdened and therefore there are wars and other annihilating processes. The earth is never overburdened. The heaviest mountains and oceans on the face of the earth hold more living entities than there are human beings, and they are not overburdened. If a census were taken of all the living beings on the surface of the earth, certainly it would be found that the number of humans is not even five percent of the total number of living beings. If the birthrate of human beings is increasing, then the birthrate of other living beings is increasing proportionately. The birthrate of lower animals—beasts, aquatics, birds, etc.—is far greater than that of human beings. There is an adequate arrangement for food for all the living beings all over the earth by the order of the Supreme Lord, and He can arrange more and more if there is actually a disproportionate increase of living beings.

Therefore, there is no question of an increase in population causing a burden. The earth became overburdened due to *dharma-glāni*, or irregular discharge of the Lord's desire. The Lord appeared on the earth to curb the increase in miscreants, and not the increase in population, as is wrongly put forward by the mundane economist. When Lord Kṛṣṇa appeared, there had been a sufficient increase in miscreants who had violated the desire of the Lord. The material creation is meant for fulfilling the desire of the Lord, and His desire is that the conditioned souls who are unfit to enter into the kingdom of God have a chance to improve their conditions for entering. The entire process of cosmic arrangement is intended just to give a chance to the conditioned souls to enter the kingdom of God, and there is an adequate arrangement for their maintenance by the nature of the Lord.

Therefore, although there may be a great increase in population on the surface of the earth, if the people are exactly in line with God consciousness and are not miscreants, such a burden on the earth is a source of pleasure for her. There are two kinds of burdens. There is the burden of the beast and the burden of love. The burden of the beast is unbearable, but the burden of love is a source of pleasure. Śrīla Viśvanātha Cakravartī describes the burden of love very practically. He says that the burden of the husband on the young wife, the burden of the child on the lap of the mother, and the burden of wealth on the businessman, although actually burdens from the viewpoint of heaviness, are sources of pleasure, and in the absence of such burdensome objects, one may feel the burden of separation, which is heavier to bear than the actual burden of love. When Lord Kṛṣṇa referred to the burden of the Yadu dynasty on the earth, He referred to something different than the burden of the beast. The large numbers of family members born of Lord Kṛṣṇa counted to some millions and were certainly a great increase in the population of the earth, but because all of them were expansions of the Lord Himself by His transcendental plenary expansions, they were a source of great pleasure for the earth. When the Lord referred to them in connection with the burden on the earth, He had in mind their imminent disappearance from the earth. All the members of the family of Lord Kṛṣṇa were incarnations of different demigods, and they were to disappear from the surface of the earth along with the Lord. When He referred to the unbearable heaviness on the earth in connection with the Yadu dynasty, He was referring to the burden of their separation. Śrīla Jīva Gosvāmī confirms this inference.

TEXT 15

मिथो यदैषां भविता विवादो
मध्वामदाताम्रविलोचनानाम् ।
नैषां वधोपाय इयानतोऽन्यो
मय्युद्यतेऽन्तर्दधते स्वयं स्म ॥१५॥

mitho yadaiṣāṁ bhavitā vivādo
madhv-āmadātāmra-vilocanānām
naiṣāṁ vadhopāya iyān ato 'nyo
mayy udyate 'ntardadhate svayaṁ sma

mithaḥ—one another; *yadā*—when; *eṣām*—of them; *bhavitā*—will take place; *vivādaḥ*—quarrel; *madhu-āmada*—intoxication by drinking; *ātāmra-vilocanānām*—of their eyes being copper-red; *na*—not; *eṣām*—of them; *vadha-upāyaḥ*—means of disappearance; *iyān*—like this; *ataḥ*—besides this; *anyaḥ*—alternative; *mayi*—on My; *udyate*—disappearance; *antaḥ-dadhate*—will disappear; *svayam*—themselves; *sma*—certainly.

TRANSLATION

When they quarrel among themselves, influenced by intoxication, with their eyes red like copper because of drinking [madhu], then only will they disappear; otherwise, it will not be possible. On My disappearance, this incident will take place.

PURPORT

The Lord and His associates appear and disappear by the will of the Lord. They are not subjected to the laws of material nature. No one was able to kill the family of the Lord, nor was there any possibility of their natural death by the laws of nature. The only means, therefore, for their disappearance was the make-show of a fight amongst themselves, as if brawling in intoxication due to drinking. That so-called fighting would also take place by the will of the Lord, otherwise there would be no cause for their fighting. Just as Arjuna was made to be illusioned by family affection and thus the *Bhagavad-gītā* was spoken, so the Yadu dynasty was made to be intoxicated by the will of the Lord, and nothing more. The devotees and associates of the Lord are completely surrendered souls. Thus they are transcendental instruments in the hands of the Lord and can be used in any way the Lord desires. The pure devotees also enjoy such pastimes of the Lord because they want to see Him happy. Devotees of the Lord never assert independent individuality; on the contrary, they utilize their individuality in pursuit of the desires of the Lord, and this cooperation of the devotees with the Lord makes a perfect scene of the Lord's pastimes.

TEXT 16

एवं सञ्चिन्त्य भगवान् स्वराज्ये स्थाप्य धर्मजम् ।
नन्दयामास सुहृदः साधूनां वर्त्म दर्शयन् ॥१६॥

evaṁ sañcintya bhagavān
sva-rājye sthāpya dharmajam
nandayām āsa suhṛdaḥ
sādhūnāṁ vartma darśayan

evam—thus; *sañcintya*—thinking within Himself; *bhagavān*—the Personality of Godhead; *sva-rājye*—in his own kingdom; *sthāpya*—installing; *dharmajam*—Mahārāja Yudhiṣṭhira; *nandayām āsa*—gladdened; *suhṛdaḥ*—the friends; *sādhūnām*—of the saints; *vartma*—the path; *darśayan*—by indicating.

TRANSLATION

Lord Śrī Kṛṣṇa, thus thinking to Himself, established Mahārāja Yudhiṣṭhira in the position of supreme control of the world in order to show the ideal of administration on the path of piety.

TEXT 17

उत्तरायां धृतः पूरोर्वंशः साध्वभिमन्युना ।
स वै द्रौण्यस्त्रसंप्लुष्टः पुनर्भगवता धृतः ॥१७॥

uttarāyāṁ dhṛtaḥ pūror
vaṁśaḥ sādhv-abhimanyunā
sa vai drauṇy-astra-sampluṣṭaḥ
punar bhagavatā dhṛtaḥ

uttarāyām—unto Uttarā; *dhṛtaḥ*—conceived; *pūroḥ*—of Pūru; *vaṁśaḥ*—descendant; *sādhu-abhimanyunā*—by the hero Abhimanyu; *saḥ*—he; *vai*—certainly; *drauṇi-astra*—by the weapon of Drauṇi, the son of Droṇa; *sampluṣṭaḥ*—being burnt; *punaḥ*—again, for the second time; *bhagavatā*—by the Personality of Godhead; *dhṛtaḥ*—was protected.

TRANSLATION

The embryo of Pūru's descendant begotten by the great hero Abhimanyu in the womb of Uttarā, his wife, was burnt by the weapon of the son of Droṇa, but later he was again protected by the Lord.

PURPORT

The embryonic body of Parīkṣit which was in formation after Uttarā's pregnancy by Abhimanyu, the great hero, was burned by the *brahmāstra* of Aśvatthāmā, but a second body was given by the Lord within the womb, and thus the descendant of Pūru was saved. This incident is the direct proof that the body and the living entity, the spiritual spark, are different. When the living entity takes shelter in the womb of a woman through the injection of the semen of a man, there is an emulsification of the man's and woman's discharges, and thus a body is formed the size of a pea, gradually developing into a complete body. But if the developing embryo is destroyed in some way or other, the living entity has to take shelter in another body or in the womb of another woman. The particular living entity who was selected to be the descendant of Mahārāja Pūru, or the Pāṇḍavas, was not an ordinary living entity, and by the superior will of the Lord he was destined to be the successor to Mahārāja Yudhiṣṭhira. Therefore, when Aśvatthāmā destroyed the embryo of Mahārāja Parīkṣit, the Lord, by His own internal potency, entered into the womb of Uttarā by His plenary portion just to give audience to the would-be Mahārāja Parīkṣit, who was in great danger. By His appearance within the womb, the Lord encouraged the child and gave him complete protection in a new body by His omnipotency. By His power of omnipresence He was present both inside and outside of Uttarā and other members of the Pāṇḍava family.

TEXT 18

अयाजयद्धर्मसुतमश्वमेधैस्त्रिभिर्विभुः ।
सोऽपि क्ष्मामनुजै रक्षन् रेमे कृष्णमनुव्रतः ॥१८॥

ayājayad dharma-sutam
aśvamedhais tribhir vibhuḥ
so 'pi kṣmām anujai rakṣan
reme kṛṣṇam anuvrataḥ

ayājayat—made to perform; *dharma-sutam*—by the son of Dharma (Mahārāja Yudhiṣṭhira); *aśvamedhaiḥ*—by horse sacrifices; *tribhiḥ*—three; *vibhuḥ*—the Supreme Lord; *saḥ*—Mahārāja Yudhiṣṭhira; *api*—also; *kṣmām*—the earth; *anujaiḥ*—assisted by his younger brothers; *rakṣan*—protecting; *reme*—enjoyed; *kṛṣṇam*—Kṛṣṇa, the Personality of Godhead; *anuvrataḥ*—constant follower.

TRANSLATION

The Supreme Lord induced the son of Dharma to perform three horse sacrifices, and Mahārāja Yudhiṣṭhira, constantly following Kṛṣṇa, the Personality of Godhead, protected and enjoyed the earth, assisted by his younger brothers.

PURPORT

Mahārāja Yudhiṣṭhira was the ideal monarchical representative on the earth because he was a constant follower of the Supreme Lord, Śrī Kṛṣṇa. As stated in the *Vedas* (*Īśopaniṣad*), the Lord is the proprietor of the entire manifested cosmic creation, which presents a chance for the conditioned souls to revive their eternal relationship with the Lord and thus go back to Godhead, back home. The whole system of the material world is arranged with that program and plan. Anyone who violates the plan is punished by the law of nature, which is acting by the direction of the Supreme Lord. Mahārāja Yudhiṣṭhira was installed on the throne of the earth as a representative of the Lord. The king is always expected to be the representative of the Lord. Perfect monarchy necessitates representation of the supreme will of the Lord, and Mahārāja Yudhiṣṭhira was the ideal monarch on this supreme principle. Both the King and the subjects were happy in the discharge of worldly duties, and thus protection of the citizens and enjoyment of natural life, with full cooperation of material nature, followed in the reign of Mahārāja Yudhiṣṭhira and his worthy descendants like Mahārāja Parīkṣit.

TEXT 19

भगवानपि विश्वात्मा लोकवेदपथानुगः ।
कामान् सिषेवे द्वार्वत्यामसक्तः सांख्यमास्थितः ॥१९॥

bhagavān api viśvātmā
loka-veda-pathānugaḥ
kāmān siṣeve dvārvatyām
asaktaḥ sāṅkhyam āsthitaḥ

bhagavān—the Personality of Godhead; *api*—also; *viśva-ātmā*—the Supersoul of the universe; *loka*—customary; *veda*—Vedic principles; *patha-anugaḥ*—follower of the path; *kāmān*—the necessities of life; *siṣeve*—enjoyed; *dvārvatyām*—in the city of Dvārakā; *asaktaḥ*—without being attached; *sāṅkhyam*—knowledge in Sāṅkhya philosophy; *āsthitaḥ*—being situated.

TRANSLATION

Simultaneously, the Personality of Godhead enjoyed life in the city of Dvārakā, strictly in conformity with the Vedic customs of society. He was situated in detachment and knowledge, as enunciated by the Sāṅkhya system of philosophy.

PURPORT

While Mahārāja Yudhiṣṭhira was the Emperor of the earth, Lord Śrī Kṛṣṇa was the King of Dvārakā and was known as Dvārakādhīśa. Like other subordinate kings, He was under the regime of Mahārāja Yudhiṣṭhira. Although Lord Śrī Kṛṣṇa is the supreme emperor of the entire creation, while He was on this earth He never violated the principles of the Vedic injunctions because they are the guide for human life. Regulated human life according to the Vedic principles, which are based on the system of knowledge called Sāṅkhya philosophy, is the real way of enjoyment of the necessities of life. Without such knowledge, detachment and custom, the so-called human civilization is no more than an animal society of eat, drink, be merry and enjoy. The Lord was acting freely, as He willed, yet by His practical example He taught not to lead a life which goes against the principles of detachment and knowledge. Attainment of knowledge and detachment, as very elaborately discussed in Sāṅkhya philosophy, is the real perfection of life. Knowledge means to know that the mission of the human form of life is to end all the miseries of material existence and that in spite of having to fulfill the bodily necessities in a regulated way, one must be detached from such animal life. Fulfilling the demands of the body is animal life, and fulfilling the mission of spirit soul is the human mission.

TEXT 20

स्निग्धस्मितावलोकेन वाचा पीयूषकल्पया ।
चरित्रेणानवद्येन श्रीनिकेतेन चात्मना ॥२०॥

snigdha-smitāvalokena
vācā pīyūṣa-kalpayā

caritreṇānavadyena
śrī-niketena cātmanā

snigdha—gentle; *smita-avalokena*—by a glance with a sweet smile; *vācā*—by words; *pīyūṣa-kalpayā*—compared to nectar; *caritreṇa*—by character; *anavadyena*—without flaw; *śrī*—fortune; *niketena*—residence; *ca*—and; *ātmanā*—by His transcendental body.

TRANSLATION

He was there in His transcendental body, the residence of the goddess of fortune, with His usual gentle and sweetly smiling face, His nectarean words and His flawless character.

PURPORT

In the previous verse it is described that Lord Kṛṣṇa, being situated in the truths of Sāṅkhya philosophy, is detached from all kinds of matter. In the present verse it is described that He is the residence of the goddess of fortune. These two things are not at all contradictory. Lord Kṛṣṇa is detached from the variegatedness of the inferior nature, but He is in eternal, blissful enjoyment of the spiritual nature, or His internal potency. One who has a poor fund of knowledge cannot understand this distinction between the external and internal potencies. In *Bhagavad-gītā*, the internal potency is described as the *parā prakṛti*. In the *Viṣṇu Purāṇa* also, the internal potency of Viṣṇu is described as *parā śakti*. The Lord is never detached from the association of *parā śakti*. This *parā śakti* and her manifestations are described in the *Brahma-saṁhitā* (5.37) as *ānanda-cinmaya-rasa-pratibhāvitābhiḥ*. The Lord is eternally joyful and cognizant in the taste derived from such transcendental bliss. Negation of the variegatedness of the inferior energy does not necessitate negation of the positive transcendental bliss of the spiritual world. Therefore the Lord's gentleness, His smile, His character and everything related to Him are all transcendental. Such manifestations of the internal potency are the reality, of which the material shadow is only a temporary representation from which everyone with proper knowledge must be detached.

TEXT 21

इमं लोकममुं चैव रमयन् सुतरां यदून् ।
रेमे क्षणदया दत्तक्षणस्त्रीक्षणसौहृदः ॥२१॥

imaṁ lokam amuṁ caiva
ramayan sutarāṁ yadūn
reme kṣaṇadayā datta-
kṣaṇa-strī-kṣaṇa-sauhṛdaḥ

imam—this; *lokam*—earth; *amum*—and the other worlds; *ca*—also; *eva*—certainly; *ramayan*—pleasing; *sutarām*—specifically; *yadūn*—the Yadus; *reme*—enjoyed; *kṣaṇadayā*—by night; *datta*—given by; *kṣaṇa*—leisure; *strī*—with women; *kṣaṇa*—conjugal love; *sauhṛdaḥ*—friendship.

TRANSLATION

The Lord enjoyed His pastimes, both in this world and in other worlds [higher planets], specifically in the association of the Yadu dynasty. At leisure hours offered by night, He enjoyed the friendship of conjugal love with women.

PURPORT

The Lord enjoyed in this world with His pure devotees. Although He is the Personality of Godhead and is transcendental to all material attachment, He nevertheless exhibited much attachment for His pure devotees on the earth, as well as for the demigods who engage in His service in the heavenly planets as powerful delegated directors in the management of all material activities. He displayed special attachment for His family members, the Yadus, as well as for His sixteen thousand wives, who had the opportunity to meet Him in the leisure hours of night. All these attachments of the Lord are manifestations of His internal potency, of which the external potency is only a shadow representation. In the *Skanda Purāṇa, Prabhāsa-khaṇḍa*, in the topics between Lord Śiva and Gaurī, there is confirmation of His internal potential manifestations. There is mention of the Lord's meeting with sixteen thousand cowherd damsels although He is the Haṁsa (transcendental) Supersoul and maintainer of all living entities. The sixteen thousand cowherd damsels are a display of sixteen varieties of internal potencies. This will be more elaborately explained in the Tenth Canto. It is said there that Lord Kṛṣṇa is just like the moon and the internal potential damsels are like the stars around the moon.

TEXT 22

तस्यैवं रममाणस्य संवत्सरगणान् बहून् ।
गृहमेधेषु योगेषु विरागः समजायत ॥२२॥

tasyaivaṁ ramamāṇasya
saṁvatsara-gaṇān bahūn
gṛhamedheṣu yogeṣu
virāgaḥ samajāyata

tasya—His; *evam*—thus; *ramamāṇasya*—enjoying; *saṁvatsara*—years; *gaṇān*—many; *bahūn*—great many; *gṛhamedheṣu*—in household life; *yogeṣu*—in sex life; *virāgaḥ*—detachment; *samajāyata*—awakened.

TRANSLATION

The Lord was thus engaged in household life for many, many years, but at last His detachment from ephemeral sex life was fully manifested.

PURPORT

Even though the Lord is never attached to any kind of material sex life, as the universal teacher He remained a householder for many, many years, just to teach others how one should live in householder life. Śrīla Viśvanātha Cakravartī Ṭhākura explains that the word *samajāyata* means "fully exhibited." In all His activities while present on the earth, the Lord exhibited detachment. This was fully displayed when He wanted to teach by example that one should not remain attached to household life for all the days of one's life. One should naturally develop detachment as a matter of course. The Lord's detachment from household life does not indicate detachment from His eternal associates, the transcendental cowherd damsels. But the Lord desired to end His so-called attachment to the three modes of material nature. He can never be detached from the service of His transcendental associates like Rukmiṇī and other goddesses of fortune, as described in the *Brahma-saṁhitā* (5.29): *lakṣmī-sahasra-śata-sambhrama-sevyamānam.*

TEXT 23

दैवाधीनेषु कामेषु दैवाधीनः स्वयं पुमान् ।
को विश्रम्भेत योगेन योगेश्वरमनुव्रतः ॥२३॥

daivādhīneṣu kāmeṣu
daivādhīnaḥ svayaṁ pumān
ko viśrambheta yogena
yogeśvaram anuvrataḥ

daiva—supernatural; *adhīneṣu*—being controlled; *kāmeṣu*—in sense enjoyment; *daiva-adhīnaḥ*—controlled by supernatural force; *svayam*—himself; *pumān*—living entity; *kaḥ*—whoever; *viśrambheta*—can have faith in; *yogena*—by devotional service; *yogeśvaram*—the Supreme Lord; *anuvrataḥ*—serving.

TRANSLATION

Every living entity is controlled by a supernatural force, and thus his sense enjoyment is also under the control of that supernatural force. No one, therefore, can put his faith in Lord Kṛṣṇa's transcendental sense activities but one who has become a devotee of the Lord by rendering devotional service.

PURPORT

As stated in *Bhagavad-gītā*, no one can understand the transcendental birth and activities of the Lord. The same fact is herein corroborated: no one but one who is enlightened by the devotional service of the Lord can understand the difference between the Lord's activities and those of others, who are controlled by the supernatural force. The sense enjoyment of all animals, men and demigods within the purview of the material universe is controlled by the supernatural force called the *prakṛti*, or *daivī-māyā*. No one is independent in obtaining sense enjoyment, and everyone in this material world is after sense enjoyment. Persons who are themselves under the control of supernatural power cannot believe that Lord Kṛṣṇa is not under any control beyond Himself in the matter of sense enjoyment. They cannot understand that His senses are transcendental. In the *Brahma-saṁhitā* the Lord's senses are described as omnipotent; i.e., with any sense He can perform the activities of the other senses. One who has limited senses cannot believe that the Lord can eat by His transcendental power of hearing and can perform the act of sex life simply by seeing. The controlled living entity cannot even dream of such sense activities in his conditional life. But simply by the activities of *bhakti-yoga*, he can understand that the Lord and His activities are always transcendental. As the Lord says in *Bhagavad-gītā* (18.55), *bhaktyā mām abhijānāti yāvān yaś cāsmi tattvataḥ:* one cannot know even a fraction of the activities of the Lord if he is not a pure devotee of the Lord.

TEXT 24

पुर्यां कदाचित्क्रीडद्भिर्यदुभोजकुमारकैः ।
कोपिता मुनयः शेपुर्भगवन्मतकोविदाः ॥२४॥

puryāṁ kadācit krīḍadbhir
yadu-bhoja-kumārakaiḥ
kopitā munayaḥ śepur
bhagavan-mata-kovidāḥ

puryām—in the city of Dvārakā; *kadācit*—once upon a time; *krīḍadbhiḥ*—by sporting activities; *yadu*—the descendants of Yadu; *bhoja*—the descendants of Bhoja; *kumārakaiḥ*—princes; *kopitāḥ*—became angry; *munayaḥ*—the great sages; *śepuḥ*—cursed; *bhagavat*—the Personality of Godhead; *mata*—desire; *kovidāḥ*—cognizant.

TRANSLATION

Once upon a time, great sages were made angry by the sporting activities of the princely descendants of the Yadu and Bhoja dynasties, and thus, as desired by the Lord, the sages cursed them.

PURPORT

The associates of the Lord who were playing the part of princely descendants of the Yadu and Bhoja dynasties were not ordinary living entities. It is not possible that they could offend any saintly man or sage, nor could the sages, who were all pure devotees of the Lord, be influenced to anger by any of the sporting activities of the princes born in the holy dynasties of Yadu or Bhoja, wherein the Lord Himself appeared as a descendant. The cursing of the princes by the sages was another transcendental pastime of the Lord to make a show of anger. The princes were cursed in order that one may know that even the descendants of the Lord, who could never be vanquished by any act of material nature, were subjected to the reactions of anger by great devotees of the Lord. One should therefore take great care and attention not to commit an offense at the feet of a devotee of the Lord.

TEXT 25

ततः कतिपयैर्मासैर्वृष्णिभोजान्धकादयः ।
ययुः प्रभासं संहृष्टा रथैर्देवविमोहिताः ॥२५॥

tataḥ katipayair māsair
vṛṣṇi-bhojāndhakādayaḥ
yayuḥ prabhāsaṁ saṁhṛṣṭā
rathair deva-vimohitāḥ

tataḥ—thereafter; *katipayaiḥ*—a few; *māsaiḥ*—months passing; *vṛṣṇi*—the descendants of Vṛṣṇi; *bhoja*—the descendants of Bhoja; *andhaka-ādayaḥ*—and others, like the sons of Andhaka; *yayuḥ*—went; *prabhāsam*—the place of pilgrimage named Prabhāsa; *saṁhṛṣṭāḥ*—with great pleasure; *rathaiḥ*—on their chariots; *deva*—by Kṛṣṇa; *vimohitāḥ*—bewildered.

TRANSLATION

A few months passed, and then, bewildered by Kṛṣṇa, all the descendants of Vṛṣṇi, Bhoja and Andhaka who were incarnations of demigods went to Prabhāsa, while those who were eternal devotees of the Lord did not leave but remained in Dvārakā.

TEXT 26

तत्र स्नात्वा पितॄन्देवानृषींश्चैव तदम्भसा ।
तर्पयित्वाथ विप्रेभ्यो गावो बहुगुणा ददुः ॥२६॥

tatra snātvā pitṝn devān
ṛṣīṁś caiva tad-ambhasā
tarpayitvātha viprebhyo
gāvo bahu-guṇā daduḥ

tatra—there; *snātvā*—by taking bath; *pitṝn*—forefathers; *devān*—demigods; *ṛṣīn*—great sages; *ca*—also; *eva*—certainly; *tat*—of that; *ambhasā*—by the water; *tarpayitvā*—by pleasing; *atha*—thereupon; *viprebhyaḥ*—unto the *brāhmaṇas; gāvaḥ*—cows; *bahu-guṇāḥ*—greatly useful; *daduḥ*—gave in charity.

TRANSLATION

After arriving there, all of them took bath, and with the water of this place of pilgrimage they offered their respects to the forefathers, demigods and great sages and thus satisfied them. They gave cows to the brāhmaṇas in royal charity.

PURPORT

Amongst the devotees of the Lord there are several divisions, mainly *nitya-siddhas* and *sādhana-siddhas.* The *nitya-siddha* devotees never fall down to the region of the material atmosphere, even though they sometimes come onto the material plane to execute the mission of the Lord. The *sādhana-siddha* devotees are chosen from the conditioned souls. Out of the *sādhana* devotees, there are mixed and pure devotees. The mixed devotees are sometimes enthusiastic about fruitive activities and are habituated to philosophical speculation. The pure devotees are free from all these mixtures and are completely absorbed in the service of the Lord, regardless of how and where they are situated. Pure devotees of the Lord are not enthusiastic to put aside their service to the Lord in order to go visit holy places of pilgrimage. A great devotee of the Lord in modern times, Śrī Narottama dāsa Ṭhākura, has sung like this: "To visit holy places of pilgrimage is another bewilderment of the mind because devotional service to the Lord at any place is the last word in spiritual perfection."

For pure devotees of the Lord who are completely satisfied with the transcendental loving service of the Lord, there is hardly any necessity to visit the various places of pilgrimage. But those who are not so advanced have the prescribed duties of visiting pilgrimage sites and regularly performing the rituals. The part of the princely order of the Yadu dynasty who went to Prabhāsa performed all duties to be done in a place of pilgrimage and offered their pious actions to their forefathers and others.

As a rule, every human being is indebted to God, the demigods, great sages, other living entities, people in general, forefathers, etc., for various contributions received from them. Thus everyone is obliged to repay the debt of gratitude. The Yadus who went to the Prabhāsa pilgrimage site performed their duties by distributing land, gold, and well-nourished cows in royal charity, as described in the following verse.

TEXT 27

हिरण्यं रजतं शय्यां वासांस्यजिनकम्बलान् ।
यानं रथानिभान् कन्या धरां वृत्तिकरीमपि ॥२७॥

hiraṇyaṁ rajataṁ śayyāṁ
vāsāṁsy ajina-kambalān
yānaṁ rathān ibhān kanyā
dharāṁ vṛtti-karīm api

hiraṇyam—gold; *rajatam*—gold coins; *śayyām*—bedding; *vāsāṁsi*—clothing; *ajina*—animal skin for seats; *kambalān*—blankets; *yānam*—horses; *rathān*—chariots; *ibhān*—elephants; *kanyāḥ*—girls; *dharām*—land; *vṛtti-karīm*—to provide livelihood; *api*—also.

TRANSLATION

The brāhmaṇas were not only given well-fed cows in charity, but also gold, gold coins, bedding, clothing, animal-skin seats, blankets, horses, elephants, girls and sufficient land for maintenance.

PURPORT

All these charities were meant for the *brāhmaṇas,* whose lives were devoted entirely to the welfare of society, both spiritually and materially. The *brāhmaṇas* were not giving their services as paid servants, but the society provided them with all necessities. It was arranged for some of the *brāhmaṇas,* who were in difficulty for marriage, to be given girls. The *brāhmaṇas,* therefore, had no economic problems. The *kṣatriya* kings and rich mercantile men would provide them with all that they needed, and in exchange the *brāhmaṇas* were completely devoted to the elevation of society. That was the way of social cooperation between the different castes. When the *brāhmaṇa* class or caste gradually became easygoing, being fed by the society although they had no brahminical qualifications, they degraded themselves into *brahma-bandhus,* or disqualified *brāhmaṇas,* and thus other members of society also gradually fell down from the social standard of progressive life. As described in *Bhagavad-gītā,* the caste system is the creation of the Lord and is arranged according to the quality of work rendered to society and not in terms of birthright, as falsely claimed in the present degraded society.

TEXT 28

अन्नं चोरुरसं तेभ्यो दत्त्वा भगवदर्पणम् ।
गोविप्रार्थासवः शूराः प्रणेमुर्भुवि मूर्धभिः ॥२८॥

annaṁ coru-rasaṁ tebhyo
dattvā bhagavad-arpaṇam
go-viprārthāsavaḥ śūrāḥ
praṇemur bhuvi mūrdhabhiḥ

annam—foodstuff; *ca*—also; *uru-rasam*—highly delicious; *tebhyaḥ*—unto the *brāhmaṇas; dattvā*—after supplying; *bhagavat-arpaṇam*—which was first offered to the Personality of Godhead; *go*—cows; *vipra*—*brāhmaṇas; artha*—purpose; *asavaḥ*—purpose of living; *śūrāḥ*—all the valiant *kṣatriyas; praṇemuḥ*—offered obeisances; *bhuvi*—touching the ground; *mūrdhabhiḥ*—with their heads.

TRANSLATION

Thereafter they offered the brāhmaṇas highly delicious foodstuffs first offered to the Personality of Godhead and offered their respectful obeisances by touching their heads to the ground. They lived perfectly by protecting the cows and the brāhmaṇas.

PURPORT

The behavior exhibited by the descendants of Yadu in the pilgrimage site of Prabhāsa was highly cultured and exactly to the point of human perfection. The perfection of human life is attained by following three principles of civilization: protecting the cows, maintaining the brahminical culture and, above all, becoming a pure devotee of the Lord. Without becoming a devotee of the Lord, one cannot perfect one's human life. The perfection of human life is to be elevated to the spiritual world, where there is no birth, no death, no disease and no old age. That is the highest perfectional aim of human life. Without this aim, any amount of material advancement in so-called comforts can only bring the defeat of the human form of life.

Brāhmaṇas and Vaiṣṇavas do not accept any foodstuff which is not first offered to the Personality of Godhead. Foodstuff offered to the Lord is accepted by the devotees as the mercy of the Lord. After all, the Lord supplies all kinds of foodstuff, both to the human being and to other animals. A human being must be conscious of the fact that all foodstuffs, namely grains, vegetables, milk, water, etc.—the prime necessities of life—are supplied for mankind by the Lord, and such foodstuffs cannot be manufactured by any scientist or materialist in a laboratory or factory established by human effort. The intelligent class of men are called *brāhmaṇas*, and those who have realized the Absolute Truth in His supreme personal feature are called Vaiṣṇavas. But both of them accept foodstuffs which are the remnants of sacrifice. Sacrifice is ultimately meant to satisfy the *yajña-puruṣa*, Viṣṇu. In *Bhagavad-gītā* (3.13) it is said that one who accepts foodstuffs as the remnants of sacrifice is freed from all sinful reactions, and one who cooks foodstuffs for maintenance of his body takes in all kinds of sins, which lead only to suffering. The foodstuffs prepared by the Yadus at the Prabhāsa pilgrimage site to offer to the bona fide *brāhmaṇas* there were all offered to the Personality of Godhead, Viṣṇu. The Yadus offered their sincere obeisances by touching their heads to the ground. The Yadus or any enlightened family in Vedic culture are trained for attainment of human perfection by total cooperation of service between the different divisions of social orders.

The word *uru-rasam* is also significant here. Hundreds of delicacies can be prepared simply by the combination of grains, vegetables and milk. All such preparations are in the mode of goodness and therefore may be offered to the Personality of Godhead. As stated in *Bhagavad-gītā* (9.26), the Lord accepts only foodstuffs which are within the range of fruits, flowers, leaves and liquids, provided they are offered in complete devotional service. Devotional service is the only criterion for a bona fide offering to the Lord. The Lord assures that He positively eats such foodstuffs offered by the devotees. So, judging from all sides, the Yadus were perfectly trained civilized persons, and their being cursed by the *brāhmaṇa* sages was only by the desire of the Lord; the whole incident was a warning to all concerned that no one should behave lightly with *brāhmaṇas* and Vaiṣṇavas.

Thus end the Bhaktivedanta purports of the Third Canto, Third Chapter, of the Śrīmad-Bhāgavatam, *entitled "The Lord's Pastimes Out of Vṛndāvana."*

CHAPTER FOUR

Vidura Approaches Maitreya

TEXT 1

उद्धव उवाच
अथ ते तदनुज्ञाता भुक्त्वा पीत्वा च वारुणीम् ।
तया विभ्रंशितज्ञाना दुरुक्तैर्मर्म पस्पृशुः ॥ १ ॥

uddhava ucāva
atha te tad-anujñātā
bhuktvā pītvā ca vāruṇīm
tayā vibhraṁśita-jñānā
duruktair marma paspṛśuḥ

uddhavaḥ uvāca—Uddhava said; *atha*—thereafter; *te*—they (the Yādavas); *tat*—by the *brāhmaṇas; anujñātāḥ*—being permitted; *bhuktvā*—after partaking; *pītvā*—drinking; *ca*—and; *vāruṇīm*—liquor; *tayā*—by that; *vibhraṁśita-jñānāḥ*—being bereft of knowledge; *duruktaiḥ*—with harsh words; *marma*—the core of the heart; *paspṛśuḥ*—touched.

TRANSLATION

Thereafter, all of them [the descendants of Vṛṣṇi and Bhoja], being permitted by the brāhmaṇas, partook of the remnants of prasāda and also drank liquor made of rice. By drinking they all became delirious, and, bereft of knowledge, they touched the cores of each other's hearts with harsh words.

PURPORT

In ceremonies when *brāhmaṇas* and Vaiṣṇavas are sumptuously fed, the host partakes of the remnants of foodstuff after the guest has given permission. So the descendants of Vṛṣṇi and Bhoja formally took permission from the *brāhmaṇas* and ate the prepared foodstuff. *Kṣatriyas* are permitted to drink at certain occasions, so they all drank a kind of light liquor made of rice. By such drinking they became delirious and bereft of sense, so much so that they forgot their relationship with one another and used harsh words which touched the cores of each other's hearts. Drinking is so harmful that even such a highly cultured family becomes affected by intoxication and can forget themselves in a drunken state. The descendants of Vṛṣṇi and Bhoja were not expected to forget themselves in this way, but by the will of the Supreme it happened, and thus they became harsh towards one another.

TEXT 2

तेषां मैरेयदोषेण विषमीकृतचेतसाम् ।
निम्लोचति रवावासीद्वेणूनामिव मर्दनम् ॥ २ ॥

teṣāṁ maireya-doṣeṇa
viṣamīkṛta-cetasām.
nimlocati ravāv
veṇūnām iva mardanam

teṣām—of them; *maireya*—of intoxication; *doṣeṇa*—by the faults; *viṣamīkṛta*—became unbalanced; *cetasām*—of those of whom the minds; *nimlocati*—sets; *ravau*—the sun; *āsīt*—takes place; *veṇūnām*—of the bamboos; *iva*—as; *mardanam*—destruction.

TRANSLATION

As by the friction of bamboos destruction takes place, so also, at sunset, by the interaction of the faults of intoxication, all their minds became unbalanced, and destruction took place.

PURPORT

When there is need of fire in the forest, by the will of the Supreme it takes place due to friction among the bamboos. Similarly, the descendants of Yadu were all destroyed by the will of the Lord by the process of self-destruction. Just as there is no possibility of a fire's occurring deep in the forest due to human effort, so also there was no power in the universe which could vanquish the descendants of Yadu, who were protected by the Lord. The Lord wanted them to be so destroyed, and thus they obeyed His order, as indicated by the word *tad-anujñāta.*

TEXT 3

भगवान् स्वात्ममायाया गतिं तामवलोक्य सः ।
सरस्वतीमुपस्पृश्य वृक्षमूलमुपाविशत् ॥ ३ ॥

bhagavān svātma-māyāyā
gatiṁ tām avalokya saḥ
sarasvatīm upaspṛśya
vṛkṣa-mūlam upāviśat

bhagavān—the Personality of Godhead; *sva-ātma-māyāyāḥ*—by His internal potency; *gatim*—the end; *tām*—that; *avalokya*—foreseeing; *saḥ*—He (Kṛṣṇa); *sarasvatīm*—the River Sarasvatī; *upaspṛśya*—after sipping water; *vṛkṣa-mūlam*—at the foot of a tree; *upāviśat*—sat down.

TRANSLATION

The Personality of Godhead, Lord Śrī Kṛṣṇa, after foreseeing the end [of His family] by His internal potency, went to the bank of the River Sarasvatī, sipped water, and sat down underneath a tree.

PURPORT

All the above-mentioned activities of the Yadus and Bhojas were executed by the internal potency of the Lord because He wanted them to be dispatched to their respective abodes after He had finished His mission of descent. They were all His sons and grandsons and were given complete protection by the paternal affection of the Lord. How they could be vanquished in the presence of the Lord is answered in this verse: everything was done by the Lord Himself (*svātma-māyāyāḥ*). The Lord's family members were either incarnations of His plenary expansions or demigods from the heavenly planets, and thus before His departure He separated them by His internal potency. Before being dispatched to their respective abodes, they were sent to the holy place of Prabhāsa, where they performed pious activities and took food and drink to their heart's content. It was then arranged for them to be sent back to their abodes so that others could see that the powerful Yadu dynasty was no longer in the world. In the previous verse, the word *anujñāta*, indicating that the whole sequence of events was arranged by the Lord, is significant. These particular pastimes of the Lord are not a manifestation of His external energy, or material nature. Such an exhibition of His internal potency is eternal, and therefore one should not conclude that the Yadus and Bhojas died in a drunken state in an ordinary fratricidal war. Śrī Jīva Gosvāmī comments on these incidents as magical performances.

TEXT 4

अहं चोक्तो भगवता प्रपन्नार्तिहरेण ह ।
बदरीं त्वं प्रयाहीति स्वकुलं संजिहीर्षुणा ॥ ४ ॥

ahaṁ cokto bhagavatā
prapannārti-hareṇa ha
badarīṁ tvaṁ prayāhīti
sva-kulaṁ sañjihīrṣuṇā

aham—I; *ca*—and; *uktaḥ*—was told; *bhagavatā*—by the Supreme Lord; *prapanna*—of the surrendered; *ārti-hareṇa*—by He who is the vanquisher of the distresses; *ha*—indeed; *badarīm*—to Badarī; *tvam*—you; *prayāhi*—should go; *iti*—thus; *sva-kulam*—His own family; *sañjihīrṣuṇā*—who desired to destroy.

TRANSLATION

The Lord is the vanquisher of the distresses of one who is surrendered unto Him. Thus He who desired to destroy His family told me previously to go to Badarikāśrama.

PURPORT

While at Dvārakā, Uddhava was warned to avoid the distresses which were to follow the disappearance of the Lord and the destruction of the Yadu dynasty. He was advised to proceed to Badarikāśrama because there he could associate with the devotees of Nara-Nārāyaṇa, and in their association of devotional service he could increase his eagerness for chanting, hearing, knowledge and detachment.

TEXT 5

तथापि तदभिप्रेतं जानन्नहमरिन्दम ।
पृष्ठतोऽन्वगमं भर्तुः पादविश्लेषणाक्षमः ॥ ५ ॥

tathāpi tad-abhipretaṁ
jānann aham arindama
pṛṣṭhato 'nvagamaṁ bhartuḥ
pāda-viśleṣaṇākṣamaḥ

tathā api—yet, in spite of; *tat-abhipretam*—His desire; *jānan*—knowing; *aham*—I; *arim-dama*—O subduer of the enemy (Vidura); *pṛṣṭhataḥ*—behind; *anvagamam*—followed; *bhartuḥ*—of the master; *pāda-viśleṣaṇa*—separation from His lotus feet; *akṣamaḥ*—not being able.

TRANSLATION

Yet in spite of my knowing His desire [to destroy the dynasty], O Arindama [Vidura], I followed Him because it was impossible for me to bear separation from the lotus feet of the master.

TEXT 6

अद्राक्षमेकमासीनं विचिन्वन् दयितं पतिम् ।
श्रीनिकेतं सरस्वत्यां कृतकेतमकेतनम् ॥ ६ ॥

adrākṣam ekam āsīnaṁ
vicinvan dayitaṁ patim
śrī-niketaṁ sarasvatyāṁ
kṛta-ketam aketanam

adrākṣam—I saw; *ekam*—alone; *āsīnam*—sitting; *vicinvan*—deeply thinking; *dayitam*—patron; *patim*—master; *śrī-niketam*—the shelter of the goddess of fortune; *sarasvatyām*—on the bank of the Sarasvatī;

kṛta-ketam—taking shelter; *aketanam*—being situated without a shelter.

TRANSLATION

Thus following, I saw my patron and master [Lord Śrī Kṛṣṇa] sitting alone and deeply thinking, taking shelter on the bank of the River Sarasvatī although He is the shelter of the goddess of fortune.

PURPORT

Those who are in the renounced order of life often take shelter underneath a tree. The Lord was found by Uddhava in that condition of taking shelter as do persons who have no shelter. Because He is the proprietor of everything, everywhere is His shelter, and everywhere is under His shelter. The entire material and spiritual cosmic manifestation is sustained by Him, and therefore He is the shelter of everything. So there was nothing astonishing in His taking shelter in the way of the unsheltered who are in the renounced order of life.

TEXT 7

श्यामावदातं विरजं प्रशान्तारुणलोचनम् ।
दोर्भिश्चतुर्भिर्विदितं पीतकौशाम्बरेण च ॥ ७ ॥

śyāmāvadātaṁ virajaṁ
praśāntāruṇa-locanam
dorbhiś caturbhir viditaṁ
pīta-kauśāmbareṇa ca

śyāma-avadātam—beautiful with black color; *virajam*—formed of pure goodness; *praśānta*—peaceful; *aruṇa*—reddish; *locanam*—eyes; *dorbhiḥ*—by the arms; *caturbhiḥ*—four; *viditam*—being recognized; *pīta*—yellow; *kauśa*—silken; *ambareṇa*—with garments; *ca*—and.

TRANSLATION

The Lord's body is blackish, but is eternal, full of bliss and knowledge, and very, very beautiful. His eyes are always peaceful,

and they are reddish like the rising morning sun. I could immediately recognize Him as the Supreme Personality of Godhead by His four hands, different symbolic representations, and yellow silk garments.

TEXT 8

वाम ऊरावधिश्रित्य दक्षिणाङ्घ्रिसरोरुहम् ।
अपाश्रितार्भकाश्वत्थमकृशं त्यक्तपिप्पलम् ॥ ८ ॥

vāma ūrāv adhiśritya
dakṣiṇāṅghri-saroruham
apāśritārbhakāśvattham
akṛśaṁ tyakta-pippalam

vāme—on the left; *ūrau*—thigh; *adhiśritya*—placed on; *dakṣiṇa-aṅghri-saroruham*—the right lotus foot; *apāśrita*—taking rest against; *arbhaka*—young; *aśvattham*—banyan tree; *akṛśam*—cheerful; *tyakta*—having left; *pippalam*—household comforts.

TRANSLATION

The Lord was sitting, taking rest against a young banyan tree, with His right lotus foot on His left thigh, and although He had left all household comforts, He looked quite cheerful in that posture.

PURPORT

According to Śrīla Viśvanātha Cakravartī Ṭhākura, the Lord's sitting posture—keeping His back against the newly grown banyan tree—is also meaningful. *Aśvattha*, the banyan tree, is so called because the tree does not die very quickly; it continues to live for many, many years. His legs and their energies are the material ingredients, which are five in all: earth, water, fire, air and sky. The material energies represented by the banyan tree are all products of His external potency and are therefore kept to His back. And because this particular universe is the smallest of all, the banyan tree is therefore designated as small, or as a child. *Tyakta-pippalam* indicates that He had now finished His pastimes in this particular small universe, but since the Lord is absolute and eternally blissful, there is no difference between His leaving or accepting something. The Lord was now prepared to leave this particular universe and go into another, just as the sun rises on one particular planet and sets in another simultaneously but does not change its own situation.

TEXT 9

तस्मिन्महाभागवतो द्वैपायनसुहृत्सखा ।
लोकाननुचरन् सिद्ध आससाद यदृच्छया ॥ ९ ॥

tasmin mahā-bhāgavato
dvaipāyana-suhṛt-sakhā
lokān anucaran siddha
āsasāda yadṛcchayā

tasmin—then; *mahā-bhāgavataḥ*—a great devotee of the Lord; *dvaipāyana*—of Kṛṣṇa-dvaipāyana Vyāsa; *suhṛt*—a well-wisher; *sakhā*—a friend; *lokān*—the three worlds; *anucaran*—traveling; *siddhe*—in that *āśrama; āsasāda*—arrived; *yadṛcchayā*—by his own perfect accord.

TRANSLATION

At that time, after traveling in many parts of the world, Maitreya, a great devotee of the Lord and a friend and well-wisher of the great sage Kṛṣṇa-dvaipāyana Vyāsa, reached that spot out of his own perfect accord.

PURPORT

Maitreya was one of the disciples of Maharṣi Parāśara, the father of Vyāsadeva. Thus Vyāsadeva and Maitreya were friends and mutual well-wishers. By some fortunate accident, Maitreya reached the place where Lord Śrī Kṛṣṇa was resting. To meet the Lord is not an ordinary incident. Maitreya was a great sage and a learned scholar-philosopher but not a pure devotee of the Lord, and therefore his meeting with the Lord at that time may have been due to *ajñāta-sukṛti*, or some unknown devotional service. Pure devotees always engage in pure devotional activities, and therefore their meeting with the Lord is natural. But when those who are not up to that standard meet the Lord, it is due to the unforeseen fortune of accidental devotional service.

TEXT 10

तस्यानुरक्तस्य मुनेर्मुकुन्दः
प्रमोदभावानतकन्धरस्य ।
आशृण्वतो मामनुरागहास-
समीक्षया विश्रमयन्नुवाच ॥१०॥

tasyānuraktasya muner mukundaḥ
pramoda-bhāvānata-kandharasya
āśṛṇvato mām anurāga-hāsa-
samīkṣayā viśramayann uvāca

tasya—his (Maitreya's); *anuraktasya*—although attached; *muneḥ*—of the sage; *mukundaḥ*—the Lord who awards salvation; *pramoda-bhāva*—in a pleasing attitude; *ānata*—lowered; *kandharasya*—of the shoulder; *āśṛṇvataḥ*—while thus hearing; *mām*—unto me; *anurāga-hāsa*—with kind smiling; *samīkṣayā*—particularly seeing me; *viśramayan*—allowing me complete rest; *uvāca*—said.

TRANSLATION

Maitreya Muni was greatly attached to Him [the Lord], and he was listening in a pleasing attitude, with his shoulder lowered. With a smile and a particular glance upon me, having allowed me to rest, the Lord spoke as follows.

PURPORT

Although both Uddhava and Maitreya were great souls, the Lord's attention was more on Uddhava because he was a spotlessly pure devotee. A *jñāna-bhakta*, or one whose devotion is mixed with the monistic viewpoint, is not a pure devotee. Although Maitreya was a devotee, his devotion was mixed. The Lord reciprocates with His devotees on the basis of transcendental love and not on the basis of philosophical knowledge or fruitive activities. In the transcendental loving service of the Lord, there is no place for monistic knowledge or fruitive activities. The *gopīs* in Vṛndāvana were neither highly learned scholars nor mystic *yogīs*. They had spontaneous love for the Lord, and thus He became their heart and soul, and the *gopīs* also became the heart and soul of the Lord. Lord Caitanya approved the relationship of the *gopīs* with the Lord as supreme. Herein the Lord's attitude towards Uddhava was more intimate than with Maitreya Muni.

TEXT 11

श्रीभगवानुवाच
वेदाहमन्तर्मनसीप्सितं ते
ददामि यत्तद् दुरवापमन्यैः ।
सत्रे पुरा विश्वसृजां वसूनां
मत्सिद्धिकामेन वसो त्वयेष्टः ॥११॥

śrī-bhagavān uvāca
vedāham antar manasīpsitaṁ te
dadāmi yat tad duravāpam anyaiḥ
satre purā viśva-sṛjāṁ vasūnāṁ
mat-siddhi-kāmena vaso tvayeṣṭaḥ

śrī-bhagavān uvāca—the Personality of Godhead said; *veda*—know; *aham*—I; *antaḥ*—within; *manasi*—the mind; *īpsitam*—what you desired; *te*—your; *dadāmi*—I give you; *yat*—which is; *tat*—that; *duravāpam*—very difficult to achieve; *anyaiḥ*—by others; *satre*—in the sacrifice; *purā*—in the days of yore; *viśva-sṛjām*—of those who expanded this creation; *vasūnām*—of the Vasus; *mat-siddhi-kāmena*—with a desire to achieve My association; *vaso*—O Vasu; *tvayā*—by you; *iṣṭaḥ*—ultimate goal of life.

TRANSLATION

O Vasu, I know from within your mind what you desired in the days of yore when the Vasus and other demigods responsible for

expanding the universal affairs performed sacrifices. You particularly desired to achieve My association. This is very difficult to obtain for others, but I award it unto you.

PURPORT

Uddhava is one of the eternal associates of the Lord, and a plenary portion of Uddhava was one of the eight Vasus in the days of yore. The eight Vasus and the demigods in the upper planetary system, who are responsible for the management of the universal affairs, performed a sacrifice in the days of yore, desiring to fulfill their respective ultimate goals in life. At that time an expansion of Uddhava, acting as one of the Vasus, desired to become an associate of the Lord. The Lord knew this because He is present in the heart of every living entity as Paramātmā, the Superconsciousness. In everyone's heart there is the representation of the Superconsciousness, who gives memory to the partial consciousness of every living entity. The living entity, as partial consciousness, forgets incidents of his past life, but the Superconsciousness reminds him how to act in terms of his past cultivation of knowledge. *Bhagavad-gītā* confirms this fact in various ways: *ye yathā māṁ prapadyante tāṁs tathaiva bhajāmy aham* (Bg. 4.11), *sarvasya cāhaṁ hṛdi sanniviṣṭo mattaḥ smṛtir jñānam apohanaṁ ca* (Bg. 15.15).

Everyone is at liberty to desire as he likes, but the desire is fulfilled by the Supreme Lord. Everyone is independent to think or desire, but the fulfillment of one's desire depends on the supreme will. This law is expressed as "Man proposes, God disposes." In the days of yore, when the demigods and Vasus performed sacrifice, Uddhava, as one of the Vasus, desired to enter into the association of the Lord, which is very difficult for those busy in empiric philosophical speculation or fruitive activities. Such persons have practically no information of the facts about becoming an associate of the Lord. Only the pure devotees can know, by the mercy of the Lord, that the personal association of the Lord is the highest perfection of life. The Lord assured Uddhava that He would fulfill his desire. It appears that when the Lord informed him by His indication to Uddhava, the great sage Maitreya finally became aware of the importance of entering into the association of the Lord.

TEXT 12

स एष साधो चरमो भवाना-
मासादितस्ते मदनुग्रहो यत् ।
यन्मां नृलोकान् रह उत्सृजन्तं
दिष्ट्या ददृश्वान् विशदानुवृत्त्या ॥१२॥

sa eṣa sādho caramo bhavānām
āsāditas te mad-anugraho yat
yan māṁ nṛlokān raha utsṛjantaṁ
diṣṭyā dadṛśvān viśadānuvṛttyā

saḥ—that; *eṣaḥ*—of those; *sādho*—O honest one; *caramaḥ*—the ultimate; *bhavānām*—of all your incarnations (as Vasu); *āsāditaḥ*—now achieved; *te*—unto you; *mat*—My; *anugrahaḥ*—mercy; *yat*—as it is; *yat*—because; *mām*—Me; *nṛ-lokān*—the planets of the conditioned souls; *rahaḥ*—in seclusion; *utsṛjantam*—while quitting; *diṣṭyā*—by seeing; *dadṛśvān*—what you have seen; *viśada-anuvṛttyā*—by unflinching devotion.

TRANSLATION

O honest one, your present life is the last and the supermost because in this term of life you have been awarded My ultimate favor. Now you can go to My transcendental abode, Vaikuṇṭha, by leaving this universe of conditioned living entities. Your visit to Me in this lonely place because of your pure and unflinching devotional service is a great boon for you.

PURPORT

When a person is fully conversant with knowledge of the Lord as far as can be known by a perfect living entity in the liberated state, he is allowed to enter into the spiritual sky, where the Vaikuṇṭha planets exist. The Lord was sitting in a lonely place just about to disappear from the vision of the inhabitants of this universe, and Uddhava was fortunate to see Him even at that time and thus receive the Lord's permission to enter Vaikuṇṭha. The Lord is everywhere at all times, and His appearance and disappearance are merely the experience of the inhabitants of a particular universe. He is just like the sun. The sun does not appear or disappear in the sky; it is only in the experience of men that in the morning the sun rises and in the evening the sun sets. The Lord is simultaneously both in Vaikuṇṭha and everywhere within and without Vaikuṇṭha.

TEXT 13

पुरा मया प्रोक्तमजाय नाभ्ये
पद्मे निषण्णाय ममादिसर्गे ।
ज्ञानं परं मन्महिमावभासं
यत्सूरयो भागवतं वदन्ति ॥१३॥

purā mayā proktam ajāya nābhye
padme niṣaṇṇāya mamādi-sarge
jñānaṁ paraṁ man-mahimāvabhāsaṁ
yat sūrayo bhāgavataṁ vadanti

purā—in the days of yore; *mayā*—by Me; *proktam*—was said; *ajāya*—unto Brahmā; *nābhye*—out of the navel; *padme*—on the lotus; *niṣaṇṇāya*—unto the one situated on; *mama*—My; *ādi-sarge*—in the beginning of creation; *jñānam*—knowledge; *param*—sublime; *mat-mahimā*—My transcendental glories; *avabhāsam*—that which clarifies; *yat*—which; *sūrayaḥ*—the great learned sages; *bhāgavatam*—*Śrīmad-Bhāgavatam; vadanti*—do say.

TRANSLATION

O Uddhava, in the lotus millennium in the days of yore, at the beginning of the creation, I spoke unto Brahmā, who is situated on the lotus that grows out of My navel, about My transcendental glories, which the great sages describe as Śrīmad-Bhāgavatam.

PURPORT

The explanation of the Supreme Self, as given to Brahmā and already explained in the Second Canto of this great literature, is further clarified herein. The Lord said that the concise form of *Śrīmad-Bhāgavatam* as explained to Brahmā was meant to elucidate His personality. The impersonal explanation of those four verses in the Second Canto is nullified herewith. Śrīdhara Svāmī also explains in this connection that the same concise form of the *Bhāgavatam* concerned the pastimes of Lord Kṛṣṇa and was never meant for impersonal indulgence.

TEXT 14

इत्यादृतोक्तः परमस्य पुंसः
प्रतिक्षणानुग्रहभाजनोऽहम् ।
स्नेहोत्थरोमा स्खलिताक्षरस्तं
मुञ्चञ्छुचः प्राञ्जलिराबभाषे ॥१४॥

ity ādṛtoktaḥ paramasya puṁsaḥ
pratikṣaṇānugraha-bhājano 'ham
snehottha-romā skhalitākṣaras taṁ
muñcañ chucaḥ prāñjalir ābabhāṣe

iti—thus; *ādṛta*—being favored; *uktaḥ*—addressed; *paramasya*—of the Supreme; *puṁsaḥ*—Personality of Godhead; *pratikṣaṇa*—every moment; *anugraha-bhājanaḥ*—object of favor; *aham*—myself; *sneha*—affection; *uttha*—eruption; *romā*—hairs on the body; *skhalita*—slackened; *akṣaraḥ*—of the eyes; *tam*—that; *muñcan*—smearing; *śucaḥ*—tears; *prāñjaliḥ*—with folded hands; *ābabhāṣe*—said.

TRANSLATION

Uddhava said: O Vidura, when I was thus favored at every moment by the Supreme Personality of Godhead and addressed by Him with great affection, my words failed in tears, and the hairs on my body erupted. After smearing my tears, I, with folded hands, spoke like this.

TEXT 15

को न्वीश ते पादसरोजभाजां
सुदुर्लभोऽर्थेषु चतुर्ष्वपीह ।

तथापि नाहं प्रवृणोमि भूमन्
भवत्पदाम्भोजनिषेवणोत्सुकः ॥१५॥

ko nv īśa te pāda-saroja-bhājāṁ
sudurlabho 'rtheṣu caturṣv apīha
tathāpi nāhaṁ pravṛṇomi bhūman
bhavat-padāmbhoja-niṣevaṇotsukaḥ

kaḥ nu īśa—O my Lord; *te*—Your; *pāda-saroja-bhājām*—of the devotees engaged in the transcendental loving service of Your lotus feet; *su-durlabhaḥ*—very difficult to obtain; *artheṣu*—in the matter of; *caturṣu*—in the four objectives; *api*—in spite of; *iha*—in this world; *tathā api*—yet; *na*—do not; *aham*—I; *pravṛṇomi*—prefer; *bhūman*—O great one; *bhavat*—Your; *pada-ambhoja*—lotus feet; *niṣevaṇa-utsukaḥ*—anxious to serve.

TRANSLATION

O my Lord, devotees who engage in the transcendental loving service of Your lotus feet have no difficulty in achieving anything within the realm of the four principles of religiosity, economic development, sense gratification and liberation. But, O great one, as far as I am concerned, I have preferred only to engage in the loving service of Your lotus feet.

PURPORT

Those who are associated with the Lord in the Vaikuṇṭha planets achieve all the bodily features of the Lord and appear to be the same as Lord Viṣṇu. Such liberation is called *sārūpya-mukti*, which is one of the five kinds of liberation. The devotees engaged in the transcendental loving service of the Lord never accept the *sāyujya-mukti*, or merging in the rays of the Lord called the *brahmajyoti*. The devotees can achieve not only liberation but any success in the realm of religiosity, economic development or sense gratification up to the standard of the demigods in the heavenly planets. But such a pure devotee as Uddhava refuses to accept all such facilities. A pure devotee wants simply to engage in the service of the Lord and does not consider his own personal benefit.

TEXT 16

कर्माण्यनीहस्य भवोऽभवस्य ते
दुर्गाश्रयोऽथारिभयात्पलायनम् ।
कालात्मनो यत्प्रमदायुताश्रमः
स्वात्मन्रतेः खिद्यति धीर्विदामिह ॥१६॥

karmāṇy anīhasya bhavo 'bhavasya te
durgāśrayo 'thāri-bhayāt palāyanam
kālātmano yat pramadā-yutāśramaḥ
svātman-rateḥ khidyati dhīr vidām iha

karmāṇi—activities; *anīhasya*—of one who has no desire; *bhavaḥ*—birth; *abhavasya*—of one who is never born; *te*—your; *durga-āśrayaḥ*—taking shelter of the fort; *atha*—thereafter; *ari-bhayāt*—out of fear of the enemies; *palāyanam*—flee; *kāla-ātmanaḥ*—of He who is the controller of eternal time; *yat*—that; *pramadā-āyuta*—in the association of women; *āśramaḥ*—household life; *sva-ātman*—in Your own Self; *rateḥ*—one who enjoys; *khidyati*—is disturbed; *dhīḥ*—intelligence; *vidām*—of the learned; *iha*—in this world.

TRANSLATION

My Lord, even the learned sages become disturbed in their intelligence when they see that Your Greatness engages in fruitive work although You are free from all desires, that You take birth although You are unborn, that You flee out of fear of the enemy and take shelter in a fort although You are the controller of invincible time, and that You enjoy householder life surrounded by many women although You enjoy in Your Self.

PURPORT

Pure devotees of the Lord are not very much concerned with philosophical speculation in regard to transcendental knowledge of the Lord. Nor is it possible to acquire complete knowledge of the Lord. Whatever little knowledge they have about the Lord is sufficient for them because devotees are simply satisfied in hearing and chanting about the transcendental pastimes of the Lord. This gives them all transcendental bliss. But some of the pastimes of the Lord appear contradictory, even to such pure devotees, and thus Uddhava asked the Lord about some of the contradictory incidents in His pastimes. The Lord is described as having nothing to do personally, and it is actually so because even in the creation and sustenance of the material world, the Lord has nothing to do. It seems contradictory, then, to hear that the Lord personally lifts the Govardhana Hill for the protection of His unalloyed devotees. The Lord is the Supreme Brahman, the Absolute Truth, the Personality of Godhead appearing like a man, but Uddhava had doubts whether He could have so many transcendental activities.

There is no difference between the Personality of Godhead and the impersonal Brahman. How then can the Lord have so many things to do, whereas the impersonal Brahman is stated to have nothing to do either materially or spiritually? If the Lord is ever unborn, how then is He born as the son of Vasudeva and Devakī? He is fearful even to *kāla*, the supreme fear, and yet the Lord is afraid of fighting Jarāsandha and takes shelter in a fort. How can one who is full in Himself take pleasure in the association of many women? How can He take wives and, just like a householder, take pleasure in the association of family members, children, relatives and parents? All these apparently contradictory happenings bewilder even the greatest learned scholars, who, thus bewildered, cannot understand whether inactivity is a fact or whether His activities are only imitations.

The solution is that the Lord has nothing to do with anything mundane. All His activities are transcendental. This cannot be understood by the mundane speculators. For the mundane speculators there is certainly a kind of bewilderment, but for the transcendental devotees there is nothing astonishing in this. The Brahman conception of the Absolute Truth is certainly the negation of all mundane activities, but the Parabrahman conception is full with transcendental activities. One who knows the distinctions between the conception of Brahman and the conception of Supreme Brahman is certainly the real transcendentalist. There is no bewilderment for such transcendentalists. The Lord Himself also declares in *Bhagavad-gītā* (10.2), "Even the great sages and demigods can know hardly anything about My activities and transcendental potencies." The right explanation of the Lord's activities is given by Grandfather Bhīṣmadeva (*Bhāg.* 1.9.16) as follows:

na hy asya karhicid rājan
pumān veda vidhitsitam
yad-vijijñāsayā yuktā
muhyanti kavayo 'pi hi

TEXT 17

मन्त्रेषु मां वा उपहूय यत्त्व-
मकुण्ठिताखण्डसदात्मबोधः ।
पृच्छेः प्रभो मुग्ध इवाप्रमत्त-
स्तन्नो मनो मोहयतीव देव ॥१७॥

mantreṣu māṁ vā upahūya yat tvam
akuṇṭhitākhaṇḍa-sadātma-bodhaḥ
pṛccheḥ prabho mugdha ivāpramattas
tan no mano mohayatīva deva

mantreṣu—in consultations; *mām*—unto me; *vai*—as either; *upahūya*—by calling; *yat*—as much as; *tvam*—Your Lordship; *akuṇṭhita*—without hesitation; *akhaṇḍa*—without being separated; *sadā*—eternally; *ātma*—self; *bodhaḥ*—intelligent; *pṛccheḥ*—asked; *prabho*—O my Lord; *mugdhaḥ*—bewildered; *iva*—as if it were so; *apramattaḥ*—although never bewildered; *tat*—that; *naḥ*—our; *manaḥ*—mind; *mohayati*—bewilders; *iva*—as it is so; *deva*—O my Lord.

TRANSLATION

O my Lord, Your eternal Self is never divided by the influence of time, and there is no limitation to Your perfect knowledge. Thus You were sufficiently able to consult with Yourself, yet You called upon me for consultation, as if bewildered, although You are never bewildered. And this act of Yours bewilders me.

PURPORT

Uddhava was never actually bewildered, but he says that all these contradictions appear to be bewildering. The whole discussion between Kṛṣṇa and Uddhava was meant for the benefit of Maitreya, who was sitting nearby. The Lord used to call Uddhava for consultation when the city was attacked by Jarāsandha and others and when He executed great sacrifices as part of His routine royal work as Lord of Dvārakā. The Lord has no past, present and future because He is unhampered by the influence of eternal time and thus nothing is hidden from Him. He is eternally self-intelligent. Therefore His calling for Uddhava to give Him enlightenment is certainly astonishing. All these actions of the Lord appear to be contradictory, although there is no contradiction in the routine activities of the Lord. Therefore it is better to see them as they are and not attempt to explain them.

TEXT 18

ज्ञानं परं स्वात्मरहःप्रकाशं
प्रोवाच कस्मै भगवान् समग्रम् ।
अपि क्षमं नो ग्रहणाय भर्त-
र्वदाञ्जसा यद् वृजिनं तरेम ॥१८॥

jñānaṁ paraṁ svātma-rahaḥ-prakāśaṁ
provāca kasmai bhagavān samagram
api kṣamaṁ no grahaṇāya bhartar
vadāñjasā yad vṛjinaṁ tarema

jñānam—knowledge; *param*—supreme; *sva-ātma*—own self; *rahaḥ*—mystery; *prakāśam*—enlightening; *provāca*—said; *kasmai*—unto Ka (Brahmājī); *bhagavān*—the Personality of Godhead; *samagram*—in sum total; *api*—if so; *kṣamam*—able; *naḥ*—unto me; *grahaṇāya*—acceptable; *bhartaḥ*—O my Lord; *vada*—say; *añjasā*—in detail; *yat*—that which; *vṛjinam*—miseries; *tarema*—can cross over.

TRANSLATION

My Lord, kindly explain to us, if You think us competent to receive it, that transcendental knowledge which gives enlightenment about Yourself and which You explained before to Brahmājī.

PURPORT

A pure devotee like Uddhava has no material afflictions because he engages constantly in the transcendental loving service of the Lord. A devotee feels afflicted without the association of the Lord. Constant remembrance of the Lord's activities keeps the devotee alive, and therefore Uddhava requested that the Lord please enlighten him with the knowledge of *Śrīmad-Bhāgavatam*, as previously instructed to Brahmājī.

TEXT 19

इत्यावेदितहार्दाय मह्यं स भगवान् परः ।
आदिदेशारविन्दाक्ष आत्मनः परमां स्थितिम् ॥१९॥

ity āvedita-hārdāya
mahyaṁ sa bhagavān paraḥ
ādideśāravindākṣa
ātmanaḥ paramāṁ sthitim

iti āvedita—thus being prayed to by me; *hārdāya*—from the core of my heart; *mahyam*—unto me; *saḥ*—He; *bhagavān*—the Personality of Godhead; *paraḥ*—Supreme; *ādideśa*—instructed; *aravinda-akṣaḥ*—the lotus-eyed; *ātmanaḥ*—of Himself; *paramām*—transcendental; *sthitim*—situation.

TRANSLATION

When I thus expressed my heartfelt desires unto the Supreme Personality of Godhead, the lotus-eyed Lord instructed me about His transcendental situation.

PURPORT

The words *paramāṁ sthitim* are significant in this verse. The Lord's transcendental situation was not even spoken of to Brahmā when the four verses of *Śrīmad-Bhāgavatam* (2.9.33–36) were explained. This transcendental situation comprises His dealings with devotees engaged in transcendental loving service, as exhibited at Dvārakā and Vṛndāvana. When the Lord explained His specific transcendental situation, it was meant for Uddhava only, and therefore Uddhava particularly said *mahyam* ("unto me"), although the great sage Maitreya was also sitting there. Such a transcendental situation is hardly understood by those whose devotion is mixed with speculative knowledge or fruitive activities. The Lord's activities in confidential love are very rarely disclosed to the general devotees who are attracted by devotion mixed with knowledge and mysticism. Such activities are the inconceivable pastimes of the Lord.

TEXT 20

स एवमाराधितपादतीर्था-
दधीततत्त्वात्मविबोधमार्गः ।
प्रणम्य पादौ परिवृत्य देव-
मिहागतोऽहं विरहातुरात्मा ॥२०॥

sa evam ārādhita-pāda-tīrthād
adhīta-tattvātma-vibodha-mārgaḥ
praṇamya pādau parivṛtya devam
ihāgato 'haṁ virahāturātmā

saḥ—so myself; *evam*—thus; *ārādhita*—worshiped; *pāda-tīrthāt*—from the Personality of Godhead; *adhīta*—studied; *tattva-ātma*—self-knowledge; *vibodha*—understanding; *mārgaḥ*—path; *praṇamya*—after saluting; *pādau*—at His lotus feet; *parivṛtya*—after circumambulating; *devam*—the Lord; *iha*—at this place; *āgataḥ*—reached; *aham*—I; *viraha*—separation; *ātura-ātmā*—aggrieved in self.

TRANSLATION

I have studied the path of understanding self-knowledge from my spiritual master, the Personality of Godhead, and thus after circumambulating Him I have come to this place, very much aggrieved due to separation.

PURPORT

Śrī Uddhava's actual life is the direct symbol of the *catuḥ-ślokī Bhāgavatam* enunciated first to Brahmājī by the Personality of Godhead.

These four very great and important verses from *Śrīmad-Bhāgavatam* are particularly taken out by the Māyāvādī speculators, who construe a different purport to suit their impersonal view of monism. Here is the proper answer to such unauthorized speculators. The verses of *Śrīmad-Bhāgavatam* are purely theistic science understandable by the post-graduate students of *Bhagavad-gītā*. The unauthorized dry speculators are offenders at the lotus feet of the Lord Śrī Kṛṣṇa because they distort the purports of *Bhagavad-gītā* and *Śrīmad-Bhāgavatam* to mislead the public and prepare a direct path to the hell known as Andhatāmisra. As confirmed in *Bhagavad-gītā* (16.20) such envious speculators are without knowledge and are surely condemned life after life. They unnecessarily take shelter of Śrīpāda Śaṅkarācārya, but he was not so drastic as to commit an offense at the lotus feet of Lord Kṛṣṇa. According to Lord Śrī Caitanya Mahāprabhu, Śrīpāda Śaṅkarācārya preached the Māyāvāda philosophy for a particular purpose. Such a philosophy was necessary to defeat the Buddhist philosophy of the nonexistence of the spirit soul, but it was never meant for perpetual acceptance. It was an emergency. Thus Lord Kṛṣṇa was accepted by Śaṅkarācārya as the Supreme Personality of Godhead in his commentation on *Bhagavad-gītā*. Since he was a great devotee of Lord Kṛṣṇa, he did not dare write any commentary on *Śrīmad-Bhāgavatam* because that would have been a direct offense at the lotus feet of the Lord. But later speculators, in the name of Māyāvāda philosophy, unnecessarily make their commentary on the *catuḥ-ślokī Bhāgavatam* without any bona fide intent.

The monistic dry speculators have no business in the *Śrīmad-Bhāgavatam* because this particular Vedic literature is forbidden for them by the great author himself. Śrīla Vyāsadeva has definitely forbidden persons engaged in religiosity, economic development, sense gratification and, finally, salvation, from trying to understand *Śrīmad-Bhāgavatam*, which is not meant for them (*Bhāg.* 1.1.2). Śrīpāda Śrīdhara Svāmī, the great commentator on *Śrīmad-Bhāgavatam*, has definitely forbidden the salvationists or monists to deal in *Śrīmad-Bhāgavatam*. It is not for them. Yet such unauthorized persons perversely try to understand *Śrīmad-Bhāgavatam*, and thus they commit offenses at the feet of the Lord, which even Śrīpāda Śaṅkarācārya dared not do. Thus they prepare for their continuation of miserable life. It should be particularly noted herein that Uddhava studied the *catuḥ-ślokī*

Bhāgavatam directly from the Lord, who spoke them first to Brahmājī, and this time the Lord explained more confidentially the self-knowledge mentioned as the *paramāṁ sthitim.* Upon learning such self-knowledge of love, Uddhava felt very much aggrieved by feelings of separation from the Lord. Unless one is awakened to the stage of Uddhava—everlastingly feeling the separation of the Lord in transcendental love, as exhibited by Lord Caitanya also—one cannot understand the real import of the four essential verses of *Śrīmad-Bhāgavatam.* One should not indulge in the unauthorized act of twisting the meaning and thereby putting himself on the dangerous path of offense.

TEXT 21

सोऽहं तद्दर्शनाह्लादवियोगार्तियुतः प्रभो ।
गमिष्ये दयितं तस्य बदर्याश्रममण्डलम् ॥२१॥

so 'haṁ tad-darśanāhlāda-
viyogārti-yutaḥ prabho
gamiṣye dayitaṁ tasya
badaryāśrama-maṇḍalam

saḥ aham—thus myself; *tat*—His; *darśana*—audience; *āhlāda*—pleasure; *viyoga*—without that; *ārti-yutaḥ*—afflicted by distress; *prabho*—my dear sir; *gamiṣye*—shall go; *dayitam*—so instructed; *tasya*—His; *badaryāśrama*—Badarikāśrama, in the Himalayas; *maṇḍalam*—association.

TRANSLATION

My dear Vidura, now I am mad for want of the pleasure of seeing Him, and just to mitigate this I am now proceeding to Badarikāśrama in the Himalayas for association, as I have been instructed by Him.

PURPORT

A pure devotee of the Lord of the standard of Uddhava constantly associates with the Lord in the double perception of simultaneous separation and meeting. The pure devotee is not for a moment unengaged in the transcendental service of the Lord. Execution of the Lord's service is the main occupation of the pure devotee. Uddhava's separation from the Lord was unbearable, and therefore he started to Badarikāśrama in obedience to the Lord's order because the order of the Lord and the Lord Himself are identical. As long as one is engaged in the execution of the order of the Lord, there is no factual separation from Him.

TEXT 22

यत्र नारायणो देवो नरश्च भगवानृषिः ।
मृदु तीव्रं तपो दीर्घं तेपाते लोकभावनौ ॥२२॥

yatra nārāyaṇo devo
naraś ca bhagavān ṛṣiḥ
mṛdu tīvraṁ tapo dīrghaṁ
tepāte loka-bhāvanau

yatra—where; *nārāyaṇaḥ*—the Personality of Godhead; *devaḥ*—by incarnation; *naraḥ*—human being; *ca*—also; *bhagavān*—the Lord; *ṛṣiḥ*—great sage; *mṛdu*—amiable to everyone; *tīvram*—severe; *tapaḥ*—penance; *dīrgham*—very long; *tepāte*—performing; *loka-bhāvanau*—welfare of all living entities.

TRANSLATION

There in Badarikāśrama the Personality of Godhead, in His incarnation as the sages Nara and Nārāyaṇa, has been undergoing great penance since time immemorial for the welfare of all amiable living entities.

PURPORT

Badarikāśrama in the Himalayas, the abode of the Nara-Nārāyaṇa sages, is a great place of pilgrimage for the Hindus. Even up to the present, hundreds and thousands of pious Hindus go to pay respects to the incarnation of Godhead Nara-Nārāyaṇa. It appears that even five thousand years ago this holy place was being visited by such a holy being as Uddhava, and even at that time the place was known to be very, very old. This particular pilgrimage site is very difficult to visit for ordinary men because of its difficult situation in the Himalayas in a place which is covered by ice almost all year. A few months during the summer season people can visit this place at great personal inconvenience. There are four *dhāmas*, or kingdoms of God, which represent the planets of the spiritual sky, which consists of the *brahmajyoti* and the Vaikuṇṭhas. These are Badarikāśrama, Rameśvara, Jagannātha Purī and Dvārakā. Faithful Hindus still visit all these holy places for perfection of spiritual realization, following in the footsteps of devotees like Uddhava.

TEXT 23

श्रीशुक उवाच

इत्युद्धवादुपाकर्ण्य सुहृदां दुःसहं वधम् ।
ज्ञानेनाशमयत्क्षत्ता शोकमुत्पतितं बुधः ॥२३॥

śrī-śuka uvāca
ity uddhavād upākarṇya
suhṛdāṁ duḥsahaṁ vadham
jñānenāśamayat kṣattā
śokam utpatitaṁ budhaḥ

śrī-śukaḥ uvāca—Śrī Śuka Gosvāmī said; *iti*—thus; *uddhavāt*—from Uddhava; *upākarṇya*—hearing; *suhṛdām*—of friends and relatives; *duḥsaham*—unbearable; *vadham*—annihilation; *jñānena*—by transcendental knowledge; *aśamayat*—pacified himself; *kṣattā*—Vidura; *śokam*—bereavement; *utpatitam*—arisen; *budhaḥ*—the learned.

TRANSLATION

Śrī Śukadeva Gosvāmī said: After hearing from Uddhava all about the annihilation of his friends and relatives, the learned Vidura pacified his overwhelming bereavement by dint of his transcendental knowledge.

PURPORT

Vidura was informed that the result of the Battle of Kurukṣetra was the annihilation of his friends and relatives as well as the destruction of the Yadu dynasty and also the passing away of the Lord. All these hurled him into bereavement for the time being, but because he was highly advanced in transcendental knowledge, he was quite competent to pacify himself by enlightenment. As it is stated in *Bhagavad-gītā*, due to our long association with bodily relationships, bereavement on account of the annihilation of friends and relatives is not at all astonishing, but one has to learn the art of subduing such bereavement with higher, transcendental knowledge. The talks between Uddhava and Vidura on the topic of Kṛṣṇa began at sunset, and Vidura was now further advanced in knowledge due to his association with Uddhava.

TEXT 24

स तं महाभागवतं व्रजन्तं कौरवर्षभः ।
विश्रम्भादभ्यधत्तेदं मुख्यं कृष्णपरिग्रहे ॥२४॥

sa taṁ mahā-bhāgavataṁ
vrajantaṁ kauravarṣabhaḥ
viśrambhād abhyadhattedaṁ
mukhyaṁ kṛṣṇa-parigrahe

saḥ—Vidura; *tam*—unto Uddhava; *mahā-bhāgavatam*—the great devotee of the Lord; *vrajantam*—while going; *kaurava-ṛṣabhaḥ*—the best amongst the Kauravas; *viśrambhāt*—out of confidence; *abhyadhatta*—submitted; *idam*—this; *mukhyam*—unto the chief; *kṛṣṇa*—Lord Kṛṣṇa; *parigrahe*—in devotional service to the Lord.

TRANSLATION

While Uddhava, the chief and most confidential amongst the devotees of the Lord, was going away, Vidura, in affection and confidence, questioned him.

PURPORT

Vidura was much older than Uddhava. By family relationship Uddhava was a contemporary brother of Kṛṣṇa's, while Vidura was as elderly as Kṛṣṇa's father Vasudeva. But although junior by age, Uddhava was much advanced in the devotional service of the Lord, and therefore he is described herein as the chief amongst the devotees of the Lord.

Vidura was confident about this, and thus he addressed Uddhava in that higher category. That is the way of courteous dealings between two devotees.

TEXT 25

विदुर उवाच
ज्ञानं परं स्वात्मरहःप्रकाशं
यदाह योगेश्वर ईश्वरस्ते ।
वक्तुं भवान्नोऽर्हति यद्धि विष्णो-
र्भृत्याः स्वभृत्यार्थकृतश्चरन्ति ॥२५॥

vidura uvāca
jñānaṁ paraṁ svātma-rahaḥ-prakāśaṁ
yad āha yogeśvara īśvaras te
vaktuṁ bhavān no 'rhati yad dhi viṣṇor
bhṛtyāḥ sva-bhṛtyārtha-kṛtaś caranti

viduraḥ uvāca—Vidura said; *jñānam*—knowledge; *param*—transcendental; *sva-ātma*—regarding the self; *rahaḥ*—mystery; *prakāśam*—enlightening; *yat*—that which; *āha*—said; *yoga-īśvaraḥ*—the master of all mystics; *īśvaraḥ*—the Lord; *te*—unto you; *vaktum*—to narrate; *bhavān*—your good self; *naḥ*—unto me; *arhati*—deserve; *yat*—for; *hi*—reason of; *viṣṇoḥ*—of Lord Viṣṇu; *bhṛtyāḥ*—servants; *sva-bhṛtya-artha-kṛtaḥ*—for the interest of their servants; *caranti*—do wander.

TRANSLATION

Vidura said: O Uddhava, because the servants of Viṣṇu, the Lord, wander in the interest of serving others, it is quite fit that you kindly describe the self-knowledge with which you have been enlightened by the Lord Himself.

PURPORT

The servants of the Lord are actually the servants of society. They have no interest in human society other than to enlighten it in transcendental knowledge; they are interested in imparting knowledge of the relationship of the living being with the Supreme Lord, the activities in that transcendental relationship, and the ultimate goal of human life. That is the real knowledge which can help society achieve the real aim of human welfare. Knowledge in the matter of the bodily necessities of eating, sleeping, mating and fearing, transformed into various branches of advancement of knowledge, is all temporary. A living being is not the material body but an eternal part and parcel of the Supreme Being, and thus revival of his self-knowledge is essential. Without this knowledge, the human life is baffled. The servants of the Lord, Viṣṇu, are entrusted with this responsible work, and so they wander over the earth and to all other planets in the universe. Thus the knowledge which was received by Uddhava directly from the Lord deserves to be distributed in human society, especially to persons like Vidura, who are highly advanced in the devotional service of the Lord.

Real transcendental knowledge descends in the disciplic succession from the Lord to Uddhava, from Uddhava to Vidura and so on. Such supreme transcendental knowledge is not possible to achieve by the process of imperfect speculation as performed by the so-called learned mundane wranglers. Vidura was anxious to know from Uddhava that confidential knowledge known as *paramāṁ sthitim*, in which the Lord is known by His transcendental pastimes. Although Vidura was older than Uddhava, he was anxious to become a servant of Uddhava in the transcendental relationship. This formula of transcendental disciplic succession is taught by Lord Caitanya also. Lord Caitanya advises that one receive transcendental knowledge from anyone—whether a *brāhmaṇa* or a *śūdra*, a householder or a *sannyāsī*—provided that person is factually conversant with the science of Kṛṣṇa. A person who knows the science of Kṛṣṇa is factually a bona fide spiritual master.

TEXT 26

उद्धव उवाच

ननु ते तत्त्वसंराध्य ऋषिः कौषारवोऽन्तिके ।
साक्षाद्भगवतादिष्टो मर्त्यलोकं जिहासता ॥२६॥

uddhava uvāca
nanu te tattva-saṁrādhya
ṛṣiḥ kauṣāravo 'ntike

sākṣād bhagavatādiṣṭo
martya-lokaṁ jihāsatā

uddhavaḥ uvāca—Uddhava said; *nanu*—however; *te*—of yourself; *tattva-saṁrādhyaḥ*—one who is worshipable for reception of transcendental knowledge; *ṛṣiḥ*—learned scholar; *kauṣāravaḥ*—unto the son of Kuṣāru (Maitreya); *antike*—staying nearby; *sākṣāt*—directly; *bhagavatā*—by the Personality of Godhead; *ādiṣṭaḥ*—instructed; *martya-lokam*—mortal world; *jihāsatā*—while quitting.

TRANSLATION

Śrī Uddhava said: You may take lessons from the great learned sage Maitreya, who is nearby and who is worshipable for reception of transcendental knowledge. He was directly instructed by the Personality of Godhead while He was about to quit this mortal world.

PURPORT

Although one may be well versed in the transcendental science, one should be careful about the offense of *maryādā-vyatikrama*, or impertinently surpassing a greater personality. According to scriptural injunction one should be very careful of transgressing the law of *maryādā-vyatikrama* because by so doing one loses his duration of life, his opulence, fame and piety and the blessings of all the world. To be well versed in the transcendental science necessitates awareness of the techniques of spiritual science. Uddhava, being well aware of all these technicalities of transcendental science, advised Vidura to approach Maitreya Ṛṣi to receive transcendental knowledge. Vidura wanted to accept Uddhava as his spiritual master, but Uddhava did not accept the post because Vidura was as old as Uddhava's father and therefore Uddhava could not accept him as his disciple, especially when Maitreya was present nearby. The rule is that in the presence of a higher personality one should not be very eager to impart instructions, even if one is competent and well versed. So Uddhava decided to send an elderly person like Vidura to Maitreya, another elderly person, but he was well versed also because he was directly instructed by the Lord while He was about to quit this mortal world. Since both Uddhava and Maitreya were directly instructed by the Lord, both had the authority to become the spiritual master of Vidura or anyone else, but Maitreya, being elderly, had the first claim to becoming the spiritual master, especially for Vidura, who was much older than Uddhava. One should not be eager to become a spiritual master cheaply for the sake of profit and fame, but should become a spiritual master only for the service of the Lord. The Lord never tolerates the impertinence of *maryādā-vyatikrama.* One should never pass over the honor due to an elderly spiritual master in the interests of one's own personal gain and fame. Impertinence on the part of the pseudo spiritual master is very risky to progressive spiritual realization.

TEXT 27

श्रीशुक उवाच

इति सह विदुरेण विश्वमूर्ते-
गुणकथया सुधया प्लावितोरुतापः ।
क्षणमिव पुलिने यमस्वसुस्तां
समुषित औपगविर्निशां ततोऽगात् ॥२७॥

śrī-śuka uvāca
iti saha vidureṇa viśva-mūrter
guṇa-kathayā sudhayā plāvitorutāpaḥ
kṣaṇam iva puline yamasvasus tāṁ
samuṣita aupagavir niśāṁ tato 'gāt

śrī-śukaḥ uvāca—Śrī Śukadeva Gosvāmī said; *iti*—thus; *saha*—along with; *vidureṇa*—Vidura; *viśva-mūrteḥ*—of the Universal Person; *guṇa-kathayā*—in the discourse of transcendental qualities; *sudhayā*—nectarean; *plāvita-uru-tāpaḥ*—overwhelmed by great affliction; *kṣaṇam*—moment; *iva*—like that; *puline*—on the bank of; *yamasvasuḥ tām*—River Yamunā; *samuṣitaḥ*—passed on; *aupagaviḥ*—the son of Aupagava (Uddhava); *niśām*—the night; *tataḥ*—thereafter; *agāt*—went away.

TRANSLATION

Śukadeva Gosvāmī said: O King, after thus discussing with Vidura the transcendental name, fame, qualities, etc., on the bank

of the Yamunā, Uddhava was overwhelmed with great affliction. He passed the night as if it were a moment, and thereafter he went away.

PURPORT

The word used here for Kṛṣṇa is *viśva-mūrti.* Both Uddhava and Vidura were in great affliction because of Lord Kṛṣṇa's departure, and the more they discussed the transcendental name, fame and qualities of the Lord, the more the picture of the Lord became visible to them everywhere. Such visualization of the transcendental form of the Lord is neither false nor imaginary but is factual Absolute Truth. When the Lord is perceived as *viśva-mūrti,* it is not that He loses His personality or transcendental eternal form, but He becomes visible in the same form everywhere.

TEXT 28

राजोवाच
निधनमुपगतेषु वृष्णिभोजे-
ष्वधिरथयूथपयूथपेषु मुख्यः ।
स तु कथमवशिष्ट उद्धवो यद्धरि-
रपि तत्यज आकृतिं त्र्यधीशः ॥२८॥

rājovāca
nidhanam upagateṣu vṛṣṇi-bhojeṣv
adhiratha-yūthapa-yūthapeṣu muhkyaḥ
sa tu katham avaśiṣṭa uddhavo yad
dharir api tatyaja ākṛtiṁ tryadhīśaḥ

rājā uvāca—the King inquired; *nidhanam*—destruction; *upagateṣu*—having overtaken; *vṛṣṇi*—of the Vṛṣṇi dynasty; *bhojeṣu*—the Bhoja dynasty; *adhiratha*—great commander; *yūtha-pa*—commander in chief; *yūtha-peṣu*—amongst them; *mukhyaḥ*—prominent; *saḥ*—he; *tu*—only; *katham*—how; *avaśiṣṭaḥ*—remained; *uddhavaḥ*—Uddhava; *yat*—whereas; *hariḥ*—the Personality of Godhead; *api*—also; *tatyaje*—finished; *ākṛtim*—complete pastimes; *tri-adhīśaḥ*—the Lord of the three worlds.

TRANSLATION

The King inquired: At the end of the pastimes of the Lord of the three worlds, Śrī Kṛṣṇa, and after the disappearance of the members of the Vṛṣṇi and Bhoja dynasties, who were the best of the great commanders, why did Uddhava alone remain?

PURPORT

According to Śrī Jīva Gosvāmī, *nidhanam* means the transcendental abode of the Lord. *Ni* means the highest, and *dhanam* means opulence. And because the abode of the Lord is the highest manifestation of transcendental opulence, His abode can therefore be called *nidhanam.* Apart from the grammatical elucidation, the real purpose of the word *nidhanam* is to indicate that all the members of the Vṛṣṇi and Bhoja dynasties were direct associates of the Lord, and after the end of His pastimes, all the associates were dispatched to their respective positions in the transcendental abode.

Śrīla Viśvanātha Cakravartī Ṭhākura elucidates the meaning of *ākṛtim* as pastimes. *Ā* means complete, and *kṛtim* means transcendental pastimes. Since the Lord is identical with His transcendental body, there is no question of His changing or quitting His body. To act in accordance with the rules and customs of the material world, the Lord seems to take His birth or leave His body, but the pure devotees of the Lord know well the actual fact. It is necessary, therefore, for the serious students of *Śrīmad-Bhāgavatam* to follow the notes and comments of the great *ācāryas* like Jīva Gosvāmī and Viśvanātha Cakravartī. To others, who are not devotees of the Lord, the comments and explanations of such *ācāryas* may appear to be grammatical jugglery, but to the students who are in the line of disciplic succession, the explanations of the great *ācāryas* are quite fit.

The word *upagateṣu* is also significant. All the members of Vṛṣṇi and Bhoja directly reached the abode of the Lord. Other devotees do not reach the abode of the Lord directly, but the pure associates of the Lord have no attraction for the opulence of any planets of the material world. Sometimes, due to inquisitiveness, devotees who are to be promoted to the abode of the Lord have some attraction for the opulence of the higher material planets above the earth, and thus they desire to see them while going up to the perfection. But the Vṛṣṇis and Bhojas were directly dispatched because they had no attraction for material planets. Śrīla Viśvanātha Cakravartī Ṭhākura also suggests that according to the *Amara-kośa* dictionary, *ākṛti* also means "signal." Lord Kṛṣṇa ordered Uddhava by signal to go to Badarikāśrama after His departure, and Uddhava, as a pure devotee of the Lord, carried out the order more faithfully than going back to Godhead, or the abode of the Lord. That was the cause of his remaining alone even after the departure of the Lord from the face of the earth.

TEXT 29

श्रीशुक उवाच
ब्रह्मशापापदेशेन कालेनामोघवाञ्छितः ।
संहृत्य स्वकुलं स्फीतं त्यक्ष्यन्देहमचिन्तयत् ॥२९॥

śrī-śuka uvāca
brahma-śāpāpadeśena
kālenāmogha-vāñchitaḥ
saṁhṛtya sva-kulaṁ sphītaṁ
tyakṣyan deham acintayat

śrī-śukaḥ uvāca—Śrī Śukadeva Gosvāmī said; *brahma-śāpa*—cursing by the *brāhmaṇas; apadeśena*—on the plea, by such a show; *kālena*—by the eternal time; *amogha*—unfailing; *vāñchitaḥ*—one who so desires; *saṁhṛtya*—closing; *sva-kulam*—own family; *sphītam*—excessively numerous; *tyakṣyan*—after giving up; *deham*—the universal form; *acintayat*—thought to Himself.

TRANSLATION

Śukadeva Gosvāmī replied: My dear King, the cursing of the brāhmaṇas was only a plea, but the actual fact was the supreme desire of the Lord. He wanted to disappear from the face of the earth after dispatching His excessively numerous family members. He thought to Himself as follows.

PURPORT

In this verse the word *tyakṣyan* is very significant in relation to Lord Śrī Kṛṣṇa's leaving His body. Since He is the eternal form of existence, knowledge and bliss, His body and His Self are identical. Therefore how is it possible that He would leave His body and then disappear from the vision of the world? There is a great controversy amongst the nondevotees or Māyāvādīs about the mysterious disappearance of the Lord, and the doubts of those men with a poor fund of knowledge have been very elaborately cleared by Śrīla Jīva Gosvāmī in his *Kṛṣṇa-sandarbha.*

According to *Brahma-saṁhitā,* the Lord has many forms. It is stated therein that the Lord has innumerable forms, and when He appears within the vision of the living entities, as Lord Kṛṣṇa actually appeared, all such forms amalgamate with Him. Besides all these infallible forms, He has His universal form, as manifested before Arjuna on the Battlefield of Kurukṣetra. Here in this verse the word *sphītam* is also used, which indicates that He left His gigantic universal form called the *virāṭ-rūpa,* not His primeval, eternal form, because there is hardly any possibility of His changing His form of *sac-cid-ānanda.* This simple understanding is at once realized by the devotees of the Lord, but those who are nondevotees, who perform hardly any devotional service to the Lord, either do not understand this simple fact or purposely raise a controversy to defeat the eternity of the transcendental body of the Lord. This is due to the defect called the cheating propensity of the imperfect living entities.

By practical experience also, it is seen, up to the present day, that the Lord's transcendental form is worshiped by devotees in different temples, and all the devotees of the Lord factually realize that the form of the Deity in the temple is nondifferent from the form of the Lord. This inconceivable performance of the internal potency of the Lord is described in *Bhagavad-gītā* (7.25): *nāhaṁ prakāśaḥ sarvasya yoga-māyā-samāvṛtaḥ.* The Lord reserves the right of not being exposed to everyone. In the *Padma Purāṇa* it is said, *ataḥ śrī-kṛṣṇa-nāmādi na bhaved grāhyam indriyaiḥ.* The name and form of the Lord cannot be perceived by the material senses, but when He appears within the vision of the mundane people He assumes the form of the *virāṭ-rūpa.* This is an additional material exhibition of form and is supported by the logic of a subject and its adjectives. In grammar, when an adjective is taken away from the subject, the subject it modifies does not change. Similarly, when the Lord quits His *virāṭ-rūpa,* His eternal form does not change, although there is no material difference between Himself and any one of His innumerable forms. In the Fifth Canto it will be seen how the Lord is worshiped in different planets in His different forms, even now, and how He is worshiped in different temples of this earth also.

Śrīla Jīva Gosvāmī and Śrīla Viśvanātha Cakravartī Ṭhākura have very elaborately explained this incident of the Lord's disappearance in their commentaries, quoting various authentic versions of Vedic literatures. We purposely do not include them all here to avoid an increase in the volume of this book. The entire matter is explained in *Bhagavad-gītā,* as quoted above: the Lord reserves the right of not being exposed to everyone. He always keeps Himself out of the vision of the nondevotees, who are devoid of love and devotion, and thus He puts them still further away from the Lord. The Lord appeared on the invitation of Brahmā, who prayed before the Kṣīrodakaśāyī Viṣṇu, and therefore when the Lord appeared, all the forms of Viṣṇu amalgamated with Him, and when the mission was fulfilled, all of them disintegrated from Him in the usual course.

TEXT 30

अस्माल्लोकादुपरते मयि ज्ञानं मदाश्रयम् ।
अर्हत्युद्धव एवाद्धा सम्प्रत्यात्मवतां वरः ॥३०॥

asmāl lokād uparate
mayi jñānaṁ mad-āśrayam
arhaty uddhava evāddhā
sampraty ātmavatāṁ varaḥ

asmāt—from this (universe); *lokāt*—earth; *uparate*—having disappeared; *mayi*—of Myself; *jñānam*—knowledge; *mat-āśrayam*—concerning Myself; *arhati*—deserves; *uddhavaḥ*—Uddhava; *eva*—certainly; *addhā*—directly; *samprati*—at the present moment; *ātmavatām*—of the devotees; *varaḥ*—foremost.

TRANSLATION

Now I shall leave the vision of this mundane world, and I see that Uddhava, the foremost of My devotees, is the only one who can be directly entrusted with knowledge about Me.

PURPORT

Jñānaṁ mad-āśrayam is significant in this verse. Transcendental knowledge has three departmental divisions, namely knowledge of impersonal Brahman, knowledge of the all-pervading Supersoul and knowledge of the Personality of Godhead. Out of the three, transcendental knowledge of the Personality of Godhead has special significance and is known as *bhagavat-tattva-vijñāna,* specific knowledge of the Personality of Godhead. This specific knowledge is realized by pure devotional service and no other means. *Bhagavad-gītā* (18.55) confirms this: *bhaktyā mām abhijānāti yāvān yaś cāsmi tattvataḥ.* "Only persons engaged in devotional service can factually know the transcendental position of the Lord." Uddhava was considered to be the best amongst all devotees of that time, and therefore he was directly instructed by the Lord's grace, so that people might take advantage of Uddhava's knowledge after the disappearance of the Lord from the vision of the world. This is one of the reasons why Uddhava was advised to go to Badarikāśrama, where the Lord is personally represented by the Nara-Nārāyaṇa Deity. One who is transcendentally advanced can gain direct inspiration from the temple Deity, and thus a devotee of the Lord always takes shelter of a recognized temple of the Lord in order to make tangible advancement in transcendental knowledge by the grace of the Lord.

TEXT 31

नोद्धवोऽण्वपि मन्न्यूनो यद्गुणैर्नार्दितः प्रभुः ।
अतो मद्वयुनं लोकं ग्राहयन्निह तिष्ठतु ॥३१॥

noddhavo 'ṇv api man-nyūno
yad guṇair nārditaḥ prabhuḥ
ato mad-vayunaṁ lokaṁ
grāhayann iha tiṣṭhatu

na—not; *uddhavaḥ*—Uddhava; *aṇu*—slightly; *api*—also; *mat*—to Myself; *nyūnaḥ*—inferior; *yat*—because; *guṇaiḥ*—by the modes of material nature; *na*—nor; *arditaḥ*—affected; *prabhuḥ*—master; *ataḥ*—therefore; *mat-vayunam*—knowledge of Me (the Personality of Godhead); *lokam*—the world; *grāhayan*—just to disseminate; *iha*—in this world; *tiṣṭhatu*—may remain.

TRANSLATION

Uddhava is not inferior to Me in any way because he is never affected by the modes of material nature. Therefore he may remain in this world in order to disseminate specific knowledge of the Personality of Godhead.

PURPORT

The specific qualification for becoming the representative of the Lord is to be unaffected by the material modes of nature. The highest qualification of a person in the material world is to be a *brāhmaṇa.* But since a *brāhmaṇa* is in the mode of goodness, to be a *brāhmaṇa* is not sufficient for becoming a representative of the Lord. One has to transcend the mode of goodness also and be situated in unalloyed goodness, unaffected by any of the qualities of material nature. This stage of transcendental qualification is called *śuddha-sattva,* or *vasudeva,* and in this stage the science of God can be realized. As the Lord is not affected by the modes of material nature, so a pure devotee of the Lord is also not affected by the modes of nature. That is the primary qualification for being one with the Lord. A person who is able to attain this transcendental qualification is called *jīvan-mukta,* or liberated, even though he is apparently in material conditions. This liberation is achieved by one who constantly engages in the transcendental loving service of the Lord. In *Bhakti-rasāmṛta-sindhu* (1.2.187) it is stated:

īhā yasya harer dāsye
karmaṇā manasā girā
nikhilāsv apy avasthāsu
jīvan-muktaḥ sa ucyate

"Anyone who, by his actions, mind and words, lives only for the transcendental loving service of the Lord, is certainly a liberated soul, even though he may appear to be in a condition of material existence." Uddhava was in such a transcendental position, and thus he was selected to be the factual representative of the Lord in His bodily absence from the vision of the world. Such a devotee of the Lord is never affected by material strength, intelligence or even renunciation. Such a devotee of the Lord can withstand all onslaughts of material nature, and therefore he is known as *gosvāmī.* Only such *gosvāmīs* can penetrate the mysteries of the Lord's transcendental loving relationships.

TEXT 32

एवं त्रिलोकगुरुणा सन्दिष्टः शब्दयोनिना ।
बदर्याश्रममासाद्य हरिमीजे समाधिना ॥३२॥

evaṁ tri-loka-guruṇā
sandiṣṭaḥ śabda-yoninā
badaryāśramam āsādya
harim īje samādhinā

evam—thus; *tri-loka*—three worlds; *guruṇā*—by the spiritual master; *sandiṣṭaḥ*—being perfectly taught; *śabda-yoninā*—by one who is the source of all Vedic knowledge; *badaryāśramam*—in the pilgrimage site of Badarikāśrama; *āsādya*—reaching; *harim*—unto the Lord; *īje*—satisfied; *samādhinā*—by trance.

TRANSLATION

Śukadeva Gosvāmī informed the King that Uddhava, being thus instructed by the Supreme Personality of Godhead, who is the source of all Vedic knowledge and the spiritual master of the three worlds, reached the pilgrimage site of Badarikāśrama and engaged himself there in trance to satisfy the Lord.

PURPORT

Lord Śrī Kṛṣṇa is factually the spiritual master of the three worlds, and He is the original source of all Vedic knowledge. It is very difficult, however, to understand the personal feature of the Absolute Truth, even from the *Vedas*. His personal instructions are needed in order to understand the Personality of Godhead as the Supreme Absolute Truth. *Bhagavad-gītā* is the evidence of such transcendental knowledge in gist. One cannot know the Supreme Lord unless one is graced by the Lord Himself. Lord Kṛṣṇa exhibited this specific mercy towards Arjuna and Uddhava while He was in the material world.

Undoubtedly *Bhagavad-gītā* was spoken by the Lord on the Battlefield of Kurukṣetra just to encourage Arjuna to fight, and yet to complete the transcendental knowledge of *Bhagavad-gītā*, the Lord instructed Uddhava. The Lord wanted Uddhava to fulfill His mission and disseminate knowledge which He had not spoken even in *Bhagavad-gītā*. Persons who are attached to the words of the *Vedas* may also know from this verse that the Lord is the source of all Vedic knowledge. One who is unable to understand the Supreme Personality of Godhead by going through the pages of the *Vedas* may take shelter of one of the Lord's devotees, such as Uddhava, in order to advance further in knowledge of the Supreme Personality of Godhead. The *Brahma-saṁhitā* says that it is very difficult to understand the Supreme Personality of Godhead from the *Vedas*, but He is easily understood from a pure devotee like Uddhava. Taking mercy on the great sages who lived at Badarikāśrama, the Lord authorized Uddhava to speak on His behalf. Unless one has such authorization, one cannot understand or preach the devotional service of the Lord.

While present on this earth, the Lord executed many uncommon activities, even traveling in space to bring down the *pārijāta* from heaven and recovering the son of His teacher (Sāndīpani Muni) from the regions of death. Uddhava was certainly informed of the conditions of life on other planets, and all the sages were anxious to know of them, just as we are anxious to know about the planets in space. Uddhava was particularly deputed to carry a message to Badarikāśrama, not only to the sages of that place of pilgrimage but also to the Nara-Nārāyaṇa Deities. Such a message must have been more confidential than the knowledge described in the pages of the *Vedas*.

The Lord is undoubtedly the source of all knowledge, and the messages dispatched through Uddhava to Nara-Nārāyaṇa and other sages were also part of the Vedic knowledge, but they were more confidential and could be sent or understood only through such a pure devotee as Uddhava. Since such confidential knowledge was known only to the Lord and Uddhava, it is said that Uddhava was as good as the Lord Himself. Every living entity can, like Uddhava, also become a confidential messenger on the same level as the Lord, provided he becomes confidential himself by dint of loving devotional service. Such confidential knowledge is entrusted, as confirmed in *Bhagavad-gītā*, only to pure devotees like Uddhava and Arjuna, and one has to learn the mystery through them, and not otherwise. One cannot understand *Bhagavad-gītā* or *Śrīmad-Bhāgavatam* without the help of such confidential devotees of the Lord. According to Śrīla Viśvanātha Cakravartī Ṭhākura, that confidential message must have concerned the mystery of His departure and the annihilation of His dynasty after the end of His appearance in the mundane world for one hundred years. Everyone must have been very anxious to know about the mystery of the annihilation of the Yadu dynasty, and that message must have been explained by the Lord to Uddhava and dispatched to Badarikāśrama for the information of Nara-Nārāyaṇa and other pure devotees of the Lord.

TEXT 33

विदुरोऽप्युद्धवाच्छ्रुत्वा कृष्णस्य परमात्मनः ।
क्रीडयोपात्तदेहस्य कर्माणि श्लाघितानि च ॥३३॥

viduro 'py uddhavāc chrutvā
kṛṣṇasya paramātmanaḥ
krīḍayopātta-dehasya
karmāṇi ślāghitāni ca

viduraḥ—Vidura; *api*—also; *uddhavāt*—from the source of Uddhava; *śrutvā*—having heard; *kṛṣṇasya*—of Lord Kṛṣṇa; *parama-ātmanaḥ*—of the Supersoul; *krīḍayā*—for the sake of pastimes in the mortal world; *upātta*—extraordinarily accepted; *dehasya*—of the body; *karmāṇi*—transcendental activities; *ślāghitāni*—most glorious; *ca*—also.

TRANSLATION

Vidura also heard from Uddhava about the appearance and disappearance of Lord Kṛṣṇa, the Supersoul, in the mortal world,

which is a subject matter sought after with great perseverance by the great sages.

PURPORT

The subject matter of the appearance and disappearance of the Supersoul, Lord Śrī Kṛṣṇa, is a mystery even for the great sages. The word *paramātmanaḥ* is significant in this verse. An ordinary living being is generally called the *ātmā*, but Lord Kṛṣṇa is never an ordinary living being because He is *paramātmā*, the Supersoul. Yet His appearance as one of the human beings and His disappearance again from the mortal world are subject matters for the research workers who execute research work with great perseverance. Such subject matters are certainly of increasing interest because the researchers have to search out the transcendental abode of the Lord, which He enters after finishing His pastimes in the mortal world. But even the great sages have no information that beyond the material sky is the spiritual sky where Śrī Kṛṣṇa eternally resides with His associates, although at the same time He exhibits His pastimes in the mortal world in all the universes one after another. This fact is confirmed in *Brahma-saṁhitā* (5.37): *goloka eva nivasaty akhilātma-bhūtaḥ.* "The Lord, by His inconceivable potency, resides in His eternal abode, Goloka, yet at the same time, as the Supersoul, He is present everywhere—in both the spiritual and material skies—by His multivarieties of manifestation." Therefore His appearance and disappearance are simultaneously going on, and no one can say definitely which of them is the beginning and which is the end. His eternal pastimes have no beginning or end, and one has to learn of them from the pure devotee only and not waste valuable time in so-called research work.

TEXT 34

देहन्यासं च तस्यैवं धीराणां धैर्यवर्धनम् ।
अन्येषां दुष्करतरं पशूनां विक्लवात्मनाम् ॥३४॥

deha-nyāsaṁ ca tasyaivaṁ
dhīrāṇāṁ dhairya-vardhanam
anyeṣāṁ duṣkarataraṁ
paśūnāṁ viklavātmanām

deha-nyāsam—entering the body; *ca*—also; *tasya*—His; *evam*—also; *dhīrāṇām*—of great sages; *dhairya*—perseverance; *vardhanam*—increasing; *anyeṣām*—for others; *duṣkara-taram*—very difficult to ascertain; *paśūnām*—of the beasts; *viklava*—disturbed; *ātmanām*—of such a mind.

TRANSLATION

The Lord's glorious acts and His acceptance of various transcendental forms for the performance of extraordinary pastimes in the mortal world are very difficult for anyone other than His devotees to understand, and for the beasts they are simply a mental disturbance.

PURPORT

The transcendental forms and pastimes of the Lord, as described in *Bhagavad-gītā*, are difficult subject matters for those who are not devotees to understand. The Lord never reveals Himself to persons like the *jñānīs* and *yogīs*. And there are others who, because of their envying the Lord from the bottom of their hearts, are classified amongst the beasts, and for such envious beasts the subject matter of the Lord's appearance and disappearance is simply a mental disturbance. As confirmed in *Bhagavad-gītā* (7.15), the miscreants who are simply concerned with material enjoyment, who work very hard like beasts of burden, can hardly know the Personality of Godhead at any stage due to *āsurika-bhāva*, or a spirit of revolt against the Supreme Lord.

The transcendental bodily expansions manifested by the Lord for His pastimes in the mortal world, and the appearance and disappearance of such transcendental expansions, are difficult subject matters, and those who are not devotees are advised not to discuss the Lord's appearance and disappearance, lest they commit further offenses at the lotus feet of the Lord. The more they discuss the transcendental appearance and disappearance of the Lord in the asuric spirit, the more they enter into the darkest region of hell, as stated in *Bhagavad-gītā* (16.20). Anyone who is against the transcendental loving service of the Lord is more or less a beastly creature, as confirmed in this verse of *Śrīmad-Bhāgavatam*.

TEXT 35

आत्मानं च कुरुश्रेष्ठ कृष्णेन मनसेक्षितम् ।
ध्यायन् गते भागवते रुरोद प्रेमविह्वलः ॥३५॥

ātmānaṁ ca kuru-śreṣṭha
kṛṣṇena manasekṣitam
dhyāyan gate bhāgavate
ruroda prema-vihvalaḥ

ātmānam—himself; *ca*—also; *kuru-śreṣṭha*—O best amongst the Kurus; *kṛṣṇena*—by Kṛṣṇa; *manasā*—by the mind; *īkṣitam*—remembered; *dhyāyan*—thus thinking of; *gate*—having gone; *bhāgavate*—of the devotee; *ruroda*—cried loudly; *prema-vihvalaḥ*—overwhelmed by the ecstasy of love.

TRANSLATION

Understanding that he was remembered by Lord Kṛṣṇa [while quitting this world], Vidura began to cry loudly, overwhelmed by the ecstasy of love.

PURPORT

Vidura was overwhelmed by the ecstasy of love when he understood that Lord Kṛṣṇa, the Supreme Personality of Godhead, thought of him at the last moment. Although he thought of himself as insignificant, he was remembered by the Lord, by His causeless mercy. Vidura accepted this as a great favor, and thus he cried. This crying is the last word in the progressive path of devotional service. One who can cry for the Lord in love is certainly successful in the line of devotional service.

TEXT 36

कालिन्द्याः कतिभिः सिद्ध अहोभिर्भरतर्षभ ।
प्रापद्यत स्वःसरितं यत्र मित्रासुतो मुनिः ॥३६॥

kālindyāḥ katibhiḥ siddha
ahobhir bharatarṣabha

prāpadyata svaḥ-saritaṁ
yatra mitrā-suto muniḥ

kālindyāḥ—on the bank of the Yamunā; *katibhiḥ*—a few; *siddhe*—being so passed; *ahobhiḥ*—days; *bharata-ṛṣabha*—O best of the Bharata dynasty; *prāpadyata*—reached; *svaḥ-saritam*—the celestial water of the Ganges; *yatra*—where; *mitrā-sutaḥ*—the son of Mitrā; *muniḥ*—sage.

TRANSLATION

After passing a few days on the bank of the River Yamunā, Vidura, the self-realized soul, reached the bank of the Ganges, where the great sage Maitreya was situated.

Thus end the Bhaktivedanta purports of the Third Canto, Fourth Chapter, of the Śrīmad-Bhāgavatam, *entitled "Vidura Approaches Maitreya."*

CHAPTER FIVE

Vidura's Talks with Maitreya

TEXT 1

श्रीशुक उवाच
द्वारि द्युनद्या ऋषभः कुरूणां
मैत्रेयमासीनमगाधबोधम् ।
क्षत्तोपसृत्याच्युतभावसिद्धः
पप्रच्छ सौशील्यगुणाभितृप्तः ॥ १ ॥

śrī-śuka uvāca
dvāri dyu-nadyā ṛṣabhaḥ kurūṇāṁ
maitreyam āsīnam agādha-bodham
kṣattopasṛtyācyuta-bhāva-siddhaḥ
papraccha sauśīlya-guṇābhitṛptaḥ

śrī-śukaḥ uvāca—Śukadeva Gosvāmī said; *dvāri*—at the source of; *dyu-nadyāḥ*—the celestial River Ganges; *ṛṣabhaḥ*—the best of the Kurus; *kurūṇām*—of the Kurus; *maitreyam*—unto Maitreya; *āsīnam*—sitting; *agādha-bodham*—of unfathomed knowledge; *kṣattā*—Vidura; *upasṛtya*—having approached nearer; *acyuta*—the infallible Lord; *bhāva*—character; *siddhaḥ*—perfect; *papraccha*—inquired; *sauśīlya*—gentleness; *guṇa-abhitṛptaḥ*—satisfied in transcendental qualities.

TRANSLATION

Śukadeva Gosvāmī said: Vidura, the best amongst the Kuru dynasty, who was perfect in devotional service to the Lord, thus reached the source of the celestial Ganges River [Hardwar], where Maitreya, the great, fathomless learned sage of the world, was seated. Vidura, who was perfect in gentleness and satisfied in transcendence, inquired from him.

PURPORT

Vidura was already perfect due to his unalloyed devotion to the infallible Lord. The Lord and the living entities are all qualitatively the same by nature, but the Lord is quantitatively much greater than any individual living entity. He is ever infallible, whereas the living entities are prone to fall under the illusory energy. Vidura had already surpassed the fallible nature of the living entity in conditional life due to his being *acyuta-bhāva*, or legitimately absorbed in the devotional service of the Lord. This stage of life is called *acyuta-bhāva-siddha*, or perfection by dint of devotional service. Anyone, therefore, who is absorbed in the devotional service of the Lord is a liberated soul and has all admirable qualities. The learned sage Maitreya was sitting in a solitary place on the bank of the Ganges at Hardwar, and Vidura, who was a perfect devotee of the Lord and possessed all good transcendental qualities, approached him for inquiry.

TEXT 2

विदुर उवाच
सुखाय कर्माणि करोति लोको
न तैः सुखं वान्यदुपारमं वा ।
विन्देत भूयस्तत एव दुःखं
यदत्र युक्तं भगवान् वदेन्नः ॥ २ ॥

vidura uvāca
sukhāya karmāṇi karoti loko
na taiḥ sukhaṁ vānyad-upāramaṁ vā
vindeta bhūyas tata eva duḥkhaṁ
yad atra yuktaṁ bhagavān vaden naḥ

viduraḥ uvāca—Vidura said; *sukhāya*—for attaining happiness; *karmāṇi*—fruitive activities; *karoti*—everyone does so; *lokaḥ*—in this world; *na*—never; *taiḥ*—by those activities; *sukham*—any happiness; *vā*—or; *anyat*—differently; *upāramam*—satiation; *vā*—either; *vindeta*—achieves; *bhūyaḥ*—on the contrary; *tataḥ*—by such activities; *eva*—certainly; *duḥkham*—miseries; *yat*—that which; *atra*—under the circumstances; *yuktam*—right course; *bhagavān*—O great one; *vadet*—may kindly enlighten; *naḥ*—us.

TRANSLATION

Vidura said: O great sage, everyone in this world engages in fruitive activities to attain happiness, but one finds neither satiation nor the mitigation of distress. On the contrary, one is only aggravated by such activities. Please, therefore, give us directions on how one should live for real happiness.

PURPORT

Vidura asked Maitreya some common questions, which was not originally his intention. Uddhava asked Vidura to approach Maitreya Muni and inquire into all the truths concerning the Lord, His name, fame, quality, form, pastimes, entourage, etc., and thus when Vidura approached Maitreya, he should have asked only about the Lord. But out of natural humility he did not immediately ask about the Lord, but inquired into a subject which would be of great importance to the common man. A common man cannot understand the Lord. He must first know the real position of his life under the influence of the illusory energy. In illusion one thinks that he can be happy only by fruitive activities, but what actually happens is that one becomes more and more entangled in the network of action and reaction and does not find any solution to the problem of life. There is a nice song in this connection: "Because of a great desire to have all happiness in life, I built this house. But unfortunately the whole scheme has turned to ashes because the house was unexpectedly set on fire." The law of nature is like that. Everyone tries to become happy by planning in the material world, but the law of nature is so cruel that it sets fire to one's schemes; the fruitive worker is not happy in his schemes, nor is there any satiation of his continuous hankering for happiness.

TEXT 3

जनस्य कृष्णाद्विमुखस्य दैवा-
दधर्मशीलस्य सुदुःखितस्य ।

अनुग्रहायेह चरन्ति नूनं
भूतानि भव्यानि जनार्दनस्य ॥ ३ ॥

janasya kṛṣṇād vimukhasya daivād
adharma-śīlasya suduḥkhitasya
anugrahāyeha caranti nūnaṁ
bhūtāni bhavyāni janārdanasya

janasya—of the common man; *kṛṣṇāt*—from the Supreme Lord, Kṛṣṇa; *vimukhasya*—of the one who has turned his face against the Lord; *daivāt*—by the influence of external energy; *adharma-śīlasya*—of one who is engaged in irreligion; *su-duḥkhitasya*—of one who is always unhappy; *anugrahāya*—due to being compassionate towards them; *iha*—in this world; *caranti*—wander; *nūnam*—certainly; *bhūtāni*—persons; *bhavyāni*—great philanthropic souls; *janārdanasya*—of the Supreme Personality of Godhead.

TRANSLATION

O my lord, great philanthropic souls travel on the earth on behalf of the Supreme Personality of Godhead to show compassion to the fallen souls who are averse to the sense of subordination to the Lord.

PURPORT

To be obedient to the wishes of the Supreme Lord is the natural position of every living entity. But due only to past misdeeds, a living being becomes averse to the sense of subordination to the Lord and suffers all the miseries of material existence. No one has anything to do but render devotional service to the Supreme Lord, Śrī Kṛṣṇa. Therefore any activity other than transcendental loving service to the Lord is more or less a rebellious action against the supreme will. All fruitive activity, empirical philosophy and mysticism are more or less against the sense of subordination to the Lord, and any living entity engaged in such rebellious activity is more or less condemned by the laws of material nature, which work under the subordination of the Lord. Great unalloyed devotees of the Lord are compassionate towards the fallen, and therefore they travel all over the world with the mission of bringing souls back to Godhead, back to home. Such pure devotees of the Lord carry the message of Godhead in order to deliver the fallen souls, and therefore the common man who is bewildered by the influence of the external energy of the Lord should avail himself of their association.

TEXT 4

तत्साधुवर्यादिश वर्त्म शं नः
संराधितो भगवान् येन पुंसाम् ।
हृदि स्थितो यच्छति भक्तिपूते
ज्ञानं सतत्त्वाधिगमं पुराणम् ॥ ४ ॥

tat sādhu-varyādiśa vartma śaṁ naḥ
saṁrādhito bhagavān yena puṁsām
hṛdi sthito yacchati bhakti-pūte
jñānaṁ sa-tattvādhigamaṁ purāṇam

tat—therefore; *sādhu-varya*—O great one amongst the saints; *ādiśa*—please instruct; *vartma*—the path; *śam*—auspicious; *naḥ*—for us; *saṁrādhitaḥ*—being perfectly served; *bhagavān*—the Personality of Godhead; *yena*—by which; *puṁsām*—of the living entity; *hṛdi sthitaḥ*—residing in the heart; *yacchati*—awards; *bhakti-pūte*—unto the unalloyed devotee; *jñānam*—knowledge; *sa*—that; *tattva*—truth; *adhigamam*—by which one learns; *purāṇam*—authorized, old.

TRANSLATION

Therefore, O great sage, please give me instruction on the transcendental devotional service of the Lord, so that He who is situated in the heart of everyone can be pleased to impart, from within, knowledge of the Absolute Truth in terms of the ancient Vedic principles delivered only to those who are purified by the process of devotional service.

PURPORT

As already explained in the First Canto of *Śrīmad-Bhāgavatam*, the Absolute Truth is realized in three different phases—although they are one and the same—in terms of the knower's capacity to understand. The most capable transcendentalist is the pure devotee of the Lord, who is without any tinge of fruitive actions or philosophical speculation. By devotional service only does one's heart become completely purified from all material coverings like *karma*, *jñāna* and *yoga*. Only in such a purified stage does the Lord, who is seated in everyone's heart with the individual soul, give instruction so that the devotee can reach the ultimate destination of going back home, back to Godhead. This is confirmed in *Bhagavad-gītā* (10.10): *teṣāṁ satata-yuktānāṁ bhajatām*. Only when the Lord is satisfied with the devotional service of the devotee does He impart knowledge, as He did for Arjuna and Uddhava.

The *jñānīs*, *yogīs* and *karmīs* cannot expect this direct cooperation of the Lord. They are not able to satisfy the Lord by transcendental loving service, nor do they believe in such service to the Lord. The *bhakti* process, as performed under the regulative principles of *vaidhī-bhakti*, or devotional service following the prescribed rules and regulations, is defined by the revealed scriptures and confirmed by great *ācāryas*. This practice can help the neophyte devotee to rise to the stage of *rāga-bhakti*, in which the Lord responds from within as the *caitya-guru*, or the spiritual master as Superconsciousness. All transcendentalists other than devotees make no distinction between the individual soul and the Supersoul because they miscalculate the Superconsciousness and the individual consciousness to be one and the same. Such miscalculation by the nondevotees makes them unfit to receive any direction from within, and therefore they are bereft of the direct cooperation of the Lord. After many, many births, when such a nondualist comes to sense that the Lord is worshipable and that the devotee is simultaneously one with and different from the Lord, then only can he surrender unto the Lord, Vāsudeva. Pure devotional service begins from that point. The process of understanding the Absolute Truth adopted by the misguided nondualist is very difficult, whereas the devotee's way of understanding the Absolute Truth comes directly from the Lord, who is pleased by devotional service. On behalf of many neophyte devotees, Vidura, at the very first instance, inquired from Maitreya about the path of devotional service, by which the Lord, who is seated within the heart, can be pleased.

TEXT 5

करोति कर्माणि कृतावतारो
यान्यात्मतन्त्रो भगवांस्त्र्यधीशः ।
यथा ससर्जाग्र इदं निरीहः
संस्थाप्य वृत्तिं जगतो विधत्ते ॥ ५ ॥

karoti karmāṇi kṛtāvatāro
yāny ātma-tantro bhagavāṁs tryadhīśaḥ
yathā sasarjāgra idaṁ nirīhaḥ
saṁsthāpya vṛttiṁ jagato vidhatte

karoti—does them; *karmāṇi*—transcendental activities; *kṛta*—by accepting; *avatāraḥ*—incarnations; *yāni*—all those; *ātma-tantraḥ*—Self-independent; *bhagavān*—the Personality of Godhead; *tri-adhīśaḥ*—the Lord of the three worlds; *yathā*—as much as; *sasarja*—created; *agre*—at first; *idam*—this cosmic manifestation; *nirīhaḥ*—although desireless; *saṁsthāpya*—by establishing; *vṛttim*—means of livelihood; *jagataḥ*—of the universes; *vidhatte*—as He regulates.

TRANSLATION

O great sage, kindly narrate how the Supreme Personality of Godhead, who is the independent, desireless Lord of the three worlds and the controller of all energies, accepts incarnations and creates the cosmic manifestation with perfectly arranged regulative principles for its maintenance.

PURPORT

Lord Kṛṣṇa is the original Personality of Godhead from whom the three creative incarnations, namely the *puruṣa-avatāras*—Kāraṇārṇavaśāyī Viṣṇu, Garbhodakaśāyī Viṣṇu and Kṣīrodakaśāyī Viṣṇu—expand. The whole material creation is conducted by the three *puruṣas* in successive stages under the external energy of the Lord, and thus material nature is controlled by Him. Thinking material nature to be independent is like seeking milk from the nipplelike bags on the neck of a goat. The Lord is independent and desireless. He does not create the material world for His own satisfaction as we create our household affairs to fulfill our material desires. Actually the material world is created for the illusory enjoyment of the conditioned souls, who have been against the transcendental service of the Lord since time immemorial. But the material universes are full in themselves. There is no scarcity for maintenance in the material world. Because of their poor fund of knowledge, the materialists are disturbed when there is an apparent increase of population on the earth. Whenever there is a living being on the earth, however, his subsistence is immediately arranged by the Lord. The other species of living entities, who far outnumber human society, are never disturbed for maintenance; they are never seen dying of starvation. It is only human society that is disturbed about the food situation and, to cover up the real fact of administrative mismanagement, takes shelter in the plea that the population is excessively increasing. If there is any scarcity in the world, it is the scarcity of God consciousness, otherwise, by the grace of the Lord, there is no scarcity of anything.

TEXT 6

यथा पुनः स्वे ख इदं निवेश्य
शेते गुहायां स निवृत्तवृत्तिः ।
योगेश्वराधीश्वर एक एत-
दनुप्रविष्टो बहुधा यथासीत् ॥ ६ ॥

yathā punaḥ sve kha idaṁ niveśya
śete guhāyāṁ sa nivṛtta-vṛttiḥ
yogeśvarādhīśvara eka etad
anupraviṣṭo bahudhā yathāsīt

yathā—as much as; *punaḥ*—again; *sve*—in His; *khe*—form of space (*virāṭ-rūpa*); *idam*—this; *niveśya*—entering into; *śete*—lies down;

guhāyām—within the universe; *saḥ*—He (the Personality of Godhead); *nivṛtta*—without endeavor; *vṛttiḥ*—means of livelihood; *yoga-īśvara*—the master of all mystic powers; *adhīśvaraḥ*—proprietor of everything; *ekaḥ*—one without a second; *etat*—this; *anupraviṣṭaḥ*—entering afterwards; *bahudhā*—by innumerable; *yathā*—as much as; *āsīt*—exists.

TRANSLATION

He lies down on His own heart spread in the form of the sky, and thus placing the whole creation in that space, He expands Himself into many living entities, which are manifested as different species of life. He does not have to endeavor for His maintenance, because He is the master of all mystic powers and the proprietor of everything. Thus He is distinct from the living entities.

PURPORT

The questions regarding creation, maintenance and destruction, which are mentioned in many parts of the *Śrīmad-Bhāgavatam*, are in relation to different millenniums (*kalpas*), and therefore they are differently described by different authorities when questioned by different students. There is no difference regarding the creative principles and the Lord's control over them, yet there are some differences in the minute details because of different *kalpas*. The gigantic sky is the material body of the Lord, called the *virāṭ-rūpa*, and all material creations are resting on the sky, or the heart of the Lord. Therefore, beginning from the sky, the first material manifestation to the gross vision, down to the earth, everything is called Brahman. *Sarvaṁ khalv idaṁ brahma:* "There is nothing but the Lord, and He is one without a second." The living entities are the superior energies, whereas matter is the inferior energy, and the combination of these energies brings about the manifestation of this material world, which is in the heart of the Lord.

TEXT 7

क्रीडन् विधत्ते द्विजगोसुराणां
क्षेमाय कर्माण्यवतारभेदैः ।

मनो न तृप्यत्यपि शृण्वतां नः
सुश्लोकमौलेश्चरितामृतानि ॥ ७ ॥

krīḍan vidhatte dvija-go-surāṇāṁ
kṣemāya karmāṇy avatāra-bhedaiḥ
mano na tṛpyaty api śṛṇvatāṁ naḥ
suśloka-mauleś caritāmṛtāni

krīḍan—manifesting pastimes; *vidhatte*—He performs; *dvija*—twice-born; *go*—cows; *surāṇām*—of the demigods; *kṣemāya*—welfare; *karmāṇi*—transcendental activities; *avatāra*—incarnations; *bhedaiḥ*—differently; *manaḥ*—mind; *na*—never; *tṛpyati*—satisfies; *api*—in spite of; *śṛṇvatām*—continuously hearing; *naḥ*—our; *su-śloka*—auspicious; *mauleh*—of the Lord; *carita*—characteristics; *amṛtāni*—undying.

TRANSLATION

You may narrate also about the auspicious characteristics of the Lord in His different incarnations for the welfare of the twice-born, the cows and the demigods. Our minds are never satisfied completely, although we continuously hear of His transcendental activities.

PURPORT

The Lord appears in this universe in different incarnations like Matsya, Kūrma, Varāha and Nṛsiṁha, and He manifests His different transcendental activities for the welfare of the twice-born, the cows and the demigods. The Lord is directly concerned with the twice-born or civilized men. A civilized man is one who has taken his birth twice. A living entity takes birth in this mundane world due to the union of male and female. A human being is born due to union of the father and mother, but a civilized human being has another birth by contact with a spiritual master, who becomes the actual father. The father and mother of the material body are so only in one birth, and in the next birth the father and mother may be a different couple. But the bona fide spiritual master, as the representative of the Lord, is the eternal father because the spiritual master has the responsibility to lead the disciple to spiritual salvation, or the ultimate goal of life. Therefore, a civilized man must be twice-born, otherwise he is no more than the lower animals.

The cow is the most important animal for developing the human body to perfection. The body can be maintained by any kind of foodstuff, but cow's milk is particularly essential for developing the finer tissues of the human brain so that one can understand the intricacies of transcendental knowledge. A civilized man is expected to live on foodstuffs comprising fruits, vegetables, grains, sugar and milk. The bull helps in the agricultural process of producing grain, etc., and thus in one sense the bull is the father of humankind, whereas the cow is the mother, for she supplies milk to human society. A civilized man is therefore expected to give all protection to the bulls and cows.

The demigods, or the living entities who live in the higher planets, are far superior to human beings. Since they have better arrangements for living conditions, they live far more luxuriously than human beings, yet they are all devotees of the Lord. The Lord incarnates in different forms, such as those of a fish, a tortoise, a hog, and a combined lion and man, just to give protection to civilized man, the cow and the demigods, who are directly responsible for the regulative life of progressive self-realization. The whole system of the material creation is planned so that the conditioned souls may have the opportunity for self-realization. One who takes advantage of such an arrangement is called a demigod or civilized man. The cow is meant to help maintain such a high standard of living.

The Lord's pastimes for the protection of the twice-born civilized men, the cows and the demigods are all transcendental. A human being is inclined to hear good narrations and stories, and therefore there are so many books, magazines and newspapers on the market to satisfy the interests of the developed soul. But the pleasure in such literature, after it is read once, becomes stale, and people do not take any interest in reading such literature repeatedly. In fact, newspapers are read for less than an hour and then thrown in the dustbins as rubbish. The case is similar with all other mundane literatures. But the beauty of transcendental literatures like *Bhagavad-gītā* and *Śrīmad-Bhāgavatam* is that they never become old. They have been read in the world by civilized man for the last five thousand years, and they have never become old. They are ever fresh to the learned scholars and devotees, and even by daily repetition of the verses of *Bhagavad-gītā* and *Śrīmad-Bhāgavatam*, there is no satiation for devotees like Vidura. Vidura might have heard the pastimes of the Lord many, many times before he met Maitreya, but still he wanted the same narrations to be repeated because he was never satiated by hearing them. That is the transcendental nature of the Lord's glorious pastimes.

TEXT 8

यैस्तत्त्वभेदैरधिलोकनाथो
लोकानलोकान् सह लोकपालान् ।
अचीक्लृपद्यत्र हि सर्वसत्त्व-
निकायभेदोऽधिकृतः प्रतीतः ॥ ८ ॥

yais tattva-bhedair adhiloka-nātho
lokān alokān saha lokapālān
acīkḷpad yatra hi sarva-sattva-
nikāya-bhedo 'dhikṛtaḥ pratītaḥ

yaiḥ—by whom; *tattva*—truth; *bhedaiḥ*—by differentiation; *adhiloka-nāthaḥ*—the King of the kings; *lokān*—planets; *alokān*—planets of the lower region; *saha*—along with; *loka-pālān*—respective kings; *acīkḷpat*—planned; *yatra*—wherein; *hi*—certainly; *sarva*—all; *sattva*—existence; *nikāya*—living entities; *bhedaḥ*—difference; *adhikṛtaḥ*—occupied; *pratītaḥ*—it so appears.

TRANSLATION

The Supreme King of all kings has created different planets and places of habitation where living entities are situated in terms of the modes of nature and work, and He has created their different kings and rulers.

PURPORT

Lord Kṛṣṇa is the chief King of all kings, and He has created different planets for all kinds of living entities. Even on this planet there are different places for inhabitation by different types of men. There are places like deserts, icelands, and valleys in mountainous countries, and in each of them there are different kinds of men born of different modes of nature according to their past deeds. There are people in the Arabian deserts and in the valleys of the Himalayan Mountains, and the inhabitants of these two places differ from one another, just as the inhabitants of the icelands also differ from them. Similarly, there are also different planets. The planets below the earth down to the Pātāla planet are full of various kinds of living beings; no planet is vacant, as wrongly imagined by the modern so-called scientist. In *Bhagavad-gītā* we find it said by the Lord that the living entities are *sarva-gata*, or present in every sphere of life. So there is no doubt that on other planets there are also inhabitants like us, sometimes with greater intelligence and greater opulence. The living conditions for those of greater intelligence are more luxurious than on this earth. There are also planets where no sunlight reaches, and there are living entities who must live there due to their past deeds. All such plans for living conditions are made by the Supreme Lord, and Vidura requested Maitreya to describe this for the sake of further enlightenment.

TEXT 9

येन प्रजानामुत आत्मकर्म-
रूपाभिधानां च भिदां व्यधत्त ।
नारायणो विश्वसृगात्मयोनि-
रेतच्च नो वर्णय विप्रवर्य ॥ ९ ॥

yena prajānām uta ātma-karma-
rūpābhidhānāṁ ca bhidāṁ vyadhatta
nārāyaṇo viśvasṛg ātma-yonir
etac ca no varṇaya vipra-varya

yena—by which; *prajānām*—of those who are born; *uta*—as also; *ātma-karma*—destined engagement; *rūpa*—form and feature; *abhidhānām*—endeavors; *ca*—also; *bhidām*—differentiation; *vyadhatta*—dispersed; *nārāyaṇaḥ*—the Supreme Personality of Godhead; *viśva-sṛk*—the creator of the universe; *ātma-yoniḥ*—self-sufficient; *etat*—all these; *ca*—also; *naḥ*—unto us; *varṇaya*—describe; *vipra-varya*—O chief amongst the *brāhmaṇas.*

TRANSLATION

O chief amongst the brāhmaṇas, please also describe how Nārāyaṇa, the creator of the universe and the self-sufficient Lord, has differently created the natures, activities, forms, features and names of the different living creatures.

PURPORT

Every living being is under the plan of his natural inclinations in terms of the modes of material nature. His work is manifested in terms of the nature of the three modes, his form and bodily features are designed according to his work, and his name is designated according to his bodily features. For example, the higher classes of men are white (*śukla*), and the lower classes of men are black. This division of white and black is in terms of one's white and black duties of life. Pious acts lead one to take birth in a good and highly placed family, to become rich, to become learned, and to acquire beautiful bodily features. Impious acts lead one to become poor by parentage, to be always in want, to become a fool or illiterate and to acquire ugly bodily features. Vidura requested Maitreya to explain these differences between all the living creatures made by Nārāyaṇa, the Supreme Personality of Godhead.

TEXT 10

परावरेषां भगवन् व्रतानि
श्रुतानि मे व्यासमुखादभीक्ष्णम् ।
अतृप्नुम क्षुल्लसुखावहानां
तेषामृते कृष्णकथामृतौघात् ॥१०॥

parāvareṣāṁ bhagavan vratāni
śrutāni me vyāsa-mukhād abhīkṣṇam
atṛpnuma kṣulla-sukhāvahānāṁ
teṣām ṛte kṛṣṇa-kathāmṛtaughāt

para—higher; *avareṣām*—of these lower; *bhagavan*—O my lord, O great one; *vratāni*—occupations; *śrutāni*—heard; *me*—by me; *vyāsa*—Vyāsa; *mukhāt*—from the mouth; *abhīkṣṇam*—repeatedly; *atṛpnuma*—

I am satisfied; *kṣulla*—little; *sukha-āvahānām*—that which causes happiness; *teṣām*—out of that; *ṛte*—without; *kṛṣṇa-kathā*—talks about the Personality of Godhead, Lord Kṛṣṇa; *amṛta-oghāt*—from the nectar.

TRANSLATION

O my lord, I have repeatedly heard about these higher and lower statuses of human society from the mouth of Vyāsadeva, and I am quite satiated with all these lesser subject matters and their happiness. They have not satisfied me with the nectar of topics about Kṛṣṇa.

PURPORT

Because people are very much interested in hearing social and historical presentations, Śrīla Vyāsadeva has compiled many books such as the *Purāṇas* and *Mahābhārata*. These books are reading matter for the mass of people, and they were compiled with a view to reviving their God consciousness, now forgotten in the conditional life of material existence. The real purpose of such literatures is not so much to present topics of historical references, but to revive the people's sense of God consciousness. For example, *Mahābhārata* is the history of the Battle of Kurukṣetra, and common people read it because it is full of topics regarding the social, political and economic problems of human society. But factually the most important part of *Mahābhārata* is *Bhagavad-gītā*, which is automatically taught to readers along with the historical narrations of the Battle of Kurukṣetra.

Vidura explained to Maitreya his position of being fully satiated with the knowledge of mundane social and political topics and having no more interest in them. He was anxious to hear transcendental topics regarding Lord Śrī Kṛṣṇa. Because there were insufficient topics directly concerning Kṛṣṇa in the *Purāṇas*, *Mahābhārata*, etc., he was not satisfied and wanted to know more about Kṛṣṇa. *Kṛṣṇa-kathā*, or topics regarding Kṛṣṇa, are transcendental, and there is no satiation in hearing such topics. *Bhagavad-gītā* is important on account of its being *kṛṣṇa-kathā*, or speeches delivered by Lord Kṛṣṇa. The story of the Battle of Kurukṣetra may be interesting for the mass of people, but to a person like Vidura, who is highly advanced in devotional service, only *kṛṣṇa-kathā* and that which is dovetailed with *kṛṣṇa-kathā* is interesting. Vidura wanted to hear of everything from Maitreya, and so he inquired from him, but he desired that all the topics be in relationship with Kṛṣṇa. As fire is never satisfied in its consumption of firewood, so a pure devotee of the Lord never hears enough about Kṛṣṇa. Historical events and other narrations concerning social and political incidents all become transcendental as soon as they are in relationship with Kṛṣṇa. That is the way to transform mundane things into spiritual identity. The whole world can be transformed into Vaikuṇṭha if all worldly activities are dovetailed with *kṛṣṇa-kathā.*

There are two important *kṛṣṇa-kathās* current in the world—*Bhagavad-gītā* and *Śrīmad-Bhāgavatam. Bhagavad-gītā* is *kṛṣṇa-kathā* because it is spoken by Kṛṣṇa, whereas *Śrīmad-Bhāgavatam* is *kṛṣṇa-kathā* because it narrates about Kṛṣṇa. Lord Caitanya advised all His disciples to preach *kṛṣṇa-kathā* all over the world without discrimination because the transcendental value of *kṛṣṇa-kathā* can purify one and all from material contamination.

TEXT 11

कस्तृप्नुयात्तीर्थपदोऽभिधानात्
सत्रेषु वः सूरिभिरीड्यमानात् ।
यः कर्णनाडीं पुरुषस्य यातो
भवप्रदां गेहरतिं छिनत्ति ॥११॥

kas tṛpnuyāt tīrtha-pado 'bhidhānāt
satreṣu vaḥ sūribhir īḍyamānāt
yaḥ karṇa-nāḍīṁ puruṣasya yāto
bhava-pradāṁ geha-ratiṁ chinatti

kaḥ—who is that man; *tṛpnuyāt*—that can be satisfied; *tīrtha-padaḥ*—whose lotus feet are all the places of pilgrimage; *abhidhānāt*—from the talks of; *satreṣu*—in human society; *vaḥ*—one who is; *sūribhiḥ*—by great devotees; *īḍyamānāt*—one who is so worshiped; *yaḥ*—who; *karṇa-nāḍīm*—in the holes of the ears; *puruṣasya*—of a man; *yātaḥ*—entering; *bhava-pradām*—that which awards births and deaths; *geha-ratim*—family affection; *chinatti*—is cut off.

TRANSLATION

Who in human society can be satisfied without hearing sufficient talk of the Lord, whose lotus feet are the sum total of all places of pilgrimage and who is worshiped by great sages and devotees? Such topics can cut off one's bondage to family affection simply by entering the holes of one's ears.

PURPORT

Kṛṣṇa-kathā is so powerful that simply by entering into a person's ear it can at once give deliverance from the bondage of family affection. Family affection is an illusory manifestation of the external energy, and it is the only impetus for all mundane activities. As long as there is mundane activity and the mind is absorbed in such engagement, one has to undergo the repetition of birth and death in the current material nescience. People are most influenced by the mode of ignorance, and some are influenced by the passionate mode of material nature, and under the spell of these two modes a living being is actuated by the material conception of life. The mundane qualities do not allow a living entity to understand his real position. The qualities of both ignorance and passion strongly bind one to the illusory bodily conception of the self. The best among the fools who are thus deluded are those who engage in altruistic activities under the spell of the material mode of passion. *Bhagavad-gītā*, which is direct *kṛṣṇa-kathā*, gives humanity the elementary lesson that the body is perishable and that the consciousness which is spread throughout the body is imperishable. The conscious being, the imperishable self, is eternally existent and cannot be killed under any circumstances, even after the dissolution of the body. Anyone who misunderstands this perishable body to be the self and who works for it in the name of sociology, politics, philanthropy, altruism, nationalism or internationalism, under the false plea of the bodily conception of life, is certainly a fool and does not know the implications of reality and unreality. Some of them are above the modes of ignorance and passion and are situated in the mode of goodness, but mundane goodness is always contaminated by tinges of ignorance and passion. Mundane goodness can enlighten one that the body and the self are different, and one in goodness is concerned with the self and not the body. But due to being contaminated, those in mundane goodness cannot understand the real nature of the self as a person. Their impersonal conception of the self as distinct from the body keeps them in the mode of goodness within material nature, and unless they are attracted by *kṛṣṇa-kathā*, they will never be liberated from the bondage of material existence. *Kṛṣṇa-kathā* is the only remedy for all people of the world because it can situate one in pure consciousness of the self and liberate one from material bondage. To preach *kṛṣṇa-kathā* all over the world, as recommended by Lord Caitanya, is the greatest missionary activity, and all sensible men and women of the world may join in this great movement started by Lord Caitanya.

TEXT 12

मुनिर्विवक्षुर्भगवद्गुणानां
सखापि ते भारतमाह कृष्णः ।
यस्मिन्नृणां ग्राम्यसुखानुवादै-
र्मतिर्गृहीता नु हरेः कथायाम् ॥१२॥

munir vivakṣur bhagavad-guṇānāṁ
sakhāpi te bhāratam āha kṛṣṇaḥ
yasmin nṛṇāṁ grāmya-sukhānuvādair
matir gṛhītā nu hareḥ kathāyām

muniḥ—the sage; *vivakṣuḥ*—described; *bhagavat*—of the Personality of Godhead; *guṇānām*—transcendental qualities; *sakhā*—friend; *api*—also; *te*—your; *bhāratam*—the *Mahābhārata;* *āha*—has described; *kṛṣṇaḥ*—Kṛṣṇa-dvaipāyana Vyāsa; *yasmin*—in which; *nṛṇām*—of the people; *grāmya*—worldly; *sukha-anuvādaiḥ*—pleasure derived from mundane topics; *matiḥ*—attention; *gṛhītā nu*—just to draw towards; *hareḥ*—of the Lord; *kathāyām*—speeches of (*Bhagavad-gītā*).

TRANSLATION

Your friend the great sage Kṛṣṇa-dvaipāyana Vyāsa has already described the transcendental qualities of the Lord in his great

work the Mahābhārata. But the whole idea is to draw the attention of the mass of people to kṛṣṇa-kathā [Bhagavad-gītā] through their strong affinity for hearing mundane topics.

PURPORT

The great sage Kṛṣṇa-dvaipāyana Vyāsa is the author of all Vedic literature, of which his works *Vedānta-sūtra*, *Śrīmad-Bhāgavatam* and *Mahābhārata* are very popular readings. As stated in *Bhāgavatam* (1.4.25), Śrīla Vyāsadeva compiled the *Mahābhārata* for the less intelligent class of men, who take more interest in mundane topics than in the philosophy of life. The *Vedānta-sūtra* was compiled for persons already above the mundane topics, who might already have tasted the bitterness of the so-called happiness of mundane affairs. The first aphorism of *Vedānta-sūtra* is *athāto brahma-jijñāsā*, i.e., only when one has finished the business of mundane inquiries in the marketplace of sense gratification can one make relevant inquiries regarding Brahman, the Transcendence. Those persons who are busy with the mundane inquiries which fill the newspapers and other such literatures are classified as *strī-śūdra-dvijabandhus*, or women, the laborer class and unworthy sons of the higher classes (*brāhmaṇa*, *kṣatriya* and *vaiśya*). Such less intelligent men cannot understand the purpose of *Vedānta-sūtra*, although they may make a show of studying the *sūtras* in a perverted way. The real purpose of *Vedānta-sūtra* is explained by the author himself in the *Śrīmad-Bhāgavatam*, and anyone trying to understand *Vedānta-sūtra* without reference to *Śrīmad-Bhāgavatam* is certainly misguided. Such misguided persons, who are interested in the mundane affairs of philanthropic and altruistic work under the misconception of the body as the self, could better take advantage of the *Mahābhārata*, which was specifically compiled by Śrīla Vyāsadeva for their benefit. The great author has compiled the *Mahābhārata* in such a way that the less intelligent class of men, who are more interested in mundane topics, may read the *Mahābhārata* with great relish and in the course of such mundane happiness can also take advantage of *Bhagavad-gītā*, the preliminary study of *Śrīmad-Bhāgavatam* or the *Vedānta-sūtra*. Śrīla Vyāsadeva had no interest in writing a history of mundane activities other than to give less intelligent persons a chance for transcendental realization through

Bhagavad-gītā. Vidura's reference to the *Mahābhārata* indicates that he had heard of the *Mahābhārata* from Vyāsadeva, his real father, while he was away from home and was touring the places of pilgrimage.

TEXT 13

सा श्रद्दधानस्य विवर्धमाना
विरक्तिमन्यत्र करोति पुंसः ।
हरेः पदानुस्मृतिनिर्वृतस्य
समस्तदुःखाप्ययमाशु धत्ते ॥१३॥

sā śraddadhānasya vivardhamānā
viraktim anyatra karoti puṁsaḥ
hareḥ padānusmṛti-nirvṛtasya
samasta-duḥkhāpyayam āśu dhatte

sā—those topics of Kṛṣṇa, or *kṛṣṇa-kathā; śraddadhānasya*—of one who is anxious to hear; *vivardhamānā*—gradually increasing; *viraktim*—indifference; *anyatra*—in other things (than such topics); *karoti*—does; *puṁsaḥ*—of one who is so engaged; *hareḥ*—of the Lord; *pada-anusmṛti*—constant remembrance of the lotus feet of the Lord; *nirvṛtasya*—one who has achieved such transcendental bliss; *samasta-duḥkha*—all miseries; *apyayam*—vanquished; *āśu*—without delay; *dhatte*—executes.

TRANSLATION

For one who is anxious to engage constantly in hearing such topics, kṛṣṇa-kathā gradually increases his indifference towards all other things. Such constant remembrance of the lotus feet of Lord Kṛṣṇa by the devotee who has achieved transcendental bliss vanquishes all his miseries without delay.

PURPORT

We must certainly know that on the absolute plane *kṛṣṇa-kathā* and Kṛṣṇa are one and the same. The Lord is the Absolute Truth, and therefore His name, form, quality, etc., which are all understood to be *kṛṣṇa-kathā,* are nondifferent from Him. *Bhagavad-gītā,* being spoken by the Lord, is as good as the Lord Himself. When a sincere devotee reads *Bhagavad-gītā,* this is as good as seeing the Lord face to face in his personal presence, but this is not so for the mundane wrangler. All the potencies of the Lord are there when one reads *Bhagavad-gītā,* provided it is read in the way recommended in the *Gītā* by the Lord Himself. One cannot foolishly manufacture an interpretation of *Bhagavad-gītā* and still bring about transcendental benefit. Anyone who tries to squeeze some artificial meaning or interpretation from *Bhagavad-gītā* for an ulterior motive is not *śraddadhāna-puṁsaḥ* (one engaged anxiously in bona fide hearing of *kṛṣṇa-kathā*). Such a person cannot derive any benefit from reading *Bhagavad-gīta,* however great a scholar he may be in the estimation of a layman. The *śraddadhāna,* or faithful devotee, can actually derive all the benefits of *Bhagavad-gītā* because by the omnipotency of the Lord he achieves the transcendental bliss which vanquishes attachment and nullifies all concomitant material miseries. Only the devotee, by his factual experience, can understand the import of this verse spoken by Vidura. The pure devotee of the Lord enjoys life by constantly remembering the lotus feet of the Lord by hearing *kṛṣṇa-kathā.* For such a devotee there is no such thing as material existence, and the much advertised bliss of *brahmānanda* is like a fig for the devotee who is in the midst of the transcendental ocean of bliss.

TEXT 14

तान्छोच्यशोच्यानविदोऽनुशोचे
हरेः कथायां विमुखानघेन ।
क्षिणोति देवोऽनिमिषस्तु येषा-
मायुर्वृथावादगतिस्मृतीनाम् ॥१४॥

tāñ chocya-śocyān avido 'nuśoce
hareḥ kathāyāṁ vimukhān aghena
kṣiṇoti devo 'nimiṣas tu yeṣām
āyur vṛthā-vāda-gati-smṛtīnām

tān—all those; *śocya*—pitiable; *śocyān*—of the pitiable; *avidaḥ*—ignorant; *anuśoce*—I pity; *hareḥ*—of the Lord; *kathāyām*—to the topics of; *vimukhān*—averse; *aghena*—because of sinful activities; *kṣiṇoti*—decaying; *devaḥ*—the Lord; *animiṣaḥ*—eternal time; *tu*—but; *yeṣām*—of whom; *āyuḥ*—duration of life; *vṛthā*—uselessly; *vāda*—philosophical speculations; *gati*—ultimate goal; *smṛtīnām*—of those following different rituals.

TRANSLATION

O sage, persons who because of their sinful activities are averse to the topics of Transcendence and thus ignorant of the purpose of the Mahābhārata [Bhagavad-gītā] are pitied by the pitiable. I also pity them because I see how their duration of life is spoiled by eternal time while they involve themselves in presentations of philosophical speculation, theoretical ultimate goals of life, and different modes of ritual.

PURPORT

According to the modes of material nature, there are three kinds of relationships between human beings and the Supreme Personality of Godhead. Those who are in the modes of ignorance and passion are averse to the existence of God, or else they formally accept the existence of God in the capacity of an order supplier. Above them are those who are in the mode of goodness. This second class of men believe the Supreme Brahman to be impersonal. They accept the cult of *bhakti,* in which hearing of *kṛṣṇa-kathā* is the first item, as a means and not the end. Above them are those who are pure devotees. They are situated in the transcendental stage above the mode of material goodness. Such persons are decidedly convinced that the name, form, fame, qualities, etc., of the Personality of Godhead are nondifferent from one another on the absolute plane. For them, hearing of the topics of Kṛṣṇa is equal to meeting with Him face to face. According to this class of men, who are situated in pure devotional service to the Lord, the highest goal of human life is *puruṣārtha,* devotional service to the Lord, the real mission of life. The impersonalists, because they engage in mental speculation and have no faith in the Personality of Godhead, have no business hearing the topics of Kṛṣṇa. Such persons are pitiable for the first-class pure devotees of the Lord. The pitiable impersonalists pity those who are influenced by the modes of ignorance and passion, but the pure devotees of the Lord take pity on them both because both waste their most valuable time in the human form of life in false pursuits, sense enjoyment and mental speculative presentations of different theories and goals of life.

TEXT 15

तदस्य कौषारव शर्मदातु-
हरेः कथामेव कथासु सारम् ।
उद्धृत्य पुष्पेभ्य इवार्तबन्धो
शिवाय नः कीर्तय तीर्थकीर्तेः ॥१५॥

tad asya kauṣārava śarma-dātur
hareḥ kathām eva kathāsu sāram
uddhṛtya puṣpebhya ivārta-bandho
śivāya naḥ kīrtaya tīrtha-kīrteḥ

tat—therefore; *asya*—His; *kauṣārava*—O Maitreya; *śarma-dātuḥ*—of one who awards good fortune; *hareḥ*—of the Lord; *kathām*—topics; *eva*—only; *kathāsu*—of all topics; *sāram*—the essence; *uddhṛtya*—by quoting; *puṣpebhyaḥ*—from the flowers; *iva*—like that; *ārta-bandho*—O friend of the distressed; *śivāya*—for welfare; *naḥ*—of us; *kīrtaya*—kindly describe; *tīrtha*—pilgrimage; *kīrteḥ*—of glorious.

TRANSLATION

O Maitreya, O friend of the distressed, the glories of the Supreme Lord can alone do good for people all over the world. Therefore, just as bees collect honey from flowers, kindly describe the essence of all topics—the topics of the Lord.

PURPORT

There are many topics for different persons in different modes of material nature, but the essential topics are those in relationship with the Supreme Lord. Unfortunately, materially affected conditioned souls are all more or less averse to topics of the Supreme Lord because some of them do not believe in the existence of God and some of them believe only in the impersonal feature of the Lord. In both cases there is nothing for them to say of God. Both the nonbelievers and the impersonalists deny the essence of all topics; therefore, they engage in topics of relativity in various ways, either in sense gratification or in mental speculation. For the pure devotees like Vidura, the topics of both the mundaners and the mental speculators are useless in all respects. Thus Vidura requested Maitreya to talk of the essence only, the talks of Kṛṣṇa, and nothing else.

TEXT 16

स विश्वजन्मस्थितिसंयमार्थे
कृतावतारः प्रगृहीतशक्तिः ।
चकार कर्माण्यतिपूरुषाणि
यानीश्वरः कीर्तय तानि मह्यम् ॥१६॥

sa viśva-janma-sthiti-saṁyamārthe
kṛtāvatāraḥ pragṛhīta-śaktiḥ
cakāra karmāṇy atipūruṣāṇi
yānīśvaraḥ kīrtaya tāni mahyam

saḥ—the Personality of Godhead; *viśva*—universe; *janma*—creation; *sthiti*—maintenance; *saṁyama-arthe*—with a view to perfect control; *kṛta*—accepted; *avatāraḥ*—incarnation; *pragṛhīta*—accomplished with; *śaktiḥ*—potency; *cakāra*—performed; *karmāṇi*—transcendental activities; *ati-pūruṣāṇi*—superhuman; *yāni*—all those; *īśvaraḥ*—the Lord; *kīrtaya*—please chant; *tāni*—all those; *mahyam*—unto me.

TRANSLATION

Kindly chant all those superhuman transcendental activities of the supreme controller, the Personality of Godhead, who accepted incarnations fully equipped with all potency for the full manifestation and maintenance of the cosmic creation.

PURPORT

Vidura was undoubtedly very eager to hear about Lord Kṛṣṇa in particular, but he was overwhelmed because Lord Kṛṣṇa had just passed away from the visible world. He therefore wanted to hear about Him in His *puruṣa* incarnations, which He manifests with full potencies for the creation and maintenance of the cosmic world. The activities of the *puruṣa* incarnations are but an extension of the activities of the Lord. This hint was given by Vidura to Maitreya because Maitreya could not decide which part of the activities of Lord Kṛṣṇa should be chanted.

TEXT 17

श्रीशुक उवाच
स एवं भगवान् पृष्टः क्षत्त्रा कौषारवो मुनिः ।
पुंसां निःश्रेयसार्थेन तमाह बहुमानयन् ॥१७॥

śrī-śuka uvāca
sa evaṁ bhagavān pṛṣṭaḥ
kṣattrā kauṣāravo muniḥ
puṁsāṁ niḥśreyasārthena
tam āha bahu-mānayan

śrī-śukaḥ uvāca—Śrī Śukadeva Gosvāmī said; *saḥ*—he; *evam*—thus; *bhagavān*—the great sage; *pṛṣṭaḥ*—being requested; *kṣattrā*—by Vidura; *kauṣāravaḥ*—Maitreya; *muniḥ*—the great sage; *puṁsām*—for all people; *niḥśreyasa*—for the greatest welfare; *arthena*—for that; *tam*—unto him; *āha*—narrated; *bahu*—greatly; *mānayan*—honoring.

TRANSLATION

Śukadeva Gosvāmī said: The great sage Maitreya Muni, after honoring Vidura very greatly, began to speak, at Vidura's request, for the greatest welfare of all people.

PURPORT

The great sage Maitreya Muni is described here as *bhagavān* because he surpassed all ordinary human beings in learning and experience. Thus his selection of the greatest welfare service for the world is considered authoritative. The all-inclusive welfare service for the entire human society is devotional service to the Lord, and, as requested by Vidura, the sage described the same very appropriately.

TEXT 18

मैत्रेय उवाच
साधु पृष्टं त्वया साधो लोकान् साध्वनुगृह्णता ।
कीर्तिं वितन्वता लोके आत्मनोऽधोक्षजात्मनः ॥१८॥

maitreya uvāca
sādhu pṛṣṭaṁ tvayā sādho
lokān sādhv anugṛhṇatā
kīrtiṁ vitanvatā loke
ātmano 'dhokṣajātmanaḥ

maitreyaḥ uvāca—Śrī Maitreya said; *sādhu*—all good; *pṛṣṭam*—I am asked; *tvayā*—by you; *sādho*—O good one; *lokān*—all the people; *sādhu anugṛhṇatā*—showing mercy in goodness; *kīrtim*—glories; *vitanvatā*—broadcasting; *loke*—in the world; *ātmanaḥ*—of the self; *adhokṣaja*—the Transcendence; *ātmanaḥ*—mind.

TRANSLATION

Śrī Maitreya said: O Vidura, all glory unto you. You have inquired from me of the greatest of all goodness, and thus you have shown your mercy both to the world and to me because your mind is always absorbed in thoughts of the Transcendence.

PURPORT

Maitreya Muni, who was experienced in the science of Transcendence, could understand that Vidura's mind was fully absorbed in Transcendence. *Adhokṣaja* means that which transcends the limits of sense perception or sensuous experience. The Lord is transcendental to our sense experience, but He reveals Himself to the sincere devotee. Because Vidura was always absorbed in thought of the Lord, Maitreya could estimate Vidura's transcendental value. He appreciated the valuable inquiries of Vidura and thus thanked him with great honor.

TEXT 19

नैतच्चित्रं त्वयि क्षत्तर्बादरायणवीर्यजे ।
गृहीतोऽनन्यभावेन यत्त्वया हरिरीश्वरः ॥१९॥

naitac citraṁ tvayi kṣattar
bādarāyaṇa-vīryaje
gṛhīto 'nanya-bhāvena
yat tvayā harir īśvaraḥ

na—never; *etat*—such inquiries; *citram*—very wonderful; *tvayi*—in you; *kṣattaḥ*—O Vidura; *bādarāyaṇa*—of Vyāsadeva; *vīrya-je*—born from the semen; *gṛhītaḥ*—accepted; *ananya-bhāvena*—without deviation from the thought; *yat*—because; *tvayā*—by you; *hariḥ*—the Personality of Godhead; *īśvaraḥ*—the Lord.

TRANSLATION

O Vidura, it is not at all wonderful that you have so accepted the Lord without deviation of thought, for you were born from the semen of Vyāsadeva.

PURPORT

The value of great parentage and noble birth is evaluated here in connection with the birth of Vidura. The culture of a human being begins when the father invests his semen in the womb of the mother. According to his status of work, a living entity is placed in a particular father's semen, and because Vidura was not an ordinary living entity, he was given the chance to be born from the semen of Vyāsa. The birth of a human being is a great science, and therefore reformation of the act of impregnation according to the Vedic ritual called *Garbhādhāna-saṁskāra* is very important for generating good population. The problem is not to check the growth of the population, but to generate good population on the level of Vidura, Vyāsa and Maitreya. There is no need to check the growth of population if the children are born as human beings with all precautions regarding their birth. So-called birth control is not only vicious but also useless.

TEXT 20

माण्डव्यशापाद्भगवान् प्रजासंयमनो यमः ।
भ्रातुः क्षेत्रे भुजिष्यायां जातः सत्यवतीसुतात् ॥२०॥

māṇḍavya-śāpād bhagavān
prajā-saṁyamano yamaḥ
bhrātuḥ kṣetre bhujiṣyāyāṁ
jātaḥ satyavatī-sutāt

māṇḍavya—the great *ṛṣi* Māṇḍavya Muni; *śāpāt*—by his curse; *bhagavān*—the greatly powerful; *prajā*—one who is born; *saṁyamanaḥ*—controller of death; *yamaḥ*—known as Yamarāja; *bhrātuḥ*—of the brother; *kṣetre*—in the wife; *bhujiṣyāyām*—kept; *jātaḥ*—born; *satyavatī*—Satyavatī (the mother of both Vicitravīrya and Vyāsadeva); *sutāt*—by the son (Vyāsadeva).

TRANSLATION

I know that you are now Vidura due to the cursing of Māṇḍavya Muni and that formerly you were King Yamarāja, the great controller of living entities after their death. You were begotten by the son of Satyavatī, Vyāsadeva, in the kept wife of his brother.

PURPORT

Māṇḍavya Muni was a great sage (cf. *Bhāg.* 1.13.1), and Vidura was formerly the controller Yamarāja, who takes charge of the living entities after death. Birth, maintenance and death are three conditional states of the living entities who are within the material world. As the appointed controller after death, Yamarāja once tried Māṇḍavya Muni for his childhood profligacy and ordered him to be pierced with a lance. Māṇḍavya, being angry at Yamarāja for awarding him undue punishment, cursed him to become a *śūdra* (member of the less intelligent laborer class). Thus Yamarāja took birth in the womb of the kept wife of Vicitravīrya from the semen of Vicitravīrya's brother, Vyāsadeva. Vyāsadeva is the son of Satyavatī by the great King Śāntanu, the father of Bhīṣmadeva. This mysterious history of Vidura was known to Maitreya Muni because he happened to be a contemporary friend of Vyāsadeva's. In spite of Vidura's birth from the womb of a kept wife, because he had otherwise high parentage and great connection he inherited the highest talent of becoming a great devotee of the Lord. To take birth in such a great family is understood to be an advantage for attaining devotional life. Vidura was given this chance due to his previous greatness.

TEXT 21

भवान् भगवतो नित्यं सम्मतः सानुगस्य ह ।
यस्य ज्ञानोपदेशाय मादिशद्भगवान्व्रजन् ॥२१॥

bhavān bhagavato nityaṁ
sammataḥ sānugasya ha
yasya jñānopadeśāya
mādiśad bhagavān vrajan

bhavān—your good self; *bhagavataḥ*—of the Personality of Godhead; *nityam*—eternal; *sammataḥ*—recognized; *sa-anugasya*—one of the associates; *ha*—have been; *yasya*—of whom; *jñāna*—knowledge; *upadeśāya*—for instructing; *mā*—unto me; *ādiśat*—so ordered; *bhagavān*—the Personality of Godhead; *vrajan*—while returning to His abode.

TRANSLATION

Your good self is one of the eternal associates of the Supreme Personality of Godhead for whose sake the Lord, while going back to His abode, left instructions with me.

PURPORT

Yamarāja, the great controller of life after death, decides the living entities' destinies in their next lives. He is surely among the most confidential representatives of the Lord. Such confidential posts are offered to great devotees of the Lord who are as good as His eternal associates in the spiritual sky. And because Vidura happened to be among them, the Lord, while returning to Vaikuṇṭha, left instructions for Vidura with Maitreya Muni. Generally the eternal associates of the Lord in the spiritual sky do not come to the material world. Sometimes they come, however, by the order of the Lord—not to hold any administrative post, but to associate with the Lord in person or to propagate the message of God in human society. Such empowered representatives are called *śaktyāveśa-avatāras*, or incarnations invested with transcendental power of attorney.

TEXT 22

अथ ते भगवल्लीला योगमायोरुबृंहिताः ।
विश्वस्थित्युद्भवान्तार्था वर्णयाम्यनुपूर्वशः ॥२२॥

atha te bhagaval-līlā
yoga-māyorubṛṁhitāḥ
viśva-sthity-udbhavāntārthā
varṇayāmy anupūrvaśaḥ

atha—therefore; *te*—unto you; *bhagavat*—pertaining to the Personality of Godhead; *līlāḥ*—pastimes; *yoga-māyā*—energy of the Lord; *uru*—greatly; *bṛṁhitāḥ*—extended by; *viśva*—of the cosmic world; *sthiti*—maintenance; *udbhava*—creation; *anta*—dissolution; *arthāḥ*—purpose; *varṇayāmi*—I shall describe; *anupūrvaśaḥ*—systematically.

TRANSLATION

I shall therefore describe to you the pastimes by which the Personality of Godhead extends His transcendental potency for the creation, maintenance and dissolution of the cosmic world as they occur one after another.

PURPORT

The omnipotent Lord, by His different energies, can perform anything and everything He likes. The creation of the cosmic world is done by His *yogamāyā* energy.

TEXT 23

भगवानेक आसेदमग्र आत्मात्मनां विभुः ।
आत्मेच्छानुगतावात्मा नानामत्युपलक्षणः ॥२३॥

bhagavān eka āsedam
agra ātmātmanāṁ vibhuḥ

ātmecchānugatāv ātmā
nānā-maty-upalakṣaṇaḥ

bhagavān—the Personality of Godhead; *ekaḥ*—one without a second; *āsa*—was there; *idam*—this creation; *agre*—prior to the creation; *ātmā*—in His own form; *ātmanām*—of the living entities; *vibhuḥ*—master; *ātmā*—Self; *icchā*—desire; *anugatau*—being merged in; *ātmā*—Self; *nānā-mati*—different vision; *upalakṣaṇaḥ*—symptoms.

TRANSLATION

The Personality of Godhead, the master of all living entities, existed prior to the creation as one without a second. It is by His will only that creation is made possible and again everything merges in Him. This Supreme Self is symptomized by different names.

PURPORT

The great sage here begins to explain the purpose of the four original verses of the *Śrīmad-Bhāgavatam.* Although they have no access to the *Śrīmad-Bhāgavatam,* the followers of the Māyāvāda (impersonalist) school sometimes screw out an imaginary explanation of the original four verses, but we must accept the actual explanation given herein by Maitreya Muni because he, along with Uddhava, personally heard it directly from the Lord. The first line of the original four verses runs, *aham evāsam evāgre.* The word *aham* is misinterpreted by the Māyāvāda school into meanings which no one but the interpreter can understand. Here *aham* is explained as the Supreme Personality of Godhead, not the individual living entities. Before the creation, there was only the Personality of Godhead; there were no *puruṣa* incarnations and certainly no living entities, nor was there the material energy, by which the manifested creation is effected. The *puruṣa* incarnations and all the different energies of the Supreme Lord were merged in Him only.

The Personality of Godhead is described herein as the master of all other living entities. He is like the sun disc, and the living entities are like the molecules of the sun's rays. This existence of the Lord before the creation is confirmed by the *śrutis: vāsudevo vā idaṁ agra āsīt na brahmā na ca śaṅkaraḥ, eko vai nārāyaṇa āsīn na brahmā neśānāḥ.*

Because everything that be is an emanation from the Personality of Godhead, He always exists alone without a second. He can so exist because He is all-perfect and omnipotent. Everything other than Him, including His plenary expansions, the *viṣṇu-tattvas,* is His part and parcel. Before the creation there were no Kāraṇārṇavaśāyī or Garbhodakaśāyī or Kṣīrodakaśāyī Viṣṇus, or was there Brahmā nor Śaṅkara. The Viṣṇu plenary expansion and the living entities beginning from Brahmā are separated parts and parcels. Although the spiritual existence was there with the Lord, the material existence was dormant in Him. By His will only is the material manifestation done and undone. The diversity of the Vaikuṇṭhaloka is one with the Lord, just as the diversity of soldiers is one with and the same as the king. As explained in *Bhagavad-gītā* (9.7), the material creation takes place at intervals by the will of the Lord, and in the periods between dissolution and creation, the living entities and the material energy remain dormant in Him.

TEXT 24

स वा एष तदा द्रष्टा नापश्यद् दृश्यमेकराट् ।
मेनेऽसन्तमिवात्मानं सुप्तशक्तिरसुप्तदृक् ॥२४॥

sa vā eṣa tadā draṣṭā
nāpaśyad dṛśyam ekarāṭ
mene 'santam ivātmānaṁ
supta-śaktir asupta-dṛk

saḥ—the Personality of Godhead; *vā*—either; *eṣaḥ*—all these; *tadā*—at that time; *draṣṭā*—the seer; *na*—did not; *apaśyat*—see; *dṛśyam*—the cosmic creation; *eka-rāṭ*—undisputed proprietor; *mene*—thought like this; *asantam*—nonexistent; *iva*—like that; *ātmānam*—plenary manifestations; *supta*—unmanifested; *śaktiḥ*—material energy; *asupta*—manifested; *dṛk*—internal potency.

TRANSLATION

The Lord, the undisputed proprietor of everything, was the only seer. The cosmic manifestation was not present at that time, and thus He felt imperfect without His plenary and separated parts

and parcels. The material energy was dormant, whereas the internal potency was manifested.

PURPORT

The Lord is the supreme seer because only by His glance did the material energy become active for cosmic manifestation. At that time the seer was there, but the external energy, over which the glance of the Lord is cast, was not present. He felt somewhat insufficient, like a husband feeling lonely in the absence of his wife. This is a poetic simile. The Lord wanted to create the cosmic manifestation to give another chance to the conditioned souls who were dormant in forgetfulness. The cosmic manifestation gives the conditioned souls a chance to go back home, back to Godhead, and that is its main purpose. The Lord is so kind that in the absence of such a manifestation He feels something wanting, and thus the creation takes place. Although the creation of the internal potency was manifested, the other potency appeared to be sleeping, and the Lord wanted to awaken her to activity, just as a husband wants to awaken his wife from the sleeping state for enjoyment. It is the compassion of the Lord for the sleeping energy that He wants to see her awaken for enjoyment like the other wives who are awake. The whole process is to enliven the sleeping conditioned souls to the real life of spiritual consciousness so that they may thus become as perfect as the ever-liberated souls in the Vaikuṇṭhalokas. Since the Lord is *sac-cid-ānanda-vigraha*, He likes every part and parcel of His different potencies to take part in the blissful *rasa* because participation with the Lord in His eternal *rāsa-līlā* is the highest living condition, perfect in spiritual bliss and eternal knowledge.

TEXT 25

सा वा एतस्य संद्रष्टुः शक्तिः सदसदात्मिका ।
माया नाम महाभाग ययेदं निर्ममे विभुः ॥२५॥

sā vā etasya saṁdraṣṭuḥ
śaktiḥ sad-asad-ātmikā
māyā nāma mahā-bhāga
yayedaṁ nirmame vibhuḥ

sā—that external energy; *vā*—is either; *etasya*—of the Lord; *saṁdraṣṭuḥ*—of the perfect seer; *śaktiḥ*—energy; *sat-asat-ātmikā*—as both the cause and the effect; *māyā nāma*—called by the name *māyā; mahā-bhāga*—O fortunate one; *yayā*—by which; *idam*—this material world; *nirmame*—constructed; *vibhuḥ*—the Almighty.

TRANSLATION

The Lord is the seer, and the external energy, which is seen, works as both cause and effect in the cosmic manifestation. O greatly fortunate Vidura, this external energy is known as māyā or illusion, and through her agency only is the entire material manifestation made possible.

PURPORT

The material nature, known as *māyā*, is both the material and efficient cause of the cosmos, but in the background the Lord is the consciousness for all activities. As in the individual body the consciousness is the source of all energies of the body, so the supreme consciousness of the Lord is the source of all energies in material nature. This is confirmed in *Bhagavad-gītā* (9.10) as follows:

mayādhyakṣeṇa prakṛtiḥ
sūyate sa-carācaram
hetunānena kaunteya
jagad viparivartate

"Throughout all the energies of material nature there is the hand of the Supreme Lord as the final superintendent. Due to this supreme cause only, the activities of material nature appear planned and systematic, and all things regularly evolve."

TEXT 26

कालवृत्त्या तु मायायां गुणमय्यामधोक्षजः ।
पुरुषेणात्मभूतेन वीर्यमाधत्त वीर्यवान् ॥२६॥

kāla-vṛttyā tu māyāyāṁ
guṇa-mayyām adhokṣajaḥ
puruṣeṇātma-bhūtena
vīryam ādhatta vīryavān

kāla—the eternal time; *vṛttyā*—by the influence of; *tu*—but; *māyāyām*—in the external energy; *guṇa-mayyām*—in the qualitative modes of nature; *adhokṣajaḥ*—the Transcendence; *puruṣeṇa*—by the *puruṣa* incarnation; *ātma-bhūtena*—who is the plenary expansion of the Lord; *vīryam*—the seeds of the living entities; *ādhatta*—impregnated; *vīryavān*—the Supreme Living Being.

TRANSLATION

The Supreme Living Being in His feature as the transcendental puruṣa incarnation, who is the Lord's plenary expansion, impregnates the material nature of three modes, and thus by the influence of eternal time the living entities appear.

PURPORT

The offspring of any living being is born after the father impregnates the mother with semen, and the living entity floating in the semen of the father takes the shape of the mother's form. Similarly, mother material nature cannot produce any living entity from her material elements unless and until she is impregnated with living entities by the Lord Himself. That is the mystery of the generation of the living entities. This impregnating process is performed by the first *puruṣa* incarnation, Kāraṇārṇavaśāyī Viṣṇu. Simply by His glance over material nature, the whole matter is accomplished.

We should not understand the process of impregnation by the Personality of Godhead in terms of our conception of sex. The omnipotent Lord can impregnate just by His eyes, and therefore He is called all-potent. Each and every part of His transcendental body can perform each and every function of the other parts. This is confirmed in the *Brahma-saṁhitā* (5.32): *aṅgāni yasya sakalendriya-vṛttimanti.* In *Bhagavad-gītā* (14.3) also, the same principle is confirmed: *mama yonir mahad-brahma tasmin garbhaṁ dadhāmy aham.* When the cosmic creation is manifested, the living entities are directly supplied from the Lord; they are never products of material nature. Thus, no scientific advancement of material science can ever produce a living being. That is the whole mystery of the material creation. The living entities are foreign to matter, and thus they cannot be happy unless they are situated in the same spiritual life as the Lord. The mistaken living being, out of forgetfulness of this original condition of life, unnecessarily wastes time trying to become happy in the material world. The whole Vedic process is to remind one of this essential feature of life. The Lord offers the conditioned soul a material body for his so-called enjoyment, but if one does not come to his senses and enter into spiritual consciousness, the Lord again puts him in the unmanifested condition as it existed in the beginning of the creation. The Lord is described here as *vīryavān*, or the greatest potent being, because He impregnates material nature with innumerable living entities who are conditioned from time immemorial.

TEXT 27

ततोऽभवन् महत्तत्त्वमव्यक्तात्कालचोदितात् ।
विज्ञानात्मात्मदेहस्थं विश्वं व्यञ्जंस्तमोनुदः ॥२७॥

tato 'bhavan mahat-tattvam
avyaktāt kāla-coditāt
vijñānātmātma-deha-sthaṁ
viśvaṁ vyañjaṁs tamo-nudaḥ

tataḥ—thereafter; *abhavat*—came into existence; *mahat*—supreme; *tattvam*—sum total; *avyaktāt*—from the unmanifested; *kāla-coditāt*—by the interaction of time; *vijñāna-ātmā*—unalloyed goodness; *ātma-deha-stham*—situated on the bodily self; *viśvam*—complete universes; *vyañjan*—manifesting; *tamaḥ-nudaḥ*—the supreme light.

TRANSLATION

Thereafter, influenced by the interactions of eternal time, the supreme sum total of matter called the mahat-tattva became manifested, and in this mahat-tattva the unalloyed goodness, the

Supreme Lord, sowed the seeds of universal manifestation out of His own body.

PURPORT

In due course of time, the impregnated material energy was manifested first as the total material ingredients. Everything takes its own time to fructify, and therefore the word *kāla-coditāt,* "influenced by time," is used herein. The *mahat-tattva* is the total consciousness because a portion of it is represented in everyone as the intellect. The *mahat-tattva* is directly connected with the supreme consciousness of the Supreme Being, but still it appears as matter. The *mahat-tattva,* or shadow of pure consciousness, is the germinating place of all creation. It is pure goodness with the slight addition of the material mode of passion, and therefore activity is generated from this point.

TEXT 28

सोऽप्यंशगुणकालात्मा भगवद्दृष्टिगोचरः ।
आत्मानं व्यकरोदात्मा विश्वस्यास्य सिसृक्षया ॥२८॥

so 'py aṁśa-guṇa-kālātmā
bhagavad-dṛṣṭi-gocaraḥ
ātmānaṁ vyakarod ātmā
viśvasyāsya sisṛkṣayā

saḥ—mahat-tattva; api—also; *aṁśa—puruṣa* plenary expansion; *guṇa*—chiefly the quality of ignorance; *kāla*—the duration of time; *ātmā*—full consciousness; *bhagavat*—the Personality of Godhead; *dṛṣṭi-gocaraḥ*—range of sight; *ātmānam*—many different forms; *vyakarot*—differentiated; *ātmā*—reservoir; *viśvasya*—the would-be entities; *asya*—of this; *sisṛkṣayā*—generates the false ego.

TRANSLATION

Thereafter the mahat-tattva differentiated itself into many different forms as the reservoir of the would-be entities. The mahat-tattva is chiefly in the mode of ignorance, and it generates

the false ego. It is a plenary expansion of the Personality of Godhead, with full consciousness of creative principles and time for fructification.

PURPORT

The *mahat-tattva* is the via medium between pure spirit and material existence. It is the junction of matter and spirit wherefrom the false ego of the living entity is generated. All living entities are differentiated parts and parcels of the Personality of Godhead. Under the pressure of false ego, the conditioned souls, although parts and parcels of the Supreme Personality of Godhead, claim to be the enjoyers of material nature. This false ego is the binding force of material existence. The Lord again and again gives a chance to the bewildered conditioned souls to get free from this false ego, and that is why the material creation takes place at intervals. He gives the conditioned souls all facilities for rectifying the activities of the false ego, but He does not interfere with their small independence as parts and parcels of the Lord.

TEXT 29

महत्तत्त्वाद्विकुर्वाणादहंतत्त्वं व्यजायत ।
कार्यकारणकर्त्रात्मा भूतेन्द्रियमनोमयः ।
वैकारिकस्तैजसश्च तामसश्चेत्यहं त्रिधा ॥२९॥

mahat-tattvād vikurvāṇād
aham-tattvam vyajāyata
kārya-kāraṇa-kartrātmā
bhūtendriya-mano-mayaḥ
vaikārikas taijasaś ca
tāmasaś cety aham tridhā

mahat—the great; *tattvāt*— from the causal truth; *vikurvāṇāt*—being transformed; *aham*—false ego; *tattvam*—material truth; *vyajāyata*—became manifested; *kārya*—effects; *kāraṇa*—cause; *kartṛ*—doer; *ātmā*—soul or source; *bhūta*—material ingredients; *indriya*—senses; *manaḥ-mayaḥ*—hovering on the mental plane; *vaikārikaḥ*—the mode of goodness; *taijasaḥ*—the mode of passion; *ca*—and; *tāmasaḥ*—the mode of ignorance; *ca*—and; *iti*—thus; *aham*—false ego; *tridhā*—three kinds.

TRANSLATION

Mahat-tattva, or the great causal truth, transforms into false ego, which is manifested in three phases—cause, effect and the doer. All such activities are on the mental plane and are based on the material elements, gross senses and mental speculation. The false ego is represented in three different modes—goodness, passion and ignorance.

PURPORT

A pure living entity in his original spiritual existence is fully conscious of his constitutional position as an eternal servitor of the Lord. All souls who are situated in such pure consciousness are liberated, and therefore they eternally live in bliss and knowledge in the various Vaikuṇṭha planets in the spiritual sky. When the material creation is manifested, it is not meant for them. The eternally liberated souls are called *nitya-muktas*, and they have nothing to do with the material creation. The material creation is meant for rebellious souls who are not prepared to accept subordination under the Supreme Lord. This spirit of false lordship is called false ego. It is manifested in three modes of material nature, and it exists in mental speculation only. Those who are in the mode of goodness think that each and every person is God, and thus they laugh at the pure devotees, who try to engage in the transcendental loving service of the Lord. Those who are puffed up by the mode of passion try to lord it over material nature in various ways. Some of them engage in altruistic activities as if they were agents appointed to do good to others by their mental speculative plans. Such men accept the standard ways of mundane altruism, but their plans are made on the basis of false ego. This false ego extends to the limit of becoming one with the Lord. The last class of egoistic conditioned souls—those in the mode of ignorance—are misguided by identification of the gross body with the self. Thus, all their activities are centered around the body only. All these persons are given the chance to play with false egoistic ideas, but at the same time the Lord is kind enough to give them a chance to take help from scriptures like *Bhagavad-gītā* and *Śrīmad-Bhāgavatam* so that they may understand the science of Kṛṣṇa and thus make their lives successful. The entire material creation, therefore, is meant for the falsely egoistic living entities hovering on the mental plane under different illusions in the modes of material nature.

TEXT 30

अहंतत्त्वाद्विकुर्वाणान्मनो वैकारिकादभूत् ।
वैकारिकाश्च ये देवा अर्थाभिव्यञ्जनं यतः ॥३०॥

aham-tattvād vikurvāṇān
mano vaikārikād abhūt
vaikārikāś ca ye devā
arthābhivyañjanaṁ yataḥ

aham-tattvāt—from the principle of false ego; *vikurvāṇāt*—by transformation; *manaḥ*—the mind; *vaikārikāt*—by interaction with the mode of goodness; *abhūt*—generated; *vaikārikāḥ*—by interaction with goodness; *ca*—also; *ye*—all these; *devāḥ*—demigods; *artha*—the phenomenon; *abhivyañjanam*—physical knowledge; *yataḥ*—the source.

TRANSLATION

The false ego is transformed into mind by interaction with the mode of goodness. All the demigods who control the phenomenal world are also products of the same principle, namely the interaction of false ego and the mode of goodness.

PURPORT

False ego interacting with the different modes of material nature is the source of all materials in the phenomenal world.

TEXT 31

तैजसानीन्द्रियाण्येव ज्ञानकर्ममयानि च ॥३१॥

taijasānīndriyāṇy eva
jñāna-karma-mayāni ca

taijasāni—the mode of passion; *indriyāṇi*—the senses; *eva*—certainly; *jñāna*—knowledge, philosophical speculations; *karma*—fruitive activities; *mayāni*—predominating; *ca*—also.

TRANSLATION

The senses are certainly products of the mode of passion in false ego, and therefore philosophical speculative knowledge and fruitive activities are predominantly products of the mode of passion.

PURPORT

The chief function of the false ego is godlessness. When a person forgets his constitutional position as an eternally subordinate part and parcel of the Supreme Personality of Godhead and wants to be happy independently, he functions mainly in two ways. He first attempts to act fruitively for personal gain or sense gratification, and after attempting such fruitive activities for a considerable time, when he is frustrated he becomes a philosophical speculator and thinks himself to be on the same level as God. This false idea of becoming one with the Lord is the last snare of the illusory energy, which traps a living entity into the bondage of forgetfulness under the spell of false ego.

The best means of liberation from the clutches of false ego is to give up the habit of philosophical speculation regarding the Absolute Truth. One should know definitely that the Absolute Truth is never realized by the philosophical speculations of the imperfect egoistic person. The Absolute Truth, or the Supreme Personality of Godhead, is realized by hearing about Him in all submission and love from a bona fide authority who is a representative of the twelve great authorities mentioned in the *Śrīmad-Bhāgavatam.* By such an attempt only can one conquer the illusory energy of the Lord, although for others she is unsurpassable, as confirmed in *Bhagavad-gītā* (7.14).

TEXT 32

तामसो भूतसूक्ष्मादिर्यतः खं लिङ्गमात्मनः ॥३२॥

tāmaso bhūta-sūkṣmādir
yataḥ khaṁ liṅgam ātmanaḥ

tāmasaḥ—from the mode of passion; *bhūta-sūkṣma-ādiḥ*—subtle sense objects; *yataḥ*—from which; *kham*—the sky; *liṅgam*—symbolic representation; *ātmanaḥ*—of the Supreme Soul.

TRANSLATION

The sky is a product of sound, and sound is the transformation of egoistic passion. In other words, the sky is the symbolic representation of the Supreme Soul.

PURPORT

In the Vedic hymns it is said, *etasmād ātmanaḥ ākāśaḥ sambhūtaḥ.* The sky is the symbolic representation of the Supreme Soul. Those who are egoistic in passion and ignorance cannot conceive of the Personality of Godhead. For them the sky is the symbolic representation of the Supreme Soul.

TEXT 33

कालमायांशयोगेन भगवद्वीक्षितं नभः ।
नभसोऽनुसृतं स्पर्शं विकुर्वन्निर्ममेऽनिलम् ॥३३॥

kāla-māyāṁśa-yogena
bhagavad-vīkṣitaṁ nabhaḥ
nabhaso 'nusṛtaṁ sparśaṁ
vikurvan nirmame 'nilam

kāla—time; *māyā*—external energy; *aṁśa-yogena*—partly mixed; *bhagavat*—the Personality of Godhead; *vīkṣitam*—glanced over; *nabhaḥ*—the sky; *nabhasaḥ*—from the sky; *anusṛtam*—being so contacted; *sparśam*—touch; *vikurvat*—being transformed; *nirmame*—was created; *anilam*—the air.

TRANSLATION

Thereafter the Personality of Godhead glanced over the sky, partly mixed with eternal time and external energy, and thus developed the touch sensation, from which the air in the sky was produced.

PURPORT

All material creations take place from subtle to gross. The entire universe has developed in that manner. From the sky developed the touch sensation, which is a mixture of eternal time, the external energy and the glance of the Personality of Godhead. The touch sensation developed into the air in the sky. Similarly, all other gross matter also developed from subtle to gross: sound developed into sky, touch developed into air, form developed into fire, taste developed into water, and smell developed into earth.

TEXT 34

अनिलोऽपि विकुर्वाणो नभसोरुबलान्वितः ।
ससर्ज रूपतन्मात्रं ज्योतिर्लोकस्य लोचनम् ॥३४॥

anilo 'pi vikurvāṇo
nabhasoru-balānvitaḥ
sasarja rūpa-tanmātraṁ
jyotir lokasya locanam

anilaḥ—air; *api*—also; *vikurvāṇaḥ*—being transformed; *nabhasā*—sky; *uru-bala-anvitaḥ*—extremely powerful; *sasarja*—created; *rūpa*—form; *tat-mātram*—sense perception; *jyotiḥ*—electricity; *lokasya*—of the world; *locanam*—light to see.

TRANSLATION

Thereafter the extremely powerful air, interacting with the sky, generated the form of sense perception, and the perception of form transformed into electricity, the light to see the world.

TEXT 35

अनिलेनान्वितं ज्योतिर्विकुर्वत्परवीक्षितम् ।
आधत्ताम्भो रसमयं कालमायांशयोगतः ॥३५॥

anilenānvitaṁ jyotir
vikurvat paravīkṣitam

ādhattāmbho rasa-mayaṁ
kāla-māyāṁśa-yogataḥ

anilena—by the air; *anvitam*—interacted; *jyotiḥ*—electricity; *vikurvat*—being transformed; *paravīkṣitam*—being glanced over by the Supreme; *ādhatta*—created; *ambhaḥ rasa-mayam*—water with taste; *kāla*—of eternal time; *māyā-aṁśa*—and external energy; *yogataḥ*—by a mixture.

TRANSLATION

When electricity was surcharged in the air and was glanced over by the Supreme, at that time, by a mixture of eternal time and external energy, there occurred the creation of water and taste.

TEXT 36

ज्योतिषाम्भोऽनुसंसृष्टं विकुर्वद्ब्रह्मवीक्षितम् ।
महीं गन्धगुणामाधात्कालमायांशयोगतः ॥३६॥

jyotiṣāmbho 'nusaṁsṛṣṭaṁ
vikurvad brahma-vīkṣitam
mahīṁ gandha-guṇām ādhāt
kāla-māyāṁśa-yogataḥ

jyotiṣā—electricity; *ambhaḥ*—water; *anusaṁsṛṣṭam*—thus created; *vikurvat*—due to transformation; *brahma*—the Supreme; *vīkṣitam*—so glanced over; *mahīm*—the earth; *gandha*—smell; *guṇām*—qualification; *ādhāt*—was created; *kāla*—eternal time; *māyā*—external energy; *aṁśa*—partially; *yogataḥ*—by intermixture.

TRANSLATION

Thereafter the water produced from electricity was glanced over by the Supreme Personality of Godhead and mixed with eternal time and external energy. Thus it was transformed into the earth, which is qualified primarily by smell.

PURPORT

From the descriptions of the physical elements in the above verses it is clear that in all stages the glance of the Supreme is needed with the other additions and alterations. In every transformation, the last finishing touch is the glance of the Lord, who acts as a painter does when he mixes different colors to transform them into a particular color. When one element mixes with another, the number of its qualities increases. For example, the sky is the cause of air. The sky has only one quality, namely sound, but by the interaction of the sky with the glance of the Lord, mixed with eternal time and external nature, the air is produced, which has two qualities—sound and touch. Similarly after the air is created, interaction of sky and air, touched by time and the external energy of the Lord, produces electricity. And after the interaction of electricity with air and sky, mixed with time, external energy and the Lord's glance over them, the water is produced. In the final stage of sky there is one quality, namely sound; in the air two qualities, sound and touch; in the electricity three qualities, namely sound, touch and form; in the water four qualities, sound, touch, form and taste; and in the last stage of physical development the result is earth, which has all five qualities—sound, touch, form, taste and smell. Although they are different mixtures of different materials, such mixtures do not take place automatically, just as a mixture of colors does not take place automatically without the touch of the living painter. The automatic system is factually activated by the glancing touch of the Lord. Living consciousness is the final word in all physical changes. This fact is mentioned in *Bhagavad-gītā* (9.10) as follows:

mayādhyakṣeṇa prakṛtiḥ
sūyate sa-carācaram
hetunānena kaunteya
jagad viparivartate

The conclusion is that the physical elements may work very wonderfully to the laymen's eyes, but their workings actually take place under the supervision of the Lord. Those who can mark only the changes of the physical elements and cannot perceive the hidden hands of the Lord behind them are certainly less intelligent persons, although they may be advertised as great material scientists.

TEXT 37

भूतानां नभ आदीनां यद्यद्भव्यावरावरम् ।
तेषां परानुसंसर्गाद्यथासंख्यं गुणान् विदुः ॥ ३७ ॥

bhūtānāṁ nabha-ādīnāṁ
yad yad bhavyāvarāvaram
teṣāṁ parānusaṁsargād
yathā saṅkhyaṁ guṇān viduḥ

bhūtānām—of all the physical elements; *nabhaḥ*—the sky; *ādīnām*—beginning from; *yat*—as; *yat*—and as; *bhavya*—O gentle one; *avara*—inferior; *varam*—superior; *teṣām*—all of them; *para*—the Supreme; *anusaṁsargāt*—last touch; *yathā*—as many; *saṅkhyam*—number; *guṇān*—qualities; *viduḥ*—you may understand.

TRANSLATION

O gentle one, of all the physical elements, beginning from the sky down to the earth, all the inferior and superior qualities are due only to the final touch of the glance of the Supreme Personality of Godhead.

TEXT 38

एते देवाः कला विष्णोः कालमायांशलिङ्गिनः ।
नानात्वात्स्वक्रियानीशाः प्रोचुः प्राञ्जलयो विभुम् ॥३८॥

ete devāḥ kalā viṣṇoḥ
kāla-māyāṁśa-liṅginaḥ
nānātvāt sva-kriyānīśāḥ
procuḥ prāñjalayo vibhum

ete—of all these physical elements; *devāḥ*—the controlling demigods; *kalāḥ*—parts and parcels; *viṣṇoḥ*—of the Supreme Personality of Godhead; *kāla*—time; *māyā*—external energy; *aṁśa*—part and parcel; *liṅginaḥ*—so embodied; *nānātvāt*—because of various; *sva-kriyā*—personal duties; *anīśāḥ*—not being able to perform; *procuḥ*—uttered; *prāñjalayaḥ*—fascinating; *vibhum*—unto the Lord.

TRANSLATION

The controlling deities of all the above-mentioned physical elements are empowered expansions of Lord Viṣṇu. They are embodied by eternal time under the external energy, and they are His parts and parcels. Because they were entrusted with different functions of universal duties and were unable to perform them, they offered fascinating prayers to the Lord as follows.

PURPORT

The conception of various controlling demigods who inhabit the higher planetary systems for the management of universal affairs is not imaginary, as proposed by persons with a poor fund of knowledge. The demigods are expanded parts and parcels of the Supreme Lord Viṣṇu, and they are embodied by time, external energy and partial consciousness of the Supreme. Human beings, animals, birds, etc., are also parts and parcels of the Lord and have different material bodies, but they are not the controlling deities of material affairs. They are, rather, controlled by such demigods. Such control is not superfluous; it is as necessary as the controlling departments in the affairs of a modern state. The demigods should not be despised by the controlled living beings. They are all great devotees of the Lord entrusted to execute certain functions of universal affairs. One may be angry with Yamarāja for his thankless task of punishing sinful souls, but Yamarāja is one of the authorized devotees of the Lord, and so are all the other demigods. A devotee of the Lord is never controlled by such deputed demigods, who function as assistants of the Lord, but he shows them all respects on account of the responsible positions to which they have been appointed by the Lord. At the same time, a devotee of the Lord does not foolishly mistake them to be the Supreme Lord. Only foolish persons accept the demigods as being on the same level as Viṣṇu; actually they are all appointed as servants of Viṣṇu.

Anyone who places the Lord and the demigods on the same level is called a *pāṣaṇḍī*, or atheist. The demigods are worshiped by persons who are more or less adherents of the processes of *jñāna*, *yoga* and *karma*, i.e., the impersonalists, meditators and fruitive workers. The devotees, however, worship only the Supreme Lord Viṣṇu. This worship is not for any material benefit, as desired by all the materialists, even up to the salvationists, mystics and fruitive workers. Devotees worship the Supreme Lord to attain unalloyed devotion to the Lord. The Lord, however, is not worshiped by others, who have no program for attaining love of God, which is the essential aim of human life. Persons averse to a loving relationship with God are more or less condemned by their own actions.

The Lord is equal to every living entity, just like the flowing Ganges. The Ganges water is meant for the purification of everyone, yet the trees on the banks of the Ganges have different values. A mango tree on the bank of the Ganges drinks the water, and the *nimba* tree also drinks the same water. But the fruits of both trees are different. One is celestially sweet, and the other is hellishly bitter. The condemned bitterness of the *nimba* is due to its own past work, just as the sweetness of the mango is also due to its own *karma*. The Lord says in *Bhagavad-gītā* (16.19):

tān ahaṁ dviṣataḥ krūrān
saṁsāreṣu narādhamān
kṣipāmy ajasram aśubhān
āsurīṣv eva yoniṣu

"The envious, the mischievous, the lowest of mankind, these do I ever put back into the ocean of material existence, into various demoniac species of life." Demigods like Yamarāja and other controllers are there for the unwanted conditioned souls who always engage in threatening the tranquillity of the kingdom of God. Since all the demigods are confidential devotee-servitors of the Lord, they are never to be condemned.

TEXT 39

देवा ऊचुः

नमाम ते देव पदारविन्दं
प्रपन्नतापोपशमातपत्रम् ।

यन्मूलकेता यतयोऽञ्जसोरु-
संसारदुःखं बहिरुत्क्षिपन्ति ॥३९॥

devā ūcuḥ
namāma te deva padāravindaṁ
prapanna-tāpopaśamātapatram
yan-mūla-ketā yatayo 'ñjasoru-
saṁsāra-duḥkhaṁ bahir utkṣipanti

devāḥ ūcuḥ—the demigods said; *namāma*—we offer our respectful obeisances; *te*—Your; *deva*—O Lord; *pada-aravindam*—lotus feet; *prapanna*—surrendered; *tāpa*—distress; *upaśama*—suppresses; *ātapatram*—umbrella; *yat-mūla-ketāḥ*—shelter of the lotus feet; *yatayaḥ*—great sages; *añjasā*—totally; *uru*—great; *saṁsāra-duḥkham*—miseries of material existence; *bahiḥ*—out; *utkṣipanti*—forcibly throw.

TRANSLATION

The demigods said: O Lord, Your lotus feet are like an umbrella for the surrendered souls, protecting them from all the miseries of material existence. All the sages under that shelter throw off all material miseries. We therefore offer our respectful obeisances unto Your lotus feet.

PURPORT

There are many sages and saints who engage in trying to conquer rebirth and all other material miseries. But of all of them, those who take shelter under the lotus feet of the Lord can completely throw off all such miseries without difficulty. Others, who are engaged in transcendental activities in different ways, cannot do so. For them it is very difficult. They may artificially think of becoming liberated without accepting the shelter of the lotus feet of the Lord, but that is not possible. One is sure to fall again to material existence from such false liberation, even though one may have undergone severe penances and austerities. This is the opinion of the demigods, who are not only well versed in Vedic knowledge but are also seers of the past, present and future. The opinions of the demigods are valuable because the demigods are authorized to hold positions in the affairs of universal management. They are appointed by the Lord as His confidential servants.

TEXT 40

धातर्यदस्मिन् भव ईश जीवा-
स्तापत्रयेणाभिहता न शर्म ।
आत्मन्लभन्ते भगवंस्तवाङ्घ्रि-
च्छायां सविद्यामत आश्रयेम ॥४०॥

dhātar yad asmin bhava īśa jīvās
tāpa-trayeṇābhihatā na śarma
ātman labhante bhagavaṁs tavāṅghri-
cchāyāṁ sa-vidyām ata āśrayema

dhātaḥ—O father; *yat*—because; *asmin*—in this; *bhave*—material world; *īśa*—O Lord; *jīvāḥ*—the living entities; *tāpa*—miseries; *trayeṇa*—by the three; *abhihatāḥ*—always embarrassed; *na*—never; *śarma*—in happiness; *ātman*—self; *labhante*—do gain; *bhagavan*—O Personality of Godhead; *tava*—Your; *aṅghri-chāyām*—shade of Your feet; *sa-vidyām*—full of knowledge; *ataḥ*—obtain; *āśrayema*—shelter.

TRANSLATION

O Father, O Lord, O Personality of Godhead, the living entities in the material world can never have any happiness because they are overwhelmed by the three kinds of miseries. Therefore they take shelter of the shade of Your lotus feet, which are full of knowledge, and we also thus take shelter of them.

PURPORT

The way of devotional service is neither sentimental nor mundane. It is the path of reality by which the living entity can attain the transcendental happiness of being freed from the three kinds of material miseries—miseries arising from the body and mind, from other living entities and from natural disturbances. Everyone who is conditioned by material existence—whether he be a man or beast or demigod or bird—must suffer from *ādhyātmika* (bodily or mental) pains, *ādhibautika* pains (those offered by living creatures), and *ādhidaivika* pains (those due to supernatural disturbances). His happiness is nothing but a hard struggle to get free from the miseries of conditional life. But there is only one way he can be rescued, and that is by accepting the shelter of the lotus feet of the Supreme Personality of Godhead.

The argument that unless one has proper knowledge one cannot be freed from material miseries is undoubtedly true. But because the lotus feet of the Lord are full of transcendental knowledge, acceptance of His lotus feet completes that necessity. We have already discussed this point in the First Canto (1.2.7):

vāsudeve bhagavati
bhakti-yogaḥ prayojitaḥ
janayaty āśu vairāgyaṁ
jñānaṁ ca yad ahaitukam

There is no want of knowledge in the devotional service of Vāsudeva, the Personality of Godhead. He, the Lord, personally takes charge of dissipating the darkness of ignorance from the heart of a devotee. He confirms this in *Bhagavad-gītā* (10.10):

teṣāṁ satata-yukatānāṁ
bhajatāṁ prīti-pūrvakam
dadāmi buddhi-yogaṁ taṁ
yena mām upayānti te

Empiric philosophical speculation cannot give one relief from the threefold miseries of material existence. Simply to endeavor for knowledge without devoting oneself to the Lord is a waste of valuable time.

TEXT 41

मार्गन्ति यत्ते मुखपद्मनीडै-
श्छन्दःसुपर्णैर्ऋषयो विविक्ते ।
यस्याघमर्षोदसरिद्वरायाः
पदं पदं तीर्थपदः प्रपन्नाः ॥४१॥

mārganti yat te mukha-padma-nīḍaiś
chandaḥ-suparṇair ṛṣayo vivikte
yasyāgha-marṣoda-sarid-varāyāḥ
padaṁ padaṁ tīrtha-padaḥ prapannāḥ

mārganti—searching after; *yat*—as; *te*—Your; *mukha-padma*—lotuslike face; *nīḍaiḥ*—by those who have taken shelter of such a lotus flower; *chandaḥ*—Vedic hymns; *suparṇaiḥ*—by the wings; *ṛṣayaḥ*—the sages; *vivikte*—in clear mind; *yasya*—whose; *agha-marṣa-uda*—that which offers freedom from all reactions to sin; *sarit*—rivers; *varāyāḥ*—in the best; *padam padam*—in every step; *tīrtha-padaḥ*—one whose lotus feet are as good as a place of pilgrimage; *prapannāḥ*—taking shelter.

TRANSLATION

The lotus feet of the Lord are by themselves the shelter of all places of pilgrimage. The great clear-minded sages, carried by the wings of the Vedas, always search after the nest of Your lotuslike face. Some of them surrender to Your lotus feet at every step by taking shelter of the best of rivers [the Ganges], which can deliver one from all sinful reactions.

PURPORT

The *paramahaṁsas* are compared to royal swans who make their nests on the petals of the lotus flower. The Lord's transcendental bodily parts are always compared to the lotus flower because in the material world the lotus flower is the last word in beauty. The most beautiful thing in the world is the *Vedas*, or *Bhagavad-gītā*, because therein knowledge is imparted by the Personality of Godhead Himself. The *paramahaṁsa* makes his nest in the lotuslike face of the Lord and always seeks shelter at His lotus feet, which are reached by the wings of Vedic wisdom. Since the Lord is the original source of all emanations, intelligent persons, enlightened by Vedic knowledge, seek the shelter of the Lord, just as birds who leave the nest again search out the nest to take complete rest. All Vedic knowledge is meant for understanding the Supreme Lord, as stated by the Lord in *Bhagavad-gītā* (15.15): *vedaiś ca sarvair aham eva vedyaḥ.* Intelligent persons, who are like swans, take shelter of the Lord by all means and do not hover on the mental plane by fruitlessly speculating on different philosophies.

The Lord is so kind that He has spread the River Ganges throughout the universe so that by taking bath in that holy river everyone can get release from the reactions of sins, which occur at every step. There are many rivers in the world which are able to evoke one's sense of God consciousness simply by one's bathing in them, and the River Ganges is chief amongst them. In India there are five sacred rivers, but the Ganges is the most sacred. The River Ganges and *Bhagavad-gītā* are chief sources of transcendental happiness for mankind, and intelligent persons can take shelter of them to go back home, back to Godhead. Even Śrīpāda Śaṅkarācārya recommends that a little knowledge in *Bhagavad-gītā* and the drinking of a little quantity of Ganges water can save one from the punishment of Yamarāja.

TEXT 42

यच्छ्रद्धया श्रुतवत्या च भक्त्या
संमृज्यमाने हृदयेऽवधाय ।
ज्ञानेन वैराग्यबलेन धीरा
व्रजेम तत्तेऽङ्घ्रिसरोजपीठम् ॥४२॥

yac chraddhayā śrutavatyā ca bhaktyā
sammṛjyamāne hṛdaye 'vadhāya
jñānena vairāgya-balena dhīrā
vrajema tat te 'ṅghri-saroja-pīṭham

yat—that which; *śraddhayā*—by eagerness; *śrutavatyā*—simply by hearing; *ca*—also; *bhaktyā*—in devotion; *sammṛjyamāne*—being cleansed; *hṛdaye*—in the heart; *avadhāya*—meditation; *jñānena*—by knowledge; *vairāgya*—detachment; *balena*—by the strength of; *dhīrāḥ*—the pacified; *vrajema*—must go to; *tat*—that; *te*—Your; *aṅghri*—feet; *saroja-pīṭham*—lotus sanctuary.

TRANSLATION

Simply by hearing about Your lotus feet with eagerness and devotion and by meditating upon them within the heart, one at once

becomes enlightened with knowledge, and on the strength of detachment one becomes pacified. We must therefore take shelter of the sanctuary of Your lotus feet.

PURPORT

The miracles of meditating on the lotus feet of the Lord with eagerness and devotion are so great that no other process can compare to it. The minds of materialistic persons are so disturbed that it is almost impossible for them to search after the Supreme Truth by personal regulative endeavors. But even such materialistic men, with a little eagerness for hearing about the transcendental name, fame, qualities, etc., can surpass all other methods of attaining knowledge and detachment. The conditioned soul is attached to the bodily conception of the self, and therefore he is in ignorance. Culture of self-knowledge can bring about detachment from material affection, and without such detachment there is no meaning to knowledge. The most stubborn attachment for material enjoyment is sex life. One who is attached to sex life is to be understood as devoid of knowledge. Knowledge must be followed by detachment. That is the way of self-realization. These two essentials for self-realization—knowledge and detachment—become manifest very quickly if one performs devotional service to the lotus feet of the Lord. The word *dhīra* is very significant in this connection. A person who is not disturbed even in the presence of cause of disturbance is called *dhīra.* Śrī Yāmunācārya says, "Since my heart has been overwhelmed by the devotional service of Lord Kṛṣṇa, I cannot even think of sex life, and if thoughts of sex come upon me I at once feel disgust." A devotee of the Lord becomes an elevated *dhīra* by the simple process of meditating in eagerness on the lotus feet of the Lord.

Devotional service entails being initiated by a bona fide spiritual master and following his instruction in regard to hearing about the Lord. Such a bona fide spiritual master is accepted by regularly hearing from him about the Lord. The improvement in knowledge and detachment can be perceived by devotees as an actual experience. Lord Śrī Caitanya Mahāprabhu strongly recommended this process of hearing from a bona fide devotee, and by following this process one can achieve the highest result, conquering all other methods.

TEXT 43

विश्वस्य जन्मस्थितिसंयमार्थे
कृतावतारस्य पदाम्बुजं ते ।
व्रजेम सर्वे शरणं यदीश
स्मृतं प्रयच्छत्यभयं स्वपुंसाम् ॥४३॥

viśvasya janma-sthiti-saṁyamārthe
kṛtāvatārasya padāmbujaṁ te
vrajema sarve śaraṇaṁ yad īśa
smṛtaṁ prayacchaty abhayaṁ sva-puṁsām

viśvasya—of the cosmic universe; *janma*—creation; *sthiti*—maintenance; *saṁyama-arthe*—for the dissolution also; *kṛta*—accepted or assumed; *avatārasya*—of the incarnations; *pada-ambujam*—lotus feet; *te*—Your; *vrajema*—let us take shelter of; *sarve*—all of us; *śaraṇam*—shelter; *yat*—that which; *īśa*—O Lord; *smṛtam*—remembrance; *prayacchati*—awarding; *abhayam*—courage; *sva-puṁsām*—of the devotees.

TRANSLATION

O Lord, You assume incarnations for the creation, maintenance and dissolution of the cosmic manifestation, and therefore we all take shelter of Your lotus feet because they always award remembrance and courage to Your devotees.

PURPORT

For the creation, maintenance and dissolution of the cosmic manifestations there are three incarnations: Brahmā, Viṣṇu and Maheśvara (Lord Śiva). They are the controllers or masters of the three modes of material nature, which cause the phenomenal manifestation. Viṣṇu is the master of the mode of goodness, Brahmā is the master of the mode of passion, and Maheśvara is the master of the mode of ignorance. There are different kinds of devotees according to the modes of nature. Persons in the mode of goodness worship Lord Viṣṇu, those in the mode of passion worship Lord Brahmā, and those in the mode of ignorance worship Lord

Śiva. All three of these deities are incarnations of the Supreme Lord Kṛṣṇa because He is the original Supreme Personality of Godhead. The demigods directly refer to the lotus feet of the Supreme Lord and not to the different incarnations. The incarnation of Viṣṇu in the material world is, however, directly worshiped by the demigods. It is learned from various scriptures that the demigods approach Lord Viṣṇu in the ocean of milk and submit their grievances whenever there is some difficulty in the administration of universal affairs. Although they are incarnations of the Lord, Lord Brahmā and Lord Śiva worship Lord Viṣṇu, and thus they are also counted amongst the demigods and not as the Supreme Personality of Godhead. Persons who worship Lord Viṣṇu are called demigods, and persons who do not do so are called *asuras*, or demons. Viṣṇu always takes the part of the demigods, but Brahmā and Śiva sometimes take the side of the demons; it is not that they become one in interest with them, but sometimes they do something in order to gain control over the demons.

TEXT 44

यत्सानुबन्धेऽसति देहगेहे
ममाहमित्यूढदुराग्रहाणाम् ।
पुंसां सुदूरं वसतोऽपि पुर्यां
भजेम तत्ते भगवन् पदाब्जम् ॥४४॥

yat sānubandhe 'sati deha-gehe
mamāham ity ūḍha-durāgrahāṇām
puṁsāṁ sudūraṁ vasato 'pi puryāṁ
bhajema tat te bhagavan padābjam

yat—because; *sa-anubandhe*—due to becoming entangled; *asati*—thus being; *deha*—the gross material body; *gehe*—in the home; *mama*—mine; *aham*—I; *iti*—thus; *ūḍha*—great, deep; *durāgrahāṇām*—undesirable eagerness; *puṁsām*—of persons; *su-dūram*—far away; *vasataḥ*—dwelling; *api*—although; *puryām*—within the body; *bhajema*—let us worship; *tat*—therefore; *te*—Your; *bhagavan*—O Lord; *pada-abjam*—lotus feet.

TRANSLATION

O Lord, persons who are entangled by undesirable eagerness for the temporary body and kinsmen, and who are bound by thoughts of "mine" and "I," are unable to see Your lotus feet, although Your lotus feet are situated within their own bodies. But let us take shelter of Your lotus feet.

PURPORT

The whole Vedic philosophy of life is that one should get rid of the material encagement of gross and subtle bodies, which only cause one to continue in a condemned life of miseries. This material body continues as long as one is not detached from the false conception of lording it over material nature. The impetus for lording it over material nature is the sense of "mine" and "I." "I am the lord of all that I survey. So many things I possess, and I shall possess more and more. Who can be richer than I in wealth and education? I am the master, and I am God. Who else is there but me?" All these ideas reflect the philosophy of *ahaṁ mama*, the conception that "I am everything." Persons conducted by such a conception of life can never get liberation from material bondage. But even a person perpetually condemned to the miseries of material existence can get relief from bondage if he simply agrees to hear only *kṛṣṇa-kathā*. In this age of Kali, the process of hearing *kṛṣṇa-kathā* is the most effective means to gain release from unwanted family affection and thus find permanent freedom in life. The age of Kali is full of sinful reactions, and people are more and more addicted to the qualities of this age, but simply by hearing and chanting of *kṛṣṇa-kathā* one is sure to go back to Godhead. Therefore, people should be trained to hear only *kṛṣṇa-kathā*—by all means—in order to get relief from all miseries.

TEXT 45

तान् वै ह्यसद्वृत्तिभिरक्षिभिर्ये
पराहृतान्तर्मनसः परेश ।
अथो न पश्यन्त्युरुगाय नूनं
ये ते पदन्यासविलासलक्ष्याः ॥४५॥

tān vai hy asad-vṛttibhir akṣibhir ye
parāhṛtāntar-manasaḥ pareśa
atho na paśyanty urugāya nūnaṁ
ye te padanyāsa-vilāsa-lakṣyāḥ

tān—the lotus feet of the Lord; *vai*—certainly; *hi*—for; *asat*—materialistic; *vṛttibhiḥ*—by those who are influenced by external energy; *akṣibhiḥ*—by the senses; *ye*—those; *parāhṛta*—missing at a distance; *antaḥ-manasaḥ*—of the internal mind; *pareśa*—O Supreme; *atho*—therefore; *na*—never; *paśyanti*—can see; *urugāya*—O great; *nūnam*—but; *ye*—those who; *te*—Your; *padanyāsa*—activities; *vilāsa*—transcendental enjoyment; *lakṣyāḥ*—those who see.

TRANSLATION

O great Supreme Lord, offensive persons whose internal vision has been too affected by external materialistic activities cannot see Your lotus feet, but they are seen by Your pure devotees, whose one and only aim is to transcendentally enjoy Your activities.

PURPORT

As stated in *Bhagavad-gītā* (18.61), the Lord is situated in everyone's heart. It is natural that one should be able to see the Lord at least within himself. But that is not possible for those whose internal vision has been covered by external activities. The pure soul, which is symptomized by consciousness, can be easily perceived even by a common man because consciousness is spread all over the body. The *yoga* system as recommended in *Bhagavad-gītā* is to concentrate the mental activities internally and thus see the lotus feet of the Lord within oneself. But there are many so-called *yogīs* who have no concern with the Lord but are only concerned with consciousness, which they accept as the final realization. Such realization of consciousness is taught by *Bhagavad-gītā* within only a few minutes, whereas the so-called *yogīs* take continuous years to realize it because of their offenses at the lotus feet of the Lord. The greatest offense is to deny the existence of the Lord as separate from the individual souls or to accept the Lord and the individual soul as one and the same. The impersonalists misinterpret the theory of reflection, and thus they wrongly accept the individual consciousness as the supreme consciousness.

The theory of the reflection of the Supreme can be clearly understood without difficulty by any sincere common man. When there is a reflection of the sky on the water, both the sky and the stars are seen within the water, but it is understood that the sky and the stars are not to be accepted on the same level. The stars are parts of the sky, and therefore they cannot be equal to the whole. The sky is the whole, and the stars are parts. They cannot be one and the same. Transcendentalists who do not accept the supreme consciousness as separate from the individual consciousness are as offensive as the materialists who deny even the existence of the Lord.

Such offenders cannot actually see the lotus feet of the Lord within themselves, nor are they even able to see the devotees of the Lord. The devotees of the Lord are so kind that they roam to all places to enlighten people in God consciousness. The offenders, however, lose the chance to receive the Lord's devotees, although the offenseless common man is at once influenced by the devotees' presence. In this connection there is an interesting story of a hunter and Devarṣi Nārada. A hunter in the forest, although a great sinner, was not an intentional offender. He was at once influenced by the presence of Nārada, and he agreed to take the path of devotion, leaving aside his hearth and home. But the offenders Nalakūvara and Maṇigrīva, even though living amongst the demigods, had to undergo the punishment of becoming trees in their next lives, although by the grace of a devotee they were later delivered by the Lord. Offenders have to wait until they receive the mercy of devotees, and then they can become eligible to see the lotus feet of the Lord within themselves. But due to their offenses and their extreme materialism, they cannot see even the devotees of the Lord. Engaged in external activities, they kill the internal vision. The Lord's devotees, however, do not mind the offenses of the foolish in their many gross and subtle bodily endeavors. The Lord's devotees continue to bestow the blessings of devotion upon all such offenders without hesitation. That is the nature of devotees.

TEXT 46

पानेन ते देव कथासुधायाः
प्रवृद्धभक्त्या विशदाशया ये ।

वैराग्यसारं प्रतिलभ्य बोधं
यथाञ्जसान्वीयुरकुण्ठधिष्ण्यम् ॥४६॥

pānena te deva kathā-sudhāyāḥ
pravṛddha-bhaktyā viśadāśayā ye
vairāgya-sāraṁ pratilabhya bodhaṁ
yathāñjasānvīyur akuṇṭha-dhiṣṇyam

pānena—by drinking; *te*—of You; *deva*—O Lord; *kathā*—topics; *sudhāyāḥ*—of the nectar; *pravṛddha*—highly enlightened; *bhaktyā*—by devotional service; *viśada-āśayāḥ*—with a greatly serious attitude; *ye*—those who; *vairāgya-sāram*—the entire purport of renunciation; *pratilabhya*—achieving; *bodham*—intelligence; *yathā*—as much as; *añjasā*—quickly; *anvīyuḥ*—achieve; *akuṇṭha-dhiṣṇyam*—Vaikuṇṭhaloka in the spiritual sky.

TRANSLATION

O Lord, persons who, because of their serious attitude, attain the stage of enlightened devotional service achieve the complete meaning of renunciation and knowledge and attain the Vaikuṇṭhaloka in the spiritual sky simply by drinking the nectar of Your topics.

PURPORT

The difference between the impersonalistic mental speculators and the pure devotees of the Lord is that the former pass through a miserable understanding of the Absolute Truth at every stage, whereas the devotees enter into the kingdom of all pleasures even from the beginning of their attempt. The devotee has only to hear about devotional activities, which are as simple as anything in ordinary life, and he also acts very simply, whereas the mental speculator has to pass through a jugglery of words, which are partially facts and partially a make-show for the maintenance of an artificial impersonal status. In spite of his strenuous efforts to attain perfect knowledge, the impersonalist attains merging into the impersonal oneness of the *brahmajyoti* of the Lord, which is also attained by the enemies of the Lord simply because of their being killed by Him. The devotees, however, attain to the highest stage of knowledge and renunciation and achieve the Vaikuṇṭhalokas, the planets in the spiritual sky. The impersonalist attains only the sky, and does not achieve any tangible transcendental bliss, whereas the devotee attains to the planets where real spiritual life prevails. With a serious attitude, the devotee throws away all achievements like so much dust, and he accepts only devotional service, the transcendental culmination.

TEXT 47

तथापरे चात्मसमाधियोग-
बलेन जित्वा प्रकृतिं बलिष्ठाम् ।
त्वामेव धीराः पुरुषं विशन्ति
तेषां श्रमः स्यान्न तु सेवया ते ॥४७॥

tathāpare cātma-samādhi-yoga-
balena jitvā prakṛtiṁ baliṣṭhām
tvām eva dhīrāḥ puruṣaṁ viśanti
teṣāṁ śramaḥ syān na tu sevayā te

tathā—as far as; *apare*—others; *ca*—also; *ātma-samādhi*—transcendental self-realization; *yoga*—means; *balena*—by the strength of; *jitvā*—conquering; *prakṛtim*—acquired nature or modes of nature; *baliṣṭhām*—very powerful; *tvām*—You; *eva*—only; *dhīrāḥ*—pacified; *puruṣam*—person; *viśanti*—enters into; *teṣām*—for them; *śramaḥ*—much labor; *syāt*—has to be taken; *na*—never; *tu*—but; *sevayā*—by serving; *te*—of You.

TRANSLATION

Others, who are pacified by means of transcendental self-realization and have conquered over the modes of nature by dint of strong power and knowledge, also enter into You, but for them there is much pain, whereas the devotee simply discharges devotional service and thus feels no such pain.

PURPORT

In terms of a labor of love and its returns, the *bhaktas*, or devotees of the Lord, always have priority over persons who are addicted to the association of *jñānīs*, or impersonalists, and *yogīs*, or mystics. The word *apare* (others) is very significant in this connection. "Others" refers to the *jñānīs* and the *yogīs*, whose only hope is to merge into the existence of the impersonal *brahmajyoti*. Although their destination is not so important in comparison to the destination of the devotees, the labor of the nondevotees is far greater than that of the *bhaktas*. One may suggest that there is sufficient labor for the devotees also in the matter of discharging devotional service. But that labor is compensated by the enhancement of transcendental pleasure. The devotees derive more transcendental pleasure while engaged continuously in the service of the Lord than when they have no such engagement. In the family combination of a man and a woman there is much labor and responsibility for both of them, yet when they are single they feel more trouble for want of their united activities.

The union of the impersonalists and the union of the devotees are not on a par. The impersonalists try to fully stop their individuality by attaining *sāyujya-mukti*, or unification by merging into oneness, whereas the devotees keep their individuality to exchange feelings in relationship with the supreme individual Lord. Such reciprocation of feelings takes place in the transcendental Vaikuṇṭha planets, and therefore the liberation sought by the impersonalists is already achieved in devotional service. The devotees attain *mukti* automatically, while continuing the transcendental pleasure of maintaining individuality. As explained in the previous verse, the destination of the devotees is Vaikuṇṭha, or *akuṇṭha-dhiṣṇya*, the place where anxieties are completely eradicated. One should not mistake the destination of the devotees and that of the impersonalists to be one and the same. The destinations are distinctly different, and the transcendental pleasure derived by the devotee is also distinct from *cin-mātra*, or spiritual feelings alone.

TEXT 48

तत्ते वयं लोकसिसृक्षयाद्य
त्वयानुसृष्टास्त्रिभिरात्मभिः स्म ।
सर्वे वियुक्ताः स्वविहारतन्त्रं
न शक्नुमस्तत्प्रतिहर्तवे ते ॥४८॥

tat te vayaṁ loka-sisṛkṣayādya
tvayānusṛṣṭās tribhir ātmabhiḥ sma
sarve viyuktāḥ sva-vihāra-tantraṁ
na śaknumas tat pratihartave te

tat—therefore; *te*—Your; *vayam*—all of us; *loka*—world; *sisṛkṣayā*—for the sake of creation; *ādya*—O Original Person; *tvayā*—by You; *anusṛṣṭāḥ*—being created one after another; *tribhiḥ*—by the three modes of nature; *ātmabhiḥ*—by one's own; *sma*—in the past; *sarve*—all; *viyuktāḥ*—separated; *sva-vihāra-tantram*—the network of activities for one's own pleasure; *na*—not; *śaknumaḥ*—could do it; *tat*—that; *pratihartave*—to award; *te*—unto Your.

TRANSLATION

O Original Person, we are therefore but Yours only. Although we are Your creatures, we are born one after another under the influence of the three modes of nature, and for this reason we are separated in action. Therefore, after the creation we could not act concertedly for Your transcendental pleasure.

PURPORT

The cosmic creation is working under the influence of the three modes of the external potency of the Lord. Different creatures are also under the same influence, and therefore they cannot act concertedly in satisfying the Lord. Because of this diverse activity, there cannot be any harmony in the material world. The best policy, therefore, is to act for the sake of the Lord. That will bring about the desired harmony.

TEXT 49

यावद्बलिं तेऽज हराम काले
यथा वयं चान्नमदाम यत्र ।
यथोभयेषां त इमे हि लोका
बलिं हरन्तोऽन्नमदन्त्यनूहाः ॥४९॥

yāvad baliṁ te 'ja harāma kāle
yathā vayaṁ cānnam adāma yatra
yathobhayeṣāṁ ta ime hi lokā
baliṁ haranto 'nnam adanty anūhāḥ

yāvat—as it may be; *balim*—offerings; *te*—Your; *aja*—O unborn one; *harāma*—shall offer; *kāle*—at the right time; *yathā*—as much as; *vayam*—we; *ca*—also; *annam*—food grains; *adāma*—shall partake; *yatra*—whereupon; *yathā*—as much as; *ubhayeṣām*—both for You and for us; *te*—all; *ime*—these; *hi*—certainly; *lokāḥ*—living entities; *balim*—offerings; *harantaḥ*—while offering; *annam*—grains; *adanti*—eat; *anūhāḥ*—without disturbance.

TRANSLATION

O unborn one, please enlighten us regarding the ways and means by which we can offer You all enjoyable grains and commodities so that both we and all other living entities in this world can maintain ourselves without disturbance and can easily accumulate the necessities of life both for You and for ourselves.

PURPORT

Developed consciousness begins from the human form of life and further increases in the forms of the demigods living in higher planets. The earth is situated almost in the middle of the universe, and the human form of life is the via medium between the life of the demigods and that of the demons. The planetary systems above the earth are especially meant for the higher intellectuals, called demigods. They are called demigods because although their standard of life is far more advanced in culture, enjoyment, luxury, beauty, education and duration of life, they are always fully God conscious. Such demigods are always ready to render service to the Supreme Lord because they are perfectly aware of the fact that every living entity is constitutionally an eternal subordinate servitor of the Lord. They also know that it is the Lord only who can maintain all living entities with all the necessities of life. The Vedic hymns, *eko bahūnāṁ yo vidadhāti kāmān, tā enam abruvann āyatanaṁ naḥ prajānīhi yasmin pratiṣṭhitā annam adāme*, etc., confirm this truth. In *Bhagavad-gītā* also, the Lord is mentioned as *bhūta-bhṛt*, or the maintainer of all living creatures.

The modern theory that starvation is due to an increase in population is not accepted by the demigods or the devotees of the Lord. The devotees or demigods are fully aware that the Lord can maintain any number of living entities, provided they are conscious of how to eat. If they want to eat like ordinary animals, who have no God consciousness, then they must live in starvation, poverty and want, like the jungle animals in the forest. The jungle animals are also maintained by the Lord with their respective foodstuffs, but they are not advanced in God consciousness. Similarly, human beings are provided with food grains, vegetables, fruits and milk by the grace of the Lord, but it is the duty of human beings to acknowledge the mercy of the Lord. As a matter of gratitude, they should feel obliged to the Lord for their supply of foodstuff, and they must first offer Him food in sacrifice and then partake of the remnants.

In *Bhagavad-gītā* (3.13) it is confirmed that one who takes foodstuff after a performance of sacrifice eats real food for proper maintenance of the body and soul, but one who cooks for himself and does not perform any sacrifice eats only lumps of sin in the shape of foodstuffs. Such sinful eating can never make one happy or free from scarcity. Famine is not due to an increase in population, as less intelligent economists think. When human society is grateful to the Lord for all His gifts for the maintenance of the living entities, then there is certainly no scarcity or want in society. But when men are unaware of the intrinsic value of such gifts from the Lord, surely they are in want. A person who has no God consciousness may live in opulence for the time being due to his past virtuous acts, but if one forgets his relationship with the Lord, certainly he must await the stage of starvation by the law of the powerful material nature. One cannot escape the vigilance of the powerful material nature unless he leads a God conscious or devotional life.

TEXT 50

त्वं नः सुराणामसि सान्वयानां
कूटस्थ आद्यः पुरुषः पुराणः ।

त्वं देव शक्त्यां गुणकर्मयोनौ
रेतस्त्वजायां कविमादधेऽजः ॥५०॥

tvaṁ naḥ surāṇām asi sānvayānāṁ
kūṭa-stha ādyaḥ puruṣaḥ purāṇaḥ
tvaṁ deva śaktyāṁ guṇa-karma-yonau
retas tv ajāyāṁ kavim ādadhe 'jaḥ

tvam—Your Lordship; *naḥ*—of us; *surāṇām*—of the demigods; *asi*—You are; *sa-anvayānām*—with different gradations; *kūṭa-sthaḥ*—one who is unchanged; *ādyaḥ*—without any superior; *puruṣaḥ*—the founder person; *purāṇaḥ*—the oldest, who has no other founder; *tvam*—You; *deva*—O Lord; *śaktyām*—unto the energy; *guṇa-karma-yonau*—unto the cause of the material modes and activities; *retaḥ*—semen of birth; *tu*—indeed; *ajāyām*—for begetting; *kavim*—the total living entities; *ādadhe*—initiated; *ajaḥ*—one who is unborn.

TRANSLATION

You are the original personal founder of all the demigods and the orders of different gradations, yet You are the oldest and are unchanged. O Lord, You have no source or superior. You have impregnated the external energy with the semen of the total living entities, yet You are unborn.

PURPORT

The Lord, the Original Person, is the father of all other living entities, beginning from Brahmā, the personality from whom all other living entities in different gradations of species are generated. Yet the supreme father has no other father. Every one of the living entities of all grades, up to Brahmā, the original creature of the universe, is begotten by a father, but He, the Lord, has no father. When He descends on the material plane, out of His causeless mercy He accepts one of His great devotees as His father to keep pace with the rules of the material world. But since He is the Lord, He is always independent in choosing who will become His father. For example, the Lord came out of a pillar in His incarnation as Nṛsiṁhadeva, and by the Lord's causeless mercy, Ahalyā came out of a stone by the touch of the lotus feet of His incarnation as Lord Śrī Rāma. He is also the companion of every living entity as the Supersoul, but He is unchanged. The living entity changes his body in the material world, but even when the Lord is in the material world, He is ever unchanged. That is His prerogative.

As confirmed in *Bhagavad-gītā* (14.3), the Lord impregnates the external or material energy, and thus the total living entities later come out in different gradations, beginning from Brahmā, the first demigod, down to the insignificant ant. All gradations of living entities are manifested by Brahmā and the external energy, but the Lord is the original father of everyone. The relationship of every living being with the Supreme Lord is certainly one of son and father and not one of equality. Sometimes in love the son is more than the father, but the relationship of father and son is one of the superior and the subordinate. Every living entity, however great he may be, even up to demigods like Brahmā and Indra, is an eternally subordinate servitor of the supreme father. The *mahat-tattva* principle is the generating source of all the modes of material nature, and the living entities take birth in the material world in bodies supplied by the mother, material nature, in terms of their previous work. The body is a gift of material nature, but the soul is originally part and parcel of the Supreme Lord.

TEXT 51

ततो वयं मत्प्रमुखा यदर्थे
बभूविमात्मन् करवाम किं ते ।
त्वं नः स्वचक्षुः परिदेहि शक्त्या
देव क्रियार्थे यदनुग्रहाणाम् ॥५१॥

tato vayaṁ mat-pramukhā yad-arthe
babhūvimātman karavāma kiṁ te
tvaṁ naḥ sva-cakṣuḥ paridehi śaktyā
deva kriyārthe yad-anugrahāṇām

tataḥ—therefore; *vayam*—all of us; *mat-pramukhāḥ*—coming from the total cosmos, the *mahat-tattva; yat-arthe*—for the purpose of which;

babhūvima—created; *ātman*—O Supreme Self; *karavāma*—shall do; *kim*—what; *te*—Your service; *tvam*—Yourself; *naḥ*—to us; *sva-cakṣuḥ*—personal plan; *paridehi*—specifically grant us; *śaktyā*—with potency to work; *deva*—O Lord; *kriyā-arthe*—for acting; *yat*—from which; *anugrahāṇām*—of those who are specifically favored.

TRANSLATION

O Supreme Self, please give us, who are created in the beginning from the mahat-tattva, the total cosmic energy, Your kind directions on how we shall act. Kindly award us Your perfect knowledge and potency so that we can render You service in the different departments of subsequent creation.

PURPORT

The Lord creates this material world and impregnates the material energy with the living entities who will act in the material world. All these actions have a divine plan behind them. The plan is to give the conditioned souls who so desire a chance to enjoy sense gratification. But there is another plan behind the creation: to help the living entities realize that they are created for the transcendental sense gratification of the Lord and not for their individual sense gratification. This is the constitutional position of the living entities. The Lord is one without a second, and He expands Himself into many for His transcendental pleasure. All the expansions—the *viṣṇu-tattvas*, the *jīva-tattvas* and the *śakti-tattvas* (the Personalities of Godhead, the living entities and the different potential energies)—are different offshoots from the same one Supreme Lord. The *jīva-tattvas* are separated expansions of the *viṣṇu-tattvas*, and although there are potential differences between them, they are all meant for the transcendental sense gratification of the Supreme Lord. Some of the *jīvas*, however, wanted to lord it over material nature in imitation of the lordship of the Personality of Godhead. Regarding when and why such propensities overcame the pure living entities, it can only be explained that the *jīva-tattvas* have infinitesimal independence and that due to misuse of this independence some of the living entities have become implicated in the conditions of cosmic creation and are therefore called *nitya-baddhas*, or eternally conditioned souls.

The expansions of Vedic wisdom also give the *nitya-baddhas*, the conditioned living entities, a chance to improve, and those who take advantage of such transcendental knowledge gradually regain their lost consciousness of rendering transcendental loving service to the Lord. The demigods are amongst the conditioned souls who have developed this pure consciousness of service to the Lord but who at the same time continue to desire to lord it over the material energy. Such mixed consciousness puts a conditioned soul in the position of managing the affairs of this creation. The demigods are entrusted leaders of the conditioned souls. As some of the old prisoners in government jails are entrusted with some responsible work of prison management, so the demigods are improved conditioned souls acting as representatives of the Lord in the material creation. Such demigods are devotees of the Lord in the material world, and when completely free from all material desire to lord it over the material energy they become pure devotees and have no desire but to serve the Lord. Therefore any living entity who desires a position in the material world may desire so in the service of the Lord and may seek power and intelligence from the Lord, as exemplified by the demigods in this particular verse. One cannot do anything unless he is enlightened and empowered by the Lord. The Lord says in *Bhagavad-gītā* (15.15), *mattaḥ smṛtir jñānam apohanaṁ ca.* All recollections, knowledge, etc., as well as all forgetfulness, are engineered by the Lord, who is sitting within the heart of everyone. The intelligent man seeks the help of the Lord, and the Lord helps the sincere devotees engaged in His multifarious services.

The demigods are entrusted by the Lord to create different species of living entities according to their past deeds. They are herein asking the favor of the Lord for the intelligence and power to carry out their task. Similarly, any conditioned soul may also engage in the service of the Lord under the guidance of an expert spiritual master and thus gradually become freed from the entanglement of material existence. The spiritual master is the manifested representative of the Lord, and anyone who puts himself under the guidance of a spiritual master and acts accordingly is said to be acting in terms of *buddhi-yoga*, as explained in *Bhagavad-gītā* (2.41):

vyavasāyātmikā buddhir
ekeha kuru-nandana

bahu-śākhā hy anantāś ca
buddhayo 'vyavasāyinām

Thus end the Bhaktivedanta purports of the Third Canto, Fifth Chapter, of the Śrīmad-Bhāgavatam, *entitled "Vidura's Talks with Maitreya."*

CHAPTER SIX

Creation of the Universal Form

TEXT 1

ऋषिरुवाच

इति तासां स्वशक्तीनां सतीनामसमेत्य सः ।
प्रसुप्तलोकतन्त्राणां निशाम्य गतिमीश्वरः ॥ १ ॥

ṛṣir uvāca
iti tāsāṁ sva-śaktīnāṁ
satīnām asametya saḥ
prasupta-loka-tantrāṇāṁ
niśāmya gatim īśvaraḥ

ṛṣiḥ uvāca—the Ṛṣi Maitreya said; *iti*—thus; *tāsām*—their; *sva-śaktīnām*—own potency; *satīnām*—so situated; *asametya*—without combination; *saḥ*—He (the Lord); *prasupta*—suspended; *loka-tantrāṇām*—in the universal creations; *niśāmya*—hearing; *gatim*—progress; *īśvaraḥ*—the Lord.

TRANSLATION

The Ṛṣi Maitreya said: The Lord thus heard about the suspension of the progressive creative functions of the universe due to the noncombination of His potencies, such as the mahat-tattva.

PURPORT

There is nothing wanting in the creation of the Lord; all the potencies are there in a dormant state. But unless they are combined by the will of the Lord, nothing can progress. The suspended progressive work of creation can only be revived by the direction of the Lord.

TEXT 2

कालसंज्ञां तदा देवीं बिभ्रच्छक्तिमुरुक्रमः ।
त्रयोविंशतितत्त्वानां गणं युगपदाविशत् ॥ २ ॥

kāla-sañjñāṁ tadā devīṁ
bibhrac-chaktim urukramaḥ
trayoviṁśati tattvānāṁ
gaṇaṁ yugapad āviśat

kāla-sañjñām—known as Kālī; *tadā*—at that time; *devīm*—the goddess; *bibhrat*—destructive; *śaktim*—potency; *urukramaḥ*—the supreme powerful; *trayaḥ-viṁśati*—twenty-three; *tattvānām*—of the elements; *gaṇam*—all of them; *yugapat*—simultaneously; *āviśat*—entered.

TRANSLATION

The Supreme Powerful Lord then simultaneously entered into the twenty-three elements with the goddess Kālī, His external energy, who alone amalgamates all the different elements.

PURPORT

The ingredients of matter are counted as twenty-three: the total material energy, false ego, sound, touch, form, taste, smell, earth, water, fire, air, sky, eye, ear, nose, tongue, skin, hand, leg, evacuating organ, genitals, speech and mind. All are combined together by the influence of time and are again dissolved in the course of time. Time, therefore, is the energy of the Lord and acts in her own way by the direction of the Lord. This energy is called Kālī and is represented by the dark destructive goddess generally worshiped by persons influenced by the mode of darkness or ignorance in material existence. In the Vedic hymn this process is described as *mūla-prakṛtir avikṛtir mahadādyāḥ prakṛti-vikṛtayaḥ sapta ṣoḍaśakas tu vikāro na prakṛtir na vikṛtiḥ puruṣaḥ.* The energy which acts as material nature in a combination of twenty-three ingredients is not the final source of creation. The Lord enters into the elements and applies His energy, called Kālī. In all other Vedic scriptures the same principle is accepted. In *Brahma-saṁhitā* (5.35) it is stated:

eko 'py asau racayituṁ jagad-aṇḍa-koṭiṁ
yac-chaktir asti jagad-aṇḍa-cayā yad-antaḥ
aṇḍāntara-stha-paramāṇu-cayāntara-sthaṁ
govindam ādi-puruṣaṁ tam ahaṁ bhajāmi

"I worship the primeval Lord, Govinda, who is the original Personality of Godhead. By His partial plenary expansion [Mahā-Viṣṇu], He enters into material nature, and then into each and every universe [as Garbhodakaśāyī Viṣṇu], and then [as Kṣīrodakaśāyī Viṣṇu] into all the elements, including every atom of matter. Such manifestations of cosmic creation are innumerable, both in the universes and in the individual atoms."

Similarly, this is confirmed in *Bhagavad-gītā* (10.42):

athavā bahunaitena
kiṁ jñātena tavārjuna
viṣṭabhyāham idaṁ kṛtsnam
ekāṁśena sthito jagat

"O Arjuna, there is no necessity of your knowing about My innumerable energies, which act in various ways. I enter into the material creation by My partial plenary expansion [Paramātmā, or the Supersoul] in all the universes and in all the elements thereof, and thus the work of creation goes on." The wonderful activities of material nature are due to Lord Kṛṣṇa, and thus He is the final cause, or the ultimate cause of all causes.

TEXT 3

सोऽनुप्रविष्टो भगवांश्चेष्टारूपेण तं गणम् ।
भिन्नं संयोजयामास सुप्तं कर्म प्रबोधयन् ॥ ३ ॥

so 'nupraviṣṭo bhagavāṁś
ceṣṭārūpeṇa taṁ gaṇam
bhinnaṁ saṁyojayām āsa
suptaṁ karma prabodhayan

saḥ—that; *anupraviṣṭaḥ*—thus entering later on; *bhagavān*—the Personality of Godhead; *ceṣṭā-rūpeṇa*—by His representation of attempt, Kālī; *tam*—them; *gaṇam*—all the living entities, including the demigods; *bhinnam*—separately; *saṁyojayām āsa*—engaged to work; *suptam*—sleeping; *karma*—work; *prabodhayan*—enlightening.

TRANSLATION

Thus when the Personality of Godhead entered into the elements by His energy, all the living entities were enlivened into different activities, just as one is engaged in his work after awakening from sleep.

PURPORT

Every individual soul remains unconscious after the dissolution of the creation and thus enters into the Lord with His material energy. These individual living entities are conditioned souls everlastingly, but in each and every material creation they are given a chance to liberate themselves and become free souls. They are all given a chance to take advantage of the Vedic wisdom and find out what is their relationship with the Supreme Lord, how they can be liberated, and what the ultimate profit is in such liberation. By properly studying the *Vedas* one becomes conscious of his position and thus takes to the transcendental devotional service of the Lord and is gradually promoted to the spiritual sky. The individual souls in the material world engage in different activities according to their past unfinished desires. After the dissolution of a particular body, the individual soul forgets everything, but the all-merciful Lord, who is situated in everyone's heart as the witness, the Supersoul, awakens him and reminds him of his past desires, and thus he begins to act accordingly in his next life. This unseen guidance is described as fate, and a sensible man can understand that this continues his material bondage in the three modes of nature.

The unconscious sleeping stage of the living entity just after the partial or total dissolution of the creation is wrongly accepted as the final stage of life by some less intelligent philosophers. After the dissolution of the partial material body, a living entity remains unconscious for only a few months, and after the total dissolution of the material creation, he remains unconscious for many millions of years. But when the creation is again revived, he is awakened to his work by the Lord. The living entity is eternal, and the wakeful state of his consciousness, manifested by activities, is his natural condition of life. He cannot stop acting while awake, and thus he acts according to his diverse desires. When his desires are trained in the transcendental service of the Lord, his life becomes perfect, and he is promoted to the spiritual sky to enjoy eternal awakened life.

TEXT 4

प्रबुद्धकर्मा दैवेन त्रयोविंशतिको गणः ।
प्रेरितोऽजनयत्स्वाभिर्मात्राभिरधिपूरुषम् ॥ ४ ॥

prabuddha-karmā daivena
trayoviṁśatiko gaṇaḥ
prerito 'janayat svābhir
mātrābhir adhipūruṣam

prabuddha—awakened; *karmā*—activities; *daivena*—by the will of the Supreme; *trayaḥ-viṁśatikaḥ*—by the twenty-three principal ingredients; *gaṇaḥ*—the combination; *preritaḥ*—induced by; *ajanayat*—manifested; *svābhiḥ*—by His personal; *mātrābhiḥ*—plenary expansion; *adhipūruṣam*—the gigantic universal form (*viśva-rūpa*).

TRANSLATION

When the twenty-three principal elements were set in action by the will of the Supreme, the gigantic universal form, or the viśva-rūpa body of the Lord, came into existence.

PURPORT

The *virāṭ-rūpa* or *viśva-rūpa*, the gigantic universal form of the Lord, which is very much appreciated by the impersonalist, is not an eternal form of the Lord. It is manifested by the supreme will of the Lord after the ingredients of material creation. Lord Kṛṣṇa exhibited this *virāṭ* or *viśva-rūpa* to Arjuna just to convince the impersonalists that He is the original Personality of Godhead. Kṛṣṇa exhibited the *virāṭ-rūpa;* it is not that Kṛṣṇa was exhibited by the *virāṭ-rūpa*. The *virāṭ-rūpa* is not, therefore, an eternal form of the Lord exhibited in the spiritual sky; it is a material manifestation of the Lord. The *arcā-vigraha,* or the worshipable Deity in the temple, is a similar manifestation of the Lord for the neophytes. But in spite of their material touch, such forms of the Lord as the *virāṭ* and *arcā* are all nondifferent from His eternal form as Lord Kṛṣṇa.

TEXT 5

परेण विशता स्वस्मिन्मात्रया विश्वसृग्गणः ।
चुक्षोभान्योन्यमासाद्य यस्मिन्लोकाश्चराचराः ॥ ५ ॥

pareṇa viśatā svasmin
mātrayā viśva-sṛg-gaṇaḥ
cukṣobhānyonyam āsādya
yasmin lokāś carācarāḥ

pareṇa—by the Lord; *viśatā*—thus entering; *svasmin*—by His own self; *mātrayā*—by a plenary portion; *viśva-sṛk*—the elements of universal creation; *gaṇaḥ*—all; *cukṣobha*—transformed; *anyonyam*—one another; *āsādya*—having obtained; *yasmin*—in which; *lokāḥ*—the planets; *cara-acarāḥ*—movable and immovable.

TRANSLATION

As the Lord, in His plenary portion, entered into the elements of the universal creation, they transformed into the gigantic form in which all the planetary systems and all movable and immovable creations rest.

PURPORT

The elements of cosmic creation are all matter and have no potency to increase in volume unless entered into by the Lord in His plenary portion. This means that matter does not increase or decrease unless it is spiritually touched. Matter is a product of spirit and increases only by the touch of spirit. The entire cosmic manifestation has not assumed its gigantic form by itself, as wrongly calculated by less intelligent persons. As long as spirit is within matter, matter can increase as needed; but without the spirit, matter stops increasing. For example, as long as there is spiritual consciousness within the material body of a living entity, the body increases to the required size, but a dead material body, which has no spiritual consciousness, stops increasing. In *Bhagavad-gītā* (Chapter Two) importance is given to the spiritual consciousness, not the body. The entire cosmic body increased by the same process that we experience in our small bodies. One should not, however, foolishly think that the individual infinitesimal soul is the cause of the gigantic manifestation of the universal form. The universal form is called the *virāṭ-rūpa* because the Supreme Lord is within it in His plenary portion.

TEXT 6

हिरण्मयः स पुरुषः सहस्रपरिवत्सरान् ।
आण्डकोश उवासाप्सु सर्वसत्त्वोपबृंहितः ॥ ६ ॥

hiraṇmayaḥ sa puruṣaḥ
sahasra-parivatsarān
āṇḍa-kośa uvāsāpsu
sarva-sattvopabṛṁhitaḥ

hiraṇmayaḥ—the Garbhodakaśāyī Viṣṇu, who also assumes the *virāṭ-rūpa; saḥ*—He; *puruṣaḥ*—incarnation of Godhead; *sahasra*—one thousand; *parivatsarān*—celestial years; *āṇḍa-kośe*—within the global universe; *uvāsa*—resided; *apsu*—on the water; *sarva-sattva*—all living entities lying with Him; *upabṛṁhitaḥ*—so spread.

TRANSLATION

The gigantic virāṭ-puruṣa, known as Hiraṇmaya, lived for one thousand celestial years on the water of the universe, and all the living entities lay with Him.

PURPORT

After the Lord entered each and every universe as the Garbhodakaśāyī Viṣṇu, half of the universe was filled with water. The cosmic manifestation of the planetary systems, outer space, etc., which are visible to us, is only one half of the complete universe. Before the manifestation takes place and after the entrance of Viṣṇu within the universe, there is a period of one thousand celestial years. All the living entities injected within the womb of the *mahat-tattva* are divided in all universes with the incarnation of Garbhodakaśāyī Viṣṇu, and all of them lie down with the Lord until Brahmā is born. Brahmā is the first living being within the universe, and from him all other demigods and living creatures are born. Manu is the original father of mankind, and therefore, in Sanskrit, mankind is called *mānuṣya.* Humanity in different bodily qualities is distributed throughout the various planetary systems.

TEXT 7

स वै विश्वसृजां गर्भो देवकर्मात्मशक्तिमान् ।
विबभाजात्मनात्मानमेकधा दशधा त्रिधा ॥ ७ ॥

sa vai viśva-sṛjāṁ garbho
deva-karmātma-śaktimān
vibabhājātmanātmānam
ekadhā daśadhā tridhā

saḥ—that; *vai*—certainly; *viśva-sṛjām*—of the gigantic *virāṭ* form; *garbhaḥ*—total energy; *deva*—living energy; *karma*—activity of life; *ātma*—self; *śaktimān*—full with potencies; *vibabhāja*—divided; *ātmanā*—by Himself; *ātmānam*—Himself; *ekadhā*—in oneness; *daśadhā*—in ten; *tridhā*—and in three.

TRANSLATION

The total energy of the mahat-tattva, in the form of the gigantic virāṭ-rūpa, divided Himself by Himself into the consciousness of the living entities, the life of activity, and self-identification, which are subdivided into one, ten and three respectively.

PURPORT

Consciousness is the sign of the living entity, or the soul. The existence of the soul is manifest in the form of consciousness, called *jñāna-śakti.* The total consciousness is that of the gigantic *virāṭ-rūpa,* and the same consciousness is exhibited in individual persons. The activity of consciousness is performed through the air of life, which is of ten divisions. The airs of life are called *prāṇa*, *apāna*, *udāna*, *vyāna* and *samāna* and are also differently qualified as *nāga*, *kūrma*, *kṛkara*, *devadatta* and *dhanañjaya.* The consciousness of the soul becomes polluted by the material atmosphere, and thus various activities are exhibited in the false ego of bodily identification. These various activities are described in *Bhagavad-gītā* (2.41) as *bahu-śākhā hy anantāś ca buddhayo 'vyavasāyinām.* The conditioned soul is bewildered into various activities for want of pure consciousness. In pure consciousness the activity is one. The consciousness of the individual soul becomes one with the supreme consciousness when there is complete synthesis between the two.

The monist believes that there is only one consciousness, whereas the *sātvatas,* or the devotees, believe that although there is undoubtedly one consciousness, they are one because there is agreement. The individual consciousness is advised to dovetail with the supreme consciousness, as instructed by the Lord in *Bhagavad-gītā* (18.66): *sarva-dharmān parityajya mām ekaṁ śaraṇaṁ vraja.* The individual consciousness (Arjuna) is advised to dovetail with the supreme consciousness and thus maintain his conscious purity. It is foolish to try to stop the activities of consciousness, but they can be purified when they are dovetailed with the Supreme. This consciousness is divided into three modes of self-identification according to the proportion of purity: *ādhyātmika,* or self-identification with the body and mind, *ādhibhautika,* or self-identification with the material products, and *ādhidaivika,* or self-identification as a servant of the Lord. Of the three, *ādhidaivika* self-identification is the beginning of purity of consciousness in pursuance of the desire of the Lord.

TEXT 8

एष ह्यशेषसत्त्वानामात्मांशः परमात्मनः ।
आद्योऽवतारो यत्रासौ भूतग्रामो विभाव्यते ॥ ८ ॥

eṣa hy aśeṣa-sattvānām
ātmāṁśaḥ paramātmanaḥ
ādyo 'vatāro yatrāsau
bhūta-grāmo vibhāvyate

eṣaḥ—this; *hi*—certainly; *aśeṣa*—unlimited; *sattvānām*—living entities; *ātmā*—Self; *aṁśaḥ*—part; *parama-ātmanaḥ*—of the Supersoul; *ādyaḥ*—the first; *avatāraḥ*—incarnation; *yatra*—whereupon; *asau*—all those; *bhūta-grāmaḥ*—the aggregate creations; *vibhāvyate*—flourish.

TRANSLATION

The gigantic universal form of the Supreme Lord is the first incarnation and plenary portion of the Supersoul. He is the Self of an unlimited number of living entities, and in Him rests the aggregate creation, which thus flourishes.

PURPORT

The Supreme Lord expands Himself in two ways, by personal plenary expansions and separated minute expansions. The personal plenary expansions are *viṣṇu-tattvas*, and the separated expansions are living entities. Since the living entities are very small, they are sometimes described as the marginal energy of the Lord. But the mystic *yogīs* consider the living entities and the Supersoul, Paramātmā, to be one and the same. It is, however, a minor point of controversy; after all, everything created rests on the gigantic *virāṭ* or universal form of the Lord.

TEXT 9

साध्यात्मः साधिदैवश्च साधिभूत इति त्रिधा ।
विराट् प्राणो दशविध एकधा हृदयेन च ॥ ९ ॥

sādhyātmaḥ sādhidaivaś ca
sādhibhūta iti tridhā
virāṭ prāṇo daśa-vidha
ekadhā hṛdayena ca

sa-ādhyātmaḥ—the body and mind with all the senses; *sa-ādhidaivaḥ*—and the controlling demigods of the senses; *ca*—and; *sa-ādhibhūtaḥ*—the present objectives; *iti*—thus; *tridhā*—three; *virāṭ*—gigantic; *prāṇaḥ*—moving force; *daśa-vidhaḥ*—ten kinds; *ekadhā*—one only; *hṛdayena*—living energy; *ca*—also.

TRANSLATION

The gigantic universal form is represented by three, ten and one in the sense that He is the body and the mind and the senses, He is the dynamic force for all movements by ten kinds of life energy, and He is the one heart where life energy is generated.

PURPORT

In *Bhagavad-gītā* (7.4–5) it is stated that the eight elements earth, water, fire, air, sky, mind, intelligence and false ego are all products of the Lord's inferior energy, whereas the living entities, who are seen to utilize the inferior energy, originally belong to the superior energy, the internal potency of the Lord. The eight inferior energies work grossly and subtly, whereas the superior energy works as the central generating force. This is experienced in the human body. The gross elements, namely, earth, etc., form the external gross body and are like a coat, whereas the subtle mind and false ego act like the inner clothing of the body.

The movements of the body are first generated from the heart, and all the activities of the body are made possible by the senses, powered by the ten kinds of air within the body. The ten kinds of air are described as follows: The main air passing through the nose in breathing is called *prāṇa.* The air which passes through the rectum as evacuated bodily air is called *apāna.* The air which adjusts the foodstuff within the stomach and which sometimes sounds as belching is called *samāna.* The air which passes through the throat and the stoppage of which constitutes suffocation is called the *udāna* air. And the total air which circulates throughout the entire body is called the *vyāna* air. Subtler than these five airs, there are others also. That which facilitates the opening of the eyes, mouth, etc., is called *nāga* air. The air which increases appetite is called *kṛkara* air. The air which helps contraction is called *kūrma* air. The air which helps relaxation by opening the mouth wide (in yawning) is called *devadatta* air, and the air which helps sustenance is called *dhanañjaya* air.

All these airs are generated from the center of the heart, which is one only. This central energy is superior energy of the Lord, who is seated within the heart with the soul of the body, who acts under the guidance of the Lord. This is explained in *Bhagavad-gītā* (15.15) as follows:

sarvasya cāhaṁ hṛdi sanniviṣṭo
mattaḥ smṛtir jñānam apohanaṁ ca
vedaiś ca sarvair aham eva vedyo
vedānta-kṛd veda-vid eva cāham

The complete central force is generated from the heart by the Lord, who is seated there and who helps the conditioned soul in remembering and forgetting. The conditioned state is due to the soul's forgetfulness of his relationship of subordination to the Lord. One who wants to continue to forget the Lord is helped by the Lord to forget Him birth after birth, but one who remembers Him, by dint of association with a devotee of the Lord, is helped to remember Him more and more. Thus the conditioned soul can ultimately go back home, back to Godhead.

This process of transcendental help by the Lord is described in *Bhagavad-gītā* (10.10) as follows:

teṣāṁ satata-yuktānāṁ
bhajatāṁ prīti-pūrvakam
dadāmi buddhi-yogaṁ taṁ
yena mām upayānti te

The *buddhi-yoga* process of self-realization with intelligence transcendental to the mind (devotional service) can alone elevate one from the conditioned state of material entanglement in the cosmic construction. The conditioned state of the living entity is like that of a person who is within the depths of a huge mechanical arrangement. The mental speculators can reach the point of *buddhi-yoga* after many, many lifetimes of speculation, but the intelligent person who begins from the platform of intelligence above the mind makes rapid progress in self-realization. Because the *buddhi-yoga* process entails no fear of deterioration or retrogression at any time, it is the guaranteed path to self-realization, as confirmed in *Bhagavad-gītā* (2.40). The mental speculators cannot understand that the two birds (*Śvetāśvatara Upaniṣad*) sitting in one tree are the soul and the Supersoul. The individual soul eats the fruit of the tree, while the other bird does not eat the fruit but only observes the activities of the eating bird. Without attachment, the witnessing bird helps the fruit-eating bird perform fruitful activities. One who cannot understand this difference between the soul and the Supersoul, or God and the living entities, is certainly still in the entanglement of the cosmic machinery and thus must still await the time when he will be free from bondage.

TEXT 10

स्मरन् विश्वसृजामीशो विज्ञापितमधोक्षजः ।
विराजमतपत्स्वेन तेजसैषां विवृत्तये ॥१०॥

smaran viśva-sṛjām īśo
vijñāpitam adhokṣajaḥ
virājam atapat svena
tejasaiṣāṁ vivṛttaye

smaran—remembering; *viśva-sṛjām*—of the demigods entrusted with the task of cosmic construction; *īśaḥ*—the Supreme Lord; *vijñāpitam*—as He was prayed for; *adhokṣajaḥ*—the Transcendence; *virājam*—the gigantic universal form; *atapat*—considered thus; *svena*—by His own; *tejasā*—energy; *eṣām*—for them; *vivṛttaye*—for understanding.

TRANSLATION

The Supreme Lord is the Supersoul of all the demigods entrusted with the task of constructing the cosmic manifestation. Being thus prayed to [by the demigods], He thought to Himself and thus manifested the gigantic form for their understanding.

PURPORT

The impersonalists are captivated by the gigantic universal form of the Supreme. They think that the control behind this gigantic manifestation is imagination. Intelligent persons, however, can estimate the value of the cause by observing the wonders of the effects. For example, the individual human body does not develop from the womb of the mother independently but because the living entity, the soul, is within the body. Without the living entity, a material body cannot automatically take shape or develop. When any material object displays development, it must be understood that there is a spiritual soul within the manifestation. The gigantic universe has developed gradually, just as the body of a child develops. The conception that the Transcendence enters within the universe is, therefore, logical. As the materialists cannot find the soul and the Supersoul within the heart, similarly, for want of sufficient knowledge, they cannot see that the Supreme Soul is the cause of the universe. The Lord is therefore described in the Vedic language as *avāṅ-mānasa-gocaraḥ*, beyond the conception of words and minds.

Due to a poor fund of knowledge, the mental speculators try to bring the Supreme within the purview of words and minds, but the Lord refuses to be so intelligible; the speculator has no adequate words or mind to gauge the infinity of the Lord. The Lord is called *adhokṣaja*, or the person who is beyond perception by the blunt, limited potency of our senses. One cannot perceive the transcendental name or form of the Lord by mental speculation. The mundane Ph.D.'s are completely unable to speculate on the Supreme with their limited senses. Such attempts by the puffed up Ph.D's are compared to the philosophy of the frog in the well. A frog in a well was informed of the gigantic Pacific Ocean, and he began to puff himself up in order to understand or measure the length and breadth of the Pacific Ocean. Ultimately the frog burst and died. The title Ph.D. can also be interpreted as Plough Department, a title meant for the tillers in the paddy field. The attempt of the tillers in the paddy field to understand the cosmic manifestation and the cause behind such wonderful work can be compared to the endeavor of the frog in the well to calculate the measurement of the Pacific Ocean.

The Lord can reveal Himself only to a person who is submissive and who engages in His transcendental loving service. The demigods controlling the elements and ingredients of universal affairs prayed to the Lord for guidance, and thus He manifested His gigantic form, as He did at the request of Arjuna.

TEXT 11

अथ तस्याभितप्तस्य कतिधायतनानि ह ।
निरभिद्यन्त देवानां तानि मे गदतः शृणु ॥११॥

atha tasyābhitaptasya
katidhāyatanāni ha

nirabhidyanta devānāṁ
tāni me gadataḥ śṛṇu

atha—therefore; *tasya*—His; *abhitaptasya*—in terms of His contemplation; *katidhā*—how many; *āyatanāni*—embodiments; *ha*—there were; *nirabhidyanta*—by separated parts; *devānām*—of the demigods; *tāni*—all those; *me gadataḥ*—described by me; *śṛṇu*—just hear.

TRANSLATION

Maitreya said: You may now hear from me how the Supreme Lord separated Himself into the diverse forms of the demigods after the manifestation of the gigantic universal form.

PURPORT

The demigods are separated parts and parcels of the Supreme Lord, as are all other living entities. The only difference between the demigods and the ordinary living entities is that when the living entities are rich in pious acts of devotional service to the Lord, and when their desire to lord it over material energy has vanished, they are promoted to the posts of demigods, who are entrusted by the Lord with executing the management of the universal affairs.

TEXT 12

तस्याग्निरास्यं निर्भिन्नं लोकपालोऽविशत्पदम् ।
वाचा स्वांशेन वक्तव्यं ययासौ प्रतिपद्यते ॥१२॥

tasyāgnir āsyaṁ nirbhinnaṁ
loka-pālo 'viśat padam
vācā svāṁśena vaktavyaṁ
yayāsau pratipadyate

tasya—His; *agniḥ*—fire; *āsyam*—mouth; *nirbhinnam*—thus separated; *loka-pālaḥ*—the directors of material affairs; *aviśat*—entered; *padam*—respective positions; *vācā*—by words; *sva-aṁśena*—by one's own part; *vaktavyam*—speeches; *yayā*—by which; *asau*—they; *pratipadyate*—express.

TRANSLATION

Agni, or heat, separated from His mouth, and all the directors of material affairs entered into it in their respective positions. By that energy the living entity expresses himself in words.

PURPORT

The mouth of the gigantic universal form of the Lord is the source of the speaking power. The director of the fire element is the controlling deity, or the *ādhidaiva*. The speeches delivered are *ādhyātma*, or bodily functions, and the subject matter of the speeches is material productions, or the *ādhibhūta* principle.

TEXT 13

निर्भिन्नं तालु वरुणो लोकपालोऽविशद्धरेः ।
जिह्वयांशेन च रसं ययासौ प्रतिपद्यते ॥१३॥

nirbhinnaṁ tālu varuṇo
loka-pālo 'viśad dhareḥ
jihvayāṁśena ca rasaṁ
yayāsau pratipadyate

nirbhinnam—separated; *tālu*—palate; *varuṇaḥ*—the deity controlling air; *loka-pālaḥ*—director of the planets; *aviśat*—entered; *hareḥ*—of the Lord; *jihvayā aṁśena*—with the part of the tongue; *ca*—also; *rasam*—tastes; *yayā*—by which; *asau*—the living entity; *pratipadyate*—expresses.

TRANSLATION

When the palate of the gigantic form was separately manifested, Varuṇa, the director of air in the planetary systems, entered therein, and thus the living entity has the facility to taste everything with his tongue.

TEXT 14

निर्भिन्ने अश्विनौ नासे विष्णोराविशतां पदम् ।
घ्राणेनांशेन गन्धस्य प्रतिपत्तिर्यतो भवेत् ॥१४॥

nirbhinne aśvinau nāse
viṣṇor āviśatāṁ padam
ghrāṇenāṁśena gandhasya
pratipattir yato bhavet

nirbhinne—thus being separated; *aśvinau*—the dual Aśvinīs; *nāse*—of the two nostrils; *viṣṇoḥ*—of the Lord; *āviśatām*—entering; *padam*—post; *ghrāṇena aṁśena*—by partially smelling; *gandhasya*—aroma; *pratipattiḥ*—experience; *yataḥ*—whereupon; *bhavet*—becomes.

TRANSLATION

When the Lord's two nostrils separately manifested themselves, the dual Aśvinī-kumāras entered them in their proper positions, and because of this the living entities can smell the aromas of everything.

TEXT 15

निर्भिन्ने अक्षिणी त्वष्टा लोकपालोऽविशद्विभोः।
चक्षुषांशेन रूपाणां प्रतिपत्तिर्यतो भवेत् ॥१५॥

nirbhinne akṣiṇī tvaṣṭā
loka-pālo 'viśad vibhoḥ
cakṣuṣāṁśena rūpāṇāṁ
pratipattir yato bhavet

nirbhinne—thus being separated; *akṣiṇī*—the eyes; *tvaṣṭā*—the sun; *loka-pālaḥ*—director of light; *aviśat*—entered; *vibhoḥ*—of the great; *cakṣuṣā aṁśena*—by the part of the eyesight; *rūpāṇām*—of the forms; *pratipattiḥ*—experience; *yataḥ*—by which; *bhavet*—becomes.

TRANSLATION

Thereafter, the two eyes of the gigantic form of the Lord were separately manifested. The sun, the director of light, entered them with the partial representation of eyesight, and thus the living entities can have vision of forms.

TEXT 16

निर्भिन्नान्यस्य चर्माणि लोकपालोऽनिलोऽविशत् ।
प्राणेनांशेन संस्पर्शं येनासौ प्रतिपद्यते ॥१६॥

nirbhinnāny asya carmāṇi
loka-pālo 'nilo 'viśat
prāṇenāṁśena saṁsparśaṁ
yenāsau pratipadyate

nirbhinnāni—being separated; *asya*—of the gigantic form; *carmāṇi*—skin; *loka-pālaḥ*—the director; *anilaḥ*—air; *aviśat*—entered; *prāṇena aṁśena*—the part of the breathing; *saṁsparśam*—touch; *yena*—by which; *asau*—the living entity; *pratipadyate*—can experience.

TRANSLATION

When there was a manifestation of skin separated from the gigantic form, Anila, the deity directing the wind, entered with partial touch, and thus the living entities can realize tactile knowledge.

TEXT 17

कर्णावस्य विनिर्भिन्नौ धिष्ण्यं स्वं विविशुर्दिशः ।
श्रोत्रेणांशेन शब्दस्य सिद्धिं येन प्रपद्यते ॥१७॥

karṇāv asya vinirbhinnau
dhiṣṇyaṁ svaṁ viviśur diśaḥ
śrotreṇāṁśena śabdasya
siddhiṁ yena prapadyate

karṇau—the ears; *asya*—of the gigantic form; *vinirbhinnau*—being thus separated; *dhiṣṇyam*—the controlling deity; *svam*—own; *viviśuḥ*—entered; *diśaḥ*—of the directions; *śrotreṇa aṁśena*—with the hearing principles; *śabdasya*—of the sound; *siddhim*—perfection; *yena*—by which; *prapadyate*—is experienced.

TRANSLATION

When the ears of the gigantic form became manifested, all the controlling deities of the directions entered into them with the hearing principles, by which all the living entities hear and take advantage of sound.

PURPORT

The ear is the most important instrument in the body of the living entity. Sound is the most important medium for carrying the message of distant and unknown things. The perfection of all sound or knowledge enters through the ear and makes one's life perfect. The entire Vedic system of knowledge is received by aural reception only, and thus sound is the most important source of knowledge.

TEXT 18

त्वचमस्य विनिर्भिन्नां विविशुर्धिष्ण्यमोषधीः ।
अंशेन रोमभिः कण्डूं यैरसौ प्रतिपद्यते ॥१८॥

tvacam asya vinirbhinnāṁ
viviśur dhiṣṇyam oṣadhīḥ
aṁśena romabhiḥ kaṇḍūṁ
yair asau pratipadyate

tvacam—skin; *asya*—of the gigantic form; *vinirbhinnām*—being separately manifested; *viviśuḥ*—entered; *dhiṣṇyam*—the controlling deity; *oṣadhīḥ*—sensations; *aṁśena*—with parts; *romabhiḥ*—through the hairs on the body; *kaṇḍūm*—itching; *yaiḥ*—by which; *asau*—the living entity; *pratipadyate*—experiences.

TRANSLATION

When there was a separate manifestation of skin, the controlling deities of sensations and their different parts entered into it, and thus the living entities feel itching and happiness due to touch.

PURPORT

For sense perception there are two principal items, touch and itching, and both of them are controlled by the skin and hairs on the body.

According to Śrī Viśvanātha Cakravartī, the controlling deity of touch is the air passing within the body, and the controlling deity of the hairs on the body is Oṣadhya. For the skin the object of perception is touch, and for the hairs on the body the object of perception is itching.

TEXT 19

मेढ्ं तस्य विनिर्भिन्नं स्वधिष्ण्यं क उपाविशत् ।
रेतसांशेन येनासावानन्दं प्रतिपद्यते ॥१९॥

meḍhraṁ tasya vinirbhinnaṁ
sva-dhiṣṇyaṁ ka upāviśat
retasāṁśena yenāsāv
ānandaṁ pratipadyate

meḍhram—genitals; *tasya*—of the gigantic form; *vinirbhinnam*—being separated; *sva-dhiṣṇyam*—own position; *kaḥ*—Brahmā, the original living creature; *upāviśat*—entered; *retasā aṁśena*—with the part of the semen; *yena*—by which; *asau*—the living entity; *ānandam*—sex pleasure; *pratipadyate*—experiences.

TRANSLATION

When the genitals of the gigantic form separately became manifest, then Prajāpati, the original living creature, entered into them with his partial semen, and thus the living entities can enjoy sex pleasure.

TEXT 20

गुदं पुंसो विनिर्भिन्नं मित्रो लोकेश आविशत् ।
पायुनांशेन येनासौ विसर्गं प्रतिपद्यते ॥२०॥

gudaṁ puṁso vinirbhinnaṁ
mitro lokeśa āviśat
pāyunāṁśena yenāsau
visargaṁ pratipadyate

gudam—evacuating outlet; *puṁsaḥ*—of the gigantic form; *vinirbhinnam*—being separately manifested; *mitraḥ*—the sun-god; *loka-īśaḥ*—the director named Mitra; *āviśat*—entered; *pāyunā aṁśena*—with the partial evacuation process; *yena*—by which; *asau*—the living entity; *visargam*—evacuation; *pratipadyate*—performs.

TRANSLATION

The evacuating channel separately became manifest, and the director named Mitra entered into it with partial organs of evacuation. Thus the living entities are able to pass stool and urine.

TEXT 21

हस्तावस्य विनिर्भिन्नाविन्द्रः स्वर्पतिराविशत् ।
वार्तयांशेन पुरुषो यया वृत्तिं प्रपद्यते ॥२१॥

hastāv asya vinirbhinnāv
indraḥ svar-patir āviśat
vārtayāṁśena puruṣo
yayā vṛttiṁ prapadyate

hastau—hands; *asya*—of the gigantic form; *vinirbhinnau*—being separately manifested; *indraḥ*—the King of heaven; *svaḥ-patiḥ*—the ruler of heavenly planets; *āviśat*—entered into it; *vārtayā aṁśena*—with partial mercantile principles; *puruṣaḥ*—the living entity; *yayā*—by which; *vṛttim*—business of livelihood; *prapadyate*—transacts.

TRANSLATION

Thereafter, when the hands of the gigantic form separately became manifested, Indra, the ruler of the heavenly planets, entered into them, and thus the living entity is able to transact business for his livelihood.

TEXT 22

पादावस्य विनिर्भिन्नौ लोकेशो विष्णुराविशत् ।
गत्या स्वांशेन पुरुषो यया प्राप्यं प्रपद्यते ॥२२॥

pādāv asya vinirbhinnau
lokeśo viṣṇur āviśat
gatyā svāṁśena puruṣo
yayā prāpyaṁ prapadyate

pādau—the legs; *asya*—of the gigantic form; *vinirbhinnau*—being manifested separately; *loka-īśaḥ viṣṇuḥ*—the demigod Viṣṇu (not the Personality of Godhead); *āviśat*—entered; *gatyā*—by the power of movement; *sva-aṁśena*—with his own parts; *puruṣaḥ*—living entity; *yayā*—by which; *prāpyam*—destination; *prapadyate*—reaches.

TRANSLATION

Thereafter the legs of the gigantic form separately became manifest, and the demigod named Viṣṇu [not the Personality of Godhead] entered with partial movement. This helps the living entity move to his destination.

TEXT 23

बुद्धिं चास्य विनिर्भिन्नां वागीशो धिष्ण्यमाविशत् ।
बोधेनांशेन बोद्धव्यम् प्रतिपत्तिर्यतो भवेत् ॥२३॥

buddhiṁ cāsya vinirbhinnāṁ
vāg-īśo dhiṣṇyam āviśat
bodhenāṁśena boddhavyam
pratipattir yato bhavet

buddhim—intelligence; *ca*—also; *asya*—of the gigantic form; *vinirbhinnām*—being separately manifested; *vāk-īśaḥ*—Brahmā, lord of the *Vedas; dhiṣṇyam*—the controlling power; *āviśat*—entered in; *bodhena aṁśena*—with his part of intelligence; *boddhavyam*—the matter of understanding; *pratipattiḥ*—understood; *yataḥ*—by which; *bhavet*—so becomes.

TRANSLATION

When the intelligence of the gigantic form separately became manifest, Brahmā, the lord of the Vedas, entered into it with the

partial power of understanding, and thus an object of understanding is experienced by the living entities.

TEXT 24

हृदयं चास्य निर्भिन्नं चन्द्रमा धिष्ण्यमाविशत् ।
मनसांशेन येनासौ विक्रियां प्रतिपद्यते ॥२४॥

hṛdayaṁ cāsya nirbhinnaṁ
candramā dhiṣṇyam āviśat
manasāṁśena yenāsau
vikriyāṁ pratipadyate

hṛdayam—heart; *ca*—also; *asya*—of the gigantic form; *nirbhinnam*—being manifested separately; *candramā*—the moon demigod; *dhiṣṇyam*—with controlling power; *āviśat*—entered into; *manasā aṁśena*—partly with mental activity; *yena*—by which; *asau*—the living entity; *vikriyām*—resolution; *pratipadyate*—transacts.

TRANSLATION

After that, the heart of the gigantic form separately manifested itself, and into it entered the moon demigod with partial mental activity. Thus the living entity can conduct his mental speculations.

TEXT 25

आत्मानं चास्य निर्भिन्नमभिमानोऽविशत्पदम् ।
कर्मणांशेन येनासौ कर्तव्यं प्रतिपद्यते ॥२५॥

ātmānaṁ cāsya nirbhinnam
abhimāno 'viśat padam
karmaṇāṁśena yenāsau
kartavyaṁ pratipadyate

ātmānam—false ego; *ca*—also; *asya*—of the gigantic form; *nirbhinnam*—being separately manifested; *abhimānaḥ*—false identification;

aviśat—entered; *padam*—in position; *karmaṇā*—activities; *aṁśena*—by the part; *yena*—by which; *asau*—the living entity; *kartavyam*—objective activities; *pratipadyate*—takes in.

TRANSLATION

Thereafter the materialistic ego of the gigantic form separately manifested itself, and into it entered Rudra, the controller of false ego, with his own partial activities, by which the living entity transacts his objective actions.

PURPORT

The false ego of materialistic identity is controlled by the demigod Rudra, an incarnation of Lord Śiva. Rudra is the incarnation of the Supreme Lord who controls the mode of ignorance within material nature. The activities of the false ego are based on the objective of the body and mind. Most persons conducted by the false ego are controlled by Lord Śiva. When one reaches a finer version of ignorance, he falsely thinks of himself as the Supreme Lord. That egoistic conviction of the conditioned soul is the last snare of the illusory energy which controls the entire material world.

TEXT 26

सत्त्वं चास्य विनिर्भिन्नं महान्धिष्ण्यमुपाविशत् ।
चित्तेनांशेन येनासौ विज्ञानं प्रतिपद्यते ॥२६॥

sattvaṁ cāsya vinirbhinnaṁ
mahān dhiṣṇyam upāviśat
cittenāṁśena yenāsau
vijñānaṁ pratipadyate

sattvam—consciousness; *ca*—also; *asya*—of the gigantic form; *vinirbhinnam*—being separately manifested; *mahān*—the total energy, *mahat-tattva; dhiṣṇyam*—with control; *upāviśat*—entered into; *cittena aṁśena*—along with His part of consciousness; *yena*—by which; *asau*—the living entity; *vijñānam*—specific knowledge; *pratipadyate*—cultivates.

TRANSLATION

Thereafter, when His consciousness separately manifested itself, the total energy, mahat-tattva, entered with His conscious part. Thus the living entity is able to conceive specific knowledge.

TEXT 27

शीर्ष्णोऽस्य द्यौर्धरा पद्भ्यां खं नाभेरुदपद्यत ।
गुणानां वृत्तयो येषु प्रतीयन्ते सुरादयः ॥२७॥

śīrṣṇo 'sya dyaur dharā padbhyāṁ
khaṁ nābher udapadyata
guṇānāṁ vṛttayo yeṣu
pratīyante surādayaḥ

śīrṣṇaḥ—head; *asya*—of the gigantic form; *dyauḥ*—the heavenly planets; *dharā*—earthly planets; *padbhyām*—on His legs; *kham*—the sky; *nābheḥ*—from the abdomen; *udapadyata*—became manifested; *guṇānām*—of the three modes of nature; *vṛttayaḥ*—reactions; *yeṣu*—in which; *pratīyante*—manifest; *sura-ādayaḥ*—the demigods and others.

TRANSLATION

Thereafter, from the head of the gigantic form, the heavenly planets were manifested, and from His legs the earthly planets and from His abdomen the sky separately manifested themselves. Within them the demigods and others also were manifested in terms of the modes of material nature.

TEXT 28

आत्यन्तिकेन सत्त्वेन दिवं देवाः प्रपेदिरे ।
धरां रजःस्वभावेन पणयो ये च ताननु ॥२८॥

ātyantikena sattvena
divaṁ devāḥ prapedire

dharāṁ rajaḥ-svabhāvena
paṇayo ye ca tān anu

ātyantikena—excessive; *sattvena*—by the mode of goodness; *divam*—in the higher planets; *devāḥ*—the demigods; *prapedire*—have been situated; *dharām*—on the earth; *rajaḥ*—the mode of passion; *svabhāvena*—by nature; *paṇayaḥ*—the human being; *ye*—all those; *ca*—also; *tān*—their; *anu*—subordinate.

TRANSLATION

The demigods, qualified by the superexcellent quality of the mode of goodness, are situated in the heavenly planets, whereas the human beings, because of their nature in the mode of passion, live on the earth in company with their subordinates.

PURPORT

In *Bhagavad-gītā* (14.14–15) it is said that those who are highly developed in the mode of goodness are promoted to the higher, heavenly planetary system, and those who are overpowered by the mode of passion are situated in the middle planetary systems—the earth and similar planets. But those who are surcharged with the mode of ignorance are degraded to the lower planetary systems or to the animal kingdom. The demigods are highly developed in the mode of goodness, and thus they are situated in the heavenly planets. Below human beings are the animals, although some of them mingle with human society; cows, horses, dogs, etc., are habituated to living under the protection of human beings.

The word *ātyantikena* is very significant in this verse. By development of the mode of goodness of material nature one can become situated in the heavenly planets. But by excessive development of the modes of passion and ignorance, the human being indulges in killing the animals who are meant to be protected by mankind. Persons who indulge in unnecessary animal killing have excessively developed in the modes of passion and ignorance and have no hope of advancing to the mode of goodness; they are destined to be degraded to lower statuses of life. The planetary systems are calculated as upper and lower in terms of the classes of living entities who live there.

TEXT 29

तार्तीयेन स्वभावेन भगवन्नाभिमाश्रिताः ।
उभयोरन्तरं व्योम ये रुद्रपार्षदां गणाः ॥२९॥

tārtīyena svabhāvena
bhagavan-nābhim āśritāḥ
ubhayor antaraṁ vyoma
ye rudra-pārṣadāṁ gaṇāḥ

tārtīyena—by excessive development of the third mode of material nature, the mode of ignorance; *svabhāvena*—by such nature; *bhagavat-nābhim*—the abdominal navel of the gigantic form of the Personality of Godhead; *āśritāḥ*—those who are so situated; *ubhayoḥ*—between the two; *antaram*—in between; *vyoma*—the sky; *ye*—all of whom; *rudra-pārṣadām*—associates of Rudra; *gaṇāḥ*—population.

TRANSLATION

Living entities who are associates of Rudra develop in the third mode of material nature, or ignorance. They are situated in the sky between the earthly planets and the heavenly planets.

PURPORT

This middle portion of the sky is called Bhuvarloka, as confirmed by both Śrīla Viśvanātha Cakravartī and Śrīla Jīva Gosvāmī. In *Bhagavad-gītā* it is stated that those who develop in the mode of passion are situated in the middle region. Those who are situated in the mode of goodness are promoted to the regions of the demigods, those who are situated in the mode of passion are placed in human society, and those who are situated in the mode of ignorance are placed in the society of animals or ghosts. There are no contradictions in this conclusion. Numerous living entities are distributed all over the universe in different planets and are so situated in terms of their own qualities in the modes of material nature.

TEXT 30

मुखतोऽवर्तत ब्रह्म पुरुषस्य कुरूद्वह ।
यस्तून्मुखत्वाद्वर्णानां मुख्योऽभूद्ब्राह्मणो गुरुः ॥३०॥

mukhato 'vartata brahma
puruṣasya kurūdvaha
yas tūnmukhatvād varṇānāṁ
mukhyo 'bhūd brāhmaṇo guruḥ

mukhataḥ—from the mouth; *avartata*—generated; *brahma*—the Vedic wisdom; *puruṣasya*—of the *virāṭ-puruṣa*, the gigantic form; *kuru-udvaha*—O chief of the Kuru dynasty; *yaḥ*—who are; *tu*—due to; *unmukhatvāt*—inclined to; *varṇānām*—of the orders of society; *mukhyaḥ*—the chief; *abhūt*—so became; *brāhmaṇaḥ*—called the *brāhmaṇas; guruḥ*—the recognized teacher or spiritual master.

TRANSLATION

O chief of the Kuru dynasty, the Vedic wisdom became manifested from the mouth of the virāṭ, the gigantic form. Those who are inclined to this Vedic knowledge are called brāhmaṇas, and they are the natural teachers and spiritual masters of all the orders of society.

PURPORT

As confirmed in *Bhagavad-gītā* (4.13), the four orders of human society developed with the order of the body of the gigantic form. The bodily divisions are the mouth, arms, waist and legs. Those who are situated on the mouth are called *brāhmaṇas*, those who are situated on the arms are called *kṣatriyas*, those who are situated on the waist are called *vaiśyas*, and those who are situated on the legs are called *śūdras*. Everyone is situated in the body of the Supreme in His gigantic *viśva-rūpa* form. In terms of the four orders, therefore, no caste is to be considered degraded because of being situated on a particular part of the body. In our own bodies we do not show any actual difference in our treatment towards the hands or legs. Each and every part of the body is important, although the mouth is the most important of the bodily parts. If other parts are cut off from the body, a man can continue his life, but if the mouth is cut off, one cannot live. Therefore, this most important part of the body of the Lord is called the sitting place of the *brāhmaṇas*, who are inclined to the Vedic wisdom. One who is not inclined to the Vedic wisdom but to mundane affairs cannot be called a *brāhmaṇa*, even if he is born of a *brāhmaṇa* family or father. To have a *brāhmaṇa* father does not qualify one as a *brāhmaṇa*. The main qualification of a *brāhmaṇa* is to be inclined to the Vedic wisdom. The *Vedas* are situated on the mouth of the Lord, and therefore anyone who is inclined to the Vedic wisdom is certainly situated on the mouth of the Lord, and he is a *brāhmaṇa*. This inclination towards Vedic wisdom is also not restricted to any particular caste or community. Anyone from any family and from any part of the world may become inclined to the Vedic wisdom, and that will qualify him as a real *brāhmaṇa*.

A real *brāhmaṇa* is the natural teacher or spiritual master. Unless one has Vedic knowledge, one cannot become a spiritual master. The perfect knowledge of the *Vedas* is to know the Lord, the Personality of Godhead, and that is the end of Vedic knowledge, or Vedānta. One who is situated in the impersonal Brahman and has no information of the Supreme Personality of Godhead may become a *brāhmaṇa*, but he cannot become a spiritual master. It is said in the *Padma Purāṇa:*

ṣaṭ-karma-nipuṇo vipro
mantra-tantra-viśāradaḥ
avaiṣṇavo gurur na syād
vaiṣṇavaḥ śva-paco guruḥ

An impersonalist can become a qualified *brāhmaṇa*, but he cannot become a spiritual master unless and until he is promoted to the stage of a Vaiṣṇava, or a devotee of the Personality of Godhead. Lord Caitanya, the great authority of Vedic wisdom in the modern age, stated:

kibā vipra, kibā nyāsī, śūdra kene naya
yei kṛṣṇa-tattva-vettā, sei 'guru' haya

A person may be a *brāhmaṇa* or a *śūdra* or a *sannyāsī*, but if he happens to be well versed in the science of Kṛṣṇa, then he is fit to become a spiritual master. (Cc. *Madhya* 8.128) The qualification, then, of a spiritual master is not to be a qualified *brāhmaṇa*, but to be well versed in the science of Kṛṣṇa.

One who is conversant with Vedic wisdom is a *brāhmaṇa.* And only a *brāhmaṇa* who is a pure Vaiṣṇava and knows all the intricacies of the science of Kṛṣṇa can become a spiritual master.

TEXT 31

बाहुभ्योऽवर्तत क्षत्रं क्षत्रियस्तदनुव्रतः ।
यो जातस्त्रायते वर्णान् पौरुषः कण्टकक्षतात् ॥३१॥

bāhubhyo 'vartata kṣatraṁ
kṣatriyas tad anuvrataḥ
yo jātas trāyate varṇān
pauruṣaḥ kaṇṭaka-kṣatāt

bāhubhyaḥ—from the arms; *avartata*—generated; *kṣatram*—the power of protection; *kṣatriyaḥ*—in relation to the power of protection; *tat*—that; *anuvrataḥ*—followers; *yaḥ*—one who; *jātaḥ*—so becomes; *trāyate*—delivers; *varṇān*—the other occupations; *pauruṣaḥ*—representative of the Personality of Godhead; *kaṇṭaka*—of disturbing elements like thieves and debauchees; *kṣatāt*—from the mischief.

TRANSLATION

Thereafter the power of protection was generated from the arms of the gigantic virāṭ form, and in relation to such power the kṣatriyas also came into existence by following the kṣatriya principle of protecting society from the disturbance of thieves and miscreants.

PURPORT

As the *brāhmaṇas* are recognized by their particular qualification of inclination towards the transcendental knowledge of Vedic wisdom, so also the *kṣatriyas* are recognized by the power to protect society from the disturbing elements of thieves and miscreants. The word *anuvrataḥ* is significant. A person who follows the *kṣatriya* principles by protecting society from thieves and miscreants is called a *kṣatriya,* not the one who is simply born a *kṣatriya.* The conception of the caste system is always based on quality and not on the qualification of birth. Birth is an extraneous consideration; it is not the main feature of the orders and divisions. In *Bhagavad-gītā* (18.41–44) the qualifications of the *brāhmaṇas*, *kṣatriyas*, *vaiśyas* and *śūdras* are specifically mentioned, and it is understood that all such qualifications are needed before one can be designated as belonging to a particular group.

Lord Viṣṇu is always mentioned as the *puruṣa* in all Vedic scriptures. Sometimes the living entities are also mentioned as *puruṣas*, although they are essentially *puruṣa-śakti* (*parā śakti* or *parā prakṛti*), the superior energy of the *puruṣa*. Illusioned by the external potency of the *puruṣa* (the Lord), the living entities falsely think of themselves as the *puruṣa* although they actually have no qualifications. The Lord has the power to protect. Of the three deities Brahmā, Viṣṇu and Maheśvara, the first has the power to create, the second has the power to protect, and the third has the power to destroy. The word *puruṣa* is significant in this verse because the *kṣatriyas* are expected to represent the *puruṣa* Lord in giving protection to the *prajās*, or all those who are born in the land and water. Protection is therefore meant for both man and the animals. In modern society the *prajās* are not protected from the hands of thieves and miscreants. The modern democratic state, which has no *kṣatriyas*, is a government of the *vaiśyas* and *śūdras*, and not of *brāhmaṇas* and *kṣatriyas* as formerly. Mahārāja Yudhiṣṭhira and his grandson, Mahārāja Parīkṣit, were typical *kṣatriya* kings, for they gave protection to all men and animals. When the personification of Kali attempted to kill a cow, Mahārāja Parīkṣit at once prepared himself to kill the miscreant, and the personification of Kali was banished from his kingdom. That is the sign of *puruṣa*, or the representative of Lord Viṣṇu. According to Vedic civilization, a qualified *kṣatriya* monarch is given the respect of the Lord because he represents the Lord by giving protection to the *prajās*. Modern elected presidents cannot even give protection from theft cases, and therefore one has to take protection from an insurance company. The problems of modern human society are due to the lack of qualified *brāhmaṇas* and *kṣatriyas* and the overinfluence of the *vaiśyas* and *śūdras* by so-called general franchise.

TEXT 32

विशोऽवर्तन्त तस्योर्वोर्लोकवृत्तिकरीर्विभोः ।
वैश्यस्तदुद्भवो वार्तां नृणां यः समवर्तयत् ॥३२॥

viśo 'vartanta tasyorvor
loka-vṛttikarīr vibhoḥ
vaiśyas tad-udbhavo vārtāṁ
nṛṇāṁ yaḥ samavartayat

viśaḥ—means of living by production and distribution; *avartanta*—generated; *tasya*—His (the gigantic form's); *ūrvoḥ*—from the thighs; *loka-vṛttikarīḥ*—means of livelihood; *vibhoḥ*—of the Lord; *vaiśyaḥ*—the mercantile community; *tat*—their; *udbhavaḥ*—orientation; *vārtām*—means of living; *nṛṇām*—of all men; *yaḥ*—one who; *samavartayat*—executed.

TRANSLATION

The means of livelihood of all persons, namely production of grains and their distribution to the prajās, was generated from the thighs of the Lord's gigantic form. The mercantile men who take charge of such execution are called vaiśyas.

PURPORT

Human society's means of living is clearly mentioned here as *viśa,* or agriculture and the business of distributing agricultural products, which involves transport, banking, etc. Industry is an artificial means of livelihood, and large-scale industry especially is the source of all the problems of society. In *Bhagavad-gītā* also the duties of the *vaiśyas,* who are engaged in *viśa,* are stated as cow protection, agriculture and business. We have already discussed that the human being can safely depend on the cow and agricultural land for his livelihood.

The exchange of produce by banking and transportation is a branch of this type of living. The *vaiśyas* are divided into many subsections: some of them are called *kṣetrī,* or landowners, some are called *kṛṣaṇa,* or land tillers, some of them are called *tila-vaṇik,* or grain raisers, some are called *gandha-vaṇik,* or merchants in spices, and some are called *suvarṇa-vaṇik,* or merchants in gold and banking. The *brāhmaṇas* are the teachers and spiritual masters, the *kṣatriyas* protect the citizens from the hands of thieves and miscreants, and the *vaiśyas* are in charge of production and distribution. The *śūdras,* the unintelligent class of men who cannot act independently in any of the above-mentioned activities, are meant for serving the three higher classes for their livelihood.

Formerly, the *brāhmaṇas* were given all the necessities of life by the *kṣatriyas* and *vaiśyas* because they had no time to spend making a living. The *kṣatriyas* would collect taxes from the *vaiśyas* and *śūdras,* but the *brāhmaṇas* were exempt from paying income tax or land revenue. That system of human society was so nice that there were no political, social and economic upheavals. The different castes, or *varṇa* classifications, are therefore essential for maintaining a peaceful human society.

TEXT 33

पद्भ्यां भगवतो जज्ञे शुश्रूषा धर्मसिद्धये ।
तस्यां जातः पुरा शूद्रो यद्वृत्त्या तुष्यते हरिः ॥३३॥

padbhyāṁ bhagavato jajñe
śuśrūṣā dharma-siddhaye
tasyāṁ jātaḥ purā śūdro
yad-vṛttyā tuṣyate hariḥ

padbhyām—from the legs; *bhagavataḥ*—of the Personality of Godhead; *jajñe*—became manifested; *śuśrūṣā*—service; *dharma*—occupational duty; *siddhaye*—for the matter of; *tasyām*—in that; *jātaḥ*—being generated; *purā*—formerly; *śūdraḥ*—the servitors; *yat-vṛttyā*—the occupation by which; *tuṣyate*—becomes satisfied; *hariḥ*—the Supreme Personality of Godhead.

TRANSLATION

Thereafter, service was manifested from the legs of the Personality of Godhead for the sake of perfecting the religious function. Situated on the legs are the śūdras, who satisfy the Lord by service.

PURPORT

Service is the real constitutional occupation of all living entities. The living entities are meant to render service to the Lord, and they can attain religious perfection by this service attitude. One cannot attain religious perfection simply by speculating to attain theoretical knowledge. The *jñānī* division of spiritualists go on speculating only to distinguish the soul from matter, but they have no information of the activities of the soul after being liberated by knowledge. It is said that persons who only mentally speculate to know things as they are and who do not engage in the transcendental loving service of the Lord are simply wasting their time.

It is clearly said here that the principle of service was generated from the legs of the Lord for the sake of perfecting the religious process, but this transcendental service is different from the idea of service in the material world. In the material world, no one wants to be a servant; everyone wants to become the master because false mastership is the basic disease of the conditioned soul. The conditioned soul in the material world wants to lord it over others. Illusioned by the external energy of the Lord, he is forced to become a servant of the material world. That is the real position of the conditioned soul. The last snare of the illusory, external energy is the conception of becoming one with the Lord, and due to this conception the illusioned soul remains in the bondage of material energy, falsely thinking himself a liberated soul and "as good as Nārāyaṇa."

It is actually better to be a *śūdra* than to be a *brāhmaṇa* and not develop the service attitude, because that attitude alone satisfies the Lord. Every living being—even if he be a *brāhmaṇa* by qualification—must take to the transcendental service of the Lord. Both *Bhagavad-gītā* and the *Śrīmad-Bhāgavatam* support that this service attitude is the perfection of the living entity. A *brāhmaṇa, kṣatriya, vaiśya* or *śūdra* can perfect his occupational duties only by rendering service unto the Lord. A *brāhmaṇa* is supposed to know this fact due to his perfection in Vedic wisdom. The other sections are supposed to follow the direction of the *brāhmaṇa* Vaiṣṇava (one who is a *brāhmaṇa* by qualification and a Vaiṣṇava by action). That will make the entire society perfect in regard to the order of its social construction. A disordered society cannot satisfy either the members of the society or the Lord. Even if one is not a perfect *brāhmaṇa, kṣatriya, vaiśya* or *śūdra* but takes to the service of the Lord, not caring for the perfection of his social position, he becomes a perfect human being simply by developing the attitude of service to the Supreme Lord.

TEXT 34

एते वर्णाः स्वधर्मेण यजन्ति स्वगुरुं हरिम् ।
श्रद्धयात्मविशुद्ध्यर्थं यज्जाताः सह वृत्तिभिः ॥३४॥

ete varṇāḥ sva-dharmeṇa
yajanti sva-gurum̐ harim
śraddhayātma-viśuddhy-artham̐
yaj-jātāḥ saha vṛttibhiḥ

ete—all these; *varṇāḥ*—orders of society; *sva-dharmeṇa*—by one's own occupational duties; *yajanti*—worship; *sva-gurum*—with the spiritual master; *harim*—the Supreme Personality of Godhead; *śraddhayā*—with faith and devotion; *ātma*—self; *viśuddhi-artham*—for purifying; *yat*—from whom; *jātāḥ*—born; *saha*—along with; *vṛttibhiḥ*—occupational duty.

TRANSLATION

All these different social divisions are born, with their occupational duties and living conditions, from the Supreme Personality of Godhead. Thus for unconditional life and self-realization one has to worship the Supreme Lord under the direction of the spiritual master.

PURPORT

Since they are born from different parts of the body of the Supreme Lord in His gigantic form, all living entities in all parts of the entire universe are supposed to be eternal servitors of the supreme body. Every part of our own body, such as the mouth, hands, thighs and legs, is meant to render service to the whole. That is their constitutional position. In subhuman life the living entities are not conscious of this constitutional position, but in the human form of life they are supposed to know this through the system of the *varṇas*, the social orders. As above mentioned, the *brāhmaṇa* is the spiritual master of all the orders of society, and thus brahminical culture, culminating in the transcendental service of the Lord, is the basic principle for purifying the soul.

In conditioned life the soul is under the impression that he can become the lord of the universe, and the last point of this misconception is to think oneself the Supreme. The foolish conditioned soul does not take into account that the Supreme cannot be conditioned by *māyā*, or illusion. If the Supreme were to become conditioned by illusion, where would be His supremacy? In that case, *māyā*, or illusion, would be the Supreme. Therefore, because the living entities are conditioned, they cannot be supreme. The actual position of the conditioned soul is explained in this verse: all the conditioned souls are impure due to contact with the material energy in three modes of nature. Therefore it is necessary that they purify themselves under the guidance of the bona fide spiritual master, who not only is a *brāhmaṇa* by qualification but must also be a Vaiṣṇava. The only self-purifying process mentioned herein is to worship the Lord under the recognized method—under the guidance of the bona fide spiritual master. That is the natural way of purification, and no other method is recommended as bona fide. The other methods of purification may be helpful to come to this stage of life, but ultimately one has to come to this last point before he attains actual perfection. *Bhagavad-gītā* (7.19) confirms this truth as follows:

bahūnāṁ janmanām ante
jñānavān māṁ prapadyate
vāsudevaḥ sarvam iti
sa mahātmā sudurlabhaḥ

TEXT 35

एतत्क्षत्तर्भगवतो दैवकर्मात्मरूपिणः ।
कः श्रद्दध्यादुपाकर्तुं योगमायाबलोदयम् ॥३५॥

etat kṣattar bhagavato
daiva-karmātma-rūpiṇaḥ
kaḥ śraddadhyād upākartuṁ
yogamāyā-balodayam

etat—this; *kṣattaḥ*—O Vidura; *bhagavataḥ*—of the Supreme Personality of Godhead; *daiva-karma-ātma-rūpiṇaḥ*—of the gigantic form of transcendental work, time and nature; *kaḥ*—who else; *śradda-*

dhyāt—can aspire; *upākartum*—measure in totality; *yogamāyā*—internal potency; *bala-udayam*—manifested by the strength of.

TRANSLATION

O Vidura, who can estimate or measure the transcendental time, work and potency of the gigantic form manifested by the internal potency of the Supreme Personality of Godhead?

PURPORT

The froggish philosophers may go on with their mental speculations on the subject matter of the *virāṭ*, the gigantic form exhibited by the *yogamāyā* internal potency of the Supreme Personality of Godhead, but factually no one can measure such a vast exhibition. In *Bhagavad-gītā* (11.16), Arjuna, the recognized devotee of the Lord, says:

aneka-bāhūdara-vaktra-netraṁ
paśyāmi tvāṁ sarvato 'nanta-rūpam
nāntaṁ na madhyaṁ na punas tavādiṁ
paśyāmi viśveśvara viśva-rūpa

"O my Lord, O gigantic *viśva-rūpa* form, O master of the universe, I see innumerable hands, bodies, mouths and eyes in all directions, and they are all unlimited. I cannot find the end of this manifestation, nor do I see the middle, nor the beginning."

Bhagavad-gītā was specifically spoken to Arjuna, and the *viśva-rūpa* was exhibited before him at his request. He was awarded the specific eyes to see this *viśva-rūpa*, yet although he was able to see the Lord's innumerable hands and mouths, he was unable to see Him completely. Since Arjuna was unable to estimate the length and breadth of the potency of the Lord, who else would be able to do so? One may only indulge in miscalculation like the frog-philosopher. The frog-philosopher wanted to estimate the length and breadth of the Pacific Ocean by his experience of a well three cubic feet large, and thus he began to puff himself up to become as big as the Pacific Ocean, but at last he burst and died by this process. This story is applicable to the mental philosophers who, under the illusion of the Lord's external energy, indulge in estimating the length and breadth of the Supreme Lord. The best path is to become a coolheaded, submissive devotee of the Lord, try to hear about the Lord from the bona fide spiritual master, and thus serve the Lord in transcendental loving service, as suggested in the previous verse.

TEXT 36

तथापि कीर्तयाम्यङ्ग यथामति यथाश्रुतम् ।
कीर्तिं हरेः स्वां सत्कर्तुं गिरमन्याभिधासतीम् ॥३६॥

tathāpi kīrtayāmy aṅga
yathā-mati yathā-śrutam
kīrtiṁ hareḥ svāṁ sat-kartuṁ
giram anyābhidhāsatīm

tathā—therefore; *api*—although it is so; *kīrtayāmi*—I do describe; *aṅga*—O Vidura; *yathā*—as much as; *mati*—intelligence; *yathā*—as much as; *śrutam*—heard; *kīrtim*—glories; *hareḥ*—of the Lord; *svām*—own; *sat-kartum*—just purify; *giram*—speeches; *anyābhidhā*—otherwise; *asatīm*—unchaste.

TRANSLATION

In spite of my inability, whatever I have been able to hear [from the spiritual master] and whatever I could assimilate I am now describing in glorification of the Lord by pure speech, for otherwise my power of speaking would remain unchaste.

PURPORT

The purification of the conditioned soul necessitates purification of his consciousness. By the presence of consciousness, the presence of the transcendental soul is verified, and as soon as consciousness leaves the body, the material body is not active. Consciousness is perceived, therefore, by activities. The theory put forward by empiric philosophers that consciousness can remain in an inactive state is the proof of their poor fund of knowledge. One should not become unchaste by stopping the activities of pure consciousness. If the activities of pure consciousness are stopped, certainly the conscious living force will be otherwise engaged because unless engaged the consciousness has no standing. Consciousness cannot be silent, even for a moment. When the body does not act, the consciousness acts in the form of dreams. Unconsciousness is artificial; by induced extraneous help it remains for a limited period, but when the intoxication of the drug is finished or when one is awake, the consciousness again acts earnestly.

Maitreya's statement is that in order to avoid unchaste conscious activities, he was trying to describe the unlimited glories of the Lord, although he did not have the ability to describe them perfectly. This glorification of the Lord is not a product of research, but the result of hearing submissively from the authority of the spiritual master. It is also not possible to repeat all that one has heard from his spiritual master, but one can narrate as far as possible by one's honest endeavor. It does not matter whether the Lord's glories are fully explained or not. One must attempt to engage one's bodily, mental and verbal activities in the transcendental glorification of the Lord, otherwise such activities will remain unchaste and impure. The existence of the conditioned soul can be purified only by the method of engaging mind and speech in the service of the Lord. The *tridaṇḍi-sannyāsī* of the Vaiṣṇava school accepts three rods, representing the vow to engage in the service of the Lord with body, mind and speech, whereas the *ekadaṇḍi-sannyāsī* takes the vow to become one with the Supreme. Since the Lord is the Absolute, there is no distinction between Him and His glories. The glories of the Lord as chanted by the Vaiṣṇava *sannyāsī* are as substantial as the Lord Himself, and thus while glorifying the Lord the devotee becomes one with Him in transcendental interest, although he remains eternally a transcendental servitor. This simultaneously one and different position of the devotee makes him eternally purified, and thus his life becomes a complete success.

TEXT 37

एकान्तलाभं वचसो नु पुंसां
सुश्लोकमौलेर्गुणवादमाहुः ।
श्रुतेश्च विद्वद्भिरुपाकृतायां
कथासुधायामुपसम्प्रयोगम् ॥३७॥

ekānta-lābhaṁ vacaso nu puṁsāṁ
suśloka-mauler guṇa-vādam āhuḥ
śruteś ca vidvadbhir upākṛtāyāṁ
kathā-sudhāyām upasamprayogam

eka-anta—the one which has no comparison; *lābham*—gain; *vacasaḥ*—by discussions; *nu puṁsām*—after the Supreme Person; *su-śloka*—pious; *mauleḥ*—activities; *guṇa-vādam*—glorification; *āhuḥ*—it is so said; *śruteḥ*—of the ear; *ca*—also; *vidvadbhiḥ*—by the learned; *upākṛtāyām*—being so edited; *kathā-sudhāyām*—in the nectar of such a transcendental message; *upasamprayogam*—serves the real purpose, being nearer to.

TRANSLATION

The highest perfectional gain of humanity is to engage in discussions of the activities and glories of the Pious Actor. Such activities are so nicely arranged in writing by the greatly learned sages that the actual purpose of the ear is served just by being near them.

PURPORT

The impersonalists are very much afraid of hearing the activities of the Lord because they think that the happiness derived from the transcendental situation of Brahman is the ultimate goal of life; they think that anyone's activity, even that of the Personality of Godhead, is mundane. But the idea of happiness indicated in this verse is different because it relates to the activities of the Supreme Personality, who has transcendental qualities. The word *guṇa-vādam* is significant because the qualities of the Lord and His activities and pastimes are the subject matter for the discussions of devotees. A *ṛṣi* like Maitreya is certainly not interested in discussing anything pertaining to mundane qualities, yet he says that the highest perfectional stage of transcendental realization is to discuss the Lord's activities. Śrīla Jīva Gosvāmī, therefore, concludes that topics regarding the transcendental activities of the Lord are far beyond the transcendental realization of *kaivalya* happiness. These transcendental activities of the Lord are so arranged in writing by the great sages that simply by hearing of those narrations one becomes perfectly self-realized, and the proper use of the ear and the tongue is also achieved.

Śrīmad-Bhāgavatam is one of such great literatures, and the highest perfectional state of life is attained simply by hearing and reciting its contents.

TEXT 38

आत्मनोऽवसितो वत्स महिमा कविनादिना ।
संवत्सरसहस्रान्ते धिया योगविपक्कया ॥३८॥

ātmano 'vasito vatsa
mahimā kavinādinā
saṁvatsara-sahasrānte
dhiyā yoga-vipakkayā

ātmanaḥ—of the Supreme Soul; *avasitaḥ*—known; *vatsa*—O my dear son; *mahimā*—glories; *kavinā*—by the poet Brahmā; *ādinā*—original; *saṁvatsara*—celestial years; *sahasra-ante*—at the end of one thousand; *dhiyā*—by intelligence; *yoga-vipakkayā*—by matured meditation.

TRANSLATION

O my son, the original poet, Brahmā, after mature meditation for one thousand celestial years, could know only that the glories of the Supreme Soul are inconceivable.

PURPORT

There are some froggish philosophers who want to know the Supreme Soul by means of philosophy and mental speculation. And when the devotees, who are to some extent in knowledge of the Supreme Lord, admit that the glories of the Lord are inestimable or inconceivable, the froggish philosophers adversely criticize them. These philosophers, like the frog in the well who tried to estimate the measurement of the Pacific Ocean, like to take trouble over fruitless mental speculation instead of taking instructions from devotees like the original poet, namely, Brahmā. Lord Brahmā underwent a severe type of meditation for one thousand celestial years, yet he said that the glories of the Lord are inconceivable. Therefore what can the froggish philosophers hope to gain from their mental speculations?

It is said in the *Brahma-saṁhitā* that the mental speculator may fly through the sky of speculation with the velocity of the mind or the wind for thousands of millions of years, and still he will find it inconceivable. The devotees, however, do not waste time in such vain searching after knowledge of the Supreme, but they submissively hear the glories of the Lord from bona fide devotees. Thus they transcendentally enjoy the process of hearing and chanting. The Lord approves of the devotional activities of the devotees or *mahātmās*, and He says:

mahātmānas tu māṁ pārtha
daivīṁ prakṛtim āśritāḥ
bhajanty ananya-manaso
jñātvā bhūtādim avyayam

satataṁ kīrtayanto māṁ
yatantaś ca dṛḍha-vratāḥ
namasyantaś ca māṁ bhaktyā
nitya-yuktā upāsate
(Bg. 9.13–14)

The pure devotees of the Lord take shelter of the *parā prakṛti*, the internal potency of the Lord called Lakṣmīdevī, Sītādevī, Śrīmatī Rādhārāṇī or Śrīmatī Rukmiṇīdevī, and thus they become actual *mahātmās*, or great souls. *Mahātmās* are not fond of indulging in mental speculations, but they actually take to the devotional service of the Lord, without the slightest deviation. Devotional service is manifested by the primary process of hearing and chanting about the activities of the Lord. This transcendental method practiced by the *mahātmās* gives them sufficient knowledge of the Lord because if the Lord can at all be known to some extent, it is only through the means of devotional service and no other way. One may go on speculating and waste the valuable time of his human life, but that will not help anyone to enter into the precincts of the Lord. The *mahātmās*, however, are not concerned with knowing the Lord by mental speculation because they enjoy hearing about His glorious activities in His transcendental dealings with His devotees or with the demons. The devotees take pleasure in both and are happy in this life and the life after.

TEXT 39

अतो भगवतो माया मायिनामपि मोहिनी ।
यत्स्वयं चात्मवर्त्मात्मा न वेद किमुतापरे ॥३९॥

ato bhagavato māyā
māyinām api mohinī
yat svayaṁ cātma-vartmātmā
na veda kim utāpare

ataḥ—therefore; *bhagavataḥ*—godly; *māyā*—potencies; *māyinām*—of the jugglers; *api*—even; *mohinī*—enchanting; *yat*—that which; *svayam*—personally; *ca*—also; *ātma-vartma*—self-sufficient; *ātmā*—self; *na*—does not; *veda*—know; *kim*—what; *uta*—to speak of; *apare*—others.

TRANSLATION

The wonderful potency of the Supreme Personality of Godhead is bewildering even to the jugglers. That potential power is unknown even to the self-sufficient Lord, so it is certainly unknown to others.

PURPORT

The froggish philosophers and mundane wranglers in science and mathematical calculation may not believe in the inconceivable potency of the Supreme Personality of Godhead, but they are sometimes puzzled by the wonderful jugglery of man and nature. Such jugglers and magicians of the mundane world are actually puzzled by the jugglery of the Lord in His transcendental activities, but they try to adjust their bewilderment by saying that it is all mythology. There is, however, nothing impossible or mythological in the Supreme Omnipotent Person. The most wonderful puzzle for the mundane wranglers is that while they remain calculating the length and breadth of the unlimited potency of the Supreme Person, His faithful devotees are set free from the bondage of material encagement simply by appreciating the wonderful jugglery of the Supreme in the practical field. The devotees of the Lord see the wonderful dexterity in everything with which they come in contact in all circumstances of eating, sleeping, working, etc. A small banyan fruit contains thousands of small seeds, and each seed holds the potency of another tree, which again holds the potency of many millions of such fruits as causes and effects. So the trees and seeds engage the devotees in meditation about the activities of the Lord, while the mundane wranglers waste time in dry speculation and mental concoction, which are fruitless in both this life and the next. In spite of their pride in speculation, they can never appreciate the simple potential activities of the banyan tree. Such speculators are poor souls destined to remain in matter perpetually.

TEXT 40

यतोऽप्राप्य न्यवर्तन्त वाचश्च मनसा सह ।
अहं चान्य इमे देवास्तस्मै भगवते नमः ॥४०॥

yato 'prāpya nyavartanta
vācaś ca manasā saha
ahaṁ cānya ime devās
tasmai bhagavate namaḥ

yataḥ—from whom; *aprāpya*—being unable to measure; *nyavartanta*—cease to try; *vācaḥ*—words; *ca*—also; *manasā*—with the mind; *saha*—with; *aham ca*—also the ego; *anye*—other; *ime*—all these; *devāḥ*—demigods; *tasmai*—unto Him; *bhagavate*—unto the Personality of Godhead; *namaḥ*—offer obeisances.

TRANSLATION

Words, mind and ego, with their respective controlling demigods, have failed to achieve success in knowing the Supreme Personality of Godhead. Therefore, we simply have to offer our respectful obeisances unto Him as a matter of sanity.

PURPORT

The froggish calculator may raise the objection that if the Absolute is unknowable even by the controlling deities of speech, mind and ego, namely the *Vedas*, Brahmā, Rudra and all the demigods headed by Bṛhaspati, then why should the devotees be so interested in this unknown object? The answer is that the transcendental ecstasy enjoyed by the devotees in delineating the pastimes of the Lord is certainly unknown to nondevotees and mental speculators. Unless one relishes transcendental joy, naturally one will come back from his speculations and concocted conclusions because he will see them as neither factual nor enjoyable. The devotees can at least know that the Absolute Truth is the Supreme Personality of Godhead Viṣṇu, as the Vedic hymns confirm: *oṁ tad viṣṇoḥ paramaṁ padaṁ sadā paśyanti sūrayaḥ. Bhagavad-gītā* (15.15) also confirms this fact: *vedaiś ca sarvair aham eva vedyaḥ.* By culture of Vedic knowledge one must know Lord Kṛṣṇa and should not falsely speculate on the word *aham,* or "I." The only method for understanding the Supreme Truth is devotional service, as stated in *Bhagavad-gītā* (18.55): *bhaktyā mām abhijānāti yāvān yaś cāsmi tattvataḥ.* Only by devotional service can one know that the ultimate truth is the Personality of Godhead and that Brahman and Paramātmā are only His partial features. This is confirmed in this verse by the great sage Maitreya. With devotion he offers his sincere surrender, *namaḥ,* to the Supreme Personality of Godhead, *bhagavate.* One has to follow in the footsteps of great sages and devotees like Maitreya and Vidura, Mahārāja Parīkṣit and Śukadeva Gosvāmī, and engage in the transcendental devotional service of the Lord if one would know His ultimate feature, which is above Brahman and Paramātmā.

Thus end the Bhaktivedanta purports of the Third Canto, Sixth Chapter, of the Śrīmad-Bhāgavatam, *entitled "Creation of the Universal Form."*

CHAPTER SEVEN

Further Inquiries by Vidura

TEXT 1

श्रीशुक उवाच
एवं ब्रुवाणं मैत्रेयं द्वैपायनसुतो बुधः ।
प्रीणयन्निव भारत्या विदुरः प्रत्यभाषत ॥ १ ॥

śrī-śuka uvāca
evaṁ bruvāṇaṁ maitreyaṁ
dvaipāyana-suto budhaḥ
prīṇayann iva bhāratyā
viduraḥ pratyabhāṣata

śrī-śukaḥ uvāca—Śrī Śukadeva Gosvāmī said; *evam*—thus; *bruvāṇam*—speaking; *maitreyam*—unto the sage Maitreya; *dvaipāyana-sutaḥ*—the son of Dvaipāyana; *budhaḥ*—learned; *prīṇayan*—in a pleasing manner; *iva*—as it was; *bhāratyā*—in the manner of a request; *viduraḥ*—Vidura; *pratyabhāṣata*—expressed.

TRANSLATION

Śrī Śukadeva Gosvāmī said: O King, while Maitreya, the great sage, was thus speaking, Vidura, the learned son of Dvaipāyana Vyāsa, expressed a request in a pleasing manner by asking this question.

TEXT 2

विदुर उवाच
ब्रह्मन् कथं भगवतश्चिन्मात्रस्याविकारिणः ।
लीलया चापि युज्येरन्निर्गुणस्य गुणाः क्रियाः ॥ २ ॥

vidura uvāca
brahman kathaṁ bhagavataś
cin-mātrasyāvikāriṇaḥ
līlayā cāpi yujyeran
nirguṇasya guṇāḥ kriyāḥ

viduraḥ uvāca—Vidura said; *brahman*—O *brāhmaṇa; katham*—how; *bhagavataḥ*—of the Personality of Godhead; *cit-mātrasya*—of the complete spiritual whole; *avikāriṇaḥ*—of the unchangeable; *līlayā*—by His pastime; *ca*—either; *api*—even though it is so; *yujyeran*—take place; *nirguṇasya*—who is without the modes of nature; *guṇāḥ*—modes of nature; *kriyāḥ*—activities.

TRANSLATION

Śrī Vidura said: O great brāhmaṇa, since the Supreme Personality of Godhead is the complete spiritual whole and is unchangeable, how is He connected with the material modes of nature and their activities? If this is His pastime, how do the activities of the unchangeable take place and exhibit qualities without the modes of nature?

PURPORT

As described in the previous chapter, the difference between the Supersoul, the Supreme Lord, and the living entities is that the activities of the Lord in creating the cosmic manifestation are performed by the Lord through the agency of His multifarious energies, but this manifestation is bewildering to the living entities. The Lord is therefore the master of the energies, whereas the living entities are subjugated by them. By asking various questions about transcendental activities, Vidura is clearing the misconception that when the Lord either descends on the earth in His incarnation or appears Himself with all His potencies, He too is subjected to the influence of *māyā*, just like an ordinary living entity. This is generally the calculation of less intelligent philosophers who consider the position of the Lord and that of the living entities to be on the same level. Vidura is hearing the great sage Maitreya refute these arguments. The Lord is described in this verse as *cin-mātra*, or completely spiritual. The Personality of Godhead has unlimited potencies to create and manifest many wonderful things, both temporary and permanent. Because this material world is the creation of His external energy, it thus appears to be temporary; it is manifested at certain intervals, maintained for some time, and again dissolved and conserved in His own energy. As described in *Bhagavad-gītā* (8.19), *bhūtvā bhūtvā pralīyate.* But the creation of His internal potency, the spiritual world, is not a temporary manifestation like the material world, but is eternal and full of transcendental knowledge, opulence, energy, strength, beauties and glories. Such manifestations of the Lord's potencies are eternal and are therefore called *nirguṇa,* or free from all tinges of the modes of material nature, even up to the mode of material goodness. The spiritual world is transcendental even to material goodness and thus is unchangeable. Since the Supreme Lord of such eternal and unchangeable qualities is never subjugated by anything like material influence, how can His activities and form be conceived to be under the influence of illusory *māyā,* as is the case with the living entities?

A juggler or magician displays many wonders with his acts and arts. He can become a cow by his magical tactics, and yet he is not that cow; but at the same time, the cow displayed by the magician is not different from him. Similarly, the material potency is not different from the Lord because it is an emanation from Him, but at the same time, that manifestation of potency is not the Supreme Lord. The Lord's transcendental knowledge and potency always remain the same; they do not change, even when displayed in the material world. As stated in *Bhagavad-gītā,* the Lord descends on the earth by His own internal potency, and therefore there is no question of His becoming materially contaminated, changed or otherwise affected by the modes of material nature. The Lord is *saguṇa* by His own internal potency, but at the same time He is *nirguṇa,* since He is not in touch with the material energy. The restrictions of the prison house are applicable to prisoners who are condemned by the king's law, but the king is never affected by such implications, although he may visit the prison house out of his good will. In the *Viṣṇu Purāṇa* the six opulences of the Lord are stated to be nondifferent from Him. The opulences of transcendental knowledge, strength, opulence, potency, beauty and renunciation are all identical with the Personality of Godhead. When He personally displays such opulences in the material world, they have no connection with the modes of material nature. The very word *cin-mātratva* is the guarantee that the Lord's activities are always transcendental, even when displayed in the material world. His activities are as good as the Supreme Personality Himself, otherwise liberated devotees like Śukadeva Gosvāmī would not have been attracted by them. Vidura inquired how the Lord's activities can be in the modes of material nature, as is sometimes miscalculated by persons with a poor fund of knowledge. The inebriety of the material qualities is due to the difference between the material body and the spirit soul. The conditioned soul's activities are displayed through the medium of the modes of material nature and are therefore perverted in appearance. However, the Lord's body and the Lord Himself are one and the same, and when the Lord's activities are displayed, they are certainly nondifferent from the Lord in all respects. The conclusion is that persons who consider the Lord's activities material are certainly mistaken.

TEXT 3

क्रीडायामुद्यमोऽर्भस्य कामश्चिक्रीडिषान्यतः ।
स्वतस्तृप्तस्य च कथं निवृत्तस्य सदान्यतः ॥ ३ ॥

krīḍāyām udyamo 'rbhasya
kāmaś cikrīḍiṣānyataḥ
svatas-tṛptasya ca kathaṁ
nivṛttasya sadānyataḥ

krīḍāyām—in the matter of playing; *udyamaḥ*—enthusiasm; *arbhasya*—of the boys; *kāmaḥ*—desire; *cikrīḍiṣā*—willingness to play; *anyataḥ*—with other boys; *svataḥ-tṛptasya*—for one who is self-satisfied; *ca*—also; *katham*—what for; *nivṛttasya*—one who is detached; *sadā*—at all times; *anyataḥ*—otherwise.

TRANSLATION

Boys are enthusiastic to play with other boys or with various diversions because they are encouraged by desire. But there is no possibility of such desire for the Lord because He is self-satisfied and detached from everything at all times.

PURPORT

Since the Supreme Personality of Godhead is one without a second, there is no possibility that anything besides Him can exist. He expands Himself by His energies in multiforms of self-expansions and separated expansions as well, just as fire expands itself by heat and light. Since there is no other existence besides the Lord Himself, the Lord's association with anything manifests His association with Himself. In *Bhagavad-gītā* (9.4) the Lord says:

mayā tatam idaṁ sarvaṁ
jagad avyakta-mūrtinā
mat-sthāni sarva-bhūtāni
na cāhaṁ teṣv avasthitaḥ

"The complete manifestation of the cosmic situation is an expansion of the Lord Himself in His impersonal feature. All things are situated in Him only, yet He is not in them." That is the opulence of the Lord's attachment and detachment. He is attached to everything, yet He is detached from all.

TEXT 4

अस्राक्षीद्भगवान् विश्वं गुणमय्यात्ममायया ।
तया संस्थापयत्येतद्भूयः प्रत्यपिधास्यति ॥ ४ ॥

asrākṣīd bhagavān viśvaṁ
guṇa-mayyātma-māyayā
tayā saṁsthāpayaty etad
bhūyaḥ pratyapidhāsyati

asrākṣīt—caused to create; *bhagavān*—the Personality of Godhead; *viśvam*—the universe; *guṇa-mayyā*—endowed with three modes of material nature; *ātma*—self; *māyayā*—by the potency; *tayā*—by her; *saṁsthāpayati*—maintains; *etat*—all these; *bhūyaḥ*—then again; *pratyapidhāsyati*—conversely dissolves also.

TRANSLATION

By His self-sheltered potency of the three modes of material nature, the Lord has caused the creation of this universe. By her

He maintains the creation and conversely dissolves it, again and again.

PURPORT

This cosmic universe is created by the Lord for those living entities who are carried away by the illusory thought of becoming one with Him by imitation. The three modes of material nature are for the further bewilderment of the conditioned souls. The conditioned living entity, bewildered by the illusory energy, considers himself a part of the material creation due to forgetfulness of his spiritual identity, and thus he becomes entangled in material activities life after life. This material world is not for the purpose of the Lord Himself, but is for the conditioned souls who wanted to be controllers due to misuse of their God-gifted minute independence. Thus the conditioned souls are subjected to repeated birth and death.

TEXT 5

देशतः कालतो योऽसाववस्थातः स्वतोऽन्यतः ।
अविलुप्तावबोधात्मा स युज्येताजया कथम् ॥ ५ ॥

deśataḥ kālato yo 'sāv
avasthātaḥ svato 'nyataḥ
aviluptāvabodhātmā
sa yujyetājayā katham

deśataḥ—circumstantial; *kālataḥ*—by the influence of time; *yaḥ*—one who; *asau*—the living entity; *avasthātaḥ*—by situation; *svataḥ*—by dream; *anyataḥ*—by others; *avilupta*—extinct; *avabodha*—consciousness; *ātmā*—pure self; *saḥ*—he; *yujyeta*—engaged; *ajayā*—with nescience; *katham*—how is it so.

TRANSLATION

The pure soul is pure consciousness and is never out of consciousness, either due to circumstances, time, situations, dreams or other causes. How then does he become engaged in nescience?

PURPORT

The consciousness of the living being is always present and never changes under any circumstances, as above mentioned. When a living man moves from one place to another, he is conscious that he has changed his position. He is always present in the past, present and future, like electricity. One can remember incidents from his past and can conjecture about his future also on the basis of past experience. He never forgets his personal identity, even though he is placed in awkward circumstances. How then can the living entity become forgetful of his real identity as pure spirit soul and identify with matter unless influenced by something beyond himself? The conclusion is that the living entity is influenced by the *avidyā* potency, as confirmed in both the *Viṣṇu Purāṇa* and the beginning of *Śrīmad-Bhāgavatam.* The living entity is mentioned in *Bhagavad-gītā* (7.5) as *parā prakṛti,* and in the *Viṣṇu Purāṇa* he is mentioned as the *parā śakti.* He is part and parcel of the Supreme Lord as potency and not as the potent. The potent can exhibit many potencies, but the potency cannot equal the potent at any stage. One potency may be overcome by another potency, but to the potent, all potencies are under control. The *jīva* potency, or the *kṣetrajña-śakti* of the Lord, has the tendency to be overpowered by the external potency, *avidyā-karma-saṁjñā,* and in this way he is placed in the awkward circumstances of material existence. The living entity cannot be forgetful of his real identity unless influenced by the *avidyā* potency. Because the living entity is prone to the influence of the *avidyā* potency, he can never equal the supreme potent.

TEXT 6

भगवानेक एवैष सर्वक्षेत्रेष्ववस्थितः ।
अमुष्य दुर्भगत्वं वा क्लेशो वा कर्मभिः कुतः ॥ ६ ॥

bhagavān eka evaiṣa
sarva-kṣetreṣv avasthitaḥ
amuṣya durbhagatvaṁ vā
kleśo vā karmabhiḥ kutaḥ

bhagavān—the Supreme Personality of Godhead; *ekaḥ*—alone; *eva eṣaḥ*—all these; *sarva*—all; *kṣetreṣu*—in the living entities; *avasthitaḥ*—situated; *amuṣya*—of the living entities; *durbhagatvam*—misfortune; *vā*—either; *kleśaḥ*—miseries; *vā*—or; *karmabhiḥ*—by activities; *kutaḥ*—what for.

TRANSLATION

The Lord, as the Supersoul, is situated in every living being's heart. Why then do the living entities' activities result in misfortune and misery?

PURPORT

The next question put forward by Vidura to Maitreya is, "Why are the living entities subjected to so many miseries and misfortunes in spite of the Lord's presence in their hearts as the Supersoul?" The body is considered a fruitful tree, and the living entity and the Lord as Supersoul are like two birds seated in that tree. The individual soul is eating the fruit of the tree, but the Supersoul, the Lord, is witnessing the activities of the other bird. A citizen of the state may be in miseries for want of sufficient supervision by the state authority, but how can it be possible that a citizen suffers from other citizens while the chief of the state is personally present? From another point of view, it is understood that the *jīva* living entity is qualitatively one with the Lord, and thus his knowledge in the pure state of life cannot be covered by nescience, especially in the presence of the Supreme Lord. How then does the living entity become subjected to ignorance and covered by the influence of *māyā?* The Lord is the father and protector of every living entity, and He is known as the *bhūta-bhṛt*, or the maintainer of the living entities. Why then should the living entity be subjected to so many sufferings and misfortunes? It should not be so, but actually we see that it happens everywhere. This question is therefore put forward by Vidura for solution.

TEXT 7

एतस्मिन्मे मनो विद्वन् खिद्यतेऽज्ञानसङ्कटे ।
तन्नः पराणुद विभो कश्मलं मानसं महत् ॥ ७ ॥

etasmin me mano vidvan
khidyate 'jñāna-saṅkaṭe
tan naḥ parāṇuda vibho
kaśmalaṁ mānasaṁ mahat

etasmin—in this; *me*—my; *manaḥ*—mind; *vidvan*—O learned one; *khidyate*—is troubling; *ajñāna*—nescience; *saṅkaṭe*—in distress; *tat*—

therefore; *naḥ*—my; *parāṇuda*—clear up; *vibho*—O great one; *kaśmalam*—illusion; *mānasam*—relating to the mind; *mahat*—great.

TRANSLATION

O great and learned one, my mind is greatly illusioned by the distress of this nescience, and I therefore request you to clear it up.

PURPORT

Such mental bewilderment as represented here by Vidura takes place for some living entities, but not for everyone, for if everyone were bewildered there would be no possibility of a solution by higher personalities.

TEXT 8

श्रीशुक उवाच
स इत्थं चोदितः क्षत्त्रा तत्त्वजिज्ञासुना मुनिः ।
प्रत्याह भगवच्चित्तः स्मयन्निव गतस्मयः ॥ ८ ॥

śrī-śuka uvāca
sa itthaṁ coditaḥ kṣattrā
tattva-jijñāsunā muniḥ
pratyāha bhagavac-cittaḥ
smayann iva gata-smayaḥ

śrī-śukaḥ uvāca—Śrī Śukadeva Gosvāmī said; *saḥ*—he (Maitreya Muni); *ittham*—in this way; *coditaḥ*—being agitated; *kṣattrā*—by Vidura; *tattva-jijñāsunā*—by one who was anxious to inquire to know the truth; *muniḥ*—the great sage; *pratyāha*—replied; *bhagavat-cittaḥ*—God conscious; *smayan*—wondering; *iva*—as if; *gata-smayaḥ*—without hesitation.

TRANSLATION

Śrī Śukadeva Gosvāmī said: O King, Maitreya, being thus agitated by the inquisitive Vidura, at first seemed astonished, but then he replied to him without hesitation, since he was fully God conscious.

PURPORT

Since the great sage Maitreya was filled with God consciousness, he had no reason to be astonished at such contradictory questions by Vidura. Therefore, although as a devotee he externally expressed surprise, as if he did not know how to reply to those questions, he immediately became perfectly settled and properly replied to Vidura. *Yasmin vijñāte sarvam evaṁ vijñātaṁ bhavati.* Anyone who is a devotee of the Lord knows about the Lord to some extent, and devotional service to the Lord makes him able to know everything by the grace of the Lord. Although a devotee may apparently express himself to be ignorant, he is full of knowledge in every intricate matter.

TEXT 9

मैत्रेय उवाच

सेयं भगवतो माया यन्नयेन विरुध्यते ।
ईश्वरस्य विमुक्तस्य कार्पण्यमुत बन्धनम् ॥ ९ ॥

maitreya uvāca
seyaṁ bhagavato māyā
yan nayena virudhyate
īśvarasya vimuktasya
kārpaṇyam uta bandhanam

maitreyaḥ uvāca—Maitreya said; *sā iyam*—such a statement; *bhagavataḥ*—of the Personality of Godhead; *māyā*—illusion; *yat*—that which; *nayena*—by logic; *virudhyate*—becomes contradictory; *īśvarasya*—of the Supreme Personality of Godhead; *vimuktasya*—of the ever liberated; *kārpaṇyam*—insufficiency; *uta*—as also, what to speak of; *bandhanam*—bondage.

TRANSLATION

Śrī Maitreya said: Certain conditioned souls put forward the theory that the Supreme Brahman, or the Personality of Godhead, is overcome by illusion, or māyā, and at the same time they maintain that He is unconditioned. This is against all logic.

PURPORT

Sometimes it appears that the Supreme Personality of Godhead, who is one hundred percent spiritual, cannot be the cause of the illusory potency which covers the knowledge of the individual soul. But factually there is no doubt that the illusory, external energy is also part and parcel of the Supreme Lord. When Vyāsadeva realized the Supreme Personality of Godhead, he saw the Lord along with His external potency, which covers the pure knowledge of the individual living entities. Why the external energy acts in this way may be considered as follows, as analyzed by great commentators like Viśvanātha Cakravartī Ṭhākura and Śrīla Jīva Gosvāmī. Although the material, illusory energy is distinct from the spiritual energy, it is one of the many energies of the Lord, and thus the material modes of nature (the mode of goodness, etc.) are surely qualities of the Lord. The energy and the energetic Personality of Godhead are not different, and although such energy is one with the Lord, He is never overpowered by it. Although the living entities are also parts and parcels of the Lord, they are overcome by the material energy. The inconceivable *yogam aiśvaram* of the Lord, as mentioned in *Bhagavad-gītā* (9.5), is misunderstood by the froggish philosophers. In order to support a theory that Nārāyaṇa (the Lord Himself) becomes a *daridra-nārāyaṇa,* a poor man, they propose that the material energy overcomes the Supreme Lord. Śrīla Jīva Gosvāmī and Śrīla Viśvanātha Cakravartī Ṭhākura, however, offer a very nice example in explanation. They say that although the sun is all light, the clouds, darkness and snowfall are all part and parcel of the sun. Without the sun there is no possibility of the sky's being overcast with clouds or darkness, nor can there be snowfall on the earth. Although life is sustained by the sun, life is also disturbed by darkness and snowfall produced by the sun. But it is also a fact that the sun itself is never overcome by darkness, clouds or snowfall; the sun is far, far away from such disturbances. Only those who have a poor fund of knowledge say that the sun is covered by a cloud or by darkness. Similarly, the Supreme Brahman, or the Parabrahman, the Personality of Godhead, is always unaffected by the influence of the material energy, although it is one of His energies (*parāsya śaktir vividhaiva śrūyate*).

There is no reason to assert that the Supreme Brahman is overpowered by the illusory energy. The clouds, darkness and snowfall can cover only a very insignificant portion of the sun's rays. Similarly, the modes of material nature may react upon the raylike living entities. It is the misfortune of the living entity, certainly not without reason, that the influence of the material energy acts on his pure consciousness and eternal bliss. This covering up of pure consciousness and eternal bliss is due to *avidyā-karmā-saṁjñā*, the energy which acts on the infinitesimal living entities who misuse their minute independence. According to *Viṣṇu Purāṇa*, *Bhagavad-gītā* and all other Vedic literatures, the living entities are generated from the *taṭasthā* energy of the Lord, and thus they are always the energy of the Lord and are not the energetic. The living entities are like the sun's rays. Although, as explained above, there is no qualitative difference between the sun and its rays, the sun's rays are sometimes overpowered by another energy of the sun, namely by clouds or by snowfall. Similarly, although the living entities are qualitatively one with the superior energy of the Lord, they have the tendency to be overpowered by the inferior, material energy. In the Vedic hymns it is said that the living entities are like the sparks of a fire. The sparks of fire also are fire, but the burning potency of the sparks is different from that of the original fire. When the sparks fly out of touch with the original fire, they come under the influence of a nonfiery atmosphere; thus they maintain the potency to be again one with the fire as sparks, but not as the original fire. The sparks can everlastingly remain within the original fire as its parts and parcels, but the moment the sparks become separated from the original fire, their misfortunes and miseries begin. The clear conclusion is that the Supreme Lord, who is the original fire, is never overpowered, but the infinitesimal sparks of the fire can become overpowered by the illusory effect of *māyā*. It is a most ludicrous argument to say that the Supreme Lord is overpowered by His own material energy. The Lord is the master of the material energy, but the living entities are in the conditioned state, controlled by the material energy. That is the version of *Bhagavad-gītā*. The froggish philosophers who put forward the argument that the Supreme Lord is overpowered by the material mode of goodness are themselves illusioned by the same material energy, although they think of themselves as liberated souls. They support their arguments by a false and laborious jugglery of words, which is a gift of the same illusory energy of the Lord. But the poor froggish philosophers, due to a false sense of knowledge, cannot understand the situation.

In the Sixth Canto, Ninth Chapter, thirty-fourth verse, of the *Śrīmad-Bhāgavatam* it is stated:

duravabodha iva tavāyaṁ vihāra-yogo yad aśaraṇo 'śarīra idam anavekṣitāsmat-samavāya ātmanaivāvikriyamāṇena saguṇam aguṇaḥ sṛjasi pāsi harasi.

Thus the demigods prayed to the Supreme Lord that although His activities are very difficult to understand, they can still be understood to some extent by those who sincerely engage in the transcendental loving service of the Lord. The demigods admitted that although the Lord is apart from the material influence or creation, He nevertheless creates, maintains and annihilates the complete cosmic manifestation by the agency of the demigods.

TEXT 10

यदर्थेन विनामुष्य पुंस आत्मविपर्ययः ।
प्रतीयत उपद्रष्टुः स्वशिरश्छेदनादिकः ॥१०॥

yad arthena vināmuṣya
puṁsa ātma-viparyayaḥ
pratīyata upadraṣṭuḥ
sva-śiraś chedanādikaḥ

yat—thus; *arthena*—a purpose or meaning; *vinā*—without; *amuṣya*—of such a one; *puṁsaḥ*—of the living entity; *ātma-viparyayaḥ*—upset about self-identification; *pratīyate*—so appear; *upadraṣṭuḥ*—of the superficial onlooker; *sva-śiraḥ*—own head; *chedana-ādikaḥ*—cutting off.

TRANSLATION

The living entity is in distress regarding his self-identity. He has no factual background, like a man who dreams that he sees his head cut off.

PURPORT

A teacher in school once threatened his pupil that he would cut off the pupil's head and hang it on the wall so that the child could see how his head had been cut off. The child became frightened and stopped his mischief. Similarly, the miseries of the pure soul and the disruption of his self-identification are managed by the external energy of the Lord, which controls those mischievous living entities who want to go against the will of the Lord. Actually there is no bondage or misery for the living entity, nor does he ever lose his pure knowledge. In his pure consciousness, when he thinks a little seriously about his position, he can understand that he is eternally subordinate to the mercy of the Supreme and that his attempt to become one with the Supreme Lord is a false illusion. Life after life the living entity falsely tries to lord it over material nature and become the lord of the material world, but there is no tangible result. At last, when frustrated, he gives up his material activities and tries to become one with the Lord and speculate with much jugglery of words, but without success.

These activities are performed under the dictation of the illusory energy. The experience is compared to the experience of one's having his head cut off in a dream. The man whose head has been cut off also *sees* that his head has been cut off. If a person's head is severed he loses his power to see. Therefore if a man sees that his head has been cut off, it means that he thinks like that in hallucination. Similarly a living entity is eternally subordinate to the Supreme Lord, and he has this knowledge with him, but, artificially, he thinks that he is God himself and that although he is God he has lost his knowledge due to *māyā*. This conception has no meaning, just as there is no meaning to seeing one's head being cut off. This is the process by which knowledge is covered. And because this artificial rebellious condition of the living entity gives him all troubles, it is to be understood that he should take to his normal life as a devotee of the Lord and be relieved from the misconception of being God. The so-called liberation of thinking oneself God is that last reaction of *avidyā* by which the living entity is entrapped. The conclusion is that a living entity deprived of eternal transcendental service to the Lord becomes illusioned in many ways. Even in his conditional life he is the eternal servant of the Lord. His servitude under the spell of illusory *māyā* is also a manifestation of his eternal condition of service. Because he has rebelled against the service of the Lord, he is therefore put in the service of the *māyā*. He is still serving, but in a perverted manner. When he wants to get out of service under material bondage, he next desires to become one with the Lord. This is another illusion. The best course, therefore, is to surrender unto the Lord and thus get rid of the illusory *māyā* for good, as confirmed in *Bhagavad-gītā* (7.14):

daivī hy eṣā guṇamayī
mama māyā duratyayā
mām eva ye prapadyante
māyām etāṁ taranti te

TEXT 11

यथा जले चन्द्रमसः कम्पादिस्तत्कृतो गुणः ।
दृश्यतेऽसन्नपि द्रष्टुरात्मनोऽनात्मनो गुणः ॥११॥

yathā jale candramasaḥ
kampādis tat-kṛto guṇaḥ
dṛśyate 'sann api draṣṭur
ātmano 'nātmano guṇaḥ

yathā—as; *jale*—in the water; *candramasaḥ*—of the moon; *kampa-ādiḥ*—quivering, etc.; *tat-kṛtaḥ*—done by the water; *guṇaḥ*—quality; *dṛśyate*—it is so seen; *asan api*—without existence; *draṣṭuḥ*—of the seer; *ātmanaḥ*—of the self; *anātmanaḥ*—of other than the self; *guṇaḥ*—quality.

TRANSLATION

As the moon reflected on water appears to the seer to tremble due to being associated with the quality of the water, so the self associated with matter appears to be qualified as matter.

PURPORT

The Supreme Soul, the Personality of Godhead, is compared to the moon in the sky, and the living entities are compared to the reflection of the moon on water. The moon in the sky is fixed and does not appear to quiver like the moon on the water. Actually, like the original moon in the sky, the moon reflected on the water should also not quiver, but because of being associated with water, the reflection appears to be quivering, although in actual fact the moon is fixed. The water moves, but the moon does not move. Similarly, the living entities appear to be tainted by material qualities like illusion, lamentation and miseries, although in the pure soul such qualities are completely absent. The word *pratīyate*, which means "apparently" and "not actually" (like the experience of having one's head cut off in a dream), is significant here. The reflection of the moon on the water is the separated rays of the moon and not the actual moon. The separated parts and parcels of the Lord entangled in the water of material existence have the quivering quality, whereas the Lord is like the actual moon in the sky, which is not at all in touch with water. The light of the sun and moon reflected on matter makes the matter bright and praiseworthy. The living symptoms are compared to the light of the sun and the moon illuminating material manifestations like trees and mountains. The reflection of the sun or moon is accepted as the real sun or moon by less intelligent men, and the pure monistic philosophy develops from these ideas. In fact, the light of the sun and the moon are actually different from the sun and moon themselves, although they are always connected. The light of the moon spread throughout the sky appears to be impersonal, but the moon planet, as it is, is personal, and the living entities on the moon planet are also personal. In the rays of the moon, different material entities appear to be comparatively more or less important. The light of the moon on the Taj Mahal appears to be more beautiful than the same light in the wilderness. Although the light of the moon is the same everywhere, due to being differently appreciated it appears different. Similarly, the light of the Lord is equally distributed everywhere, but due to being differently received, it appears to be different. One should not, therefore, accept the reflection of the moon on the water as actual and misunderstand the whole situation through monistic philosophy. The quivering quality of the moon is also variable. When the water is standing still, there is no quivering: A more settled conditioned soul quivers less, but due to material connection the quivering quality is more or less present everywhere.

TEXT 12

स वै निवृत्तिधर्मेण वासुदेवानुकम्पया ।
भगवद्भक्तियोगेन तिरोधत्ते शनैरिह ॥१२॥

sa vai nivṛtti-dharmeṇa
vāsudevānukampayā
bhagavad-bhakti-yogena
tirodhatte śanair iha

saḥ—that; *vai*—also; *nivṛtti*—detachment; *dharmeṇa*—by engagement; *vāsudeva*—the Supreme Personality of Godhead; *anukampayā*—by the mercy of; *bhagavat*—in relation with the Personality of Godhead; *bhakti-yogena*—by linking up; *tirodhatte*—diminishes; *śanaiḥ*—gradually; *iha*—in this existence.

TRANSLATION

But that misconception of self-identity can be diminished gradually by the mercy of the Personality of Godhead, Vāsudeva, through the process of devotional service to the Lord in the mode of detachment.

PURPORT

The quivering quality of material existence, which comes from identification with matter or from thinking oneself, under the material influence of philosophical speculation, to be God, can be eradicated by devotional service to the Lord, by the mercy of the Personality of Godhead, Vāsudeva. As discussed in the First Canto, because the application of devotional service to Lord Vāsudeva invites pure knowledge, it quickly detaches one from the material conception of life and thus revives one's normal condition of spiritual existence, even in this life, and frees one from the material winds which cause one to quiver. Only knowledge in devotional service can elevate one towards the path of liberation. The development of knowledge for the purpose of knowing everything, without rendering devotional service, is considered fruitless labor, and one cannot get the desired result by such labor of love. Lord Vāsudeva is pleased by devotional service only, and thus His mercy is realized by association with pure devotees of the Lord. Pure devotees of the Lord are transcendental to all material desires, including the desire for the results of fruitive activities and philosophical speculation. If one wants to acquire the mercy of the Lord, he has to associate with pure devotees. Such association alone can, by degrees, release one from the quivering elements.

TEXT 13

यदेन्द्रियोपरामोऽथ द्रष्ट्रात्मनि परे हरौ ।
विलीयन्ते तदा क्लेशाः संसुप्तस्येव कृत्स्नशः ॥१३॥

yadendriyoparāmo 'tha
draṣṭrātmani pare harau
vilīyante tadā kleśāḥ
saṁsuptasyeva kṛtsnaśaḥ

yadā—when; *indriya*—senses; *uparāmaḥ*—satiated; *atha*—thus; *draṣṭṛ-ātmani*—unto the seer, the Supersoul; *pare*—in the Transcendence; *harau*—unto the Supreme Personality of Godhead; *vilīyante*—become merged in; *tadā*—at that time; *kleśāḥ*—miseries; *saṁsuptasya*—one who has enjoyed sound sleep; *iva*—like; *kṛtsnaśaḥ*—completely.

TRANSLATION

When the senses are satisfied in the seer-Supersoul, the Personality of Godhead, and merge in Him, all miseries are completely vanquished, as after a sound sleep.

PURPORT

The quivering of the living entity as described above is due to the senses. Since the entire material existence is meant for sense gratification, the senses are the medium of material activities, and they cause the quivering of the steady soul. Therefore, these senses are to be detached from all such material activities. According to the impersonalists the senses are stopped from work by merging the soul in the Supersoul Brahman. The devotees, however, do not stop the material senses from acting, but they engage their transcendental senses in the service of the Transcendence, the Supreme Personality of Godhead. In either case, the activities of the senses in the material field are to be stopped by cultivation of knowledge, and, if possible, they can be engaged in the service of the Lord. The senses are transcendental in nature, but their activities become polluted when contaminated by matter. We have to treat the senses to cure them of the material disease, not stop them from acting, as suggested by the impersonalist. In *Bhagavad-gītā* (2.59) it is said that one ceases all material activities only when satisfied by contact with a better engagement. Consciousness is active by nature and cannot be stopped from working. Artificially stopping a mischievous child is not the real remedy. The child must be given some better engagement so that he will automatically stop causing mischief. In the same way, the mischievous activities of the senses can be stopped only by better engagement in relation with the Supreme Personality of Godhead. When the eyes are engaged in seeing the beautiful form of the Lord, the tongue engaged in tasting *prasāda*, or remnants of foodstuff offered to the Lord, the ears are engaged in hearing His glories, the hands engaged in cleaning the temple of the Lord, the legs engaged in visiting His temples—or when all the senses are engaged in transcendental variegatedness—then only can the transcendental senses become satiated and eternally free from material engagement. The Lord, as the Supersoul residing in everyone's heart and as the Supreme Personality of Godhead in the transcendental world far beyond the material creation, is the seer of all our activities. Our activities must be so transcendentally saturated that the Lord will be kind enough to look upon us favorably and engage us in His transcendental service; then only can the senses be satisfied completely and be no longer troubled by material attraction.

TEXT 14

अशेषसंक्लेशशमं विधत्ते गुणानुवादश्रवणं मुरारेः ।
किं वा पुनस्तच्चरणारविन्दपरागसेवारतिरात्मलब्धा ॥१४॥

aśeṣa-saṅkleśa-śamaṁ vidhatte
guṇānuvāda-śravaṇaṁ murāreḥ
kiṁ vā punas tac-caraṇāravinda-
parāga-sevā-ratir ātma-labdhā

aśeṣa—unlimited; *saṅkleśa*—miserable conditions; *śamam*—cessation; *vidhatte*—can perform; *guṇa-anuvāda*—of the transcendental name, form, qualities, pastimes, entourage and paraphernalia, etc.; *śravaṇam*—hearing and chanting; *murāreḥ*—of Murāri (Śrī Kṛṣṇa), the Personality of Godhead; *kim vā*—what to speak of; *punaḥ*—again; *tat*—His; *caraṇa-aravinda*—lotus feet; *parāga-sevā*—to the service of the flavorful dust; *ratiḥ*—attraction; *ātma-labdhā*—those who have gained such self-achievement.

TRANSLATION

Simply by chanting and hearing of the transcendental name, form, etc., of the Personality of Godhead, Śrī Kṛṣṇa, one can achieve the cessation of unlimited miserable conditions. Therefore what to speak of those who have attained attraction for serving the flavor of the dust of the Lord's lotus feet?

PURPORT

Two different methods for controlling the material senses are recommended in the Vedic scriptural wisdom. One of them is the process of *jñāna*, or the path of philosophical understanding of the Supreme—Brahma, Paramātmā and Bhagavān. The other is that of direct engagement in the transcendental loving devotional service of the Lord. Of these two most popular methods, the path of devotional service is recommended here as the best because one on the path of devotional service does not have to wait for the attainment of the fruitive results of pious activities or for the results of knowledge. The two stages of executing devotional service are, first, the stage of practicing devotional service with our present senses under the regulations of the recognized scriptures and, second, attaining sincere attachment for serving the particles of the dust of the lotus feet of the Lord. The first stage is called *sādhana-bhakti*, or devotional service for the neophyte, which is rendered under the direction of a pure devotee, and the second stage is called *rāga-bhakti*, in which the mature devotee automatically takes to the various services of the Lord out of sincere attachment. The great sage Maitreya now gives the final answer to all the questions of Vidura: devotional service to the Lord is the ultimate means to mitigate all the miserable conditions of material existence. The path of knowledge or that of mystic gymnastics may be adopted as a means for the purpose, but unless mixed with *bhakti*, or devotional service, they are unable to award the desired result. By practicing *sādhana-bhakti* one may gradually rise to the point of *rāga-bhakti*, and by performing *rāga-bhakti* in loving transcendental service one can even control the Supreme Powerful Lord.

TEXT 15

विदुर उवाच
संछिन्नः संशयो मह्यं तव सूक्तासिना विभो ।
उभयत्रापि भगवन्मनो मे सम्प्रधावति ॥१५॥

vidura uvāca
sañchinnaḥ saṁśayo mahyaṁ
tava sūktāsinā vibho
ubhayatrāpi bhagavan
mano me sampradhāvati

viduraḥ uvāca—Vidura said; *sañchinnaḥ*—cut off; *saṁśayaḥ*—doubts; *mahyam*—unto me; *tava*—your; *sūkta-asinā*—by the weapon of convincing words; *vibho*—O my lord; *ubhayatra api*—both in God and in the living entity; *bhagavan*—O powerful one; *manaḥ*—mind; *me*—my; *sampradhāvati*—perfectly entering.

TRANSLATION

Vidura said: O powerful sage, my lord, all my doubts about the Supreme Personality of Godhead and the living entities have now been removed by your convincing words. My mind is now perfectly entering into them.

PURPORT

The science of Kṛṣṇa, or the science of God and the living entities, is so subtle that even a personality like Vidura has to consult persons like the sage Maitreya. Doubts about the eternal relationship of the Lord and the living entity are created by mental speculators in different ways, but the conclusive fact is that the relationship of God and the living entity is one of the predominator and the predominated. The Lord is the eternal predominator, and the living entities are eternally predominated. Real knowledge of this relationship entails reviving the lost consciousness to this standard, and the process for such revival is devotional service to the Lord. By clearly understanding from authorities like the sage Maitreya, one can become situated in real knowledge, and the disturbed mind can thus be fixed on the progressive path.

TEXT 16

साध्वेतद् व्याहृतं विद्वन्नात्ममायायनं हरेः ।
आभात्यपार्थं निर्मूलं विश्वमूलं न यद्बहिः ॥१६॥

sādhv etad vyāhṛtaṁ vidvan
nātma-māyāyanaṁ hareḥ
ābhāty apārthaṁ nirmūlaṁ
viśva-mūlaṁ na yad bahiḥ

sādhu—as good as it should be; *etat*—all these explanations; *vyāhṛtam*—thus spoken; *vidvan*—O learned one; *na*—not; *ātma*—the self; *māyā*—energy; *ayanam*—movement; *hareḥ*—of the Personality of Godhead; *ābhāti*—appears; *apārtham*—without meaning; *nirmūlam*—without basis; *viśva-mūlam*—the origin is the Supreme; *na*—not; *yat*—which; *bahiḥ*—outside.

TRANSLATION

O learned sage, your explanations are very good, as they should be. Disturbances to the conditioned soul have no other basis than the movement of the external energy of the Lord.

PURPORT

A living entity's unlawful desire to become one with the Lord in every respect is the root cause of the entire material manifestation, for otherwise the Lord has no need to create such a manifestation, even for His pastimes. The conditioned soul, under the spell of the external energy of the Lord, falsely suffers many unfortunate incidents in material life. The Lord is the predominator of the external energy, *māyā*, whereas the living entity is predominated by the same *māyā* under the material condition. The false attempt of the living entity to occupy the predominating post of the Lord is the cause of his material bondage, and the conditioned soul's attempt to become one with the Lord is the last snare of *māyā*.

TEXT 17

यश्च मूढतमो लोके यश्च बुद्धेः परं गतः ।
तावुभौ सुखमेधेते क्लिश्यत्यन्तरितो जनः ॥१७॥

yaś ca mūḍhatamo loke
yaś ca buddheḥ paraṁ gataḥ
tāv ubhau sukham edhete
kliśyaty antarito janaḥ

yaḥ—one who is; *ca*—also; *mūḍha-tamaḥ*—the lowest of the fools; *loke*—in the world; *yaḥ ca*—and one who is; *buddheḥ*—of intelligence; *param*—transcendental; *gataḥ*—gone; *tau*—of them; *ubhau*—both; *sukham*—happiness; *edhete*—enjoy; *kliśyati*—suffer; *antaritaḥ*—situated between; *janaḥ*—persons.

TRANSLATION

Both the lowest of fools and he who is transcendental to all intelligence enjoy happiness, whereas persons between them suffer the material pangs.

PURPORT

The lowest of fools do not understand material miseries; they pass their lives merrily and do not inquire into the miseries of life. Such persons are almost on the level of the animals, who, although in the eyes of superiors are always miserable in life, are unaware of material distresses. A hog's life is degraded in its standard of happiness, which entails living in a filthy place, engaging in sex enjoyment at every opportune moment, and laboring hard in a struggle for existence, but this is unknown to the hog. Similarly, human beings who are unaware of the miseries of material existence and are happy in sex life and hard labor are the lowest of fools. Yet because they have no sense of miseries, they supposedly enjoy so-called happiness. The other class of men, those who are liberated and are situated in the transcendental position above intelligence, are really happy and are called *paramahaṁsas.* But persons who are neither like hogs and dogs nor on the level of the *paramahaṁsas* feel the material pangs, and for them inquiry about the Supreme Truth is necessary. The *Vedānta-sūtra* states, *athāto brahma-jijñāsā:* "Now one should inquire about Brahman." This inquiry is necessary for those who are between the *paramahaṁsas* and the fools who have forgotten the question of self-realization in the midst of life in sense gratification.

TEXT 18

अर्थाभावं विनिश्चित्य प्रतीतस्यापि नात्मनः ।
तां चापि युष्मच्चरणसेवयाहं पराणुदे ॥१८॥

arthābhāvaṁ viniścitya
pratītasyāpi nātmanaḥ
tāṁ cāpi yuṣmac-caraṇa-
sevayāhaṁ parāṇude

artha-abhāvam—without substance; *viniścitya*—being ascertained; *pratītasya*—of the apparent values; *api*—also; *na*—never; *ātmanaḥ*—of the self; *tām*—that; *ca*—also; *api*—thus; *yuṣmat*—your; *caraṇa*—feet; *sevayā*—by service; *aham*—myself; *parāṇude*—shall be able to give up.

TRANSLATION

But, my dear sir, I am obliged to you because now I can understand that this material manifestation is without substance, although it appears real. I am confident that by serving your feet it will be possible for me to give up the false idea.

PURPORT

The sufferings of the conditioned soul are superficial and have no intrinsic value, like the cutting off of one's head in a dream. Yet although this statement is theoretically very true, it is very difficult for the common man or the neophyte on the transcendental path to realize practically. However, by serving the feet of great transcendentalists like Maitreya Muni and by constantly associating with them, one is enabled to give up the false idea that the soul suffers from material pangs.

TEXT 19

यत्सेवया भगवतः कूटस्थस्य मधुद्विषः ।
रतिरासो भवेत्तीव्रः पादयोर्व्यसनार्दनः ॥१९॥

yat-sevayā bhagavataḥ
kūṭa-sthasya madhu-dviṣaḥ

rati-rāso bhavet tīvraḥ
pādayor vyasanārdanaḥ

yat—to whom; *sevayā*—by service; *bhagavataḥ*—of the Personality of Godhead; *kūṭa-sthasya*—of the unchangeable; *madhu-dviṣaḥ*—the enemy of the Madhu *asura; rati-rāsaḥ*—attachment in different relationships; *bhavet*—develops; *tīvraḥ*—highly ecstatic; *pādayoḥ*—of the feet; *vyasana*—distresses; *ardanaḥ*—vanquishing.

TRANSLATION

By serving the feet of the spiritual master, one is enabled to develop transcendental ecstasy in the service of the Personality of Godhead, who is the unchangeable enemy of the Madhu demon and whose service vanquishes one's material distresses.

PURPORT

The association of a bona fide spiritual master like the sage Maitreya can be of absolute help in achieving transcendental attachment for the direct service of the Lord. The Lord is the enemy of the Madhu demon, or in other words He is the enemy of the sufferings of His pure devotee. The word *rati-rāsaḥ* is significant in this verse. Service to the Lord is rendered in different transcendental mellows (relationships): neutral, active, friendly, parental and nuptial. A living entity in the liberated position of transcendental service to the Lord becomes attracted to one of the above-mentioned mellows, and when one is engaged in transcendental loving service to the Lord, one's service attachment in the material world is automatically vanquished. As stated in *Bhagavad-gītā* (2.59), *rasa-varjaṁ raso 'py asya paraṁ dṛṣṭvā nivartate.*

TEXT 20

दुरापा ह्यल्पतपसः सेवा वैकुण्ठवर्त्मसु ।
यत्रोपगीयते नित्यं देवदेवो जनार्दनः ॥२०॥

durāpā hy alpa-tapasaḥ
sevā vaikuṇṭha-vartmasu

yatropagīyate nityaṁ
deva-devo janārdanaḥ

durāpā—rarely obtainable; *hi*—certainly; *alpa-tapasaḥ*—of one whose austerity is meager; *sevā*—service; *vaikuṇṭha*—the transcendental kingdom of God; *vartmasu*—on the path of; *yatra*—wherein; *upagīyate*—is glorified; *nityam*—always; *deva*—of the demigods; *devaḥ*—the Lord; *jana-ardanaḥ*—the controller of the living entities.

TRANSLATION

Persons whose austerity is meager can hardly obtain the service of the pure devotees who are progressing on the path back to the kingdom of Godhead, the Vaikuṇṭhas. Pure devotees engage one hundred percent in glorifying the Supreme Lord, who is the Lord of the demigods and the controller of all living entities.

PURPORT

The path of liberation, as recommended by all authorities, is to serve the *mahātmā* transcendentalists. As far as *Bhagavad-gītā* is concerned, the *mahātmās* are the pure devotees who are on the path to Vaikuṇṭha, the kingdom of God, and who always chant and hear the glories of the Lord rather than talk of dry, profitless philosophy. This system of association has been recommended since time immemorial, but in this age of quarrel and hypocrisy it is especially recommended by Lord Śrī Caitanya Mahāprabhu. Even if one has no assets of favorable austerity, if he nevertheless takes shelter of the *mahātmās*, who are engaged in chanting and hearing the glories of the Lord, he is sure to make progress on the path back home, back to Godhead.

TEXT 21

सृष्ट्वाग्रे महदादीनि सविकाराण्यनुक्रमात् ।
तेभ्यो विराजमुद्धृत्य तमनु प्राविशद्विभुः ॥२१॥

sṛṣṭvāgre mahad-ādīni
sa-vikārāṇy anukramāt

tebhyo virājam uddhṛtya
tam anu prāviśad vibhuḥ

sṛṣṭvā—after creating; *agre*—in the beginning; *mahat-ādīni*—the total material energy; *sa-vikārāṇi*—along with the sense organs; *anukramāt*—by a gradual process of differentiation; *tebhyaḥ*—out of that; *virājam*—the gigantic universal form; *uddhṛtya*—manifesting; *tam*—unto that; *anu*—later; *prāviśat*—entered; *vibhuḥ*—the Supreme.

TRANSLATION

After creating the total material energy, the mahat-tattva, and thereby manifesting the gigantic universal form with senses and sense organs, the Supreme Lord entered within it.

PURPORT

Fully satisfied by the answers of the sage Maitreya, Vidura wanted to understand the remaining portions of the creative function of the Lord, and he took the clue from the previous topics.

TEXT 22

यमाहुराद्यं पुरुषं सहस्राङ्घ्र्यूरुबाहुकम् ।
यत्र विश्व इमे लोकाः सविकाशं त आसते ॥२२॥

yam āhur ādyaṁ puruṣaṁ
sahasrāṅghry-ūru-bāhukam
yatra viśva ime lokāḥ
sa-vikāśaṁ ta āsate

yam—who; *āhuḥ*—is called; *ādyam*—original; *puruṣam*—incarnation for cosmic manifestation; *sahasra*—thousand; *aṅghri*—legs; *ūru*—thighs; *bāhukam*—hands; *yatra*—wherein; *viśvaḥ*—the universe; *ime*—all these; *lokāḥ*—planets; *sa-vikāśam*—with respective developments; *te*—all of them; *āsate*—living.

TRANSLATION

The puruṣa incarnation lying on the Causal Ocean is called the original puruṣa in the material creations, and in His virāṭ form, in whom all the planets and their inhabitants live, He has many thousands of legs and hands.

PURPORT

The first *puruṣa* is Kāraṇodakaśāyī Viṣṇu, the second *puruṣa* is Garbhodakaśāyī Viṣṇu, and the third *puruṣa* is Kṣīrodakaśāyī Viṣṇu, in whom is contemplated the *virāṭ-puruṣa,* the gigantic form in which all the planets with their different developments and inhabitants are floating.

TEXT 23

यस्मिन् दशविधः प्राणः सेन्द्रियार्थेन्द्रियस्त्रिवृत् ।
त्वयेरितो यतो वर्णास्तद्विभूतीर्वदस्व नः ॥२३॥

yasmin daśa-vidhaḥ prāṇaḥ
sendriyārthendriyas tri-vṛt
tvayerito yato varṇās
tad-vibhūtīr vadasva naḥ

yasmin—in which; *daśa-vidhaḥ*—ten kinds of; *prāṇaḥ*—air of life; *sa*—with; *indriya*—senses; *artha*—interest; *indriyaḥ*—of the senses; *tri-vṛt*—three kinds of life vigor; *tvayā*—by you; *īritaḥ*—explained; *yataḥ*—wherefrom; *varṇāḥ*—four specific divisions; *tat-vibhūtīḥ*—prowess; *vadasva*—please describe; *naḥ*—unto me.

TRANSLATION

O great brāhmaṇa, you have told me that the gigantic virāṭ form and His senses, sense objects and ten kinds of life air exist with three kinds of life vigor. Now, if you will, kindly explain to me the different powers of the specific divisions.

TEXT 24

यत्र पुत्रैश्च पौत्रैश्च नप्तृभिः सह गोत्रजैः ।
प्रजा विचित्राकृतय आसन् याभिरिदं ततम् ॥२४॥

yatra putraiś ca pautraiś ca
naptṛbhiḥ saha gotrajaiḥ
prajā vicitrākṛtaya
āsan yābhir idaṁ tatam

yatra—wherein; *putraiḥ*—along with sons; *ca*—and; *pautraiḥ*—along with grandsons; *ca*—also; *naptṛbhiḥ*—with grandsons from daughters; *saha*—along with; *gotra-jaiḥ*—of the same family; *prajāḥ*—generations; *vicitra*—of different kinds; *ākṛtayaḥ*—so done; *āsan*—exist; *yābhiḥ*—by whom; *idam*—all these planets; *tatam*—spread.

TRANSLATION

O my lord, I think that the prowess manifest in the forms of sons, grandsons and family members has spread all over the universe in different varieties and species.

TEXT 25

प्रजापतीनां स पतिश्चक्लृपे कान् प्रजापतीन् ।
सर्गांश्चैवानुसर्गांश्च मनून्मन्वन्तराधिपान् ॥२५॥

prajāpatīnāṁ sa patiś
cakḷpe kān prajāpatīn
sargāṁś caivānusargāṁś ca
manūn manvantarādhipān

prajā-patīnām—of the demigods like Brahmā and others; *saḥ*—he; *patiḥ*—leader; *cakḷpe*—decided; *kān*—whomsoever; *prajāpatīn*—fathers of the living entities; *sargān*—generations; *ca*—also; *eva*—certainly; *anusargān*—later generations; *ca*—and; *manun*—the Manus; *manvantara-adhipān*—and the changes of such.

TRANSLATION

O learned brāhmaṇa, please describe how the leader of all the demigods, namely Prajāpati, Brahmā, decided to establish the various Manus, the heads of the ages. Please describe the Manus also, and please describe the descendants of those Manus.

PURPORT

The human race, or *manuṣya-sara*, descends from the Manus, sons and grandsons of the Prajāpati, Brahmā. The descendants of Manu reside in all the different planets and rule all the universe.

TEXT 26

उपर्यधश्च ये लोका भूमेर्मित्रात्मजासते ।
तेषां संस्थां प्रमाणं च भूर्लोकस्य च वर्णय ॥२६॥

upary adhaś ca ye lokā
bhūmer mitrātmajāsate
teṣāṁ saṁsthāṁ pramāṇaṁ ca
bhūr-lokasya ca varṇaya

upari—on the head; *adhaḥ*—underneath; *ca*—also; *ye*—which; *lokāḥ*—planets; *bhūmeḥ*—of the earth; *mitra-ātmaja*—O son of Mitrā (Maitreya Muni); *āsate*—do exist; *teṣām*—their; *saṁsthām*—situation; *pramāṇam ca*—also their measurement; *bhūḥ-lokasya*—of the earthly planets; *ca*—also; *varṇaya*—please describe.

TRANSLATION

O son of Mitrā, kindly describe how the planets are situated above the earth as well as underneath it, and also please mention their measurement as well as that of the earthly planets.

PURPORT

Yasmin vijñāte sarvam evaṁ vijñātaṁ bhavati. This Vedic hymn declares emphatically that the devotee of the Lord knows everything material and spiritual in relationship with the Lord. Devotees are not simply emotional, as is ill conceived by certain less intelligent men. Their direction is practical. They know everything that is and all the details of the Lord's domination over the different creations.

TEXT 27

तिर्यङ्मानुषदेवानां सरीसृपपतत्त्रिणाम् ।
वद नः सर्गसंव्यूहं गार्भस्वेदद्विजोद्भिदाम् ॥२७॥

tiryaṅ-mānuṣa-devānāṁ
sarīsṛpa-patattriṇām
vada naḥ sarga-saṁvyūhaṁ
gārbha-sveda-dvijodbhidām

tiryak—subhuman; *mānuṣa*—human beings; *devānām*—of the superhuman beings, or demigods; *sarīsṛpa*—reptiles; *patattriṇām*—of the birds; *vada*—kindly describe; *naḥ*—unto me; *sarga*—generation; *saṁvyūham*—specific divisions; *gārbha*—embryonic; *sveda*—perspiration; *dvija*—twice-born; *udbhidām*—of the planets, etc.

TRANSLATION

Also please describe the living beings under different classifications: subhumans, humans, those born of the embryo, those born of perspiration, those who are twice-born [birds], and the plants and vegetables. Kindly describe their generations and subdivisions also.

TEXT 28

गुणावतारैर्विश्वस्य सर्गस्थित्यप्ययाश्रयम् ।
सृजतः श्रीनिवासस्य व्याचक्ष्वोदारविक्रमम् ॥२८॥

guṇāvatārair viśvasya
sarga-sthity-apyayāśrayam
sṛjataḥ śrīnivāsasya
vyācakṣvodāra-vikramam

guṇa—modes of material nature; *avatāraiḥ*—of the incarnations; *viśvasya*—of the universe; *sarga*—creation; *sthiti*—maintenance; *apyaya*—destruction; *āśrayam*—and ultimate rest; *sṛjataḥ*—of the one who creates; *śrīnivāsasya*—of the Personality of Godhead; *vyācakṣva*—kindly describe; *udāra*—magnanimous; *vikramam*—specific activities.

TRANSLATION

Please also describe the incarnations of the material modes of nature—Brahmā, Viṣṇu and Maheśvara—and please describe the incarnation of the Supreme Personality of Godhead and His magnanimous activities.

PURPORT

Although Brahmā, Viṣṇu and Maheśvara, the three incarnations of the material modes of nature, are the principal deities for the creation, maintenance and destruction of the cosmic manifestation, they are not the final authority. The Supreme Personality of Godhead Lord Kṛṣṇa is the ultimate goal, the cause of all causes. He is the *āśraya*, or the final rest of everything.

TEXT 29

वर्णाश्रमविभागांश्च रूपशीलस्वभावतः ।
ऋषीणां जन्मकर्माणि वेदस्य च विकर्षणम् ॥२९॥

varṇāśrama-vibhāgāṁś ca
rūpa-śīla-svabhāvataḥ
ṛṣīṇāṁ janma-karmāṇi
vedasya ca vikarṣaṇam

varṇa-āśrama—the four divisions of social statuses and orders of spiritual culture; *vibhāgān*—respective divisions; *ca*—also; *rūpa*—personal features; *śīla-svabhāvataḥ*—personal character; *ṛṣīṇām*—of the sages; *janma*—birth; *karmāṇi*—activities; *vedasya*—of the *Vedas; ca*—and; *vikarṣaṇam*—categorical divisions.

TRANSLATION

O great sage, kindly describe the divisions and orders of human society in terms of symptoms, behavior and the characteristics of mental equilibrium and sense control. Also please describe the births of the great sages and the categorical divisions of the Vedas.

PURPORT

The four statuses and orders of human society—*brāhmaṇas, kṣatriyas, vaiśyas* and *śūdras*, as well as *brahmacārīs, gṛhasthas, vānaprasthas* and *sannyāsīs*—are all divisions of quality, education, culture and spiritual advancement attained by practicing control of the mind and the senses. All these divisions are based on the particular nature of each individual person, not on the principle of birth. Birth is not mentioned in this verse because birth is immaterial. Vidura is famous in history as born of a *śūdrāṇī* mother, yet he is more than a *brāhmaṇa* by qualification because he is seen here to be the disciple of a great sage, Maitreya Muni. Unless one achieves at least the brahminical qualifications, one cannot understand the Vedic hymns. *Mahābhārata* is also a division of the *Vedas*, but it is meant for women, *śūdras* and *dvija-bandhus*, the worthless children of the higher section. The less intelligent section of society can avail themselves of the Vedic instructions simply by studying the *Mahābhārata*.

TEXT 30

यज्ञस्य च वितानानि योगस्य च पथः प्रभो ।
नैष्कर्म्यस्य च सांख्यस्य तन्त्रं वा भगवत्स्मृतम् ॥३०॥

yajñasya ca vitānāni
yogasya ca pathaḥ prabho
naiṣkarmyasya ca sāṅkhyasya
tantraṁ vā bhagavat-smṛtam

yajñasya—of sacrifices; *ca*—also; *vitānāni*—expansions; *yogasya*—of the mystic powers; *ca*—also; *pathaḥ*—ways; *prabho*—O my lord; *naiṣkarmyasya*—of knowledge; *ca*—and; *sāṅkhyasya*—of analytical studies; *tantram*—the path of devotional service; *vā*—as well as; *bhagavat*—in relation with the Personality of Godhead; *smṛtam*—regulative principles.

TRANSLATION

Please also describe the expansions of different sacrifices and the paths of mystic powers, analytical study of knowledge, and devotional service, all with their respective regulations.

PURPORT

The word *tantram* is significant herein. Sometimes *tantram* is misunderstood to be the black spiritual science of materialistic persons engaged in sense gratification, but here *tantram* means the science of devotional service compiled by Śrīla Nārada Muni. One can take advantage of such regulative explanations of the path of devotional service and make progressive advancement in the devotional service of the Lord. Sāṅkhya philosophy is the basic principle of acquiring knowledge, as will be explained by the sage Maitreya. The Sāṅkhya philosophy enunciated by Kapiladeva, the son of Devahūti, is the real source of knowledge about the Supreme Truth. Knowledge not based on the Sāṅkhya philosophy is mental speculation and can yield no tangible profit.

TEXT 31

पाषण्डपथवैषम्यं प्रतिलोमनिवेशनम् ।
जीवस्य गतयो याश्च यावतीर्गुणकर्मजाः ॥३१॥

pāṣaṇḍa-patha-vaiṣamyaṁ
pratiloma-niveśanam
jīvasya gatayo yāś ca
yāvatīr guṇa-karmajāḥ

pāṣaṇḍa-patha—the path of the faithless; *vaiṣamyam*—imperfection by contradiction; *pratiloma*—crossbreeding; *niveśanam*—situation; *jīvasya*—of the living entities; *gatayaḥ*—movements; *yāḥ*—as they are; *ca*—also; *yāvatīḥ*—as many as; *guṇa*—modes of material nature; *karma-jāḥ*—generated by different work.

TRANSLATION

Please also describe the imperfections and contradictions of the faithless atheists, the situation of crossbreeding, and the movements of the living entities in various species of life according to their particular modes of nature and work.

PURPORT

The combination of living entities in different modes of material nature is called crossbreeding. The faithless atheists do not believe in the existence of God, and thus their paths of philosophy are contradictory. Atheistic philosophies never agree with one another. Different species of life are evidence of varieties of mixtures of the modes of material nature.

TEXT 32

धर्मार्थकाममोक्षाणां निमित्तान्यविरोधतः ।
वार्तया दण्डनीतेश्च श्रुतस्य च विधिं पृथक् ॥३२॥

dharmārtha-kāma-mokṣāṇāṁ
nimittāny avirodhataḥ
vārtāyā daṇḍa-nīteś ca
śrutasya ca vidhiṁ pṛthak

dharma—religiosity; *artha*—economic development; *kāma*—sense gratification; *mokṣāṇām*—salvation; *nimittāni*—causes; *avirodhataḥ*—without being contradictory; *vārtāyāḥ*—on the principles of the means of livelihood; *daṇḍa-nīteḥ*—of law and order; *ca*—also; *śrutasya*—of the codes of scriptures; *ca*—also; *vidhim*—regulations; *pṛthak*—different.

TRANSLATION

You may also describe the noncontradictory causes of religiosity, economic development, sense gratification and salvation and also the different means of livelihood and different processes of law and order as mentioned in the revealed scriptures.

TEXT 33

श्राद्धस्य च विधिं ब्रह्मन् पितॄणां सर्गमेव च ।
ग्रहनक्षत्रताराणां कालावयवसंस्थितिम् ॥३३॥

śrāddhasya ca vidhiṁ brahman
pitṝṇāṁ sargam eva ca
graha-nakṣatra-tārāṇāṁ
kālāvayava-saṁsthitim

śrāddhasya—of the periodical offerings of respects; *ca*—also; *vidhim*—regulations; *brahman*—O *brāhmaṇa; pitṝṇām*—of the forefathers; *sargam*—creation; *eva*—as; *ca*—also; *graha*—planetary system; *nakṣatra*—the stars; *tārāṇām*—luminaries; *kāla*—time; *avayava*—duration; *saṁsthitim*—situations.

TRANSLATION

Please also explain the regulations for offering respects to the forefathers, the creation of the Pitṛloka, the time schedule in the planets, stars and luminaries, and their respective situations.

PURPORT

The time durations of day and night as well as months and years are different in the different planets, stars and luminaries. The higher planets like the moon and Venus have time measurements different from those of the earth. It is said that six months of this planet earth equal one day of the higher planets. In *Bhagavad-gītā* the duration of one day in Brahmaloka is measured to be 1,000 times the four *yugas,* or 4,300,000 years multiplied by 1,000. And the month and year in Brahmaloka are calculated in that measure.

TEXT 34

दानस्य तपसो वापि यच्चेष्टापूर्तयोः फलम् ।
प्रवासस्थस्य यो धर्मो यश्च पुंस उतापदि ॥३४॥

dānasya tapaso vāpi
yac ceṣṭā-pūrtayoḥ phalam
pravāsa-sthasya yo dharmo
yaś ca puṁsa utāpadi

dānasya—of charity; *tapasaḥ*—of penance; *vāpi*—lake; *yat*—that which; *ca*—and; *iṣṭā*—endeavor; *pūrtayoḥ*—of reservoirs of water; *phalam*—fruitive result; *pravāsa-sthasya*—one who is away from home; *yaḥ*—that which; *dharmaḥ*—duty; *yaḥ ca*—and which; *puṁsaḥ*—of man; *uta*—described; *āpadi*—in danger.

TRANSLATION

Please also describe the fruitive results of charity and penance and of digging reservoirs of water. Please describe the situation of persons who are away from home and also the duty of a man in an awkward position.

PURPORT

The digging of reservoirs of water for public use is a great work of charity, and retiring from family life after fifty years of age is a great act of penance performed by the sober human being.

TEXT 35

येन वा भगवांस्तुष्येद्धर्मयोनिर्जनार्दनः ।
सम्प्रसीदति वा येषामेतदाख्याहि मेऽनघ ॥३५॥

yena vā bhagavāṁs tuṣyed
dharma-yonir janārdanaḥ
samprasīdati vā yeṣām
etad ākhyāhi me 'nagha

yena—by which; *vā*—either; *bhagavān*—the Personality of Godhead; *tuṣyet*—is satisfied; *dharma-yoniḥ*—the father of all religion; *janārdanaḥ*—the controller of all living beings; *samprasīdati*—completely satisfied; *vā*—either, or; *yeṣām*—of those; *etat*—all these; *ākhyāhi*—kindly describe; *me*—unto me; *anagha*—O sinless one.

TRANSLATION

O sinless one, because the Personality of Godhead, the controller of all living entities, is the father of all religion and all those who are candidates for religious activities, kindly describe how He can be completely satisfied.

PURPORT

All religious activities are meant ultimately to satisfy the Supreme Personality of Godhead. The Lord is the father of all religious principles. As stated in *Bhagavad-gītā* (7.16), four kinds of pious men—the needy, the distressed, the enlightened and the inquisitive—approach the Lord in devotional service, and their devotion is mixed with material affection. But above them are the pure devotees, whose devotion is not tainted by any material tinges of fruitive work or speculative knowledge. Those who are only miscreants throughout their lives are compared to demons

(Bg. 7.15). They are bereft of all knowledge, in spite of any academic educational career they may pursue. Such miscreants are never candidates for satisfying the Lord.

TEXT 36

अनुव्रतानां शिष्याणां पुत्राणां च द्विजोत्तम ।
अनापृष्टमपि ब्रूयुर्गुरवो दीनवत्सलाः ॥३६॥

anuvratānāṁ śiṣyāṇāṁ
putrāṇāṁ ca dvijottama
anāpṛṣṭam api brūyur
guravo dīna-vatsalāḥ

anuvratānām—the followers; *śiṣyāṇām*—of the disciples; *putrāṇām*—of the sons; *ca*—also; *dvija-uttama*—O best amongst the *brāhmaṇas; anāpṛṣṭam*—that which is not asked for; *api*—in spite of; *brūyuḥ*—please describe; *guravaḥ*—the spiritual masters; *dīna-vatsalāḥ*—who are kind to the needy.

TRANSLATION

O best among the brāhmaṇas, those who are spiritual masters are very kind to the needy. They are always kind to their followers, disciples and sons, and without being asked by them, the spiritual master describes all that is knowledge.

PURPORT

There are many subjects to be known from the bona fide spiritual master. The followers, disciples and sons are all on one level for the bona fide spiritual master, and he is always kind to them and always speaks to them on transcendental subjects, even though he is not asked by them. That is the nature of the bona fide spiritual master. Vidura appealed to Maitreya Muni to speak on subjects about which he might not have asked.

TEXT 37

तत्त्वानां भगवंस्तेषां कतिधा प्रतिसंक्रमः ।
तत्रेमं क उपासीरन् क उ स्विदनुशेरते ॥३७॥

tattvānāṁ bhagavaṁs teṣāṁ
katidhā pratisaṅkramaḥ
tatremaṁ ka upāsīran
ka u svid anuśerate

tattvānām—of the elements of nature; *bhagavan*—O great sage; *teṣām*—of them; *katidhā*—how many; *pratisaṅkramaḥ*—dissolutions; *tatra*—thereupon; *imam*—unto the Supreme Lord; *ke*—who are they; *upāsīran*—being saved; *ke*—who are they; *u*—who; *svit*—may; *anuśerate*—serve the Lord while He sleeps.

TRANSLATION

Please describe how many dissolutions there are for the elements of material nature and who survives after the dissolutions to serve the Lord while He is asleep.

PURPORT

In the *Brahma-saṁhitā* (5.47–48) it is said that all the material manifestations with innumerable universes appear and disappear with the breathing of Mahā-Viṣṇu lying in *yoga-nidrā*, or mystic sleep.

yaḥ kāraṇārṇava-jale bhajati sma yoga-
nidrām ananta-jagad-aṇḍa-saroma-kūpaḥ
ādhāra-śaktim avalambya parāṁ sva-mūrtiṁ
govindam ādi-puruṣaṁ tam ahaṁ bhajāmi

yasyaika-niśvasita-kālam athāvalambya
jīvanti loma-vilajā jagad-aṇḍa-nāthāḥ
viṣṇur mahān sa iha yasya kalā-viśeṣo
govindam ādi-puruṣaṁ tam ahaṁ bhājami

"Govinda, the ultimate and Supreme Personality of Godhead [Lord Kṛṣṇa], lies sleeping unlimitedly on the Causal Ocean in order to create unlimited numbers of universes during that sleep. He lies on the water by His own internal potency, and I worship that original Supreme Godhead.

"Due to His breathing, innumerable universes come into existence, and when He withdraws His breath there occurs the dissolution of all the lords of the universes. That plenary portion of the Supreme Lord is called Mahā-Viṣṇu, and He is a part of the part of Lord Kṛṣṇa. I worship Govinda, the original Lord."

After the dissolution of the material manifestations, the Lord and His kingdom beyond the Causal Ocean do not disappear, nor do the inhabitants, the Lord's associates. The associates of the Lord are far more numerous than the living entities who have forgotten the Lord due to material association. The impersonalist's explanation of the word *aham* in the four verses of the original *Bhāgavatam—aham evāsam evāgre* etc.—is refuted here. The Lord and His eternal associates remain after the dissolution. Vidura's inquiry about such persons is a clear indication of the existence of all the paraphernalia of the Lord. This is also confirmed in the *Kāśī-khaṇḍa*, as quoted by both Jīva Gosvāmī and Śrīla Viśvanātha Cakravartī, who follow in the footsteps of Śrīla Śrīdhara Svāmī.

na cyavante hi yad-bhaktā
mahatyāṁ pralayāpadi
ato 'cyuto 'khile loke
sa ekaḥ sarva-go 'vyayaḥ

"The devotees of the Lord never annihilate their individual existences even after the dissolution of the entire cosmic manifestation. The Lord and the devotees who associate with Him are always eternal, in both the material and spiritual worlds."

TEXT 38

पुरुषस्य च संस्थानं स्वरूपं वा परस्य च ।
ज्ञानं च नैगमं यत्तद्गुरुशिष्यप्रयोजनम् ॥३८॥

puruṣasya ca saṁsthānaṁ
svarūpaṁ vā parasya ca
jñānaṁ ca naigamaṁ yat tad
guru-śiṣya-prayojanam

puruṣasya—of the living entity; *ca*—also; *saṁsthānam*—existence; *svarūpam*—identity; *vā*—either, or; *parasya*—of the Supreme; *ca*—also; *jñānam*—knowledge; *ca*—also; *naigamam*—in the matter of the *Upaniṣads; yat*—that; *tat*—the same; *guru*—spiritual master; *śiṣya*—disciple; *prayojanam*—necessity.

TRANSLATION

What are the truths regarding the living entities and the Supreme Personality of Godhead? What are their identities? What are the specific values in the knowledge in the Vedas, and what are the necessities for the spiritual master and his disciples?

PURPORT

The living entities are constitutionally servitors of the Lord, who can accept all kinds of service from everyone. It is clearly declared (Bg. 5.29) that the Lord is the supreme enjoyer of the benefits of all sacrifices and penances, the proprietor of all that is manifested and the friend of all living entities. That is His real identity. Therefore, when the living entity accepts this supreme proprietorship of the Lord and acts in that attitude, he resumes his real identity. In order to elevate the living entity to this standard of knowledge, there is the necessity of spiritual association. The bona fide spiritual master desires that his disciples know the process of rendering transcendental service to the Lord, and the disciples also know that they have to learn about the eternal relationship between God and the living entity from a self-realized soul. To disseminate transcendental knowledge one must retire from mundane activities on the strength of enlightenment in knowledge in terms of Vedic wisdom. That is the sum and substance of all the questions in this verse.

TEXT 39

निमित्तानि च तस्येह प्रोक्तान्यनघसूरिभिः ।
स्वतो ज्ञानं कुतः पुंसां भक्तिर्वैराग्यमेव वा ॥३९॥

nimittāni ca tasyeha
proktāny anagha-sūribhiḥ

svato jñānaṁ kutaḥ puṁsāṁ
bhaktir vairāgyam eva vā

nimittāni—the source of knowledge; *ca*—also; *tasya*—of such knowledge; *iha*—in this world; *proktāni*—mentioned; *anagha*—spotless; *sūribhiḥ*—by devotees; *svataḥ*—self-sufficient; *jñānam*—knowledge; *kutaḥ*—how; *puṁsām*—of the living entity; *bhaktiḥ*—devotional service; *vairāgyam*—detachment; *eva*—certainly; *vā*—also.

TRANSLATION

Spotless devotees of the Lord have mentioned the source of such knowledge. How could one have knowledge of devotional service and detachment without the help of such devotees?

PURPORT

There are many inexperienced persons who advocate self-realization without the help of a spiritual master. They decry the necessity of the spiritual master and try themselves to take his place by propagating the theory that a spiritual master is not necessary. *Śrīmad-Bhāgavatam*, however, does not approve this viewpoint. Even the great transcendental scholar Vyāsadeva had need of a spiritual master, and under the instruction of his spiritual master, Nārada, he prepared this sublime literature, *Śrīmad-Bhāgavatam*. Even Lord Caitanya, although He is Kṛṣṇa Himself, accepted a spiritual master; even Lord Kṛṣṇa accepted a spiritual master, Sāndīpani Muni, in order to be enlightened; and all the *ācāryas* and saints of the world had spiritual masters. In *Bhagavad-gītā* Arjuna accepted Lord Kṛṣṇa as his spiritual master, although there was no necessity of such a formal declaration. So, in all cases, there is no question about the necessity of accepting a spiritual master. The only stipulation is that the spiritual master should be bona fide; i.e., the spiritual master must be in the proper chain of disciplic succession, called the *paramparā* system.

Sūris are great scholars, but they may not always be *anagha*, or spotless. The *anagha-sūri* is one who is a pure devotee of the Lord. Those who are not pure devotees of the Lord, or who want to be on an equal level with Him, are not *anagha-sūri*. Pure devotees have prepared many books of knowledge on the basis of authorized scriptures. Śrīla Rūpa Gosvāmī and his assistants, under the instructions of Lord Śrī Caitanya Mahāprabhu, have all written various literatures for the guidance of prospective devotees, and anyone who is very serious about raising himself to the standard of a pure devotee of the Lord must take advantage of those literatures.

TEXT 40

एतान्मे पृच्छतः प्रश्नान् हरेः कर्मविवित्सया ।
ब्रूहि मेऽज्ञस्य मित्रत्वादजया नष्टचक्षुषः ॥४०॥

etān me pṛcchataḥ praśnān
hareḥ karma-vivitsayā
brūhi me 'jñasya mitratvād
ajayā naṣṭa-cakṣuṣaḥ

etān—all these; *me*—my; *pṛcchataḥ*—of one who inquires; *praśnān*—questions; *hareḥ*—of the Supreme Lord; *karma*—pastimes; *vivitsayā*—desiring to know; *brūhi*—kindly describe; *me*—unto me; *ajñasya*—of one who is ignorant; *mitratvāt*—because of friendship; *ajayā*—by the external energy; *naṣṭa-cakṣuṣaḥ*—those who have lost their vision.

TRANSLATION

My dear sage, I have put all these questions before you with a view to knowing the pastimes of Hari, the Supreme Personality of Godhead. You are the friend of all, so kindly describe them for all those who have lost their vision.

PURPORT

Vidura put forward many varieties of questions with a view to understanding the principles of transcendental loving service to the Lord. As stated in *Bhagavad-gītā* (2.41), devotional service to the Lord is one, and the mind of the devotee is not diverted to the many branches of uncertainties. Vidura's purpose was to be situated in that service to the Lord, wherein one merges undivertedly. He claimed the friendship of Maitreya Muni, not because he was Maitreya's son but because Maitreya was actually the friend of all who have lost their spiritual vision due to material influence.

TEXT 41

सर्वे वेदाश्च यज्ञाश्च तपो दानानि चानघ ।
जीवाभयप्रदानस्य न कुर्वीरन् कलामपि ॥४१॥

sarve vedāś ca yajñāś ca
tapo dānāni cānagha
jīvābhaya-pradānasya
na kurvīran kalām api

sarve—all kinds of; *vedāḥ*—divisions of the *Vedas; ca*—also; *yajñāḥ*—sacrifices; *ca*—also; *tapaḥ*—penances; *dānāni*—charities; *ca*—and; *anagha*—O spotless one; *jīva*—the living entity; *abhaya*—immunity from material pangs; *pradānasya*—of one who gives such assurance; *na*—not; *kurvīran*—can be equalized; *kalām*—even partially; *api*—certainly.

TRANSLATION

O spotless one, your answers to all these questions will grant immunity from all material miseries. Such charity is greater than all Vedic charities, sacrifices, penances, etc.

PURPORT

The highest perfectional work of charity is to give people in general immunity from the anxieties of material existence. This can be done only by performing activities in devotional service to the Lord. Such knowledge is incomparable. Cultivation of the knowledge in the *Vedas*, performance of sacrifice, and distribution of munificent charities all together cannot form even a part of the immunity from the pangs of material existence that is gained from devotional service. The charity of Maitreya not only will help Vidura, but, due to its universal nature, will deliver all others in all times. Thus Maitreya is immortal.

TEXT 42

श्रीशुक उवाच

स इत्थमापृष्टपुराणकल्पः कुरुप्रधानेन मुनिप्रधानः ।
प्रवृद्धहर्षो भगवत्कथायां सञ्चोदितस्तं प्रहसन्निवाह ॥४२॥

śrī-śuka uvāca
sa ittham āpṛṣṭa-purāṇa-kalpaḥ
kuru-pradhānena muni-pradhānaḥ
pravṛddha-harṣo bhagavat-kathāyāṁ
sañcoditas taṁ prahasann ivāha

śrī-śukaḥ uvāca—Śrī Śukadeva Gosvāmī said; *saḥ*—he; *ittham*—thus; *āpṛṣṭa*—being questioned; *purāṇa-kalpaḥ*—one who knows how to explain the supplements of the *Vedas* (the *Purāṇas*); *kuru-pradhānena*—by the chief of the Kurus; *muni-pradhānaḥ*—the chief amongst the sages; *pravṛddha*—sufficiently enriched; *harṣaḥ*—satisfaction; *bhagavat*—the Personality of Godhead; *kathāyām*—in the topics of; *sañcoditaḥ*—being so infused; *tam*—unto Vidura; *prahasan*—with smiles; *iva*—like that; *āha*—replied.

TRANSLATION

Śrī Śukadeva Gosvāmī said: Thus the chief of the sages, who was always enthusiastic about describing topics regarding the Personality of Godhead, began to narrate the descriptive explanation of the Purāṇas, being so infused by Vidura. He was very much enlivened by speaking on the transcendental activities of the Lord.

PURPORT

Great learned sages like Maitreya Muni are always very enthusiastic about describing the transcendental activities of the Lord. Maitreya Muni, being thus invited by Vidura to speak, appeared to be smiling because he actually felt transcendental bliss.

Thus end the Bhaktivedanta purports of the Third Canto, Seventh Chapter, of the Śrīmad-Bhāgavatam, *entitled "Further Inquiries by Vidura."*

CHAPTER EIGHT

Manifestation of Brahmā From Garbhodakaśāyī Viṣṇu

TEXT 1

मैत्रेय उवाच
सत्सेवनीयो बत पूरुवंशो
यल्लोकपालो भगवत्प्रधानः ।
बभूविथेहाजितकीर्तिमालां
पदे पदे नूतनयस्यभीक्ष्णम् ॥ १ ॥

maitreya uvāca
sat-sevanīyo bata pūru-vaṁśo
yal loka-pālo bhagavat-pradhānaḥ
babhūvithehājita-kīrti-mālāṁ
pade pade nūtanayasy abhīkṣṇam

maitreyaḥ uvāca—Śrī Maitreya Muni said; *sat-sevanīyaḥ*—worthy to serve the pure devotees; *bata*—oh, certainly; *pūru-vaṁśaḥ*—the descendants of King Pūru; *yat*—because; *loka-pālaḥ*—the kings are; *bhagavat-pradhānaḥ*—chiefly devoted to the Personality of Godhead; *babhūvitha*—you are also born; *iha*—in this; *ajita*—the Lord, who is unconquerable; *kīrti-mālām*—chain of transcendental activities; *pade pade*—step by step; *nūtanayasi*—becoming newer and newer; *abhīkṣṇam*—always.

TRANSLATION

The great sage Maitreya Muni said to Vidura: The royal dynasty of King Pūru is worthy to serve the pure devotees because all the descendants of that family are devoted to the Personality of Godhead. You are also born in that family, and it is wonderful that

because of your attempt the transcendental pastimes of the Lord are becoming newer and newer at every moment.

PURPORT

The great sage Maitreya thanked Vidura and praised him by reference to his family glories. The Pūru dynasty was full of devotees of the Personality of Godhead and was therefore glorious. Because they were not attached to impersonal Brahman or to the localized Paramātmā but were directly attached to Bhagavān, the Personality of Godhead, they were worthy to render service to the Lord and His pure devotees. Because Vidura was one of the descendants of that family, naturally he engaged in spreading wide the ever-new glories of the Lord. Maitreya felt happy to have such glorious company as Vidura. He considered the company of Vidura most desirable because such association can accelerate one's dormant propensities for devotional service.

TEXT 2

सोऽहं नृणां क्षुल्लसुखाय दुःखं
महद्गतानां विरमाय तस्य ।
प्रवर्तये भागवतं पुराणं
यदाह साक्षाद्भगवानृषिभ्यः ॥ २ ॥

so 'haṁ nṛṇāṁ kṣulla-sukhāya duḥkhaṁ
mahad gatānāṁ viramāya tasya
pravartaye bhāgavataṁ purāṇaṁ
yad āha sākṣād bhagavān ṛṣibhyaḥ

saḥ—that; *aham*—I; *nṛṇām*—of the human being; *kṣulla*—very little; *sukhāya*—for happiness; *duḥkham*—distress; *mahat*—great; *gatānām*—entered into; *viramāya*—for mitigation; *tasya*—his; *pravartaye*—in beginning; *bhāgavatam*—*Śrīmad-Bhāgavatam*; *purāṇam*—Vedic supplement; *yat*—which; *āha*—said; *sākṣāt*—directly; *bhagavān*—the Personality of Godhead; *ṛṣibhyaḥ*—unto the sages.

TRANSLATION

Let me now begin speaking on the Bhāgavata Purāṇa, which was directly spoken to the great sages by the Personality of Godhead for the benefit of those who are entangled in extreme miseries for the sake of very little pleasure.

PURPORT

The sage Maitreya proposed to speak on *Śrīmad-Bhāgavatam* because it was especially compiled, and traditionally comes down in the disciplic succession, for the solution of all the problems of human society. Only one who is fortunate can have the opportunity to hear *Śrīmad-Bhāgavatam* in the association of pure devotees of the Lord. Under the spell of material energy, the living entities are entrapped in the bondage of many difficulties simply for the sake of a little bit of material happiness. They engage in fruitive activities, not knowing the implications. Under the false impression that the body is the self, the living entities foolishly relate to so many false attachments. They think that they can engage with materialistic paraphernalia forever. This gross misconception of life is so strong that a person suffers continually, life after life, under the external energy of the Lord. If one comes in contact with the book *Bhāgavatam* as well as with the devotee *bhāgavata,* who knows what the *Bhāgavatam* is, then such a fortunate man gets out of the material entanglement. Therefore Śrī Maitreya Muni, out of compassion for the suffering men in the world, proposes to speak on the *Śrīmad-Bhāgavatam* first and last.

TEXT 3

आसीनमुर्व्यां भगवन्तमाद्यं
सङ्कर्षणं देवमकुण्ठसत्त्वम् ।
विवित्सवस्तत्त्वमतः परस्य
कुमारमुख्या मुनयोऽन्वपृच्छन् ॥ ३ ॥

āsīnam urvyāṁ bhagavantam ādyaṁ
saṅkarṣaṇaṁ devam akuṇṭha-sattvam

vivitsavas tattvam ataḥ parasya
kumāra-mukhyā munayo 'nvapṛcchan

āsīnam—seated; *urvyām*—in the bottom of the universe; *bhagavantam*—unto the Lord; *ādyam*—the original; *saṅkarṣaṇam*—Saṅkarṣaṇa; *devam*—the Personality of Godhead; *akuṇṭha-sattvam*—undeterred knowledge; *vivitsavaḥ*—being inquisitive to know; *tattvam ataḥ*—truth like this; *parasya*—regarding the Supreme Personality of Godhead; *kumāra*—the boy-saint; *mukhyāḥ*—headed by; *munayaḥ*—great sages; *anvapṛcchan*—inquired like this.

TRANSLATION

Some time ago, being inquisitive to know, Sanat-kumāra, the chief of the boy-saints, accompanied by other great sages, inquired exactly like you about the truths regarding Vāsudeva, the Supreme, from Lord Saṅkarṣaṇa, who is seated at the bottom of the universe.

PURPORT

This is in clarification of the statement that the Lord spoke directly on the *Śrīmad-Bhāgavatam.* When and unto whom the *Bhāgavatam* was spoken is explained herewith. Questions similar to those put forward by Vidura were asked by great sages like Sanat-kumāra, and Lord Saṅkarṣaṇa, the plenary expansion of the Supreme Lord Vāsudeva, answered them.

TEXT 4

स्वमेव धिष्ण्यं बहु मानयन्तं
यद्वासुदेवाभिधमामनन्ति ।
प्रत्यग्धृताक्षाम्बुजकोशमीष-
दुन्मीलयन्तं विबुधोदयाय ॥ ४ ॥

svam eva dhiṣṇyaṁ bahu mānayantaṁ
yad vāsudevābhidham āmananti
pratyag-dhṛtākṣāmbuja-kośam īṣad
unmīlayantaṁ vibudhodayāya

svam—Himself; *eva*—thus; *dhiṣṇyam*—situated; *bahu*—greatly; *mānayantam*—esteemed; *yat*—that which; *vāsudeva*—Lord Vāsudeva; *abhidham*—by the name; *āmananti*—acknowledge; *pratyak-dhṛta-akṣa*—eyes settled for introspection; *ambuja-kośam*—lotuslike eye; *īṣat*—slightly; *unmīlayantam*—opened; *vibudha*—of the greatly learned sages; *udayāya*—for the sake of advancement.

TRANSLATION

At that time Lord Saṅkarṣaṇa was meditating upon His Supreme Lord, whom the learned esteem as Lord Vāsudeva, but for the sake of the advancement of the great learned sages He slightly opened His lotuslike eyes and began to speak.

TEXT 5

स्वर्धुन्युदार्द्रैः स्वजटाकलापै-
रुपस्पृशन्तश्चरणोपधानम् ।
पद्मं यदर्चन्त्यहिराजकन्याः
सप्रेमनानाबलिभिर्वरार्थाः ॥ ५ ॥

svardhuny-udārdraiḥ sva-jaṭā-kalāpair
upaspṛśantaś caraṇopadhānam
padmaṁ yad arcanty ahi-rāja-kanyāḥ
sa-prema nānā-balibhir varārthāḥ

svardhunī-uda—by the water of the Ganges; *ārdraiḥ*—being moistened; *sva-jaṭā*—bunch of hairs; *kalāpaiḥ*—situated on the head; *upaspṛśantaḥ*—by so touching; *caraṇa-upadhānam*—the shelter of His feet; *padmam*—the lotus shelter; *yat*—that which; *arcanti*—worships; *ahi-rāja*—the serpent-king; *kanyāḥ*—daughters; *sa-prema*—with great devotion; *nānā*—various; *balibhiḥ*—paraphernalia; *vara-arthāḥ*—being desirous of husbands.

TRANSLATION

The sages came from the highest planets down to the lower region through the water of the Ganges, and therefore the hair on

their heads was wet. They touched the lotus feet of the Lord, which are worshiped with various paraphernalia by the daughters of the serpent-king when they desire good husbands.

PURPORT

The Ganges water flows directly from the lotus feet of Viṣṇu, and its course runs from the highest planet of the universe down to the lowest. The sages came down from Satyaloka by taking advantage of the flowing water, a process of transportation made possible by the power of mystic *yoga.* If a river flows thousands and thousands of miles, a perfect *yogī* can at once transport himself from one place to another simply by dipping in its water. The Ganges is the only celestial river which flows throughout the universe, and great sages travel all over the universe via this sacred river. The statement that their hair was wet indicates that it was directly moistened by the water originating from the lotus feet of Viṣṇu (the Ganges). Whoever touches the water of the Ganges to his head surely touches the lotus feet of the Lord directly and can become free from all effects of sinful acts. If after taking a bath in the Ganges or being washed of all sins, a man guards himself against committing further sinful acts, then certainly he is delivered. But if he again takes up sinful activities, his bath in the Ganges is as good as that of the elephant, who nicely takes his bath in a river but later spoils the whole thing by covering himself with dust on the land.

TEXT 6

मुहुर्गृणन्तो वचसानुराग-
स्खलत्पदेनास्य कृतानि तज्ज्ञाः ।
किरीटसाहस्रमणिप्रवेक-
प्रद्योतितोद्दामफणासहस्रम् ॥ ६ ॥

muhur gṛṇanto vacasānurāga-
skhalat-padenāsya kṛtāni taj-jñāḥ
kirīṭa-sāhasra-maṇi-praveka-
pradyotitoddāma-phaṇā-sahasram

muhuḥ—again and again; *gṛṇantaḥ*—glorifying; *vacasā*—by words; *anurāga*—with great affection; *skhalat-padena*—with symmetrical rhythm; *asya*—of the Lord; *kṛtāni*—activities; *tat-jñāḥ*—those who know the pastimes; *kirīṭa*—helmets; *sāhasra*—thousands; *maṇi-praveka*—glowing effulgence of the valuable stones; *pradyotita*—emanating from; *uddāma*—raised; *phaṇā*—hoods; *sahasram*—thousands.

TRANSLATION

The four Kumāras, headed by Sanat-kumāra, who all knew the transcendental pastimes of the Lord, glorified the Lord in rhythmic accents with selected words full of affection and love. At that time Lord Saṅkarṣaṇa, with His thousands of raised hoods, began to radiate an effulgence from the glowing stones on His head.

PURPORT

The Lord is sometimes addressed as *uttamaśloka*, which means "one who is worshiped with selected words by devotees." A profusion of such selected words comes from a devotee who is fully absorbed in affection and love for the devotional service of the Lord. There are many instances in which even a small boy who was a great devotee of the Lord could offer excellent prayers in the choicest words for glorification of the pastimes of the Lord. In other words, without the development of fine affection and love, one cannot offer prayers to the Lord very suitably.

TEXT 7

प्रोक्तं किलैतद्भगवत्तमेन
निवृत्तिधर्माभिरताय तेन ।
सनत्कुमाराय स चाह पृष्टः
सांख्यायनायाङ्ग धृतव्रताय ॥ ७ ॥

proktaṁ kilaitad bhagavattamena
nivṛtti-dharmābhiratāya tena

sanat-kumārāya sa cāha pṛṣṭaḥ
sāṅkhyāyanāyāṅga dhṛta-vratāya

proktam—was said; *kila*—certainly; *etat*—this; *bhagavattamena*—by Lord Saṅkarṣaṇa; *nivṛtti*—renunciation; *dharma-abhiratāya*—unto one who has taken this religious vow; *tena*—by Him; *sanat-kumārāya*—unto Sanat-kumāra; *saḥ*—he; *ca*—also; *āha*—said; *pṛṣṭaḥ*—when inquired of; *sāṅkhyāyanāya*—unto the great sage Sāṅkhyāyana; *aṅga*—my dear Vidura; *dhṛta-vratāya*—unto one who has taken such a vow.

TRANSLATION

Lord Saṅkarṣaṇa thus spoke the purport of Śrīmad-Bhāgavatam to the great sage Sanat-kumāra, who had already taken the vow of renunciation. Sanat-kumāra also, in his turn, when inquired of by Sāṅkhyāyana Muni, explained Śrīmad-Bhāgavatam as he had heard it from Saṅkarṣaṇa.

PURPORT

This is the way of the *paramparā* system. Although Sanat-kumāra, the well-known great saintly Kumāra, was in the perfect stage of life, still he heard the message of *Śrīmad-Bhāgavatam* from Lord Saṅkarṣaṇa. Similarly, when he was questioned by Sāṅkhyāyana Ṛṣi, he spoke to him the same message he had heard from Lord Saṅkarṣaṇa. In other words, unless one hears from the proper authority one cannot become a preacher. In devotional service, therefore, two items out of the nine, namely hearing and chanting, are most important. Without hearing nicely, one cannot preach the message of Vedic knowledge.

TEXT 8

सांख्यायनः पारमहंस्यमुख्यो
विवक्षमाणो भगवद्विभूतीः ।
जगाद सोऽस्मद्गुरवेऽन्विताय
पराशरायाथ बृहस्पतेश्च ॥ ८ ॥

sāṅkhyāyanaḥ pāramahaṁsya-mukhyo
vivakṣamāṇo bhagavad-vibhūtīḥ
jagāda so 'smad-gurave 'nvitāya
parāśarāyātha bṛhaspateś ca

sāṅkhyāyanaḥ—the great sage Sāṅkhyāyana; *pāramahaṁsya-mukhyaḥ*—the chief of all transcendentalists; *vivakṣamāṇaḥ*—while reciting; *bhagavat-vibhūtīḥ*—the glories of the Lord; *jagāda*—explained; *saḥ*—he; *asmat*—of me; *gurave*—unto the spiritual master; *anvitāya*—followed; *parāśarāya*—unto the sage Parāśara; *atha bṛhaspateḥ ca*—also to Bṛhaspati.

TRANSLATION

The great sage Sāṅkhyāyana was the chief amongst the transcendentalists, and when he was describing the glories of the Lord in terms of Śrīmad-Bhāgavatam, it so happened that my spiritual master, Parāśara, and Bṛhaspati both heard him.

TEXT 9

प्रोवाच मह्यं स दयालुरुक्तो
मुनिः पुलस्त्येन पुराणमाद्यम् ।
सोऽहं तवैतत्कथयामि वत्स
श्रद्धालवे नित्यमनुव्रताय ॥ ९ ॥

provāca mahyaṁ sa dayālur ukto
muniḥ pulastyena purāṇam ādyam
so 'haṁ tavaitat kathayāmi vatsa
śraddhālave nityam anuvratāya

provāca—said; *mahyam*—unto me; *saḥ*—he; *dayāluḥ*—kindhearted; *uktaḥ*—aforementioned; *muniḥ*—sage; *pulastyena*—by the sage Pulastya; *purāṇam ādyam*—the foremost of all the *Purāṇas; saḥ aham*—that also I; *tava*—unto you; *etat*—this; *kathayāmi*—shall speak; *vatsa*—my dear son; *śraddhālave*—unto one who is faithful; *nityam*—always; *anuvratāya*—unto one who is a follower.

TRANSLATION

The great sage Parāśara, as aforementioned, being so advised by the great sage Pulastya, spoke unto me the foremost of the Purāṇas [Bhāgavatam]. I shall also describe this before you, my dear son, in terms of my hearing, because you are always my faithful follower.

PURPORT

The great sage of the name Pulastya is the father of all demoniac descendants. Once upon a time Parāśara began a sacrifice in which all the demons were to be burnt to death because his father had been killed and devoured by one of them. The great sage Vasiṣṭha Muni arrived at the sacrifice and requested Parāśara to stop the deadly action, and because of Vasiṣṭha's position and respect in the community of sages, Parāśara could not deny the request. Parāśara having stopped the sacrifice, Pulastya, the father of the demons, appreciated his brahminical temperament and gave the blessing that in the future he would be a great speaker on the Vedic literatures called the *Purāṇas*, the supplements of the *Vedas*. Parāśara's action was appreciated by Pulastya because Parāśara had forgiven the demons out of his brahminical power of forgiveness. Parāśara was able to demolish all the demons in the sacrifice, but he considered, "Demons are so made that they devour living creatures, men and animals, but why on that account should I withdraw my brahminical qualification of forgiveness?" As the great speaker of the *Purāṇas*, Parāśara first of all spoke on the *Śrīmad-Bhāgavata Purāṇa* because it is the foremost of all the *Purāṇas.* Maitreya Muni desired to narrate the same *Bhāgavatam* he had heard from Parāśara, and Vidura was qualified to hear it because of his faithfulness and his following the instructions received from superiors. So *Śrīmad-Bhāgavatam* was being narrated from time immemorial by the disciplic succession, even before the time of Vyāsadeva. The so-called historians calculate the *Purāṇas* to be only a few hundred years old, but factually the *Purāṇas* existed from time immemorial, before all historical calculations by the mundaners and speculative philosophers.

TEXT 10

उदाप्लुतं विश्वमिदं तदासीद्
यन्निद्रयामीलितदृङ् न्यमीलयत् ।

अहीन्द्रतल्पेऽधिशयान एकः
कृतक्षणः स्वात्मरतौ निरीहः ॥१०॥

udāplutaṁ viśvam idaṁ tadāsīd
yan nidrayāmīlita-dṛṅ nyamīlayat
ahīndra-talpe 'dhiśayāna ekaḥ
kṛta-kṣaṇaḥ svātma-ratau nirīhaḥ

uda—water; *āplutam*—submerged in; *viśvam*—the three worlds; *idam*—this; *tadā*—at that time; *āsīt*—it so remained; *yat*—in which; *nidrayā*—in slumber; *amīlita*—closed; *dṛk*—eyes; *nyamīlayat*—not completely closed; *ahi-indra*—the great snake Ananta; *talpe*—on the bed of; *adhiśayānaḥ*—lying on; *ekaḥ*—alone; *kṛta-kṣaṇaḥ*—being engaged; *sva-ātma-ratau*—enjoying in His internal potency; *nirīhaḥ*—without any part of external energy.

TRANSLATION

At that time when the three worlds were submerged in water, Garbhodakaśāyī Viṣṇu was alone, lying on His bedstead, the great snake Ananta, and although He appeared to be in slumber in His own internal potency, free from the action of the external energy, His eyes were not completely closed.

PURPORT

The Lord is eternally enjoying transcendental bliss by His internal potency, whereas the external potency is suspended during the time of the dissolution of the cosmic manifestation.

TEXT 11

सोऽन्तःशरीरेऽर्पितभूतसूक्ष्मः
कालात्मिकां शक्तिमुदीरयाणः ।
उवास तस्मिन् सलिले पदे स्वे
यथानलो दारुणि रुद्धवीर्यः ॥११॥

so 'ntaḥ śarīre 'rpita-bhūta-sūkṣmaḥ
kālātmikāṁ śaktim udīrayāṇaḥ

uvāsa tasmin salile pade sve
yathānalo dāruṇi ruddha-vīryaḥ

saḥ—the Supreme Lord; *antaḥ*—within; *śarīre*—in the transcendental body; *arpita*—kept; *bhūta*—material elements; *sūkṣmaḥ*—subtle; *kāla-ātmikām*—the form of time; *śaktim*—energy; *udīrayāṇaḥ*—invigorating; *uvāsa*—resided; *tasmin*—therein; *salile*—in the water; *pade*—in the place; *sve*—His own; *yathā*—as much as; *analaḥ*—fire; *dāruṇi*—in the fuel wood; *ruddha-vīryaḥ*—submerged strength.

TRANSLATION

Just like the strength of fire within fuel wood, the Lord remained within the water of dissolution, submerging all the living entities in their subtle bodies. He lay in the self-invigorated energy called kāla.

PURPORT

After the three worlds—the upper, lower and middle planetary systems—merged into the water of dissolution, the living entities of all the three worlds remained in their subtle bodies by dint of the energy called *kāla.* In this dissolution, the gross bodies became unmanifest, but the subtle bodies existed, just like the water of the material creation. Thus the material energy was not completely wound up, as is the case in the full dissolution of the material world.

TEXT 12

चतुर्युगानां च सहस्रमप्सु
स्वपन् स्वयोदीरितया स्वशक्त्या ।
कालाख्ययासादितकर्मतन्त्रो
लोकानपीतान्ददृशे स्वदेहे ॥१२॥

catur-yugānāṁ ca sahasram apsu
svapan svayodīritayā sva-śaktyā
kālākhyayāsādita-karma-tantro
lokān apītān dadṛśe sva-dehe

catuḥ—four; *yugānām*—of the millenniums; *ca*—also; *sahasram*—one thousand; *apsu*—in the water; *svapan*—dreaming in sleep; *svayā*—with His internal potency; *udīritayā*—for further development; *sva-śaktyā*—by His own energy; *kāla-ākhyayā*—by the name *kāla; āsādita*—being so engaged; *karma-tantraḥ*—in the matter of fruitive activities; *lokān*—the total living entities; *apītān*—bluish; *dadṛśe*—saw it so; *sva-dehe*—in His own body.

TRANSLATION

The Lord lay down for four thousand yuga cycles in His internal potency, and by His external energy He appeared to be sleeping within the water. When the living entities were coming out for further development of their fruitive activities, actuated by the energy called kāla-śakti, He saw His transcendental body as bluish.

PURPORT

In the *Viṣṇu Purāṇa*, *kāla-śakti* is mentioned as *avidyā*. The symptom of the influence of the *kāla-śakti* is that one has to work in the material world for fruitive results. The fruitive workers are described in *Bhagavad-gītā* as *mūḍhas*, or foolish. Such foolish living entities are very enthusiastic to work for some temporary benefit within perpetual bondage. One thinks himself very clever throughout his life if he is able to leave behind him a great asset of wealth for his children, and to achieve this temporary benefit he takes the risk of all sinful activities, without knowledge that such activities will keep him perpetually bound by the shackles of material bondage. Due to this polluted mentality and due to material sins, the aggregate combination of living entities appeared to be bluish. Such an impetus of activity for fruitive result is made possible by the dictation of the external energy of the Lord, *kāla*.

TEXT 13

तस्यार्थसूक्ष्माभिनिविष्टदृष्टे-
रन्तर्गतोऽर्थो रजसा तनीयान् ।
गुणेन कालानुगतेन विद्धः
सूष्यंस्तदाभिद्यत नाभिदेशात् ॥१३॥

tasyārtha-sūkṣmābhiniviṣṭa-dṛṣṭer
antar-gato 'rtho rajasā tanīyān
guṇena kālānugatena viddhaḥ
sūṣyaṁs tadābhidyata nābhi-deśāt

tasya—His; *artha*—subject; *sūkṣma*—subtle; *abhiniviṣṭa-dṛṣṭeḥ*—of one whose attention was fixed; *antaḥ-gataḥ*—internal; *arthaḥ*—purpose; *rajasā*—by the mode of passion of material nature; *tanīyān*—very subtle; *guṇena*—by the qualities; *kāla-anugatena*—in due course of time; *viddhaḥ*—agitated; *sūṣyan*—generating; *tadā*—then; *abhidyata*—pierced through; *nābhi-deśāt*—from the abdomen.

TRANSLATION

The subtle subject matter of creation, on which the Lord's attention was fixed, was agitated by the material mode of passion, and thus the subtle form of creation pierced through His abdomen.

TEXT 14

स पद्मकोशः सहसोदतिष्ठत्
कालेन कर्मप्रतिबोधनेन ।
स्वरोचिषा तत्सलिलं विशालं
विद्योतयन्नर्क इवात्मयोनिः ॥१४॥

sa padma-kośaḥ sahasodatiṣṭhat
kālena karma-pratibodhanena
sva-rociṣā tat salilaṁ viśālaṁ
vidyotayann arka ivātma-yoniḥ

saḥ—that; *padma-kośaḥ*—bud of a lotus flower; *sahasā*—suddenly; *udatiṣṭhat*—appeared; *kālena*—by time; *karma*—fruitive activities; *pratibodhanena*—awakening; *sva-rociṣā*—by its own effulgence; *tat*—that; *salilam*—water of devastation; *viśālam*—vast; *vidyotayan*—illuminating; *arkaḥ*—the sun; *iva*—like; *ātma-yoniḥ*—generating from the Personality of Viṣṇu.

TRANSLATION

Piercing through, this sum total form of the fruitive activity of the living entities took the shape of the bud of a lotus flower generated from the Personality of Viṣṇu, and by His supreme will it illuminated everything, like the sun, and dried up the vast waters of devastation.

TEXT 15

तल्लोकपद्मं स उ एव विष्णुः
प्रावीविशत्सर्वगुणावभासम् ।
तस्मिन् स्वयं वेदमयो विधाता
स्वयम्भुवं यं स्म वदन्ति सोऽभूत् ॥१५॥

tal loka-padmaṁ sa u eva viṣṇuḥ
prāvīviśat sarva-guṇāvabhāsam
tasmin svayaṁ vedamayo vidhātā
svayambhuvaṁ yaṁ sma vadanti so 'bhūt

tat—that; *loka*—universal; *padmam*—lotus flower; *saḥ*—He; *u*—certainly; *eva*—factually; *viṣṇuḥ*—the Lord; *prāvīviśat*—entered into; *sarva*—all; *guṇa-avabhāsam*—reservoir of all modes of nature; *tasmin*—in which; *svayam*—in person; *veda-mayaḥ*—the personality of Vedic wisdom; *vidhātā*—controller of the universe; *svayam-bhuvam*—self-born; *yam*—whom; *sma*—in the past; *vadanti*—do say; *saḥ*—he; *abhūt*—generated.

TRANSLATION

Into that universal lotus flower Lord Viṣṇu personally entered as the Supersoul, and when it was thus impregnated with all the modes of material nature, the personality of Vedic wisdom, whom we call the self-born, was generated.

PURPORT

This lotus flower is the universal *virāṭ* form, or the gigantic form of the Lord in the material world. It becomes amalgamated in the Personality of Godhead Viṣṇu, in His abdomen, at the time of dissolution, and it becomes manifest at the time of creation. This is due to Garbhodakaśāyī Viṣṇu, who enters into each of the universes. In this form is the sum total of all the fruitive activities of the living entities conditioned by material nature, and the first of them, namely Brahmā, or the controller of the universe, is generated from this lotus flower. This first-born living being, unlike all the others, has no material father, and thus he is called self-born, or *svayambhū.* He goes to sleep with Nārāyaṇa at the time of devastation, and when there is another creation, he is born in this way. From this description we have the conception of three—the gross *virāṭ* form, the subtle Hiraṇyagarbha and the material creative force, Brahmā.

TEXT 16

तस्यां स चाम्भोरुहकर्णिकाया-
मवस्थितो लोकमपश्यमानः ।
परिक्रमन् व्योम्नि विवृत्तनेत्र-
श्चत्वारि लेभेऽनुदिशं मुखानि ॥१६॥

tasyāṁ sa cāmbho-ruha-karṇikāyām
avasthito lokam apaśyamānaḥ
parikraman vyomni vivṛtta-netraś
catvāri lebhe 'nudiśaṁ mukhāni

tasyām—in that; *ca*—and; *ambhaḥ*—water; *ruha-karṇikāyām*—whorl of the lotus; *avasthitaḥ*—being situated; *lokam*—the world; *apaśyamānaḥ*—without being able to see; *parikraman*—circumambulating; *vyomni*—in space; *vivṛtta-netraḥ*—while moving the eyes; *catvāri*—four; *lebhe*—achieved; *anudiśam*—in terms of direction; *mukhāni*—heads.

TRANSLATION

Brahmā, born out of the lotus flower, could not see the world, although he was situated in the whorl. He therefore circumambulated all of space, and while moving his eyes in all directions he achieved four heads in terms of the four directions.

TEXT 17

तस्माद्युगान्तश्वसनावघूर्ण-
जलोर्मिचक्रात्सलिलाद्विरूढम् ।
उपाश्रितः कञ्जमु लोकतत्त्वं
नात्मानमद्धाविददादिदेवः ॥१७॥

tasmād yugānta-śvasanāvaghūrṇa-
jalormi-cakrāt salilād virūḍham
upāśritaḥ kañjam u loka-tattvaṁ
nātmānam addhāvidad ādi-devaḥ

tasmāt—from there; *yuga-anta*—at the end of the millennium; *śvasana*—the air of devastation; *avaghūrṇa*—because of movement; *jala*—water; *ūrmi-cakrāt*—out of the circle of waves; *salilāt*—from the water; *virūḍham*—situated on them; *upāśritaḥ*—having the shelter of; *kañjam*—lotus flower; *u*—in astonishment; *loka-tattvam*—the mystery of creation; *na*—not; *ātmānam*—himself; *addhā*—perfectly; *avidat*—could understand; *ādi-devaḥ*—the first demigod.

TRANSLATION

Lord Brahmā, situated in that lotus, could not perfectly understand the creation, the lotus or himself. At the end of the millennium the air of devastation began to move the water and the lotus in great circular waves.

PURPORT

Lord Brahmā was perplexed about his creation, the lotus and the world, even though he tried to understand them for one millennium, which is beyond calculation in the solar years of human beings. No one, therefore, can know the mystery of the creation and cosmic manifestation simply by mental speculation. The human being is so limited in his capacity that without the help of the Supreme he can hardly understand the mystery of the will of the Lord in terms of creation, continuance and destruction.

TEXT 18

क एष योऽसावहमब्जपृष्ठ
एतत्कुतो वाब्जमनन्यदप्सु ।
अस्ति ह्यधस्तादिह किञ्चनैत-
दधिष्ठितं यत्र सता नु भाव्यम् ॥१८॥

ka eṣa yo 'sāv aham abja-pṛṣṭha
etat kuto vābjam ananyad apsu
asti hy adhastād iha kiñcanaitad
adhiṣṭhitaṁ yatra satā nu bhāvyam

kaḥ—who; *eṣaḥ*—this; *yaḥ asau aham*—that I am; *abja-pṛṣṭhe*—on top of the lotus; *etat*—this; *kutaḥ*—wherefrom; *vā*—either; *abjam*—lotus flower; *ananyat*—otherwise; *apsu*—in the water; *asti*—there is; *hi*—certainly; *adhastāt*—from below; *iha*—in this; *kiñcana*—anything; *etat*—this; *adhiṣṭhitam*—situated; *yatra*—wherein; *satā*—automatically; *nu*—or not; *bhāvyam*—must be.

TRANSLATION

Lord Brahmā, in his ignorance, contemplated: Who am I that am situated on the top of this lotus? Wherefrom has it sprouted? There must be something downwards, and that from which this lotus has grown must be within the water.

PURPORT

The subject matter of the speculations of Brahmā in the beginning regarding the creation of the cosmic manifestation is still a subject matter for mental speculators. The most intelligent man is he who tries to find the cause of his personal existence and that of the whole cosmic creation and thus tries to find the ultimate cause. If his attempt is properly executed with penances and perseverance, it is sure to be crowned with success.

TEXT 19

स इत्थमुद्वीक्ष्य तदब्जनाल-
नाडीभिरन्तर्जलमाविवेश ।

नार्वाग्गतस्तत्खरनालनाल-
नाभिं विचिन्वंस्तदविन्दताजः ॥१९॥

sa ittham udvīkṣya tad-abja-nāla-
nāḍībhir antar-jalam āviveśa
nārvāg-gatas tat-khara-nāla-nāla-
nābhiṁ vicinvaṁs tad avindatājaḥ

saḥ—he (Brahmā); *ittham*—in this way; *udvīkṣya*—contemplating; *tat*—that; *abja*—lotus; *nāla*—stem; *nāḍībhiḥ*—by the pipe; *antaḥ-jalam*—within the water; *āviveśa*—entered into; *na*—not; *arvāk-gataḥ*—in spite of going inside; *tat-khara-nāla*—the stem of the lotus; *nāla*—pipe; *nābhim*—of the navel; *vicinvan*—thinking much of it; *tat*—that; *avindata*—understood; *ajaḥ*—the self-born.

TRANSLATION

Lord Brahmā, thus contemplating, entered the water through the channel of the stem of the lotus. But in spite of entering the stem and going nearer to the navel of Viṣṇu, he could not trace out the root.

PURPORT

By dint of one's personal endeavor one may go nearer to the Lord, but without the Lord's mercy one cannot reach the ultimate point. Such understanding of the Lord is possible only by devotional service, as confirmed in *Bhagavad-gītā* (18.55): *bhaktyā mām abhijānāti yāvān yaś cāsmi tattvataḥ.*

TEXT 20

तमस्यपारे विदुरात्मसर्गं
विचिन्वतोऽभूत्सुमहांस्त्रिणेमिः ।
यो देहभाजां भयमीरयाणः
परिक्षिणोत्यायुरजस्य हेतिः ॥२०॥

tamasy apāre vidurātma-sargaṁ
vicinvato 'bhūt sumahāṁs tri-ṇemiḥ

yo deha-bhājāṁ bhayam īrayāṇaḥ
parikṣiṇoty āyur ajasya hetiḥ

tasmasi apāre—because of an ignorant way of searching; *vidura*—O Vidura; *ātma-sargam*—the cause of his creation; *vicinvataḥ*—while contemplating; *abhūt*—it so became; *su-mahān*—very great; *tri-nemiḥ*—time of three dimensions; *yaḥ*—which; *deha-bhājām*—of the embodied; *bhayam*—fearfulness; *īrayāṇaḥ*—generating; *parikṣiṇoti*—diminishing the one hundred years; *āyuḥ*—duration of life; *ajasya*—of the self-born; *hetiḥ*—the wheel of eternal time.

TRANSLATION

O Vidura, while searching in that way about his existence, Brahmā reached his ultimate time, which is the eternal wheel in the hand of Viṣṇu and which generates fear in the mind of the living entity like the fear of death.

TEXT 21

ततो निवृत्तोऽप्रतिलब्धकामः
स्वधिष्ण्यमासाद्य पुनः स देवः ।
शनैर्जितश्वासनिवृत्तचित्तो
न्यषीददारूढसमाधियोगः ॥२१॥

tato nivṛtto 'pratilabdha-kāmaḥ
sva-dhiṣṇyam āsādya punaḥ sa devaḥ
śanair jita-śvāsa-nivṛtta-citto
nyaṣīdad ārūḍha-samādhi-yogaḥ

tataḥ—thereafter; *nivṛttaḥ*—retired from that endeavor; *aprati-labdha-kāmaḥ*—without achievement of the desired destination; *sva-dhiṣṇyam*—own seat; *āsādya*—reaching; *punaḥ*—again; *saḥ*—he; *devaḥ*—the demigod; *śanaiḥ*—without delay; *jita-śvāsa*—controlling the breathing; *nivṛtta*—retired; *cittaḥ*—intelligence; *nyaṣīdat*—sat down; *ārūḍha*—in confidence; *samādhi-yogaḥ*—in meditation on the Lord.

TRANSLATION

Thereafter, being unable to achieve the desired destination, he retired from such searching and came back again to the top of the lotus. Thus, controlling all objectives, he concentrated his mind on the Supreme Lord.

PURPORT

Samādhi involves concentrating the mind upon the supreme cause of all, even if one is unaware of whether His actual nature is personal, impersonal or localized. Concentration of the mind on the Supreme is certainly a form of devotional service. To cease from personal sense endeavors and to concentrate on the supreme cause is a sign of self-surrender, and when self-surrender is present, that is a sure sign of devotional service. Each and every living entity needs to engage in devotional service to the Lord if he wishes to understand the ultimate cause of his existence.

TEXT 22

कालेन सोऽजः पुरुषायुषाभि-
प्रवृत्तयोगेन विरूढबोधः ।
स्वयं तदन्तर्हृदयेऽवभात-
मपश्यतापश्यत यन्न पूर्वम् ॥२२॥

kālena so 'jaḥ puruṣāyuṣābhi-
pravṛtta-yogena virūḍha-bodhaḥ
svayaṁ tad antar-hṛdaye 'vabhātam
apaśyatāpaśyata yan na pūrvam

kālena—in due course of time; *saḥ*—he; *ajaḥ*—the self-born Brahmā; *puruṣa-āyuṣā*—by the duration of his age; *abhipravṛtta*—being engaged; *yogena*—in meditation; *virūḍha*—developed; *bodhaḥ*—intelligence; *svayam*—automatically; *tat antaḥ-hṛdaye*—in the heart; *avabhātam*—manifested; *apaśyata*—saw; *apaśyata*—did see; *yat*—which; *na*—not; *pūrvam*—before.

TRANSLATION

At the end of Brahmā's one hundred years, when his meditation was complete, he developed the required knowledge, and as a result he could see in his heart the Supreme within himself, whom he could not see before with the greatest endeavor.

PURPORT

The Supreme Lord can be experienced only through the process of devotional service and not by one's personal endeavor in mental speculation. The age of Brahmā is calculated in terms of *divya* years, which are distinct from the solar years of human beings. The *divya* years are calculated in *Bhagavad-gītā* (8.17): *sahasra-yuga-paryantam ahar yad brahmaṇo viduḥ*. Brahmā's one day is equal to one thousand times the aggregate of the four *yugas* (calculated to be 4,300,000 years). On that basis, Brahmā meditated for one hundred years before he could understand the supreme cause of all causes, and then he wrote the *Brahma-saṁhitā*, which is approved and recognized by Lord Caitanya and in which he sings, *govindam ādi-puruṣaṁ tam ahaṁ bhajāmi.* One has to wait for the mercy of the Lord before one can either render service unto Him or know Him as He is.

TEXT 23

मृणालगौरायतशेषभोग-
पर्यङ्क एकं पुरुषं शयानम् ।
फणातपत्रायुतमूर्धरत्न-
द्युभिर्हतध्वान्तयुगान्ततोये ॥२३॥

mṛṇāla-gaurāyata-śeṣa-bhoga-
paryaṅka ekaṁ puruṣaṁ śayānam
phaṇātapatrāyuta-mūrdha-ratna-
dyubhir hata-dhvānta-yugānta-toye

mṛṇāla—lotus flower; *gaura*—white all over; *āyata*—gigantic; *śeṣa-bhoga*—body of Śeṣa-nāga; *paryaṅke*—on the bed; *ekam*—alone; *puruṣam*—the Supreme Person; *śayānam*—was lying; *phaṇa-*

ātapatra—umbrella of a serpent hood; *āyuta*—bedecked with; *mūrdha*—head; *ratna*—jewels; *dyubhiḥ*—by the rays; *hata-dhvānta*—darkness dissipated; *yuga-anta*—devastation; *toye*—in the water.

TRANSLATION

Brahmā could see that on the water there was a gigantic lotuslike white bedstead, the body of Śeṣa-nāga, on which the Personality of Godhead was lying alone. The whole atmosphere was illuminated by the rays of the jewels bedecking the hood of Śeṣa-nāga, and that illumination dissipated all the darkness of those regions.

TEXT 24

प्रेक्षां क्षिपन्तं हरितोपलाद्रेः
सन्ध्याभ्रनीवेरुरुरुक्ममूर्ध्नः ।
रत्नोदधारौषधिसौमनस्य
वनस्रजो वेणुभुजाङ्घ्रिपाङ्घ्रेः ॥२४॥

prekṣāṁ kṣipantaṁ haritopalādreḥ
sandhyābhra-nīver uru-rukma-mūrdhnaḥ
ratnodadhārauṣadhi-saumanasya
vana-srajo veṇu-bhujāṅghripāṅghreḥ

prekṣām—the panorama; *kṣipantam*—deriding; *harita*—green; *upala*—coral; *adreḥ*—of the hell; *sandhyā-abra-nīveḥ*—of the dress of the evening sky; *uru*—great; *rukma*—gold; *mūrdhnaḥ*—on the summit; *ratna*—jewels; *udadhāra*—waterfalls; *auṣadhi*—herbs; *saumanasya*—of the scenery; *vana-srajaḥ*—flower garland; *veṇu*—dress; *bhuja*—hands; *aṅghripa*—trees; *aṅghreḥ*—legs.

TRANSLATION

The luster of the transcendental body of the Lord mocked the beauty of the coral mountain. The coral mountain is very beautifully dressed by the evening sky, but the yellow dress of the Lord mocked its beauty. There is gold on the summit of the mountain, but the Lord's helmet, bedecked with jewels, mocked it.

The mountain's waterfalls, herbs, etc., with a panorama of flowers, seem like garlands, but the Lord's gigantic body, and His hands and legs, decorated with jewels, pearls, tulasī leaves and flower garlands, mocked the scene on the mountain.

PURPORT

The panoramic beauty of nature, which strikes one with wonder, may be taken as a perverted reflection of the transcendental body of the Lord. One who is therefore attracted by the beauty of the Lord is no longer attracted by the beauty of material nature, although he does not minimize its beauty. In *Bhagavad-gītā* (2.59) it is described that one who is attracted by *param*, the Supreme, is no longer attracted by anything inferior.

TEXT 25

आयामतो विस्तरतः स्वमान-
देहेन लोकत्रयसंग्रहेण ।
विचित्रदिव्याभरणांशुकानां
कृतश्रियापाश्रितवेषदेहम् ॥२५॥

āyāmato vistarataḥ sva-māna-
dehena loka-traya-saṅgraheṇa
vicitra-divyābharaṇāṁśukānāṁ
kṛta-śriyāpāśrita-veṣa-deham

āyāmataḥ—by length; *vistarataḥ*—by breadth; *sva-māna*—by His own measurement; *dehena*—by the transcendental body; *loka-traya*—the three (upper, middle and lower) planetary systems; *saṅgraheṇa*—by total absorption; *vicitra*—variegated; *divya*—transcendental; *ābharaṇa-aṁśukānām*—rays of the ornaments; *kṛta-śriyā apāśrita*—beauty created by those dresses and ornaments; *veṣa*—dressed; *deham*—transcendental body.

TRANSLATION

His transcendental body, unlimited in length and breadth, occupied the three planetary systems, upper, middle and lower. His

body was self-illuminated by unparalleled dress and variegatedness and was properly ornamented.

PURPORT

The length and breadth of the transcendental body of the Supreme Personality of Godhead could only be measured by His own measurement because He is all-pervading throughout the complete cosmic manifestation. The beauty of material nature is due to His personal beauty, yet He is always magnificently dressed and ornamented to prove His transcendental variegatedness, which is so important in the advancement of spiritual knowledge.

TEXT 26

पुंसां स्वकामाय विविक्तमार्गै-
रभ्यर्चतां कामदुघाङ्घ्रिपद्मम् ।
प्रदर्शयन्तं कृपया नखेन्दु-
मयूखभिन्नाङ्गुलिचारुपत्रम् ॥२६॥

puṁsāṁ sva-kāmāya vivikta-mārgair
abhyarcatāṁ kāma-dughāṅghri-padmam
pradarśayantaṁ kṛpayā nakhendu-
mayūkha-bhinnāṅguli-cāru-patram

puṁsām—of the human being; *sva-kāmāya*—according to the desire; *vivikta-mārgaiḥ*—by the path of devotional service; *abhyarcatām*—worshiped; *kāma-dugha-aṅghri-padmam*—the lotus feet of the Lord, which can award all desired fruits; *pradarśayantam*—while showing them; *kṛpayā*—by causeless mercy; *nakha*—nails; *indu*—moonlike; *mayūkha*—rays; *bhinna*—divided; *aṅguli*—figures; *cāru-patram*—very beautiful.

TRANSLATION

The Lord showed His lotus feet by raising them. His lotus feet are the source of all awards achieved by devotional service free from material contamination. Such awards are for those who

worship Him in pure devotion. The splendor of the transcendental rays from His moonlike toenails and fingernails appeared like the petals of a flower.

PURPORT

The Lord fulfills the desires of everyone just as one desires. Pure devotees are interested in achieving the transcendental service of the Lord, which is nondifferent from Him. Therefore, the Lord is the only desire of the pure devotees, and devotional service is the only spotless process for achieving His favor. Śrīla Rūpa Gosvāmī says in his *Bhakti-rasāmṛta-sindhu* (1.1.11) that pure devotional service is *jñāna-karmādy-anāvṛtam:* pure devotional service is without any tinge of speculative knowledge and fruitive activities. Such devotional service is able to award the pure devotee the highest result, namely direct association with the Supreme Personality of Godhead, Lord Kṛṣṇa. According to the *Gopāla-tāpanī Upaniṣad*, the Lord showed one of the many thousands of petals of His lotus feet. It is said: *brāhmaṇo 'sāv anavaratam me dhyātaḥ stutaḥ parārdhānte so 'budhyata gopa-veśo me purastāt āvirbabhūva.* After penetrating for millions of years, Lord Brahmā could understand the transcendental form of the Lord as Śrī Kṛṣṇa, in the dress of a cowherd boy, and thus he recorded his experience in the *Brahma-saṁhitā* in the famous prayer, *govindam ādi-puruṣaṁ tam ahaṁ bhajāmi.*

TEXT 27

मुखेन लोकार्तिहरस्मितेन
परिस्फुरत्कुण्डलमण्डितेन ।
शोणायितेनाधरबिम्बभासा
प्रत्यर्हयन्तं सुनसेन सुभ्र्वा ॥२७॥

mukhena lokārti-hara-smitena
parisphurat-kuṇḍala-maṇḍitena
śoṇāyitenādhara-bimba-bhāsā
pratyarhayantaṁ sunasena subhrvā

mukhena—by a gesture of the face; *loka-ārti-hara*—vanquisher of the distress of the devotees; *smitena*—by smiling; *parisphurat*—dazzling; *kuṇḍala*—earrings; *maṇḍitena*—decorated with; *śoṇāyitena*—acknowledging; *adhara*—of His lips; *bimba*—reflection; *bhāsā*—rays; *pratyarhayantam*—reciprocating; *su-nasena*—by His pleasing nose; *su-bhrvā*—and pleasing eyebrows.

TRANSLATION

He also acknowledged the service of the devotees and vanquished their distress by His beautiful smile. The reflection of His face, decorated with earrings, was so pleasing because it dazzled with the rays from His lips and the beauty of His nose and eyebrows.

PURPORT

Devotional service to the Lord is very much obliging to Him. There are many transcendentalists in different fields of spiritual activities, but devotional service to the Lord is unique. Devotees do not ask anything from the Lord in exchange for their service. Even the most desirable liberation is refused by devotees, although offered by the Lord. Thus the Lord becomes a kind of debtor to the devotees, and He can only try to repay the devotees' service with His ever-enchanting smile. The devotees are ever satisfied by the smiling face of the Lord, and they become enlivened. And by seeing the devotees so enlivened, the Lord Himself is further satisfied. So there is continuous transcendental competition between the Lord and His devotees by such reciprocation of service and acknowledgment.

TEXT 28

कदम्बकिञ्जल्कपिशङ्गवाससा
स्वलंकृतं मेखलया नितम्बे ।
हारेण चानन्तधनेन वत्स
श्रीवत्सवक्षःस्थलवल्लभेन ॥२८॥

kadamba-kiñjalka-piśaṅga-vāsasā
svalaṅkṛtaṁ mekhalayā nitambe

hāreṇa cānanta-dhanena vatsa
śrīvatsa-vakṣaḥ-sthala-vallabhena

kadamba-kiñjalka—saffron dust of the *kadamba* flower; *piśaṅga*—dress of the color; *vāsasā*—by clothing; *su-alaṅkṛtam*—well decorated; *mekhalayā*—by the belt; *nitambe*—on the waist; *hāreṇa*—by the garland; *ca*—also; *ananta*—highly; *dhanena*—valuable; *vatsa*—my dear Vidura; *śrīvatsa*—of the transcendental marking; *vakṣaḥ-sthala*—on the chest; *vallabhena*—very pleasing.

TRANSLATION

O my dear Vidura, the Lord's waist was covered with yellow cloth resembling the saffron dust of the kadamba flower, and it was encircled by a well-decorated belt. His chest was decorated with the śrīvatsa marking and a necklace of unlimited value.

TEXT 29

परार्ध्यकेयूरमणिप्रवेक-
पर्यस्तदोर्दण्डसहस्रशाखम् ।
अव्यक्तमूलं भुवनाङ्घ्रिपेन्द्र-
महीन्द्रभोगैरधिवीतवल्शम् ॥२९॥

parārdhya-keyūra-maṇi-praveka-
paryasta-dordaṇḍa-sahasra-śākham
avyakta-mūlaṁ bhuvanāṅghripendram
ahīndra-bhogair adhivīta-valśam

parārdhya—very valuable; *keyūra*—ornaments; *maṇi-praveka*—highly valuable jewels; *paryasta*—disseminating; *dordaṇḍa*—arms; *sahasra-śākham*—with thousands of branches; *avyakta-mūlam*—self-situated; *bhuvana*—universal; *aṅghripa*—trees; *indram*—the Lord; *ahi-indra*—Anantadeva; *bhogaiḥ*—by hoods; *adhivīta*—surrounded; *valśam*—shoulders.

TRANSLATION

As a sandalwood tree is decorated with fragrant flowers and branches, the Lord's body was decorated with valuable jewels and

pearls. He was the self-situated tree, the Lord of all others in the universe. And as a sandalwood tree is covered with many snakes, so the Lord's body was also covered by the hoods of Ananta.

PURPORT

The word *avyakta-mūlam* is significant here. Generally, no one can see the roots of a tree. But as far as the Lord is concerned, He is the root of Himself because there is no other separate cause of His standing but He Himself. In the *Vedas* it is said that the Lord is *svāśrayāśraya;* He is His own support, and there is no other support for Him. Therefore, *avyakta* means the Supreme Lord Himself and no one else.

TEXT 30

चराचरौको भगवन्महीध्र-
महीन्द्रबन्धुं सलिलोपगूढम् ।
किरीटसाहस्रहिरण्यशृङ्ग-
माविर्भवत्कौस्तुभरत्नगर्भम् ॥३०॥

carācarauko bhagavan-mahīdhram
ahīndra-bandhuṁ salilopagūḍham
kirīṭa-sāhasra-hiraṇya-śṛṅgam
āvirbhavat kaustubha-ratna-garbham

cara—moving animals; *acara*—nonmoving trees; *okaḥ*—the place or situation; *bhagavat*—the Personality of Godhead; *mahīdram*—the mountain; *ahi-indra*—Śrī Anantadeva; *bandhum*—friend; *salila*—water; *upagūḍham*—submerged; *kirīṭa*—helmets; *sāhasra*—thousands; *hiraṇya*—gold; *śṛṅgam*—peaks; *āvirbhavat*—manifested; *kaustubha*—the Kaustubha jewel; *ratna-garbham*—ocean.

TRANSLATION

Like a great mountain, the Lord stands as the abode for all moving and nonmoving living entities. He is the friend of the snakes because Lord Ananta is His friend. As a mountain has thousands of golden peaks, so the Lord was seen with the thousands of golden-helmeted hoods of Ananta-nāga; and as a mountain is sometimes

filled with jewels, so also His transcendental body was fully decorated with valuable jewels. As a mountain is sometimes submerged in the ocean water, so the Lord is sometimes submerged in the water of devastation.

TEXT 31

निवीतमाम्नायमधुव्रतश्रिया
स्वकीर्तिमय्या वनमालया हरिम् ।
सूर्येन्दुवाय्वग्न्यगमं त्रिधामभिः
परिक्रमत्प्राधनिकैर्दुरासदम् ॥३१॥

nivītam āmnāya-madhu-vrata-śriyā
sva-kīrti-mayyā vana-mālayā harim
sūryendu-vāyv-agny-agamaṁ tri-dhāmabhiḥ
parikramat-prādhanikair durāsadam

nivītam—so being enclosed; *āmnāya*—Vedic wisdom; *madhu-vrata-śriyā*—sweet sound in beauty; *sva-kīrti-mayyā*—by His own glories; *vana-mālayā*—flower garland; *harim*—unto the Lord; *sūrya*—the sun; *indu*—the moon; *vāyu*—the air; *agni*—the fire; *agamam*—unapproachable; *tri-dhāmabhiḥ*—by the three planetary systems; *parikramat*—circumambulating; *prādhanikaiḥ*—for fighting; *durāsadam*—very difficult to reach.

TRANSLATION

Lord Brahmā, thus looking upon the Lord in the shape of a mountain, concluded that He was Hari, the Personality of Godhead. He saw that the garland of flowers on His chest glorified Him with Vedic wisdom in sweet songs and looked very beautiful. He was protected by the Sudarśana wheel for fighting, and even the sun, moon, air, fire, etc., could not have access to Him.

TEXT 32

तर्ह्येव तन्नाभिसरःसरोज-
मात्मानमम्भः श्वसनं वियच्च ।

दद‍र्श देवो जगतो विधाता
नातः परं लोकविसर्गदृष्टिः ॥३२॥

tarhy eva tan-nābhi-saraḥ-sarojam
ātmānam ambhaḥ śvasanaṁ viyac ca
dadarśa devo jagato vidhātā
nātaḥ paraṁ loka-visarga-dṛṣṭiḥ

tarhi—therefore; *eva*—certainly; *tat*—His; *nābhi*—navel; *saraḥ*—lake; *sarojam*—lotus flower; *ātmānam*—Brahmā; *ambhaḥ*—the devastating water; *śvasanam*—the drying air; *viyat*—the sky; *ca*—also; *dadarśa*—looked upon; *devaḥ*—demigod; *jagataḥ*—of the universe; *vidhātā*—maker of the destination; *na*—not; *ataḥ param*—beyond; *loka-visarga*—creation of the cosmic manifestation; *dṛṣṭiḥ*—glance.

TRANSLATION

When Lord Brahmā, the maker of the universal destination, thus saw the Lord, he simultaneously glanced over creation. Lord Brahmā saw the lake in Lord Viṣṇu's navel, and the lotus flower, as well as the devastating water, the drying air and the sky. All became visible to him.

TEXT 33

स कर्मबीजं रजसोपरक्तः
प्रजाः सिसृक्षन्नियदेव दृष्ट्वा ।
अस्तौद्विसर्गाभिमुखस्तमीड्य-
मव्यक्तवर्त्मन्यभिवेशितात्मा ॥३३॥

sa karma-bījaṁ rajasoparaktaḥ
prajāḥ sisṛkṣann iyad eva dṛṣṭvā
astaud visargābhimukhas tam īḍyam
avyakta-vartmany abhiveśitātmā

saḥ—he (Brahmā); *karma-bījam*—seed of worldly activities; *rajasā uparaktaḥ*—initiated by the mode of passion; *prajāḥ*—living entities;

sisṛkṣan—willing to create progeny; *iyat*—all the five causes of creation; *eva*—thus; *dṛṣṭvā*—looking on; *astaut*—prayed for; *visarga*—creation after the creation by the Lord; *abhimukhaḥ*—towards; *tam*—that; *īḍyam*—worshipable; *avyakta*—transcendental; *vartmani*—on the path of; *abhiveśita*—fixed; *ātmā*—mind.

TRANSLATION

Lord Brahmā, thus being surcharged with the mode of passion, became inclined to create, and after seeing the five causes of creation indicated by the Personality of Godhead, he began to offer his respectful prayers on the path of the creative mentality.

PURPORT

Even if one is in the material mode of passion, to create something in the world he has to take shelter of the Supreme for the necessary energy. That is the path of the successful termination of any attempt.

Thus end the Bhaktivedanta purports of the Third Canto, Eighth Chapter, of the Śrīmad-Bhāgavatam, *entitled "Manifestation of Brahmā from Garbhodakaśāyī Viṣṇu."*

CHAPTER NINE

Brahmā's Prayers for Creative Energy

TEXT 1

ब्रह्मोवाच
ज्ञातोऽसि मेऽद्य सुचिरान्ननु देहभाजां
न ज्ञायते भगवतो गतिरित्यवद्यम् ।
नान्यत्त्वदस्ति भगवन्नपि तन्न शुद्धं
मायागुणव्यतिकराद्यदुरुर्विभासि ॥ १ ॥

brahmovāca
jñāto 'si me 'dya sucirān nanu deha-bhājāṁ
na jñāyate bhagavato gatir ity avadyam
nānyat tvad asti bhagavann api tan na śuddhaṁ
māyā-guṇa-vyatikarād yad urur vibhāsi

brahmā uvāca—Lord Brahmā said; *jñātaḥ*—known; *asi*—You are; *me*—by me; *adya*—today; *sucirāt*—after a long time; *nanu*—but; *deha-bhājām*—of one who has a material body; *na*—not; *jñāyate*—is known; *bhagavataḥ*—of the Personality of Godhead; *gatiḥ*—course; *iti*—so it is; *avadyam*—great offense; *na anyat*—none beyond; *tvat*—You; *asti*—there is; *bhagavan*—O my Lord; *api*—even though there is; *tat*—anything that may be; *na*—never; *śuddham*—absolute; *māyā*—material energy; *guṇa-vyatikarāt*—because of the mixture of the modes of; *yat*—to which; *uruḥ*—transcendental; *vibhāsi*—You are.

TRANSLATION

Lord Brahmā said: O my Lord, today, after many, many years of penance, I have come to know about You. Oh, how unfortunate the embodied living entities are that they are unable to know Your personality! My Lord, You are the only knowable object because

there is nothing supreme beyond You. If there is anything supposedly superior to You, it is not the Absolute. You exist as the Supreme by exhibiting the creative energy of matter.

PURPORT

The highest peak of the ignorance of the living entities who are conditioned by material bodies is that they are unaware of the supreme cause of the cosmic manifestation. Different people have different theories regarding the supreme cause, but none of them are genuine. The only supreme cause is Viṣṇu, and the intervening impediment is the illusory energy of the Lord. The Lord has employed His wonderful material energy in manifesting many, many wonderful distractions in the material world, and the conditioned souls, illusioned by the same energy, are thus unable to know the supreme cause. The most stalwart scientists and philosophers, therefore, cannot be accepted as wonderful. They only appear wonderful because they are instruments in the hands of the illusory energy of the Lord. Under illusion, the general mass of people deny the existence of the Supreme Lord and accept the foolish products of illusory energy as supreme.

One can know the supreme cause, the Personality of Godhead, by the causeless mercy of the Lord, which is bestowed upon the Lord's pure devotees like Brahmā and those in his disciplic succession. By acts of penance only was Lord Brahmā able to see the Garbhodakaśāyī Viṣṇu, and by realization only could he understand the Lord as He is. Brahmā was extremely satisfied upon observing the magnificent beauty and opulence of the Lord, and he admitted that nothing can be comparable to Him. Only by penance can one appreciate the beauty and opulence of the Lord, and when one is acquainted with that beauty and opulence, he is no longer attracted by any other. This is confirmed in *Bhagavad-gītā* (2.59): *paraṁ dṛṣṭvā nivartate.*

Foolish human beings who do not endeavor to investigate the supreme beauty and opulence of the Lord are here condemned by Brahmā. It is imperative that every human being try for such knowledge, and if anyone does not do so, his life is spoiled. Anything that is beautiful and opulent in the material sense is enjoyed by those living entities who are like crows. Crows always engage in picking at rejected garbage, whereas the white ducks do not mix with the crows. Rather, they take pleasure in transparent lakes with lotus flowers, surrounded by beautiful orchards. Both crows and ducks are undoubtedly birds by birth, but they are not of the same feather.

TEXT 2

रूपं यदेतदवबोधरसोदयेन
शश्वन्निवृत्ततमसः सदनुग्रहाय ।
आदौ गृहीतमवतारशतैकबीजं
यन्नाभिपद्मभवनादहमाविरासम् ॥ २ ॥

rūpaṁ yad etad avabodha-rasodayena
śaśvan-nivṛtta-tamasaḥ sad-anugrahāya
ādau gṛhītam avatāra-śataika-bījaṁ
yan-nābhi-padma-bhavanād aham āvirāsam

rūpam—form; *yat*—which; *etat*—that; *avabodha-rasa*—of Your internal potency; *udayena*—with the manifestation; *śaśvat*—forever; *nivṛtta*—freed from; *tamasaḥ*—material contamination; *sat-anugrahāya*—for the sake of the devotees; *ādau*—original in the creative energy of matter; *gṛhītam*—accepted; *avatāra*—of incarnations; *śata-eka-bījam*—the root cause of hundreds; *yat*—that which; *nābhi-padma*—the navel lotus flower; *bhavanāt*—from the home; *aham*—myself; *āvirāsam*—generated.

TRANSLATION

The form which I see is eternally freed from material contamination and has advented to show mercy to the devotees as a manifestation of internal potency. This incarnation is the origin of many other incarnations, and I am born from the lotus flower grown from Your navel home.

PURPORT

The three deities Brahmā, Viṣṇu and Maheśvara (Śiva), the executive heads of the three modes of material nature (passion, goodness and ignorance), are all generated from Garbhodakaśāyī Viṣṇu, who is described herein by Brahmā. From the Kṣīrodakaśāyī Viṣṇu, many Viṣṇu incarnations expand at different ages in the duration of the cosmic manifestation. They are expanded only for the transcendental happiness of the pure devotees. The incarnations of Viṣṇu, who appear at different ages and times, are never to be compared to the conditioned souls. The *viṣṇu-tattvas* are not to be compared to deities like Brahmā and Śiva, nor are they on the same level. Anyone who compares them is called a *pāṣaṇḍī*, or infidel. *Tamasaḥ*, mentioned herein, is the material nature, and the spiritual nature has a completely separate existence from *tamaḥ*. Therefore, spiritual nature is called *avabodha-rasa*, or *avarodha-rasa*. *Avarodha* means "that which completely nullifies." In the Transcendence there is no chance of material contact by any means. Brahmā is the first living being, and therefore he mentions his birth from the lotus flower generated from the abdomen of Garbhodakaśāyī Viṣṇu.

TEXT 3

नातः परं परम यद्भवतः स्वरूप-
मानन्दमात्रमविकल्पमविद्धवर्चः ।
पश्यामि विश्वसृजमेकमविश्वमात्मन्
भूतेन्द्रियात्मकमदस्त उपाश्रितोऽस्मि ॥३॥

nātaḥ paraṁ parama yad bhavataḥ svarūpam
ānanda-mātram avikalpam aviddha-varcaḥ
paśyāmi viśva-sṛjam ekam aviśvam ātman
bhūtendriyātmaka-madas ta upāśrito 'smi

na—do not; *ataḥ param*—hereafter; *parama*—O Supreme; *yat*—that which; *bhavataḥ*—of Your Lordship; *svarūpam*—eternal form; *ānanda-mātram*—impersonal Brahman effulgence; *avikalpam*—without changes; *aviddha-varcaḥ*—without deterioration of potency; *paśyāmi*—do I see; *viśva-sṛjam*—creator of the cosmic manifestation; *ekam*—one without a second; *aviśvam*—and yet not of matter; *ātman*—O Supreme Cause; *bhūta*—body; *indriya*—senses; *ātmaka*—on such identification; *madaḥ*—pride; *te*—unto You; *upāśritaḥ*—surrendered; *asmi*—I am.

TRANSLATION

O my Lord, I do not see a form superior to Your present form of eternal bliss and knowledge. In Your impersonal Brahman effulgence in the spiritual sky, there is no occasional change and no deterioration of internal potency. I surrender unto You because whereas I am proud of my material body and senses, Your Lordship is the cause of the cosmic manifestation and yet You are untouched by matter.

PURPORT

As stated in *Bhagavad-gītā* (18.55), *bhaktyā mām abhijānāti yāvān yaś cāsmi tattvataḥ:* the Supreme Personality of Godhead can only be partially known, and only by the process of devotional service to the Lord. Lord Brahmā became aware that the Supreme Lord Kṛṣṇa has many, many eternal, blissful forms of knowledge. He has described such expansions of the Supreme Lord, Govinda, in his *Brahma-saṁhitā* (5.33), as follows:

advaitam acyutam anādim ananta-rūpam
ādyaṁ purāṇa-puruṣaṁ nava-yauvanaṁ ca
vedeṣu durlabham adurlabham ātma-bhaktau
govindam ādi-puruṣaṁ tam ahaṁ bhajāmi

"I worship Govinda, the primeval Lord, who is nondual and infallible. He is the original cause of all causes, even though He expands in many, many forms. Although He is the oldest personality, He is ever youthful, unaffected by old age. The Supreme Personality of Godhead cannot be known by the academic wisdom of the *Vedas;* one has to approach the devotee of the Lord to understand Him."

The only way to understand the Lord as He is, is by devotional service to the Lord, or by approaching the devotee of the Lord who always has the Lord in his heart. By devotional perfection one can understand that the impersonal *brahmajyoti* is only a partial representation of the Supreme Personality of Godhead, Lord Kṛṣṇa, and that the three *puruṣa* expansions in the material creation are His plenary portions. In the spiritual sky of the *brahmajyoti* there is no change of various *kalpas* or millenniums, and there are no creative activities in the Vaikuṇṭha worlds. The influence of time is conspicuous by its absence. The rays of the transcendental body of the Lord, the unlimited *brahmajyoti,* are undeterred by the influence of material energy. In the material world also, the initial creator is the Lord Himself. He brings about the creation of Brahmā, who becomes the subsequent creator, empowered by the Lord.

TEXT 4

तद्वा इदं भुवनमङ्गल मङ्गलाय
ध्याने स्म नो दर्शितं त उपासकानाम् ।
तस्मै नमो भगवतेऽनुविधेम तुभ्यं
योऽनादृतो नरकभाग्भिरसत्प्रसङ्गैः ॥ ४ ॥

tad vā idaṁ bhuvana-maṅgala maṅgalāya
dhyāne sma no darśitaṁ ta upāsakānām
tasmai namo bhagavate 'nuvidhema tubhyaṁ
yo 'nādṛto naraka-bhāgbhir asat-prasaṅgaiḥ

tat—the Supreme Personality of Godhead, Śrī Kṛṣṇa; *vā*—or; *idam*—this present form; *bhuvana-maṅgala*—O You who are all-auspicious for all the universes; *maṅgalāya*—for the sake of all prosperity; *dhyāne*—in meditation; *sma*—as it were; *naḥ*—unto us; *darśitam*—manifested; *te*—Your; *upāsakānām*—of the devotees; *tasmai*—unto Him; *namaḥ*—my respectful obeisances; *bhagavate*—unto the Personality of Godhead; *anuvidhema*—I perform; *tubhyam*—unto You; *yaḥ*—which; *anādṛtaḥ*—is neglected; *naraka-bhāgbhiḥ*—by persons destined for hell; *asat-prasaṅgaiḥ*—by material topics.

TRANSLATION

This present form, or any transcendental form expanded by the Supreme Personality of Godhead, Śrī Kṛṣṇa, is equally auspicious for all the universes. Since You have manifested this eternal personal form upon whom Your devotees meditate, I therefore offer my respectful obeisances unto You. Those who are destined to be

dispatched to the path of hell neglect Your personal form because of speculating on material topics.

PURPORT

Regarding the personal and impersonal features of the Supreme Absolute Truth, the personal forms exhibited by the Lord in His different plenary expansions are all for the benediction of all the universes. The personal form of the Lord is also worshiped in meditation as Supersoul, Paramātmā, but the impersonal *brahmajyoti* is not worshiped. Persons who are addicted to the impersonal feature of the Lord, whether in meditation or otherwise, are all pilgrims to hell because, as stated in *Bhagavad-gītā* (12.5), impersonalists simply waste their time in mundane mental speculation because they are addicted more to false arguments than to reality. Therefore, the association of the impersonalists is condemned herewith by Brahmā.

All the plenary expansions of the Personality of Godhead are equally potent, as confirmed in the *Brahma-saṁhitā* (5.46):

dīpārcir eva hi daśāntaram abhyupetya
dīpāyate vivṛta-hetu-samāna-dharmā
yas tādṛg eva hi ca viṣṇutayā vibhāti
govindam ādi-puruṣaṁ tam ahaṁ bhajāmi

The Lord expands Himself as the flames of a fire expand one after another. Although the original flame, or Śrī Kṛṣṇa, is accepted as Govinda, the Supreme Person, all other expansions, such as Rāma, Nṛsiṁha and Varāha, are as potent as the original Lord. All such expanded forms are transcendental. In the beginning of *Śrīmad-Bhāgavatam* it is made clear that the Supreme Truth is eternally uncontaminated by material touch. There is no jugglery of words and activities in the transcendental kingdom of the Lord. All the Lord's forms are transcendental, and such manifestations are ever identical. The particular form of the Lord exhibited to a devotee is not mundane, even though the devotee may retain material desire, nor is it manifest under the influence of material energy, as is foolishly considered by the impersonalists. Impersonalists who consider the transcendental forms of the Lord to be products of the material world are surely destined for hell.

TEXT 5

ये तु त्वदीयचरणाम्बुजकोशगन्धं
जिघ्रन्ति कर्णविवरैः श्रुतिवातनीतम् ।
भक्त्या गृहीतचरणः परया च तेषां
नापैषि नाथ हृदयाम्बुरुहात्स्वपुंसाम् ॥५॥

ye tu tvadīya-caraṇāmbuja-kośa-gandhaṁ
jighranti karṇa-vivaraiḥ śruti-vāta-nītam
bhaktyā gṛhīta-caraṇaḥ parayā ca teṣāṁ
nāpaiṣi nātha hṛdayāmburuhāt sva-puṁsām

ye—those who; *tu*—but; *tvadīya*—Your; *caraṇa-ambuja*—lotus feet; *kośa*—inside; *gandham*—flavor; *jighranti*—smell; *karṇa-vivaraiḥ*—through the channel of the ears; *śruti-vāta-nītam*—carried by the air of Vedic sound; *bhaktyā*—by devotional service; *gṛhīta-caraṇaḥ*—accepting the lotus feet; *parayā*—transcendental; *ca*—also; *teṣām*—for them; *na*—never; *apaiṣi*—separate; *nātha*—O my Lord; *hṛdaya*—heart; *ambu-ruhāt*—from the lotus of; *sva-puṁsām*—of Your own devotees.

TRANSLATION

O my Lord, persons who smell the aroma of Your lotus feet, carried by the air of Vedic sound through the holes of the ears, accept Your devotional service. For them You are never separated from the lotus of their hearts.

PURPORT

For the pure devotee of the Lord there is nothing beyond the lotus feet of the Lord, and the Lord knows that such devotees do not wish anything more than that. The word *tu* specifically establishes this fact. The Lord also does not wish to be separated from the lotus hearts of those pure devotees. That is the transcendental relationship between the pure devotees and the Personality of Godhead. Because the Lord does not wish to separate Himself from the hearts of such pure devotees, it is understood that they are specifically dearer than the impersonalists. The relationship of the pure devotees with the Lord develops because of devotional service to the Lord on the authentic basis of Vedic authority. Such pure devotees are not mundane sentimentalists, but are factually realists because their activities are supported by the Vedic authorities who have given aural reception to the facts mentioned in the Vedic literatures.

The word *parayā* is very significant. *Parā bhakti*, or spontaneous love of God, is the basis of an intimate relationship with the Lord. This highest stage of relationship with the Lord can be attained simply by hearing about Him (His name, form, quality, etc.) from authentic sources like *Bhagavad-gītā* and *Śrīmad-Bhāgavatam*, recited by pure, unalloyed devotees of the Lord.

TEXT 6

तावद्भयं द्रविणदेहसुहृन्निमित्तं
शोकः स्पृहा परिभवो विपुलश्च लोभः ।
तावन्ममेत्यसदवग्रह आर्तिमूलं
यावन्न तेऽङ्घ्रिमभयं प्रवृणीत लोकः ॥६॥

tāvad bhayaṁ draviṇa-deha-suhṛn-nimittaṁ
śokaḥ spṛhā paribhavo vipulaś ca lobhaḥ
tāvan mamety asad-avagraha ārti-mūlaṁ
yāvan na te 'ṅghrim abhayaṁ pravṛṇīta lokaḥ

tāvat—until then; *bhayam*—fear; *draviṇa*—wealth; *deha*—body; *suhṛt*—relatives; *nimittam*—for the matter of; *śokaḥ*—lamentation; *spṛhā*—desire; *paribhavaḥ*—paraphernalia; *vipulaḥ*—very great; *ca*—also; *lobhaḥ*—avarice; *tāvat*—up to that time; *mama*—mine; *iti*—thus; *asat*—perishable; *avagrahaḥ*—undertaking; *ārti-mūlam*—full of anxieties; *yāvat*—as long as; *na*—do not; *te*—Your; *aṅghrim abhayam*—safe lotus feet; *pravṛṇīta*—take shelter; *lokaḥ*—the people of the world.

TRANSLATION

O my Lord, the people of the world are embarrassed by all material anxieties—they are always afraid. They always try to protect wealth, body and friends, they are filled with lamentation and

unlawful desires and paraphernalia, and they avariciously base their undertakings on the perishable conceptions of "my" and "mine." As long as they do not take shelter of Your safe lotus feet, they are full of such anxieties.

PURPORT

One may question how one can always think of the Lord in regard to His name, fame, quality, etc., if one is embarrassed by thoughts of family affairs. Everyone in the material world is full of thoughts about how to maintain his family, how to protect his wealth, how to keep pace with friends and relatives, etc. Thus he is always in fear and lamentation, trying to keep up with the status quo. In answer to this question, this verse spoken by Brahmā is very appropriate.

A pure devotee of the Lord never thinks of himself as the proprietor of his home. He surrenders everything unto the supreme control of the Lord, and thus he has no fear for maintaining his family or protecting the interests of his family. Because of this surrender, he no longer has any attraction for wealth. Even if there is attraction for wealth, it is not for sense enjoyment, but for the service of the Lord. A pure devotee may be attracted to accumulating wealth just like an ordinary man, but the difference is that a devotee acquires money for the service of the Lord, whereas the ordinary man acquires money for his sense enjoyment. Thus the acquisition of wealth by a devotee is not a source of anxieties, as is the case for a worldly man. And because a pure devotee accepts everything in the sense of serving the Lord, the poisonous teeth of accumulation of wealth are extracted. If a snake has its poison removed and bites a man, there is no fatal effect. Similarly, wealth accumulated in the cause of the Lord has no poisonous teeth, and the effect is not fatal. A pure devotee is never entangled in material worldly affairs even though he may remain in the world like an ordinary man.

TEXT 7

दैवेन ते हतधियो भवतः प्रसङ्गा-
त्सर्वाशुभोपशमनाद्विमुखेन्द्रिया ये ।
कुर्वन्ति कामसुखलेशलवाय दीना
लोभाभिभूतमनसोऽकुशलानि शश्वत् ॥७॥

daivena te hata-dhiyo bhavataḥ prasaṅgāt
sarvāśubhopaśamanād vimukhendriyā ye
kurvanti kāma-sukha-leśa-lavāya dīnā
lobhābhibhūta-manaso 'kuśalāni śaśvat

daivena—by fate of misfortune; *te*—they; *hata-dhiyaḥ*—bereft of memory; *bhavataḥ*—of You; *prasaṅgāt*—from the topics; *sarva*—all; *aśubha*—inauspiciousness; *upaśamanāt*—curbing down; *vimukha*—turned against; *indriyāḥ*—senses; *ye*—those; *kurvanti*—act; *kāma*—sense gratification; *sukha*—happiness; *leśa*—brief; *lavāya*—for a moment only; *dīnāḥ*—poor fellows; *lobha-abhibhūta*—overwhelmed by greed; *manasaḥ*—of one whose mind; *akuśalāni*—inauspicious activities; *śaśvat*—always.

TRANSLATION

O my Lord, persons who are bereft of the all-auspicious performance of chanting and hearing about Your transcendental activities are certainly unfortunate and are also bereft of good sense. They engage in inauspicious activities, enjoying sense gratification for a very little while.

PURPORT

The next question is why people are against such auspicious activities as chanting and hearing the glories and pastimes of the Lord, which can bring total freedom from the cares and anxieties of material existence. The only answer to this question is that they are unfortunate because of supernatural control due to their offensive activities performed simply for the sake of sense gratification. The Lord's pure devotees, however, take compassion upon such unfortunate persons and, in a missionary spirit, try to persuade them into the line of devotional service. Only by the grace of pure devotees can such unfortunate men be elevated to the position of transcendental service.

TEXT 8

क्षुत्तृट्त्रिधातुभिरिमा मुहुरर्द्यमानाः
शीतोष्णवातवरषैरितरेतराच्च ।

कामाग्निनाच्युत रुषा च सुदुर्भरेण
सम्पश्यतो मन उरुक्रम सीदते मे ॥ ८ ॥

kṣut-tṛṭ-tridhātubhir imā muhur ardyamānāḥ
śītoṣṇa-vāta-varaṣair itaretarāc ca
kāmāgninācyuta-ruṣā ca sudurbhareṇa
sampaśyato mana urukrama sīdate me

kṣut—hunger; *tṛṭ*—thirst; *tri-dhātubhiḥ*—three humors, namely mucus, bile and wind; *imāḥ*—all of them; *muhuḥ*—always; *ardyamānāḥ*—perplexed; *śīta*—winter; *uṣṇa*—summer; *vāta*—wind; *varaṣaiḥ*—by rains; *itara-itarāt*—and many other disturbances; *ca*—also; *kāma-agninā*—by strong sex urges; *acyuta-ruṣā*—indefatigable anger; *ca*—also; *sudurbhareṇa*—most unbearable; *sampaśyataḥ*—so observing; *manaḥ*—mind; *urukrama*—O great actor; *sīdate*—becomes despondent; *me*—my.

TRANSLATION

O great actor, my Lord, all these poor creatures are constantly perplexed by hunger, thirst, severe cold, secretion and bile, attacked by coughing winter, blasting summer, rains and many other disturbing elements, and overwhelmed by strong sex urges and indefatigable anger. I take pity on them, and I am very much aggrieved for them.

PURPORT

A pure devotee of the Lord like Brahmā and persons in his disciplic succession are always unhappy to see the perplexities of the conditioned souls, who are suffering the onslaughts of the threefold miseries which pertain to the body and mind, to the disturbances of material nature, and to many other such material disadvantages. Not knowing adequate measures for relieving such difficulties, suffering persons sometimes pose themselves as leaders of the people, and the unfortunate followers are put into further disadvantages under such so-called leadership. This is like a blind man's leading another blind man to fall into a ditch. Therefore, unless the devotees of the Lord take pity on them and teach them the right path, their lives are hopeless failures. The devotees of the

Lord who voluntarily take the responsibility of raising the foolish materialistic sense enjoyers are as confidential to the Lord as Lord Brahmā.

TEXT 9

यावत्पृथक्त्वमिदमात्मन इन्द्रियार्थ-
मायाबलं भगवतो जन ईश पश्येत् ।
तावन्न संसृतिरसौ प्रतिसंक्रमेत
व्यर्थापि दुःखनिवहं वहती क्रियार्था ॥९॥

yāvat pṛthaktvam idam ātmana indriyārtha-
māyā-balaṁ bhagavato jana īśa paśyet
tāvan na saṁsṛtir asau pratisaṅkrameta
vyarthāpi duḥkha-nivahaṁ vahatī kriyārthā

yāvat—as long as; *pṛthaktvam*—separatism; *idam*—this; *ātmanaḥ*—of the body; *indriya-artha*—for sense gratification; *māyā-balam*—influence of external energy; *bhagavataḥ*—of the Personality of Godhead; *janaḥ*—a person; *īśa*—O my Lord; *paśyet*—sees; *tāvat*—so long; *na*—not; *saṁsṛtiḥ*—the influence of material existence; *asau*—that man; *pratisaṅkrameta*—can overcome; *vyarthā api*—although without meaning; *duḥkha-nivaham*—multiple miseries; *vahatī*—bringing; *kriyā-arthā*—for fruitive activities.

TRANSLATION

O my Lord, the material miseries are without factual existence for the soul. Yet as long as the conditioned soul sees the body as meant for sense enjoyment, he cannot get out of the entanglement of material miseries, being influenced by Your external energy.

PURPORT

The whole trouble of the living entity in material existence is that he has an independent conception of life. He is always dependent on the rules of the Supreme Lord, in both the conditioned and liberated states, but by the influence of the external energy the conditioned soul thinks himself independent of the supremacy of the Personality of Godhead.

His constitutional position is to dovetail himself with the desire of the supreme will, but as long as he does not do so, he is sure to drag on in the shackles of material bondage. As stated in *Bhagavad-gītā* (2.55), *prajahāti yadā kāmān sarvān pārtha mano-gatān:* he has to give up all sorts of plans manufactured by mental concoction. The living entity has to dovetail himself with the supreme will. That will help him to get out of the entanglement of material existence.

TEXT 10

अह्न्याप्तार्तकरणा निशि निःशयाना
नानामनोरथधिया क्षणभग्ननिद्राः ।
दैवाहतार्थरचना ऋषयोऽपि देव
युष्मत्प्रसङ्गविमुखा इह संसरन्ति ॥१०॥

ahny āpṛtārta-karaṇā niśi niḥśayānā
nānā-manoratha-dhiyā kṣaṇa-bhagna-nidrāḥ
daivāhatārtha-racanā ṛṣayo 'pi deva
yuṣmat-prasaṅga-vimukhā iha saṁsaranti

ahni—during the daytime; *āpṛta*—engaged; *ārta*—distressing engagement; *karaṇāḥ*—senses; *niśi*—at night; *niḥśayānāḥ*—insomnia; *nānā*—various; *manoratha*—mental speculations; *dhiyā*—by intelligence; *kṣaṇa*—constantly; *bhagna*—broken; *nidrāḥ*—sleep; *daiva*—superhuman; *āhata-artha*—frustrated; *racanāḥ*—plans; *ṛṣayaḥ*—great sages; *api*—also; *deva*—O my Lord; *yuṣmat*—Your Lordship's; *prasaṅga*—topic; *vimukhāḥ*—turned against; *iha*—in this (material world); *saṁsaranti*—do rotate.

TRANSLATION

Such nondevotees engage their senses in very troublesome and extensive work, and they suffer insomnia at night because their intelligence constantly breaks their sleep with various mental speculations. They are frustrated in all their various plans by supernatural power. Even great sages, if they are against Your transcendental topics, must rotate in this material world.

PURPORT

As described in the previous verse, people who have no taste for the devotional service of the Lord are occupied in material engagements. Most of them engage during the daytime in hard physical labor; their senses are engaged very extensively in troublesome duties in the gigantic plants of heavy industrial enterprise. The owners of such factories are engaged in finding a market for their industrial products, and the laborers are engaged in extensive production involving huge mechanical arrangements. "Factory" is another name for hell. At night, hellishly engaged persons take advantage of wine and women to satisfy their tired senses, but they are not even able to have sound sleep because their various mental speculative plans constantly interrupt their sleep. Because they suffer from insomnia sometimes they feel sleepy in the morning for lack of sufficient rest. By the arrangement of supernatural power, even the great scientists and thinkers of the world suffer frustration of their various plans and thus rot in the material world birth after birth. A great scientist may make discoveries in atomic energy for the quick destruction of the world and may be awarded the best prize in recognition of his service (or disservice), but he also has to undergo the reactions of his work by rotating in the cycle of repeated births and deaths under the superhuman law of material nature. All these people who are against the principle of devotional service are destined to rotate in this material world without fail.

This verse particularly mentions that even sages who are averse to the principles of devotional service to the Lord are also condemned to undergo the terms of material existence. Not only in this age, but formerly also, there were many sages who tried to invent their own systems of religion without reference to devotional service to the Supreme Lord, but there cannot be any religious principle without devotional service to the Lord. The Supreme Lord is the leader of the entire range of living entities, and no one can be equal to or greater than Him. Even the Lord's impersonal feature and all-pervading localized feature cannot be on an equal level with the Supreme Personality of Godhead. Therefore, there cannot be any religion or system of genuine philosophy for the advancement of the living entities without the principle of devotional service.

The impersonalists, who take much trouble in penance and austerity for self-liberation, may approach the impersonal *brahmajyoti*, but ultimately, because of not being situated in devotional service, they glide down again to the material world to undergo another term of material existence. This is confirmed as follows:

ye 'nye 'ravindākṣa vimukta-māninas
tvayy asta-bhāvād aviśuddha-buddhayaḥ
āruhya kṛcchreṇa paraṁ padaṁ tataḥ
patanty adho 'nādṛta-yuṣmad-aṅghrayaḥ

"Persons who are falsely under the impression of being liberated, without devotional service to the Lord, may reach the goal of the *brahmajyoti*, but because of their impure consciousness and for want of shelter in the Vaikuṇṭhalokas, such so-called liberated persons again fall down into material existence." (*Bhāg.* 10.2.32)

Therefore, no one can manufacture any system of religion without the principle of devotional service to the Lord. As we find in the Sixth Canto of *Śrīmad-Bhāgavatam*, the initiator of religious principles is the Lord Himself. In *Bhagavad-gītā* also we find that the Lord condemns all forms of religion other than that which entails the process of surrendering unto the Supreme. Any system which leads one to the devotional service of the Lord, and nothing else, is actually religion or philosophy. In the Sixth Canto we find the following statements of Yamarāja, the controller of all unfaithful living entities:

dharmaṁ tu sākṣād bhagavat-praṇītaṁ
na vai vidur ṛṣayo nāpi devāḥ
na siddha-mukhyā asurā manuṣyāḥ
kuto nu vidyādhara-cāraṇādayaḥ

svayambhūr nāradaḥ śambhuḥ
kumāraḥ kapilo manuḥ
prahlādo janako bhīṣmo
balir vaiyāsakir vayam

dvādaśaite vijānīmo
dharmaṁ bhāgavataṁ bhaṭāḥ

guhyaṁ viśuddhaṁ durbodhaṁ
yaṁ jñātvāmṛtam aśnute

"The principles of religion are initiated by the Supreme Personality of Godhead, and no one else, including the sages and demigods, can manufacture any such principles. Since even great sages and demigods are unauthorized to inaugurate such principles of religion, what to speak of others—the so-called mystics, demons, human beings, Vidyādharas and Cāraṇas living in the lower planets? Twelve personalities—Brahmā, Nārada, Lord Śiva, Kumāra, Kapila, Manu, Prahlāda Mahārāja, Janaka Mahārāja, Bhīṣma, Bali, Śukadeva Gosvāmī and Yamarāja—are agents of the Lord authorized to speak and propagate the principles of religion." (*Bhāg.* 6.3.19–21)

The principles of religion are not open to any ordinary living entity. They are just to bring the human being onto the platform of morality. Nonviolence, etc., are necessary for misguided persons because unless one is moral and nonviolent one cannot understand the principles of religion. To understand what is actually religion is very difficult even if one is situated in the principles of morality and nonviolence. It is very confidential because as soon as one is conversant with the real principles of religion, he is at once liberated to the eternal life of bliss and knowledge. Therefore, one who is not situated in the principles of devotional service to the Lord should not pose himself as a religious leader of the innocent public. The *Īśopaniṣad* emphatically forbids this nonsense in the following *mantra:*

andhaṁ tamaḥ praviśanti
ye 'sambhūtim upāsate
tato bhūya iva te tamo
ya u sambhūtyāṁ ratāḥ
(*Īśopaniṣad* 12)

A person in ignorance of the principles of religion who therefore does nothing in the matter of religion is far better than a person who misguides others in the name of religion without reference to the factual religious principles of devotional service. Such so-called leaders of religion are sure to be condemned by Brahmā and other great authorities.

TEXT 11

त्वं भक्तियोगपरिभावितहृत्सरोज
आस्से श्रुतेक्षितपथो ननु नाथ पुंसाम् ।
यद्यद्धिया त उरुगाय विभावयन्ति
तत्तद्वपुः प्रणयसे सदनुग्रहाय ॥११॥

tvaṁ bhakti-yoga-paribhāvita-hṛt-saroja
āsse śruteksita-patho nanu nātha puṁsām
yad-yad-dhiyā ta urugāya vibhāvayanti
tat-tad-vapuḥ praṇayase sad-anugrahāya

tvam—unto You; *bhakti-yoga*—in devotional service; *paribhāvita*—being one hundred percent engaged; *hṛt*—of the heart; *saroje*—on the lotus; *āsse*—You reside; *śruta-īkṣita*—seen through the ear; *pathaḥ*—the path; *nanu*—now; *nātha*—O my Lord; *puṁsām*—of the devotees; *yat-yat*—whichever; *dhiyā*—by meditating; *te*—Your; *urugāya*—O multiglorious; *vibhāvayanti*—they specifically think of; *tat-tat*—the very same; *vapuḥ*—transcendental form; *praṇayase*—do You manifest; *sat-anugrahāya*—to show Your causeless mercy.

TRANSLATION

O my Lord, Your devotees can see You through the ears by the process of bona fide hearing, and thus their hearts become cleansed, and You take Your seat there. You are so merciful to Your devotees that You manifest Yourself in the particular eternal form of transcendence in which they always think of You.

PURPORT

The statement here that the Lord manifests Himself before the devotee in the form in which the devotee likes to worship Him indicates that the Lord becomes subordinate to the desire of the devotee—so much so that He manifests His particular form as the devotee demands. This demand of the devotee is satisfied by the Lord because He is pliable in terms of the transcendental loving service of the devotee. This is also confirmed in *Bhagavad-gītā* (4.11): *ye yathā māṁ prapadyante tāṁs tathaiva bhajāmy aham.* We should note, however, that the Lord is never the order supplier of the devotee. Here in this verse it is particularly mentioned: *tvaṁ bhakti-yoga-paribhāvita.* This indicates the efficiency achieved through execution of matured devotional service, or *premā,* love of Godhead. This state of *premā* is achieved by the gradual process of development from faith to love. On faith one associates with bona fide devotees, and by such association one can become engaged in bona fide devotional service, which includes proper initiation and the execution of the primary devotional duties prescribed in the revealed scriptures. This is clearly indicated herein by the word *śrutekṣita.* The *śrutekṣita* path is to hear from bona fide devotees who are conversant with Vedic wisdom, free from mundane sentiment. By this bona fide hearing process, the neophyte devotee becomes cleansed of all material rubbish, and thus he becomes attached to one of the many transcendental forms of the Lord, as described in the *Vedas.*

This attachment of the devotee to a particular form of the Lord is due to natural inclination. Each and every living entity is originally attached to a particular type of transcendental service because he is eternally the servitor of the Lord. Lord Caitanya says that the living entity is eternally a servitor of the Supreme Personality of Godhead, Śrī Kṛṣṇa. Therefore, every living entity has a particular type of service relationship with the Lord, eternally. This particular attachment is invoked by practice of regulative devotional service to the Lord, and thus the devotee becomes attached to the eternal form of the Lord, exactly like one who is already eternally attached. This attachment for a particular form of the Lord is called *svarūpa-siddhi.* The Lord sits on the lotus heart of the devotee in the eternal form the pure devotee desires, and thus the Lord does not part from the devotee, as confirmed in the previous verse. The Lord, however, does not disclose Himself to a casual or inauthentic worshiper to be exploited. This is confirmed in *Bhagavad-gītā* (7.25): *nāhaṁ prakāśaḥ sarvasya yoga-māyā-samāvṛtaḥ.* Rather, by *yoga-māyā,* the Lord remains concealed to the nondevotees or casual devotees who are serving their sense gratification. The Lord is never visible to the pseudodevotees who worship the demigods in charge of universal affairs. The conclusion is that the Lord cannot become the order supplier of a pseudodevotee, but He is always prepared to respond to the desires of a pure, unconditional devotee, who is free from all tinges of material infection.

TEXT 12

नातिप्रसीदति तथोपचितोपचारै-
राराधितः सुरगणैर्हृदिबद्धकामैः ।
यत्सर्वभूतदययासदलभ्ययैको
नानाजनेष्ववहितः सुहृदन्तरात्मा ॥१२॥

nātiprasīdati tathopacitopacārair
ārādhitaḥ sura-gaṇair hṛdi baddha-kāmaiḥ
yat sarva-bhūta-dayayāsad-alabhyayaiko
nānā-janeṣv avahitaḥ suhṛd antar-ātmā

na—never; *ati*—very much; *prasīdati*—become satisfied; *tathā*—as much as; *upacita*—by pompous arrangement; *upacāraiḥ*—with much worshipable paraphernalia; *ārādhitaḥ*—being worshiped; *sura-gaṇaiḥ*—by the celestial demigods; *hṛdi baddha-kāmaiḥ*—with hearts full of all sorts of material desires; *yat*—that which; *sarva*—all; *bhūta*—living entities; *dayayā*—to show them causeless mercy; *asat*—nondevotee; *alabhyayā*—not being achieved; *ekaḥ*—one without a second; *nānā*—various; *janeṣu*—in living entities; *avahitaḥ*—perceived; *suhṛt*—well-wishing friend; *antaḥ*—within; *ātmā*—Supersoul.

TRANSLATION

My Lord, You are not very much satisfied by the worship of the demigods, who arrange for Your worship very pompously, with various paraphernalia, but who are full of material hankerings. You are situated in everyone's heart as the Supersoul just to show Your causeless mercy, and You are the eternal well-wisher, but You are unavailable for the nondevotee.

PURPORT

The demigods in the celestial heavenly planets, who are appointed administrators of the material affairs, are also devotees of the Lord. But, at the same time, they have desires for material opulence and sense gratification. The Lord is so kind that He awards them all sorts of material happiness, more than they can desire, but He is not satisfied with them because they are not pure devotees. The Lord does not want any one of His innumerable sons (the living entities) to remain in the material world of threefold miseries to perpetually suffer the material pangs of birth, death, old age and disease. The demigods in the heavenly planets, and many devotees on this planet also, want to remain in the material world as devotees of the Lord and take advantage of material happiness. They do so at a risk of falling down to the lower status of existence, and this makes the Lord dissatisfied with them.

Pure devotees are not desirous of any material enjoyment, nor are they averse to it. They completely dovetail their desires with the desires of the Lord and perform nothing on their personal account. Arjuna is a good example. On his own sentiment, due to family affection, Arjuna did not want to fight, but finally, after hearing *Śrīmad Bhagavad-gītā*, he agreed to fight in the interests of the Lord. Therefore, the Lord is very much satisfied with pure devotees because they do not act for sense gratification but only in terms of the Lord's desire. As Paramātmā, or Supersoul, He is situated in everyone's heart, always giving everyone the chance of good counsel. Thus everyone should take the opportunity and render transcendental loving service to Him wholly and solely.

The nondevotees, however, are neither like the demigods nor like the pure devotees, but are averse to the transcendental relationship with the Lord. They have revolted against the Lord and must perpetually undergo the reactions of their own activities.

Bhagavad-gītā (4.11) states: *ye yathā māṁ prapadyante tāṁs tathaiva bhajāmy aham.* "Although the Lord is equally kind to every living being, the living beings, for their own part, are able to please the Lord to either a greater or lesser extent." The demigods are called *sakāma* devotees, or devotees with material desires in mind, while the pure devotees are called *niṣkāma* devotees because they have no desires for their personal interests. The *sakāma* devotees are self-interested because they do not think of others, and therefore they are not able to satisfy the Lord perfectly, whereas the pure devotees take the missionary responsibility of turning nondevotees into devotees, and they are therefore able to satisfy the Lord more than the demigods. The Lord is unmindful of the nondevotees, although He is sitting within everyone's heart as well-wisher and Supersoul. However, He also gives them the chance to receive His mercy through His pure devotees who are engaged in missionary activities. Sometimes the Lord Himself descends for missionary activities, as He did in the form of Lord Caitanya, but mostly He sends His bona fide representatives, and thus He shows His causeless mercy towards the nondevotees. The Lord is so satisfied with His pure devotees that He wants to give them the credit for missionary success, although He could do the work personally. This is the sign of His satisfaction with His pure, *niṣkāma* devotees, compared to the *sakāma* devotees. By such transcendental activities the Lord simultaneously becomes free from the charge of partiality and exhibits His pleasure with the devotees.

Now a question arises: If the Lord is sitting in the hearts of nondevotees, why are they not moved to become devotees? It may be answered that the stubborn nondevotees are like the barren land or alkaline field, where no agricultural activities can be successful. As part and parcel of the Lord, every individual living entity has a minute quantity of independence, and by misuse of this minute independence, the nondevotees commit offense after offense, to both the Lord and His pure devotees engaged in missionary work. As a result of such acts, they become as barren as an alkaline field, where there is no strength to produce.

TEXT 13

पुंसामतो विविधकर्मभिरध्वराद्यै-
दानेन चोग्रतपसा परिचर्यया च ।
आराधनं भगवतस्तव सत्क्रियार्थो
धर्मोऽर्पितः कर्हिचिद्म्रियते न यत्र ॥१३॥

puṁsām ato vividha-karmabhir adhvarādyair
dānena cogra-tapasā paricaryayā ca
ārādhanaṁ bhagavatas tava sat-kriyārtho
dharmo 'rpitaḥ karhicid mriyate na yatra

puṁsām—of the people; *ataḥ*—therefore; *vividha-karmabhiḥ*—by various fruitive activities; *adhvara-ādyaiḥ*—by performance of Vedic rituals; *dānena*—by charities; *ca*—and; *ugra*—very hard; *tapasā*—austerity; *paricaryayā*—by transcendental service; *ca*—also; *ārādhanam*—worship; *bhagavataḥ*—of the Personality of Godhead; *tava*—

Your; *sat-kriyā-arthaḥ*—simply for pleasing Your Lordship; *dharmaḥ*—religion; *arpitaḥ*—so offered; *karhicit*—at any time; *mriyate*—vanquishes; *na*—never; *yatra*—there.

TRANSLATION

But the pious activities of the people, such as performance of Vedic rituals, charity, austere penances, and transcendental service, performed with a view to worship You and satisfy You by offering You the fruitive results, are also beneficial. Such acts of religion never go in vain.

PURPORT

Absolute devotional service, conducted in nine different spiritual activities—hearing, chanting, remembering, worshiping, praying, etc.—does not always appeal to people with a pompous nature; they are more attracted by the Vedic superficial rituals and other costly performances of social religious shows. But the process according to the Vedic injunctions is that the fruits of all pious activities should be offered to the Supreme Lord. In *Bhagavad-gītā* (9.27), the Lord demands that whatever one may do in one's daily activities, such as worship, sacrifice, and offering charity, all the results should be offered to Him only. This offering of the results of pious acts unto the Supreme Lord is a sign of devotional service to the Lord and is of permanent value, whereas enjoying the same results for oneself is only temporary. Anything done on account of the Lord is a permanent asset and accumulates in the form of unseen piety for gradual promotion to the unalloyed devotional service of the Lord. These undetected pious activities will one day result in full-fledged devotional service by the grace of the Supreme Lord. Therefore, any pious act done on account of the Supreme Lord is also recommended here for those who are not pure devotees.

TEXT 14

शश्वत्स्वरूपमहसैव निपीतभेद-
मोहाय बोधधिषणाय नमः परस्मै ।
विश्वोद्भवस्थितिलयेषु निमित्तलीला-
रासाय ते नम इदं चकृमेश्वराय ॥१४॥

śaśvat svarūpa-mahasaiva nipīta-bheda-
mohāya bodha-dhiṣaṇāya namaḥ parasmai
viśvodbhava-sthiti-layeṣu nimitta-līlā-
rāsāya te nama idaṁ cakṛmeśvarāya

śaśvat—eternally; *svarūpa*—transcendental form; *mahasā*—by the glories; *eva*—certainly; *nipīta*—distinguished; *bheda*—differentiation; *mohāya*—unto the illusory conception; *bodha*—self-knowledge; *dhiṣaṇāya*—intelligence; *namaḥ*—obeisances; *parasmai*—unto the Transcendence; *viśva-udbhava*—creation of the cosmic manifestation; *sthiti*—maintenance; *layeṣu*—also destruction; *nimitta*—for the matter of; *līlā*—by such pastimes; *rāsāya*—for enjoyment; *te*—unto You; *namaḥ*—obeisances; *idam*—this; *cakṛma*—do I perform; *īśvarāya*—unto the Supreme.

TRANSLATION

Let me offer my obeisances unto the Supreme Transcendence, who is eternally distinguished by His internal potency. His indistinguishable impersonal feature is realized by intelligence for self-realization. I offer my obeisances unto Him who by His pastimes enjoys the creation, maintenance and dissolution of the cosmic manifestation.

PURPORT

The Supreme Lord is eternally distinguished from the living entities by His internal potency, although He is also understood in His impersonal feature by self-realized intelligence. Devotees of the Lord, therefore, offer all respectful obeisances unto the impersonal feature of the Lord. The word *rāsa* is significant herein. The *rāsa* dance is performed by Lord Kṛṣṇa in the company of the cowherd damsels at Vṛndāvana, and the Personality of Godhead Garbhodakaśāyī Viṣṇu is also engaged in *rāsa* enjoyment with His external potency, by which He creates, maintains and dissolves the entire material manifestation. Indirectly, Lord Brahmā offers his respectful obeisances unto Lord Śrī Kṛṣṇa, who is factually ever engaged in *rāsa* enjoyment with the *gopīs*, as confirmed in the *Gopāla-tāpanī Upaniṣad* in the following words: *parārdhānte so 'budhyata gopa-veśo me puruṣaḥ purastād āvirbabhūva.*

The distinction between the Lord and the living entity is definitely experienced when there is sufficient intelligence to understand His internal potency, as distinguished from the external potency by which He makes possible the material manifestation.

TEXT 15

यस्यावतारगुणकर्मविडम्बनानि
नामानि येऽसुविगमे विवशा गृणन्ति ।
तेऽनैकजन्मशमलं सहसैव हित्वा
संयान्त्यपावृतामृतं तमजं प्रपद्ये ॥१५॥

yasyāvatāra-guṇa-karma-viḍambanāni
nāmāni ye 'su-vigame vivaśā gṛṇanti
te 'naika-janma-śamalaṁ sahasaiva hitvā
saṁyānty apāvṛtāmṛtaṁ tam ajaṁ prapadye

yasya—whose; *avatāra*—incarnations; *guṇa*—transcendental qualities; *karma*—activities; *viḍambanāni*—all mysterious; *nāmāni*—transcendental names; *ye*—those; *asu-vigame*—while quitting this life; *vivaśāḥ*—automatically; *gṛṇanti*—invoke; *te*—they; *anaika*—many; *janma*—births; *śamalam*—accumulated sins; *sahasā*—immediately; *eva*—certainly; *hitvā*—giving up; *saṁyānti*—obtain; *apāvṛta*—open; *amṛtam*—immortality; *tam*—Him; *ajam*—the unborn; *prapadye*—I take shelter.

TRANSLATION

Let me take shelter of the lotus feet of Him whose incarnations, qualities and activities are mysterious imitations of worldly affairs. One who invokes His transcendental names, even unconsciously, at the time he quits this life, is certainly washed immediately of the sins of many, many births and attains Him without fail.

PURPORT

The activities of the incarnations of the Supreme Personality of Godhead are a kind of imitation of the activities going on in the material world. He is just like an actor on a stage. An actor imitates the activities of a king on stage, although actually he is not the king. Similarly, when the Lord incarnates, He imitates parts with which He has nothing to do. In *Bhagavad-gītā* (4.14), it is said that the Lord has nothing to do with the activities in which He is supposedly engaged: *na māṁ karmāṇi limpanti na me karma-phale spṛhā.* The Lord is omnipotent; simply by His will He can perform anything and everything. When the Lord appeared as Lord Kṛṣṇa, He played the part of the son of Yaśodā and Nanda, and He lifted the Govardhana Hill, although lifting a hill is not His concern. He can lift millions of Govardhana Hills by His simple desire; He does not need to lift it with His hand. But He imitates the ordinary living entity by this lifting, and at the same time He exhibits His supernatural power. Thus His name is chanted as the lifter of Govardhana Hill, or Śrī Govardhanadhārī. Therefore, His acts in His incarnations and His partiality to the devotees are all imitations only, just like the stage makeup of an expert dramatical player. His acts in that capacity, however, are all omnipotent, and the remembrance of such activities of the incarnations of the Supreme Personality of Godhead is as powerful as the Lord Himself. Ajāmila remembered the holy name of the Lord, Nārāyaṇa, by merely calling the name of his son Nārāyaṇa, and that gave him a complete opportunity to achieve the highest perfection of life.

TEXT 16

योे वा अहं च गिरिशश्च विभुः स्वयं च
स्थित्युद्भवप्रलयहेतव आत्ममूलम् ।
भित्त्वा त्रिपाद्ववृध एक उरुप्ररोह-
स्तस्मै नमो भगवते भुवनद्रुमाय ॥१६॥

yo vā ahaṁ ca giriśaś ca vibhuḥ svayaṁ ca
sthity-udbhava-pralaya-hetava ātma-mūlam
bhittvā tri-pād vavṛdha eka uru-prarohas
tasmai namo bhagavate bhuvana-drumāya

yaḥ—one who; *vai*—certainly; *aham ca*—also I; *giriśaḥ ca*—also Śiva; *vibhuḥ*—the Almighty; *svayam*—personality (as Viṣṇu); *ca*—

and; *sthiti*—maintenance; *udbhava*—creation; *pralaya*—dissolution; *hetavaḥ*—the causes; *ātma-mūlam*—self-rooted; *bhittvā*—having penetrated; *tri-pāt*—three trunks; *vavṛdhe*—grew; *ekaḥ*—one without a second; *uru*—many; *prarohaḥ*—branches; *tasmai*—unto Him; *namaḥ*—obeisances; *bhagavate*—unto the Personality of Godhead; *bhuvana-drumāya*—unto the tree of the planetary system.

TRANSLATION

Your Lordship is the prime root of the tree of the planetary systems. This tree has grown by first penetrating the material nature in three trunks—as me, Śiva and You, the Almighty—for creation, maintenance and dissolution, and we three have grown with many branches. Therefore I offer my obeisances unto You, the tree of the cosmic manifestation.

PURPORT

The cosmic manifestation is grossly divided into three worlds, the upper, lower and middle planetary systems, and then it broadens into the cosmos of fourteen planetary systems, with the manifestation of the Supreme Personality of Godhead as the supreme root. Material nature, which appears to be the cause of the cosmic manifestation, is only the agency or energy of the Lord. This is confirmed in *Bhagavad-gītā* (9.10): *mayādhyakṣeṇa prakṛtiḥ sūyate sa-carācaram.* "Only under the superintendence of the Supreme Lord does material nature appear to be the cause of all creation, maintenance and dissolution." The Lord expands Himself into three—Viṣṇu, Brahmā and Śiva—for maintenance, creation and destruction respectively. Of the three principal agents controlling the three modes of material nature, Viṣṇu is the Almighty; even though He is within material nature for the purpose of maintenance, He is not controlled by the laws of material nature. The other two, Brahmā and Śiva, although almost as greatly powerful as Viṣṇu, are within the control of the material energy of the Supreme Lord. The conception of many gods controlling the many departments of material nature is ill conceived of by the foolish pantheist. God is one without a second, and He is the primal cause of all causes. As there are many departmental heads of governmental affairs, so there are many heads of management of the universal affairs.

Due to a poor fund of knowledge, the impersonalist does not believe in the personal management of things as they are. But in this verse it is clearly explained that everything is personal and nothing is impersonal. We have already discussed this point in the Introduction, and it is confirmed here in this verse. The tree of the material manifestation is described in the Fifteenth Chapter of *Bhagavad-gītā* as an *aśvattha* tree whose root is upward. We have actual experience of such a tree when we see the shadow of a tree on the bank of a reservoir of water. The reflection of the tree on the water appears to hang down from its upward roots. The tree of creation described here is only a shadow of the reality which is Parabrahman, Viṣṇu. In the internal potential manifestation of the Vaikuṇṭhalokas, the actual tree exists, and the tree reflected in the material nature is only the shadow of this actual tree. The impersonalists' theory that Brahman is void of all variegatedness is false because the shadow-tree described in *Bhagavad-gītā* cannot exist without being the reflection of a real tree. The real tree is situated in the eternal existence of spiritual nature, full of transcendental varieties, and Lord Viṣṇu is the root of that tree also. The root is the same—the Lord—both for the real tree and the false, but the false tree is only the perverted reflection of the real tree. The Lord, being the real tree, is here offered obeisances by Brahmā on his own behalf and also on behalf of Lord Śiva.

TEXT 17

लोको विकर्मनिरतः कुशले प्रमत्तः
कर्मण्ययं त्वदुदिते भवदर्चने स्वे ।
यस्तावदस्य बलवानिह जीविताशां
सद्यश्छिनत्त्यनिमिषाय नमोऽस्तु तस्मै ॥१७॥

loko vikarma-ratah kuśale pramattaḥ
karmaṇy ayaṁ tvad-udite bhavad-arcane sve
yas tāvad asya balavān iha jīvitāśāṁ
sadyaś chinatty animiṣāya namo 'stu tasmai

lokaḥ—people in general; *vikarma*—work without sense; *nirataḥ*—engaged in; *kuśale*—in beneficial activity; *pramattaḥ*—negligent; *karmaṇi*—in activity; *ayam*—this; *tvat*—by You; *udite*—enunciated;

bhavat—of You; *arcane*—in worship; *sve*—their own; *yaḥ*—who; *tāvat*—as long as; *asya*—of the people in general; *balavān*—very strong; *iha*—this; *jīvita-āśām*—struggle for existence; *sadyaḥ*—directly; *chinatti*—is cut to pieces; *animiṣāya*—by the eternal time; *namaḥ*—my obeisances; *astu*—let there be; *tasmai*—unto Him.

TRANSLATION

People in general all engage in foolish acts, not in the really beneficial activities enunciated directly by You for their guidance. As long as their tendency for foolish work remains powerful, all their plans in the struggle for existence will be cut to pieces. I therefore offer my obeisances unto Him who acts as eternal time.

PURPORT

People in general are all engaged in senseless work. They are systematically unmindful of the real beneficial work, which is the devotional service of the Lord, technically called the *arcanā* regulations. The *arcanā* regulations are directly instructed by the Lord in the *Nārada-pañcarātra* and are strictly followed by the intelligent men, who know well that the highest perfectional goal of life is to reach Lord Viṣṇu, who is the root of the tree called the cosmic manifestation. Also, in the *Bhāgavatam* and in *Bhagavad-gītā* such regulative activities are clearly mentioned. Foolish people do not know that their self-interest is in realization of Viṣṇu. The *Bhāgavatam* (7.5.30–32) says:

matir na kṛṣṇe parataḥ svato vā
mitho 'bhipadyeta gṛha-vratānām
adānta-gobhir viśatāṁ tamisraṁ
punaḥ punaś carvita-carvaṇānām

na te viduḥ svārtha-gatiṁ hi viṣṇuṁ
durāśayā ye bahir-artha-māninaḥ
andhā yathāndhair upanīyamānās
te 'pīśa-tantryām uru-dāmni baddhāḥ

naiṣāṁ matis tāvad urukramāṅghriṁ
spṛśaty anarthāpagamo yad-arthaḥ

mahīyasāṁ pāda-rajo-'bhiṣekaṁ
niṣkiñcanānāṁ na vṛṇīta yāvat

"Persons who are determined to totally rot in false, material happiness cannot become Kṛṣṇa-minded either by instructions from teachers, by self-realization or by parliamentary discussions. They are dragged by the unbridled senses into the darkest region of ignorance, and thus they madly engage in what is called 'chewing the chewed.'

"Because of their foolish activities, they are unaware that the ultimate goal of human life is to achieve Viṣṇu, the Lord of the cosmic manifestation, and so their struggle for existence is in the wrong direction of material civilization, which is under the external energy. They are led by similar foolish persons, just as one blind man is led by another blind man and both fall in the ditch.

"Such foolish men cannot be attracted towards the activities of the Supreme Powerful, who is actually the neutralizing measure for their foolish activities, unless and until they have the good sense to be guided by the great souls who are completely freed from material attachment."

In *Bhagavad-gītā* the Lord asks everyone to give up all other occupational duties and absolutely engage in *arcanā* activities, or in pleasing the Lord. But almost no one is attracted to such *arcanā* activity. Everyone is more or less attracted by activities which are conditions of rebellion against the Supreme Lord. The systems of *jñāna* and *yoga* are also indirectly rebellious acts against the Lord. There is no auspicious activity except *arcanā* of the Lord. *Jñāna* and *yoga* are sometimes accepted within the purview of *arcanā* when the ultimate aim is Viṣṇu, and not otherwise. The conclusion is that only the devotees of the Lord are bona fide human beings eligible for salvation. Others are vainly struggling for existence without any actual benefit.

TEXT 18

यस्माद्बिभेम्यहमपि द्विपरार्धधिष्ण्य-
मध्यासितः सकललोकनमस्कृतं यत् ।
तेपे तपो बहुसवोऽवरुरुत्समान-
स्तस्मै नमो भगवतेऽधिमखाय तुभ्यम् ॥१८॥

yasmād bibhemy aham api dviparārdha-dhiṣṇyam
adhyāsitaḥ sakala-loka-namaskṛtaṁ yat
tepe tapo bahu-savo 'varurutsamānas
tasmai namo bhagavate 'dhimakhāya tubhyam

yasmāt—from whom; *bibhemi*—fear; *aham*—I; *api*—also; *dvi-parārdha*—up to the limit of 4,300,000,000 X 2 X 30 X 12 X 100 solar years; *dhiṣṇyam*—place; *adhyāsitaḥ*—situated in; *sakala-loka*—all other planets; *namaskṛtam*—honored by; *yat*—that; *tepe*—underwent; *tapaḥ*—penances; *bahu-savaḥ*—many, many years; *avarurutsamānaḥ*—desiring to obtain You; *tasmai*—unto Him; *namaḥ*—I do offer my obeisances; *bhagavate*—unto the Supreme Personality of Godhead; *adhimakhāya*—unto Him who is the enjoyer of all sacrifices; *tubhyam*—unto Your Lordship.

TRANSLATION

Your Lordship, I offer my respectful obeisances unto You who are indefatigable time and the enjoyer of all sacrifices. Although I am situated in an abode which will continue to exist for a time duration of two parārdhas, although I am the leader of all other planets in the universe, and although I have undergone many, many years of penance for self-realization, still I offer my respects unto You.

PURPORT

Brahmā is the greatest personality in the universe because he has the longest duration of life. He is the most respectable personality because of his penance, influence, prestige, etc., and still he has to offer his respectful obeisances unto the Lord. Therefore, it is incumbent upon all others, who are far, far below the standard of Brahmā, to do as he did and offer respects as a matter of duty.

TEXT 19

तिर्यङ्मनुष्यविबुधादिषु जीवयोनि-
ष्वात्मेच्छयात्मकृतसेतुपरीप्सया यः ।

रेमे निरस्तविषयोऽप्यवरुद्धदेह-
स्तस्मै नमो भगवते पुरुषोत्तमाय ॥१९॥

tiryaṅ-manuṣya-vibudhādiṣu jīva-yoniṣv
ātmecchayātma-kṛta-setu-parīpsayā yaḥ
reme nirasta-viṣayo 'py avaruddha-dehas
tasmai namo bhagavate puruṣottamāya

tiryak—animals lower than human beings; *manuṣya*—human beings, etc.; *vibudha-ādiṣu*—amongst the demigods; *jīva-yoniṣu*—in different species of life; *ātma*—self; *icchayā*—by the will; *ātma-kṛta*—self-created; *setu*—obligations; *parīpsayā*—desiring to preserve; *yaḥ*—who; *reme*—performing transcendental pastimes; *nirasta*—not being affected; *viṣayaḥ*—material contamination; *api*—certainly; *avaruddha*—manifested; *dehaḥ*—transcendental body; *tasmai*—unto Him; *namaḥ*—my obeisances; *bhagavate*—unto the Personality of Godhead; *puruṣottamāya*—the primeval Lord.

TRANSLATION

O my Lord, by Your own will You appear in the various species of living entities, among animals lower than human beings as well as among the demigods, to perform Your transcendental pastimes. You are not affected by material contamination. You come just to fulfill the obligations of Your own principles of religion, and therefore, O Supreme Personality, I offer my obeisances unto You for manifesting such different forms.

PURPORT

The Lord's incarnations in different species of life are all transcendental. He appears as a human being in His incarnations of Kṛṣṇa, Rāma, etc., but He is not a human being. Anyone who mistakes Him for an ordinary human being is certainly not very intelligent, as confirmed in *Bhagavad-gītā* (9.11): *avajānanti māṁ mūḍhā mānuṣīṁ tanum āśritam.* The same principle is applicable when He appears as the hog or fish incarnations. They are transcendental forms of the Lord and are manifested under certain necessities of His own pleasure and pastimes.

Such manifestations of the transcendental forms of the Lord are accepted by Him mostly to enliven His devotees. All His incarnations are manifested whenever there is a need to deliver His devotees and maintain His own principles.

TEXT 20

योऽविद्ययानुपहतोऽपि दशार्धवृत्त्या
निद्रामुवाह जठरीकृतलोकयात्रः ।
अन्तर्जलेऽहिकशिपुस्पर्शानुकूलां
भीमोर्मिमालिनि जनस्य सुखं विवृण्वन् ॥२०॥

yo 'vidyayānupahato 'pi daśārdha-vṛttyā
nidrām uvāha jaṭharī-kṛta-loka-yātraḥ
antar-jale 'hi-kaśipu-sparśānukūlāṁ
bhīmormi-mālini janasya sukhaṁ vivṛṇvan

yaḥ—one; *avidyayā*—influenced by nescience; *anupahataḥ*—without being affected; *api*—in spite of; *daśa-ardha*—five; *vṛttyā*—interaction; *nidrām*—sleep; *uvāha*—accepted; *jaṭharī*—within the abdomen; *kṛta*—doing so; *loka-yātraḥ*—maintenance of the different entities; *antaḥ-jale*—within the water of devastation; *ahi-kaśipu*—on the snake bed; *sparśa-anukūlām*—happy for the touch; *bhīma-ūrmi*—violent waves; *mālini*—chain of; *janasya*—of the intelligent person; *sukham*—happiness; *vivṛṇvan*—showing.

TRANSLATION

My Lord, You accept the pleasure of sleeping in the water of devastation, where there are violent waves, and You enjoy pleasure on the bed of snakes, showing the happiness of Your sleep to intelligent persons. At that time, all the universal planets are stationed within Your abdomen.

PURPORT

Persons who cannot think of anything beyond the limit of their own power are like frogs in a well who cannot imagine the length and breadth of the great Pacific Ocean. Such people take it as legendary when they hear that the Supreme Lord is lying on His bed within the great ocean of the universe. They are surprised that one can lie down within water and sleep very happily. But a little intelligence can mitigate this foolish astonishment. There are many living entities within the bed of the ocean who also enjoy the material bodily activities of eating, sleeping, defending and mating. If such insignificant living entities can enjoy life within the water, why can't the Supreme Lord, who is all-powerful, sleep on the cool body of a serpent and enjoy in the turmoil of violent ocean waves? The distinction of the Lord is that His activities are all transcendental, and He is able to do anything and everything without being deterred by limitations of time and space. He can enjoy His transcendental happiness regardless of material considerations.

TEXT 21

यन्नाभिपद्मभवनादहमासमीड्य
लोकत्रयोपकरणो यदनुग्रहेण ।
तस्मै नमस्त उदरस्थभवाय योग-
निद्रावसानविकसन्नलिनेक्षणाय ॥२१॥

yan-nābhi-padma-bhavanād aham āsam īḍya
loka-trayopakaraṇo yad-anugraheṇa
tasmai namas ta udara-stha-bhavāya yoga-
nidrāvasāna-vikasan-nalinekṣaṇāya

yat—whose; *nābhi*—navel; *padma*—lotus; *bhavanāt*—from the house of; *aham*—I; *āsam*—became manifested; *īḍya*—O worshipable one; *loka-traya*—the three worlds; *upakaraṇaḥ*—helping in the creation of; *yat*—whose; *anugraheṇa*—by the mercy; *tasmai*—unto Him; *namaḥ*—my obeisances; *te*—unto You; *udara-stha*—situated within the abdomen; *bhavāya*—having the universe; *yoga-nidrā-avasāna*—after the end of that transcendental sleep; *vikasat*—blossoming; *nalina-īkṣaṇāya*—unto Him whose opening eyes are like lotuses.

TRANSLATION

O object of my worship, I am born from the house of Your lotus navel for the purpose of creating the universe by Your mercy. All

these planets of the universe were stationed within Your transcendental abdomen while You were enjoying sleep. Now, Your sleep having ended, Your eyes are open like blossoming lotuses in the morning.

PURPORT

Brahmā is teaching us the beginning of *arcanā* regulations from morning (four o'clock) to night (ten o'clock). Early in the morning, the devotee has to rise from his bed and pray to the Lord, and there are other regulative principles for offering *maṅgala-ārati* early in the morning. Foolish nondevotees, not understanding the importance of *arcanā*, criticize the regulative principles, but they have no eyes to see that the Lord also sleeps, by His own will. The impersonal conception of the Supreme is so detrimental to the path of devotional service that it is very difficult to associate with the stubborn nondevotees, who always think in terms of material conceptions.

Impersonalists always think backwards. They think that because there is form in matter, spirit should be formless; because in matter there is sleep, in spirit there cannot be sleep; and because the sleeping of the Deity is accepted in *arcanā* worship, the *arcanā* is *māyā.* All these thoughts are basically material. To think either positively or negatively is still thinking materially. Knowledge accepted from the superior source of the *Vedas* is standard. Here in these verses of the *Śrīmad-Bhāgavatam*, we find that *arcanā* is recommended. Before Brahmā took up the task of creation, he found the Lord sleeping on the serpent bed in the waves of the water of devastation. Therefore, sleeping exists in the internal potency of the Lord, and this is not denied by pure devotees of the Lord like Brahmā and his disciplic succession. It is clearly said here that the Lord slept very happily within the violent waves of the water, manifesting thereby that He is able to do anything and everything by His transcendental will and not be hampered by any circumstances. The Māyāvādī cannot think beyond this material experience, and thus he denies the Lord's ability to sleep within the water. His mistake is that he compares the Lord to himself—and that comparison is also a material thought. The whole philosophy of the Māyāvāda school, based on "not this, not that" (*neti, neti*), is basically material. Such thought cannot give one the chance to know the Supreme Personality of Godhead as He is.

TEXT 22

सोऽयं समस्तजगतां सुहृदेक आत्मा
सत्त्वेन यन्मृडयते भगवान् भगेन ।
तेनैव मे दृशमनुस्पृशताद्यथाहं
स्रक्ष्यामि पूर्ववदिदं प्रणतप्रियोऽसौ ॥२२॥

so 'yaṁ samasta-jagatāṁ suhṛd eka ātmā
sattvena yan mṛḍayate bhagavān bhagena
tenaiva me dṛśam anuspṛśatād yathāhaṁ
srakṣyāmi pūrvavad idaṁ praṇata-priyo 'sau

saḥ—He; *ayam*—the Lord; *samasta-jagatām*—of all the universes; *suhṛt ekaḥ*—the one friend and philosopher; *ātmā*—the Supersoul; *sattvena*—by the mode of goodness; *yat*—one who; *mṛḍayate*—causes happiness; *bhagavān*—the Personality of Godhead; *bhagena*—with six opulences; *tena*—by Him; *eva*—certainly; *me*—to me; *dṛśam*—power of introspection; *anuspṛśatāt*—let Him give; *yathā*—as; *aham*—I; *srakṣyāmi*—will be able to create; *pūrva-vat*—as before; *idam*—this universe; *praṇata*—surrendered; *priyaḥ*—dear; *asau*—He (the Lord).

TRANSLATION

Let the Supreme Lord be merciful towards me. He is the one friend and soul of all living entities in the world, and He maintains all, for their ultimate happiness, by His six transcendental opulences. May He be merciful towards me so that I, as before, may be empowered with the introspection to create, for I am also one of the surrendered souls who are dear to the Lord.

PURPORT

The Supreme Lord, Puruṣottama, or Śrī Kṛṣṇa, is the maintainer of all, in both the transcendental and material worlds. He is the life and friend of all because there is eternally natural affection and love between the living entities and the Lord. He is the one friend and well-wisher for all, and He is one without a second. The Lord maintains all the living entities everywhere by His six transcendental opulences, for which He is known as *bhagavān*, or the Supreme Personality of Godhead. Lord Brahmā prayed for His mercy so that he might be able to create the universal affairs as he did before; only by the Lord's causeless mercy could he create both material and spiritual personalities like Marīci and Nārada respectively. Brahmā prayed to the Lord because He is very much dear to the surrendered soul. The surrendered soul knows nothing but the Lord, and therefore the Lord is very affectionate towards him.

TEXT 23

एष प्रपन्नवरदो रमयात्मशक्त्या
यद्यत्करिष्यति गृहीतगुणावतारः ।
तस्मिन् स्वविक्रममिदं सृजतोऽपि चेतो
युञ्जीत कर्मशमलं च यथा विजह्याम् ॥२३॥

eṣa prapanna-varado ramayātma-śaktyā
yad yat kariṣyati gṛhīta-guṇāvatāraḥ
tasmin sva-vikramam idaṁ sṛjato 'pi ceto
yuñjīta karma-śamalaṁ ca yathā vijahyām

eṣaḥ—this; *prapanna*—one who is surrendered; *vara-daḥ*—benefactor; *ramayā*—enjoying always with the goddess of fortune (Lakṣmī); *ātma-śaktyā*—with His internal potency; *yat yat*—whatever; *kariṣyati*—He may act; *gṛhīta*—accepting; *guṇa-avatāraḥ*—incarnation of the mode of goodness; *tasmin*—unto Him; *sva-vikramam*—with omnipotency; *idam*—this cosmic manifestation; *sṛjataḥ*—creating; *api*—in spite of; *cetaḥ*—heart; *yuñjīta*—be engaged; *karma*—work; *śamalam*—material affection; *ca*—also; *yathā*—as much as; *vijahyām*—I can give up.

TRANSLATION

The Supreme Lord, the Personality of Godhead, is always the benefactor of the surrendered souls. His activities are always enacted through His internal potency, Ramā, or the goddess of fortune. I pray only to engage in His service in the creation of the material world, and I pray that I not be materially affected by my

works, for thus I may be able to give up the false prestige of being the creator.

PURPORT

In the matter of material creation, maintenance and destruction, there are three incarnations of the material modes of nature—Brahmā, Viṣṇu and Maheśvara. But the Lord's incarnation as Viṣṇu, in His internal potency, is the supreme energy for the total activities. Brahmā, who is only an assistant in the modes of creation, wanted to remain in his actual position as an instrument of the Lord instead of becoming puffed up by the false prestige of thinking himself the creator. That is the way of becoming dear to the Supreme Lord and receiving His benediction. Foolish men want to take credit for all creations made by them, but intelligent persons know very well that not a blade of grass can move without the will of the Lord; thus all the credit for wonderful creations must go to Him. By spiritual consciousness only can one be free from the contamination of material affection and receive the benedictions offered by the Lord.

TEXT 24

नाभिह्रदादिह सतोऽम्भसि यस्य पुंसो
विज्ञानशक्तिरहमासमनन्तशक्तेः ।
रूपं विचित्रमिदमस्य विवृण्वतो मे
मा रीरिषीष्ट निगमस्य गिरां विसर्गः ॥२४॥

nābhi-hradād iha sato 'mbhasi yasya puṁso
vijñāna-śaktir aham āsam ananta-śakteḥ
rūpaṁ vicitram idam asya vivṛṇvato me
mā rīriṣīṣṭa nigamasya girāṁ visargaḥ

nābhi-hradāt—from the navel lake; *iha*—in this millennium; *sataḥ*—lying; *ambhasi*—in the water; *yasya*—one whose; *puṁsaḥ*—of the Personality of Godhead; *vijñāna*—of the total universe; *śaktiḥ*—energy; *aham*—I; *āsam*—was born; *ananta*—unlimited; *śakteḥ*—of the powerful; *rūpam*—form; *vicitram*—variegated; *idam*—this; *asya*—His; *vivṛṇvataḥ*—manifesting; *me*—unto me; *mā*—may not; *rīriṣīṣṭa*—vanish; *nigamasya*—of the *Vedas;* *girām*—of the sounds; *visargaḥ*—vibration.

TRANSLATION

The Lord's potencies are innumerable. As He lies down in the water of devastation, I am born as the total universal energy from the navel lake in which the lotus sprouts. I am now engaged in manifesting His diverse energies in the form of the cosmic manifestation. I therefore pray that in the course of my material activities I may not be deviated from the vibration of the Vedic hymns.

PURPORT

Every person engaged in the transcendental loving service of the Lord in this material world is prone to so many material activities, and if one is not strong enough to protect himself against the onslaught of material affection, he may be diverted from the spiritual energy. In the material creation Brahmā has to create all kinds of living entities with bodies suitable to their material conditions. Brahmā wants to be protected by the Lord because he has to contact many, many vicious living entities. An ordinary *brāhmaṇa* may fall from the *brahma-tejas*, or the power of brahminical excellence, due to his association with many fallen, conditioned souls. Brahmā, as the supermost *brāhmaṇa*, is afraid of such a falldown, and therefore he prays to the Lord for protection. This is a warning for one and all in the spiritual advancement of life. Unless one is sufficiently protected by the Lord, he may fall down from his spiritual position; therefore one has to pray constantly to the Lord for protection and the blessing to carry out one's duty. Lord Caitanya also entrusted His missionary work to His devotees and assured them of His protection against the onslaught of material affection. The path of spiritual life is stated in the *Vedas* to be like the edge of a sharpened razor. A little inattentiveness may at once create havoc and bloodshed, but one who is a completely surrendered soul, always seeking protection from the Lord in the discharge of his entrusted duties, has no fear of falling into material contamination.

TEXT 25

सोऽसावदभ्रकरुणो भगवान् विवृद्ध-
प्रेमस्मितेन नयनाम्बुरुहं विजृम्भन् ।
उत्थाय विश्वविजयाय च नो विषादं
माध्व्या गिरापनयतात्पुरुषः पुराणः ॥२५॥

so 'sāv adabhra-karuṇo bhagavān vivṛddha-
prema-smitena nayanāmburuhaṁ vijṛmbhan
utthāya viśva-vijayāya ca no viṣādaṁ
mādhvyā girāpanayatāt puruṣaḥ purāṇaḥ

saḥ—He (the Lord); *asau*—that; *adabhra*—unlimited; *karuṇaḥ*—merciful; *bhagavān*—the Personality of Godhead; *vivṛddha*—excessive; *prema*—love; *smitena*—by smiling; *nayana-amburuham*—the lotus eyes; *vijṛmbhan*—by opening; *utthāya*—for flourishing; *viśva-vijayāya*—for glorifying the cosmic creation; *ca*—as also; *naḥ*—our; *viṣādam*—dejection; *mādhvyā*—by sweet; *girā*—words; *apanayatāt*—let Him kindly remove; *puruṣaḥ*—the Supreme; *purāṇaḥ*—oldest.

TRANSLATION

The Lord, who is supreme and is the oldest of all, is unlimitedly merciful. I wish that He may smilingly bestow His benediction upon me by opening His lotus eyes. He can uplift the entire cosmic creation and remove our dejection by kindly speaking His directions.

PURPORT

The Lord is ever increasingly merciful upon the fallen souls of this material world. The whole cosmic manifestation is a chance for all to improve themselves in devotional service to the Lord, and everyone is meant for that purpose. The Lord expands Himself into many personalities who are either self-expansions or separated expansions. The personalities of the individual souls are His separated expansions, whereas the self-expansions are the Lord Himself. The self-expansions are predominators, and the separated expansions are predominated for reciprocation of transcendental bliss with the supreme form of bliss and knowledge. The liberated souls can join in this blissful reciprocation of predominator and predominated without materially concocted ideas. The typical example of such a transcendental exchange between the predominator and the predominated is the Lord's *rāsa-līlā* with the *gopīs*. The *gopīs* are predominated expansions of the internal potency, and therefore the Lord's participation in the *rāsa-līlā* dance is never to be considered like the mundane relationship of man and woman. It is, rather, the highest perfectional stage of the exchange of feelings between the Lord and the living entities. The Lord gives the fallen souls the chance for this highest perfection of life. Lord Brahmā is entrusted with the management of the complete cosmic show, and therefore he prays that the Lord bestow His blessings upon him so that he may execute its purpose.

TEXT 26

मैत्रेय उवाच
स्वसम्भवं निशाम्यैवं तपोविद्यासमाधिभिः ।
यावन्मनोवचः स्तुत्वा विरराम स खिन्नवत् ॥२६॥

maitreya uvāca
sva-sambhavaṁ niśāmyaivaṁ
tapo-vidyā-samādhibhiḥ
yāvan mano-vacaḥ stutvā
virarāma sa khinnavat

maitreyaḥ uvāca—the great sage Maitreya said; *sva-sambhavam*—the source of his appearance; *niśāmya*—by seeing; *evam*—thus; *tapaḥ*—penance; *vidyā*—knowledge; *samādhibhiḥ*—as also by concentration of the mind; *yāvat*—as far as possible; *manaḥ*—mind; *vacaḥ*—words; *stutvā*—having prayed; *virarāma*—became silent; *saḥ*—he (Brahmā); *khinna-vat*—as if tired.

TRANSLATION

The sage Maitreya said: O Vidura, after observing the source of his appearance, namely the Personality of Godhead, Brahmā prayed for His mercy as far as his mind and words would permit him. Thus having prayed, he became silent, as if tired from his activities of penance, knowledge and mental concentration.

PURPORT

Brahmā's enlightenment in knowledge was due to the Lord sitting within his heart. After being created, Brahmā could not ascertain the source of his appearance, but after penance and mental concentration he could see the source of his birth, and thus he became enlightened through his heart. The spiritual master outside and the spiritual master within are both representations of the Lord. Unless one has contact with such bona fide representations, one cannot claim to be a spiritual master. Lord Brahmā had no opportunity to take the help of a spiritual master from outside because at that time Brahmā himself was the only creature in the universe. Therefore, on becoming satisfied by the prayers of Brahmā, the Lord enlightened him about everything from within.

TEXTS 27–28

अथाभिप्रेतमन्वीक्ष्य ब्रह्मणो मधुसूदनः ।
विषण्णचेतसं तेन कल्पव्यतिकराम्भसा ॥२७॥
लोकसंस्थानविज्ञान आत्मनः परिखिद्यतः ।
तमाहागाधया वाचा कश्मलं शमयन्निव ॥२८॥

athābhipretam anvīkṣya
brahmaṇo madhusūdanaḥ
viṣaṇṇa-cetasaṁ tena
kalpa-vyatikarāmbhasā

loka-saṁsthāna-vijñāna
ātmanaḥ parikhidyataḥ
tam āhāgādhayā vācā
kaśmalaṁ śamayann iva

atha—thereupon; *abhipretam*—intention; *anvīkṣya*—observing; *brahmaṇaḥ*—of Brahmā; *madhusūdanaḥ*—the killer of the Madhu demon; *viṣaṇṇa*—depressed; *cetasam*—of the heart; *tena*—by him; *kalpa*—millennium; *vyatikara-ambhasā*—devastating water; *loka-saṁsthāna*—situation of the planetary system; *vijñāne*—in the science; *ātmanaḥ*—of himself; *parikhidyataḥ*—sufficiently anxious; *tam*—unto him; *āha*—said; *agādhayā*—deeply thoughtful; *vācā*—by words; *kaśmalam*—impurities; *śamayan*—removing; *iva*—like that.

TRANSLATION

The Lord saw that Brahmā was very anxious about the planning and construction of the different planetary systems and was

depressed upon seeing the devastating water. He could understand the intention of Brahmā, and thus He spoke in deep, thoughtful words, removing all the illusion that had arisen.

PURPORT

The devastating water was so fearful that even Brahmā was perturbed at its appearance and became very anxious about how to situate the different planetary systems in outer space to accommodate the different kinds of living entities, such as the human beings, those lower than the human beings, and the superhuman beings. All the planets in the universe are situated according to the different grades of living entities under the influence of the modes of material nature. There are three modes of material nature, and when they are mixed with one another they become nine. When the nine are mixed they become eighty-one, and the eighty-one also become mixed, and thus we ultimately do not know how the delusion increases and increases. Lord Brahmā had to accommodate different places and situations for the requisite bodies of the conditioned souls. The task was meant only for Brahmā, and no one in the universe can even understand how difficult it was. But by the grace of the Lord, Brahmā was able to execute the tremendous task so perfectly that everyone is amazed to see the workmanship of the *vidhātā*, or the regulator.

TEXT 29

श्रीभगवानुवाच

मा वेदगर्भ गास्तन्द्रीं सर्ग उद्यममावह ।
तन्मयापादितं ह्यग्रे यन्मां प्रार्थयते भवान् ॥२९॥

śrī-bhagavān uvāca
mā veda-garbha gās tandrīṁ
sarga udyamam āvaha
tan mayāpāditaṁ hy agre
yan māṁ prārthayate bhavān

śrī-bhagavān uvāca—the Lord, the Personality of Godhead, said; *mā*—do not; *veda-garbha*—O You who have the depth of all Vedic wisdom; *gāḥ tandrīm*—become dejected; *sarge*—for creation;

udyamam—enterprises; *āvaha*—you just undertake; *tat*—that (which you want); *mayā*—by Me; *āpāditam*—executed; *hi*—certainly; *agre*—previously; *yat*—which; *mām*—from Me; *prārthayate*—begging; *bhavān*—you.

TRANSLATION

The Supreme Personality of Godhead then said: O Brahmā, O depth of Vedic wisdom, be neither depressed nor anxious about the execution of creation. What you are begging from Me has already been granted before.

PURPORT

Any person authorized by either the Lord or by His bona fide representative is already blessed, as is the work entrusted to him. Of course, the person entrusted with such a responsibility should always be aware of his incapability and must always look for the mercy of the Lord for the successful execution of his duty. One should not be puffed up because he is entrusted with certain executive work. Fortunate is he who is so entrusted, and if he is always fixed in the sense of being subordinate to the will of the Supreme, he is sure to come out successful in the discharge of his work. Arjuna was entrusted with the work of fighting on the Battlefield of Kurukṣetra, and before he was so entrusted, the Lord had already arranged for his victory. But Arjuna was always conscious of his position as subordinate to the Lord, and thus he accepted Him as the supreme guide in his responsibility. Anyone who takes pride in doing responsible work but does not give credit to the Supreme Lord is certainly falsely proud and cannot execute anything nicely. Brahmā and persons in the line of his disciplic succession who follow in his footsteps are always successful in the discharge of loving transcendental service to the Supreme Lord.

TEXT 30

भूयस्त्वं तप आतिष्ठ विद्यां चैव मदाश्रयाम् ।
ताभ्यामन्तर्हृदि ब्रह्मन् लोकान्द्रक्ष्यस्यपावृतान् ॥३०॥

bhūyas tvaṁ tapa ātiṣṭha
vidyāṁ caiva mad-āśrayām

tābhyām antar-hṛdi brahman
lokān drakṣyasy apāvṛtān

bhūyaḥ—again; *tvam*—yourself; *tapaḥ*—penance; *ātiṣṭha*—be situated; *vidyām*—in the knowledge; *ca*—also; *eva*—certainly; *mat*—My; *āśrayām*—under the protection; *tābhyām*—by those qualifications; *antaḥ*—within; *hṛdi*—in the heart; *brahman*—O *brāhmaṇa; lokān*—all the worlds; *drakṣyasi*—you will see; *apāvṛtān*—all disclosed.

TRANSLATION

O Brahmā, situate yourself in penance and meditation and follow the principles of knowledge to receive My favor. By these actions you will be able to understand everything from within your heart.

PURPORT

The mercy the Lord bestows upon a particular person engaged in executing the responsible work entrusted unto him is beyond imagination. But His mercy is received due to our penance and perseverance in executing devotional service. Brahmā was entrusted with the work of creating the planetary systems. The Lord instructed him that when he meditated he would very easily know where and how the planetary systems must be arranged. The directions were to come from within, and there was no necessity for anxiety in that task. Such instructions of *buddhi-yoga* are directly imparted by the Lord from within, as confirmed in *Bhagavad-gītā* (10.10).

TEXT 31

तत आत्मनि लोके च भक्तियुक्तः समाहितः ।
द्रष्टासि मां ततं ब्रह्मन्मयि लोकांस्त्वमात्मनः ॥३१॥

tata ātmani loke ca
bhakti-yuktaḥ samāhitaḥ
draṣṭāsi māṁ tataṁ brahman
mayi lokāṁs tvam ātmanaḥ

tataḥ—thereafter; *ātmani*—in yourself; *loke*—in the universe; *ca*—also; *bhakti-yuktaḥ*—being situated in devotional service; *samāhitaḥ*—being completely absorbed; *draṣṭā asi*—you shall see; *mām*—Me; *tatam*—spread throughout; *brahman*—O Brahmā; *mayi*—in Me; *lokān*—all the universe; *tvam*—you; *ātmanaḥ*—the living entities.

TRANSLATION

O Brahmā, when you are absorbed in devotional service, in the course of your creative activities, you will see Me in you and throughout the universe, and you will see that you yourself, the universe and the living entities are all in Me.

PURPORT

It is cited herein by the Lord that during his daytime Brahmā would see Him as Lord Śrī Kṛṣṇa. He would appreciate how the Lord expanded Himself into all the calves during His childhood at Vṛndāvana, he would know how Yaśodāmayī saw all the universes and planetary systems within the mouth of Kṛṣṇa during His playful childhood pastimes, and he would also see that there are many millions of Brahmās during the appearance of Lord Kṛṣṇa in Brahmā's daytime. But all these manifestations of the Lord, appearing everywhere in His eternal, transcendental forms, cannot be understood by anyone but the pure devotees, who are always engaged in devotional service to the Lord and are fully absorbed in the Lord. The high qualifications of Brahmā are also indicated herein.

TEXT 32

यदा तु सर्वभूतेषु दारुष्वग्निमिव स्थितम् ।
प्रतिचक्षीत मां लोको जह्यात्तर्ह्येव कश्मलम् ॥३२॥

yadā tu sarva-bhūteṣu
dāruṣv agnim iva sthitam
praticakṣīta māṁ loko
jahyāt tarhy eva kaśmalam

yadā—when; *tu*—but; *sarva*—all; *bhūteṣu*—in the living entities; *dāruṣu*—in wood; *agnim*—fire; *iva*—like; *sthitam*—situated; *pra-*

ticakṣīta—you shall see; *mām*—Me; *lokaḥ*—and the universe; *jahyāt*—can give up; *tarhi*—then at once; *eva*—certainly; *kaśmalam*—illusion.

TRANSLATION

You will see Me in all living entities as well as all over the universe, just as fire is situated in wood. Only in that state of transcendental vision will you be able to be free from all kinds of illusion.

PURPORT

Brahmā prayed that he might not forget his eternal relationship with the Lord during the course of his material activities. In answer to that prayer, the Lord said that he should not think of existing without a relationship with His omnipotency. The example is given of the fire in wood. The fire kindled in wood is always the same, although the wood may be of different types. Similarly, the bodies within the material creation may be specifically different according to shape and quality, but the spirit souls within them are not different from one another. The quality of fire, warmth, is the same everywhere, and the spiritual spark, or part and parcel of the Supreme Spirit, is the same in every living being; thus the potency of the Lord is distributed all over His creation. This transcendental knowledge alone can save one from the contamination of material illusion. Since the Lord's potency is distributed everywhere, a pure soul, or devotee of the Lord, can see everything in relationship with the Lord, and therefore he has no affection for the outer coverings. That pure spiritual conception makes him immune to all contamination of material association. The pure devotee never forgets the touch of the Lord in all circumstances.

TEXT 33

यदा रहितमात्मानं भूतेन्द्रियगुणाशयैः ।
स्वरूपेण मयोपेतं पश्यन् स्वाराज्यमृच्छति ॥३३॥

yadā rahitam ātmānaṁ
bhūtendriya-guṇāśayaiḥ
svarūpeṇa mayopetaṁ
paśyan svārājyam ṛcchati

yadā—when; *rahitam*—freed from; *ātmānam*—self; *bhūta*—material elements; *indriya*—material senses; *guṇa-āśayaiḥ*—under the influence of the material modes of nature; *svarūpeṇa*—in pure existence; *mayā*—by Me; *upetam*—approaching; *paśyan*—by seeing; *svārājyam*—spiritual kingdom; *ṛcchati*—enjoy.

TRANSLATION

When you are free from the conception of gross and subtle bodies and when your senses are free from all influences of the modes of material nature, you will realize your pure form in My association. At that time you will be situated in pure consciousness.

PURPORT

In the *Bhakti-rasāmṛta-sindhu* it is said that a person whose only desire is to render transcendental loving service to the Lord is a free person in any condition of material existence. That service attitude is the *svarūpa*, or real form, of the living entity. Lord Śrī Caitanya Mahāprabhu, in the *Caitanya-caritāmṛta*, also confirms this statement by declaring that the real, spiritual form of the living entity is eternal servitorship to the Supreme Lord. The Māyāvāda school shudders at the thought of a service attitude in the living entity, not knowing that in the transcendental world the service of the Lord is based on transcendental love. Transcendental loving service is never to be compared to the forced service of the material world. In the material world, even if one is under the conception that he is no one's servant, he is still the servant of his senses, under the dictation of the material modes. Factually no one is master here in the material world, and therefore the servants of the senses have a very bad experience of servitude. They shudder at the thought of service because they have no knowledge of the transcendental position. In transcendental loving service, the servitor is as free as the Lord. The Lord is *svarāṭ*, or fully independent, and the servant is also fully independent, or *svarāṭ*, in the spiritual atmosphere because there is no forced service. There the transcendental loving service is due to spontaneous love. A reflected glimpse of such service is experienced in the service of the mother unto the son, the friend's service unto the friend, or the wife's service unto the husband. These reflections of service by friends, parents or wives are not forced, but are due only to love. Here in this material world, however, the loving service is only a reflection. The real service, or service in *svarūpa*, is present in the transcendental world, in association with the Lord. The very same service in transcendental love can be practiced in devotion here.

This verse is also applicable to the *jñānī* school. The enlightened *jñānī*, when free from all material contaminations, namely the gross and subtle bodies together with the senses of the material modes of nature, is placed in the Supreme and is thus liberated from material bondage. The *jñānīs* and the devotees are actually in agreement up to the point of liberation from material contamination. But whereas the *jñānīs* remain pacified on the platform of simple understanding, the devotees develop further spiritual advancement in loving service. The devotees develop a spiritual individuality in their spontaneous service attitude, which is enhanced on and on, up to the point of *mādhurya-rasa*, or transcendental loving service reciprocated between the lover and the beloved.

TEXT 34

नानाकर्मवितानेन प्रजा बह्वीः सिसृक्षतः ।
नात्मावसीदत्यस्मिंस्ते वर्षीयान्मदनुग्रहः ॥३४॥

nānā-karma-vitānena
prajā bahvīḥ sisṛkṣataḥ
nātmāvasīdaty asmiṁs te
varṣīyān mad-anugrahaḥ

nānā-karma—varieties of service; *vitānena*—by expansion of; *prajāḥ*—population; *bahvīḥ*—innumerable; *sisṛkṣataḥ*—desiring to increase; *na*—never; *ātmā*—self; *avasīdati*—will be bereaved; *asmin*—in the matter; *te*—of you; *varṣīyān*—always increasing; *mat*—My; *anugrahaḥ*—causeless mercy.

TRANSLATION

Since you have desired to increase the population innumerably and expand your varieties of service, you shall never be deprived in this matter because My causeless mercy upon you will always increase for all time.

PURPORT

A pure devotee of the Lord, being cognizant of the facts of the particular time, object and circumstances, always desires to expand the number of devotees of the Lord in various ways. Such expansions of transcendental service may appear to be material to the materialist, but factually they are expansions of the causeless mercy of the Lord towards the devotee. Plans for such activities may appear to be material activities, but they are different in potency, being engaged in the satisfaction of the transcendental senses of the Supreme.

TEXT 35

ऋषिमाद्यं न बध्नाति पापीयांस्त्वां रजोगुणः ।
यन्मनो मयि निर्बद्धं प्रजाः संसृजतोऽपि ते ॥३५॥

ṛṣim ādyaṁ na badhnāti
pāpīyāṁs tvāṁ rajo-guṇaḥ
yan mano mayi nirbaddhaṁ
prajāḥ saṁsṛjato 'pi te

ṛṣim—unto the great sage; *ādyam*—the first of the kind; *na*—never; *badhnāti*—encroaches; *pāpīyān*—vicious; *tvām*—you; *rajaḥ-guṇaḥ*—the material mode of passion; *yat*—because; *manaḥ*—mind; *mayi*—in Me; *nirbaddham*—compact in; *prajāḥ*—progeny; *saṁsṛjataḥ*—generating; *api*—in spite of; *te*—your.

TRANSLATION

You are the original ṛṣi, and because your mind is always fixed on Me, even though you will be engaged in generating various progeny, the vicious mode of passion will never encroach upon you.

PURPORT

The same assurance is given to Brahmā in the Second Canto, Chapter Nine, verse 36. Being so favored by the Lord, Brahmā's schemes and plans are all infallible. If sometimes Brahmā is seen to be bewildered, as, in the Tenth Canto, he is bewildered by seeing the action of the internal potency, that is also for his further advancement in transcendental service. Arjuna is found to be similarly bewildered. All such bewilderment of the pure devotees of the Lord is specifically meant for their further advancement in knowledge of the Lord.

TEXT 36

ज्ञातोऽहं भवता त्वद्य दुर्विज्ञेयोऽपि देहिनाम् ।
यन्मां त्वं मन्यसेऽयुक्तं भूतेन्द्रियगुणात्मभिः ॥३६॥

jñāto 'haṁ bhavatā tv adya
durvijñeyo 'pi dehinām
yan māṁ tvaṁ manyase 'yuktaṁ
bhūtendriya-guṇātmabhiḥ

jñātaḥ—known; *aham*—Myself; *bhavatā*—by you; *tu*—but; *adya*—today; *duḥ*—difficult; *vijñeyaḥ*—to be known; *api*—in spite of; *dehinām*—for the conditioned soul; *yat*—because; *mām*—Me; *tvam*—you; *manyase*—understand; *ayuktam*—without being made of; *bhūta*—material elements; *indriya*—material senses; *guṇa*—material modes; *ātmabhiḥ*—and false ego like the conditioned soul.

TRANSLATION

Although I am not easily knowable by the conditioned soul, you have known Me today because you know that My personality is not constituted of anything material, and specifically not of the five gross and three subtle elements.

PURPORT

Knowledge of the Supreme Absolute Truth does not necessitate negation of the material manifestation but understanding of spiritual existence as it is. To think that because material existence is realized in forms therefore spiritual existence must be formless is only a negative material conception of spirit. The real spiritual conception is that spiritual form is not material form. Brahmā appreciated the eternal form of the Lord in that way, and the Personality of Godhead approved of Brahmā's spiritual conception. In *Bhagavad-gītā* the Lord condemned the material conception of Kṛṣṇa's body which arises because He is apparently present like a man. The Lord may appear in any of His many, many spiritual forms, but He is not materially composed, nor has He any difference between body and self. That is the way of conceiving the spiritual form of the Lord.

TEXT 37

तुभ्यं मद्विचिकित्सायामात्मा मे दर्शितोऽबहिः ।
नालेन सलिले मूलं पुष्करस्य विचिन्वतः ॥३७॥

tubhyaṁ mad-vicikitsāyām
ātmā me darśito 'bahiḥ
nālena salile mūlaṁ
puṣkarasya vicinvataḥ

tubhyam—unto you; *mat*—Me; *vicikitsāyām*—on your trying to know; *ātmā*—self; *me*—of Myself; *darśitaḥ*—exhibited; *abahiḥ*—from within; *nālena*—through the stem; *salile*—in the water; *mūlam*—root; *puṣkarasya*—of the lotus, the primeval source; *vicinvataḥ*—contemplating.

TRANSLATION

When you were contemplating whether there was a source to the stem of the lotus of your birth and you even entered into that stem, you could not trace out anything. But at that time I manifested My form from within.

PURPORT

The Personality of Godhead can be experienced only by His causeless mercy, not by mental speculation or with the help of the material senses. Material senses cannot approach the transcendental understanding of the Supreme Personality of Godhead. He can be appreciated only by submissive devotional service when He reveals Himself before the devotee. Only by love of Godhead can one know God, and not otherwise. The Personality of Godhead cannot be seen with the material eyes, but He can be seen from within by spiritual eyes opened by the ointment of love of

Godhead. As long as one's spiritual eyes are closed due to the dirty covering of matter, one cannot see the Lord. But when the dirt is removed by the process of devotional service, one can see the Lord, without a doubt. Brahmā's personal endeavor to see the root of the lotus pipe failed, but when the Lord was satisfied by his penance and devotion, He revealed Himself from within with no external endeavor.

TEXT 38

यच्चकर्थाङ्ग मत्स्तोत्रं मत्कथाभ्युदयाङ्कितम् ।
यद्वा तपसि ते निष्ठा स एष मदनुग्रहः ॥३८॥

yac cakarthāṅga mat-stotraṁ
mat-kathābhyudayāṅkitam
yad vā tapasi te niṣṭhā
sa eṣa mad-anugrahaḥ

yat—that which; *cakartha*—performed; *aṅga*—O Brahmā; *mat-stotram*—prayers for Me; *mat-kathā*—words regarding My activities; *abhyudaya-aṅkitam*—enumerating My transcendental glories; *yat*—or that; *vā*—either; *tapasi*—in penance; *te*—your; *niṣṭhā*—faith; *saḥ*—that; *eṣaḥ*—all these; *mat*—My; *anugrahaḥ*—causeless mercy.

TRANSLATION

O Brahmā, the prayers that you have chanted praising the glories of My transcendental activities, the penances you have undertaken to understand Me, and your firm faith in Me—all these are to be considered My causeless mercy.

PURPORT

When a living entity desires to serve the Lord in transcendental loving service, the Lord helps the devotee in so many ways as the *caitya-guru*, or the spiritual master within, and thus the devotee can perform many wonderful activities beyond material estimation. By the mercy of the Lord even a layman can compose prayers of the highest spiritual perfection. Such spiritual perfection is not limited by material qualifications but is developed by dint of one's sincere endeavor to render transcendental service. Voluntary endeavor is the only qualification for spiritual perfection. Material acquisitions of wealth or education are not considered.

TEXT 39

प्रीतोऽहमस्तु भद्रं ते लोकानां विजयेच्छया ।
यदस्तौषीर्गुणमयं निर्गुणं मानुवर्णयन् ॥३९॥

prīto 'ham astu bhadraṁ te
lokānāṁ vijayecchayā
yad astauṣīr guṇamayaṁ
nirguṇaṁ mānuvarṇayan

prītaḥ—pleased; *aham*—Myself; *astu*—let it be so; *bhadram*—all benediction; *te*—unto you; *lokānām*—of the planets; *vijaya*—for glorification; *icchayā*—by your desire; *yat*—that which; *astauṣīḥ*—you prayed for; *guṇa-mayam*—describing all transcendental qualities; *nirguṇam*—although I am free from all material qualities; *mā*—Me; *anuvarṇayan*—nicely describing.

TRANSLATION

I am very much pleased by your description of Me in terms of My transcendental qualities, which appear mundane to the mundaners. I grant you all benedictions in your desire to glorify all the planets by your activities.

PURPORT

A pure devotee of the Lord like Brahmā and those in his line of disciplic succession always desire that the Lord be known all over the universe by each and every one of the living entities. That desire of the devotee is always blessed by the Lord. The impersonalist sometimes prays for the mercy of the Personality of Godhead Nārāyaṇa as the embodiment of material goodness, but such prayers do not satisfy the Lord because He is not thereby glorified in terms of His actual transcendental qualities. The pure devotees of the Lord are always most dear to Him, although He is always kind and merciful to all living entities. Here the word *guṇamayam* is significant because it indicates the Lord's possessing transcendental qualities.

TEXT 40

य एतेन पुमान्नित्यं स्तुत्वा स्तोत्रेण मां भजेत् ।
तस्याशु सम्प्रसीदेयं सर्वकामवरेश्वरः ॥४०॥

ya etena pumān nityaṁ
stutvā stotreṇa māṁ bhajet
tasyāśu samprasīdeyaṁ
sarva-kāma-vareśvaraḥ

yaḥ—anyone who; *etena*—by this; *pumān*—human being; *nityam*—regularly; *stutvā*—praying; *stotreṇa*—by the verses; *mām*—Me; *bhajet*—may worship; *tasya*—his; *āśu*—very soon; *samprasīdeyam*—I shall fulfill; *sarva*—all; *kāma*—desires; *vara-īśvaraḥ*—the Lord of all benediction.

TRANSLATION

Any human being who prays like Brahmā, and who thus worships Me, shall very soon be blessed with the fulfillment of all his desires, for I am the Lord of all benediction.

PURPORT

The prayers offered by Brahmā cannot be chanted by anyone who desires to fulfill his own sense gratification. Such prayers can be selected only by a person who wants to satisfy the Lord in His service. The Lord certainly fulfills all desires in regard to transcendental loving service, but He cannot fulfill the whims of nondevotees, even when such casual devotees offer Him the best of prayers.

TEXT 41

पूर्तेन तपसा यज्ञैर्दानैर्योगसमाधिना ।
राद्धं निःश्रेयसं पुंसां मत्प्रीतिस्तत्त्वविन्मतम् ॥४१॥

pūrtena tapasā yajñair
dānair yoga-samādhinā
rāddhaṁ niḥśreyasaṁ puṁsāṁ
mat-prītis tattvavin-matam

pūrtena—by traditional good work; *tapasā*—by penances; *yajñaiḥ*—by sacrifices; *dānaiḥ*—by charities; *yoga*—by mysticism; *samādhinā*—by trance; *rāddham*—success; *niḥśreyasam*—ultimately beneficial; *puṁsām*—of the human being; *mat*—of Me; *prītiḥ*—satisfaction; *tattva-vit*—expert transcendentalist; *matam*—opinion.

TRANSLATION

It is the opinion of expert transcendentalists that the ultimate goal of performing all traditional good works, penances, sacrifices, charities, mystic activities, trances, etc., is to invoke My satisfaction.

PURPORT

There are many traditionally pious activities in human society, such as altruism, philanthropy, nationalism, internationalism, charity, sacrifice, penance, and even meditation in trance, and all of them can be fully beneficial only when they lead to the satisfaction of the Supreme Personality of Godhead. The perfection of any activity—social, political, religious or philanthropic—is to satisfy the Supreme Lord. This secret of success is known to the devotee of the Lord, as exemplified by Arjuna on the Battlefield of Kurukṣetra. As a good, nonviolent man, Arjuna did not want to fight with his kinsmen, but when he understood that Kṛṣṇa wanted the fight and had arranged it at Kurukṣetra, he gave up his own satisfaction and fought for the satisfaction of the Lord. That is the right decision for all intelligent men. One's only concern should be to satisfy the Lord by one's activities. If the Lord is satisfied by an action, whatever it may be, then it is successful. Otherwise, it is simply a waste of time. That is the standard of all sacrifice, penance, austerity, mystic trance and other good and pious work.

TEXT 42

अहमात्मात्मनां धातः प्रेष्ठः सन् प्रेयसामपि ।
अतो मयि रतिं कुर्याद्देहादिर्यत्कृते प्रियः ॥४२॥

aham ātmātmanāṁ dhātaḥ
preṣṭhaḥ san preyasām api
ato mayi ratiṁ kuryād
dehādir yat-kṛte priyaḥ

aham—I am; *ātmā*—the Supersoul; *ātmanām*—of all other souls; *dhātaḥ*—director; *preṣṭhaḥ*—the dearest; *san*—being; *preyasām*—of all dear things; *api*—certainly; *ataḥ*—therefore; *mayi*—unto Me; *ratim*—attachment; *kuryāt*—one should do; *deha-ādiḥ*—the body and mind; *yat-kṛte*—on whose account; *priyaḥ*—very dear.

TRANSLATION

I am the Supersoul of every individual. I am the supreme director and the dearest. People are wrongly attached to the gross and subtle bodies, but they should be attached to Me only.

PURPORT

The Supreme Lord, the Personality of Godhead, is the dearest in both the conditioned and liberated states. When a person does not know that the Lord is the only dearmost object, then he is in the conditioned state of life, and when one knows perfectly well that the Lord is the only dearmost object, he is considered to be liberated. There are degrees of knowing one's relationship with the Lord, depending on the degree of realization as to why the Supreme Lord is the dearmost object of every living being. The real reason is clearly stated in *Bhagavad-gītā* (15.7). *Mamaivāṁśo jīva-loke jīva-bhūtaḥ sanātanaḥ:* the living entities are eternally parts and parcels of the Supreme Lord. The living entity is called the *ātmā*, and the Lord is called the Paramātmā. The living entity is called Brahman, and the Lord is called the Parabrahman, or the Parameśvara. *Īśvaraḥ paramaḥ kṛṣṇaḥ.* The conditioned souls, who do not have self-realization, accept the material body as the dearmost. The idea of the dearmost is then spread all over the body, both concentrated and extended. The attachment for one's own body and its extensions like children and relatives is actually developed on the basis of the real living entity. As soon as the real living entity is out of the body, even the body of the most dear son is no longer attractive. Therefore the living spark, or eternal part of the Supreme, is the real basis of affection, and not the body. Because the living entities are also parts of the whole living entity, that supreme living entity is the factual basis of affection for all. One who has forgotten the basic principle of his love for everything has only flickering love because he is in *māyā.* The more one is affected by the principle of *māyā,* the more he is detached from the basic principle of love. One cannot factually love anything unless he is fully developed in the loving service of the Lord.

In the present verse, stress is given to focusing love upon the Supreme Personality of Godhead. The word *kuryāt* is significant here. This means "one must have it." It is just to stress that we must have more and more attachment to the principle of love. The influence of *māyā* is experienced by the part and parcel spiritual entity, but it cannot influence the Supersoul, the Paramātmā. The Māyāvādī philosophers, accepting the influence of *māyā* on the living entity, want to become one with the Paramātmā. But because they have no actual love for Paramātmā, they remain ever entrapped by the influence of *māyā* and are unable to approach the vicinity of Paramātmā. This inability is due to their lack of affection for the Paramātmā. A rich miser does not know how to utilize his wealth, and therefore, in spite of his being very rich, his miserly behavior keeps him everlastingly a poor man. On the other hand, a person who knows how to utilize wealth can quickly become a rich man, even with a small credit balance.

The eyes and the sun are very intimately related because without sunlight the eyes are unable to see. But the other parts of the body, being attached to the sun as a source of warmth, take more advantage of the sun than do the eyes. Without possessing affection for the sun, the eyes cannot bear the rays of the sun; or, in other words, such eyes have no capacity to understand the utility of the sun's rays. Similarly, the empiric philosophers, despite their theoretical knowledge of Brahman, cannot utilize the mercy of the Supreme Brahman because they lack affection. So many impersonal philosophers remain everlastingly under the influence of *māyā* because, although they indulge in theoretical knowledge of Brahman, they do not develop affection for Brahman nor do they have any scope for development of affection because of their defective method. A devotee of the sun-god, even though devoid of eyesight, can see the sun-god as he is even from this planet, whereas one who is not a devotee of the sun cannot even bear the glaring sunlight. Similarly, by devotional service, even though one is not on the level of a *jñānī*, one can see the Personality of Godhead within himself due to his development of pure love. In all circumstances one should try to develop love of Godhead, and that will solve all contending problems.

TEXT 43

सर्ववेदमयेनेदमात्मनात्मात्मयोनिना ।
प्रजाः सृज यथापूर्वं याश्च मय्यनुशेरते ॥४३॥

sarva-veda-mayenedam
ātmanātmātma-yoninā
prajāḥ sṛja yathā-pūrvaṁ
yāś ca mayy anuśerate

sarva—all; *veda-mayena*—under complete Vedic wisdom; *idam*—this; *ātmanā*—by the body; *ātmā*—you; *ātma-yoninā*—directly born of the Lord; *prajāḥ*—living entities; *sṛja*—generate; *yathā-pūrvam*—as it was hereinbefore; *yāḥ*—which; *ca*—also; *mayi*—in Me; *anuśerate*—lie.

TRANSLATION

By following My instructions you can now generate the living entities as before, by dint of your complete Vedic wisdom and the body you have directly received from Me, the supreme cause of everything.

TEXT 44

मैत्रेय उवाच
तस्मा एवं जगत्स्रष्ट्रे प्रधानपुरुषेश्वरः ।
व्यज्येदं स्वेन रूपेण कञ्जनाभस्तिरोदधे ॥४४॥

maitreya uvāca
tasmā evaṁ jagat-sraṣṭre
pradhāna-puruṣeśvaraḥ
vyajyedaṁ svena rūpeṇa
kañja-nābhas tirodadhe

maitreyaḥ uvāca—the sage Maitreya said; *tasmai*—unto him; *evam*—thus; *jagat-sraṣṭre*—unto the creator of the universe; *pradhāna-puruṣa-īśvaraḥ*—the primeval Lord, the Personality of Godhead; *vyajya idam*—after instructing this; *svena*—in His person; *rūpeṇa*—by the form; *kañja-nābhaḥ*—the Personality of Godhead Nārāyaṇa; *tirodadhe*—disappeared.

TRANSLATION

The sage Maitreya said: After instructing Brahmā, the creator of the universe, to expand, the primeval Lord, the Personality of Godhead in His personal form as Nārāyaṇa, disappeared.

PURPORT

Before his activity in creating the universe, Brahmā saw the Lord. That is the explanation of the *catuḥ-ślokī Bhāgavatam.* When the creation awaited Brahmā's activity, Brahmā saw the Lord, and therefore the Lord existed in His personal form before the creation. His eternal form is not created by the attempt of Brahmā, as imagined by less intelligent men. The Personality of Godhead appeared as He is before Brahmā, and He disappeared from him in the same form, which is not materially tinged.

Thus end the Bhaktivedanta purports of the Third Canto, Ninth Chapter, of the Śrīmad-Bhāgavatam, *entitled "Brahmā's Prayers for Creative Energy."*

CHAPTER TEN

Divisions of the Creation

TEXT 1

विदुर उवाच
अन्तर्हिते भगवति ब्रह्मा लोकपितामहः ।
प्रजाः ससर्ज कतिधा दैहिकीर्मानसीर्विभुः ॥ १ ॥

vidura uvāca
antarhite bhagavati
brahmā loka-pitāmahaḥ
prajāḥ sasarja katidhā
daihikīr mānasīr vibhuḥ

viduraḥ uvāca—Śrī Vidura said; *antarhite*—after the disappearance; *bhagavati*—of the Personality of Godhead; *brahmā*—the first created living being; *loka-pitāmahaḥ*—the grandfather of all planetary inhabitants; *prajāḥ*—generations; *sasarja*—created; *katidhāḥ*—how many; *daihikīḥ*—from his body; *mānasīḥ*—from his mind; *vibhuḥ*—the great.

TRANSLATION

Śrī Vidura said: O great sage, please let me know how Brahmā, the grandfather of the planetary inhabitants, created the bodies of the living entities from his own body and mind after the disappearance of the Supreme Personality of Godhead.

TEXT 2

ये च मे भगवन् पृष्टास्त्वय्यर्था बहुवित्तम ।
तान् वदस्वानुपूर्व्येण छिन्धि नः सर्वसंशयान् ॥२॥

ye ca me bhagavan pṛṣṭās
tvayy arthā bahuvittama

tān vadasvānupūrvyeṇa
chindhi naḥ sarva-saṁśayān

ye—all those; *ca*—also; *me*—by me; *bhagavan*—O powerful one; *pṛṣṭāḥ*—inquired; *tvayi*—unto you; *arthāḥ*—purpose; *bahu-vit-tama*—O greatly learned one; *tān*—all of them; *vadasva*—kindly describe; *ānupūrvyeṇa*—from beginning to end; *chindhi*—kindly eradicate; *naḥ*—my; *sarva*—all; *saṁśayān*—doubts.

TRANSLATION

O greatly learned one, kindly eradicate all my doubts, and let me know of all that I have inquired from you from the beginning to the end.

PURPORT

Vidura asked all relevant questions of Maitreya because he knew well that Maitreya was the right person to reply to all the points of his inquiries. One must be confident about the qualifications of his teacher; one should not approach a layman for replies to specific spiritual inquiries. Such inquiries, when replied to with imaginative answers by the teacher, are a program for wasting time.

TEXT 3

सूत उवाच
एवं सञ्चोदितस्तेन क्षत्त्रा कौषारविर्मुनिः ।
प्रीतः प्रत्याह तान् प्रश्नान् हृदिस्थानथ भार्गव ॥३॥

sūta uvāca
evaṁ sañcoditas tena
kṣattrā kauṣāravir muniḥ
prītaḥ pratyāha tān praśnān
hṛdi-sthān atha bhārgava

sūtaḥ uvāca—Śrī Sūta Gosvāmī said; *evam*—thus; *sañcoditaḥ*—being enlivened; *tena*—by him; *kṣattrā*—by Vidura; *kauṣāraviḥ*—the son of Kuṣāra; *muniḥ*—great sage; *prītaḥ*—being pleased; *pratyāha*—replied;

tān—those; *praśnān*—questions; *hṛdi-sthān*—from the core of his heart; *atha*—thus; *bhārgava*—O son of Bhṛgu.

TRANSLATION

Sūta Gosvāmī said: O son of Bhṛgu, the great sage Maitreya Muni, thus hearing from Vidura, felt very much enlivened. Everything was in his heart, and thus he began to reply to the questions one after another.

PURPORT

The phrase *sūta uvāca* ("Sūta Gosvāmī said") appears to indicate a break in the discourse between Mahārāja Parīkṣit and Śukadeva Gosvāmī. While Śukadeva Gosvāmī was speaking to Mahārāja Parīkṣit, Sūta Gosvāmī was only one member of a large audience. But Sūta Gosvāmī was speaking to the sages of Naimiṣāraṇya, headed by the sage Śaunaka, a descendant of Śukadeva Gosvāmī. This, however, does not make any substantial difference in the topics under discussion.

TEXT 4

मैत्रेय उवाच
विरिञ्चोऽपि तथा चक्रे दिव्यं वर्षशतं तपः ।
आत्मन्यात्मानमावेश्य यथाह भगवानजः ॥ ४ ॥

maitreya uvāca
viriñco 'pi tathā cakre
divyaṁ varṣa-śataṁ tapaḥ
ātmany ātmānam āveśya
yathāha bhagavān ajaḥ

maitreyaḥ uvāca—the great sage Maitreya said; *viriñcaḥ*—Brahmā; *api*—also; *tathā*—in that manner; *cakre*—performed; *divyam*—celestial; *varṣa-śatam*—one hundred years; *tapaḥ*—penances; *ātmani*—unto the Lord; *ātmānam*—his own self; *āveśya*—engaging; *yathā āha*—as it was spoken; *bhagavān*—the Personality of Godhead; *ajaḥ*—the unborn.

TRANSLATION

The greatly learned sage Maitreya said: O Vidura, Brahmā thus engaged himself in penances for one hundred celestial years, as advised by the Personality of Godhead, and applied himself in devotional service to the Lord.

PURPORT

That Brahmā engaged himself for the Personality of Godhead, Nārāyaṇa, means that he engaged himself in the service of the Lord; that is the highest penance one can perform for any number of years. There is no retirement from such service, which is eternal and ever encouraging.

TEXT 5

तद्विलोक्याब्जसम्भूतो वायुना यदधिष्ठितः ।
पद्ममम्भश्च तत्कालकृतवीर्येण कम्पितम् ॥ ५ ॥

tad vilokyābja-sambhūto
vāyunā yad-adhiṣṭhitaḥ
padmam ambhaś ca tat-kāla-
kṛta-vīryeṇa kampitam

tat vilokya—looking into that; *abja-sambhūtaḥ*—whose source of birth was a lotus; *vāyunā*—by the air; *yat*—that; *adhiṣṭhitaḥ*—on which he was situated; *padmam*—lotus; *ambhaḥ*—water; *ca*—also; *tat-kāla-kṛta*—which was effected by eternal time; *vīryeṇa*—by its inherent force; *kampitam*—trembling.

TRANSLATION

Thereafter Brahmā saw that both the lotus on which he was situated and the water on which the lotus was growing were trembling due to a strong, violent wind.

PURPORT

The material world is called illusory because it is a place of forgetfulness of the transcendental service of the Lord. Thus one engaged in the

the Lord's devotional service in the material world may sometimes be very much disturbed by awkward circumstances. There is a declaration of war between the two parties, the illusory energy and the devotee, and sometimes the weak devotees fall victim to the onslaught of the powerful illusory energy. Lord Brahmā, however, was sufficiently strong, by the causeless mercy of the Lord, and he could not be victimized by the material energy, although it gave him cause for anxiety when it managed to totter the existence of his position.

TEXT 6

तपसा ह्येधमानेन विद्यया चात्मसंस्थया ।
विवृद्धविज्ञानबलो न्यपाद् वायुं सहाम्भसा ॥ ६ ॥

tapasā hy edhamānena
vidyayā cātma-saṁsthayā
vivṛddha-vijñāna-balo
nyapād vāyuṁ sahāmbhasā

tapasā—by penance; *hi*—certainly; *edhamānena*—increasing; *vidyayā*—by transcendental knowledge; *ca*—also; *ātma*—self; *saṁsthayā*—situated in the self; *vivṛddha*—matured; *vijñāna*—practical knowledge; *balaḥ*—power; *nyapāt*—drank; *vāyum*—the wind; *saha ambhasā*—along with the water.

TRANSLATION

Long penance and transcendental knowledge of self-realization had matured Brahmā in practical knowledge, and thus he drank the wind completely, along with the water.

PURPORT

Lord Brahmā's struggle for existence is a personal example of the continued fight between the living entities in the material world and the illusory energy called *māyā*. Beginning from Brahmā down to this age, the living entities are struggling with the forces of material nature. By advanced knowledge in science and transcendental realization, one can try to control the material energy, which works against our endeavors, and in the modern age advanced material scientific knowledge and penance have played very wonderful roles in controlling the powers of the material energy. Such control of the material energy, however, can be most successfully carried out if one is a soul surrendered unto the Supreme Personality of Godhead and carries out His order in the spirit of loving transcendental service.

TEXT 7

तद्विलोक्य वियद्व्यापि पुष्करं यदधिष्ठितम् ।
अनेन लोकान् प्राग्लीनान् कल्पितास्मीत्यचिन्तयत् ॥ ७ ॥

tad vilokya viyad-vyāpi
puṣkaraṁ yad-adhiṣṭhitam
anena lokān prāg-līnān
kalpitāsmīty acintayat

tat vilokya—looking into that; *viyat-vyāpi*—extensively widespread; *puṣkaram*—the lotus; *yat*—that which; *adhiṣṭhitam*—he was situated; *anena*—by this; *lokān*—all the planets; *prāk-līnān*—previously merged in dissolution; *kalpitā asmi*—I shall create; *iti*—thus; *acintayat*—he thought.

TRANSLATION

Thereafter he saw that the lotus on which he was situated was spread throughout the universe, and he contemplated how to create all the planets, which were previously merged in that very same lotus.

PURPORT

The seeds of all the planets in the universe were impregnated in the lotus on which Brahmā was situated. All the planets were already generated by the Lord, and all the living entities were also born in Brahmā. The material world and the living entities were all already generated in seedling forms by the Supreme Personality of Godhead, and Brahmā was to disseminate the same seedlings all over the universe. The real creation is therefore called *sarga*, and, later on, the manifestation by Brahmā is called *visarga.*

TEXT 8

पद्मकोशं तदाविश्य भगवत्कर्मचोदितः ।
एकं व्यभाङ्क्षीदुरुधा त्रिधा भाव्यं द्विसप्तधा ॥ ८ ॥

padma-kośaṁ tadāviśya
bhagavat-karma-coditaḥ
ekaṁ vyabhāṅkṣīd urudhā
tridhā bhāvyaṁ dvi-saptadhā

padma-kośam—the whorl of the lotus; *tadā*—then; *āviśya*—entering into; *bhagavat*—by the Supreme Personality of Godhead; *karma*—in activities; *coditaḥ*—being encouraged by; *ekam*—one; *vyabhāṅkṣīt*—divided into; *urudhā*—great division; *tridhā*—three divisions; *bhāvyam*—capable of further creation; *dvi-saptadhā*—fourteen divisions.

TRANSLATION

Thus engaged in the service of the Supreme Personality of Godhead, Lord Brahmā entered into the whorl of the lotus, and as it spread all over the universe he divided it into three divisions of worlds and later into fourteen divisions.

TEXT 9

एतावाञ्जीवलोकस्य संस्थाभेदः समाहृतः ।
धर्मस्य ह्यनिमित्तस्य विपाकः परमेष्ठ्यसौ ॥ ९ ॥

etāvāñ jīva-lokasya
saṁsthā-bhedaḥ samāhṛtaḥ
dharmasya hy animittasya
vipākaḥ parameṣṭhy asau

etāvān—up to this; *jīva-lokasya*—of the planets inhabited by the living entities; *saṁsthā-bhedaḥ*—different situations of habitation; *samāhṛtaḥ*—performed completely; *dharmasya*—of religion; *hi*—certainly; *animittasya*—of causelessness; *vipākaḥ*—mature stage; *parameṣṭhī*—the highest personality in the universe; *asau*—that.

TRANSLATION

Lord Brahmā is the most exalted personality in the universe because of his causeless devotional service unto the Lord in mature transcendental knowledge. He therefore created all the fourteen planetary divisions for inhabitation by the different types of living entities.

PURPORT

The Supreme Lord is the reservoir of all the qualities of the living entities. The conditioned souls in the material world reflect only part of those qualities, and therefore they are sometimes called *pratibimbas.* These *pratibimba* living entities, as parts and parcels of the Supreme Lord, have inherited different proportions of His original qualities, and in terms of their inheritance of these qualities, they appear as different species of life and are accommodated in different planets according to the plan of Brahmā. Brahmā is the creator of the three worlds, namely the lower planets, called the Pātālalokas, the middle planets, called the Bhūrlokas, and the upper planets, called the Svarlokas. Still higher planets, such as Maharloka, Tapoloka, Satyaloka and Brahmaloka, do not dissolve in the devastating water. This is because of the causeless devotional service rendered unto the Lord by their inhabitants, whose existence continues up to the end of *dvi-parārdha* time, when they are generally liberated from the chain of birth and death in the material world.

TEXT 10

विदुर उवाच
यथात्थ बहुरूपस्य हरेरद्भुतकर्मणः ।
कालाख्यं लक्षणं ब्रह्मन् यथा वर्णय नः प्रभो ॥१०॥

vidura uvāca
yathāttha bahu-rūpasya
harer adbhuta-karmaṇaḥ
kālākhyaṁ lakṣaṇaṁ brahman
yathā varṇaya naḥ prabho

viduraḥ uvāca—Vidura said; *yathā*—as; *āttha*—you have said; *bahu-rūpasya*—having varieties of forms; *hareḥ*—of the Lord;

adbhuta—wonderful; *karmaṇaḥ*—of the actor; *kāla*—time; *ākhyam*—of the name; *lakṣaṇam*—symptoms; *brahman*—O learned *brāhmaṇa;* *yathā*—as it is; *varṇaya*—please describe; *naḥ*—unto us; *prabho*—O lord.

TRANSLATION

Vidura inquired from Maitreya: O my lord, O greatly learned sage, kindly describe eternal time, which is another form of the Supreme Lord, the wonderful actor. What are the symptoms of that eternal time? Please describe them to us in detail.

PURPORT

The complete universe is a manifestation of varieties of entities, beginning from the atoms up to the gigantic universe itself, and all is under the control of the Supreme Lord in His form of *kāla*, or eternal time. The controlling time has different dimensions in relation to particular physical embodiments. There is a time for atomic dissolution and a time for the universal dissolution. There is a time for the annihilation of the body of the human being, and there is a time for the annihilation of the universal body. Also, growth, development and resultant actions all depend on the time factor. Vidura wanted to know in detail the different physical manifestations and their times of annihilation.

TEXT 11

मैत्रेय उवाच
गुणव्यतिकराकारो निर्विशेषोऽप्रतिष्ठितः ।
पुरुषस्तदुपादानमात्मानं लीलयासृजत् ॥११॥

maitreya uvāca
guṇa-vyatikarākāro
nirviśeṣo 'pratiṣṭhitaḥ
puruṣas tad-upādānam
ātmānaṁ līlayāsṛjat

maitreyaḥ uvāca—Maitreya said; *guṇa-vyatikara*—of the interactions of the modes of material nature; *ākāraḥ*—source; *nirviśeṣaḥ*—

without diversity; *apratiṣṭhitaḥ*—unlimited; *puruṣaḥ*—of the Supreme Person; *tat*—that; *upādānam*—instrument; *ātmānam*—the material creation; *līlayā*—by pastimes; *asṛjat*—created.

TRANSLATION

Maitreya said: Eternal time is the primeval source of the interactions of the three modes of material nature. It is unchangeable and limitless, and it works as the instrument of the Supreme Personality of Godhead for His pastimes in the material creation.

PURPORT

The impersonal time factor is the background of the material manifestation as the instrument of the Supreme Lord. It is the ingredient of assistance offered to material nature. No one knows where time began and where it ends, and it is time only which can keep a record of the creation, maintenance and destruction of the material manifestation. This time factor is the material cause of creation and is therefore a self-expansion of the Personality of Godhead. Time is considered the impersonal feature of the Lord.

The time factor is also explained by modern men in various ways. Some accept it almost as it is explained in the *Śrīmad-Bhāgavatam*. For example, in Hebrew literature time is accepted, in the same spirit, as a representation of God. It is stated therein: "God, who at sundry times and in diverse manners spake in time past unto the fathers by the prophets. . . ." Metaphysically, time is distinguished as absolute and real. Absolute time is continuous and is unaffected by the speed or slowness of material things. Time is astronomically and mathematically calculated in relation to the speed, change and life of a particular object. Factually, however, time has nothing to do with the relativities of things; rather, everything is shaped and calculated in terms of the facility offered by time. Time is the basic measurement of the activity of our senses, by which we calculate past, present and future; but in factual calculation, time has no beginning and no end. Paṇḍita Cāṇakya says that even a slight fraction of time cannot be purchased with millions of dollars, and therefore even a moment of time lost without profit must be calculated as the greatest loss in life. Time is not subject to any form of psychology, nor are the moments objective realities in themselves, but they are dependent on particular experiences.

Therefore, Śrīla Jīva Gosvāmī concludes that the time factor is intermixed with the activities—actions and reactions—of the external energy of the Lord. The external energy, or material nature, works under the superintendence of the time factor as the Lord Himself, and that is why material nature appears to have produced so many wonderful things in the cosmic manifestation. *Bhagavad-gītā* (9.10) confirms this conclusion as follows:

mayādhyakṣeṇa prakṛtiḥ
sūyate sa-carācaram
hetunānena kaunteya
jagad viparivartate

TEXT 12

विश्वं वै ब्रह्मतन्मात्रं संस्थितं विष्णुमायया ।
ईश्वरेण परिच्छिन्नं कालेनाव्यक्तमूर्तिना ॥१२॥

viśvaṁ vai brahma-tan-mātraṁ
saṁsthitaṁ viṣṇu-māyayā
īśvareṇa paricchinnaṁ
kālenāvyakta-mūrtinā

viśvam—the material phenomenon; *vai*—certainly; *brahma*—the Supreme; *tat-mātram*—the same as; *saṁsthitam*—situated; *viṣṇu-māyayā*—by the energy of Viṣṇu; *īśvareṇa*—by the Personality of Godhead; *paricchinnam*—separated; *kālena*—by the eternal time; *avyakta*—unmanifested; *mūrtinā*—by such a feature.

TRANSLATION

This cosmic manifestation is separated from the Supreme Lord as material energy by means of kāla, which is the unmanifested, impersonal feature of the Lord. It is situated as the objective manifestation of the Lord under the influence of the same material energy of Viṣṇu.

PURPORT

As stated previously by Nārada before Vyāsadeva (*Bhāg.* 1.5.20), *idaṁ hi viśvaṁ bhagavān ivetaraḥ:* this unmanifested world is the selfsame Personality of Godhead, but it appears to be something else beyond or besides the Lord. It appears so because of its being separated from the Lord by means of *kāla.* It is something like the tape-recorded voice of a person who is now separated from the voice. As the tape recording is situated on the tape, so the whole cosmic manifestation is situated on the material energy and appears separate by means of *kāla.* The material manifestation is therefore the objective manifestation of the Supreme Lord and exhibits His impersonal feature so much adored by impersonalist philosophers.

TEXT 13

यथेदानीं तथाग्रे च पश्चादप्येतदीदृशम् ॥१३॥

yathedānīṁ tathāgre ca
paścād apy etad īdṛśam

yathā—as it is; *idānīm*—at present; *tathā*—so it was; *agre*—in the beginning; *ca*—and; *paścāt*—at the end; *api*—also; *etat īdṛśam*—it continues to be the same.

TRANSLATION

This cosmic manifestation is as it is now, it was the same in the past, and it will continue in the same way in the future.

PURPORT

There is a systematic schedule for the perpetual manifestation, maintenance and annihilation of the material world, as stated in *Bhagavad-gītā* (9.8): *bhūta-grāmam imaṁ kṛtsnam avaśaṁ prakṛter vaśāt.* As it is created now and as it will be destroyed later on, so also it existed in the past and again will be created, maintained and destroyed in due course of time. Therefore, the systematic activities of the time factor are perpetual and eternal and cannot be stated to be false. The manifestation is temporary and occasional, but it is not false as claimed by the Māyāvādī philosophers.

TEXT 14

सर्गो नवविधस्तस्य प्राकृतो वैकृतस्तु यः ।
कालद्रव्यगुणैरस्य त्रिविधः प्रतिसंक्रमः ॥१४॥

sargo nava-vidhas tasya
prākṛto vaikṛtas tu yaḥ
kāla-dravya-guṇair asya
tri-vidhaḥ pratisaṅkramaḥ

sargaḥ—creation; *nava-vidhaḥ*—of nine different kinds; *tasya*—its; *prākṛtaḥ*—material; *vaikṛtaḥ*—by the modes of material nature; *tu*—but; *yaḥ*—that which; *kāla*—eternal time; *dravya*—matter; *guṇaiḥ*—qualities; *asya*—its; *tri-vidhaḥ*—three kinds; *pratisaṅkramaḥ*—annihilation.

TRANSLATION

There are nine different kinds of creations besides the one which naturally occurs due to the interactions of the modes. There are three kinds of annihilations due to eternal time, the material elements and the quality of one's work.

PURPORT

The scheduled creations and annihilations take place in terms of the supreme will. There are other creations due to interactions of material elements which take place by the intelligence of Brahmā. Later these will be more explicitly explained. At present, only preliminary information is given. The three kinds of annihilations are (1) due to the scheduled time of the annihilation of the entire universe, (2) due to a fire which emanates from the mouth of Ananta, and (3) due to one's qualitative actions and reactions.

TEXT 15

आद्यस्तु महतः सर्गो गुणवैषम्यमात्मनः ।
द्वितीयस्त्वहमो यत्र द्रव्यज्ञानक्रियोदयः ॥१५॥

ādyas tu mahataḥ sargo
guṇa-vaiṣamyam ātmanaḥ

dvitīyas tv ahamo yatra
dravya-jñāna-kriyodayaḥ

ādyaḥ—the first; *tu*—but; *mahataḥ*—of the total emanation from the Lord; *sargaḥ*—creation; *guṇa-vaiṣamyam*—interaction of the material modes; *ātmanaḥ*—of the Supreme; *dvitīyaḥ*—the second; *tu*—but; *ahamaḥ*—false ego; *yatra*—wherein; *dravya*—material ingredients; *jñāna*—material knowledge; *kriyā-udayaḥ*—awakening of activities (work).

TRANSLATION

Of the nine creations, the first one is the creation of the mahat-tattva, or the sum total of the material ingredients, wherein the modes interact due to the presence of the Supreme Lord. In the second, the false ego is generated in which the material ingredients, material knowledge and material activities arise.

PURPORT

The first emanation from the Supreme Lord for material creation is called the *mahat-tattva.* The interaction of the material modes is the cause of false identification, or the sense that a living being is made of material elements. This false ego is the cause of identifying the body and mind with the soul proper. Material resources and the capacity and knowledge to work are all generated in the second term of creation, after the *mahat-tattva. Jñāna* indicates the senses which are sources of knowledge, and their controlling deities. Work entails the working organs and their controlling deities. All these are generated in the second creation.

TEXT 16

भूतसर्गस्तृतीयस्तु तन्मात्रो द्रव्यशक्तिमान् ।
चतुर्थ ऐन्द्रियः सर्गो यस्तु ज्ञानक्रियात्मकः ॥ १६ ॥

bhūta-sargas tṛtīyas tu
tan-mātro dravya-śaktimān

caturtha aindriyaḥ sargo
yas tu jñāna-kriyātmakaḥ

bhūta-sargaḥ—creation of matter; *tṛtīyaḥ*—is the third; *tu*—but; *tat-mātraḥ*—sense perception; *dravya*—of the elements; *śaktimān*—generator; *caturthaḥ*—the fourth; *aindriyaḥ*—in the matter of the senses; *sargaḥ*—creation; *yaḥ*—that which; *tu*—but; *jñāna*—knowledge-acquiring; *kriyā*—working; *ātmakaḥ*—basically.

TRANSLATION

The sense perceptions are created in the third creation, and from these the elements are generated. The fourth creation is the creation of knowledge and of working capacity.

TEXT 17

वैकारिको देवसर्गः पञ्चमो यन्मयं मनः ।
षष्ठस्तु तमसः सर्गो यस्त्वबुद्धिकृतः प्रभोः ॥१७॥

vaikāriko deva-sargaḥ
pañcamo yan-mayaṁ manaḥ
ṣaṣṭhas tu tamasaḥ sargo
yas tv abuddhi-kṛtaḥ prabhoḥ

vaikārikaḥ—interaction of the mode of goodness; *deva*—the demigods, or controlling deities; *sargaḥ*—creation; *pañcamaḥ*—fifth; *yat*—that which; *mayam*—sum total; *manaḥ*—mind; *ṣaṣṭhaḥ*—sixth; *tu*—but; *tamasaḥ*—of darkness; *sargaḥ*—creation; *yaḥ*—that which; *tu*—expletive; *abuddhi-kṛtaḥ*—made foolish; *prabhoḥ*—of the master.

TRANSLATION

The fifth creation is that of the controlling deities by the interaction of the mode of goodness, of which the mind is the sum total. The sixth creation is the ignorant darkness of the living entity, by which the master acts as a fool.

PURPORT

The demigods in the higher planets are called *devas* because they are all devotees of Lord Viṣṇu. *Viṣṇu-bhaktaḥ smṛto daiva āsuras tad-viparyayaḥ:* all the devotees of Lord Viṣṇu are *devas,* or demigods, whereas all others are *asuras.* That is the division of the *devas* and the *asuras. Devas* are situated in the mode of goodness of material nature, whereas the *asuras* are situated in the modes of passion or ignorance. The demigods, or controlling deities, are entrusted with departmental management of all the different functions of the material world. For example, one of our sense organs, the eye, is controlled by light, light is distributed by the sun rays, and their controlling deity is the sun. Similarly, mind is controlled by the moon. All other senses, both for working and for acquiring knowledge, are controlled by the different demigods. The demigods are assistants of the Lord in the management of material affairs.

After the creation of the demigods, all entities are covered by the darkness of ignorance. Each and every living being in the material world is conditioned by his mentality of lording it over the resources of material nature. Although a living entity is the master of the material world, he is conditioned by ignorance, by the false impression of being the proprietor of material things.

The energy of the Lord called *avidyā* is the bewildering factor of the conditioned souls. The material nature is called *avidyā,* or ignorance, but to the devotees of the Lord engaged in pure devotional service, this energy becomes *vidyā,* or pure knowledge. This is confirmed in *Bhagavad-gītā.* The energy of the Lord transforms from *mahāmāyā* to *yogamāyā* and appears to pure devotees in her real feature. The material nature therefore appears to function in three phases: as the creative principle of the material world, as ignorance and as knowledge. As disclosed in the previous verse, in the fourth creation the power of knowledge is also created. The conditioned souls are not originally fools, but by the influence of the *avidyā* function of material nature they are made fools, and thus they are unable to utilize knowledge in the proper channel.

By the influence of darkness, the conditioned soul forgets his relationship with the Supreme Lord and is overwhelmed by attachment, hatred, pride, ignorance and false identification, the five kinds of illusion that cause material bondage.

TEXT 18

षडिमे प्राकृताः सर्गा वैकृतानपि मे शृणु ।
रजोभाजो भगवतो लीलेयं हरिमेधसः ॥१८॥

ṣaḍ ime prākṛtāḥ sargā
vaikṛtān api me śṛṇu
rajo-bhājo bhagavato
līleyaṁ hari-medhasaḥ

ṣaṭ—six; *ime*—all these; *prākṛtāḥ*—of the material energy; *sargāḥ*—creations; *vaikṛtān*—secondary creations by Brahmā; *api*—also; *me*—from me; *śṛṇu*—just hear; *rajaḥ-bhājaḥ*—of the incarnation of the mode of passion (Brahmā); *bhagavataḥ*—of the greatly powerful; *līlā*—pastime; *iyam*—this; *hari*—the Supreme Personality of Godhead; *medhasaḥ*—of one who has such a brain.

TRANSLATION

All the above are natural creations by the external energy of the Lord. Now hear from me about the creations by Brahmā, who is an incarnation of the mode of passion and who, in the matter of creation, has a brain like that of the Personality of Godhead.

TEXT 19

सप्तमो मुख्यसर्गस्तु षड्विधस्तस्थुषां च यः ।
वनस्पत्योषधिलतात्वक्सारा वीरुधो द्रुमाः ॥१९॥

saptamo mukhya-sargas tu
ṣaḍ-vidhas tasthuṣāṁ ca yaḥ
vanaspaty-oṣadhi-latā-
tvaksārā vīrudho drumāḥ

saptamaḥ—the seventh; *mukhya*—principle; *sargaḥ*—creation; *tu*—indeed; *ṣaṭ-vidhaḥ*—six kinds of; *tasthuṣām*—of those who do not move; *ca*—also; *yaḥ*—those; *vanaspati*—fruit trees without flowers; *oṣadhi*—trees and plants existing until the fruit is ripe; *latā*—creepers;

tvaksārāḥ—pipe plants; *vīrudhaḥ*—creepers without support; *drumāḥ*—trees with flowers and fruits.

TRANSLATION

The seventh creation is that of the immovable entities, which are of six kinds: the fruit trees without flowers, trees and plants which exist until the fruit is ripe, creepers, pipe plants, creepers which have no support, and trees with flowers and fruits.

TEXT 20

उत्स्रोतसस्तमःप्राया अन्तःस्पर्शा विशेषिणः ॥२०॥

utsrotasas tamaḥ-prāyā
antaḥ-sparśā viśeṣiṇaḥ

utsrotasaḥ—they seek their subsistence upwards; *tamaḥ-prāyāḥ*—almost unconscious; *antaḥ-sparśāḥ*—slightly feeling within; *viśeṣiṇaḥ*—with varieties of manifestation.

TRANSLATION

All the immovable trees and plants seek their subsistence upwards. They are almost unconscious but have feelings of pain within. They are manifested in variegatedness.

TEXT 21

तिरश्चामष्टमः सर्गः सोऽष्टाविंशद्विधो मतः ।
अविदो भूरितमसो घ्राणज्ञा हृद्यवेदिनः ॥२१॥

tiraścām aṣṭamaḥ sargaḥ
so 'ṣṭāviṁśad-vidho mataḥ
avido bhūri-tamaso
ghrāṇa-jñā hṛdy avedinaḥ

tiraścām—species of lower animals; *aṣṭamaḥ*—the eighth; *sargaḥ*—creation; *saḥ*—they are; *aṣṭāviṁśat*—twenty-eight; *vidhaḥ*—varieties; *mataḥ*—considered; *avidaḥ*—without knowledge of tomorrow; *bhūri*—

extensively; *tamasaḥ*—ignorant; *ghrāṇa-jñāḥ*—can know desirables by smell; *hṛdi avedinaḥ*—can remember very little in the heart.

TRANSLATION

The eighth creation is that of the lower species of life, and they are of different varieties, numbering twenty-eight. They are all extensively foolish and ignorant. They know their desirables by smell, but are unable to remember anything within the heart.

PURPORT

In the *Vedas* the symptoms of the lower animals are described as follows: *athetareṣāṁ paśūnāḥ aśanāpipāse evābhivijñānaṁ na vijñātaṁ vadanti na vijñātaṁ paśyanti na viduḥ śvastanaṁ na lokālokāv iti; yad vā, bhūri-tamaso bahu-ruṣaḥ ghrāṇenaiva jānanti hṛdyaṁ prati svapriyaṁ vastv eva vindanti bhojana-śayanādy-arthaṁ gṛhṇanti.* "Lower animals have knowledge only of their hunger and thirst. They have no acquired knowledge, no vision. Their behavior exhibits no dependence on formalities. Extensively ignorant, they can know their desirables only by smell, and by such intelligence only can they understand what is favorable and unfavorable. Their knowledge is concerned only with eating and sleeping." Therefore, even the most ferocious lower animals, such as tigers, can be tamed simply by regularly supplying meals and accommodations for sleeping. Only snakes cannot be tamed by such an arrangement.

TEXT 22

गौरजो महिषः कृष्णः सूकरो गवयो रुरुः ।
द्विशफाः पशवश्चेमे अविरुष्ट्रश्च सत्तम ॥२२॥

gaur ajo mahiṣaḥ kṛṣṇaḥ
sūkaro gavayo ruruḥ
dvi-śaphāḥ paśavaś ceme
avir uṣṭraś ca sattama

gauḥ—the cow; *ajaḥ*—the goat; *mahiṣaḥ*—the buffalo; *kṛṣṇaḥ*—a kind of stag; *sūkaraḥ*—hog; *gavayaḥ*—a species of animal; *ruruḥ*—

deer; *dvi-śaphāḥ*—having two hooves; *paśavaḥ*—animals; *ca*—also; *ime*—all these; *aviḥ*—lamb; *uṣṭraḥ*—camel; *ca*—and; *sattama*—O purest.

TRANSLATION

O purest Vidura, of the lower animals the cow, goat, buffalo, kṛṣṇa-stag, hog, gavaya animal, deer, lamb and camel all have two hooves.

TEXT 23

खरोऽश्वोऽश्वतरो गौरः शरभश्चमरी तथा ।
एते चैकशफाः क्षत्तः शृणु पञ्चनखान् पशून् ॥२३॥

kharo 'śvo 'śvataro gauraḥ
śarabhaś camarī tathā
ete caika-śaphāḥ kṣattaḥ
śṛṇu pañca-nakhān paśūn

kharaḥ—ass; *aśvaḥ*—horse; *aśvataraḥ*—mule; *gauraḥ*—white deer; *śarabhaḥ*—bison; *camarī*—wild cow; *tathā*—thus; *ete*—all these; *ca*—and; *eka*—only one; *śaphāḥ*—hoof; *kṣattaḥ*—O Vidura; *śṛṇu*—just hear now; *pañca*—five; *nakhān*—nails; *paśūn*—animals.

TRANSLATION

The horse, mule, ass, gaura, śarabha bison and wild cow all have only one hoof. Now you may hear from me about the animals who have five nails.

TEXT 24

श्वा सृगालो वृको व्याघ्रो मार्जारः शशशल्लकौ ।
सिंहः कपिर्गजः कूर्मो गोधा च मकरादयः ॥२४॥

śvā sṛgālo vṛko vyāghro
mārjāraḥ śaśa-śallakau
siṁhaḥ kapir gajaḥ kūrmo
godhā ca makarādayaḥ

śvā—dog; *sṛgālaḥ*—jackal; *vṛkaḥ*—fox; *vyāghraḥ*—tiger; *mārjāraḥ*—cat; *śaśa*—rabbit; *śallakau*—*sajāru* (with thorns on the body); *siṁhaḥ*—lion; *kapiḥ*—monkey; *gajaḥ*—elephant; *kūrmaḥ*—tortoise; *godhā*—*gosāpa* (snake with four legs); *ca*—also; *makara-ādayaḥ*—the alligator and others.

TRANSLATION

The dog, jackal, tiger, fox, cat, rabbit, sajāru, lion, monkey, elephant, tortoise, alligator, gosāpa, etc., all have five nails in their claws. They are known as pañca-nakhas, or animals having five nails.

TEXT 25

कङ्कगृध्रबकश्येनभासभल्लूकबर्हिणः ।
हंससारसचक्राह्वकाकोलूकादयः खगाः ॥२५॥

kaṅka-gṛdhra-baka-śyena-
bhāsa-bhallūka-barhiṇaḥ
haṁsa-sārasa-cakrāhva-
kākolūkādayaḥ khagāḥ

kaṅka—heron; *gṛdhra*—vulture; *baka*—crane; *śyena*—hawk; *bhāsa*—the *bhāsa; bhallūka*—the *bhallūka; barhiṇaḥ*—the peacock; *haṁsa*—swan; *sārasa*—the *sārasa; cakrāhva*—the *cakravāka; kāka*—crow; *ulūka*—owl; *ādayaḥ*—and others; *khagāḥ*—the birds.

TRANSLATION

The heron, vulture, crane, hawk, bhāsa, bhallūka, peacock, swan, sārasa, cakravāka, crow, owl and others are the birds.

TEXT 26

अर्वाक्स्रोतस्तु नवमः क्षत्तरेकविधो नृणाम् ।
रजोऽधिकाः कर्मपरा दुःखे च सुखमानिनः ॥२६॥

arvāk-srotas tu navamaḥ
kṣattar eka-vidho nṛṇām

rajo 'dhikāḥ karma-parā
duḥkhe ca sukha-māninaḥ

arvāk—downwards; *srotaḥ*—passage of food; *tu*—but; *navamaḥ*—the ninth; *kṣattaḥ*—O Vidura; *eka-vidhaḥ*—one species; *nṛṇām*—of human beings; *rajaḥ*—the mode of passion; *adhikāḥ*—very prominent; *karma-parāḥ*—interested in working; *duḥkhe*—in misery; *ca*—but; *sukha*—happiness; *māninaḥ*—thinking.

TRANSLATION

The creation of the human beings, who are of one species only and who stock their eatables in the belly, is the ninth in the rotation. In the human race, the mode of passion is very prominent. Humans are always busy in the midst of miserable life, but they think themselves happy in all respects.

PURPORT

The human being is more passionate than the animals, and thus the sex life of the human being is more irregular. The animals have their due time for sexual intercourse, but the human being has no regular time for such activities. The human being is endowed with a higher, advanced stage of consciousness for getting relief from the existence of material miseries, but due to his ignorance he thinks that his higher consciousness is meant for advancing in the material comforts of life. Thus his intelligence is misused in the animal propensities—eating, sleeping, defending and mating—instead of spiritual realization. By advancing in material comforts the human being puts himself into a more miserable condition, but, illusioned by the material energy, he always thinks himself happy, even while in the midst of misery. Such misery of human life is distinct from the natural comfortable life enjoyed even by the animals.

TEXT 27

वैकृतास्त्रय एवैते देवसर्गश्च सत्तम ।
वैकारिकस्तु यः प्रोक्तः कौमारस्तूभयात्मकः ॥२७॥

vaikṛtās traya evaite
deva-sargaś ca sattama
vaikārikas tu yaḥ proktaḥ
kaumāras tūbhayātmakaḥ

vaikṛtāḥ—creations of Brahmā; *trayaḥ*—three kinds; *eva*—certainly; *ete*—all these; *deva-sargaḥ*—appearance of the demigods; *ca*—also; *sattama*—O good Vidura; *vaikārikaḥ*—creation of demigods by nature; *tu*—but; *yaḥ*—which; *proktaḥ*—described before; *kaumāraḥ*—the four Kumāras; *tu*—but; *ubhaya-ātmakaḥ*—both ways (namely *vaikṛta* and *prākṛta*).

TRANSLATION

O good Vidura, these last three creations and the creation of demigods (the tenth creation) are vaikṛta creations, which are different from the previously described prākṛta (natural) creations. The appearance of the Kumāras is both.

TEXTS 28–29

देवसर्गश्चाष्टविधो विबुधाः पितरोऽसुराः ।
गन्धर्वाप्सरसः सिद्धा यक्षरक्षांसि चारणाः ॥२८॥
भूतप्रेतपिशाचाश्च विद्याध्राः किन्नरादयः ।
दशैते विदुराख्याताः सर्गास्ते विश्वसृक्कृताः ॥२९॥

deva-sargaś cāṣṭa-vidho
vibudhāḥ pitaro 'surāḥ
gandharvāpsarasaḥ siddhā
yakṣa-rakṣāṁsi cāraṇāḥ

bhūta-preta-piśācāś ca
vidyādhrāḥ kinnarādayaḥ
daśaite vidurākhyātāḥ
sargās te viśva-sṛk-kṛtāḥ

deva-sargaḥ—creation of the demigods; *ca*—also; *aṣṭa-vidhaḥ*—eight kinds; *vibudhāḥ*—the demigods; *pitaraḥ*—the forefathers; *asurāḥ*—the demons; *gandharva*—the expert artisans in the higher planets; *apsarasaḥ*—the angels; *siddhāḥ*—persons who are perfect in mystic powers; *yakṣa*—the superprotectors; *rakṣāṁsi*—giants; *cāraṇāḥ*—the celestial singers; *bhūta*—jinn; *preta*—evil spirits; *piśācāḥ*—attendant spirits; *ca*—also; *vidyādhrāḥ*—the celestial denizens named Vidyādharas; *kinnara*—superhuman beings; *ādayaḥ*—and others; *daśa ete*—all these ten (creations); *vidura*—O Vidura; *ākhyātāḥ*—described; *sargāḥ*—creations; *te*—unto you; *viśva-sṛk*—the creator of the universe (Brahmā); *kṛtāḥ*—done by him.

TRANSLATION

The creation of the demigods is of eight varieties: (1) the demigods, (2) the forefathers, (3) the asuras, or demons, (4) the Gandharvas and Apsarās, or angels, (5) the Yakṣas and Rākṣasas, (6) the Siddhas, Cāraṇas and Vidyādharas, (7) the Bhūtas, Pretas and Piśācas, and (8) the superhuman beings, celestial singers, etc. All are created by Brahmā, the creator of the universe.

PURPORT

As explained in the Second Canto of *Śrīmad-Bhāgavatam*, the Siddhas are inhabitants of Siddhaloka, where the residents travel in space without vehicles. At their mere will they can pass from one planet to another without difficulty. Therefore, in the upper planets the inhabitants are far superior to the inhabitants of this planet in all matters of art, culture and science, since they possess brains superior to those of human beings. The spirits and jinn mentioned in this connection are also counted among the demigods because they are able to perform uncommon functions not possible for men.

TEXT 30

अतः परं प्रवक्ष्यामि वंशान्मन्वन्तराणि च ।
एवं रजःप्लुतः स्रष्टा कल्पादिष्वात्मभूर्हरिः ।
सृजत्यमोघसङ्कल्प आत्मैवात्मानमात्मना ॥३०॥

ataḥ paraṁ pravakṣyāmi
vaṁśān manvantarāṇi ca

evaṁ rajaḥ-plutaḥ sraṣṭā
kalpādiṣv ātmabhūr hariḥ
sṛjaty amogha-saṅkalpa
ātmaivātmānam ātmanā

ataḥ—here; *param*—after; *pravakṣyāmi*—I shall explain; *vaṁśān*—descendants; *manvantarāṇi*—different advents of Manus; *ca*—and; *evam*—thus; *rajaḥ-plutaḥ*—infused with the mode of passion; *sraṣṭā*—the creator; *kalpa-ādiṣu*—in different millenniums; *ātma-bhūḥ*—self-advent; *hariḥ*—the Personality of Godhead; *sṛjati*—creates; *amogha*—unfailing; *saṅkalpaḥ*—determination; *ātmā eva*—He Himself; *ātmānam*—Himself; *ātmanā*—by His own energy.

TRANSLATION

Now I shall describe the descendants of the Manus. The creator, Brahmā, as the incarnation of the passion mode of the Personality of Godhead, creates the universal affairs with unfailing desires in every millennium by the force of the Lord's energy.

PURPORT

The cosmic manifestation is an expansion of one of the many energies of the Supreme Personality of Godhead; the creator and the created are both emanations of the same Supreme Truth, as stated in the beginning of the *Bhāgavatam: janmādy asya yataḥ.*

Thus end the Bhaktivedanta purports of the Third Canto, Tenth Chapter, of the Śrīmad-Bhāgavatam, *entitled "Divisions of the Creation."*

CHAPTER ELEVEN

Calculation of Time, From the Atom

TEXT 1

मैत्रेय उवाच

चरमः सद्विशेषाणामनेकोऽसंयुतः सदा ।
परमाणुः स विज्ञेयो नृणामैक्यभ्रमो यतः

maitreya uvāca
caramaḥ sad-viśeṣāṇām
aneko 'saṁyutaḥ sadā
paramāṇuḥ sa vijñeyo
nṛṇām aikya-bhramo yataḥ

maitreyaḥ uvāca—Maitreya said; *caramaḥ*—ultimate; *sat*—effect; *viśeṣāṇām*—symptoms; *anekaḥ*—innumerable; *asaṁyutaḥ*—unmixed; *sadā*—always; *parama-aṇuḥ*—atoms; *saḥ*—that; *vijñeyaḥ*—should be understood; *nṛṇām*—of men; *aikya*—oneness; *bhramaḥ*—mistaken; *yataḥ*—from which.

TRANSLATION

The material manifestation's ultimate particle, which is indivisible and not formed into a body, is called the atom. It exists always as an invisible identity, even after the dissolution of all forms. The material body is but a combination of such atoms, but it is misunderstood by the common man.

PURPORT

The atomic description of the *Śrīmad-Bhāgavatam* is almost the same as the modern science of atomism, and this is further described in the Paramāṇu-vāda of Kaṇāda. In modern science also, the atom is accepted as the ultimate indivisible particle of which the universe is composed.

Śrīmad-Bhāgavatam is the full text of all descriptions of knowledge, including the theory of atomism. The atom is the minute subtle form of eternal time.

TEXT 2

सत एव पदार्थस्य स्वरूपावस्थितस्य यत् ।
कैवल्यं परममहानविशेषो निरन्तरः ॥ २ ॥

sata eva padārthasya
svarūpāvasthitasya yat
kaivalyaṁ parama-mahān
aviśeṣo nirantaraḥ

sataḥ—of the effective manifestation; *eva*—certainly; *pada-arthasya*—of physical bodies; *svarūpa-avasthitasya*—staying in the same form even to the time of dissolution; *yat*—that which; *kaivalyam*—oneness; *parama*—the supreme; *mahān*—unlimited; *aviśeṣaḥ*—forms; *nirantaraḥ*—eternally.

TRANSLATION

Atoms are the ultimate state of the manifest universe. When they stay in their own forms without forming different bodies, they are called the unlimited oneness. There are certainly different bodies in physical forms, but the atoms themselves form the complete manifestation.

TEXT 3

एवं कालोऽप्यनुमितः सौक्ष्म्ये स्थौल्ये च सत्तम ।
संस्थानभुक्त्या भगवानव्यक्तो व्यक्तभुग्विभुः ॥ ३ ॥

evaṁ kālo 'py anumitaḥ
saukṣmye sthaulye ca sattama
saṁsthāna-bhuktyā bhagavān
avyakto vyakta-bhug vibhuḥ

evam—thus; *kālaḥ*—time; *api*—also; *anumitaḥ*—measured; *saukṣmye*—in the subtle; *sthaulye*—in the gross forms; *ca*—also; *sat-*

tama—O best; *saṁsthāna*—combinations of the atoms; *bhuktyā*—by the motion; *bhagavān*—the Supreme Personality of Godhead; *avyaktaḥ*—unmanifested; *vyakta-bhuk*—controlling all physical movement; *vibhuḥ*—the great potential.

TRANSLATION

One can estimate time by measuring the movement of the atomic combination of bodies. Time is the potency of the almighty Personality of Godhead, Hari, who controls all physical movement although He is not visible in the physical world.

TEXT 4

स कालः परमाणुर्वै यो भुङ्क्ते परमाणुताम् ।
सतोऽविशेषभुग्यस्तु स कालः परमो महान् ॥ ४ ॥

sa kālaḥ paramāṇur vai
yo bhuṅkte paramāṇutām
sato 'viśeṣa-bhug yas tu
sa kālaḥ paramo mahān

saḥ—that; *kālaḥ*—eternal time; *parama-aṇuḥ*—atomic; *vai*—certainly; *yaḥ*—which; *bhuṅkte*—passes through; *parama-aṇutām*—the space of an atom; *sataḥ*—of the entire aggregate; *aviśeṣa-bhuk*—passing through the nondual exhibition; *yaḥ tu*—which; *saḥ*—that; *kālaḥ*—time; *paramaḥ*—the supreme; *mahān*—the great.

TRANSLATION

Atomic time is measured according to its covering a particular atomic space. That time which covers the unmanifest aggregate of atoms is called the great time.

PURPORT

Time and space are two correlative terms. Time is measured in terms of its covering a certain space of atoms. Standard time is calculated in terms of the movement of the sun. The time covered by the sun in passing over an atom is calculated as atomic time. The greatest time of all covers the entire existence of the nondual manifestation. All the planets rotate and cover space, and space is calculated in terms of atoms. Each planet has its particular orbit for rotating, in which it moves without deviation, and similarly the sun has its orbit. The complete calculation of the time of creation, maintenance and dissolution, measured in terms of the circulation of the total planetary systems until the end of creation, is known as the supreme *kāla*.

TEXT 5

अणुर्द्वौ परमाणू स्यात्त्रसरेणुस्त्रयः स्मृतः ।
जालार्करश्म्यवगतः खमेवानुपतन्नगात् ॥ ५ ॥

aṇur dvau paramāṇū syāt
trasareṇus trayaḥ smṛtaḥ
jālārka-raśmy-avagataḥ
kham evānupatann agāt

aṇuḥ—double atom; *dvau*—two; *parama-aṇu*—atoms; *syāt*—become; *trasareṇuḥ*—hexatom; *trayaḥ*—three; *smṛtaḥ*—considered; *jāla-arka*—of sunshine through the holes of a window screen; *raśmi*—by the rays; *avagataḥ*—can be known; *kham eva*—towards the sky; *anupatan agāt*—going up.

TRANSLATION

The division of gross time is calculated as follows: two atoms make one double atom, and three double atoms make one hexatom. This hexatom is visible in the sunshine which enters through the holes of a window screen. One can clearly see that the hexatom goes up towards the sky.

PURPORT

The atom is described as an invisible particle, but when six such atoms combine together, they are called a *trasareṇu*, and this is visible in the sunshine pouring through the holes of a window screen.

TEXT 6

त्रसरेणुत्रिकं भुङ्क्ते यः कालः स त्रुटिः स्मृतः।
शतभागस्तु वेधः स्यात्तैस्त्रिभिस्तु लवः स्मृतः ॥ ६ ॥

trasareṇu-trikaṁ bhuṅkte
yaḥ kālaḥ sa truṭiḥ smṛtaḥ
śata-bhāgas tu vedhaḥ syāt
tais tribhis tu lavaḥ smṛtaḥ

trasareṇu-trikam—combination of three hexatoms; *bhuṅkte*—as they take time to integrate; *yaḥ*—that which; *kālaḥ*—duration of time; *saḥ*—that; *truṭiḥ*—by the name *truṭi; smṛtaḥ*—is called; *śata-bhāgaḥ*—one hundred *truṭis; tu*—but; *vedhaḥ*—called a *vedha; syāt*—it so happens; *taiḥ*—by them; *tribhiḥ*—three times; *tu*—but; *lavaḥ*—*lava; smṛtaḥ*—so called.

TRANSLATION

The time duration needed for the integration of three trasareṇus is called a truṭi, and one hundred truṭis make one vedha. Three vedhas make one lava.

PURPORT

It is calculated that if a second is divided into 1687.5 parts, each part is the duration of a *truṭi*, which is the time occupied in the integration of eighteen atomic particles. Such a combination of atoms into different bodies creates the calculation of material time. The sun is the central point for calculating all different durations.

TEXT 7

निमेषस्त्रिलवो ज्ञेय आम्नातस्ते त्रयः क्षणः ।
क्षणान् पञ्च विदुः काष्ठां लघु ता दश पञ्च च ॥ ७ ॥

nimeṣas tri-lavo jñeya
āmnātas te trayaḥ kṣaṇaḥ
kṣaṇān pañca viduḥ kāṣṭhāṁ
laghu tā daśa pañca ca

nimeṣaḥ—the duration of time called a *nimeṣa; tri-lavaḥ*—the duration of three *lavas; jñeyaḥ*—is to be known; *āmnātaḥ*—it is so called; *te*—they; *trayaḥ*—three; *kṣaṇaḥ*—the duration of time called a *kṣaṇa; kṣaṇān*—such *kṣaṇas; pañca*—five; *viduḥ*—one should understand; *kāṣṭhām*—the duration of time called a *kāṣṭhā; laghu*—the duration of time called a *laghu; tāḥ*—those; *daśa pañca*—fifteen; *ca*—also.

TRANSLATION

The duration of time of three lavas is equal to one nimeṣa, the combination of three nimeṣas makes one kṣaṇa, five kṣaṇas combined together make one kāṣṭhā, and fifteen kāṣṭhās make one laghu.

PURPORT

By calculation it is found that one *laghu* is equal to two minutes. The atomic calculation of time in terms of Vedic wisdom may be converted into present time with this understanding.

TEXT 8

लघूनि वै समाम्नाता दश पञ्च च नाडिका ।
ते द्वे मुहूर्तः प्रहरः षड्यामः सप्त वा नृणाम् ॥ ८ ॥

laghūni vai samāmnātā
daśa pañca ca nāḍikā
te dve muhūrtaḥ praharaḥ
ṣaḍ yāmaḥ sapta vā nṛṇām

laghūni—such *laghus* (each of two minutes); *vai*—exactly; *samāmnātā*—is called; *daśa pañca*—fifteen; *ca*—also; *nāḍikā*—a *nāḍikā; te*—of them; *dve*—two; *muhūrtaḥ*—a moment; *praharaḥ*—three hours; *ṣaṭ*—six; *yāmaḥ*—one fourth of a day or night; *sapta*—seven; *vā*—or; *nṛṇām*—of human calculation.

TRANSLATION

Fifteen laghus make one nāḍikā, which is also called a daṇḍa. Two daṇḍas make one muhūrta, and six or seven daṇḍas make one fourth of a day or night, according to human calculation.

TEXT 9

द्वादशार्धपलोन्मानं चतुर्भिश्चतुरङ्गुलैः ।
स्वर्णमाषैः कृतच्छिद्रं यावत्प्रस्थजलप्लुतम् ॥ ९ ॥

dvādaśārdha-palonmānaṁ
caturbhiś catur-aṅgulaiḥ
svarṇa-māṣaiḥ kṛta-cchidraṁ
yāvat prastha-jala-plutam

dvādaśa-ardha—six; *pala*—of the scale of weight; *unmānam*—measuring pot; *caturbhiḥ*—by weight of four; *catuḥ-aṅgulaiḥ*—four fingers by measure; *svarṇa*—of gold; *māṣaiḥ*—of the weight; *kṛta-chidram*—making a hole; *yāvat*—as long as; *prastha*—measuring one *prastha; jala-plutam*—filled by water.

TRANSLATION

The measuring pot for one nāḍikā, or daṇḍa, can be prepared with a six-pala-weight [fourteen ounce] pot of copper, in which a hole is bored with a gold probe weighing four māṣa and measuring four fingers long. When the pot is placed on water, the time before the water overflows in the pot is called one daṇḍa.

PURPORT

It is advised herein that the bore in the copper measuring pot must be made with a probe weighing not more than four *māṣa* and measuring not longer than four fingers. This regulates the diameter of the hole. The pot is submerged in water, and the overflooding time is called a *daṇḍa.* This is another way of measuring the duration of a *daṇḍa,* just as time is measured by sand in a glass. It appears that in the days of Vedic civilization there was no dearth of knowledge in physics, chemistry or higher mathematics. Measurements were calculated in different ways, as simply as could be done.

TEXT 10

यामाश्चत्वारश्चत्वारो मर्त्यानामहनी उभे ।
पक्षः पञ्चदशाहानि शुक्लः कृष्णश्च मानद ॥१०॥

yāmāś catvāraś catvāro
martyānām ahanī ubhe
pakṣaḥ pañca-daśāhāni
śuklaḥ kṛṣṇaś ca mānada

yāmāḥ—three hours; *catvāraḥ*—four; *catvāraḥ*—and four; *martyānām*—of the human beings; *ahanī*—duration of day; *ubhe*—both day and night; *pakṣaḥ*—fortnight; *pañca-daśa*—fifteen; *ahāni*—days; *śuklaḥ*—white; *kṛṣṇaḥ*—black; *ca*—also; *mānada*—measured.

TRANSLATION

It is calculated that there are four praharas, which are also called yāmas, in the day and four in the night of the human being. Similarly, fifteen days and nights are a fortnight, and there are two fortnights, white and black, in a month.

TEXT 11

तयोः समुच्चयो मासः पितॄणां तदहर्निशम् ।
द्वौ तावृतुः षडयनं दक्षिणं चोत्तरं दिवि ॥११॥

tayoḥ samuccayo māsaḥ
pitṝṇāṁ tad ahar-niśam
dvau tāv ṛtuḥ ṣaḍ ayanaṁ
dakṣiṇaṁ cottaraṁ divi

tayoḥ—of them; *samuccayaḥ*—aggregate; *māsaḥ*—month; *pitṝṇām*—of the Pitā planets; *tat*—that (month); *ahaḥ-niśam*—day and night; *dvau*—two; *tau*—months; *ṛtuḥ*—a season; *ṣaṭ*—six; *ayanam*—the movement of the sun in six months; *dakṣiṇam*—southern; *ca*—also; *uttaram*—northern; *divi*—in the heavens.

TRANSLATION

The aggregate of two fortnights is one month, and that period is one complete day and night for the Pitā planets. Two of such months comprise one season, and six months comprise one complete movement of the sun from south to north.

TEXT 12

अयने चाहनी प्राहुर्वत्सरो द्वादश स्मृतः ।
संवत्सरशतं नृणां परमायुर्निरूपितम् ॥१२॥

ayane cāhanī prāhur
vatsaro dvādaśa smṛtaḥ
saṁvatsara-śataṁ nṛṇāṁ
paramāyur nirūpitam

ayane—in the solar movement (of six months); *ca*—and; *ahanī*—a day of the demigods; *prāhuḥ*—it is said; *vatsaraḥ*—one calendar year; *dvādaśa*—twelve months; *smṛtaḥ*—is so called; *saṁvatsara-śatam*—one hundred years; *nṛṇām*—of human beings; *parama-āyuḥ*—duration of life; *nirūpitam*—is estimated.

TRANSLATION

Two solar movements make one day and night of the demigods, and that combination of day and night is one complete calendar year for the human being. The human being has a duration of life of one hundred years.

TEXT 13

ग्रहर्क्षताराचक्रस्थः परमाण्वादिना जगत् ।
संवत्सरावसानेन पर्येत्यनिमिषो विभुः ॥१३॥

graharkṣa-tārā-cakra-sthaḥ
paramāṇv-ādinā jagat
saṁvatsarāvasānena
paryety animiṣo vibhuḥ

graha—influential planets like the moon; *ṛkṣa*—luminaries like Aśvinī; *tārā*—stars; *cakra-sthaḥ*—in the orbit; *parama-aṇu-ādinā*—along with the atoms; *jagat*—the entire universe; *saṁvatsara-avasānena*—by the end of one year; *paryeti*—completes its orbit; *animiṣaḥ*—the eternal time; *vibhuḥ*—the Almighty.

TRANSLATION

Influential stars, planets, luminaries and atoms all over the universe are rotating in their respective orbits under the direction of the Supreme, represented by eternal kāla.

PURPORT

In the *Brahma-saṁhitā* it is stated that the sun is the eye of the Supreme and it rotates in its particular orbit of time. Similarly, beginning from the sun down to the atom, all bodies are under the influence of the *kāla-cakra*, or the orbit of eternal time, and each of them has a scheduled orbital time of one *saṁvatsara.*

TEXT 14

संवत्सरः परिवत्सर इडावत्सर एव च ।
अनुवत्सरो वत्सरश्च विदुरैवं प्रभाष्यते ॥१४॥

saṁvatsaraḥ parivatsara
iḍā-vatsara eva ca
anuvatsaro vatsaraś ca
viduraivaṁ prabhāṣyate

saṁvatsaraḥ—orbit of the sun; *parivatsaraḥ*—circumambulation of Bṛhaspati; *iḍā-vatsaraḥ*—orbit of the stars; *eva*—as they are; *ca*—also; *anuvatsaraḥ*—orbit of the moon; *vatsaraḥ*—one calendar year; *ca*—also; *vidura*—O Vidura; *evam*—thus; *prabhāṣyate*—they are so told.

TRANSLATION

There are five different names for the orbits of the sun, moon, stars and luminaries in the firmament, and they each have their own saṁvatsara.

PURPORT

The subject matters of physics, chemistry, mathematics, astronomy, time and space dealt with in the above verses of *Śrīmad-Bhāgavatam* are certainly very interesting to students of the particular subject, but as far as we are concerned, we cannot explain them very thoroughly in terms of technical knowledge. The subject is summarized by the statement that above all the different branches of knowledge is the supreme control of *kāla*, the plenary representation of the Supreme Personality of Godhead. Nothing exists without Him, and therefore everything, however wonderful it may appear to our meager knowledge, is but the work of the magical wand of the Supreme Lord. As far as time is concerned, we beg to subjoin herewith a table of timings in terms of the modern clock.

One *truṭi* -	8/13,500	second	One *laghu*	- 2	minutes
One *vedha* -	8/135	second	One *daṇḍa*	- 30	minutes
One *lava* -	8/45	second	One *prahara*	- 3	hours
One *nimeṣa* -	8/15	second	One day	- 12	hours
One *kṣaṇa* -	8/5	second	One night	- 12	hours
One *kāṣṭhā* -	8	seconds	One *pakṣa*	- 15	days

Two *pakṣas* comprise one month, and twelve months comprise one calendar year, or one full orbit of the sun. A human being is expected to live up to one hundred years. That is the way of the controlling measure of eternal time.

The *Brahma-saṁhitā* (5.52) affirms this control in this way:

yac-cakṣur eṣa savitā sakala-grahāṇāṁ
rājā samasta-sura-mūrtir aśeṣa-tejāḥ
yasyājñayā bhramati saṁbhṛta-kāla-cakro
govindam ādi-puruṣaṁ tam ahaṁ bhajāmi

"I worship Govinda, the primeval Lord, the Supreme Personality of Godhead, under whose control even the sun, which is considered to be the eye of the Lord, rotates within the fixed orbit of eternal time. The sun is the king of all planetary systems and has unlimited potency in heat and light."

TEXT 15

यः सृज्यशक्तिमुरुधोच्छ्वसयन् स्वशक्त्या
पुंसोऽभ्रमाय दिवि धावति भूतभेदः ।

कालाख्यया गुणमयं क्रतुभिर्वितन्वं-
स्तस्मै बलिं हरत वत्सरपञ्चकाय ॥१५॥

yaḥ sṛjya-śaktim urudhocchvasayan sva-śaktyā
puṁso 'bhramāya divi dhāvati bhūta-bhedaḥ
kālākhyayā guṇamayaṁ kratubhir vitanvaṁs
tasmai baliṁ harata vatsara-pañcakāya

yaḥ—one who; *sṛjya*—of creation; *śaktim*—the seeds; *urudhā*—in various ways; *ucchvasayan*—invigorating; *sva-śaktyā*—by his own energy; *puṁsaḥ*—of the living entity; *abhramāya*—to dissipate darkness; *divi*—during the daytime; *dhāvati*—moves; *bhūta-bhedaḥ*—distinct from all other material form; *kāla-ākhyayā*—by the name eternal time; *guṇa-mayam*—the material results; *kratubhiḥ*—by offerings; *vitanvan*—enlarging; *tasmai*—unto him; *balim*—ingredients of offerings; *harata*—one should offer; *vatsara-pañcakāya*—offerings every five years.

TRANSLATION

O Vidura, the sun enlivens all living entities with his unlimited heat and light. He diminishes the duration of life of all living entities in order to release them from their illusion of material attachment, and he enlarges the path of elevation to the heavenly kingdom. He thus moves in the firmament with great velocity, and therefore everyone should offer him respects once every five years with all ingredients of worship.

TEXT 16

विदुर उवाच

पितृदेवमनुष्याणामायुः परमिदं स्मृतम् ।
परेषां गतिमाचक्ष्व ये स्युःकल्पाद् बहिर्विदः ॥१६॥

vidura uvāca
pitṛ-deva-manuṣyāṇām
āyuḥ param idaṁ smṛtam

pareṣāṁ gatim ācakṣva
ye syuḥ kalpād bahir vidaḥ

viduraḥ uvāca—Vidura said; *pitṛ*—the Pitā planets; *deva*—the heavenly planets; *manuṣyāṇām*—and that of the human beings; *āyuḥ*—duration of life; *param*—final; *idam*—in their own measurement; *smṛtam*—calculated; *pareṣām*—of the superior living entities; *gatim*—duration of life; *ācakṣva*—kindly calculate; *ye*—all those who; *syuḥ*—are; *kalpāt*—from the millennium; *bahiḥ*—outside; *vidaḥ*—greatly learned.

TRANSLATION

Vidura said: I now understand the life durations of the residents of the Pitā planets and heavenly planets as well as that of the human beings. Now kindly inform me of the durations of life of those greatly learned living entities who are beyond the range of a kalpa.

PURPORT

The partial dissolution of the universe that takes place at the end of Brahmā's day does not affect all the planetary systems. The planets of highly learned living entities like the sages Sanaka and Bhṛgu are not affected by the dissolutions of the millenniums. All the planets are of different types, and each is controlled by a different *kāla-cakra*, or schedule of eternal time. The time of the earth planet is not applicable to other, more elevated planets. Therefore, Vidura herein inquires about the duration of life on other planets.

TEXT 17

भगवान् वेद कालस्य गतिं भगवतो ननु ।
विश्वं विचक्षते धीरा योगराद्धेन चक्षुषा ॥१७॥

bhagavān veda kālasya
gatiṁ bhagavato nanu
viśvaṁ vicakṣate dhīrā
yoga-rāddhena cakṣuṣā

bhagavān—O spiritually powerful one; *veda*—you know; *kālasya*—of the eternal time; *gatim*—movements; *bhagavataḥ*—of the Supreme Personality of Godhead; *nanu*—as a matter of course; *viśvam*—the whole universe; *vicakṣate*—see; *dhīrāḥ*—those who are self-realized; *yoga-rāddhena*—by dint of mystic vision; *cakṣuṣā*—by the eyes.

TRANSLATION

O spiritually powerful one, you can understand the movements of eternal time, which is the controlling form of the Supreme Personality of Godhead. Because you are a self-realized person, you can see everything by the power of mystic vision.

PURPORT

Those who have reached the highest perfectional stage of mystic power and can see everything in the past, present and future are called *tri-kāla-jñas.* Similarly, the devotees of the Lord can see everything clearly that is in the revealed scriptures. The devotees of Lord Śrī Kṛṣṇa can very easily understand the science of Kṛṣṇa, as well as the situation of the material and spiritual creations, without difficulty. Devotees do not have to endeavor for any *yoga-siddhi,* or perfection in mystic powers. They are competent to understand everything by the grace of the Lord, who is sitting in everyone's heart.

TEXT 18

मैत्रेय उवाच
कृतं त्रेता द्वापरं च कलिश्चेति चतुर्युगम् ।
दिव्यैर्द्वादशभिर्वर्षैः सावधानं निरूपितम् ॥१८॥

maitreya uvāca
kṛtaṁ tretā dvāparaṁ ca
kaliś ceti catur-yugam
divyair dvādaśabhir varṣaiḥ
sāvadhānaṁ nirūpitam

maitreyaḥ uvāca—Maitreya said; *kṛtam*—the age of Satya; *tretā*—the age of Tretā; *dvāparam*—the age of Dvāpara; *ca*—also; *kaliḥ*—the age of Kali; *ca*—and; *iti*—thus; *catuḥ-yugam*—four millenniums; *divyaiḥ*—of the demigods; *dvādaśabhiḥ*—twelve; *varṣaiḥ*—thousands of years; *sa-avadhānam*—approximately; *nirūpitam*—ascertained.

TRANSLATION

Maitreya said: O Vidura, the four millenniums are called the Satya, Tretā, Dvāpara and Kali yugas. The aggregate number of years of all of these combined is equal to twelve thousand years of the demigods.

PURPORT

The years of the demigods are equal to 360 years of humankind. As will be clarified in the subsequent verses, 12,000 of the demigods' years, including the transitional periods which are called *yuga-sandhyās*, comprise the total of the aforementioned four millenniums. Thus the aggregate of the above-mentioned four millenniums is 4,320,000 years.

TEXT 19

चत्वारि त्रीणि द्वे चैकं कृतादिषु यथाक्रमम् ।
संख्यातानि सहस्राणि द्विगुणानि शतानि च ॥१९॥

catvāri trīṇi dve caikaṁ
kṛtādiṣu yathā-kramam
saṅkhyātāni sahasrāṇi
dvi-guṇāni śatāni ca

catvāri—four; *trīṇi*—three; *dve*—two; *ca*—also; *ekam*—one; *kṛta-ādiṣu*—in the Satya-yuga; *yathā-kramam*—and subsequently others; *saṅkhyātāni*—numbering; *sahasrāṇi*—thousands; *dvi-guṇāni*—twice; *śatāni*—hundreds; *ca*—also.

TRANSLATION

The duration of the Satya millennium equals 4,800 years of the demigods; the duration of the Tretā millennium equals 3,600 years of the demigods; the duration of the Dvāpara millennium

equals 2,400 years; and that of the Kali millennium is 1,200 years of the demigods.

PURPORT

As aforementioned, one year of the demigods is equal to 360 years of the human beings. The duration of the Satya-yuga is therefore 4,800 X 360, or 1,728,000 years. The duration of the Tretā-yuga is 3,600 X 360, or 1,296,000 years. The duration of the Dvāpara-yuga is 2,400 X 360, or 864,000 years. And the last, the Kali-yuga, is 1,200 X 360, or 432,000 years.

TEXT 20

संध्यासंध्यांशयोरन्तर्यः कालः शतसंख्ययोः ।
तमेवाहुर्युगं तज्ज्ञा यत्र धर्मो विधीयते ॥२०॥

sandhyā-sandhyāṁśayor antar
yaḥ kālaḥ śata-saṅkhyayoḥ
tam evāhur yugaṁ taj-jñā
yatra dharmo vidhīyate

sandhyā—transitional period before; *sandhyā-aṁśayoḥ*—and transitional period after; *antaḥ*—within; *yaḥ*—that which; *kālaḥ*—duration of time; *śata-saṅkhyayoḥ*—hundreds of years; *tam eva*—that period; *āhuḥ*—they call; *yugam*—millennium; *tat-jñāḥ*—the expert astronomers; *yatra*—wherein; *dharmaḥ*—religion; *vidhīyate*—is performed.

TRANSLATION

The transitional periods before and after every millennium, which are a few hundred years as aforementioned, are known as yuga-sandhyās, or the conjunctions of two millenniums, according to the expert astronomers. In those periods all kinds of religious activities are performed.

TEXT 21

धर्मश्चतुष्पान्मनुजान् कृते समनुवर्तते ।
स एवान्येष्वधर्मेण व्येति पादेन वर्धता ॥२१॥

dharmaś catuṣ-pān manujān
kṛte samanuvartate
sa evānyeṣv adharmeṇa
vyeti pādena vardhatā

dharmaḥ—religion; *catuḥ-pāt*—complete four dimensions; *manujān*—mankind; *kṛte*—in the Satya-yuga; *samanuvartate*—properly maintained; *saḥ*—that; *eva*—certainly; *anyeṣu*—in other; *adharmeṇa*—by the influence of irreligion; *vyeti*—declined; *pādena*—by one part; *vardhatā*—gradually increasing proportionately.

TRANSLATION

O Vidura, in the Satya millennium mankind properly and completely maintained the principles of religion, but in other millenniums religion gradually decreased by one part as irreligion was proportionately admitted.

PURPORT

In the Satya millennium, complete execution of religious principles prevailed. Gradually, the principles of religion decreased by one part in each of the subsequent millenniums. In other words, at present there is one part religion and three parts irreligion. Therefore people in this age are not very happy.

TEXT 22

त्रिलोक्या युगसाहस्रं बहिराब्रह्मणो दिनम् ।
तावत्येव निशा तात यन्निमीलति विश्वसृक् ॥२२॥

tri-lokyā yuga-sāhasraṁ
bahir ābrahmaṇo dinam
tāvaty eva niśā tāta
yan nimīlati viśva-sṛk

tri-lokyāḥ—of the three worlds; *yuga*—the four *yugas; sāhasram*—one thousand; *bahiḥ*—outside of; *ābrahmaṇaḥ*—up to Brahmaloka; *dinam*—is a day; *tāvatī*—a similar (period); *eva*—certainly; *niśā*—is night; *tāta*—O dear one; *yat*—because; *nimīlati*—goes to sleep; *viśva-sṛk*—Brahmā.

TRANSLATION

Outside of the three planetary systems [Svarga, Martya and Pātāla], the four yugas multiplied by one thousand comprise one day on the planet of Brahmā. A similar period comprises a night of Brahmā, in which the creator of the universe goes to sleep.

PURPORT

When Brahmā goes to sleep in his nighttime, the three planetary systems below Brahmaloka are all submerged in the water of devastation. In his sleeping condition, Brahmā dreams about the Garbhodakaśāyī Viṣṇu and takes instruction from the Lord for the rehabilitation of the devastated area of space.

TEXT 23

निशावसान आरब्धो लोककल्पोऽनुवर्तते ।
यावद्दिनं भगवतो मनून् भुञ्जंश्चतुर्दश ॥२३॥

niśāvasāna ārabdho
loka-kalpo 'nuvartate
yāvad dinaṁ bhagavato
manūn bhuñjaṁś catur-daśa

niśā—night; *avasāne*—termination; *ārabdhaḥ*—beginning from; *loka-kalpaḥ*—further creation of the three worlds; *anuvartate*—follows; *yāvat*—until; *dinam*—the daytime; *bhagavataḥ*—of the lord (Brahmā); *manūn*—the Manus; *bhuñjan*—existing through; *catuḥ-daśa*—fourteen.

TRANSLATION

After the end of Brahmā's night, the creation of the three worlds begins again in the daytime of Brahmā, and they continue to exist through the life durations of fourteen consecutive Manus, or fathers of mankind.

PURPORT

At the end of the life of each Manu there are shorter dissolutions also.

TEXT 24

स्वं स्वं कालं मनुर्भुङ्क्ते साधिकां ह्येकसप्ततिम् ॥२४॥

svaṁ svaṁ kālaṁ manur bhuṅkte
sādhikāṁ hy eka-saptatim

svam—own; *svam*—accordingly; *kālam*—duration of life; *manuḥ*—Manu; *bhuṅkte*—enjoys; *sa-adhikām*—a little more than; *hi*—certainly; *eka-saptatim*—seventy-one.

TRANSLATION

Each and every Manu enjoys a life of a little more than seventy-one sets of four millenniums.

PURPORT

The duration of life of a Manu comprises seventy-one sets of four millenniums, as described in the *Viṣṇu Purāṇa.* The duration of life of one Manu is about 852,000 years in the calculation of the demigods, or, in the calculation of human beings, 306,720,000 years.

TEXT 25

मन्वन्तरेषु मनवस्तद्वंश्या ऋषयः सुराः ।
भवन्ति चैव युगपत्सुरेशाश्चानु ये च तान् ॥२५॥

manvantareṣu manavas
tad-vaṁśyā ṛṣayaḥ surāḥ
bhavanti caiva yugapat
sureśāś cānu ye ca tān

manu-antareṣu—after the dissolution of each and every Manu; *manavaḥ*—other Manus; *tat-vaṁśyāḥ*—and their descendants; *ṛṣayaḥ*—the seven famous sages; *surāḥ*—devotees of the Lord;

bhavanti—flourish; *ca eva*—also all of them; *yugapat*—simultaneously; *sura-īśāḥ*—demigods like Indra; *ca*—and; *anu*—followers; *ye*—all; *ca*—also; *tān*—them.

TRANSLATION

After the dissolution of each and every Manu, the next Manu comes in order, along with his descendants, who rule over the different planets; but the seven famous sages, and demigods like Indra and their followers, such as the Gandharvas, all appear simultaneously with Manu.

PURPORT

There are fourteen Manus in one day of Brahmā, and each of them has different descendants.

TEXT 26

एष दैनन्दिनः सर्गो ब्राह्मस्त्रैलोक्यवर्तनः ।
तिर्यङ्नृपितृदेवानां सम्भवो यत्र कर्मभिः ॥२६॥

eṣa dainan-dinaḥ sargo
brāhmas trailokya-vartanaḥ
tiryaṅ-nṛ-pitṛ-devānāṁ
sambhavo yatra karmabhiḥ

eṣaḥ—all these creations; *dainam-dinaḥ*—daily; *sargaḥ*—creation; *brāhmaḥ*—in terms of the days of Brahmā; *trailokya-vartanaḥ*—revolution of the three worlds; *tiryak*—animals lower than the human beings; *nṛ*—human beings; *pitṛ*—of the Pitā planets; *devānām*—of the demigods; *sambhavaḥ*—appearance; *yatra*—wherein; *karmabhiḥ*—in the cycle of fruitive activities.

TRANSLATION

In the creation, during Brahmā's day, the three planetary systems—Svarga, Martya and Pātāla—revolve, and the inhabitants, including the lower animals, human beings, demigods and Pitās, appear and disappear in terms of their fruitive activities.

TEXT 27

मन्वन्तरेषु भगवान् बिभ्रत्सत्त्वं स्वमूर्तिभिः ।
मन्वादिभिरिदं विश्वमवत्युदितपौरुषः ॥२७॥

manvantareṣu bhagavān
bibhrat sattvaṁ sva-mūrtibhiḥ
manv-ādibhir idaṁ viśvam
avaty udita-pauruṣaḥ

manu-antareṣu—in each change of Manu; *bhagavān*—the Personality of Godhead; *bibhrat*—manifesting; *sattvam*—His internal potency; *sva-mūrtibhiḥ*—by His different incarnations; *manu-ādibhiḥ*—as Manus; *idam*—this; *viśvam*—the universe; *avati*—maintains; *udita*—discovering; *pauruṣaḥ*—divine potencies.

TRANSLATION

In each and every change of Manu, the Supreme Personality of Godhead appears by manifesting His internal potency in different incarnations, as Manu and others. Thus He maintains the universe by discovered power.

TEXT 28

तमोमात्रामुपादाय प्रतिसंरुद्धविक्रमः ।
कालेनानुगताशेष आस्ते तूष्णीं दिनात्यये ॥२८॥

tamo-mātrām upādāya
pratisaṁruddha-vikramaḥ
kālenānugatāśeṣa
āste tūṣṇīṁ dinātyaye

tamaḥ—the mode of ignorance, or the darkness of night; *mātrām*—an insignificant portion only; *upādāya*—accepting; *pratisaṁruddha-vikramaḥ*—suspending all power of manifestation; *kālena*—by means of the eternal *kāla; anugata*—merged in; *aśeṣaḥ*—innumerable living entities; *āste*—remains; *tūṣṇīm*—silent; *dina-atyaye*—at the end of the day.

TRANSLATION

At the end of the day, under the insignificant portion of the mode of darkness, the powerful manifestation of the universe merges in the darkness of night. By the influence of eternal time, the innumerable living entities remain merged in that dissolution, and everything is silent.

PURPORT

This verse is an explanation of the night of Brahmā, which is the effect of the influence of time in touch with an insignificant portion of the modes of material nature in darkness. The dissolution of the three worlds is effected by the incarnation of darkness, Rudra, represented by the fire of eternal time which blazes over the three worlds. These three worlds are known as Bhūḥ, Bhuvaḥ and Svaḥ (Pātāla, Martya and Svarga). The innumerable living entities merge into that dissolution, which appears to be the dropping of the curtain of the scene of the Supreme Lord's energy, and so everything becomes silent.

TEXT 29

तमेवान्वपिधीयन्ते लोका भूरादयस्त्रयः ।
निशायामनुवृत्तायां निर्मुक्तशशिभास्करम् ॥२९॥

tam evānv api dhīyante
lokā bhūr-ādayas trayaḥ
niśāyām anuvṛttāyāṁ
nirmukta-śaśi-bhāskaram

tam—that; *eva*—certainly; *anu*—after; *api dhīyante*—are out of sight; *lokāḥ*—the planets; *bhūḥ-ādayaḥ*—the three worlds, Bhūḥ, Bhuvaḥ and Svaḥ; *trayaḥ*—three; *niśāyām*—in the night; *anuvṛt-tāyām*—ordinary; *nirmukta*—without glare; *śaśi*—the moon; *bhāskaram*—the sun.

TRANSLATION

When the night of Brahmā ensues, all the three worlds are out of sight, and the sun and the moon are without glare, just as in the due course of an ordinary night.

PURPORT

It is understood that the glare of the sun and moon disappear from the sphere of the three worlds, but the sun and the moon themselves do not vanish. They appear in the remaining portion of the universe, which is beyond the sphere of the three worlds. The portion in dissolution remains without sunrays or moonglow. It all remains dark and full of water, and there are indefatigable winds, as explained in the following verses.

TEXT 30

त्रिलोक्यां दह्यमानायां शक्त्या सङ्कर्षणाग्निना ।
यान्त्यूष्मणा महर्लोकाज्जनं भृग्वादयोऽर्दिताः ॥३०॥

tri-lokyāṁ dahyamānāyāṁ
śaktyā saṅkarṣaṇāgninā
yānty ūṣmaṇā maharlokāj
janaṁ bhṛgv-ādayo 'rditāḥ

tri-lokyām—when the spheres of the three worlds; *dahyamānāyām*—being set ablaze; *śaktyā*—by the potency; *saṅkarṣaṇa*—from the mouth of Saṅkarṣaṇa; *agninā*—by the fire; *yānti*—they go; *ūṣmaṇā*—heated by the warmth; *mahaḥ-lokāt*—from Maharloka; *janam*—to Janaloka; *bhṛgu*—the sage Bhṛgu; *ādayaḥ*—and others; *arditāḥ*—being so distressed.

TRANSLATION

The devastation takes place due to the fire emanating from the mouth of Saṅkarṣaṇa, and thus great sages like Bhṛgu and other inhabitants of Maharloka transport themselves to Janaloka, being distressed by the warmth of the blazing fire which rages through the three worlds below.

TEXT 31

तावत्त्रिभुवनं सद्यः कल्पान्तैधितसिन्धवः ।
प्लावयन्त्युत्कटाटोपचण्डवातेरितोर्मयः ॥३१॥

tāvat tri-bhuvanaṁ sadyaḥ
kalpāntaidhita-sindhavaḥ
plāvayanty utkaṭāṭopa-
caṇḍa-vāteritormayaḥ

tāvat—then; *tri-bhuvanam*—all the three worlds; *sadyaḥ*—immediately after; *kalpa-anta*—in the beginning of the devastation; *edhita*—inflated; *sindhavaḥ*—all the oceans; *plāvayanti*—inundate; *utkaṭa*—violent; *āṭopa*—agitation; *caṇḍa*—hurricane; *vāta*—by winds; *īrita*—blown; *ūrmayaḥ*—waves.

TRANSLATION

At the beginning of the devastation all the seas overflow, and hurricane winds blow very violently. Thus the waves of the seas become ferocious, and in no time at all the three worlds are full of water.

PURPORT

It is said that the blazing fire from the mouth of Saṅkarṣaṇa rages for one hundred years of the demigods, or 36,000 human years. Then for another 36,000 years there are torrents of rain, accompanied by violent winds and waves, and the seas and oceans overflow. These reactions of 72,000 years are the beginning of the partial devastation of the three worlds. People forget all these devastations of the worlds and think themselves happy in the material progress of civilization. This is called *māyā*, or "that which is not."

TEXT 32

अन्तः स तस्मिन् सलिल आस्तेऽनन्तासनो हरिः ।
योगनिद्रानिमीलाक्षः स्तूयमानो जनालयैः ॥३२॥

antaḥ sa tasmin salila
āste 'nantāsano hariḥ
yoga-nidrā-nimīlākṣaḥ
stūyamāno janālayaiḥ

antaḥ—within; *saḥ*—that; *tasmin*—in that; *salile*—water; *āste*—there is; *ananta*—Ananta; *āsanaḥ*—on the seat of; *hariḥ*—the Lord;

yoga—mystic; *nidrā*—sleep; *nimīla-akṣaḥ*—eyes closed; *stūya-mānaḥ*—being glorified; *jana-ālayaiḥ*—by the inhabitants of the Janaloka planets.

TRANSLATION

The Supreme Lord, the Personality of Godhead, lies down in the water on the seat of Ananta, with His eyes closed, and the inhabitants of the Janaloka planets offer their glorious prayers unto the Lord with folded hands.

PURPORT

We should not understand the sleeping condition of the Lord to be the same as our sleep. Here the word *yoga-nidrā* is specifically mentioned, which indicates that the Lord's sleeping condition is also a manifestation of His internal potency. Whenever the word *yoga* is used it should be understood to refer to that which is transcendental. In the transcendental stage all activities are always present, and they are glorified by prayers of great sages like Bhṛgu.

TEXT 33

एवंविधैरहोरात्रैः कालगत्योपलक्षितैः ।
अपक्षितमिवास्यापि परमायुर्वयःशतम् ॥३३॥

evaṁ-vidhair aho-rātraiḥ
kāla-gatyopalakṣitaiḥ
apakṣitam ivāsyāpi
paramāyur vayaḥ-śatam

evam—thus; *vidhaiḥ*—by the process of; *ahaḥ*—days; *rātraiḥ*—by nights; *kāla-gatyā*—advancement of time; *upalakṣitaiḥ*—by such symptoms; *apakṣitam*—declined; *iva*—just like; *asya*—his; *api*—although; *parama-āyuḥ*—duration of life; *vayaḥ*—years; *śatam*—one hundred.

TRANSLATION

Thus the process of the exhaustion of the duration of life exists for every one of the living beings, including Lord Brahmā. One's

life endures for only one hundred years, in terms of the times in the different planets.

PURPORT

Every living being lives for one hundred years in terms of the times in different planets for different entities. These one hundred years of life are not equal in every case. The longest duration of one hundred years belongs to Brahmā, but although the life of Brahmā is very long, it expires in the course of time. Brahmā is also afraid of his death, and thus he performs devotional service to the Lord, just to release himself from the clutches of illusory energy. Animals, of course, have no sense of responsibility, but even humans, who have developed a sense of responsibility, while away their valuable time without engaging in devotional service to the Lord; they live merrily, unafraid of impending death. This is the madness of human society. The madman has no responsibility in life. Similarly, a human being who does not develop a sense of responsibility before he dies is no better than the madman who tries to enjoy material life very happily without concern for the future. It is necessary that every human being be responsible in preparing himself for the next life, even if he has a duration of life like that of Brahmā, the greatest of all living creatures within the universe.

TEXT 34

यदर्धमायुषस्तस्य परार्धमभिधीयते ।
पूर्वः परार्धोऽपक्रान्तो ह्यपरोऽद्य प्रवर्तते ॥३४॥

yad ardham āyuṣas tasya
parārdham abhidhīyate
pūrvaḥ parārdho 'pakrānto
hy aparo 'dya pravartate

yat—that which; *ardham*—half; *āyuṣaḥ*—of the duration of life; *tasya*—his; *parārdham*—a *parārdha; abhidhīyate*—is called; *pūrvaḥ*—the former; *para-ardhaḥ*—half of the duration of life; *apakrāntaḥ*—having passed; *hi*—certainly; *aparaḥ*—the latter; *adya*—in this millennium; *pravartate*—shall begin.

TRANSLATION

The one hundred years of Brahmā's life are divided into two parts, the first half and the second half. The first half of the duration of Brahmā's life is already over, and the second half is now current.

PURPORT

The duration of one hundred years in the life of Brahmā has already been discussed in many places in this work, and it is described in *Bhagavad-gītā* (8.17) also. Fifty years of the life of Brahmā are already over, and fifty years are yet to be completed; then, for Brahmā also, death is inevitable.

TEXT 35

पूर्वस्यादौ परार्धस्य ब्राह्मो नाम महानभूत् ।
कल्पो यत्राभवद्ब्रह्मा शब्दब्रह्मेति यं विदुः ॥३५॥

pūrvasyādau parārdhasya
brāhmo nāma mahān abhūt
kalpo yatrābhavad brahmā
śabda-brahmeti yaṁ viduḥ

pūrvasya—of the first half; *ādau*—in the beginning; *para-ardhasya*—of the superior half; *brāhmaḥ*—Brāhma-kalpa; *nāma*—of the name; *mahān*—very great; *abhūt*—was manifest; *kalpaḥ*—millennium; *yatra*—whereupon; *abhavat*—appeared; *brahmā*—Lord Brahmā; *śabda-brahma iti*—the sounds of the *Vedas;* *yam*—which; *viduḥ*—they know.

TRANSLATION

In the beginning of the first half of Brahmā's life, there was a millennium called Brāhma-kalpa, wherein Lord Brahmā appeared. The birth of the Vedas was simultaneous with Brahmā's birth.

PURPORT

According to *Padma Purāṇa* (*Prabhāsa-khaṇḍa*), in thirty days of Brahmā many *kalpas* take place, such as the Varāha-kalpa and Pitṛ-kalpa. Thirty days make one month of Brahmā, beginning from the full moon to the disappearance of the moon. Twelve such months complete one year, and fifty years complete one *parārdha*, or one half the duration of the life of Brahmā. The Śveta-varāha appearance of the Lord is the first birthday of Brahmā. The birth date of Brahmā is in the month of March, according to Hindu astronomical calculation. This statement is reproduced from the explanation of Śrīla Viśvanātha Cakravartī Ṭhākura.

TEXT 36

तस्यैव चान्ते कल्पोऽभूद् यं पाद्ममभिचक्षते ।
यद्धरेर्नाभिसरस आसील्लोकसरोरुहम् ॥३६॥

tasyaiva cānte kalpo 'bhūd
yaṁ pādmam abhicakṣate
yad dharer nābhi-sarasa
āsīl loka-saroruham

tasya—of the Brāhma-kalpa; *eva*—certainly; *ca*—also; *ante*—at the end of; *kalpaḥ*—millennium; *abhūt*—came into existence; *yam*—which; *pādmam*—Pādma; *abhicakṣate*—is called; *yat*—in which; *hareḥ*—of the Personality of Godhead; *nābhi*—in the navel; *sarasaḥ*—from the reservoir of water; *āsīt*—there was; *loka*—of the universe; *saroruham*—lotus.

TRANSLATION

The millennium which followed the first Brāhma millennium is known as the Pādma-kalpa because in that millennium the universal lotus flower grew out of the navel reservoir of water of the Personality of Godhead, Hari.

PURPORT

The millennium following the Brāhma-kalpa is known as the Pādma-kalpa because the universal lotus grows in that millennium. The Pādma-kalpa is also called the Pitṛ-kalpa in certain *Purāṇas*.

TEXT 37

अयं तु कथितः कल्पो द्वितीयस्यापि भारत ।
वाराह इति विख्यातो यत्रासीच्छूकरो हरिः ॥३७॥

ayaṁ tu kathitaḥ kalpo
dvitīyasyāpi bhārata
vārāha iti vikhyāto
yatrāsīc chūkaro hariḥ

ayam—this; *tu*—but; *kathitaḥ*—known as; *kalpaḥ*—the current millennium; *dvitīyasya*—of the second half; *api*—certainly; *bhārata*—O descendant of Bharata; *vārāhaḥ*—Vāraha; *iti*—thus; *vikhyātaḥ*—is celebrated; *yatra*—in which; *āsīt*—appeared; *śūkaraḥ*—hog shape; *hariḥ*—the Personality of Godhead.

TRANSLATION

O descendant of Bharata, the first millennium in the second half of the life of Brahmā is also known as the Vārāha millennium because the Personality of Godhead appeared in that millennium as the hog incarnation.

PURPORT

The different millenniums known as the Brāhma, Pādma and Vārāha *kalpas* appear a little puzzling for the layman. There are some scholars who think these *kalpas* to be one and the same. According to Śrīla Viśvanātha Cakravartī, the Brāhma-kalpa in the beginning of the first half appears to be the Pādma-kalpa. We can, however, simply abide by the text and understand that the present millennium is in the second half of the duration of the life of Brahmā.

TEXT 38

कालोऽयं द्विपरार्धाख्यो निमेष उपचर्यते ।
अव्याकृतस्यानन्तस्य ह्यनादेर्जगदात्मनः ॥३८॥

kālo 'yaṁ dvi-parārdhākhyo
nimeṣa upacaryate
avyākṛtasyānantasya
hy anāder jagad-ātmanaḥ

kālaḥ—eternal time; *ayam*—this (as measured by Brahmā's duration of life); *dvi-parārdha-ākhyaḥ*—measured by the two halves of Brahmā's life; *nimeṣaḥ*—less than a second; *upacaryate*—is so measured; *avyākṛtasya*—of one who is unchanged; *anantasya*—of the unlimited; *hi*—certainly; *anādeḥ*—of the beginningless; *jagat-ātmanaḥ*—of the soul of the universe.

TRANSLATION

The duration of the two parts of Brahmā's life, as above mentioned, is calculated to be equal to one nimeṣa [less than a second] for the Supreme Personality of Godhead, who is unchanging and unlimited and is the cause of all causes of the universe.

PURPORT

The great sage Maitreya has given a considerable description of the time of different dimensions, beginning from the atom up to the duration of the life of Brahmā. Now he attempts to give some idea of the time of the unlimited Personality of Godhead. He just gives a hint of His unlimited time by the standard of the life of Brahmā. The entire duration of the life of Brahmā is calculated to be less than a second of the Lord's time, and it is explained in the *Brahma-saṁhitā* (5.48) as follows:

yasyaika-niśvasita-kālam athāvalambya
jīvanti loma-vilajā jagad-aṇḍa-nāthāḥ
viṣṇur mahān sa iha yasya kalā-viśeṣo
govindam ādi-puruṣaṁ tam ahaṁ bhajāmi

"I worship Govinda, the Supreme Personality of Godhead, the cause of all causes, whose plenary portion is Mahā-Viṣṇu. All the heads of the innumerable universes [the Brahmās] live only by taking shelter of the time occupied by one of His breaths." The impersonalists do not believe in the form of the Lord, and thus they would hardly believe in the Lord's sleeping. Their idea is obtained by a poor fund of knowledge; they calculate everything in terms of man's capacity. They think that the existence of the Supreme is just the opposite of active human existence; because the human being has senses, the Supreme must be without sense perception; because the human being has a form, the Supreme must be formless; and because the human being sleeps, the Supreme must not sleep. *Śrīmad-Bhāgavatam*, however, does not agree with such impersonalists. It is clearly stated herein that the Supreme Lord rests in *yoga-*

nidrā, as previously discussed. And because He sleeps, naturally He must breathe, and the *Brahma-saṁhitā* confirms that within His breathing period innumerable Brahmās take birth and die.

There is complete agreement between *Śrīmad-Bhāgavatam* and the *Brahma-saṁhitā*. Eternal time is never lost along with the life of Brahmā. It continues, but it has no ability to control the Supreme Personality of Godhead because the Lord is the controller of time. In the spiritual world there is undoubtedly time, but it has no control over activities. Time is unlimited, and the spiritual world is also unlimited, since everything there exists on the absolute plane.

TEXT 39

कालोऽयं परमाण्वादिर्द्विपरार्धान्त ईश्वरः ।
नैवेशितुं प्रभुर्भूम्न ईश्वरो धाममानिनाम् ॥३९॥

kālo 'yaṁ paramāṇv-ādir
dvi-parārdhānta īśvaraḥ
naiveśituṁ prabhur bhūmna
īśvaro dhāma-māninām

kālaḥ—the eternal time; *ayam*—this; *parama-aṇu*—atom; *ādiḥ*—beginning from; *dvi-parārdha*—two superdurations of time; *antaḥ*—to the end; *īśvaraḥ*—controller; *na*—never; *eva*—certainly; *īśitum*—to control; *prabhuḥ*—capable; *bhūmnaḥ*—of the Supreme; *īśvaraḥ*—controller; *dhāma-māninām*—of those who are body conscious.

TRANSLATION

Eternal time is certainly the controller of different dimensions, from that of the atom up to the superdivisions of the duration of Brahmā's life; but, nevertheless, it is controlled by the Supreme. Time can control only those who are body conscious, even up to the Satyaloka or the other higher planets of the universe.

TEXT 40

विकारैः सहितो युक्तैर्विशेषादिभिरावृतः ।
आण्डकोशो बहिरयं पञ्चाशत्कोटिविस्तृतः ॥४०॥

vikāraiḥ sahito yuktair
viśeṣādibhir āvṛtaḥ
āṇḍakośo bahir ayaṁ
pañcāśat-koṭi-vistṛtaḥ

vikāraiḥ—by the transformation of the elements; *sahitaḥ*—along with; *yuktaiḥ*—being so amalgamated; *viśeṣa*—manifestations; *ādibhiḥ*—by them; *āvṛtaḥ*—covered; *āṇḍa-kośaḥ*—the universe; *bahiḥ*—outside; *ayam*—this; *pañcāśat*—fifty; *koṭi*—ten million; *vistṛtaḥ*—widespread.

TRANSLATION

This phenomenal material world is expanded to a diameter of four billion miles, as a combination of eight material elements transformed into sixteen further categories, within and without, as follows.

PURPORT

As explained before, the entire material world is a display of sixteen diversities and eight material elements. The analytical studies of the material world are the subject matter of Sāṅkhya philosophy. The first sixteen diversities are the eleven senses and five sense objects, and the eight elements are the gross and subtle matter, namely earth, water, fire, air, sky, mind, intelligence and ego. All these combined together are distributed throughout the entire universe, which extends diametrically to four billion miles. Besides this universe of our experience, there are innumerable other universes. Some of them are bigger than the present one, and all of them are clustered together under similar material elements as described below.

TEXT 41

दशोत्तराधिकैर्यत्र प्रविष्टः परमाणुवत् ।
लक्ष्यतेऽन्तर्गताश्चान्ये कोटिशो ह्यण्डराशयः ॥४१॥

daśottarādhikair yatra
praviṣṭaḥ paramāṇuvat
lakṣyate 'ntar-gatāś cānye
koṭiśo hy aṇḍa-rāśayaḥ

daśa-uttara-adhikaiḥ—with ten times greater thickness; *yatra*—in which; *praviṣṭaḥ*—entered; *parama-aṇu-vat*—like atoms; *lakṣyate*—it (the mass of universes) appears; *antaḥ-gatāḥ*—come together; *ca*—and; *anye*—in the other; *koṭiśaḥ*—clustered; *hi*—for; *aṇḍa-rāśayaḥ*—huge combination of universes.

TRANSLATION

The layers of elements covering the universes are each ten times thicker than the one before, and all the universes clustered together appear like atoms in a huge combination.

PURPORT

The coverings of the universes are also constituted of the elements of earth, water, fire, air and ether, and each is ten times thicker than the one before. The first covering of the universe is earth, and it is ten times thicker than the universe itself. If the universe is four billion miles in size, then the size of the earthly covering of the universe is four billion times ten. The covering of water is ten times greater than the earthly covering, the covering of fire is ten times greater than the watery covering, the covering of air is ten times greater than that of the fire, the covering of ether is ten times greater still than that of air, and so on. The universe within the coverings of matter appears to be like an atom in comparison to the coverings, and the number of universes is unknown even to those who can estimate the coverings of the universes.

TEXT 42

तदाहुरक्षरं ब्रह्म सर्वकारणकारणम् ।
विष्णोर्धाम परं साक्षात्पुरुषस्य महात्मनः ॥४२॥

tad āhur akṣaraṁ brahma
sarva-kāraṇa-kāraṇam
viṣṇor dhāma paraṁ sākṣāt
puruṣasya mahātmanaḥ

tat—that; *āhuḥ*—is said; *akṣaram*—infallible; *brahma*—the supreme; *sarva-kāraṇa*—all causes; *kāraṇam*—the supreme cause;

viṣṇoḥ dhāma—the spiritual abode of Viṣṇu; *param*—the supreme; *sākṣāt*—without doubt; *puruṣasya*—of the *puruṣa* incarnation; *mahātmanaḥ*—of the Mahā-Viṣṇu.

TRANSLATION

The Supreme Personality of Godhead, Śrī Kṛṣṇa, is therefore said to be the original cause of all causes. Thus the spiritual abode of Viṣṇu is eternal without a doubt, and it is also the abode of Mahā-Viṣṇu, the origin of all manifestations.

PURPORT

Lord Mahā-Viṣṇu, who is resting in *yoga-nidrā* on the Causal Ocean and creating innumerable universes by His breathing process, only temporarily appears in the *mahat-tattva* for the temporary manifestation of the material worlds. He is a plenary portion of Lord Śrī Kṛṣṇa, and thus although He is nondifferent from Lord Kṛṣṇa, His formal appearance in the material world as an incarnation is temporary. The original form of the Personality of Godhead is actually the *svarūpa*, or real form, and He eternally resides in the Vaikuṇṭha world (Viṣṇuloka). The word *mahātmanaḥ* is used here to indicate Mahā-Viṣṇu, and His real manifestation is Lord Kṛṣṇa, who is called *parama*, as confirmed in the *Brahma-saṁhitā:*

īśvaraḥ paramaḥ kṛṣṇaḥ
sac-cid-ānanda-vigrahaḥ
anādir ādir govindaḥ
sarva-kāraṇa-kāraṇam

"The Supreme Lord is Kṛṣṇa, the original Personality of Godhead known as Govinda. His form is eternal, full of bliss and knowledge, and He is the original cause of all causes."

Thus end the Bhaktivedanta purports of the Third Canto, Eleventh Chapter, of the Śrīmad-Bhāgavatam, *entitled "Calculation of Time, From the Atom."*

CHAPTER TWELVE

Creation of the Kumāras and Others

TEXT 1

मैत्रेय उवाच
इति ते वर्णितः क्षत्तः कालाख्यः परमात्मनः ।
महिमा वेदगर्भोऽथ यथास्राक्षीन्निबोध मे ॥ १ ॥

maitreya uvāca
iti te varṇitaḥ kṣattaḥ
kālākhyaḥ paramātmanaḥ
mahimā veda-garbho 'tha
yathāsrākṣīn nibodha me

maitreyaḥ uvāca—Śrī Maitreya said; *iti*—thus; *te*—unto you; *varṇitaḥ*—described; *kṣattaḥ*—O Vidura; *kāla-ākhyaḥ*—by the name eternal time; *paramātmanaḥ*—of the Supersoul; *mahimā*—glories; *veda-garbhaḥ*—Lord Brahmā, the reservoir of the *Vedas; atha*—hereafter; *yathā*—as it is; *asrākṣīt*—did create; *nibodha*—just try to understand; *me*—from me.

TRANSLATION

Śrī Maitreya said: O learned Vidura, so far I have explained to you the glories of the form of the Supreme Personality of Godhead in His feature of kāla. Now you can hear from me about the creation of Brahmā, the reservoir of all Vedic knowledge.

TEXT 2

ससर्जाग्रेऽन्धतामिस्रमथ तामिस्रमादिकृत् ।
महामोहं च मोहं च तमश्चाज्ञानवृत्तयः ॥ २ ॥

sasarjāgre 'ndha-tāmisram
atha tāmisram ādi-kṛt

mahāmohaṁ ca mohaṁ ca
tamaś cājñāna-vṛttayaḥ

sasarja—created; *agre*—at first; *andha-tāmisram*—the sense of death; *atha*—then; *tāmisram*—anger upon frustration; *ādi-kṛt*—all these; *mahā-moham*—ownership of enjoyable objects; *ca*—also; *moham*—illusory conception; *ca*—also; *tamaḥ*—darkness in self-knowledge; *ca*—as well as; *ajñāna*—nescience; *vṛttayaḥ*—engagements.

TRANSLATION

Brahmā first created the nescient engagements like self-deception, the sense of death, anger after frustration, the sense of false ownership, and the illusory bodily conception, or forgetfulness of one's real identity.

PURPORT

Before the factual creation of the living entities in different varieties of species, the conditions under which a living being in the material world has to live were created by Brahmā. Unless a living entity forgets his real identity, it is impossible for him to live in the material conditions of life. Therefore the first condition of material existence is forgetfulness of one's real identity. And by forgetting one's real identity, one is sure to be afraid of death, although a pure living soul is deathless and birthless. This false identification with material nature is the cause of false ownership of things which are offered by the arrangement of superior control. All material resources are offered to the living entity for his peaceful living and for the discharge of the duties of self-realization in conditioned life. But due to false identification, the conditioned soul becomes entrapped by the sense of false ownership of the property of the Supreme Lord. It is evident from this verse that Brahmā himself is a creation of the Supreme Lord, and the five kinds of nescience which condition the living entities in material existence are creations of Brahmā. It is simply ludicrous to think the living entity to be equal with the Supreme Being when one can understand that the conditioned souls are under the influence of Brahmā's magic wand. Patañjali also accepts that there are five kinds of nescience, as mentioned herein.

TEXT 3

दृष्ट्वा पापीयसीं सृष्टिं नात्मानं बह्वमन्यत ।
भगवद्ध्यानपूतेन मनसान्यां ततोऽसृजत् ॥ ३ ॥

dṛṣṭvā pāpīyasīṁ sṛṣṭiṁ
nātmānaṁ bahv amanyata
bhagavad-dhyāna-pūtena
manasānyāṁ tato 'sṛjat

dṛṣṭvā—by seeing; *pāpīyasīm*—sinful; *sṛṣṭim*—creation; *na*—did not; *ātmānam*—unto himself; *bahu*—much pleasure; *amanyata*—felt; *bhagavat*—on the Personality of Godhead; *dhyāna*—meditation; *pūtena*—purified by that; *manasā*—by such a mentality; *anyām*—another; *tataḥ*—thereafter; *asṛjat*—created.

TRANSLATION

Seeing such a misleading creation as a sinful task, Brahmā did not feel much pleasure in his activity, and therefore he purified himself by meditation on the Personality of Godhead. Then he began another term of creation.

PURPORT

Although he created the different influences of nescience, Lord Brahmā was not satisfied in performing such a thankless task, but he had to do it because most of the conditioned souls wanted it to be so. Lord Kṛṣṇa says in *Bhagavad-gītā* (15.15) that He is present in everyone's heart and is helping everyone to either remember or forget. The question may be raised why the Lord, who is all-merciful, helps one to remember and another to forget. Actually, His mercy is not exhibited in partiality towards one and enmity towards another. The living entity, as part and parcel of the Lord, is partially independent because he partially possesses all the qualities of the Lord. Anyone who has some independence may sometimes misuse it due to ignorance. When the living entity prefers to misuse his independence and glide down towards nescience, the all-merciful Lord first of all tries to protect him from the trap, but when the living entity persists in gliding down to hell, the Lord helps him to forget his real position. The Lord helps the falling living entity glide down to the lowest point, just to give him the chance to see if he is happy by misusing his independence.

Almost all the conditioned souls who are rotting in the material world are misusing their independence, and therefore five kinds of nescience are imposed upon them. As an obedient servitor of the Lord, Brahmā creates all these as a matter of necessity, but he is not happy in doing so because a devotee of the Lord naturally does not like to see anyone falling down from his real position. Persons who do not care for the path of realization get full facilities from the Lord for executing their proclivities to the fullest extent, and Brahmā helps in that procedure without fail.

TEXT 4

सनकं च सनन्दं च सनातनमथात्मभूः ।
सनत्कुमारं च मुनीन्निष्क्रियानूर्ध्वरेतसः ॥ ४ ॥

sanakaṁ ca sanandaṁ ca
sanātanam athātmabhūḥ
sanat-kumāraṁ ca munīn
niṣkriyān ūrdhva-retasaḥ

sanakam—Sanaka; *ca*—also; *sanandam*—Sananda; *ca*—and; *sanātanam*—Sanātana; *atha*—thereafter; *ātma-bhūḥ*—Brahmā, who is self-born; *sanat-kumāram*—Sanat-kumāra; *ca*—also; *munīn*—the great sages; *niṣkriyān*—free from all fruitive action; *ūrdhva-retasaḥ*—those whose semen flows upwards.

TRANSLATION

In the beginning, Brahmā created four great sages named Sanaka, Sananda, Sanātana and Sanat-kumāra. All of them were unwilling to adopt materialistic activities because they were highly elevated due to their semen's flowing upwards.

PURPORT

Although Brahmā created the principles of nescience as a matter of necessity for those living entities who were destined to ignorance by the will of the Lord, he was not satisfied in performing such a thankless task. He therefore created four principles of knowledge: *sāṅkhya*, or empirical philosophy for the analytical study of material conditions; *yoga*, or mysticism for liberation of the pure soul from material bondage; *vairāgya*, the acceptance of complete detachment from material enjoyment in life to elevate oneself to the highest spiritual understanding; and *tapas*, or the various kinds of voluntary austerities performed for spiritual perfection. Brahmā created the four great sages Sanaka, Sananda, Sanātana and Sanat to entrust them with these four principles of spiritual advancement, and they inaugurated their own spiritual party, or *sampradāya*, known as the Kumāra-sampradāya, or later on as the Nimbārka-sampradāya, for the advancement of *bhakti*. All of these great sages became great devotees, for without devotional service to the Personality of Godhead one cannot achieve success in any activity of spiritual value.

TEXT 5

तान् बभाषे स्वभूः पुत्रान् प्रजाः सृजत पुत्रकाः ।
तन्नैच्छन्मोक्षधर्माणो वासुदेवपरायणाः ॥ ५ ॥

tān babhāṣe svabhūḥ putrān
prajāḥ sṛjata putrakāḥ
tan naicchan mokṣa-dharmāṇo
vāsudeva-parāyaṇāḥ

tān—unto the Kumāras, as above mentioned; *babhāṣe*—addressed; *svabhūḥ*—Brahmā; *putrān*—unto the sons; *prajāḥ*—generations; *sṛjata*—to create; *putrakāḥ*—O my sons; *tat*—that; *na*—not; *aicchan*—desired; *mokṣa-dharmāṇaḥ*—pledged to the principles of liberation; *vāsudeva*—the Personality of Godhead; *parāyaṇāḥ*—who are so devoted.

TRANSLATION

Brahmā spoke to his sons after generating them. "My dear sons," he said, "now generate progeny." But due to their being attached to Vāsudeva, the Supreme Personality of Godhead, they aimed at liberation, and therefore they expressed their unwillingness.

PURPORT

The four sons of Brahmā, the Kumāras, declined to become family men even on the request of their great father, Brahmā. Those who are serious about gaining release from material bondage should not be entangled in the false relationship of family bondage. People may ask how the Kumāras could refuse the orders of Brahmā, who was their father and above all the creator of the universe. The reply is that one who is *vāsudeva-parāyaṇa*, or seriously engaged in the devotional service of the Personality of Godhead, Vāsudeva, need not care for any other obligation. It is enjoined in the *Bhāgavatam* (11.5.41):

devarṣi-bhūtāpta-nṛṇāṁ pitṝṇāṁ
na kiṅkaro nāyam ṛṇī ca rājan
sarvātmanā yaḥ śaraṇaṁ śaraṇyaṁ
gato mukundaṁ parihṛtya kartam

"Anyone who has completely given up all worldly relationships and has taken absolute shelter of the lotus feet of the Lord, who gives us salvation and who alone is fit to be taken shelter of, is no longer a debtor or servant of anyone, including the demigods, forefathers, sages, other living entities, relatives and members of human society." Thus there was nothing wrong in the acts of the Kumāras when they refused their great father's request that they become family men.

TEXT 6

सोऽवध्यातः सुतैरेवं प्रत्याख्यातानुशासनैः ।
क्रोधं दुर्विषहं जातं नियन्तुमुपचक्रमे ॥ ६ ॥

so 'vadhyātaḥ sutair evaṁ
pratyākhyātānuśāsanaiḥ
krodhaṁ durviṣahaṁ jātaṁ
niyantum upacakrame

saḥ—he (Brahmā); *avadhyātaḥ*—thus being disrespected; *sutaiḥ*—by the sons; *evam*—thus; *pratyākhyāta*—refusing to obey; *anuśāsanaiḥ*—the order of their father; *krodham*—anger; *durviṣaham*—too much to be tolerated; *jātam*—thus generated; *niyantum*—to control; *upacakrame*—tried his best.

TRANSLATION

On the refusal of the sons to obey the order of their father, there was much anger generated in the mind of Brahmā, which he tried to control and not express.

PURPORT

Brahmā is the director in charge of the mode of passion of material nature. Therefore it was natural for him to become angry on the refusal of his sons to obey his order. Although the Kumāras were right in such acts of refusal, Brahmā, being absorbed in the mode of passion, could not check his passionate anger. He did not express it, however, because he knew that his sons were far enlightened in spiritual advancement and thus he should not express his anger before them.

TEXT 7

धिया निगृह्यमाणोऽपि भ्रुवोर्मध्यात्प्रजापतेः ।
सद्योऽजायत तन्मन्युः कुमारो नीललोहितः ॥ ७ ॥

dhiyā nigṛhyamāṇo 'pi
bhruvor madhyāt prajāpateḥ
sadyo 'jāyata tan-manyuḥ
kumāro nīla-lohitaḥ

dhiyā—by intelligence; *nigṛhyamāṇaḥ*—being controlled; *api*—in spite of; *bhruvoḥ*—of the eyebrows; *madhyāt*—from between; *prajāpateḥ*—of Brahmā; *sadyaḥ*—at once; *ajāyata*—generated; *tat*—his; *manyuḥ*—anger; *kumāraḥ*—a child; *nīla-lohitaḥ*—mixture of blue and red.

TRANSLATION

Although he tried to curb his anger, it came out from between his eyebrows, and a child of mixed blue and red was immediately generated.

PURPORT

The face of anger is the same whether exhibited due to ignorance or knowledge. Although Brahmā tried to curb his anger, he could not do so, even though he is the supreme being. Such anger in its true color came from between the eyebrows of Brahmā as Rudra, in a mixed color of blue (ignorance) and red (passion), because anger is the product of passion and ignorance.

TEXT 8

स वै रुरोद देवानां पूर्वजो भगवान् भवः ।
नामानि कुरु मे धातः स्थानानि च जगद्गुरो ॥ ८ ॥

sa vai ruroda devānāṁ
pūrvajo bhagavān bhavaḥ
nāmāni kuru me dhātaḥ
sthānāni ca jagad-guro

saḥ—he; *vai*—certainly; *ruroda*—cried loudly; *devānām pūrvajaḥ*—the eldest of all demigods; *bhagavān*—the most powerful; *bhavaḥ*—Lord Śiva; *nāmāni*—different names; *kuru*—designate; *me*—my; *dhātaḥ*—O destiny maker; *sthānāni*—places; *ca*—also; *jagat-guro*—O teacher of the universe.

TRANSLATION

After his birth he began to cry: O destiny maker, teacher of the universe, kindly designate my name and place.

TEXT 9

इति तस्य वचः पाद्मो भगवान् परिपालयन् ।
अभ्यधाद्भद्रया वाचा मा रोदीस्तत्करोमि ते ॥ ९ ॥

iti tasya vacaḥ pādmo
bhagavān paripālayan
abhyadhād bhadrayā vācā
mā rodīs tat karomi te

iti—thus; *tasya*—his; *vacaḥ*—request; *pādmaḥ*—one who is born from the lotus flower; *bhagavān*—the powerful; *paripālayan*—accepting the request; *abhyadhāt*—pacified; *bhadrayā*—by gentle; *vācā*—words; *mā*—do not; *rodīḥ*—cry; *tat*—that; *karomi*—I shall do it; *te*—as desired by you.

TRANSLATION

The all-powerful Brahmā, who was born from the lotus flower, pacified the boy with gentle words, accepting his request, and said: Do not cry. I shall certainly do as you desire.

TEXT 10

यदरोदीः सुरश्रेष्ठ सोद्वेग इव बालकः ।
ततस्त्वामभिधास्यन्ति नाम्ना रुद्र इति प्रजाः ॥१०॥

yad arodīḥ sura-śreṣṭha
sodvega iva bālakaḥ
tatas tvām abhidhāsyanti
nāmnā rudra iti prajāḥ

yat—as much as; *arodīḥ*—cried loudly; *sura-śreṣṭha*—O chief of the demigods; *sa-udvegaḥ*—with great anxiety; *iva*—like; *bālakaḥ*—a boy; *tataḥ*—therefore; *tvām*—you; *abhidhāsyanti*—will call; *nāmnā*—by the name; *rudraḥ*—Rudra; *iti*—thus; *prajāḥ*—people.

TRANSLATION

Thereafter Brahmā said: O chief of the demigods, you shall be called by the name Rudra by all people because you have so anxiously cried.

TEXT 11

हृदिन्द्रियाण्यसुर्व्योम वायुरग्निर्जलं मही ।
सूर्यश्चन्द्रस्तपश्चैव स्थानान्यग्रे कृतानि ते ॥११॥

hṛd indriyāṇy asur vyoma
vāyur agnir jalaṁ mahī

sūryaś candras tapaś caiva
sthānāny agre kṛtāni te

hṛt—the heart; *indriyāṇi*—the senses; *asuḥ*—life air; *vyoma*—the sky; *vāyuḥ*—the air; *agniḥ*—fire; *jalam*—water; *mahī*—the earth; *sūryaḥ*—the sun; *candraḥ*—the moon; *tapaḥ*—austerity; *ca*—as well as; *eva*—certainly; *sthānāni*—all these places; *agre*—hereinbefore; *kṛtāni*—already made; *te*—for you.

TRANSLATION

My dear boy, I have already selected the following places for your residence: the heart, the senses, the air of life, the sky, the air, the fire, the water, the earth, the sun, the moon and austerity.

PURPORT

The creation of Rudra from between the eyebrows of Brahmā as the result of his anger, generated from the mode of passion partly touched by ignorance, is very significant. In *Bhagavad-gītā* (3.37) the principle of Rudra is described. *Krodha* (anger) is the product of *kāma* (lust), which is the result of the mode of passion. When lust and hankering are unsatisfied, the element of *krodha* appears, which is the formidable enemy of the conditioned soul. This most sinful and inimical passion is represented as *ahaṅkāra*, or the false egocentric attitude of thinking oneself to be all in all. Such an egocentric attitude on the part of the conditioned soul, who is completely under the control of material nature, is described in *Bhagavad-gītā* as foolish. The egocentric attitude is a manifestation of the Rudra principle in the heart, wherein *krodha* (anger) is generated. This anger develops in the heart and is further manifested through various senses, like the eyes, hands and legs. When a man is angry he expresses such anger with red-hot eyes and sometimes makes a display of clenching his fists or kicking his legs. This exhibition of the Rudra principle is the proof of Rudra's presence in such places. When a man is angry he breathes very rapidly, and thus Rudra is represented in the air of life, or in the activities of breathing. When the sky is overcast with dense clouds and roars in anger, and when the wind blows very fiercely, the Rudra principle is manifested, and so also when the seawater is infuriated by the wind it appears in a gloomy feature of Rudra, which is very fearful to the common man. When fire is ablaze we can also experience the presence of Rudra, and when there is an inundation over the earth we can understand that this is also the representation of Rudra.

There are many earthly creatures who constantly represent the Rudra element. The snake, tiger and lion are always representations of Rudra. Sometimes, because of the extreme heat of the sun, there are cases of heatstroke, and due to the extreme coldness created by the moon there are cases of collapse. There are many sages empowered with the influence of austerity and many *yogīs*, philosophers and renouncers who sometimes exhibit their acquired power under the influence of the Rudra principles of anger and passion. The great *yogī* Durvāsā, under the influence of this Rudra principle, picked a quarrel with Mahārāja Ambarīṣa, and a *brāhmaṇa* boy exhibited the Rudra principle by cursing the great King Parīkṣit. When the Rudra principle is exhibited by persons who are not engaged in the devotional service of the Supreme Personality of Godhead, the angry person falls down from the peak of his improved position. This is confirmed as follows:

ye 'nye 'ravindākṣa vimukta-māninas
tvayy asta-bhāvād aviśuddha-buddhayaḥ
āruhya kṛcchreṇa paraṁ padaṁ tataḥ
patanty adho 'nādṛta-yuṣmad-aṅghrayaḥ
(*Bhāg.* 10.2.32)

The most lamentable falldown of the impersonalist is due to his false and unreasonable claim of being one with the Supreme.

TEXT 12

मन्युर्मनुर्महिनसो महाञ्छिव ऋतध्वजः ।
उग्ररेता भवः कालो वामदेवो धृतव्रतः ॥१२॥

manyur manur mahinaso
mahāñ chiva ṛtadhvajaḥ
ugraretā bhavaḥ kālo
vāmadevo dhṛtavrataḥ

manyuḥ, manuḥ, mahinasaḥ, mahān, śivaḥ, ṛtadhvajaḥ, ugraretāḥ, bhavaḥ, kālaḥ, vāmadevaḥ, dhṛtavrataḥ—all names of Rudra.

TRANSLATION

Lord Brahmā said: My dear boy Rudra, you have eleven other names: Manyu, Manu, Mahinasa, Mahān, Śiva, Ṛtadhvaja, Ugraretā, Bhava, Kāla, Vāmadeva and Dhṛtavrata.

TEXT 13

धीर्धृतिरसलोमा च नियुत्सर्पिरिलाम्बिका ।
इरावती स्वधा दीक्षा रुद्राण्यो रुद्र ते स्त्रियः ॥१३॥

dhīr dhṛti-rasalomā ca
niyut sarpir ilāmbikā
irāvatī svadhā dīkṣā
rudrāṇyo rudra te striyaḥ

dhīḥ, dhṛti, rasalā, umā, niyut, sarpiḥ, ilā, ambikā, irāvatī, svadhā, dīkṣā rudrāṇyaḥ—the eleven Rudrāṇīs; *rudra*—O Rudra; *te*—unto you; *striyaḥ*—wives.

TRANSLATION

O Rudra, you also have eleven wives, called the Rudrāṇīs, and they are as follows: Dhī, Dhṛti, Rasalā, Umā, Niyut, Sarpi, Ilā, Ambikā, Irāvatī, Svadhā and Dīkṣā.

TEXT 14

गृहाणैतानि नामानि स्थानानि च सयोषणः ।
एभिः सृज प्रजा बह्वीः प्रजानामसि यत्पतिः ॥१४॥

gṛhāṇaitāni nāmāni
sthānāni ca sa-yoṣaṇaḥ
ebhiḥ sṛja prajā bahvīḥ
prajānām asi yat patiḥ

gṛhāṇa—just accept; *etāni*—all these; *nāmāni*—different names; *sthānāni*—as well as places; *ca*—also; *sa-yoṣaṇaḥ*—along with wives;

ebhiḥ—with them; *sṛja*—just generate; *prajāḥ*—progeny; *bahvīḥ*—on a large scale; *prajānām*—of the living entities; *asi*—you are; *yat*—since; *patiḥ*—the master.

TRANSLATION

My dear boy, you may now accept all the names and places designated for you and your different wives, and since you are now one of the masters of the living entities, you may increase the population on a large scale.

PURPORT

Brahmā, as the father of Rudra, selected the wives of his son, his living places, and his names as well. It is natural that one should accept the wife selected by one's father, just as a son accepts the name given by the father or as he accepts the property offered by the father. That is the general course in increasing the population of the world. On the other hand, the Kumāras did not accept the offering of their father because they were elevated far beyond the business of generating a great number of sons. As the son can refuse the order of the father for higher purposes, so the father can refuse to maintain his sons in increasing population because of higher purposes.

TEXT 15

इत्यादिष्टः स्वगुरुणा भगवान्नीललोहितः ।
सत्त्वाकृतिस्वभावेन ससर्जात्मसमाः प्रजाः ॥१५॥

ity ādiṣṭaḥ sva-guruṇā
bhagavān nīla-lohitaḥ
sattvākṛti-svabhāvena
sasarjātma-samāḥ prajāḥ

iti—thus; *ādiṣṭaḥ*—being ordered; *sva-guruṇā*—by his own spiritual master; *bhagavān*—the most powerful; *nīla-lohitaḥ*—Rudra, whose color is mixed blue and red; *sattva*—power; *ākṛti*—bodily features; *svabhāvena*—and with a very furious mode of nature; *sasarja*—created; *ātma-samāḥ*—like his own prototype; *prajāḥ*—generations.

TRANSLATION

The most powerful Rudra, whose bodily color was blue mixed with red, created many offspring exactly resembling him in features, strength and furious nature.

TEXT 16

रुद्राणां रुद्रसृष्टानां समन्ताद् ग्रसतां जगत् ।
निशाम्यासंख्यशो यूथान् प्रजापतिरशङ्कत ॥१६॥

rudrāṇāṁ rudra-sṛṣṭānāṁ
samantād grasatāṁ jagat
niśāmyāsaṅkhyaśo yūthān
prajāpatir aśaṅkata

rudrāṇām—of the sons of Rudra; *rudra-sṛṣṭānām*—who were generated by Rudra; *samantāt*—being assembled together; *grasatām*—while devouring; *jagat*—the universe; *niśāmya*—by observing their activities; *asaṅkhyaśaḥ*—unlimited; *yūthān*—assembly; *prajā-patiḥ*—the father of the living entities; *aśaṅkata*—became afraid of.

TRANSLATION

The sons and grandsons generated by Rudra were unlimited in number, and when they assembled together they attempted to devour the entire universe. When Brahmā, the father of the living entities, saw this, he became afraid of the situation.

PURPORT

The generations of Rudra, the incarnation of anger, were so dangerous to the maintenance of universal affairs that even Brahmā, the father of the living entities, became afraid of them. The so-called devotees or followers of Rudra are also a menace. They are sometimes dangerous even to Rudra himself. Descendants of Rudra sometimes make plans to kill Rudra—by the grace of Rudra. That is the nature of his devotees.

TEXT 17

अलं प्रजाभिः सृष्टाभिरीदृशीभिः सुरोत्तम ।
मया सह दहन्तीभिर्दिशश्चक्षुर्भिरुल्बणैः ॥१७॥

alaṁ prajābhiḥ sṛṣṭābhir
īdṛśībhiḥ surottama
mayā saha dahantībhir
diśaś cakṣurbhir ulbaṇaiḥ

alam—unnecessary; *prajābhiḥ*—by such living entities; *sṛṣṭābhiḥ*—generated; *īdṛśībhiḥ*—of this type; *sura-uttama*—O best among the demigods; *mayā*—me; *saha*—along with; *dahantībhiḥ*—who are burning; *diśaḥ*—all sides; *cakṣurbhiḥ*—by the eyes; *ulbaṇaiḥ*—fiery flames.

TRANSLATION

Brahmā told Rudra: O best among the demigods, there is no need for you to generate living entities of this nature. They have begun to devastate everything on all sides with the fiery flames from their eyes, and they have even attacked me.

TEXT 18

तप आतिष्ठ भद्रं ते सर्वभूतसुखावहम् ।
तपसैव यथापूर्वं स्रष्टा विश्वमिदं भवान् ॥१८॥

tapa ātiṣṭha bhadraṁ te
sarva-bhūta-sukhāvaham
tapasaiva yathā pūrvaṁ
sraṣṭā viśvam idaṁ bhavān

tapaḥ—penance; *ātiṣṭha*—be situated; *bhadram*—auspicious; *te*—unto you; *sarva*—all; *bhūta*—living entities; *sukha-āvaham*—bringing happiness; *tapasā*—by penance; *eva*—only; *yathā*—as much as; *pūrvam*—before; *sraṣṭā*—will create; *viśvam*—the universe; *idam*—this; *bhavān*—yourself.

TRANSLATION

My dear son, you had better situate yourself in penance, which is auspicious for all living entities and which will bring all benediction upon you. By penance only shall you be able to create the universe as it was before.

PURPORT

In the creation, maintenance and dissolution of the cosmic manifestation, the three deities Brahmā, Viṣṇu and Maheśvara, or Śiva, are respectively in charge. Rudra was advised not to destroy while the period of creation and maintenance was going on, but to situate himself in penance and wait for the time of dissolution, when his services would be called for.

TEXT 19

तपसैव परं ज्योतिर्भगवन्तमधोक्षजम् ।
सर्वभूतगुहावासमञ्जसा विन्दते पुमान् ॥१९॥

tapasaiva paraṁ jyotir
bhagavantam adhokṣajam
sarva-bhūta-guhāvāsam
añjasā vindate pumān

tapasā—by penance; *eva*—only; *param*—the supreme; *jyotiḥ*—light; *bhagavantam*—unto the Personality of Godhead; *adhokṣajam*—He who is beyond the approach of the senses; *sarva-bhūta-guhā-āvāsam*—residing in the heart of all living entities; *añjasā*—completely; *vindate*—can know; *pumān*—a person.

TRANSLATION

By penance only can one even approach the Personality of Godhead, who is within the heart of every living entity and at the same time beyond the reach of all senses.

PURPORT

Rudra was advised by Brahmā to perform penance as an example to his sons and followers that penance is necessary for attaining the favor of the Supreme Personality of Godhead. In *Bhagavad-gītā* it is said that the common mass of people follow the path shown by an authority. Thus Brahmā, disgusted with the Rudra generations and afraid of being devoured by the increase of population, asked Rudra to stop producing such an unwanted generation and take to penance for attaining the favor of the Supreme Lord. We find, therefore, in pictures, that Rudra is always sitting in meditation for the attainment of the favor of the Lord. Indirectly, the sons and followers of Rudra are advised to stop the business of annihilation, following the Rudra principle while the peaceful creation of Brahmā is going on.

TEXT 20

मैत्रेय उवाच

एवमात्मभुवादिष्टः परिक्रम्य गिरां पतिम् ।
बाढमित्यमुमामन्त्र्य विवेश तपसे वनम् ॥२०॥

maitreya uvāca
evam ātmabhuvādiṣṭaḥ
parikramya girāṁ patim
bāḍham ity amum āmantrya
viveśa tapase vanam

maitreyaḥ uvāca—Śrī Maitreya said; *evam*—thus; *ātma-bhuvā*—by Brahmā; *ādiṣṭaḥ*—being so requested; *parikramya*—by circumambulating; *girām*—of the *Vedas; patim*—unto the master; *bāḍham*—that is right; *iti*—thus; *amum*—unto Brahmā; *āmantrya*—thus addressing; *viveśa*—entered into; *tapase*—for the matter of penance; *vanam*—into the forest.

TRANSLATION

Śrī Maitreya said: Thus Rudra, having been ordered by Brahmā, circumambulated his father, the master of the Vedas. Addressing him with words of assent, he entered the forest to perform austere penances.

TEXT 21

अथाभिध्यायतः सर्गं दश पुत्राः प्रजज्ञिरे ।
भगवच्छक्तियुक्तस्य लोकसन्तानहेतवः ॥२१॥

athābhidhyāyataḥ sargaṁ
daśa putrāḥ prajajñire
bhagavac-chakti-yuktasya
loka-santāna-hetavaḥ

atha—thus; *abhidhyāyataḥ*—while thinking of; *sargam*—creation; *daśa*—ten; *putrāḥ*—sons; *prajajñire*—were begotten; *bhagavat*—regarding the Personality of Godhead; *śakti*—potency; *yuktasya*—empowered with; *loka*—the world; *santāna*—generation; *hetavaḥ*—the causes.

TRANSLATION

Brahmā, who was empowered by the Supreme Personality of Godhead, thought of generating living entities and begot ten sons for the extension of the generations.

TEXT 22

मरीचिरत्र्यङ्गिरसौ पुलस्त्यः पुलहः क्रतुः ।
भृगुर्वसिष्ठो दक्षश्च दशमस्तत्र नारदः ॥२२॥

marīcir atry-aṅgirasau
pulastyaḥ pulahaḥ kratuḥ
bhṛgur vasiṣṭho dakṣaś ca
daśamas tatra nāradaḥ

marīciḥ, atri, aṅgirasau, pulastyaḥ, pulahaḥ, kratuḥ, bhṛguḥ, vasiṣṭhaḥ, dakṣaḥ—names of sons of Brahmā; *ca*—and; *daśamaḥ*—the tenth; *tatra*—there; *nāradaḥ*—Nārada.

TRANSLATION

Marīci, Atri, Aṅgirā, Pulastya, Pulaha, Kratu, Bhṛgu, Vasiṣṭha, Dakṣa, and the tenth son, Nārada, were thus born.

PURPORT

The whole process of the creation, maintenance and dissolution of the cosmic manifestation is meant to give the conditioned souls a chance to go back home, back to Godhead. Brahmā created Rudra to help him in his creative endeavor, but from the very beginning Rudra began to devour the whole creation, and thus he had to be stopped from such devastating activities. Brahmā therefore created another set of good children, who were mostly in favor of worldly fruitive activities. He knew very well, however, that without devotional service to the Lord there is hardly any benefit for the conditioned souls, and therefore he at last created his worthy son Nārada, who is the supreme spiritual master of all transcendentalists. Without devotional service to the Lord one cannot make progress in any department of activity, although the path of devotional service is always independent of anything material. Only the transcendental loving service of the Lord can deliver the real goal of life, and thus the service rendered by Śrīman Nārada Muni is the highest among all the sons of Brahmā.

TEXT 23

उत्सङ्गान्नारदो जज्ञे दक्षोऽङ्गुष्ठात्स्वयम्भुवः ।
प्राणाद्वसिष्ठः सञ्जातो भृगुस्त्वचि करात्क्रतुः ॥२३॥

utsaṅgān nārado jajñe
dakṣo 'ṅguṣṭhāt svayambhuvaḥ
prāṇād vasiṣṭhaḥ sañjāto
bhṛgus tvaci karāt kratuḥ

utsaṅgāt—by transcendental deliberation; *nāradaḥ*—Mahāmuni Nārada; *jajñe*—was generated; *dakṣaḥ*—Dakṣa; *aṅguṣṭhāt*—from the thumb; *svayambhuvaḥ*—of Brahmā; *prāṇāt*—from the life air, or breathing; *vasiṣṭhaḥ*—Vasiṣṭha; *sañjātaḥ*—was born; *bhṛguḥ*—the sage Bhṛgu; *tvaci*—from the touch; *karāt*—from the hand; *kratuḥ*—the sage Kratu.

TRANSLATION

Nārada was born from the deliberation of Brahmā, which is the best part of his body. Vasiṣṭha was born from his breathing, Dakṣa from a thumb, Bhṛgu from his touch, and Kratu from his hand.

PURPORT

Nārada was born from the best deliberation of Brahmā because Nārada was able to deliver the Supreme Lord to anyone he liked. The Supreme Personality of Godhead cannot be realized by any amount of Vedic knowledge or by any number of penances. But a pure devotee of the Lord like Nārada can deliver the Supreme Lord by his good will. The very name Nārada suggests that he can deliver the Supreme Lord. *Nāra* means the "Supreme Lord," and *da* means "one who can deliver." That he can deliver the Supreme Lord does not mean that the Lord is like a commodity that can be delivered to any person. But Nārada can deliver to anyone the transcendental loving service of the Lord as a servitor, friend, parent or lover, as one may desire out of one's own transcendental love for the Lord. In other words, it is Nārada only who can deliver the path of *bhakti-yoga*, the highest mystic means for attainment of the Supreme Lord.

TEXT 24

पुलहो नाभितो जज्ञे पुलस्त्यः कर्णयोर्ऋषिः ।
अङ्गिरा मुखतोऽक्ष्णोऽत्रिर्मरीचिर्मनसोऽभवत् ॥२४॥

pulaho nābhito jajñe
pulastyaḥ karṇayor ṛṣiḥ
aṅgirā mukhato 'kṣṇo 'trir
marīcir manaso 'bhavat

pulahaḥ—the sage Pulaha; *nābhitaḥ*—from the navel; *jajñe*—generated; *pulastyaḥ*—the sage Pulastya; *karṇayoḥ*—from the ears; *ṛṣiḥ*—the great sage; *aṅgirāḥ*—the sage Aṅgirā; *mukhataḥ*—from the mouth; *akṣṇaḥ*—from the eyes; *atriḥ*—the sage Atri; *marīciḥ*—the sage Marīci; *manasaḥ*—from the mind; *abhavat*—appeared.

TRANSLATION

Pulastya was generated from the ears, Aṅgirā from the mouth, Atri from the eyes, Marīci from the mind and Pulaha from the navel of Brahmā.

TEXT 25

धर्मः स्तनाद्दक्षिणतो यत्र नारायणः स्वयम् ।
अधर्मः पृष्ठतो यस्मान्मृत्युर्लोकभयङ्करः ॥२५॥

dharmaḥ stanād dakṣiṇato
yatra nārāyaṇaḥ svayam

adharmaḥ pṛṣṭhato yasmān
mṛtyur loka-bhayaṅkaraḥ

dharmaḥ—religion; *stanāt*—from the breast; *dakṣiṇataḥ*—on the right side; *yatra*—wherein; *nārāyaṇaḥ*—the Supreme Lord; *svayam*—personally; *adharmaḥ*—irreligion; *pṛṣṭhataḥ*—from the back; *yasmāt*—from which; *mṛtyuḥ*—death; *loka*—to the living entity; *bhayam-karaḥ*—horrible.

TRANSLATION

Religion was manifested from the breast of Brahmā, wherein is seated the Supreme Personality of Godhead Nārāyaṇa, and irreligion appeared from his back, where horrible death takes place for the living entity.

PURPORT

That religion was manifested from the place where the Personality of Godhead is personally situated is very significant because religion means devotional service to the Personality of Godhead, as confirmed in *Bhagavad-gītā* as well as the *Bhāgavatam.* In *Bhagavad-gītā* the last instruction is to give up all other engagements in the name of religion and take shelter of the Personality of Godhead. *Śrīmad-Bhāgavatam* also confirms that the highest perfection of religion is that which leads to the devotional service of the Lord, unmotivated and unhampered by material impediments. Religion in its perfect form is the devotional service of the Lord, and irreligion is just the opposite. The heart is the most important part of the body, whereas the back is the most neglected part. When one is attacked by an enemy one is apt to endure attacks from the back and protect himself carefully from all attacks on the chest. All types of irreligion spring from the back of Brahmā, whereas real religion, the devotional service of the Lord, is generated from the chest, the seat of Nārāyaṇa. Anything which does not lead to the devotional service of the Lord is irreligion, and anything which leads to the devotional service of the Lord is called religion.

TEXT 26

हृदि कामो भ्रुवः क्रोधो लोभश्चाधरदच्छदात् ।
आस्याद्वाक्सिन्धवो मेढ्रान्निर्ऋतिः पायोरघाश्रयः ॥२६॥

hṛdi kāmo bhruvaḥ krodho
lobhaś cādhara-dacchadāt
āsyād vāk sindhavo meḍhrān
nirṛtiḥ pāyor aghāśrayaḥ

hṛdi—from the heart; *kāmaḥ*—lust; *bhruvaḥ*—from the eyebrows; *krodhaḥ*—anger; *lobhaḥ*—greed; *ca*—also; *adhara-dacchadāt*—from between the lips; *āsyāt*—from the mouth; *vāk*—speaking; *sindhavaḥ*—the seas; *meḍhrāt*—from the penis; *nirṛtiḥ*—low activities; *pāyoḥ*—from the anus; *agha-āśrayaḥ*—reservoir of all vices.

TRANSLATION

Lust and desire became manifested from the heart of Brahmā, anger from between his eyebrows, greed from between his lips, the power of speaking from his mouth, the ocean from his penis, and low and abominable activities from his anus, the source of all sins.

PURPORT

A conditioned soul is under the influence of mental speculation. However great one may be in the estimation of mundane education and learning, he cannot be free from the influence of psychic activities. Therefore it is very difficult to give up lust and the desires for low activities until one is in the line of devotional service to the Lord. When one is frustrated in lust and low desires, anger is generated from the mind and expressed from between the eyebrows. Ordinary men are therefore advised to concentrate the mind by focusing on the place between the eyebrows, whereas the devotees of the Lord are already practiced to place the Supreme Personality of Godhead on the seat of their minds. The theory of becoming desireless is untenable because the mind cannot be made desireless. When it is recommended that one be desireless, it is understood that one should not desire things which are destructive to spiritual values. A devotee of the Lord always has the Lord in his mind, and thus he does not need to be desireless because all his desires are in relationship with the service of the Lord. The power of speaking is called Sarasvatī, or the goddess of learning, and the birthplace of the goddess of learning is the mouth of Brahmā. Even if a man is endowed with the favor of the goddess of learning, it is quite possible for his heart to be full of lust and material desire and his eyebrows to display symptoms of anger. One may be very learned in the mundane estimation, but that does not mean that he is free from all low activities of lust and anger. Good qualifications can be expected only from a pure devotee, who is always engaged in the thought of the Lord, or in *samādhi*, with faith.

TEXT 27

छायायाः कर्दमो जज्ञे देवहूत्याः पतिः प्रभुः ।
मनसो देहतश्चेदं जज्ञे विश्वकृतो जगत् ॥२७॥

chāyāyāḥ kardamo jajñe
devahūtyāḥ patiḥ prabhuḥ
manaso dehataś cedaṁ
jajñe viśva-kṛto jagat

chāyāyāḥ—by the shadow; *kardamaḥ*—Kardama Muni; *jajñe*—became manifested; *devahūtyāḥ*—of Devahūti; *patiḥ*—husband; *prabhuḥ*—the master; *manasaḥ*—from the mind; *dehataḥ*—from the body; *ca*—also; *idam*—this; *jajñe*—developed; *viśva*—the universe; *kṛtaḥ*—of the creator; *jagat*—cosmic manifestation.

TRANSLATION

Sage Kardama, husband of the great Devahūti, was manifested from the shadow of Brahmā. Thus all became manifested from either the body or the mind of Brahmā.

PURPORT

Although one of the three modes of material nature is always prominent, they are never represented unalloyed by one another. Even in the most prominent existence of the two lower qualities, the modes of passion and ignorance, there is sometimes a tinge of the mode of goodness. Therefore all the sons generated from the body or the mind of Brahmā were in the modes of passion and ignorance, but some of them, like

Kardama, were born in the mode of goodness. Nārada was born in the transcendental state of Brahmā.

TEXT 28

वाचं दुहितरं तन्वीं स्वयम्भूर्हरतीं मनः ।
अकामां चकमे क्षत्तः सकाम इति नः श्रुतम् ॥२८॥

vācaṁ duhitaraṁ tanvīm
svayambhūr haratīṁ manaḥ
akāmāṁ cakame kṣattaḥ
sa-kāma iti naḥ śrutam

vācam—Vāk; *duhitaram*—unto the daughter; *tanvīm*—born of his body; *svayambhūḥ*—Brahmā; *haratīm*—attracting; *manaḥ*—his mind; *akāmām*—without being sexually inclined; *cakame*—desired; *kṣattaḥ*—O Vidura; *sa-kāmaḥ*—being sexually inclined; *iti*—thus; *naḥ*—we; *śrutam*—have heard.

TRANSLATION

O Vidura, we have heard that Brahmā had a daughter named Vāk who was born from his body and who attracted his mind toward sex, although she was not sexually inclined towards him.

PURPORT

Balavān indriya-grāmo vidvāṁsam api karṣati (*Bhāg.* 9.19.17). It is said that the senses are so mad and strong that they can bewilder even the most sensible and learned man. Therefore it is advised that one should not indulge in living alone even with one's mother, sister or daughter. *Vidvāṁsam api karṣati* means that even the most learned also become victims of the sensuous urge. Maitreya hesitated to state this anomaly on the part of Brahmā, who was sexually inclined to his own daughter, but still he mentioned it because sometimes it so happens, and the living example is Brahmā himself, although he is the primeval living being and the most learned within the whole universe. If Brahmā could be a victim of the sexual urge, then what of others, who are prone to so many mundane frailties? This extraordinary immorality on the part of

Brahmā was heard to have occurred in some particular *kalpa*, but it could not have happened in the *kalpa* in which Brahmā heard directly from the Lord the four essential verses of *Śrīmad-Bhāgavatam* because the Lord benedicted Brahmā, after giving him lessons on the *Bhāgavatam*, that he would never be bewildered in any *kalpa* whatsoever. This indicates that before the hearing of *Śrīmad-Bhāgavatam* he might have fallen a victim to such sensuality, but after hearing *Śrīmad-Bhāgavatam* directly from the Lord, there was no possibility of such failures.

One should, however, take serious note of this incident. The human being is a social animal, and his unrestricted mixing with the fair sex leads to downfall. Such social freedom of man and woman, especially among the younger section, is certainly a great stumbling block on the path of spiritual progress. Material bondage is due only to sexual bondage, and therefore unrestricted association of man and woman is surely a great impediment. Maitreya cited this example on the part of Brahmā just to bring to our notice this great danger.

TEXT 29

तमधर्मे कृतमतिं विलोक्य पितरं सुताः ।
मरीचिमुख्या मुनयो विश्रम्भात्प्रत्यबोधयन् ॥२९॥

tam adharme kṛta-matiṁ
vilokya pitaraṁ sutāḥ
marīci-mukhyā munayo
viśrambhāt pratyabodhayan

tam—unto him; *adharme*—in the matter of immorality; *kṛta-matim*—the mind being so given; *vilokya*—seeing thus; *pitaram*—unto the father; *sutāḥ*—sons; *marīci-mukhyāḥ*—headed by Marīci; *munayaḥ*—sages; *viśrambhāt*—with due respect; *pratyabodhayan*—submitted as follows.

TRANSLATION

Thus, finding their father so deluded in an act of immorality, the sages headed by Marīci, all sons of Brahmā, spoke as follows with great respect.

PURPORT

The sages like Marīci were not in the wrong in submitting their protests against the acts of their great father. They knew very well that even though their father committed a mistake, there must have been some great purpose behind the show, otherwise such a great personality could not have committed such a mistake. It might be that Brahmā wanted to warn his subordinates about human frailties in their dealings with women. This is always very dangerous for persons who are on the path of self-realization. Therefore, great personalities like Brahmā, even when in the wrong, should not be neglected, nor could the great sages headed by Marīci show any disrespect because of his extraordinary behavior.

TEXT 30

नैतत्पूर्वैः कृतं त्वद्ये न करिष्यन्ति चापरे ।
यस्त्वं दुहितरं गच्छेरनिगृह्याङ्गजं प्रभुः ॥३०॥

naitat pūrvaiḥ kṛtaṁ tvad ye
na kariṣyanti cāpare
yas tvaṁ duhitaraṁ gaccher
anigṛhyāṅgajaṁ prabhuḥ

na—never; *etat*—such a thing; *pūrvaiḥ*—by any other Brahmā, or yourself in any previous *kalpa; kṛtam*—performed; *tvat*—by you; *ye*—that which; *na*—nor; *kariṣyanti*—will do; *ca*—also; *apare*—anyone else; *yaḥ*—that which; *tvam*—you; *duhitaram*—unto the daughter; *gaccheḥ*—would go; *anigṛhya*—without controlling; *aṅgajam*—sex desire; *prabhuḥ*—O father.

TRANSLATION

O father, this performance in which you are endeavoring to complicate yourself was never attempted by any other Brahmā, nor by anyone else, nor by you in previous kalpas, nor will anyone dare to attempt it in the future. You are the supreme being in the universe, so how is it that you want to have sex with your daughter and cannot control your desire?

PURPORT

The post of Brahmā is the supermost post in the universe, and it appears that there are many Brahmās and many universes besides the one in which we are situated. One who fills this post must be ideal in behavior, for Brahmā sets the example for all living entities. Brahmā, the living entity who is the most pious and spiritually elevated, is entrusted with a post next to that of the Personality of Godhead.

TEXT 31

तेजीयसामपि ह्येतन्न सुश्लोक्यं जगद्गुरो ।
यद्वृत्तमनुतिष्ठन् वै लोकः क्षेमाय कल्पते ॥३१॥

tejīyasām api hy etan
na suślokyaṁ jagad-guro
yad-vṛttam anutiṣṭhan vai
lokaḥ kṣemāya kalpate

tejīyasām—of the most powerful; *api*—also; *hi*—certainly; *etat*—such an act; *na*—not suitable; *su-ślokyam*—good behavior; *jagat-guro*—O spiritual master of the universe; *yat*—whose; *vṛttam*—character; *anutiṣṭhan*—following; *vai*—certainly; *lokaḥ*—the world; *kṣemāya*—for prosperity; *kalpate*—becomes eligible.

TRANSLATION

Even though you are the most powerful being, this act does not suit you because your character is followed for spiritual improvement by people in general.

PURPORT

It is said that a supremely powerful living entity can do anything and everything he likes and such acts do not affect him in any way. For example, the sun, the most powerful fiery planet in the universe, can evaporate water from anywhere and still remain as powerful. The sun evaporates water from filthy places and yet is not infected with the quality of the filth. Similarly, Brahmā remains unimpeachable in all conditions. But still, since he is the spiritual master of all living entities, his behavior and character should be so ideal that people will follow such sublime behavior and derive the highest spiritual benefit. Therefore, he should not have acted as he did.

TEXT 32

तस्मै नमो भगवते य इदं स्वेन रोचिषा ।
आत्मस्थं व्यञ्जयामास स धर्मं पातुमर्हति ॥३२॥

tasmai namo bhagavate
ya idaṁ svena rociṣā
ātma-sthaṁ vyañjayām āsa
sa dharmaṁ pātum arhati

tasmai—unto Him; *namaḥ*—obeisances; *bhagavate*—unto the Personality of Godhead; *yaḥ*—who; *idam*—this; *svena*—by His own; *rociṣā*—effulgence; *ātma-stham*—situated in Himself; *vyañjayām āsa*—has manifested; *saḥ*—He; *dharmam*—religion; *pātum*—for protection; *arhati*—may kindly do so.

TRANSLATION

Let us offer our respectful obeisances unto the Personality of Godhead, who, by His own effulgence, while situated in Himself, has manifested this cosmos. May He also protect religion for all goodness.

PURPORT

Lust for sexual intercourse is so strong that it appears herein that Brahmā could not be dissuaded from his determination in spite of the appeal by his great sons like Marīci. Therefore, the great sons began to pray to the Supreme Lord for the good sense of Brahmā. It is only by the grace of the Supreme Lord that one can be protected from the allurement of lusty material desires. The Lord gives protection to devotees who are always engaged in His transcendental loving service, and by His causeless mercy He forgives the accidental fall of a devotee. Therefore, sages like Marīci prayed for the mercy of the Lord, and their prayer was fruitful.

TEXT 33

**स इत्थं गृणतः पुत्रान् पुरो दृष्ट्वा प्रजापतीन् ।
प्रजापतिपतिस्तन्वं तत्याज व्रीडितस्तदा ।
तां दिशो जगृहुर्घोरां नीहारं यद्विदुस्तमः ॥३३॥**

sa ittham gṛṇataḥ putrān
puro dṛṣṭvā prajāpatīn
prajāpati-patis tanvaṁ
tatyāja vrīḍitas tadā
tāṁ diśo jagṛhur ghorāṁ
nīhāraṁ yad vidus tamaḥ

saḥ—he (Brahmā); *ittham*—thus; *gṛṇataḥ*—speaking; *putrān*—sons; *puraḥ*—before; *dṛṣṭvā*—seeing; *prajā-patīn*—all the progenitors of living entities; *prajāpati-patiḥ*—the father of all of them (Brahmā); *tanvam*—body; *tatyāja*—quit; *vrīḍitaḥ*—ashamed; *tadā*—at that time; *tām*—that body; *diśaḥ*—all directions; *jagṛhuḥ*—accepted; *ghorām*—blamable; *nīhāram*—fog; *yat*—which; *viduḥ*—they know as; *tamaḥ*—darkness.

TRANSLATION

The father of all Prajāpatis, Brahmā, thus seeing all his Prajāpati sons speaking in that way, became very much ashamed and at once gave up the body he had accepted. Later that body appeared in all directions as the dangerous fog in darkness.

PURPORT

The best way to compensate for one's sinful acts is to give up one's body at once, and Brahmā, the leader of the living entities, showed this by his personal example. Brahmā has a fabulous duration of life, but he was obliged to give up his body due to his grievous sin, even though he had merely contemplated it in his mind without having actually done it.

This is a lesson for the living entities, showing how sinful an act it is to indulge in unrestricted sex life. Even to think of abominable sex life is sinful, and to compensate for such sinful acts, one has to give up his body. In other words, one's duration of life, blessings, opulence, etc., are decreased by sinful acts, and the most dangerous type of sinful act is unrestricted sex.

Ignorance is the cause of sinful life, or sinful life is the cause of gross ignorance. The feature of ignorance is darkness or fog. Darkness or fog still covers the whole universe, and the sun is the only counteracting principle. One who takes shelter of the Lord, the perpetual light, has no fear of being annihilated in the darkness of fog or ignorance.

TEXT 34

कदाचिद् ध्यायतः स्रष्टुर्वेदा आसंश्चतुर्मुखात् ।
कथं स्रक्ष्याम्यहं लोकान् समवेतान् यथा पुरा ॥३४॥

kadācid dhyāyataḥ sraṣṭur
vedā āsaṁś catur-mukhāt
kathaṁ srakṣyāmy ahaṁ lokān
samavetān yathā purā

kadācit—once upon a time; *dhyāyataḥ*—while contemplating; *sraṣṭuḥ*—of Brahmā; *vedāḥ*—the Vedic literature; *āsan*—became manifested; *catuḥ-mukhāt*—from the four mouths; *katham srakṣyāmi*—how shall I create; *aham*—myself; *lokān*—all these worlds; *samavetān*—assembled; *yathā*—as they were; *purā*—in the past.

TRANSLATION

Once upon a time, when Brahmā was thinking of how to create the worlds as in the past millennium, the four Vedas, which contain all varieties of knowledge, became manifested from his four mouths.

PURPORT

As a fire can consume anything and everything without being contaminated, so, by the grace of the Lord, the fire of Brahmā's greatness consumed his desire for the sinful act of sex with his daughter. The *Vedas* are the source of all knowledge, and they were first revealed to Brahmā by the mercy of the Supreme Personality of Godhead while

Brahmā was thinking of re-creating the material world. Brahmā is powerful by dint of his devotional service unto the Lord, and the Lord is always ready to forgive His devotee if by chance he falls down from the noble path of devotional service. The *Śrīmad-Bhāgavatam* (11.5.42) confirms this as follows:

sva-pāda-mūlaṁ bhajataḥ priyasya
tyaktvānya-bhāvasya hariḥ pareśaḥ
vikarma yac cotpatitaṁ kathañ-cid
dhunoti sarvaṁ hṛdi sanniviṣṭaḥ

"Any person who is engaged one hundred percent in the transcendental loving service of the Lord, at His lotus feet, is very dear to the Personality of Godhead Hari, and the Lord, being situated in the heart of the devotee, excuses all kinds of sins committed by chance." It was never expected that a great personality like Brahmā would ever think of sex indulgence with his daughter. The example shown by Brahmā only suggests that the power of material nature is so strong that it can act upon everyone, even Brahmā. Brahmā was saved by the mercy of the Lord with a little punishment, but by the grace of the Lord he did not lose his prestige as the great Brahmā.

TEXT 35

चातुर्होत्रं कर्मतन्त्रमुपवेदनयैः सह ।
धर्मस्य पादाश्चत्वारस्तथैवाश्रमवृत्तयः ॥३५॥

cātur-hotraṁ karma-tantram
upaveda-nayaiḥ saha
dharmasya pādāś catvāras
tathaivāśrama-vṛttayaḥ

cātuḥ—four; *hotram*—paraphernalia for sacrifice; *karma*—action; *tantram*—expansions of such activities; *upaveda*—supplementary to the *Vedas; nayaiḥ*—by logical conclusions; *saha*—along with; *dharmasya*—of religiosity; *pādāḥ*—principles; *catvāraḥ*—four; *tathā eva*—in the same way; *āśrama*—social orders; *vṛttayaḥ*—occupations.

TRANSLATION

The four kinds of paraphernalia for conducting the fire sacrifice became manifest: the performer [the chanter], the offerer, the fire, and the action performed in terms of the supplementary Vedas. Also the four principles of religiosity [truth, austerity, mercy and cleanliness] and the duties in the four social orders all became manifest.

PURPORT

Eating, sleeping, defending and mating are the four principles of material bodily demands which are common to both the animals and human society. To distinguish human society from the animals there is the performance of religious activities in terms of the social statuses and orders of life. They are all clearly mentioned in the Vedic literatures and were manifested by Brahmā when the four *Vedas* were generated from his four mouths. Thus the duties of humankind in terms of the statuses and social orders were established to be observed by the civilized man. Those who traditionally follow these principles are called Āryans, or progressive human beings.

TEXT 36

विदुर उवाच

स वै विश्वसृजामीशो वेदादीन् मुखतोऽसृजत् ।
यद् यद् येनासृजद् देवस्तन्मे ब्रूहि तपोधन ॥३६॥

vidura uvāca
sa vai viśva-sṛjām īśo
vedādīn mukhato 'sṛjat
yad yad yenāsṛjad devas
tan me brūhi tapo-dhana

viduraḥ uvāca—Vidura said; *saḥ*—he (Brahmā); *vai*—certainly; *viśva*—the universe; *sṛjām*—of those who created; *īśaḥ*—the controller; *veda-ādīn*—the *Vedas*, etc.; *mukhataḥ*—from the mouth; *asṛjat*—established; *yat*—that; *yat*—which; *yena*—by which; *asṛjat*—created; *devaḥ*—the god; *tat*—that; *me*—unto me; *brūhi*—please explain; *tapaḥ-dhana*—O sage whose only wealth is penance.

TRANSLATION

Vidura said: O great sage whose only wealth is penance, kindly explain to me how and with whose help Brahmā established the Vedic knowledge which emanated from his mouth.

TEXT 37

मैत्रेय उवाच
ऋग्यजुःसामाथर्वाख्यान् वेदान् पूर्वादिभिर्मुखैः ।
शास्त्रमिज्यां स्तुतिस्तोमं प्रायश्चित्तं व्यधात्क्रमात् ॥३७॥

maitreya uvāca
ṛg-yajuḥ-sāmātharvākhyān
vedān pūrvādibhir mukhaiḥ
śāstram ijyāṁ stuti-stomaṁ
prāyaścittaṁ vyadhāt kramāt

maitreyaḥ uvāca—Maitreya said; *ṛk-yajuḥ-sāma-atharva*—the four *Vedas; ākhyān*—of the name; *vedān*—Vedic literatures; *pūrva-ādibhiḥ*—beginning with the front; *mukhaiḥ*—by the mouths; *śāstram*—Vedic hymns not pronounced before; *ijyām*—priestly rituals; *stuti-stomam*—the subject matter of the reciters; *prāyaścittam*—transcendental activities; *vyadhāt*—established; *kramāt*—one after another.

TRANSLATION

Maitreya said: Beginning from the front face of Brahmā, gradually the four Vedas—Ṛk, Yajur, Sāma and Atharva—became manifest. Thereafter, Vedic hymns which had not been pronounced before, priestly rituals, the subject matters of the recitation, and transcendental activities were all established, one after another.

TEXT 38

आयुर्वेदं धनुर्वेदं गान्धर्वं वेदमात्मनः ।
स्थापत्यं चासृजद् वेदं क्रमात्पूर्वादिभिर्मुखैः ॥३८॥

āyur-vedaṁ dhanur-vedaṁ
gāndharvaṁ vedam ātmanaḥ

sthāpatyaṁ cāsṛjad vedaṁ
kramāt pūrvādibhir mukhaiḥ

āyuḥ-vedam—medical science; *dhanuḥ-vedam*—military science; *gāndharvam*—musical art; *vedam*—they are all Vedic knowledge; *ātmanaḥ*—of his own; *sthāpatyam*—architectural; *ca*—also; *asṛjat*—created; *vedam*—knowledge; *kramāt*—respectively; *pūrva-ādibhiḥ*—beginning from the front face; *mukhaiḥ*—by the mouths.

TRANSLATION

He also created the medical science, military art, musical art and architectural science, all from the Vedas. They all emanated one after another, beginning from the front face.

PURPORT

The *Vedas* contain perfect knowledge, which includes all kinds of knowledge necessary for the human society, not only on this particular planet but on other planets as well. It is understood that military art is also necessary knowledge for the upkeep of social order, as is the art of music. All these groups of knowledge are called the *Upapurāṇa*, or supplements of the *Vedas*. Spiritual knowledge is the main topic of the *Vedas*, but to help the human being's spiritual pursuit of knowledge, the other information, as above mentioned, forms necessary branches of the Vedic knowledge.

TEXT 39

इतिहासपुराणानि पञ्चमं वेदमीश्वरः ।
सर्वेभ्य एव वक्त्रेभ्यः ससृजे सर्वदर्शनः ॥३९॥

itihāsa-purāṇāni
pañcamaṁ vedam īśvaraḥ
sarvebhya eva vaktrebhyaḥ
sasṛje sarva-darśanaḥ

itihāsa—histories; *purāṇāni*—the *Purāṇas* (supplementary *Vedas*); *pañcamam*—the fifth; *vedam*—the Vedic literature; *īśvaraḥ*—the Lord;

sarvebhyaḥ—all together; *eva*—certainly; *vaktrebhyaḥ*—from his mouths; *sasṛje*—created; *sarva*—all around; *darśanaḥ*—one who can see all time.

TRANSLATION

Then he created the fifth Veda—the Purāṇas and the histories—from all his mouths, since he could see all the past, present and future.

PURPORT

There are histories of particular countries and nations and of the world, but the *Purāṇas* are the histories of the universe, not only in one millennium, but in many *kalpas*. Brahmā has knowledge of those historical facts, and therefore all the *Purāṇas* are histories. As originally composed by Brahmā, they are part of the *Vedas* and are called the fifth *Veda*.

TEXT 40

षोडश्युक्थौ पूर्ववक्त्रात्पुरीष्यग्निष्टुतावथ ।
आप्तोर्यामातिरात्रौ च वाजपेयं सगोसवम् ॥४०॥

ṣoḍaśy-ukthau pūrva-vaktrāt
purīṣy-agniṣṭutāv atha
āptoryāmātirātrau ca
vājapeyaṁ sagosavam

ṣoḍaśī-ukthau—types of sacrifice; *pūrva-vaktrāt*—from the eastern mouth; *purīṣi-agniṣṭutau*—types of sacrifice; *atha*—then; *āptoryāma-atirātrau*—types of sacrifice; *ca*—and; *vājapeyam*—type of sacrifice; *sa-gosavam*—type of sacrifice.

TRANSLATION

All the different varieties of fire sacrifices [ṣoḍaśī, uktha, purīṣi, agniṣṭoma, āptoryāma, atirātra, vājapeya and gosava] became manifested from the eastern mouth of Brahmā.

TEXT 41

विद्या दानं तपः सत्यं धर्मस्येति पदानि च ।
आश्रमांश्च यथासंख्यमसृजत्सह वृत्तिभिः ॥४१॥

vidyā dānaṁ tapaḥ satyaṁ
dharmasyeti padāni ca
āśramāṁś ca yathā-saṅkhyam
asṛjat saha vṛttibhiḥ

vidyā—education; *dānam*—charity; *tapaḥ*—penance; *satyam*—truth; *dharmasya*—of religion; *iti*—thus; *padāni*—four legs; *ca*—also; *āśramān*—orders of life; *ca*—also; *yathā*—as they are; *saṅkhyam*—in number; *asṛjat*—created; *saha*—along with; *vṛttibhiḥ*—by vocations.

TRANSLATION

Education, charity, penance and truth are said to be the four legs of religion, and to learn this there are four orders of life with different classifications of castes according to vocation. Brahmā created all these in systematic order.

PURPORT

The nucleus of the four social orders—*brahmacarya*, or student life, *gṛhastha*, or household family life, *vānaprastha*, or retired life for practicing penance, and *sannyāsa*, or renounced life for preaching the truth—is the four legs of religion. The vocational divisions are the *brāhmaṇas*, or the intelligent class, the *kṣatriyas*, or administrative class, the *vaiśyas*, or mercantile productive class, and the *śūdras*, or general laborer class who have no specific qualifications. All were systematically planned and created by Brahmā for the regular promotion of self-realization. Student life is meant for acquiring the best education; household family life is meant for gratifying the senses, provided it is performed with a charitable disposition of mind, retirement from household life is meant for penance, for advancement in spiritual life, and renounced life is meant for preaching the Absolute Truth to the people in general. The combined actions of all members of society make the whole situation favorable for the upliftment of the mission of human life. The beginning of this social institution is based on education meant for purifying the animal propensities of the human being. The highest purificatory process is knowledge of the Supreme Personality of Godhead, the purest of the pure.

TEXT 42

सावित्रं प्राजापत्यं च ब्राह्मं चाथ बृहत्तथा ।
वार्तासञ्चयशालीनशिलोञ्छ इति वै गृहे ॥४२॥

sāvitraṁ prājāpatyaṁ ca
brāhmaṁ cātha bṛhat tathā
vārtā sañcaya-śālīna-
śiloñcha iti vai gṛhe

sāvitram—the thread ceremony of the twice-born; *prājāpatyam*—to execute the vow for one year; *ca*—and; *brāhmam*—acceptance of the *Vedas; ca*—and; *atha*—also; *bṛhat*—complete abstinence from sex life; *tathā*—then; *vārtā*—vocation in terms of Vedic sanction; *sañcaya*—professional duty; *śālīna*—livelihood without asking anyone for cooperation; *śila-uñchaḥ*—picking up rejected grains; *iti*—thus; *vai*—even though; *gṛhe*—in household life.

TRANSLATION

Then the thread ceremony for the twice-born was inaugurated, as were the rules to be followed for at least one year after acceptance of the Vedas, rules for observing complete abstinence from sex life, vocations in terms of Vedic injunctions, various professional duties in household life, and the method of maintaining a livelihood without anyone's cooperation by picking up rejected grains.

PURPORT

During student life the *brahmacārīs* were given full instructions about the importance of the human form of life. Thus the basic education was designed to encourage the student in becoming free from family encumbrances. Only students unable to accept such a vow in life were allowed to go home and marry a suitable wife. Otherwise, the student would remain a permanent *brahmacārī*, observing complete abstinence from sex life for his whole life. It all depended on the quality of the student's training. We had the opportunity to meet an avowed *brahmacārī* in the personality of our spiritual master, Oṁ Viṣṇupāda Śrī Śrīmad Bhaktisiddhānta Gosvāmī Mahārāja. Such a great soul is called a *naiṣṭhika-brahmacārī.*

TEXT 43

वैखानसा वालखिल्यौदुम्बराः फेनपा वने ।
न्यासे कुटीचकः पूर्वं बह्वोदो हंसनिष्क्रियौ ॥४३॥

vaikhānasā vālakhilyau-
dumbarāḥ phenapā vane
nyāse kuṭīcakaḥ pūrvaṁ
bahvodo haṁsa-niṣkriyau

vaikhānasāḥ—the section of men who retire from active life and live on half-boiled meals; *vālakhilya*—one who quits his former stock of grains on receipt of more; *audumbarāḥ*—one who lives on what he gets from the direction towards which he starts after rising from bed; *phenapāḥ*—one who lives on the fruits which automatically fall from the tree; *vane*—in the forest; *nyāse*—in the order of renunciation; *kuṭīcakaḥ*—life in the family without attachment; *pūrvam*—in the beginning; *bahvodaḥ*—giving up all material activities and engaging fully in transcendental service; *haṁsa*—fully engaged in transcendental knowledge; *niṣkriyau*—stopping all kinds of activities.

TRANSLATION

The four divisions of retired life are the vaikhānasas, vālakhilyas, audumbaras and phenapas. The four divisions of the renounced order of life are the kuṭīcakas, bahvodas, haṁsas and niṣkriyas. All these were manifested from Brahmā.

PURPORT

The *varṇāśrama-dharma,* or the institution of the four divisions and orders of social and spiritual life, is not a new invention of the modern age, as proposed by the less intelligent. It is an institution established by Brahmā from the beginning of the creation. This is also confirmed in the *Bhagavad-gītā* (4.13): *cātur-varṇyaṁ mayā sṛṣṭam.*

TEXT 44

आन्वीक्षिकी त्रयी वार्ता दण्डनीतिस्तथैव च ।
एवं व्याहृतयश्चासन् प्रणवो ह्यस्य दहतः ॥४४॥

ānvīkṣikī trayī vārtā
daṇḍa-nītis tathaiva ca
evaṁ vyāhṛtayaś cāsan
praṇavo hy asya dahrataḥ

ānvīkṣikī—logic; *trayī*—the three goals, namely religion, economy and salvation; *vārtā*—sense gratification; *daṇḍa*—law and order; *nītiḥ*—moral codes; *tathā*—as also; *eva ca*—respectively; *evam*—thus; *vyāhṛtayaḥ*—the celebrated hymns *bhūḥ, bhuvaḥ* and *svaḥ; ca*—also; *āsan*—came into existence; *praṇavaḥ*—the *oṁkāra; hi*—certainly; *asya*—of him (Brahmā); *dahrataḥ*—from the heart.

TRANSLATION

The science of logical argument, the Vedic goals of life, and also law and order, moral codes, and the celebrated hymns bhūḥ, bhuvaḥ and svaḥ all became manifested from the mouths of Brahmā, and the praṇava oṁkāra was manifested from his heart.

TEXT 45

तस्योष्णिगासील्लोमभ्यो गायत्री च त्वचो विभोः ।
त्रिष्टुम्मांसात्स्नुतोऽनुष्टुब्जगत्यस्थ्नः प्रजापतेः ॥४५॥

tasyoṣṇig āsīl lomabhyo
gāyatrī ca tvaco vibhoḥ
triṣṭum māṁsāt snuto 'nuṣṭub
jagaty asthnaḥ prajāpateḥ

tasya—his; *uṣṇik*—one of the Vedic meters; *āsīt*—generated; *lomabhyaḥ*—from the hairs on the body; *gāyatrī*—the principal Vedic hymn; *ca*—also; *tvacaḥ*—from the skin; *vibhoḥ*—of the lord; *triṣṭup*—a particular type of poetic meter; *māṁsāt*—from the flesh; *snutaḥ*—from the sinews; *anuṣṭup*—another type of poetic meter; *jagatī*—another type of poetic meter; *asthnaḥ*—from the bones; *prajāpateḥ*—of the father of the living entities.

TRANSLATION

Thereafter the art of literary expression, uṣṇik, was generated from the hairs on the body of the almighty Prajāpati. The principal Vedic hymn, gāyatrī, was generated from the skin, triṣṭup from the flesh, anuṣṭup from the veins, and jagatī from the bones of the lord of the living entities.

TEXT 46

मज्जायाः पङ्क्तिरुत्पन्ना बृहती प्राणतोऽभवत् : ॥४६॥

majjāyāḥ paṅktir utpannā
bṛhatī prāṇato 'bhavat

majjāyāḥ—from the bone marrow; *paṅktiḥ*—a particular type of verse; *utpannā*—became manifested; *bṛhatī*—another type of verse; *prāṇataḥ*—out of the life-breathing; *abhavat*—generated.

TRANSLATION

The art of writing verse, paṅkti, became manifested from the bone marrow, and that of bṛhatī, another type of verse, was generated from the life-breath of the lord of the living entities.

TEXT 47

स्पर्शस्तस्याभवज्जीवः स्वरो देह उदाहृत ।
ऊष्माणमिन्द्रियाण्याहुरन्तःस्था बलमात्मनः ।
स्वराः सप्त विहारेण भवन्ति स्म प्रजापतेः ॥४७॥

sparśas tasyābhavaj jīvaḥ
svaro deha udāhṛta
ūṣmāṇam indriyāṇy āhur
antaḥ-sthā balam ātmanaḥ
svarāḥ sapta vihāreṇa
bhavanti sma prajāpateḥ

sparśaḥ—the set of letters from *ka* to *ma; tasya*—his; *abhavat*—became; *jīvaḥ*—the soul; *svaraḥ*—vowels; *dehaḥ*—his body; *udāhṛtaḥ*—are expressed; *ūṣmāṇam*—the letters *śa, ṣa, sa* and *ha; indriyāṇi*—the senses; *āhuḥ*—are called; *antaḥ-sthāḥ*—the set of letters so known (*ya, ra, la* and *va*); *balam*—energy; *ātmanaḥ*—of his self; *svarāḥ*—music; *sapta*—seven; *vihāreṇa*—by the sensual activities; *bhavanti sma*—became manifested; *prajāpateḥ*—of the lord of the living entities.

TRANSLATION

Brahmā's soul was manifested as the touch alphabets, his body as the vowels, his senses as the sibilant alphabets, his strength as the intermediate alphabets and his sensual activities as the seven notes of music.

PURPORT

In Sanskrit there are thirteen vowels and thirty-five consonants. The vowels are *a, ā, i, ī, u, ū, ṛ, ṝ, ḷ, e, ai, o, au*, and the consonants are *ka, kha, ga, gha*, etc. Amongst the consonants, the first twenty-five letters are called the *sparśas*. There are also four *antaḥ-sthas*. Of the *ūṣmas* there are three *s*'s, called *tālavya, mūrdhanya* and *dantya*. The musical notes are *ṣa, ṛ, gā, ma, pa, dha* and *ni*. All these sound vibrations are originally called *śabda-brahma*, or spiritual sound. It is said, therefore, that Brahmā was created in the Mahā-kalpa as the incarnation of spiritual sound. The *Vedas* are spiritual sound, and therefore there is no need of material interpretation for the sound vibration of the Vedic literature. The *Vedas* should be vibrated as they are, although they are symbolically represented with letters which are known to us materially. In the ultimate issue there is nothing material because everything has its origin in the spiritual world. The material manifestation is therefore called illusion in the proper sense of the term. For those who are realized souls there is nothing but spirit.

TEXT 48

शब्दब्रह्मात्मनस्तस्य व्यक्providedाव्यक्तात्मनः परः ।
ब्रह्मावभाति विततो नानाशक्त्युपबृंहितः ॥४८॥

śabda-brahmātmanas tasya
vyaktāvyaktātmanaḥ paraḥ

brahmāvabhāti vitato
nānā-śakty-upabṛṁhitaḥ

śabda-brahma—transcendental sound; *ātmanaḥ*—of the Supreme Lord; *tasya*—His; *vyakta*—manifested; *avyakta-ātmanaḥ*—of the unmanifested; *paraḥ*—transcendental; *brahmā*—the Absolute; *avabhāti*—completely manifested; *vitataḥ*—distributing; *nānā*—multifarious; *śakti*—energies; *upabṛṁhitaḥ*—invested with.

TRANSLATION

Brahmā is the personal representation of the Supreme Personality of Godhead as the source of transcendental sound and is therefore above the conception of manifested and unmanifested. Brahmā is the complete form of the Absolute Truth and is invested with multifarious energies.

PURPORT

The post of Brahmā is the highest responsible post within the universe, and it is offered to the most perfect personality of the universe. Sometimes the Supreme Personality of Godhead has to become Brahmā when there is no suitable living being to occupy the post. In the material world, Brahmā is the complete representation of the Supreme Personality of Godhead, and transcendental sound, *praṇava*, comes from him. He is therefore invested with multifarious energies, from which all the demigods like Indra, Candra and Varuṇa are manifested. His transcendental value is not to be minimized, even though he exhibited a tendency to enjoy his own daughter. There is a purpose for the exhibition of such a tendency by Brahmā, and he is not to be condemned like an ordinary living entity.

TEXT 49

ततोऽपरामुपादाय स सर्गाय मनो दधे ॥४९॥

tato 'parām upādāya
sa sargāya mano dadhe

tataḥ—thereafter; *aparām*—another; *upādāya*—having accepted; *saḥ*—he; *sargāya*—in the matter of creation; *manaḥ*—mind; *dadhe*—gave attention.

TRANSLATION

Thereafter Brahmā accepted another body, in which sex life was not forbidden, and thus he engaged himself in the matter of further creation.

PURPORT

In his former body, which was transcendental, affection for sex life was forbidden, and Brahmā therefore had to accept another body to allow himself to be connected with sex. He thus engaged himself in the matter of creation. His former body transformed into fog, as previously described.

TEXT 50

ऋषीणां भूरिवीर्याणामपि सर्गमविस्तृतम् ।
ज्ञात्वा तद्धृदये भूयश्चिन्तयामास कौरव ॥५०॥

ṛṣīṇāṁ bhūri-vīryāṇām
api sargam avistṛtam
jñātvā tad dhṛdaye bhūyaś
cintayām āsa kaurava

ṛṣīṇām—of the great sages; *bhūri-vīryāṇām*—with great potential power; *api*—in spite of; *sargam*—the creation; *avistṛtam*—not extended; *jñātvā*—knowing; *tat*—that; *hṛdaye*—in his heart; *bhūyaḥ*—again; *cintayām āsa*—he began to consider; *kaurava*—O son of the Kurus.

TRANSLATION

O son of the Kurus, when Brahmā saw that in spite of the presence of sages of great potency there was no sufficient increase in population, he seriously began to consider how the population could be increased.

TEXT 51

अहो अद्भुतमेतन्मे व्यापृतस्यापि नित्यदा ।
न ह्येधन्ते प्रजा नूनं दैवमत्र विघातकम् ॥५१॥

aho adbhutam etan me
vyāpṛtasyāpi nityadā

na hy edhante prajā nūnaṁ
daivam atra vighātakam

aho—alas; *adbhutam*—it is wonderful; *etat*—this; *me*—for me; *vyāpṛtasya*—being busy; *api*—although; *nityadā*—always; *na*—does not; *hi*—certainly; *edhante*—generate; *prajāḥ*—living entities; *nūnam*—however; *daivam*—destiny; *atra*—herein; *vighātakam*—against.

TRANSLATION

Brahmā thought to himself: Alas, it is wonderful that in spite of my being scattered all over, there is still insufficient population throughout the universe. There is no other cause for this misfortune but destiny.

TEXT 52

एवं युक्तकृतस्तस्य दैवञ्चावेक्षतस्तदा ।
कस्य रूपमभूद् द्वेधा यत्कायमभिचक्षते ॥५२॥

evaṁ yukta-kṛtas tasya
daivaṁ cāvekṣatas tadā
kasya rūpam abhūd dvedhā
yat kāyam abhicakṣate

evam—thus; *yukta*—contemplating; *kṛtaḥ*—while doing so; *tasya*—his; *daivam*—supernatural power; *ca*—also; *avekṣataḥ*—observing; *tadā*—at that time; *kasya*—of Brahmā; *rūpam*—form; *abhūt*—became manifested; *dvedhā*—twofold; *yat*—which is; *kāyam*—his body; *abhicakṣate*—is said to be.

TRANSLATION

While he was thus absorbed in contemplation and was observing the supernatural power, two other forms were generated from his body. They are still celebrated as the body of Brahmā.

PURPORT

Two bodies came out from the body of Brahmā. One had a mustache, and the other had swollen breasts. No one can explain the source of their manifestation, and therefore until today they are known as the *kāyam*, or the body of Brahmā, with no indication of their relationship as his son or daughter.

TEXT 53

ताभ्यां रूपविभागाभ्यां मिथुनं समपद्यत ॥५३॥

tābhyāṁ rūpa-vibhāgābhyāṁ
mithunaṁ samapadyata

tābhyām—of them; *rūpa*—form; *vibhāgābhyām*—thus being divided; *mithunam*—sex relation; *samapadyata*—perfectly executed.

TRANSLATION

The two newly separated bodies united together in a sexual relationship.

TEXT 54

यस्तु तत्र पुमान् सोऽभून्मनुः स्वायम्भुवः स्वराट् ।
स्त्री यासीच्छतरूपाख्या महिष्यस्य महात्मनः ॥५४॥

yas tu tatra pumān so 'bhūn
manuḥ svāyambhuvaḥ svarāṭ
strī yāsīc chatarūpākhyā
mahiṣy asya mahātmanaḥ

yaḥ—one who; *tu*—but; *tatra*—there; *pumān*—the male; *saḥ*—he; *abhūt*—became; *manuḥ*—the father of mankind; *svāyambhuvaḥ*—of the name Svāyambhuva; *sva-rāṭ*—fully independent; *strī*—the woman; *yā*—one who; *āsīt*—there was; *śatarūpā*—of the name Śatarūpā; *ākhyā*—known as; *mahiṣī*—the queen; *asya*—of him; *mahātmanaḥ*—the great soul.

TRANSLATION

Out of them, the one who had the male form became known as the Manu named Svāyambhuva, and the woman became known as Śatarūpā, the queen of the great soul Manu.

TEXT 55

तदा मिथुनधर्मेण प्रजा ह्येधाम्बभूविरे ॥५५॥

tadā mithuna-dharmeṇa
prajā hy edhām babhūvire

tadā—at that time; *mithuna*—sex life; *dharmeṇa*—according to regulative principles; *prajāḥ*—generations; *hi*—certainly; *edhām*—increased; *babhūvire*—took place.

TRANSLATION

Thereafter, by sex indulgence, they gradually increased generations of population one after another.

TEXT 56

स चापि शतरूपायां पञ्चापत्यान्यजीजनत् ।
प्रियव्रतोत्तानपादौ तिस्रः कन्याश्च भारत ।
आकूतिर्देवहूतिश्च प्रसूतिरिति सत्तम ॥५६॥

sa cāpi śatarūpāyāṁ
pañcāpatyāny ajījanat
priyavratottānapādau
tisraḥ kanyāś ca bhārata
ākūtir devahūtiś ca
prasūtir iti sattama

saḥ—he (Manu); *ca*—also; *api*—in due course; *śatarūpāyām*—unto Śatarūpā; *pañca*—five; *apatyāni*—children; *ajījanat*—begot; *priyavrata*—Priyavrata; *uttānapādau*—Uttānapāda; *tisraḥ*—three in number; *kanyāḥ*—daughters; *ca*—also; *bhārata*—O son of Bharata; *ākūtiḥ*—Ākūti; *devahūtiḥ*—Devahūti; *ca*—and; *prasūtiḥ*—Prasūti; *iti*—thus; *sattama*—O best of all.

TRANSLATION

O son of Bharata, in due course of time he [Manu] begot in Śatarūpā five children—two sons, Priyavrata and Uttānapāda, and three daughters, Ākūti, Devahūti and Prasūti.

TEXT 57

आकूतिं रुचये प्रादात्कर्दमाय तु मध्यमाम् ।
दक्षायादात्प्रसूतिं च यत आपूरितं जगत् ॥५७॥

ākūtiṁ rucaye prādāt
kardamāya tu madhyamām
dakṣāyādāt prasūtiṁ ca
yata āpūritaṁ jagat

ākūtim—the daughter named Ākūti; *rucaye*—unto the sage Ruci; *prādāt*—handed over; *kardamāya*—unto the sage Kardama; *tu*—but; *madhyamām*—the middle one (Devahūti); *dakṣāya*—unto Dakṣa; *adāt*—handed over; *prasūtim*—the youngest daughter; *ca*—also; *yataḥ*—wherefrom; *āpūritam*—is fulfilled; *jagat*—the whole world.

TRANSLATION

The father, Manu, handed over his first daughter, Ākūti, to the sage Ruci, the middle daughter, Devahūti, to the sage Kardama, and the youngest, Prasūti, to Dakṣa. From them, all the world filled with population.

PURPORT

The history of the creation of the population of the universe is given herewith. Brahmā is the original living creature in the universe, from whom were generated the Manu Svāyambhuva and his wife Śatarūpā. From Manu, two sons and three daughters were born, and from them all the population in different planets has sprung up until now. Therefore, Brahmā is known as the grandfather of everyone, and the Personality of Godhead, being the father of Brahmā, is known as the great-grandfather of all living beings. This is confirmed in *Bhagavad-gītā* (11.39) as follows:

vāyur yamo 'gnir varuṇaḥ śaśāṅkaḥ
prajāpatis tvaṁ prapitāmahaś ca
namo namas te 'stu sahasra-kṛtvaḥ
punaś ca bhūyo 'pi namo namas te

"You are the Lord of air, the supreme justice Yama, the fire, and the Lord of rains. You are the moon, and You are the great-grandfather. Therefore I offer my respectful obeisances unto You again and again."

Thus end the Bhaktivedanta purports of the Third Canto, Twelfth Chapter, of the Śrīmad-Bhāgavatam, *entitled "Creation of the Kumāras and Others."*

CHAPTER THIRTEEN

The Appearance of Lord Varāha

TEXT 1

श्रीशुक उवाच
निशम्य वाचं वदतो मुनेः पुण्यतमां नृप ।
भूयः पप्रच्छ कौरव्यो वासुदेवकथादृतः ॥ १ ॥

śrī-śuka uvāca
niśamya vācaṁ vadato
muneḥ puṇyatamāṁ nṛpa
bhūyaḥ papraccha kauravyo
vāsudeva-kathādṛtaḥ

śrī-śukaḥ uvāca—Śrī Śukadeva Gosvāmī said; *niśamya*—after hearing; *vācam*—talks; *vadataḥ*—while speaking; *muneḥ*—of Maitreya Muni; *puṇya-tamām*—the most virtuous; *nṛpa*—O King; *bhūyaḥ*—then again; *papraccha*—inquired; *kauravyaḥ*—the best amongst the Kurus (Vidura); *vāsudeva-kathā*—topics on the subject of the Personality of Godhead, Vāsudeva; *ādṛtaḥ*—one who so adores.

TRANSLATION

Śrī Śukadeva Gosvāmī said: O King, after hearing all these most virtuous topics from the sage Maitreya, Vidura inquired further on the topics of the Supreme Personality of Godhead, which he adored to hear.

PURPORT

The word *ādṛtaḥ* is significant because it indicates that Vidura had a natural inclination for hearing the transcendental message of the Supreme Personality of Godhead, and he was never fully satisfied though continuing to hear those topics. He wanted to hear more and more so that he could be more and more blessed by the transcendental message.

TEXT 2

विदुर उवाच

स वै स्वायम्भुवः सम्राट् प्रियः पुत्रः स्वयम्भुवः ।
प्रतिलभ्य प्रियां पत्नीं किं चकार ततो मुने ॥ २ ॥

vidura uvāca
sa vai svāyambhuvaḥ samrāṭ
priyaḥ putraḥ svayambhuvaḥ
pratilabhya priyāṁ patnīṁ
kiṁ cakāra tato mune

viduraḥ uvāca—Vidura said; *saḥ*—he; *vai*—easily; *svāyambhuvaḥ*—Svāyambhuva Manu; *samrāṭ*—the king of all kings; *priyaḥ*—dear; *putraḥ*—son; *svayambhuvaḥ*—of Brahmā; *pratilabhya*—after obtaining; *priyām*—most loving; *patnīm*—wife; *kim*—what; *cakāra*—did; *tataḥ*—thereafter; *mune*—O great sage.

TRANSLATION

Vidura said: O great sage, what did Svāyambhuva, the dear son of Brahmā, do after obtaining his very loving wife?

TEXT 3

चरितं तस्य राजर्षेरादिराजस्य सत्तम ।
ब्रूहि मे श्रद्दधानाय विष्वक्सेनाश्रयो ह्यसौ ॥ ३ ॥

caritaṁ tasya rājarṣer
ādi-rājasya sattama
brūhi me śraddadhānāya
viṣvaksenāśrayo hy asau

caritam—character; *tasya*—his; *rājarṣeḥ*—of the saintly king; *ādi-rājasya*—of the original king; *sattama*—O most pious one; *brūhi*—kindly speak; *me*—unto me; *śraddadhānāya*—unto one eager to receive; *viṣvaksena*—of the Personality of Godhead; *āśrayaḥ*—one who has taken shelter; *hi*—certainly; *asau*—that king.

TRANSLATION

O best of the virtuous, the original king of kings [Manu] was a great devotee of the Personality of Godhead Hari, and thus it is worth hearing of his sublime character and activities. Please describe them. I am very eager to hear.

PURPORT

Śrīmad-Bhāgavatam is full of the transcendental topics of the Personality of Godhead and His pure devotees. In the absolute world there is no difference in quality between the Supreme Lord and His pure devotee. Therefore, hearing the topics of the Lord and hearing of the character and activities of the pure devotee have the same result, namely, the development of devotional service.

TEXT 4

श्रुतस्य पुंसां सुचिरश्रमस्य
नन्वञ्जसा सूरिभिरीडितोऽर्थः ।
तत्तद्गुणानुश्रवणं मुकुन्द-
पादारविन्दं हृदयेषु येषाम् ॥ ४ ॥

śrutasya puṁsāṁ sucira-śramasya
nanv añjasā sūribhir īḍito 'rthaḥ
tat-tad-guṇānuśravaṇaṁ mukunda-
pādāravindaṁ hṛdayeṣu yeṣām

śrutasya—of persons who are in the process of hearing; *puṁsām*—of such persons; *sucira*—for a long time; *śramasya*—laboring very hard; *nanu*—certainly *añjasā*—elaborately; *sūribhiḥ*—by pure devotees; *īḍitaḥ*—explained by; *arthaḥ*—statements; *tat*—that; *tat*—that; *guṇa*—transcendental qualities; *anuśravaṇam*—thinking; *mukunda*—the Personality of Godhead, who awards liberation; *pāda-aravindam*—the lotus feet; *hṛdayeṣu*—within the heart; *yeṣām*—of them.

TRANSLATION

Persons who hear from a spiritual master with great labor and for a long time must hear from the mouths of pure devotees about

the character and activities of pure devotees. Pure devotees always think within their hearts of the lotus feet of the Personality of Godhead, who awards His devotees liberation.

PURPORT

Transcendental students are those who undergo great penance in being trained by hearing the *Vedas* from a bona fide spiritual master. Not only must they hear about the activities of the Lord, but they must also hear about the transcendental qualities of the devotees who are constantly thinking of the lotus feet of the Lord within their hearts. A pure devotee of the Lord cannot be separated from the lotus feet of the Lord for even a moment. Undoubtedly the Lord is always within the hearts of all living creatures, but they hardly know about it because they are deluded by the illusory material energy. The devotees, however, realize the presence of the Lord, and therefore they can always see the lotus feet of the Lord within their hearts. Such pure devotees of the Lord are as glorious as the Lord; they are, in fact, recommended by the Lord as more worshipable then He Himself. Worship of the devotee is more potent than worship of the Lord. It is therefore the duty of the transcendental students to hear of pure devotees, as explained by similar devotees of the Lord, because one cannot explain about the Lord or His devotee unless one happens to be a pure devotee himself.

TEXT 5

श्रीशुक उवाच

इति ब्रुवाणं विदुरं विनीतं
सहस्रशीर्ष्णश्चरणोपधानम् ।
प्रहृष्टरोमा भगवत्कथायां
प्रणीयमानो मुनिरभ्यचष्ट ॥ ५ ॥

śrī-śuka uvāca
iti bruvāṇaṁ viduraṁ vinītaṁ
sahasra-śīrṣṇaś caraṇopadhānam
prahṛṣṭa-romā bhagavat-kathāyāṁ
praṇīyamāno munir abhyacaṣṭa

śrī-śukaḥ uvāca—Śrī Śukadeva Gosvāmī said; *iti*—thus; *bruvāṇam*—speaking; *viduram*—unto Vidura; *vinītam*—very gentle; *sahasra-śīrṣṇaḥ*—the Personality of Godhead Kṛṣṇa; *caraṇa*—lotus feet; *upadhānam*—pillow; *prahṛṣṭa-romā*—hairs standing in ecstasy; *bhagavat*—in relationship with the Personality of Godhead; *kathāyām*—in the words; *praṇīyamānaḥ*—being influenced by such spirit; *muniḥ*—the sage; *abhyacaṣṭa*—attempted to speak.

TRANSLATION

Śrī Śukadeva Gosvāmī said: The Personality of Godhead Śrī Kṛṣṇa was pleased to place His lotus feet on the lap of Vidura because Vidura was very meek and gentle. The sage Maitreya was very pleased with Vidura's words, and, being influenced by his spirit, he attempted to speak.

PURPORT

The word *sahasra-śīrṣṇaḥ* is very significant. One who has diverse energies and activities and a wonderful brain is known as the *sahasra-śīrṣṇaḥ.* This qualification is applicable only to the Personality of Godhead, Śrī Kṛṣṇa, and no one else. The Personality of Godhead was pleased to dine sometimes with Vidura at his home, and while resting He placed His lotus feet on the lap of Vidura. Maitreya was inspired by the thought of Vidura's wonderful fortune. The hairs of his body stood on end, and he was pleased to narrate the topics of the Personality of Godhead with great delight.

TEXT 6

मैत्रेय उवाच
यदा स्वभार्यया सार्धं जातः स्वायम्भुवो मनुः ।
प्राञ्जलिः प्रणतश्चेदं वेदगर्भमभाषत ॥ ६ ॥

maitreya uvāca
yadā sva-bhāryayā sārdhaṁ
jātaḥ svāyambhuvo manuḥ
prāñjaliḥ praṇataś cedaṁ
veda-garbham abhāṣata

maitreyaḥ uvāca—Maitreya said; *yadā*—when; *sva-bhāryayā*—along with his wife; *sārdham*—accompanied by; *jātaḥ*—appeared; *svāyambhuvaḥ*—Svāyambhuva Manu; *manuḥ*—the father of mankind; *prāñjaliḥ*—with folded hands; *praṇataḥ*—in obeisances; *ca*—also; *idam*—this; *veda-garbham*—unto the reservoir of Vedic wisdom; *abhāṣata*—addressed.

TRANSLATION

The sage Maitreya said to Vidura: After his appearance, Manu, the father of mankind, along with his wife, thus addressed the reservoir of Vedic wisdom, Brahmā, with obeisances and folded hands.

TEXT 7

त्वमेकः सर्वभूतानां जन्मकृद् वृत्तिदः पिता ।
तथापि नः प्रजानां ते शुश्रूषा केन वा भवेत् ॥ ७ ॥

tvam ekaḥ sarva-bhūtānāṁ
janma-kṛd vṛttidaḥ pitā
tathāpi naḥ prajānāṁ te
śuśrūṣā kena vā bhavet

tvam—you; *ekaḥ*—one; *sarva*—all; *bhūtānām*—living entities; *janma-kṛt*—progenitor; *vṛtti-daḥ*—source of subsistence; *pitā*—the father; *tathā api*—yet; *naḥ*—ourselves; *prajānām*—of all who are born; *te*—of you; *śuśrūṣā*—service; *kena*—how; *vā*—either; *bhavet*—may be possible.

TRANSLATION

You are the father of all living entities and the source of their subsistence because they are all born of you. Please order us how we may be able to render service unto you.

PURPORT

A son's duty is not only to make the father the source of supply for all his needs, but also, when he is grown up, to render service unto him. That is the law of creation beginning from the time of Brahmā. A father's duty is to bring up the son until he is grown, and when the son is grown up, it is his duty to render service unto the father.

TEXT 8

तद्विधेहि नमस्तुभ्यं कर्मस्वीड्यात्मशक्तिषु ।
यत्कृत्वेह यशो विष्वगमुत्र च भवेद्गतिः ॥ ८ ॥

tad vidhehi namas tubhyaṁ
karmasv īḍyātma-śaktiṣu
yat kṛtveha yaśo viṣvag
amutra ca bhaved gatiḥ

tat—that; *vidhehi*—give direction; *namaḥ*—my obeisances; *tubhyam*—unto you; *karmasu*—in duties; *īḍya*—O worshipful one; *ātma-śaktiṣu*—within our working capacity; *yat*—which; *kṛtvā*—doing; *iha*—in this world; *yaśaḥ*—fame; *viṣvak*—everywhere; *amutra*—in the next world; *ca*—and; *bhavet*—it should be; *gatiḥ*—progress.

TRANSLATION

O worshipful one, please give us your direction for the execution of duty within our working capacity so that we can follow it for fame in this life and progress in the next.

PURPORT

Brahmā is the direct recipient of Vedic knowledge from the Personality of Godhead, and anyone discharging his entrusted duties in disciplic succession from Brahmā is sure to gain fame in this life and salvation in the next. The disciplic succession from Brahmā is called the Brahma-sampradāya, and it descends as follows: Brahmā, Nārada, Vyāsa, Madhva Muni (Pūrṇaprajña), Padmanābha, Nṛhari, Mādhava, Akṣobhya, Jayatīrtha, Jñānasindhu, Dayānidhi, Vidyānidhi, Rājendra, Jayadharma, Puruṣottama, Brahmaṇyatīrtha, Vyāsatīrtha, Lakṣmīpati, Mādhavendra Purī, Īśvara Purī, Śrī Caitanya Mahāprabhu, Svarūpa Dāmodara and Śrī Rūpa Gosvāmī and others, Śrī Raghunātha dāsa Gosvāmī, Kṛṣṇadāsa Gosvāmī, Narottama dāsa Ṭhākura, Viśvanātha Cakravartī, Jagannātha dāsa Bābājī, Bhaktivinoda Ṭhākura, Gaurakiśora dāsa Bābājī, Śrīmad Bhaktisiddhānta Sarasvatī, A. C. Bhaktivedanta Swami.

This line of disciplic succession from Brahmā is spiritual, whereas the genealogical succession from Manu is material, but both are on the progressive march towards the same goal of Kṛṣṇa consciousness.

TEXT 9

ब्रह्मोवाच
प्रीतस्तुभ्यमहं तात स्वस्ति स्ताद्वां क्षितीश्वर ।
यन्निर्व्यलीकेन हृदा शाधि मेत्यात्मनार्पितम् ॥ ९ ॥

brahmovāca
prītas tubhyam ahaṁ tāta
svasti stād vāṁ kṣitīśvara
yan nirvyalīkena hṛdā
śādhi mety ātmanārpitam

brahmā uvāca—Brahmā said; *prītaḥ*—pleased; *tubhyam*—unto you; *aham*—I; *tāta*—my dear son; *svasti*—all blessings; *stāt*—let there be; *vām*—unto you both; *kṣiti-īśvara*—O lord of the world; *yat*—because; *nirvyalīkena*—without reservation; *hṛdā*—by the heart; *śādhi*—give instruction; *mā*—unto me; *iti*—thus; *ātmanā*—by self; *arpitam*—surrendered.

TRANSLATION

Lord Brahmā said: My dear son, O lord of the world, I am very pleased with you, and I desire all blessings for both you and your wife. You have without reservation surrendered yourself unto me with your heart for my instructions.

PURPORT

The relationship between the father and the son is always sublime. The father is naturally disposed with good will towards the son, and he is always ready to help the son in his progress in life. But in spite of the father's good will, the son is sometimes misguided because of his misuse of personal independence. Every living entity, however small or big he may be, has the choice of independence. If the son is unreservedly willing to be guided by the father, the father is ten times more eager to instruct and guide him by all means. The father and son relationship as exhibited here in the dealings of Brahmā and Manu is excellent. Both the father and the son are well qualified, and their example should be followed by all humankind. Manu, the son, unreservedly asked the father, Brahmā, to instruct him, and the father, who was full of Vedic wisdom, was very glad to instruct. The example of the father of mankind may be rigidly followed by mankind, and that will advance the cause of the relationship of fathers and sons.

TEXT 10

एतावत्यात्मजैर्वीर कार्या ह्यपचितिर्गुरौ ।
शक्त्याप्रमत्तैर्गृह्येत सादरं गतमत्सरैः ॥१०॥

etāvaty ātmajair vīra
kāryā hy apacitir gurau
śaktyāpramattair gṛhyeta
sādaraṁ gata-matsaraiḥ

etāvatī—just exactly like this; *ātmajaiḥ*—by the offspring; *vīra*—O hero; *kāryā*—should be performed; *hi*—certainly; *apacitiḥ*—worship; *gurau*—unto the superior; *śaktyā*—with full capacity; *apramattaiḥ*—by the sane; *gṛhyeta*—should be accepted; *sa-ādaram*—with great delight; *gata-matsaraiḥ*—by those who are beyond the limit of envy.

TRANSLATION

O hero, your example is quite befitting a son in relationship with his father. This sort of adoration for the superior is required. One who is beyond the limit of envy and who is sane accepts the order of his father with great delight and executes it to his full capacity.

PURPORT

When the four previous sons of Brahmā, the sages Sanaka, Sanātana, Sanandana and Sanat-kumāra, refused to obey their father, Brahmā was mortified, and his anger was manifested in the shape of Rudra. That incident was not forgotten by Brahmā, and therefore the obedience of Manu Svāyambhuva was very encouraging. From the material point of view, the four sages' disobedience to the order of their father was certainly abominable, but because such disobedience was for a higher purpose, they were free from the reaction of disobedience. Those who disobey their fathers on material grounds, however, are surely subjected to disciplinary reaction for such disobedience. Manu's obedience to his father on material grounds was certainly free from envy, and in the material world it is imperative for ordinary men to follow the example of Manu.

TEXT 11

स त्वमस्यामपत्यानि सदृशान्यात्मनो गुणैः ।
उत्पाद्य शास धर्मेण गां यज्ञैः पुरुषं यज ॥११॥

sa tvam asyām apatyāni
sadṛśāny ātmano guṇaiḥ
utpādya śāsa dharmeṇa
gāṁ yajñaiḥ puruṣaṁ yaja

saḥ—therefore that obedient son; *tvam*—as you are; *asyām*—in her; *apatyāni*—children; *sadṛśāni*—equally qualified; *ātmanaḥ*—of yourself; *guṇaiḥ*—with the characteristics; *utpādya*—having begotten; *śāsa*—rule; *dharmeṇa*—on the principles of devotional service; *gām*—the world; *yajñaiḥ*—by sacrifices; *puruṣam*—the Supreme Personality of Godhead; *yaja*—worship.

TRANSLATION

Since you are my very obedient son, I ask you to beget children qualified like yourself in the womb of your wife. Rule the world in pursuance of the principles of devotional service unto the Supreme Personality of Godhead, and thus worship the Lord by performances of yajña.

PURPORT

The purpose of the material creation by Brahmā is clearly described herein. Every human being should beget nice children in the womb of his wife, as a sacrifice for the purpose of worshiping the Supreme Personality of Godhead in devotional service. In the *Viṣṇu Purāṇa* (3.8.9) it is stated:

varṇāśramācāravatā
puruṣeṇa paraḥ pumān
viṣṇur ārādhyate panthā
nānyat tat-toṣa-kāraṇam

"One can worship the Supreme Personality of Godhead, Viṣṇu, by proper discharge of the principles of *varṇa* and *āśrama.* There is no alternative to pacifying the Lord by execution of the principles of the *varṇāśrama* system."

Viṣṇu worship is the ultimate aim of human life. Those who take the license of married life for sense enjoyment must also take the responsibility to satisfy the Supreme Personality of Godhead, Viṣṇu, and the first stepping-stone is the *varṇāśrama-dharma* system. *Varṇāśrama-dharma* is the systematic institution for advancing in worship of Viṣṇu. However, if one directly engages in the process of devotional service to the Supreme Personality of Godhead, it may not be necessary to undergo the disciplinary system of *varṇāśrama-dharma.* The other sons of Brahmā, the Kumāras, directly engaged in devotional service, and thus they had no need to execute the principles of *varṇāśrama-dharma.*

TEXT 12

परं शुश्रूषणं मह्यं स्यात्प्रजारक्षया नृप ।
भगवांस्ते प्रजाभर्तुर्हृषीकेशोऽनुतुष्यति ॥१२॥

paraṁ śuśrūṣaṇaṁ mahyaṁ
syāt prajā-rakṣayā nṛpa
bhagavāṁs te prajā-bhartur
hṛṣīkeśo 'nutuṣyati

param—the greatest; *śuśrūṣaṇam*—devotional service; *mahyam*—unto me; *syāt*—should be; *prajā*—the living entities born in the material world; *rakṣayā*—by saving them from being spoiled; *nṛpa*—O King; *bhagavān*—the Personality of Godhead; *te*—with you; *prajā-bhartuḥ*—with the protector of the living beings; *hṛṣīkeśaḥ*—the Lord of the senses; *anutuṣyati*—is satisfied.

TRANSLATION

O King, if you can give proper protection to the living beings in the material world, that will be the best service for me. When the Supreme Lord sees you to be a good protector of the conditioned souls, certainly the master of the senses will be very pleased with you.

PURPORT

The whole administrative system is arranged for the purpose of going back home, back to Godhead. Brahmā is the representative of the Supreme Personality of Godhead, and Manu is the representative of Brahmā. Similarly, all other kings on different planets of the universe are representatives of Manu. The lawbook for the entire human society is the *Manu-saṁhitā*, which directs all activities towards the transcendental service of the Lord. Every king, therefore, must know that his responsibility in administration is not merely to exact taxes from the citizens but to see personally that the citizens under him are being trained in Viṣṇu worship. Everyone must be educated in Viṣṇu worship and engaged in the devotional service of Hṛṣīkeśa, the owner of the senses. The conditioned souls are meant not to satisfy their material senses but to satisfy the senses of Hṛṣīkeśa, the Supreme Personality of Godhead. That is the purpose of the complete administrative system. One who knows this secret, as disclosed here in the version of Brahmā, is the perfect administrative head. One who does not know this is a show-bottle administrator. By training the citizens in the devotional service of the Lord, the head of a state can be free in his responsibility, otherwise he will fail in the onerous duty entrusted to him and thus be punishable by the supreme authority. There is no other alternative in the discharge of administrative duty.

TEXT 13

येषां न तुष्टो भगवान् यज्ञलिङ्गो जनार्दनः ।
तेषां श्रमो ह्यपार्थाय यदात्मा नादृतः स्वयम् ॥१३॥

yeṣāṁ na tuṣṭo bhagavān
yajña-liṅgo janārdanaḥ
teṣāṁ śramo hy apārthāya
yad ātmā nādṛtaḥ svayam

yeṣām—of those with whom; *na*—never; *tuṣṭaḥ*—satisfied; *bhagavān*—the Personality of Godhead; *yajña-liṅgaḥ*—the form of sacrifice; *janārdanaḥ*—Lord Kṛṣṇa, or the *viṣṇu-tattva; teṣām*—of them; *śramaḥ*—labor; *hi*—certainly; *apārthāya*—without profit; *yat*—because; *ātmā*—the Supreme Soul; *na*—not; *ādṛtaḥ*—respected; *svayam*—his own self.

TRANSLATION

The Supreme Personality of Godhead, Janārdana [Lord Kṛṣṇa], is the form to accept all the results of sacrifice. If He is not satisfied, then one's labor for advancement is futile. He is the ultimate Self, and therefore one who does not satisfy Him certainly neglects his own interests.

PURPORT

Brahmā is deputed as the supreme head of universal affairs, and he in his turn deputes Manu and others as *chargés d'affaires* of the material manifestation, but the whole show is for the satisfaction of the Supreme Personality of Godhead. Brahmā knows how to satisfy the Lord, and similarly persons engaged in the line of Brahmā's plan of activities also know how to satisfy the Lord. The Lord is satisfied by the process of devotional service, consisting of the ninefold process of hearing, chanting, etc. It is in one's own self-interest to execute prescribed devotional service, and anyone who neglects this process neglects his own self-interest. Everyone wants to satisfy his senses, but above the senses is the mind, above the mind is the intelligence, above the intelligence is the individual self, and above the individual self is the Superself. Above even the Superself is the Supreme Personality of Godhead, *viṣṇu-tattva.* The primeval Lord and the cause of all causes is Śrī Kṛṣṇa. The complete process of perfectional service is to render service for the satisfaction of the transcendental senses of Lord Kṛṣṇa, who is known as Janārdana.

TEXT 14

मनुरुवाच

आदेशेऽहं भगवतो वर्तेयामीवसूदन ।
स्थानं त्विहानुजानीहि प्रजानां मम च प्रभो ॥१४॥

manur uvāca
ādeśe 'haṁ bhagavato
varteyāmīva-sūdana
sthānaṁ tv ihānujānīhi
prajānāṁ mama ca prabho

manuḥ uvāca—Śrī Manu said; *ādeśe*—under the order; *aham*—I; *bhagavataḥ*—of your powerful self; *varteya*—shall stay; *amīva-sūdana*—O killer of all sins; *sthānam*—the place; *tu*—but; *iha*—in this world; *anujānīhi*—please let me know; *prajānām*—of the living entities born from me; *mama*—my; *ca*—also; *prabho*—O lord.

TRANSLATION

Śrī Manu said: O all-powerful lord, O killer of all sins, I shall abide by your order. Now please let me know my place and that of the living entities born of me.

TEXT 15

यदोकः सर्वभूतानां मही मग्ना महाम्भसि ।
अस्या उद्धरणे यत्नो देव देव्या विधीयताम् ॥१५॥

yad okaḥ sarva-bhūtānāṁ
mahī magnā mahāmbhasi
asyā uddharaṇe yatno
deva devyā vidhīyatām

yat—because; *okaḥ*—the dwelling place; *sarva*—for all; *bhūtānām*—living entities; *mahī*—the earth; *magnā*—merged; *mahā-ambhasi*—in the great water; *asyāḥ*—of this; *uddharaṇe*—in the lifting; *yatnaḥ*—attempt; *deva*—O master of the demigods; *devyāḥ*—of this earth; *vidhīyatām*—let it be done.

TRANSLATION

O master of the demigods, please attempt to lift the earth, which is merged in the great water, because it is the dwelling place for all

the living entities. It can be done by your endeavor and by the mercy of the Lord.

PURPORT

The great water mentioned in this connection is the Garbhodaka Ocean, which fills half of the universe.

TEXT 16

मैत्रेय उवाच

परमेष्ठी त्वपां मध्ये तथा सन्नामवेक्ष्य गाम् ।
कथमेनां समुन्नेष्य इति दध्यौ धिया चिरम् ॥१६॥

maitreya uvāca
parameṣṭhī tv apāṁ madhye
tathā sannām avekṣya gām
katham enāṁ samunneṣya
iti dadhyau dhiyā ciram

maitreyaḥ uvāca—Śrī Maitreya Muni said; *parameṣṭhī*—Brahmā; *tu*—also; *apām*—the water; *madhye*—within; *tathā*—thus; *sannām*—situated; *avekṣya*—seeing; *gām*—the earth; *katham*—how; *enām*—this; *samunneṣye*—I shall lift; *iti*—thus; *dadhyau*—gave attention; *dhiyā*—by intelligence; *ciram*—for a long time.

TRANSLATION

Śrī Maitreya said: Thus, seeing the earth merged in the water, Brahmā gave his attention for a long time to how it could be lifted.

PURPORT

According to Jīva Gosvāmī, the topics delineated here are of different millenniums. The present topics are of the Śveta-varāha millennium, and topics regarding the Cākṣuṣa millennium will also be discussed in this chapter.

TEXT 17

सृजतो मे क्षितिर्वार्भिः प्लाव्यमाना रसां गता ।
अथात्र किमनुष्ठेयमस्माभिः सर्गयोजितैः ।
यस्याहं हृदयादासं स ईशो विदधातु मे ॥१७॥

sṛjato me kṣitir vārbhiḥ
plāvyamānā rasāṁ gatā
athātra kim anuṣṭheyam
asmābhiḥ sarga-yojitaiḥ
yasyāhaṁ hṛdayād āsaṁ
sa īśo vidadhātu me

sṛjataḥ—while engaged in creation; *me*—of me; *kṣitiḥ*—the earth; *vārbhiḥ*—by the water; *plāvyamānā*—being inundated; *rasām*—depth of water; *gatā*—gone down; *atha*—therefore; *atra*—in this matter; *kim*—what; *anuṣṭheyam*—is right to be attempted; *asmābhiḥ*—by us; *sarga*—creation; *yojitaiḥ*—engaged in; *yasya*—the one from whose; *aham*—I; *hṛdayāt*—from the heart; *āsam*—born; *saḥ*—He; *īśaḥ*—the Lord; *vidadhātu*—may direct; *me*—unto me.

TRANSLATION

Brahmā thought: While I have been engaged in the process of creation, the earth has been inundated by a deluge and has gone down into the depths of the ocean. What can we do who are engaged in this matter of creation? It is best to let the Almighty Lord direct us.

PURPORT

The devotees of the Lord, who are all confidential servitors, are sometimes perplexed in the discharge of their respective duties, but they are never discouraged. They have full faith in the Lord, and He paves the way for the smooth progress of the devotee's duty.

TEXT 18

इत्यभिध्यायतो नासाविवरात्सहसानघ ।
वराहतोको निरगादङ्गुष्ठपरिमाणकः ॥१८॥

ity abhidhyāyato nāsā-
vivarāt sahasānagha
varāha-toko niragād
aṅguṣṭha-parimāṇakaḥ

iti—thus; *abhidhyāyataḥ*—while thinking; *nāsā-vivarāt*—from the nostrils; *sahasā*—all of a sudden; *anagha*—O sinless one; *varāha-tokaḥ*—a minute form of Varāha (a boar); *niragāt*—came out; *aṅguṣṭha*—the upper portion of the thumb; *parimāṇakaḥ*—of the measurement.

TRANSLATION

O sinless Vidura, all of a sudden, while Brahmā was engaged in thinking, a small form of a boar came out of his nostril. The measurement of the creature was not more than the upper portion of a thumb.

TEXT 19

तस्याभिपश्यतः खस्थः क्षणेन किल भारत ।
गजमात्रः प्रववृधे तदद्भुतमभून्महत् ॥१९॥

tasyābhipaśyataḥ kha-sthaḥ
kṣaṇena kila bhārata
gaja-mātraḥ pravavṛdhe
tad adbhutam abhūn mahat

tasya—his; *abhipaśyataḥ*—while thus observing; *kha-sthaḥ*—situated in the sky; *kṣaṇena*—suddenly; *kila*—verily; *bhārata*—O descendant of Bharata; *gaja-mātraḥ*—just like an elephant; *pravavṛdhe*—thoroughly expanded; *tat*—that; *adbhutam*—extraordinary; *abhūt*—transformed; *mahat*—into a gigantic body.

TRANSLATION

O descendant of Bharata, while Brahmā was observing Him, that boar became situated in the sky in a wonderful manifestation as gigantic as a great elephant.

TEXT 20

मरीचिप्रमुखैर्विप्रैः कुमारैर्मनुना सह ।
दृष्ट्वा तत्सौकरं रूपं तर्कयामास चित्रधा ॥२०॥

marīci-pramukhair vipraiḥ
kumārair manunā saha
dṛṣṭvā tat saukaraṁ rūpaṁ
tarkayām āsa citradhā

marīci—the great sage Marīci; *pramukhaiḥ*—headed by; *vipraiḥ*—all *brāhmaṇas; kumāraiḥ*—with the four Kumāras; *manunā*—and with Manu; *saha*—with; *dṛṣṭvā*—seeing; *tat*—that; *saukaram*—appearance like a boar; *rūpam*—form; *tarkayām āsa*—argued among themselves; *citradhā*—in various ways.

TRANSLATION

Struck with wonder at observing the wonderful boarlike form in the sky, Brahmā, with great brāhmaṇas like Marīci, as well as the Kumāras and Manu, began to argue in various ways.

TEXT 21

किमेतत्सूकरव्याजं सत्त्वं दिव्यमवस्थितम् ।
अहो बताश्चर्यमिदं नासाया मे विनिःसृतम् ॥२१॥

kim etat sūkara-vyājaṁ
sattvaṁ divyam avasthitam
aho batāścaryam idaṁ
nāsāyā me viniḥsṛtam

kim—what; *etat*—this; *sūkara*—boar; *vyājam*—pretention; *sattvam*—entity; *divyam*—extraordinary; *avasthitam*—situated; *aho bata*—oh, it is; *āścaryam*—very wonderful; *idam*—this; *nāsāyāḥ*—from the nose; *me*—my; *viniḥsṛtam*—came out.

TRANSLATION

Is this some extraordinary entity come in the pretense of a boar? It is very wonderful that He has come from my nose.

TEXT 22

दृष्टोऽङ्गुष्ठशिरोमात्रः क्षणाद्गण्डशिलासमः ।
अपि स्विद्भगवानेष यज्ञो मे खेदयन्मनः ॥२२॥

dṛṣṭo 'ṅguṣṭha-śiro-mātraḥ
kṣaṇād gaṇḍa-śilā-samaḥ
api svid bhagavān eṣa
yajño me khedayan manaḥ

dṛṣṭaḥ—just seen; *aṅguṣṭha*—thumb; *śiraḥ*—tip; *mātraḥ*—only; *kṣaṇāt*—immediately; *gaṇḍa-śilā*—large stone; *samaḥ*—like; *api svit*—whether; *bhagavān*—the Personality of Godhead; *eṣaḥ*—this; *yajñaḥ*—Viṣṇu; *me*—my; *khedayan*—perturbing; *manaḥ*—mind.

TRANSLATION

First of all this boar was seen no bigger than the tip of a thumb, and within a moment He was as large as a stone. My mind is perturbed. Is He the Supreme Personality of Godhead, Viṣṇu?

PURPORT

Since Brahmā is the supermost person in the universe and he had never before experienced such a form, he could guess that the wonderful appearance of the boar was an incarnation of Viṣṇu. The uncommon features symptomatic of the incarnation of Godhead can bewilder even the mind of Brahmā.

TEXT 23

इति मीमांसतस्तस्य ब्रह्मणः सह सूनुभिः ।
भगवान् यज्ञपुरुषो जगर्जागेन्द्रसन्निभः ॥२३॥

iti mīmāṁsatas tasya
brahmaṇaḥ saha sūnubhiḥ
bhagavān yajña-puruṣo
jagarjāgendra-sannibhaḥ

iti—thus; *mīmāṁsataḥ*—while deliberating; *tasya*—his; *brahmaṇaḥ*—of Brahmā; *saha*—along with; *sūnubhiḥ*—his sons; *bhagavān*—the Personality of Godhead; *yajña*—Lord Viṣṇu; *puruṣaḥ*—the Supreme Person; *jagarja*—resounded; *aga-indra*—great mountain; *sannibhaḥ*—like.

TRANSLATION

While Brahmā was deliberating with his sons, the Supreme Personality of Godhead, Viṣṇu, roared tumultuously like a great mountain.

PURPORT

It appears that great hills and mountains also have their roaring power because they are also living entities. The volume of the sound vibrated is in proportion to the size of the material body. While Brahmā was guessing about the appearance of the Lord's incarnation as a boar, the Lord confirmed Brahmā's contemplation by roaring with His gorgeous voice.

TEXT 24

ब्रह्माणं हर्षयामास हरिस्तांश्च द्विजोत्तमान् ।
स्वगर्जितेन ककुभः प्रतिस्वनयता विभुः ॥२४॥

brahmāṇaṁ harṣayām āsa
haris tāṁś ca dvijottamān
sva-garjitena kakubhaḥ
pratisvanayatā vibhuḥ

brahmāṇam—unto Brahmā; *harṣayām āsa*—enlivened; *hariḥ*—the Personality of Godhead; *tān*—all of them; *ca*—also; *dvija-uttamān*—highly elevated *brāhmaṇas; sva-garjitena*—by His uncommon voice; *kakubhaḥ*—all directions; *pratisvanayatā*—which echoed; *vibhuḥ*—the omnipotent.

TRANSLATION

The omnipotent Supreme Personality of Godhead enlivened Brahmā and the other highly elevated brāhmaṇas by again roaring with His uncommon voice, which echoed in all directions.

PURPORT

Brahmā and other enlightened *brāhmaṇas* who know the Supreme Personality of Godhead are enlivened by the appearance of the Lord in any of His multi-incarnations. The appearance of the wonderful and gigantic incarnation of Viṣṇu as the mountainlike boar did not fill them with any kind of fear, although the Lord's resounding voice was tumultuous and echoed horribly in all directions as an open threat to all demons who might challenge His omnipotency.

TEXT 25

निशम्य ते घर्घरितं स्वखेद-
क्षयिष्णु मायामयसूकरस्य ।
जनस्तपःसत्यनिवासिनस्ते
त्रिभिः पवित्रैर्मुनयोऽगृणन् स्म ॥२५॥

niśamya te ghargharitaṁ sva-kheda-
kṣayiṣṇu māyāmaya-sūkarasya
janas-tapaḥ-satya-nivāsinas te
tribhiḥ pavitrair munayo 'gṛṇan sma

niśamya—just after hearing; *te*—those; *ghargharitam*—the tumultuous sound; *sva-kheda*—personal lamentation; *kṣayiṣṇu*—destroying; *māyā-maya*—all-merciful; *sūkarasya*—of Lord Boar; *janaḥ*—the Janaloka planet; *tapaḥ*—the Tapoloka planet; *satya*—the Satyaloka planet; *nivāsinaḥ*—residents; *te*—all of them; *tribhiḥ*—from the three *Vedas; pavitraiḥ*—by the all-auspicious *mantras; munayaḥ*—great thinkers and sages; *agṛṇan sma*—chanted.

TRANSLATION

When the great sages and thinkers who are residents of Janaloka, Tapoloka and Satyaloka heard the tumultuous voice of

Lord Boar, which was the all-auspicious sound of the all-merciful Lord, they chanted auspicious chants from the three Vedas.

PURPORT

The word *māyāmaya* is very significant in this verse. *Māyā* means "mercy," "specific knowledge" and also "illusion." Therefore Lord Boar is everything; He is merciful, He is all knowledge, and He is illusion also. The sound which He vibrated as the boar incarnation was answered by the Vedic hymns of the great sages in the planets Janaloka, Tapoloka and Satyaloka. The highest intellectual and pious living entities live in those planets, and when they heard the extraordinary voice of the boar, they could understand that the specific sound was vibrated by the Lord and no one else. Therefore they replied by praying to the Lord with Vedic hymns. The earth planet was submerged in the mire, but on hearing the sound of the Lord, the inhabitants of the higher planets were all jubilant because they knew that the Lord was there to deliver the earth. Therefore Brahmā and all the sages, such as Bhṛgu, Brahmā's other sons, and learned *brāhmaṇas*, were enlivened, and they concertedly joined in praising the Lord with the transcendental vibrations of the Vedic hymns. The most important is the *Bṛhan-nāradīya Purāṇa* verse Hare Kṛṣṇa, Hare Kṛṣṇa, Kṛṣṇa Kṛṣṇa, Hare Hare/ Hare Rāma, Hare Rāma, Rāma Rāma, Hare Hare.

TEXT 26

तेषां सतां वेदवितानमूर्ति-
ब्रह्मावधार्यात्मगुणानुवादम् ।
विनद्य भूयो विबुधोदयाय
गजेन्द्रलीलो जलमाविवेश ॥२६॥

teṣāṁ satāṁ veda-vitāna-mūrtir
brahmāvadhāryātma-guṇānuvādam
vinadya bhūyo vibudhodayāya
gajendra-līlo jalam āviveśa

teṣām—of them; *satām*—of the great devotees; *veda*—all knowledge; *vitāna-mūrtiḥ*—the form of expansion; *brahma*—Vedic sound;

avadhārya—knowing it well; *ātma*—of Himself; *guṇa-anuvādam*—transcendental glorification; *vinadya*—resounding; *bhūyaḥ*—again; *vibudha*—of the transcendentally learned; *udayāya*—for the elevation or benefit; *gajendra-līlaḥ*—playing like an elephant; *jalam*—the water; *āviveśa*—entered.

TRANSLATION

Playing like an elephant, He entered into the water after roaring again in reply to the Vedic prayers by the great devotees. The Lord is the object of the Vedic prayers, and thus He understood that the devotees' prayers were meant for Him.

PURPORT

The form of the Lord in any shape is always transcendental and full of knowledge and mercy. The Lord is the destroyer of all material contamination because His form is personified Vedic knowledge. All the *Vedas* worship the transcendental form of the Lord. In the Vedic *mantras* the devotees request the Lord to remove the glaring effulgence because it covers His real face. That is the version of the *Īśopaniṣad.* The Lord has no material form, but His form is always understood in terms of the *Vedas.* The *Vedas* are said to be the breath of the Lord, and that breath was inhaled by Brahmā, the original student of the *Vedas.* The breathing from the nostril of Brahmā caused the appearance of Lord Boar, and therefore the boar incarnation of the Lord is the personified *Vedas.* The glorification of the incarnation by the sages on the higher planets consisted of factual Vedic hymns. Whenever there is glorification of the Lord, it is to be understood that Vedic *mantras* are being rightly vibrated. The Lord was therefore pleased when such Vedic *mantras* were chanted, and to encourage His pure devotees, He roared once more and entered the water to rescue the submerged earth.

TEXT 27

उत्क्षिप्तवालः खचरः कठोरः
सटा विधुन्वन् खररोमशत्वक् ।
खुराहताभ्रः सितदंष्ट्र ईक्षा-
ज्योतिर्बभासे भगवान्महीध्रः ॥२७॥

utkṣipta-vālaḥ kha-caraḥ kaṭhoraḥ
saṭā vidhunvan khara-romaśa-tvak
khurāhatābhraḥ sita-daṁṣṭra īkṣā-
jyotir babhāse bhagavān mahīdhraḥ

utkṣipta-vālaḥ—slashing with the tail; *kha-caraḥ*—in the sky; *kaṭhoraḥ*—very hard; *saṭāḥ*—hairs on the shoulder; *vidhunvan*—quivering; *khara*—sharp; *romaśa-tvak*—skin full of hairs; *khura-āhata*—struck by the hooves; *abhraḥ*—the clouds; *sita-daṁṣṭraḥ*—white tusks; *īkṣā*—glance; *jyotiḥ*—luminous; *babhāse*—began to emit an effulgence; *bhagavān*—the Personality of Godhead; *mahī-dhraḥ*—the supporter of the world.

TRANSLATION

Before entering the water to rescue the earth, Lord Boar flew in the sky, slashing His tail, His hard hairs quivering. His very glance was luminous, and He scattered the clouds in the sky with His hooves and His glittering white tusks.

PURPORT

When the Lord is offered prayers by His devotees, His transcendental activities are described. Here are some of the transcendental features of Lord Boar. As the residents of the upper three planetary systems offered their prayers to the Lord, it is understood that His body expanded throughout the sky, beginning from the topmost planet, Brahmaloka, or Satyaloka. It is stated in the *Brahma-saṁhitā* that His eyes are the sun and the moon; therefore His very glance over the sky was as illuminating as the sun or the moon. The Lord is described herein as *mahīdhrah*, which means either a "big mountain" or the "sustainer of the earth." In other words, the Lord's body was as big and hard as the Himalayan Mountains; otherwise how was it possible that He kept the entire earth on the support of His white tusks? The poet Jayadeva, a great devotee of the Lord, has sung of the incident in his prayers for the incarnations:

vasati daśana-śikhare dharaṇī tava lagnā
śaśini kalaṅka-kaleva nimagnā
keśava dhṛta-śūkara-rūpa jaya jagadīśa hare

"All glories to Lord Keśava [Kṛṣṇa], who appeared as the boar. The earth was held between His tusks, which appeared like the scars on the moon."

TEXT 28

घ्राणेन पृथ्व्याः पदवीं विजिघ्रन्
क्रोडापदेशः स्वयमध्वराङ्गः ।
करालदंष्ट्रोऽप्यकरालदृग्भ्या-
मुद्वीक्ष्य विप्रान् गृणतोऽविशत्कम् ॥२८॥

ghrāṇena pṛthvyāḥ padavīṁ vijighran
kroḍāpadeśaḥ svayam adhvarāṅgaḥ
karāla-daṁṣṭro 'py akarāla-dṛgbhyām
udvīkṣya viprān gṛṇato 'viśat kam

ghrāṇena—by smelling; *pṛthvyāḥ*—of the earth; *padavīm*—situation; *vijighran*—searching after the earth; *kroḍa-apadeśaḥ*—assuming the body of a hog; *svayam*—personally; *adhvara*—transcendental; *aṅgaḥ*—body; *karāla*—fearful; *daṁṣṭraḥ*—teeth (tusks); *api*—in spite of; *akarāla*—not fearful; *dṛgbhyām*—by His glance; *udvīkṣya*—glancing over; *viprān*—all the *brāhmaṇa*-devotees; *gṛṇataḥ*—who were engaged in prayers; *aviśat*—entered; *kam*—the water.

TRANSLATION

He was personally the Supreme Lord Viṣṇu and was therefore transcendental, yet because He had the body of a hog, He searched after the earth by smell. His tusks were fearful, and He glanced over the devotee-brāhmaṇas engaged in offering prayers. Thus He entered the water.

PURPORT

We should always remember that although the body of a hog is material, the hog form of the Lord was not materially contaminated. It is not possible for an earthly hog to assume a gigantic form spreading throughout the sky, beginning from the Satyaloka. His body is always transcendental in all circumstances; therefore, the assumption of the form of a boar is only His pastime. His body is all *Vedas*, or transcendental. But since He had assumed the form of a boar, He began to search out the earth by smelling, just like a hog. The Lord can perfectly play the part of any living entity. The gigantic feature of the boar was certainly very fearful for all nondevotees, but to the pure devotees of the Lord He was not at all fearful; on the contrary, He was so pleasingly glancing upon His devotees that all of them felt transcendental happiness.

TEXT 29

स वज्रकूटाङ्गनिपातवेग-
विशीर्णकुक्षिः स्तनयन्नुदन्वान् ।
उत्सृष्टदीर्घोर्मिभुजैरिवार्त-
श्चुक्रोश यज्ञेश्वर पाहि मेति ॥२९॥

sa vajra-kūṭāṅga-nipāta-vega-
viśīrṇa-kukṣiḥ stanayann udanvān
utsṛṣṭa-dīrghormi-bhujair ivārtaś
cukrośa yajñeśvara pāhi meti

saḥ—that; *vajra-kūṭa-aṅga*—body like a great mountain; *nipāta-vega*—the force of diving; *viśīrṇa*—bifurcating; *kukṣiḥ*—the middle portion; *stanayan*—resounding like; *udanvān*—the ocean; *utsṛṣṭa*—creating; *dīrgha*—high; *ūrmi*—waves; *bhujaiḥ*—by the arms; *iva ārtaḥ*—like a distressed person; *cukrośa*—prayed loudly; *yajña-īśvara*—O master of all sacrifices; *pāhi*—please protect; *mā*—unto me; *iti*—thus.

TRANSLATION

Diving into the water like a giant mountain, Lord Boar divided the middle of the ocean, and two high waves appeared as the arms of the ocean, which cried loudly as if praying to the Lord, "O Lord of all sacrifices, please do not cut me in two! Kindly give me protection!"

PURPORT

Even the great ocean was perturbed by the falling of the mountainlike body of the transcendental boar, and it appeared to be frightened, as if death were imminent.

TEXT 30

खुरैः क्षुरप्रैर्दरयंस्तदाप
उत्पारपारं त्रिपरू रसायाम् ।
ददर्श गां तत्र सुषुप्सुरग्रे
यां जीवधानीं स्वयमभ्यधत्त ॥३०॥

khuraiḥ kṣuraprair darayaṁs tad āpa
utpāra-pāraṁ tri-parū rasāyām
dadarśa gāṁ tatra suṣupsur agre
yāṁ jīva-dhānīṁ svayam abhyadhatta

khuraiḥ—by the hooves; *kṣurapraiḥ*—compared to a sharp weapon; *darayan*—penetrating; *tat*—that; *āpaḥ*—water; *utpāra-pāram*—found the limitation of the unlimited; *tri-paruḥ*—the master of all sacrifices; *rasāyām*—within the water; *dadarśa*—found; *gām*—the earth; *tatra*—there; *suṣupsuḥ*—lying; *agre*—in the beginning; *yām*—whom; *jīva-dhānīm*—the resting place for all living entities; *svayam*—personally; *abhyadhatta*—uplifted.

TRANSLATION

Lord Boar penetrated the water with His hooves, which were like sharp arrows, and found the limits of the ocean, although it was unlimited. He saw the earth, the resting place for all living beings, lying as it was in the beginning of creation, and He personally lifted it.

PURPORT

The word *rasāyām* is sometimes interpreted to mean Rasātala, the lowest planetary system, but that is not applicable in this connection, according to Viśvanātha Cakravartī Ṭhākura. The earth is seven times superior to the other planetary systems, namely Tala, Atala, Talātala, Vitala, Rasātala, Pātāla, etc. Therefore the earth cannot be situated in the Rasātala planetary system. It is described in the *Viṣṇu-dharma:*

pātāla-mūleśvara-bhoga-saṁhatau
vinyasya pādau pṛthivīṁ ca bibhrataḥ
yasyopamāno na babhūva so 'cyuto
mamāstu māṅgalya-vivṛddhaye hariḥ

Therefore the Lord found the earth on the bottom of the Garbhodaka Ocean, where the planets rest during the devastation at the end of Brahmā's day.

TEXT 31

स्वदंष्ट्रयोद्धृत्य महीं निमग्नां
स उत्थितः संरुरुचे रसायाः ।
तत्रापि दैत्यं गदयापतन्तं
सुनाभसन्दीपिततीव्रमन्युः ॥३१॥

sva-daṁṣṭrayoddhṛtya mahīṁ nimagnāṁ
sa utthitaḥ saṁruruce rasāyāḥ
tatrāpi daityaṁ gadayāpatantaṁ
sunābha-sandīpita-tīvra-manyuḥ

sva-daṁṣṭrayā—by His own tusks; *uddhṛtya*—raising; *mahīm*—the earth; *nimagnām*—submerged; *saḥ*—He; *utthitaḥ*—getting up; *saṁruruce*—appeared very splendid; *rasāyāḥ*—from the water; *tatra*—there; *api*—also; *daityam*—unto the demon; *gadayā*—with the club; *āpatantam*—rushing towards Him; *sunābha*—the wheel of Kṛṣṇa; *sandīpita*—glowing; *tīvra*—fierce; *manyuḥ*—anger.

TRANSLATION

Lord Boar very easily took the earth on His tusks and got it out of the water. Thus He appeared very splendid. Then, His anger glowing like the Sudarśana wheel, He immediately killed the demon [Hiraṇyākṣa], although he tried to fight with the Lord.

PURPORT

According to Śrīla Jīva Gosvāmī, the Vedic literatures describe the incarnation of Lord Varāha (Boar) in two different devastations, namely the Cākṣuṣa devastation and the Svāyambhuva devastation. This particular appearance of the boar incarnation actually took place in the Svāyambhuva devastation, when all planets other than the higher ones—Jana, Mahar and Satya—merged in the water of devastation. This particular incarnation of the boar was seen by the inhabitants of the planets mentioned above. Śrīla Viśvanātha Cakravartī suggests that the sage Maitreya amalgamated both the boar incarnations in different devastations and summarized them in his description to Vidura.

TEXT 32

जघान रुन्धानमसह्यविक्रमं
स लीलयेभं मृगराडिवाम्भसि ।
तद्रक्तपङ्काङ्कितगण्डतुण्डो
यथा गजेन्द्रो जगतीं विभिन्दन् ॥३२॥

jaghāna rundhānam asahya-vikramaṁ
sa līlayebhaṁ mṛgarāḍ ivāmbhasi
tad-rakta-paṅkāṅkita-gaṇḍa-tuṇḍo
yathā gajendro jagatīṁ vibhindan

jaghāna—killed; *rundhānam*—the obstructive enemy; *asahya*—unbearable; *vikramam*—prowess; *saḥ*—He; *līlayā*—easily; *ibham*—the elephant; *mṛga-rāṭ*—the lion; *iva*—like; *ambhasi*—in the water; *tat-rakta*—of his blood; *paṅka-aṅkita*—smeared by the pool; *gaṇḍa*—cheeks; *tuṇḍaḥ*—tongue; *yathā*—as if; *gajendraḥ*—the elephant; *jagatīm*—earth; *vibhindan*—digging.

TRANSLATION

Thereupon Lord Boar killed the demon within the water, just as a lion kills an elephant. The cheeks and tongue of the Lord became smeared with the blood of the demon, just as an elephant becomes reddish from digging in the purple earth.

TEXT 33

तमालनीलं सितदन्तकोट्या
क्ष्मामुत्क्षिपन्तं गजलीलयाङ्ग ।
प्रज्ञाय बद्धाञ्जलयोऽनुवाकै-
र्विरिञ्चिमुख्या उपतस्थुरीशम् ॥३३॥

tamāla-nīlaṁ sita-danta-koṭyā
kṣmām utkṣipantaṁ gaja-līlayāṅga
prajñāya baddhāñjalayo 'nuvākair
viriñci-mukhyā upatasthur īśam

tamāla—a blue tree named the *tamāla; nīlam*—bluish; *sita*—white; *danta*—tusks; *koṭyā*—with the curved edge; *kṣmām*—the earth; *utkṣipantam*—while suspending; *gaja-līlayā*—playing like an elephant; *aṅga*—O Vidura; *prajñāya*—after knowing it well; *baddha*—folded; *añjalayaḥ*—hands; *anuvākaiḥ*—by Vedic hymns; *viriñci*—Brahmā; *mukhyāḥ*—headed by; *upatasthuḥ*—offered prayers; *īśam*—unto the Supreme Lord.

TRANSLATION

Then the Lord, playing like an elephant, suspended the earth on the edge of His curved white tusks. He assumed a bluish complexion like that of a tamāla tree, and thus the sages, headed by Brahmā, could understand Him to be the Supreme Personality of Godhead and offered respectful obeisances unto the Lord.

TEXT 34

ऋषय ऊचुः

जितं जितं तेऽजित यज्ञभावन
त्रयीं तनुं स्वां परिधुन्वते नमः ।
यद्रोमगर्तेषु निलिल्युरद्धय-
स्तस्मै नमः कारणसूकराय ते ॥३४॥

ṛṣaya ūcuḥ
jitaṁ jitaṁ te 'jita yajña-bhāvana
trayīṁ tanuṁ svāṁ paridhunvate namaḥ
yad-roma-garteṣu nililyur addhayas
tasmai namaḥ kāraṇa-sūkarāya te

ṛṣayaḥ ūcuḥ—the glorified sages uttered; *jitam*—all glories; *jitam*—all victories; *te*—unto You; *ajita*—O unconquerable one; *yajña-bhāvana*—one who is understood by performances of sacrifice; *trayīm*—personified *Vedas;* *tanum*—such a body; *svām*—own; *paridhunvate*—shaking; *namaḥ*—all obeisances; *yat*—whose; *roma*—hairs; *garteṣu*—in the holes; *nililyuḥ*—submerged; *addhayaḥ*—the oceans; *tasmai*—unto Him; *namaḥ*—offering obeisances; *kāraṇa-sūkarāya*—unto the hog form assumed for reasons; *te*—unto You.

TRANSLATION

All the sages uttered with great respect: O unconquerable enjoyer of all sacrifices, all glories and all victories unto You! You are moving in Your form of the personified Vedas, and in the hair holes of Your body the oceans are submerged. For certain reasons [to uplift the earth] You have now assumed the form of a boar.

PURPORT

The Lord can assume any form He likes, and in all circumstances He is the cause of all causes. Since His form is transcendental, He is always the Supreme Personality of Godhead, as He is in the Causal Ocean in the form of Mahā-Viṣṇu. Innumerable universes generate from the holes of His bodily hairs, and thus His transcendental body is the *Vedas* personified. He is the enjoyer of all sacrifices, and He is the unconquerable Supreme Personality of Godhead. He is never to be misunderstood to be other than the Supreme Lord because of His assuming the form of a boar to lift the earth. That is the clear understanding of sages and great personalities like Brahmā and other residents of the higher planetary systems.

TEXT 35

रूपं तवैतन्ननु दुष्कृतात्मनां
दुर्दर्शनं देव यदध्वरात्मकम् ।
छन्दांसि यस्य त्वचि बर्हिरोम-
स्वाज्यं दृशि त्वङ्घ्रिषु चातुर्होत्रम् ॥३५॥

rūpaṁ tavaitan nanu duṣkṛtātmanāṁ
durdarśanaṁ deva yad adhvarātmakam
chandāṁsi yasya tvaci barhi-romasv
ājyaṁ dṛśi tv aṅghriṣu cātur-hotram

rūpam—form; *tava*—Your; *etat*—this; *nanu*—but; *duṣkṛta-ātmanām*—of souls who are simply miscreants; *durdarśanam*—very difficult to see; *deva*—O Lord; *yat*—that; *adhvara-ātmakam*—worshipable by performances of sacrifice; *chandāṁsi*—the Gāyatrī *mantra* and others; *yasya*—whose; *tvaci*—touch of the skin; *barhiḥ*—sacred grass called *kuśa; romasu*—hairs on the body; *ājyam*—clarified butter; *dṛśi*—in the eyes; *tu*—also; *aṅghriṣu*—on the four legs; *cātuḥ-hotram*—four kinds of fruitive activities.

TRANSLATION

O Lord, Your form is worshipable by performances of sacrifice, but souls who are simply miscreants are unable to see it. All the Vedic hymns, Gāyatrī and others, are in the touch of Your skin. In Your bodily hairs is the kuśa grass, in Your eyes is the clarified butter, and in Your four legs are the four kinds of fruitive activities.

PURPORT

There is a class of miscreants who are known in the words of *Bhagavad-gītā* as *veda-vādī*, or so-called strict followers of the *Vedas.* They do not believe in the incarnation of the Lord, what to speak of the Lord's incarnation as the worshipable hog. They describe worship of the different forms or incarnations of the Lord as anthropomorphism. In the estimation of *Śrīmad-Bhāgavatam* these men are miscreants, and in

Bhagavad-gītā (7.15) they are called not only miscreants but also fools and the lowest of mankind, and it is said that their knowledge has been plundered by illusion due to their atheistic temperament. For such condemned persons, the Lord's incarnation as the gigantic hog is invisible. These strict followers of the *Vedas* who despise the eternal forms of the Lord may know from *Śrīmad-Bhāgavatam* that such incarnations are personified forms of the *Vedas*. Lord Boar's skin, His eyes and His bodily hair holes are all described here as different parts of the *Vedas*. He is therefore the personified form of the Vedic hymns, and specifically the Gāyatrī *mantra*.

TEXT 36

स्रक्तुण्ड आसीत्स्रुव ईश नासयो-
रिडोदरे चमसाः कर्णरन्ध्रे ।
प्राशित्रमास्ये ग्रसने ग्रहास्तु ते
यच्चर्वणं ते भगवन्नग्निहोत्रम् ॥३६॥

srak tuṇḍa āsīt sruva īśa nāsayor
iḍodare camasāḥ karṇa-randhre
prāśitram āsye grasane grahās tu te
yac carvaṇaṁ te bhagavann agni-hotram

srak—the plate for sacrifice; *tuṇḍe*—on the tongue; *āsīt*—there is; *sruvaḥ*—another plate for sacrifice; *īśa*—O Lord; *nāsayoḥ*—of the nostrils; *iḍā*—the plate for eating; *udare*—in the belly; *camasāḥ*—another plate for sacrifices; *karṇa-randhre*—in the holes of the ears; *prāśitram*—the plate called the Brahmā plate; *āsye*—in the mouth; *grasane*—in the throat; *grahāḥ*—the plates known as *soma* plates; *tu*—but; *te*—Your; *yat*—that which; *carvaṇam*—chewing; *te*—Your; *bhagavan*—O my Lord; *agni-hotram*—is Your eating through Your sacrificial fire.

TRANSLATION

O Lord, Your tongue is a plate of sacrifice, Your nostril is another plate of sacrifice, in Your belly is the eating plate of

sacrifice, and another plate of sacrifice is the holes of Your ears. In Your mouth is the Brahmā plate of sacrifice, Your throat is the plate of sacrifice known as soma, and whatever You chew is known as agni-hotra.

PURPORT

The *veda-vādīs* say that there is nothing more than the *Vedas* and the performances of sacrifice mentioned in the *Vedas.* They have recently made a rule in their group to formally observe daily sacrifice; they simply ignite a small fire and offer something whimsically, but they do not strictly follow the sacrificial rules and regulations mentioned in the *Vedas.* It is understood that by regulation there are different plates of sacrifice required, such as *srak, sruvā, barhis, cātur-hotra, iḍā, camasa, prāśitra, graha* and *agni-hotra.* One cannot achieve the results of sacrifice unless one observes the strict regulations. In this age there is practically no facility for performing sacrifices in strict discipline. Therefore, in this age of Kali there is a stricture regarding such sacrifices: it is explicitly directed that one should perform *saṅkīrtana-yajña* and nothing more. The incarnation of the Supreme Lord is Yajñeśvara, and unless one has respect for the incarnation of the Lord, he cannot perfectly perform sacrifice. In other words, taking shelter of the Lord and rendering service unto Him is the factual performance of all sacrifices, as explained herein. Different plates of sacrifice correspond to the different parts of the body of the Lord's incarnation. In the *Śrīmad-Bhāgavatam*, Eleventh Canto, it is explicitly directed that one should perform *saṅkīrtana-yajña* to please the Lord's incarnation as Śrī Caitanya Mahāprabhu. This should be rigidly followed in order to achieve the result of *yajña* performance.

TEXT 37

दीक्षानुजन्मोपसदः शिरोधरं
त्वं प्रायणीयोदयनीयदंष्ट्रः ।
जिह्वा प्रवर्ग्यस्तव शीर्षकं क्रतोः
सत्यावसथ्यं चितयोऽसवो हि ते ॥३७॥

dīkṣānujanmopasadaḥ śirodharaṁ
tvaṁ prāyaṇīyodayanīya-daṁṣṭraḥ
jihvā pravargyas tava śīrṣakaṁ kratoḥ
satyāvasathyaṁ citayo 'savo hi te

dīkṣā—initiation; *anujanma*—spiritual birth, or repeated incarnations; *upasadaḥ*—three kinds of desires (relationship, activities and ultimate goal); *śiraḥ-dharam*—the neck; *tvam*—You; *prāyaṇīya*—after the result of initiation; *udayanīya*—the last rites of desires; *daṁṣṭraḥ*—the tusks; *jihvā*—the tongue; *pravargyaḥ*—prior activities; *tava*—Your; *śīrṣakam*—head; *kratoḥ*—of the sacrifice; *satya*—fire without sacrifice; *āvasathyam*—fire of worship; *citayaḥ*—aggregate of all desires; *asavaḥ*—life breath; *hi*—certainly; *te*—Your.

TRANSLATION

Moreover, O Lord, the repetition of Your appearance is the desire for all kinds of initiation. Your neck is the place for three desires, and Your tusks are the result of initiation and the end of all desires. Your tongue is the prior activities of initiation, Your head is the fire without sacrifice as well as the fire of worship, and Your living forces are the aggregate of all desires.

TEXT 38

सोमस्तु रेतः सवनान्यवस्थितिः
संस्थाविभेदास्तव देव धातवः ।
सत्राणि सर्वाणि शरीरसन्धि-
स्त्वं सर्वयज्ञक्रतुरिष्टिबन्धनः ॥३८॥

somas tu retaḥ savanāny avasthitiḥ
saṁsthā-vibhedās tava deva dhātavaḥ
satrāṇi sarvāṇi śarīra-sandhis
tvaṁ sarva-yajña-kratur iṣṭi-bandhanaḥ

somaḥ tu retaḥ—Your semen is the sacrifice called *soma; savanāni*—ritualistic performances of the morning; *avasthitiḥ*—different statuses of bodily growth; *saṁsthā-vibhedāḥ*—seven varieties of sacrifices; *tava*—Your; *deva*—O Lord; *dhātavaḥ*—ingredients of the body such as skin and flesh; *satrāṇi*—sacrifices performed over twelve days; *sarvāṇi*—all of them; *śarīra*—the bodily; *sandhiḥ*—joints; *tvam*—Your Lordship; *sarva*—all; *yajña*—*asoma* sacrifices; *kratuḥ*—*soma* sacrifices; *iṣṭi*—the ultimate desire; *bandhanaḥ*—attachment.

TRANSLATION

O Lord, Your semen is the sacrifice called soma-yajña. Your growth is the ritualistic performances of the morning. Your skin and touch sensations are the seven elements of the agniṣṭoma sacrifice. Your bodily joints are symbols of various other sacrifices performed in twelve days. Therefore You are the object of all sacrifices called soma and asoma, and You are bound by yajñas only.

PURPORT

There are seven kinds of routine *yajñas* performed by all followers of the Vedic rituals, and they are called *agniṣṭoma, atyagniṣṭoma, uktha, ṣoḍaśī, vājapeya, atirātra* and *āptoryāma.* Anyone performing such *yajñas* regularly is supposed to be situated with the Lord. But anyone who is in contact with the Supreme Lord by discharging devotional service is understood to have performed all different varieties of *yajñas.*

TEXT 39

नमो नमस्तेऽखिलमन्त्रदेवता-
द्रव्याय सर्वक्रतवे क्रियात्मने ।
वैराग्यभक्त्यात्मजयानुभावित-
ज्ञानाय विद्यागुरवे नमो नमः ॥३९॥

namo namas te 'khila-mantra-devatā-
dravyāya sarva-kratave kriyātmane
vairāgya-bhaktyātmajayānubhāvita-
jñānāya vidyā-gurave namo namaḥ

namaḥ namaḥ—obeisances unto You; *te*—unto You, who are worshipable; *akhila*—all-inclusive; *mantra*—hymns; *devatā*—the Supreme Lord; *dravyāya*—unto all ingredients for performing sacrifices; *sarva-kratave*—unto all kinds of sacrifices; *kriyā-ātmane*—unto You, the supreme form of all sacrifices; *vairāgya*—renunciation; *bhaktyā*—by devotional service; *ātma-jaya-anubhāvita*—perceivable by conquering the mind; *jñānāya*—such knowledge; *vidyā-gurave*—the supreme spiritual master of all knowledge; *namaḥ namaḥ*—again I offer my respectful obeisances.

TRANSLATION

O Lord, You are the Supreme Personality of Godhead and are worshipable by universal prayers, Vedic hymns and sacrificial ingredients. We offer our obeisances unto You. You can be realized by the pure mind freed from all visible and invisible material contamination. We offer our respectful obeisances to You as the supreme spiritual master of knowledge in devotional service.

PURPORT

The qualification of *bhakti,* or devotional service to the Lord, is that the devotee should be free from all material contaminations and desires. This freedom is called *vairāgya,* or renouncement of material desires. One who engages in devotional service to the Lord according to regulative principles is automatically freed from material desires, and in that pure state of mind one can realize the Personality of Godhead. The Personality of Godhead, being situated in everyone's heart, instructs the devotee regarding pure devotional service so that he may ultimately achieve the association of the Lord. This is confirmed in *Bhagavad-gītā* (10.10) as follows:

teṣāṁ satata-yuktānāṁ
bhajatāṁ prīti-pūrvakam
dadāmi buddhi-yogaṁ taṁ
yena mām upayānti te

"To one who constantly engages in the devotional service of the Lord with faith and love, the Lord certainly gives the intelligence to achieve Him at the ultimate end."

One has to conquer the mind, and one may do it by following the Vedic rituals and by performing different types of sacrifice. The ultimate end of all those performances is to attain *bhakti*, or the devotional service of the Lord. Without *bhakti* one cannot understand the Supreme Personality of Godhead. The original Personality of Godhead or His innumerable expansions of Viṣṇu are the only objects of worship by all the Vedic rituals and sacrificial performances.

TEXT 40

दंष्ट्राग्रकोट्या भगवंस्त्वया धृता
विराजते भूधर भूः सभूधरा ।
यथा वनान्निःसरतो दता धृता
मतङ्गजेन्द्रस्य सपत्रपद्मिनी ॥४०॥

daṁṣṭrāgra-koṭyā bhagavaṁs tvayā dhṛtā
virājate bhūdhara bhūḥ sa-bhūdharā
yathā vanān niḥsarato datā dhṛtā
mataṅ-gajendrasya sa-patra-padminī

daṁṣṭra-agra—the tips of the tusks; *koṭyā*—by the edges; *bhagavan*—O Personality of Godhead; *tvayā*—by You; *dhṛtā*—sustained; *virājate*—is so beautifully situated; *bhū-dhara*—O lifter of the earth; *bhūḥ*—the earth; *sa-bhūdharā*—with mountains; *yathā*—as much as; *vanāt*—from the water; *niḥsarataḥ*—coming out; *datā*—by the tusk; *dhṛtā*—captured; *matam-gajendrasya*—infuriated elephant; *sa-patra*—with leaves; *padminī*—the lotus flower.

TRANSLATION

O lifter of the earth, the earth with its mountains, which You have lifted with Your tusks, is situated as beautifully as a lotus flower with leaves sustained by an infuriated elephant just coming out of the water.

PURPORT

The fortune of the earth planet is praised because of its being specifically sustained by the Lord; its beauty is appreciated and compared to that of a lotus flower situated on the trunk of an elephant. As a lotus flower with leaves is very beautifully situated, so the world, with its many beautiful mountains, appeared on the tusks of the Lord Boar.

TEXT 41

त्रयीमयं रूपमिदं च सौकरं
भूमण्डलेनाथ दता धृतेन ते ।
चकास्ति शृङ्गोढघनेन भूयसा
कुलाचलेन्द्रस्य यथैव विभ्रमः ॥४१॥

trayīmayaṁ rūpam idaṁ ca saukaraṁ
bhū-maṇḍalenātha datā dhṛtena te
cakāsti śṛṅgoḍha-ghanena bhūyasā
kulācalendrasya yathaiva vibhramaḥ

trayī-mayam—*Vedas* personified; *rūpam*—form; *idam*—this; *ca*—also; *saukaram*—the boar; *bhū-maṇḍalena*—by the earth planet; *atha*—now; *datā*—by the tusk; *dhṛtena*—sustained by; *te*—Your; *cakāsti*—is glowing; *śṛṅga-ūḍha*—sustained by the peaks; *ghanena*—by the clouds; *bhūyasā*—more glorified; *kula-acala-indrasya*—of the great mountains; *yathā*—as much as; *eva*—certainly; *vibhramaḥ*—decoration.

TRANSLATION

O Lord, as the peaks of great mountains become beautiful when decorated with clouds, Your transcendental body has become beautiful because of Your lifting the earth on the edge of Your tusks.

PURPORT

The word *vibhramaḥ* is significant. *Vibhramaḥ* means "illusion" as well as "beauty." When a cloud rests on the peak of a great mountain, it appears to be sustained by the mountain, and at the same time it looks very beautiful. Similarly, the Lord has no need to sustain the earth on His tusks, but when He does so the world becomes beautiful, just as the

Lord becomes more beautiful because of His pure devotees on the earth. Although the Lord is the transcendental personification of the Vedic hymns, He has become more beautiful because of His appearance to sustain the earth.

TEXT 42

संस्थापयैनां जगतां सतस्थुषां
लोकाय पत्नीमसि मातरं पिता ।
विधेम चास्यै नमसा सह त्वया
यस्यां स्वतेजोऽग्निमिवारणावधाः ॥४२॥

saṁsthāpayaināṁ jagatāṁ sa-tasthuṣāṁ
lokāya patnīm asi mātaraṁ pitā
vidhema cāsyai namasā saha tvayā
yasyāṁ sva-tejo 'gnim ivāraṇāv adhāḥ

saṁsthāpaya enām—raise this earth; *jagatām*—both the moving and; *sa-tasthuṣām*—nonmoving; *lokāya*—for their residence; *patnīm*—wife; *asi*—You are; *mātaram*—the mother; *pitā*—the father; *vidhema*—do we offer; *ca*—also; *asyai*—unto the mother; *namasā*—with all obeisances; *saha*—along with; *tvayā*—with You; *yasyām*—in whom; *sva-tejaḥ*—by Your own potency; *agnim*—fire; *iva*—likened; *araṇau*—in the *araṇi* wood; *adhāḥ*—invested.

TRANSLATION

O Lord, for the residential purposes of all inhabitants, both moving and nonmoving, this earth is Your wife, and You are the supreme father. We offer our respectful obeisances unto You, along with mother earth, in whom You have invested Your own potency, just as an expert sacrificer puts fire in the araṇi wood.

PURPORT

The so-called law of gravitation which sustains the planets is described herein as the potency of the Lord. This potency is invested by the Lord in the way that an expert sacrificial *brāhmaṇa* puts fire in the *araṇi* wood by the potency of Vedic *mantras.* By this arrangement the world becomes habitable for both the moving and nonmoving creatures. The conditioned souls, who are residents of the material world, are put in the womb of mother earth in the same way the seed of a child is put by the father in the womb of the mother. This conception of the Lord and the earth as father and mother is explained in *Bhagavad-gītā* (14.4). Conditioned souls are devoted to the motherland in which they take their birth, but they do not know their father. The mother is not independent in producing children. Similarly, material nature cannot produce living creatures unless in contact with the supreme father, the Supreme Personality of Godhead. *Śrīmad-Bhāgavatam* teaches us to offer obeisances unto the mother along with the Father, the Supreme Lord, because it is the Father only who impregnates the mother with all energies for the sustenance and maintenance of all living beings, both moving and nonmoving.

TEXT 43

कः श्रद्दधीतान्यतमस्तव प्रभो
रसां गताया भुव उद्विबर्हणम् ।
न विस्मयोऽसौ त्वयि विश्वविस्मये
यो माययेदं ससृजेऽतिविस्मयम् ॥४३॥

kaḥ śraddadhītānyatamas tava prabho
rasāṁ gatāyā bhuva udvibarhaṇam
na vismayo 'sau tvayi viśva-vismaye
yo māyayedaṁ sasṛje 'tivismayam

kaḥ—who else; *śraddadhīta*—can endeavor; *anyatamaḥ*—anyone besides Yourself; *tava*—Your; *prabho*—O Lord; *rasām*—in the water; *gatāyāḥ*—while lying in; *bhuvaḥ*—of the earth; *udvibarhaṇam*—deliverance; *na*—never; *vismayaḥ*—wonderful; *asau*—such an act; *tvayi*—unto You; *viśva*—universal; *vismaye*—full of wonders; *yaḥ*—one who; *māyayā*—by potencies; *idam*—this; *sasṛje*—created; *ati-vismayam*—surpassing all wonders.

TRANSLATION

Who else but You, the Supreme Personality of Godhead, could deliver the earth from within the water? It is not very wonderful for You, however, because You acted most wonderfully in the creation of the universe. By Your energy You have created this wonderful cosmic manifestation.

PURPORT

When a scientist discovers something impressive to the ignorant mass of people, the common man, without inquiry, accepts such a discovery as wonderful. But the intelligent man is not struck with wonder by such discoveries. He gives all credit to the person who created the wonderful brain of the scientist. A common man is also struck with wonder by the wonderful action of material nature, and he gives all credit to the cosmic manifestation. The learned Kṛṣṇa conscious person, however, knows well that behind the cosmic manifestation is the brain of Kṛṣṇa, as confirmed in *Bhagavad-gītā* (9.10): *mayādhyakṣeṇa prakṛtiḥ sūyate sa-carācaram.* Since Kṛṣṇa can direct the wonderful cosmic manifestation, it is not at all wonderful for Him to assume the gigantic form of a boar and thus deliver the earth from the mire of the water. A devotee is therefore not astonished to see the wonderful boar because he knows that the Lord is able to act far more wonderfully by His potencies, which are inconceivable to the brain of even the most erudite scientist.

TEXT 44

विधुन्वता वेदमयं निजं वपु-
र्जनस्तपःसत्यनिवासिनो वयम् ।
सटाशिखोद्धूतशिवाम्बुबिन्दुभि-
र्विमृज्यमाना भृशमीश पाविताः ॥४४॥

vidhunvatā vedamayaṁ nijaṁ vapur
janas-tapaḥ-satya-nivāsino vayam
saṭā-śikhoddhūta-śivāmbu-bindubhir
vimṛjyamānā bhṛśam īśa pāvitāḥ

vidhunvatā—while shaking; *veda-mayam*—personified *Vedas; nijam*—own; *vapuḥ*—body; *janaḥ*—the Janaloka planetary system; *tapaḥ*—the Tapoloka planetary system; *satya*—the Satyaloka planetary system; *nivāsinaḥ*—the inhabitants; *vayam*—we; *saṭā*—hairs on the shoulder; *śikha-uddhūta*—sustained by the tip of the hair; *śiva*—auspicious; *ambu*—water; *bindubhiḥ*—by the particles; *vimṛjyamānāḥ*—we are thus sprinkled by; *bhṛśam*—highly; *īśa*—O Supreme Lord; *pāvitāḥ*—purified.

TRANSLATION

O Supreme Lord, undoubtedly we are inhabitants of the most pious planets—the Jana, Tapas and Satya lokas—but still we have been purified by the drops of water sprinkled from Your shoulder hairs by the shaking of Your body.

PURPORT

Ordinarily the body of a hog is considered impure, but one should not consider that the hog incarnation assumed by the Lord is also impure. That form of the Lord is the personified *Vedas* and is transcendental. The inhabitants of the Jana, Tapas and Satya *lokas* are the most pious persons in the material world, but because those planets are situated in the material world, there are so many material impurities there also. Therefore, when the drops of water from the tips of the Lord's shoulder hairs were sprinkled upon the bodies of the inhabitants of the higher planets, they felt purified. The Ganges water is pure because of its emanating from the toe of the Lord, and there is no difference between the water emanating from the toe and that from the tips of the hair on the shoulder of Lord Boar. They are both absolute and transcendental.

TEXT 45

स वै बत भ्रष्टमतिस्तवैषते
यः कर्मणां पारमपारकर्मणः ।
यद्योगमायागुणयोगमोहितं
विश्वं समस्तं भगवन् विधेहि शम् ॥४५॥

sa vai bata bhraṣṭa-matis tavaiṣate
yaḥ karmaṇāṁ pāram apāra-karmaṇaḥ
yad-yogamāyā-guṇa-yoga-mohitaṁ
viśvaṁ samastaṁ bhagavan vidhehi śam

saḥ—he; *vai*—certainly; *bata*—alas; *bhraṣṭa-matiḥ*—nonsense; *tava*—Your; *eṣate*—desires; *yaḥ*—one who; *karmaṇām*—of activities; *pāram*—limit; *apāra-karmaṇaḥ*—of one who has unlimited activities; *yat*—by whom; *yoga*—mystic power; *māyā*—potency; *guṇa*—modes of material nature; *yoga*—mystic power; *mohitam*—bewildered; *viśvam*—the universe; *samastam*—in total; *bhagavan*—O Supreme Personality of Godhead; *vidhehi*—just be pleased to bestow; *śam*—good fortune.

TRANSLATION

O Lord, there is no limit to Your wonderful activities. Anyone who desires to know the limit of Your activities is certainly nonsensical. Everyone in this world is conditioned by the powerful mystic potencies. Please bestow Your causeless mercy upon these conditioned souls.

PURPORT

Mental speculators who want to understand the limit of the Unlimited are certainly nonsensical. Every one of them is captivated by the external potencies of the Lord. The best thing for them is to surrender unto Him, knowing Him to be inconceivable, for thus they can receive His causeless mercy. This prayer was offered by the inhabitants of the higher planetary systems, namely the Jana, Tapas and Satya *lokas*, who are far more intelligent and powerful than humans.

Viśvaṁ samastam is very significant here. There are the material world and the spiritual world. The sages pray: "Both worlds are bewildered by Your different energies. Those who are in the spiritual world are absorbed in Your loving service, forgetting themselves and You also, and those in the material world are absorbed in material sense gratification and therefore also forget You. No one can know You, because You are unlimited. It is best not to try to know You by unnecessary mental speculation. Rather, kindly bless us so that we can worship You with causeless devotional service."

TEXT 46

मैत्रेय उवाच

इत्युपस्थीयमानोऽसौ मुनिभिर्ब्रह्मवादिभिः ।
सलिले स्वखुराक्रान्त उपाधत्ताविताविनिम् ॥४६॥

maitreya uvāca
ity upasthīyamāno 'sau
munibhir brahma-vādibhiḥ
salile sva-khurākrānta
upādhattāvitāvanim

maitreyaḥ uvāca—the sage Maitreya said; *iti*—thus; *upasthīyamānaḥ*—being praised by; *asau*—Lord Boar; *munibhiḥ*—by the great sages; *brahma-vādibhiḥ*—by the transcendentalists; *salile*—on the water; *sva-khura-ākrānte*—touched by His own hooves; *upādhatta*—placed; *avitā*—the maintainer; *avanim*—the earth.

TRANSLATION

The sage Maitreya said: The Lord, being thus worshiped by all the great sages and transcendentalists, touched the earth with His hooves and placed it on the water.

PURPORT

The earth was placed on the water by His inconceivable potency. The Lord is all-powerful, and therefore He can sustain the huge planets either on the water or in the air, as He likes. The tiny human brain cannot conceive how these potencies of the Lord can act. Man can give some vague explanation of the laws by which such phenomena are made possible, but actually the tiny human brain is unable to conceive of the activities of the Lord, which are therefore called inconceivable. Yet the frog-philosophers still try to give some imaginary explanation.

TEXT 47

स इत्थं भगवानुर्वीं विष्वक्सेनः प्रजापतिः ।
रसाया लीलयोन्नीतामप्सु न्यस्य ययौ हरिः ॥४७॥

sa ittham bhagavān urvīṁ
viṣvaksenaḥ prajāpatiḥ
rasāyā līlayonnītām
apsu nyasya yayau hariḥ

saḥ—He; *ittham*—in this manner; *bhagavān*—the Personality of Godhead; *urvīm*—the earth; *viṣvaksenaḥ*—another name of Viṣṇu; *prajā-patiḥ*—the Lord of the living entities; *rasāyāḥ*—from within the water; *līlayā*—very easily; *unnītām*—raised; *apsu*—on the water; *nyasya*—placing; *yayau*—returned to His own abode; *hariḥ*—the Personality of Godhead.

TRANSLATION

In this manner the Personality of Godhead, Lord Viṣṇu, the maintainer of all living entities, raised the earth from within the water, and having placed it afloat on the water, He returned to His own abode.

PURPORT

The Personality of Godhead Lord Viṣṇu descends by His will to the material planets in His innumerable incarnations for particular purposes, and again He goes back to His own abode. When He descends He is called an *avatāra* because *avatāra* means "one who descends." Neither the Lord Himself nor His specific devotees who come to this earth are ordinary living entities like us.

TEXT 48

य एवमेतां हरिमेधसो हरेः
कथां सुभद्रां कथनीयमायिनः ।
शृण्वीत भक्त्या श्रवयेत वोशतीं
जनार्दनोऽस्याशु हृदि प्रसीदति ॥४८॥

ya evam etāṁ hari-medhaso hareḥ
kathāṁ subhadrāṁ kathanīya-māyinaḥ
śṛṇvīta bhaktyā śravayeta vośatīṁ
janārdano 'syāśu hṛdi prasīdati

yaḥ—one who; *evam*—thus; *etām*—this; *hari-medhasaḥ*—who destroys the material existence of the devotee; *hareḥ*—of the Personality of Godhead; *kathām*—narration; *su-bhadrām*—auspicious; *kathanīya*—worthy to narrate; *māyinaḥ*—of the merciful by His internal potency; *śṛṇvīta*—hears; *bhaktyā*—in devotion; *śravayeta*—also allows others to hear; *vā*—either; *uśatīm*—very pleasing; *janārdanaḥ*—the Lord; *asya*—his; *āśu*—very soon; *hṛdi*—within the heart; *prasīdati*—becomes very pleased.

TRANSLATION

If one hears and describes in a devotional service attitude this auspicious narration of Lord Boar, which is worthy of description, the Lord, who is within the heart of everyone, is very pleased.

PURPORT

In His various incarnations, the Lord appears, acts and leaves behind Him a narrative history which is as transcendental as He Himself. Every one of us is fond of hearing some wonderful narration, but most stories are neither auspicious nor worth hearing because they are of the inferior quality of material nature. Every living entity is of superior quality, spirit soul, and nothing material can be auspicious for him. Intelligent persons should therefore hear personally and cause others to hear the descriptive narrations of the Lord's activities, for that will destroy the pangs of material existence. Out of His causeless mercy only, the Lord comes to this earth and leaves behind His merciful activities so that the devotees may derive transcendental benefit.

TEXT 49

तस्मिन् प्रसन्ने सकलाशिषां प्रभौ
किं दुर्लभं ताभिरलं लवात्मभिः ।
अनन्यदृष्ट्या भजतां गुहाशयः
स्वयं विधत्ते स्वगतिं परः पराम् ॥४९॥

tasmin prasanne sakalāśiṣāṁ prabhau
kiṁ durlabhaṁ tābhir alaṁ lavātmabhiḥ
ananya-dṛṣṭyā bhajatāṁ guhāśayaḥ
svayaṁ vidhatte sva-gatiṁ paraḥ parām

tasmin—unto Him; *prasanne*—being pleased; *sakala-āśiṣām*—of all benediction; *prabhau*—unto the Lord; *kim*—what is that; *durlabham*—very difficult to obtain; *tābhiḥ*—with them; *alam*—away; *lava-ātmabhiḥ*—with insignificant gains; *ananya-dṛṣṭyā*—by nothing but devotional service; *bhajatām*—of those who are engaged in devotional service; *guhā-āśayaḥ*—residing within the heart; *svayam*—personally; *vidhatte*—executes; *sva-gatim*—in His own abode; *paraḥ*—the supreme; *parām*—transcendental.

TRANSLATION

Nothing remains unachieved when the Supreme Personality of Godhead is pleased with someone. By transcendental achievement one understands everything else to be insignificant. One who engages in transcendental loving service is elevated to the highest perfectional stage by the Lord Himself, who is seated in everyone's heart.

PURPORT

As stated in *Bhagavad-gītā* (10.10), the Lord gives intelligence to the pure devotees so that they may be elevated to the highest perfectional stage. It is confirmed herein that a pure devotee, who constantly engages in the loving service of the Lord, is awarded all knowledge necessary to reach the Supreme Personality of Godhead. For such a devotee there is nothing valuable to be achieved but the Lord's service. If one serves faithfully, there is no possibility of frustration because the Lord Himself takes charge of the devotee's advancement. The Lord is seated in everyone's heart, and He knows the devotee's motive and arranges everything achievable. In other words, the pseudo devotee, who is anxious to achieve material gains, cannot attain the highest perfectional stage because the Lord is in knowledge of his motive. One merely has to become sincere in his purpose, and then the Lord is there to help in every way.

TEXT 50

को नाम लोके पुरुषार्थसारवित्
पुराकथानां भगवत्कथासुधाम् ।
आपीय कर्णाञ्जलिभिर्भवापहा-
महो विरज्येत विना नरेतरम् ॥५०॥

ko nāma loke puruṣārtha-sāravit
purā-kathānāṁ bhagavat-kathā-sudhām
āpīya karṇāñjalibhir bhavāpahām
aho virajyeta vinā naretaram

kaḥ—who; *nāma*—indeed; *loke*—in the world; *puruṣa-artha*—goal of life; *sāra-vit*—one who knows the essence of; *purā-kathānām*—of all past histories; *bhagavat*—regarding the Personality of Godhead; *kathā-sudhām*—the nectar of the narrations about the Personality of Godhead; *āpīya*—by drinking; *karṇa-añjalibhiḥ*—by aural reception; *bhava-apahām*—that which kills all material pangs; *aho*—alas; *virajyeta*—could refuse; *vinā*—except; *nara-itaram*—other than the human being.

TRANSLATION

Who, other than one who is not a human being, can exist in this world and not be interested in the ultimate goal of life? Who can refuse the nectar of narrations about the Personality of Godhead's activities, which by itself can deliver one from all material pangs?

PURPORT

The narration of the activities of the Personality of Godhead is like a constant flow of nectar. No one can refuse to drink such nectar except one who is not a human being. Devotional service to the Lord is the highest goal of life for every human being, and such devotional service begins by hearing about the transcendental activities of the Personality of Godhead. Only an animal, or a man who is almost an animal in behavior, can refuse to take an interest in hearing the transcendental message of the Lord. There are many books of stories and histories in the world, but except for the histories or narrations on the topics of the Personality of Godhead, none are capable of diminishing the burden of material pangs. Therefore one who is serious about eliminating material existence must chant and hear of the transcendental activities of the Personality of Godhead. Otherwise one must be compared to the nonhumans.

Thus end the Bhaktivedanta purports of the Third Canto, Thirteenth Chapter, of the Śrīmad-Bhāgavatam, *entitled "The Appearance of Lord Varāha."*

CHAPTER FOURTEEN

Pregnancy of Diti in the Evening

TEXT 1

श्रीशुक उवाच
निशम्य कौषारविणोपवर्णितां
हरेः कथां कारणसूकरात्मनः ।
पुनः स पप्रच्छ तमुद्यताञ्जलि-
र्न चातितृप्तो विदुरो धृतव्रतः ॥ १ ॥

śrī-śuka uvāca
niśamya kauṣāraviṇopavarṇitāṁ
hareḥ kathāṁ kāraṇa-sūkarātmanaḥ
punaḥ sa papraccha tam udyatāñjalir
na cātitṛpto viduro dhṛta-vrataḥ

śrī-śukaḥ uvāca—Śrī Śukadeva Gosvāmī said; *niśamya*—after hearing; *kauṣāraviṇā*—by the sage Maitreya; *upavarṇitām*—described; *hareḥ*—of the Personality of Godhead; *kathām*—narrations; *kāraṇa*—for the reason of lifting the earth; *sūkara-ātmanaḥ*—of the boar incarnation; *punaḥ*—again; *saḥ*—he; *papraccha*—inquired; *tam*—from him (Maitreya); *udyata-añjaliḥ*—with folded hands; *na*—never; *ca*—also; *ati-tṛptaḥ*—very much satisfied; *viduraḥ*—Vidura; *dhṛta-vrataḥ*—taken to a vow.

TRANSLATION

Śukadeva Gosvāmī said: After hearing from the great sage Maitreya about the Lord's incarnation as Varāha, Vidura, who had taken a vow, begged him with folded hands to please narrate further transcendental activities of the Lord, since he [Vidura] did not yet feel satisfied.

TEXT 2

विदुर उवाच
तेनैव तु मुनिश्रेष्ठ हरिणा यज्ञमूर्तिना ।
आदिदैत्यो हिरण्याक्षो हत इत्यनुशुश्रुम ॥ २ ॥

vidura uvāca
tenaiva tu muni-śreṣṭha
hariṇā yajña-mūrtinā
ādi-daityo hiraṇyākṣo
hata ity anuśuśruma

viduraḥ uvāca—Śrī Vidura said; *tena*—by Him; *eva*—certainly; *tu*—but; *muni-śreṣṭha*—O chief among the sages; *hariṇā*—by the Personality of Godhead; *yajña-mūrtinā*—the form of sacrifices; *ādi*—original; *daityaḥ*—demon; *hiraṇyākṣaḥ*—by the name Hiraṇyākṣa; *hataḥ*—slain; *iti*—thus; *anuśuśruma*—heard in succession.

TRANSLATION

Śrī Vidura said: O chief amongst the great sages, I have heard by disciplic succession that Hiraṇyākṣa, the original demon, was slain by the same form of sacrifices, the Personality of Godhead [Lord Boar].

PURPORT

As referred to previously, the boar incarnation was manifested in two millenniums—namely Svāyambhuva and Cākṣuṣa. In both millenniums there was a boar incarnation of the Lord, but in the Svāyambhuva millennium He lifted the earth from within the water of the universe, whereas in the Cākṣuṣa millennium He killed the first demon, Hiraṇyākṣa. In the Svāyambhuva millennium He assumed the color white, and in the Cākṣuṣa millennium He assumed the color red. Vidura had already heard about one of them, and he proposed to hear about the other. The two different boar incarnations described are the one Supreme Personality of Godhead.

TEXT 3

तस्य चोद्धरतः क्षौणीं स्वदंष्ट्राग्रेण लीलया ।
दैत्यराजस्य च ब्रह्मन् कस्माद्धेतोरभून्मृधः ॥ ३ ॥

tasya coddharataḥ kṣauṇīṁ
sva-daṁṣṭrāgreṇa līlayā
daitya-rājasya ca brahman
kasmād dhetor abhūn mṛdhaḥ

tasya—His; *ca*—also; *uddharataḥ*—while lifting; *kṣauṇīm*—the earth planet; *sva-daṁṣṭra-agreṇa*—by the edge of His tusks; *līlayā*—in His pastimes; *daitya-rājasya*—of the king of demons; *ca*—and; *brahman*—O *brāhmaṇa; kasmāt*—from what; *hetoḥ*—reason; *abhūt*—there was; *mṛdhaḥ*—fight.

TRANSLATION

What was the reason, O brāhmaṇa, for the fight between the demon king and Lord Boar while the Lord was lifting the earth as His pastime?

TEXT 4

श्रद्दधानाय भक्ताय ब्रूहि तज्जन्मविस्तरम् ।
ऋषे न तृप्यति मनः परं कौतूहलं हि मे ॥ ४ ॥

śraddadhānāya bhaktāya
brūhi taj-janma-vistaram
ṛṣe na tṛpyati manaḥ
paraṁ kautūhalaṁ hi me

śraddadhānāya—unto a faithful person; *bhaktāya*—unto a devotee; *brūhi*—please narrate; *tat*—His; *janma*—appearance; *vistaram*—in detail; *ṛṣe*—O great sage; *na*—not; *tṛpyati*—become satisfied; *manaḥ*—mind; *param*—very much; *kautūhalam*—inquisitive; *hi*—certainly; *me*—my.

TRANSLATION

My mind has become very inquisitive, and therefore I am not satisfied with hearing the narration of the Lord's appearance. Please, therefore, speak more and more to a devotee who is faithful.

PURPORT

One who is actually faithful and inquisitive is qualified to hear the transcendental pastimes of the appearance and disappearance of the Supreme Personality of Godhead. Vidura was a suitable candidate to receive such transcendental messages.

TEXT 5

मैत्रेय उवाच

साधु वीर त्वया पृष्टमवतारकथां हरेः ।
यत्त्वं पृच्छसि मर्त्यानां मृत्युपाशविशातनीम् ॥ ५ ॥

maitreya uvāca
sādhu vīra tvayā pṛṣṭam
avatāra-kathāṁ hareḥ
yat tvaṁ pṛcchasi martyānāṁ
mṛtyu-pāśa-viśātanīm

maitreyaḥ uvāca—Maitreya said; *sādhu*—devotee; *vīra*—O warrior; *tvayā*—by you; *pṛṣṭam*—inquired; *avatāra-kathām*—topics on the incarnation of the Lord; *hareḥ*—of the Personality of Godhead; *yat*—that which; *tvam*—your good self; *pṛcchasi*—asking me; *martyānām*—of those who are destined for death; *mṛtyu-pāśa*—the chain of birth and death; *viśātanīm*—source of liberation.

TRANSLATION

The great sage Maitreya said: O warrior, the inquiry made by you is just befitting a devotee because it concerns the incarnation of the Personality of Godhead. He is the source of liberation from the chain of birth and death for all those who are otherwise destined to die.

PURPORT

The great sage Maitreya addressed Vidura as a warrior not only because Vidura belonged to the Kuru family but because he was anxious to hear about the chivalrous activities of the Lord in His incarnations of Varāha and Nṛsiṁha. Because the inquiries concerned the Lord, they were perfectly befitting a devotee. A devotee has no taste for hearing anything mundane. There are many topics of mundane warfare, but a devotee is not inclined to hear them. The topics of the warfare in which the Lord engages do not concern the war of death but the war against the chain of *māyā* which obliges one to accept repeated birth and death. In other words, one who takes delight in hearing the war topics of the Lord is relieved from the chains of birth and death. Foolish people are suspicious of Kṛṣṇa's taking part in the Battle of Kurukṣetra, not knowing that His taking part insured liberation for all who were present on the battlefield. It is said by Bhīṣmadeva that all who were present on the Battlefield of Kurukṣetra attained their original spiritual existences after death. Therefore, hearing the war topics of the Lord is as good as any other devotional service.

TEXT 6

यथोत्तानपदः पुत्रो मुनिना गीतयार्भकः ।
मृत्योः कृत्वैव मूर्ध्न्यङ्घ्रिमारुरोह हरेः पदम् ॥ ६ ॥

yayottānapadaḥ putro
muninā gītayārbhakaḥ
mṛtyoḥ kṛtvaiva mūrdhny aṅghrim
āruroha hareḥ padam

yayā—by which; *uttānapadaḥ*—of King Uttānapāda; *putraḥ*—son; *muninā*—by the sage; *gītayā*—being sung; *arbhakaḥ*—a child; *mṛtyoḥ*—of death; *kṛtvā*—placing; *eva*—certainly; *mūrdhni*—on the head; *aṅghrim*—feet; *āruroha*—ascended; *hareḥ*—of the Personality of Godhead; *padam*—to the abode.

TRANSLATION

By hearing these topics from the sage [Nārada], the son of King Uttānapāda [Dhruva] was enlightened regarding the Personality of

Godhead, and he ascended to the abode of the Lord, placing his feet over the head of death.

PURPORT

While quitting his body, Mahārāja Dhruva, the son of King Uttānapāda, was attended by personalities like Sunanda and others, who received him in the kingdom of God. He left this world at an early age, as a young boy, although he had attained the throne of his father and had several children of his own. Because he was due to quit this world, death was waiting for him. He did not care for death, however, and even with his present body he boarded a spiritual airplane and went directly to the planet of Viṣṇu because of his association with the great sage Nārada, who had spoken to him the narration of the pastimes of the Lord.

TEXT 7

अथात्रापीतिहासोऽयं श्रुतो मे वर्णितः पुरा ।
ब्रह्मणा देवदेवेन देवानामनुपृच्छताम् ॥ ७ ॥

athātrāpītihāso 'yaṁ
śruto me varṇitaḥ purā
brahmaṇā deva-devena
devānām anupṛcchatām

atha—now; *atra*—in this matter; *api*—also; *itihāsaḥ*—history; *ayam*—this; *śrutaḥ*—heard; *me*—by me; *varṇitaḥ*—described; *purā*—years ago; *brahmaṇā*—by Brahmā; *deva-devena*—the foremost of the demigods; *devānām*—by the demigods; *anupṛcchatām*—asking.

TRANSLATION

This history of the fight between the Lord as a boar and the demon Hiraṇyākṣa was heard by me in a year long ago as it was described by the foremost of the demigods, Brahmā, when he was questioned by the other demigods.

TEXT 8

दितिर्दाक्षायणी क्षत्तर्मारीचं कश्यपं पतिम् ।
अपत्यकामा चकमे सन्ध्यायां हृच्छयार्दिता ॥ ८ ॥

ditir dākṣāyaṇī kṣattar
mārīcaṁ kaśyapaṁ patim
apatya-kāmā cakame
sandhyāyāṁ hṛc-chayārditā

ditiḥ—Diti; *dākṣāyaṇī*—the daughter of Dakṣa; *kṣattaḥ*—O Vidura; *mārīcam*—the son of Marīci; *kaśyapam*—Kaśyapa; *patim*—her husband; *apatya-kāmā*—desirous of having a child; *cakame*—longed for; *sandhyāyām*—in the evening; *hṛt-śaya*—by sex desires; *arditā*—distressed.

TRANSLATION

Diti, daughter of Dakṣa, being afflicted with sex desire, begged her husband, Kaśyapa, the son of Marīci, to have intercourse with her in the evening in order to beget a child.

TEXT 9

इष्ट्वाग्निजिह्वं पयसा पुरुषं यजुषां पतिम् ।
निम्लोचत्यर्क आसीनमग्न्यगारे समाहितम् ॥ ९ ॥

iṣṭvāgni-jihvaṁ payasā
puruṣaṁ yajuṣāṁ patim
nimlocaty arka āsīnam
agny-agāre samāhitam

iṣṭvā—after worshiping; *agni*—fire; *jihvam*—tongue; *payasā*—by oblation; *puruṣam*—unto the Supreme Person; *yajuṣām*—of all sacrifices; *patim*—master; *nimlocati*—while setting; *arke*—the sun; *āsīnam*—sitting; *agni-agāre*—in the sacrificial hall; *samāhitam*—completely in trance.

TRANSLATION

The sun was setting, and the sage was sitting in trance after offering oblations to the Supreme Personality of Godhead, Viṣṇu, whose tongue is the sacrificial fire.

PURPORT

Fire is considered to be the tongue of the Personality of Godhead Viṣṇu, and oblations of grains and clarified butter offered to the fire are thus accepted by Him. That is the principle of all sacrifices, of which Lord Viṣṇu is the master. In other words, the satisfaction of Lord Viṣṇu includes the satisfaction of all demigods and other living beings.

TEXT 10

दितिरुवाच
एष मां त्वत्कृते विद्वन् काम आत्तशरासनः ।
दुनोति दीनां विक्रम्य रम्भामिव मतङ्गजः ॥१०॥

ditir uvāca
eṣa māṁ tvat-kṛte vidvan
kāma ātta-śarāsanaḥ
dunoti dīnāṁ vikramya
rambhām iva mataṅgajaḥ

ditiḥ uvāca—beautiful Diti said; *eṣaḥ*—all these; *mām*—unto me; *tvat-kṛte*—for you; *vidvan*—O learned one; *kāmaḥ*—Cupid; *ātta-śarāsanaḥ*—taking his arrows; *dunoti*—distresses; *dīnām*—poor me; *vikramya*—attacking; *rambhām*—banana tree; *iva*—like; *matam-gajaḥ*—mad elephant.

TRANSLATION

In that place the beautiful Diti expressed her desire: O learned one, Cupid is taking his arrows and distressing me forcibly, as a mad elephant troubles a banana tree.

PURPORT

Beautiful Diti, seeing her husband absorbed in trance, began to speak loudly, not attempting to attract him by bodily expressions. She frankly said that her whole body was distressed by sex desire because of her husband's presence, just as a banana tree is troubled by a mad elephant. It was not natural for her to agitate her husband when he was in trance, but she could not control her strong sexual appetite. Her sex desire was like a mad elephant, and therefore it was the prime duty of her husband to give her all protection by fulfilling her desire.

TEXT 11

तद्भवान्दह्यमानायां सपत्नीनां समृद्धिभिः ।
प्रजावतीनां भद्रं ते मय्यायुङ्क्तामनुग्रहम् ॥११॥

tad bhavān dahyamānāyāṁ
sa-patnīnāṁ samṛddhibhiḥ
prajāvatīnāṁ bhadraṁ te
mayy āyuṅktām anugraham

tat—therefore; *bhavān*—your good self; *dahyamānāyām*—being distressed; *sa-patnīnām*—of the co-wives; *samṛddhibhiḥ*—by the prosperity; *prajā-vatīnām*—of those who have children; *bhadram*—all prosperity; *te*—unto you; *mayi*—unto me; *āyuṅktām*—do unto me, in all respects; *anugraham*—favor.

TRANSLATION

Therefore you should be kind towards me by showing me complete mercy. I desire to have sons, and I am much distressed by seeing the opulence of my co-wives. By performing this act, you will become happy.

PURPORT

In *Bhagavad-gītā* sexual intercourse for begetting children is accepted as righteous. A person sexually inclined for simple sense gratification, however, is unrighteous. In Diti's appeal to her husband for sex, it was not exactly that she was afflicted by sex desires, but she desired sons. Since she had no sons, she felt poorer than her co-wives. Therefore Kaśyapa was supposed to satisfy his bona fide wife.

TEXT 12

भर्तर्याप्तोरुमानानां लोकानाविशते यशः ।
पतिर्भवद्विधो यासां प्रजया ननु जायते ॥१२॥

bhartary āptorumānānāṁ
lokān āviśate yaśaḥ
patir bhavad-vidho yāsāṁ
prajayā nanu jāyate

bhartari—by the husband; *āpta-urumānānām*—of those who are beloved; *lokān*—in the world; *āviśate*—spreads; *yaśaḥ*—fame; *patiḥ*—husband; *bhavat-vidhaḥ*—like your good self; *yāsām*—of those whose; *prajayā*—by children; *nanu*—certainly; *jāyate*—expands.

TRANSLATION

A woman is honored in the world by the benediction of her husband, and a husband like you will become famous by having children because you are meant for the expansion of living entities.

PURPORT

According to Ṛṣabhadeva, one should not become a father or mother unless one is confident that he can beget children whom he can deliver from the clutches of birth and death. Human life is the only opportunity to get out of the material scene, which is full of the miseries of birth, death, old age and diseases. Every human being should be given the opportunity to take advantage of his human form of life, and a father like Kaśyapa is supposed to beget good children for the purpose of liberation.

TEXT 13

पुरा पिता नो भगवान्दक्षो दुहितृवत्सलः ।
कं वृणीत वरं वत्सा इत्यपृच्छत नः पृथक् ॥१३॥

purā pitā no bhagavān
dakṣo duhitṛ-vatsalaḥ
kaṁ vṛṇīta varaṁ vatsā
ity apṛcchata naḥ pṛthak

purā—in days long ago; *pitā*—father; *naḥ*—our; *bhagavān*—the most opulent; *dakṣaḥ*—Dakṣa; *duhitṛ-vatsalaḥ*—affectionate to his daughters; *kam*—unto whom; *vṛṇīta*—you want to accept; *varam*—your husband; *vatsāḥ*—O my children; *iti*—thus; *apṛcchata*—inquired; *naḥ*—us; *pṛthak*—separately.

TRANSLATION

In days long ago, our father, the most opulent Dakṣa, who was affectionate to his daughters, asked each of us separately whom we would prefer to select as our husband.

PURPORT

It appears from this verse that free selection of a husband was allowed by the father, but not by free association. The daughters were asked separately to submit their selection of a husband who was famous for his acts and personality. The ultimate selection depended on the choice of the father.

TEXT 14

स विदित्वात्मजानां नो भावं सन्तानभावनः ।
त्रयोदशाददात्तासां यास्ते शीलमनुव्रताः ॥१४॥

sa viditvātmajānāṁ no
bhāvaṁ santāna-bhāvanaḥ
trayodaśādadāt tāsāṁ
yās te śīlam anuvratāḥ

saḥ—Dakṣa; *viditvā*—understanding; *ātma-jānām*—of the daughters; *naḥ*—our; *bhāvam*—indication; *santāna*—children; *bhāvanaḥ*—well-wisher; *trayodaśa*—thirteen; *adadāt*—handed over; *tāsām*—of all of them; *yāḥ*—those who are; *te*—your; *śīlam*—behavior; *anuvratāḥ*—all faithful.

TRANSLATION

Our well-wishing father, Dakṣa, after knowing our intentions, handed over thirteen of his daughters unto you, and since then we have all been faithful.

PURPORT

Generally the daughters were too shy to express their opinions before their father, but the father would accept the daughters' intentions through someone else, such as a grandmother to whom the grandchildren had free access. King Dakṣa collected the opinions of his daughters and thus handed over thirteen to Kaśyapa. Every one of Diti's sisters was a mother of children. Therefore, since she was equally faithful to the same husband, why should she remain without children?

TEXT 15

अथ मे कुरु कल्याणं कामं कमललोचन ।
आर्तोपसर्पणं भूमन्नमोघं हि महीयसि ॥१५॥

atha me kuru kalyāṇaṁ
kāmaṁ kamala-locana
ārtopasarpaṇaṁ bhūmann
amoghaṁ hi mahīyasi

atha—therefore; *me*—unto me; *kuru*—kindly do; *kalyāṇam*—benediction; *kāmam*—desire; *kamala-locana*—O lotus-eyed one; *ārta*—of the distressed; *upasarpaṇam*—the approaching; *bhūman*—O great one; *amogham*—without failure; *hi*—certainly; *mahīyasi*—to a great person.

TRANSLATION

O lotus-eyed one, kindly bless me by fulfilling my desire. When someone in distress approaches a great person, his pleas should never go in vain.

PURPORT

Diti knew well that her request might be rejected because of the untimely situation, but she pleaded that when there is an emergency or a distressful condition, there is no consideration of time or situation.

TEXT 16

इति तां वीर मारीचः कृपणां बहुभाषिणीम् ।
प्रत्याहानुनयन् वाचा प्रवृद्धानङ्गकश्मलाम् ॥१६॥

iti tāṁ vīra mārīcaḥ
kṛpaṇāṁ bahu-bhāṣiṇīm
pratyāhānunayan vācā
pravṛddhānaṅga-kaśmalām

iti—thus; *tām*—unto her; *vīra*—O hero; *mārīcaḥ*—the son of Marīci (Kaśyapa); *kṛpaṇām*—unto the poor; *bahu-bhāṣiṇīm*—too talkative; *pratyāha*—replied; *anunayan*—pacifying; *vācā*—by words; *pravṛddha*—highly agitated; *anaṅga*—lust; *kaśmalām*—contaminated.

TRANSLATION

O hero [Vidura], Diti, being thus afflicted by the contamination of lust, and therefore poor and talkative, was pacified by the son of Marīci in suitable words.

PURPORT

When a man or woman is afflicted by the lust of sex desire, it is to be understood as sinful contamination. Kaśyapa was engaged in his spiritual activities, but he did not have sufficient strength to refuse his wife, who was thus afflicted. He could have refused her with strong words expressing impossibility, but he was not as spiritually strong as Vidura. Vidura is addressed here as a hero because no one is stronger in self-control than a devotee of the Lord. It appears that Kaśyapa was already inclined to have sexual enjoyment with his wife, and because he was not a strong man he tried to dissuade her only with pacifying words.

TEXT 17

एष तेऽहं विधास्यामि प्रियं भीरु यदिच्छसि ।
तस्याः कामं न कः कुर्यात्सिद्धिस्त्रैवर्गिकी यतः ॥१७॥

eṣa te 'haṁ vidhāsyāmi
priyaṁ bhīru yad icchasi

tasyāḥ kāmaṁ na kaḥ kuryāt
siddhis traivargikī yataḥ

eṣaḥ—this; *te*—your request; *aham*—I; *vidhāsyāmi*—shall execute; *priyam*—very dear; *bhīru*—O afflicted one; *yat*—what; *icchasi*—you are desiring; *tasyāḥ*—her; *kāmam*—desires; *na*—not; *kaḥ*—who; *kuryāt*—would perform; *siddhiḥ*—perfection of liberation; *traivargikī*—three; *yataḥ*—from whom.

TRANSLATION

O afflicted one, I shall forthwith gratify whatever desire is dear to you, for who else but you is the source of the three perfections of liberation?

PURPORT

The three perfections of liberation are religiosity, economic development and sense gratification. For a conditioned soul, the wife is considered to be the source of liberation because she offers her service to the husband for his ultimate liberation. Conditional material existence is based on sense gratification, and if someone has the good fortune to get a good wife, he is helped by the wife in all respects. If one is disturbed in his conditional life, he becomes more and more entangled in material contamination. A faithful wife is supposed to cooperate with her husband in fulfilling all material desires so that he can then become comfortable and execute spiritual activities for the perfection of life. If, however, the husband is progressive in spiritual advancement, the wife undoubtedly shares in his activities, and thus both the wife and the husband profit in spiritual perfection. It is essential, therefore, that girls as well as boys be trained to discharge spiritual duties so that at the time of cooperation both will be benefited. The training of the boy is *brahmacarya*, and the training of the girl is chastity. A faithful wife and spiritually trained *brahmacārī* are a good combination for advancement of the human mission.

TEXT 18

सर्वाश्रमानुपादाय स्वाश्रमेण कलत्रवान् ।
व्यसनार्णवमत्येति जलयानैर्यथार्णवम् ॥१८॥

sarvāśramān upādāya
svāśrameṇa kalatravān
vyasanārṇavam atyeti
jala-yānair yathārṇavam

sarva—all; *āśramān*—social orders; *upādāya*—completing; *sva*—own; *āśrameṇa*—by the social orders; *kalatra-vān*—a person living with a wife; *vyasana-arṇavam*—the dangerous ocean of material existence; *atyeti*—one can cross over; *jala-yānaiḥ*—with seagoing vessels; *yathā*—as; *arṇavam*—the ocean.

TRANSLATION

As one can cross over the ocean with seagoing vessels, one can cross the dangerous situation of the material ocean by living with a wife.

PURPORT

There are four social orders for cooperation in the endeavor for liberation from material existence. The orders of *brahmacarya*, or pious student life, household life with a wife, retired life and renounced life all depend for successful advancement on the householder who lives with a wife. This cooperation is essential for the proper functioning of the institution of the four social orders and the four spiritual orders of life. This Vedic *varṇāśrama* system is generally known as the caste system. The man who lives with a wife has a great responsibility in maintaining the members of the other social orders—the *brahmacārīs*, *vānaprasthas* and *sannyāsīs*. Except for the *gṛhasthas*, or the householders, everyone is supposed to engage in the spiritual advancement of life, and therefore the *brahmacārī*, the *vānaprastha* and the *sannyāsī* have very little time to earn a livelihood. They therefore collect alms from the *gṛhasthas*, and thus they secure the bare necessities of life and cultivate spiritual understanding. By helping the other three sections of society cultivate spiritual values, the householder also makes advancement in spiritual life. Ultimately every member of society automatically becomes spiritually advanced and easily crosses the ocean of nescience.

TEXT 19

यामाहुरात्मनो ह्यर्धं श्रेयस्कामस्य मानिनि ।
यस्यां स्वधुरमध्यस्य पुमांश्चरति विज्वरः ॥१९॥

yām āhur ātmano hy ardhaṁ
śreyas-kāmasya mānini
yasyāṁ sva-dhuram adhyasya
pumāṁś carati vijvaraḥ

yām—the wife who; *āhuḥ*—is said; *ātmanaḥ*—of the body; *hi*—thus; *ardham*—half; *śreyaḥ*—welfare; *kāmasya*—of all desires; *mānini*—O respectful one; *yasyām*—in whom; *sva-dhuram*—all responsibilities; *adhyasya*—entrusting; *pumān*—a man; *carati*—moves; *vijvaraḥ*—without anxiety.

TRANSLATION

O respectful one, a wife is so helpful that she is called the better half of a man's body because of her sharing in all auspicious activities. A man can move without anxiety entrusting all responsibilities to his wife.

PURPORT

By the Vedic injunction, the wife is accepted as the better half of a man's body because she is supposed to be responsible for discharging half of the duties of the husband. A family man has a responsibility to perform five kinds of sacrifices, called *pañca-yajña*, in order to get relief from all kinds of unavoidable sinful reaction incurred in the course of his affairs. When a man becomes qualitatively like the cats and dogs, he forgets his duties in cultivating spiritual values, and thus he accepts his wife as a sense gratificatory agency. When the wife is accepted as a sense gratificatory agency, personal beauty is the main consideration, and as soon as there is a break in personal sense gratification, there is disruption or divorce. But when husband and wife aim at spiritual advancement by mutual cooperation, there is no consideration of personal beauty or the disruption of so-called love. In the material world there is no question of love. Marriage is actually a duty performed in mutual cooperation as directed in the authoritative scriptures for spiritual advancement. Therefore marriage is essential in order to avoid the life of cats and dogs, who are not meant for spiritual enlightenment.

TEXT 20

यामाश्रित्येन्द्रियारातीन्दुर्जयानितराश्रमैः ।
वयं जयेम हेलाभिर्दस्यून्दुर्गपतिर्यथा ॥२०॥

yām āśrityendriyārātīn
durjayān itarāśramaiḥ
vayaṁ jayema helābhir
dasyūn durga-patir yathā

yām—whom; *āśritya*—taking shelter of; *indriya*—senses; *arātīn*—enemies; *durjayān*—difficult to conquer; *itara*—other than the householders; *āśramaiḥ*—by orders of society; *vayam*—we; *jayema*—can conquer; *helābhiḥ*—easily; *dasyūn*—invading plunderers; *durga-patiḥ*—a fort commander; *yathā*—as.

TRANSLATION

As a fort commander very easily conquers invading plunderers, by taking shelter of a wife one can conquer the senses, which are unconquerable in the other social orders.

PURPORT

Of the four orders of human society—the student, or *brahmacārī* order, the householder, or *gṛhastha* order, the retired, or *vānaprastha* order, and the renounced, or *sannyāsī* order—the householder is on the safe side. The bodily senses are considered plunderers of the fort of the body. The wife is supposed to be the commander of the fort, and therefore whenever there is an attack on the body by the senses, it is the wife who protects the body from being smashed. The sex demand is inevitable for everyone, but one who has a fixed wife is saved from the onslaught of the sense enemies. A man who possesses a good wife does not create a disturbance in society by corrupting virgin girls. Without a fixed wife, a man becomes a debauchee of the first order and is a nuisance in society—unless he is a trained *brahmacārī*, *vānaprastha* or *sannyāsī*. Unless there is rigid and systematic training of the *brahmacārī* by the expert spiritual master, and unless the student is obedient, it is sure that the so-called *brahmacārī* will fall prey to the attack of sex. There are so many instances of falldown, even for great *yogīs* like Viśvāmitra. A *gṛhastha* is saved, however, because of his faithful wife. Sex life is the cause of material bondage, and therefore it is prohibited in three *āśramas* and is allowed only in the *gṛhastha-āśrama*. The *gṛhastha* is responsible for producing first-quality *brahmacārīs*, *vānaprasthas* and *sannyāsīs*.

TEXT 21

न वयं प्रभवस्तां त्वामनुकर्तुं गृहेश्वरि ।
अप्यायुषा वा कार्त्स्न्येन ये चान्ये गुणगृध्नवः ॥२१॥

na vayaṁ prabhavas tāṁ tvām
anukartuṁ gṛheśvari
apy āyuṣā vā kārtsnyena
ye cānye guṇa-gṛdhnavaḥ

na—never; *vayam*—we; *prabhavaḥ*—are able; *tām*—that; *tvām*—unto you; *anukartum*—do the same; *gṛha-īśvari*—O queen of the home; *api*—in spite of; *āyuṣā*—by duration of life; *vā*—or (in the next life); *kārtsnyena*—entire; *ye*—who; *ca*—also; *anye*—others; *guṇa-gṛdhnavaḥ*—those who are able to appreciate qualities.

TRANSLATION

O queen of the home, we are not able to act like you, nor could we repay you for what you have done, even if we worked for our entire life or even after death. To repay you is not possible, even for those who are admirers of personal qualities.

PURPORT

So much glorification of a woman by her husband indicates that he is henpecked or is talking lightly in joke. Kaśyapa meant that householders living with wives enjoy the heavenly blessings of sense enjoyment and at the same time have no fear of going down to hell. The man in the renounced order of life has no wife and may be driven by sex desire to seek another woman or another's wife and thus go to hell. In other words, the so-called man of the renounced order, who has left his house and wife, goes to hell if he again desires sexual pleasure, knowingly or unknowingly. In that way the householders are on the side of safety. Therefore husbands as a class cannot repay their debt to women either in this life or in the next. Even if they engage themselves in repaying the women throughout their whole lives, it is still not possible. Not all husbands are as able to appreciate the good qualities of their wives, but even though one is able to appreciate these qualities, it is still not possible to repay the debt to the wife. Such extraordinary praises by a husband for his wife are certainly in the mode of joking.

TEXT 22

अथापि काममेतं ते प्रजात्यै करवाण्यलम् ।
यथा मां नातिरोचन्ति मुहूर्तं प्रतिपालय ॥२२॥

athāpi kāmam etaṁ te
prajātyai karavāṇy alam
yathā māṁ nātirocanti
muhūrtaṁ pratipālaya

atha api—even though (it is not possible); *kāmam*—this sex desire; *etam*—as it is; *te*—your; *prajātyai*—for the sake of children; *karavāṇi*—let me do; *alam*—without delay; *yathā*—as; *mām*—unto me; *na*—may not; *atirocanti*—reproach; *muhūrtam*—a few seconds; *pratipālaya*—wait for.

TRANSLATION

Even though it is not possible to repay you, I shall satisfy your sex desire immediately for the sake of begetting children. But you must wait for only a few seconds so that others may not reproach me.

PURPORT

The henpecked husband may not be able to repay his wife for all the benefits that he derives from her, but as for begetting children by fulfilling sexual desire, it is not at all difficult for any husband unless he is thoroughly impotent. This is a very easy task for a husband under normal conditions. In spite of Kaśyapa's being very eager, he requested her to wait for a few seconds so that others might not reproach him. He explains his position as follows.

TEXT 23

एषा घोरतमा वेला घोराणां घोरदर्शना ।
चरन्ति यस्यां भूतानि भूतेशानुचराणि ह ॥२३॥

eṣā ghoratamā velā
ghorāṇāṁ ghora-darśanā
caranti yasyāṁ bhūtāni
bhūteśānucarāṇi ha

eṣā—this time; *ghora-tamā*—most horrible; *velā*—period; *ghorāṇām*—of the horrible; *ghora-darśanā*—horrible looking; *caranti*—move; *yasyām*—in which; *bhūtāni*—ghosts; *bhūta-īśa*—the lord of the ghosts; *anucarāṇi*—constant companions; *ha*—indeed.

TRANSLATION

This particular time is most inauspicious because at this time the horrible-looking ghosts and constant companions of the lord of the ghosts are visible.

PURPORT

Kaśyapa has already told his wife Diti to wait for a while, and now he warns her that failure to consider the particular time will result in punishment from the ghosts and evil spirits who move during this time, along with their master, Lord Rudra.

TEXT 24

एतस्यां साध्वि सन्ध्यायां भगवान् भूतभावनः ।
परीतो भूतपर्षद्भिर्वृषेणाटति भूतराट् ॥२४॥

etasyāṁ sādhvi sandhyāyāṁ
bhagavān bhūta-bhāvanaḥ

parīto bhūta-parṣadbhir
vṛṣeṇāṭati bhūtarāṭ

etasyām—in this period; *sādhvi*—O chaste one; *sandhyāyām*—at the junction of day and night (evening); *bhagavān*—the Personality of God; *bhūta-bhāvanaḥ*—the well-wisher of the ghostly characters; *parītaḥ*—surrounded by; *bhūta-parṣadbhiḥ*—by ghostly companions; *vṛṣeṇa*—on the back of the bull carrier; *aṭati*—travels; *bhūta-rāṭ*—the king of the ghosts.

TRANSLATION

Lord Śiva, the king of the ghosts, sitting on the back of his bull carrier, travels at this time, accompanied by ghosts who follow him for their welfare.

PURPORT

Lord Śiva, or Rudra, is the king of the ghosts. Ghostly characters worship Lord Śiva to be gradually guided toward a path of self-realization. Māyāvādī philosophers are mostly worshipers of Lord Śiva, and Śrīpāda Śaṅkarācārya is considered to be the incarnation of Lord Śiva for preaching godlessness to the Māyāvādī philosophers. Ghosts are bereft of a physical body because of their grievously sinful acts, such as suicide. The last resort of the ghostly characters in human society is to take shelter of suicide, either material or spiritual. Material suicide causes loss of the physical body, and spiritual suicide causes loss of the individual identity. Māyāvādī philosophers desire to lose their individuality and merge into the impersonal spiritual *brahmajyoti* existence. Lord Śiva, being very kind to the ghosts, sees that although they are condemned, they get physical bodies. He places them into the wombs of women who indulge in sexual intercourse regardless of the restrictions on time and circumstance. Kaśyapa wanted to impress this fact upon Diti so that she might wait for a while.

TEXT 25

श्मशानचक्रानिलधूलिधूम्र-
विकीर्णविद्योतजटाकलापः ।

भस्मावगुण्ठामलरुक्मदेहो
देवस्त्रिभिः पश्यति देवरस्ते ॥२५॥

śmaśāna-cakrānila-dhūli-dhūmra-
vikīrṇa-vidyota-jaṭā-kalāpaḥ
bhasmāvaguṇṭhāmala-rukma-deho
devas tribhiḥ paśyati devaras te

śmaśāna—burning crematorium; *cakra-anila*—whirlwind; *dhūli*—dust; *dhūmra*—smoky; *vikīrṇa-vidyota*—thus smeared over beauty; *jaṭā-kalāpaḥ*—bunches of matted hair; *bhasma*—ashes; *avaguṇṭha*—covered by; *amala*—stainless; *rukma*—reddish; *dehaḥ*—body; *devaḥ*—the demigod; *tribhiḥ*—with three eyes; *paśyati*—sees; *devaraḥ*—younger brother of the husband; *te*—your.

TRANSLATION

Lord Śiva's body is reddish, and he is unstained, but he is covered with ashes. His hair is dusty from the whirlwind dust of the burning crematorium. He is the younger brother of your husband, and he sees with his three eyes.

PURPORT

Lord Śiva is not an ordinary living entity, nor is he in the category of Viṣṇu, or the Supreme Personality of Godhead. He is far more powerful than any living entity up to the standard of Brahmā, yet he is not on an equal level with Viṣṇu. Since he is almost like Lord Viṣṇu, Śiva can see past, present and future. One of his eyes is like the sun, another is like the moon, and his third eye, which is between his eyebrows, is like fire. He can generate fire from his middle eye, and he is able to vanquish any powerful living entity, including Brahmā, yet he does not live pompously in a nice house, etc., nor does he possess any material properties, although he is master of the material world. He lives mostly in the crematorium, where dead bodies are burnt, and the whirlwind dust of the crematorium is his bodily dress. He is unstained by material contamination. Kaśyapa took him as his younger brother because the youngest sister of Diti (Kaśyapa's wife) was married to Lord Śiva. The husband of one's sister is considered one's brother. By that social relationship, Lord Śiva happened to be the younger brother of Kaśyapa. Kaśyapa warned his wife that because Lord Śiva would see their sex indulgence, the time was not appropriate. Diti might argue that they would enjoy sex life in a private place, but Kaśyapa reminded her that Lord Śiva has three eyes, called the sun, moon and fire, and one cannot escape his vigilance any more than one can escape Viṣṇu. Although seen by the police, a criminal is sometimes not immediately punished; the police wait for the proper time to apprehend him. The forbidden time for sexual intercourse would be noted by Lord Śiva, and Diti would meet with proper punishment by giving birth to a child of ghostly character or a godless impersonalist. Kaśyapa foresaw this, and thus he warned his wife Diti.

TEXT 26

न यस्य लोके स्वजनः परो वा
नात्यादृतो नोत कश्चिद्विगर्ह्यः ।
वयं व्रतैर्यच्चरणापविद्धा-
माशास्महेऽजां बत भुक्तभोगाम् ॥२६॥

na yasya loke sva-janaḥ paro vā
nātyādṛto nota kaścid vigarhyaḥ
vayaṁ vratair yac-caraṇāpaviddhām
āśāsmahe 'jāṁ bata bhukta-bhogām

na—never; *yasya*—of whom; *loke*—in the world; *sva-janaḥ*—kinsman; *paraḥ*—unconnected; *vā*—nor; *na*—neither; *ati*—greater; *ādṛtaḥ*—favorable; *na*—not; *uta*—or; *kaścit*—anyone; *vigarhyaḥ*—criminal; *vayam*—we; *vrataiḥ*—by vows; *yat*—whose; *caraṇa*—feet; *apaviddhām*—rejected; *āśāsmahe*—respectfully worship; *ajām*—*mahā-prasāda; bata*—certainly; *bhukta-bhogām*—remnants of foodstuff.

TRANSLATION

Lord Śiva regards no one as his relative, yet there is no one who is not connected with him; he does not regard anyone as very

favorable or abominable. We respectfully worship the remnants of his foodstuff, and we vow to accept what is rejected by him.

PURPORT

Kaśyapa informed his wife that just because Lord Śiva happened to be his brother-in-law, that should not encourage her in her offense towards him. Kaśyapa warned her that actually Lord Śiva is not connected with anyone, nor is anyone his enemy. Since he is one of the three controllers of the universal affairs, he is equal to everyone. His greatness is incomparable because he is a great devotee of the Supreme Personality of Godhead. It is said that among all the devotees of the Personality of Godhead, Lord Śiva is the greatest. Thus the remnants of foodstuff left by him are accepted by other devotees as *mahā-prasāda*, or great spiritual foodstuff. The remnants of foodstuff offered to Lord Kṛṣṇa are called *prasāda*, but when the same *prasāda* is eaten by a great devotee like Lord Śiva, it is called *mahā-prasāda*. Lord Śiva is so great that he does not care for the material prosperity for which every one of us is so eager. Pārvatī, who is the powerful material nature personified, is under his full control as his wife, yet he does not use her even to build a residential house. He prefers to remain without shelter, and his great wife also agrees to live with him humbly. People in general worship goddess Durgā, the wife of Lord Śiva, for material prosperity, but Lord Śiva engages her in his service without material desire. He simply advises his great wife that of all kinds of worship, the worship of Viṣṇu is the highest, and greater than that is the worship of a great devotee or anything in relation with Viṣṇu.

TEXT 27

यस्यानवद्याचरितं मनीषिणो
गृणन्त्यविद्यापटलं बिभित्सवः ।
निरस्तसाम्यातिशयोऽपि यत्स्वयं
पिशाचचर्यामचरद्गतिः सताम् ॥२७॥

yasyānavadyācaritaṁ manīṣiṇo
gṛṇanty avidyā-paṭalaṁ bibhitsavaḥ
nirasta-sāmyātiśayo 'pi yat svayaṁ
piśāca-caryām acarad gatiḥ satām

yasya—whose; *anavadya*—unimpeachable; *ācaritam*—character; *manīṣiṇaḥ*—great sages; *gṛṇanti*—follow; *avidyā*—nescience; *paṭalam*—mass; *bibhitsavaḥ*—desiring to dismantle; *nirasta*—nullified; *sāmya*—equality; *atiśayaḥ*—greatness; *api*—in spite of; *yat*—as; *svayam*—personally; *piśāca*—devil; *caryām*—activities; *acarat*—performed; *gatiḥ*—destination; *satām*—of the devotees of the Lord.

TRANSLATION

Although no one in the material world is equal to or greater than Lord Śiva, and although his unimpeachable character is followed by great souls to dismantle the mass of nescience, he nevertheless remains as if a devil to give salvation to all devotees of the Lord.

PURPORT

Lord Śiva's uncivilized, devilish characteristics are never abominable because he teaches the sincere devotees of the Lord how to practice detachment from material enjoyment. He is called Mahādeva, or the greatest of all demigods, and no one is equal to or greater than him in the material world. He is almost equal with Lord Viṣṇu. Although he always associates with Māyā, Durgā, he is above the reactionary stage of the three modes of material nature, and although he is in charge of devilish characters in the mode of ignorance, he is not affected by such association.

TEXT 28

हसन्ति यस्याचरितं हि दुर्भगाः
स्वात्मन्-रतस्याविदुषः समीहितम् ।
यैर्वस्त्रमाल्याभरणानुलेपनैः
श्वभोजनं स्वात्मतयोपलालितम् ॥२८॥

hasanti yasyācaritaṁ hi durbhagāḥ
svātman-ratasyāviduṣaḥ samīhitam
yair vastra-mālyābharaṇānulepanaiḥ
śva-bhojanaṁ svātmatayopalālitam

hasanti—laugh at; *yasya*—whose; *ācaritam*—activity; *hi*—certainly; *durbhagāḥ*—the unfortunate; *sva-ātman*—in the self; *ratasya*—of one engaged; *aviduṣaḥ*—not knowing; *samīhitam*—his purpose; *yaiḥ*—by whom; *vastra*—clothing; *mālya*—garlands; *ābharaṇa*—ornaments; *anu*—such luxurious; *lepanaiḥ*—with ointments; *śva-bhojanam*—eatable by the dogs; *sva-ātmatayā*—as if the self; *upalālitam*—fondled.

TRANSLATION

Unfortunate, foolish persons, not knowing that he is engaged in his own self, laugh at him. Such foolish persons engage in maintaining the body—which is eatable by dogs—with dresses, ornaments, garlands and ointments.

PURPORT

Lord Śiva never accepts any luxurious dress, garland, ornament or ointment. But those who are addicted to the decoration of the body, which is finally eatable by dogs, very luxuriously maintain it as the self. Such persons do not understand Lord Śiva, but they approach him for luxurious material comforts. There are two kinds of devotees of Lord Śiva. One class is the gross materialist seeking only bodily comforts from Lord Śiva, and the other class desires to become one with him. They are mostly impersonalists and prefer to chant *śivo 'ham*, "I am Śiva," or "After liberation I shall become one with Lord Śiva." In other words, the *karmīs* and *jñānīs* are generally devotees of Lord Śiva, but they do not properly understand his real purpose in life. Sometimes so-called devotees of Lord Śiva imitate him in using poisonous intoxicants. Lord Śiva once swallowed an ocean of poison, and thus his throat became blue. The imitation Śivas try to follow him by indulging in poisons, and thus they are ruined. The real purpose of Lord Śiva is to serve the Soul of the soul, Lord Kṛṣṇa. He desires that all luxurious articles, such as nice garments, garlands, ornaments and cosmetics, be given to Lord Kṛṣṇa only, because Kṛṣṇa is the real enjoyer. He refuses to accept such luxurious items himself because they are only meant for Kṛṣṇa. However, since they do not know this purpose of Lord Śiva, foolish persons either laugh at him or profitlessly try to imitate him.

TEXT 29

ब्रह्मादयो यत्कृतसेतुपाला
यत्कारणं विश्वमिदं च माया ।
आज्ञाकरी यस्य पिशाचचर्या
अहो विभूम्नश्चरितं विडम्बनम् ॥२९॥

brahmādayo yat-kṛta-setu-pālā
yat-kāraṇaṁ viśvam idaṁ ca māyā
ājñā-karī yasya piśāca-caryā
aho vibhūmnaś caritaṁ viḍambanam

brahma-ādayaḥ—demigods like Brahmā; *yat*—whose; *kṛta*—activities; *setu*—religious rites; *pālāḥ*—observers; *yat*—one who is; *kāraṇam*—the origin of; *viśvam*—the universe; *idam*—this; *ca*—also; *māyā*—material energy; *ājñā-karī*—order carrier; *yasya*—whose; *piśāca*—devilish; *caryā*—activity; *aho*—O my lord; *vibhūmnaḥ*—of the great; *caritam*—character; *viḍambanam*—simply imitation.

TRANSLATION

Demigods like Brahmā also follow the religious rites observed by him. He is the controller of the material energy, which causes the creation of the material world. He is great, and therefore his devilish characteristics are simply imitation.

PURPORT

Lord Śiva is the husband of Durgā, the controller of the material energy. Durgā is personified material energy, and Lord Śiva, being her husband, is the controller of the material energy. He is also the incarnation of the mode of ignorance and one of the three deities representing the Supreme Lord. As His representative, Lord Śiva is identical with the Supreme Personality of Godhead. He is very great, and his renunciation of all material enjoyment is an ideal example of how one should be materially unattached. One should therefore follow in his footsteps and be unattached to matter, not imitate his uncommon acts like drinking poison.

TEXT 30

मैत्रेय उवाच

सैवं संविदिते भर्त्रा मन्मथोन्मथितेन्द्रिया ।
जग्राह वासो ब्रह्मर्षेर्वृषलीव गतत्रपा ॥३०॥

maitreya uvāca
saivaṁ saṁvidite bhartrā
manmathonmathitendriyā
jagrāha vāso brahmarṣer
vṛṣalīva gata-trapā

maitreyaḥ uvāca—Maitreya said; *sā*—she; *evam*—thus; *saṁvidite*—in spite of being informed; *bhartrā*—by her husband; *manmatha*—by Cupid; *unmathita*—being pressed; *indriyā*—senses; *jagrāha*—caught hold of; *vāsaḥ*—clothing; *brahma-ṛṣeḥ*—of the great *brāhmaṇa*-sage; *vṛṣalī*—public prostitute; *iva*—like; *gata-trapā*—without shame.

TRANSLATION

Maitreya said: Diti was thus informed by her husband, but she was pressed by Cupid for sexual satisfaction. She caught hold of the clothing of the great brāhmaṇa-sage, just like a shameless public prostitute.

PURPORT

The difference between a married wife and a public prostitute is that one is restrained in sex life by the rules and regulations of the scriptures, whereas the other is unrestricted in sex life and is conducted solely by the strong sex urge. Although very enlightened, Kaśyapa, the great sage, became a victim of his prostitute wife. Such is the strong force of material energy.

TEXT 31

स विदित्वाथ भार्यायास्तं निर्बन्धं विकर्मणि ।
नत्वा दिष्टाय रहसि तयाथोपविवेश हि ॥३१॥

sa viditvātha bhāryāyās
taṁ nirbandhaṁ vikarmaṇi

natvā diṣṭāya rahasi
tayāthopaviveśa hi

saḥ—he; *viditvā*—understanding; *atha*—thereupon; *bhāryāyāḥ*—of the wife; *tam*—that; *nirbandham*—obstinacy; *vikarmaṇi*—in the forbidden act; *natvā*—offering obeisances; *diṣṭāya*—unto worshipable fate; *rahasi*—in a secluded place; *tayā*—with her; *atha*—thus; *upaviveśa*—lay; *hi*—certainly.

TRANSLATION

Understanding his wife's purpose, he was obliged to perform the forbidden act, and thus after offering his obeisances unto worshipable fate, he lay with her in a secluded place.

PURPORT

It appears from the talks of Kaśyapa with his wife that he was a worshiper of Lord Śiva, and although he knew that Lord Śiva would not be pleased with him for such a forbidden act, he was obliged to act by his wife's desire, and thus he offered his obeisances unto fate. He knew that the child born of such untimely sexual intercourse would certainly not be a good child, but could not protect himself because he was too obligated to his wife. In a similar case, however, when Ṭhākura Haridāsa was tempted by a public prostitute at the dead of night, he avoided the allurement because of his perfection in Kṛṣṇa consciousness. That is the difference between a Kṛṣṇa conscious person and others. Kaśyapa Muni was greatly learned and enlightened, and he knew all the rules and regulations of systematic life, yet he failed to protect himself from the attack of sex desire. Ṭhākura Haridāsa was not born of a *brāhmaṇa* family, nor was he himself *brāhmaṇa*, yet he could protect himself from such an attack due to his being Kṛṣṇa conscious. Ṭhākura Haridāsa used to chant the holy name of the Lord three hundred thousand times daily.

TEXT 32

अथोपस्पृश्य सलिलं प्राणानायम्य वाग्यतः ।
ध्यायञ्जजाप विरजं ब्रह्म ज्योतिः सनातनम् ॥३२॥

athopaspṛśya salilaṁ
prāṇān āyamya vāg-yataḥ
dhyāyañ jajāpa virajaṁ
brahma jyotiḥ sanātanam

atha—thereafter; *upaspṛśya*—touching or taking bath in water; *salilam*—water; *prāṇān āyamya*—practicing trance; *vāk-yataḥ*—controlling speech; *dhyāyan*—meditating; *jajāpa*—chanted within the mouth; *virajam*—pure; *brahma*—Gāyatrī hymns; *jyotiḥ*—effulgence; *sanātanam*—eternal.

TRANSLATION

Thereafter the brāhmaṇa took his bath in the water and controlled his speech by practicing trance, meditating on the eternal effulgence and chanting the holy Gāyatrī hymns within his mouth.

PURPORT

As one has to take bath after using the toilet, so one has to wash himself with water after sexual intercourse, especially when at a forbidden time. Kaśyapa Muni meditated on the impersonal *brahmajyoti* by chanting the Gāyatrī *mantra* within his mouth. When a Vedic *mantra* is chanted within the mouth so that only the chanter can hear, the chanting is called *japa.* But when such *mantras* are chanted loudly, it is called *kīrtana.* The Vedic hymn Hare Kṛṣṇa, Hare Kṛṣṇa, Kṛṣṇa Kṛṣṇa, Hare Hare/ Hare Rāma, Hare Rāma, Rāma Rāma, Hare Hare can be chanted both softly to oneself or loudly; therefore it is called the *mahā-mantra,* or the great hymn.

Kaśyapa Muni appears to be an impersonalist. Comparing his character with that of Ṭhākura Haridāsa as referred to above, it is clear that the personalist is stronger in sense control than the impersonalist. This is explained in *Bhagavad-gītā* as *paraṁ dṛṣṭvā nivartate;* i.e., one ceases to accept lower grade things when one is situated in a superior condition. One is supposed to be purified after taking bath and chanting Gāyatrī, but the *mahā-mantra* is so powerful that one can chant loudly or softly, in any condition, and he is protected from all the evils of material existence.

TEXT 33

दितिस्तु व्रीडिता तेन कर्मावद्येन भारत ।
उपसङ्गम्य विप्रर्षिमधोमुख्यभ्यभाषत ॥३३॥

ditis tu vrīḍitā tena
karmāvadyena bhārata
upasaṅgamya viprarṣim
adho-mukhy abhyabhāṣata

ditiḥ—Diti, the wife of Kaśyapa; *tu*—but; *vrīḍitā*—ashamed; *tena*—by that; *karma*—act; *avadyena*—faulty; *bhārata*—O son of the Bharata family; *upasaṅgamya*—going nearer to; *vipra-ṛṣim*—the *brāhmaṇa*-sage; *adhaḥ-mukhī*—with her face lowered; *abhyabhāṣata*—politely said.

TRANSLATION

O son of the Bharata family, Diti, after this, went nearer to her husband, her face lowered because of her faulty action. She spoke as follows.

PURPORT

When one is ashamed of an abominable action, one naturally becomes down-faced. Diti came to her senses after the abominable sexual intercourse with her husband. Such sexual intercourse is condemned as prostitution. In other words, sex life with one's wife is equal to prostitution if the regulations are not properly followed.

TEXT 34

दितिरुवाच
न मे गर्भमिमं ब्रह्मन् भूतानामृषभोऽवधीत् ।
रुद्रः पतिर्हि भूतानां यस्याकरवमंहसम् ॥३४॥

ditir uvāca
na me garbham imaṁ brahman
bhūtānām ṛṣabho 'vadhīt

rudraḥ patir hi bhūtānāṁ
yasyākaravam aṁhasam

ditiḥ uvāca—the beautiful Diti said; *na*—not; *me*—my; *garbham*—pregnancy; *imam*—this; *brahman*—O *brāhmaṇa; bhūtānām*—of all living entities; *ṛṣabhaḥ*—the noblest of all living entities; *avadhīt*—let him kill; *rudraḥ*—Lord Śiva; *patiḥ*—master; *hi*—certainly; *bhūtānām*—of all living entities; *yasya*—whose; *akaravam*—I have done; *aṁhasam*—offense.

TRANSLATION

The beautiful Diti said: My dear brāhmaṇa, kindly see that my embryo is not killed by Lord Śiva, the lord of all living entities, because of the great offense I have committed against him.

PURPORT

Diti was conscious of her offense and was anxious to be excused by Lord Śiva. Lord Śiva has two popular names, Rudra and Āśutoṣa. He is very prone to anger as well as quickly pacified. Diti knew that because of his being quickly angered he might spoil the pregnancy she had so unlawfully achieved. But because he was also Āśutoṣa, she implored her *brāhmaṇa*-husband to help her in pacifying Lord Śiva, for her husband was a great devotee of Lord Śiva. In other words, Lord Śiva might have been angry with Diti because she obliged her husband to transgress the law, but he would not refuse her husband's prayer. Therefore the application for excuse was submitted through her husband. She prayed to Lord Śiva as follows.

TEXT 35

नमो रुद्राय महते देवायोग्राय मीढुषे ।
शिवाय न्यस्तदण्डाय धृतदण्डाय मन्यवे ॥३५॥

namo rudrāya mahate
devāyogrāya mīḍhuṣe
śivāya nyasta-daṇḍāya
dhṛta-daṇḍāya manyave

namaḥ—all obeisances unto; *rudrāya*—unto the angry Lord Śiva; *mahate*—unto the great; *devāya*—unto the demigod; *ugrāya*—unto the ferocious; *mīḍhuṣe*—unto the fulfiller of all material desires; *śivāya*—unto the all-auspicious; *nyasta-daṇḍāya*—unto the forgiving; *dhṛta-daṇḍāya*—unto the immediate chastiser; *manyave*—unto the angry.

TRANSLATION

Let me offer my obeisances unto the angry Lord Śiva, who is simultaneously the very ferocious great demigod and the fulfiller of all material desires. He is all-auspicious and forgiving, but his anger can immediately move him to chastise.

PURPORT

Diti prayed for the mercy of Lord Śiva very cleverly. She prayed: "The lord can cause me to cry, but if he likes he can also stop my crying because he is Āśutoṣa. He is so great that if he likes he can immediately destroy my pregnancy, but by his mercy he can also fulfill my desire that my pregnancy not be spoiled. Because he is all-auspicious, it is not difficult for him to excuse me from being punished, although he is now ready to punish me because I have moved his great anger. He appears like a man, but he is the lord of all men."

TEXT 36

स नः प्रसीदतां भामो भगवानुर्वनुग्रहः ।
व्याधस्याप्यनुकम्प्यानां स्त्रीणां देवः सतीपतिः ॥३६॥

sa naḥ prasīdatāṁ bhāmo
bhagavān urv-anugrahaḥ
vyādhasyāpy anukampyānāṁ
strīṇāṁ devaḥ satī-patiḥ

saḥ—he; *naḥ*—with us; *prasīdatām*—be pleased; *bhāmaḥ*—brother-in-law; *bhagavān*—the personality of all opulences; *uru*—very great; *anugrahaḥ*—merciful; *vyādhasya*—of the hunter; *api*—also; *anukampyānām*—of the objects of mercy; *strīṇām*—of the women;

devaḥ—the worshipable lord; *satī-patiḥ*—the husband of Satī (the chaste).

TRANSLATION

Let him be pleased with us, since he is my brother-in-law, the husband of my sister Satī. He is also the worshipable lord of all women. He is the personality of all opulences and can show mercy towards women, who are excused even by the uncivilized hunters.

PURPORT

Lord Śiva is the husband of Satī, one of the sisters of Diti. Diti invoked the pleasure of her sister Satī so that Satī would request her husband to excuse her. Besides that, Lord Śiva is the worshipable lord of all women. He is naturally very kind towards women, on whom even the uncivilized hunters also show their mercy. Since Lord Śiva is himself associated with women, he knows very well their defective nature, and he might not take very seriously Diti's unavoidable offense, which occurred due to her faulty nature. Every virgin girl is supposed to be a devotee of Lord Śiva. Diti remembered her childhood worship of Lord Śiva and begged his mercy.

TEXT 37

मैत्रेय उवाच

स्वसर्गस्याशिषं लोक्यामाशासानां प्रवेपतीम् ।
निवृत्तसन्ध्यानियमो भार्यामाह प्रजापतिः ॥३७॥

maitreya uvāca
sva-sargasyāśiṣaṁ lokyām
āśāsānāṁ pravepatīm
nivṛtta-sandhyā-niyamo
bhāryām āha prajāpatiḥ

maitreyaḥ uvāca—the great sage Maitreya said; *sva-sargasya*—of her own children; *āśiṣam*—welfare; *lokyām*—in the world; *āśāsānām*—desiring; *pravepatīm*—while trembling; *nivṛtta*—averted from;

sandhyā-niyamaḥ—the rules and regulations of evening; *bhāryām*—unto the wife; *āha*—said; *prajāpatiḥ*—the progenitor.

TRANSLATION

Maitreya said: The great sage Kaśyapa thus addressed his wife, who was trembling because of fear that her husband was offended. She understood that he had been dissuaded from his daily duties of offering evening prayers, yet she desired the welfare of her children in the world.

TEXT 38

कश्यप उवाच
अप्रायत्यादात्मनस्ते दोषान्मौहूर्तिकादुत ।
मन्निदेशातिचारेण देवानां चातिहेलनात् ॥३८॥

kaśyapa uvāca
aprāyatyād ātmanas te
doṣān mauhūrtikād uta
man-nideśāticāreṇa
devānāṁ cātihelanāt

kaśyapaḥ uvāca—the learned *brāhmaṇa* Kaśyapa said; *aprāyatyāt*—because of the pollution; *ātmanaḥ*—of the mind; *te*—your; *doṣāt*—because of defilement; *mauhūrtikāt*—in terms of the moment; *uta*—also; *mat*—my; *nideśa*—direction; *aticāreṇa*—being too neglectful; *devānām*—of the demigods; *ca*—also; *atihelanāt*—being too apathetic.

TRANSLATION

The learned Kaśyapa said: Because of your mind's being polluted, because of defilement of the particular time, because of your negligence of my directions, and because of your being apathetic to the demigods, everything was inauspicious.

PURPORT

The conditions for having good progeny in society are that the husband should be disciplined in religious and regulative principles and the wife should be faithful to the husband. In *Bhagavad-gītā* (7.11) it is said that sexual intercourse according to religious principles is a representation of Kṛṣṇa consciousness. Before engaging in sexual intercourse, both the husband and the wife must consider their mental condition, the particular time, the husband's direction, and obedience to the demigods. According to Vedic society, there is a suitable auspicious time for sex life, which is called the time for *garbhādhāna.* Diti neglected all the principles of scriptural injunction, and therefore, although she was very anxious for auspicious children, she was informed that her children would not be worthy to be the sons of a *brāhmaṇa.* There is a clear indication herein that a *brāhmaṇa*'s son is not always a *brāhmaṇa.* Personalities like Rāvaṇa and Hiraṇyakaśipu were actually born of *brāhmaṇas*, but they were not accepted as *brāhmaṇas* because their fathers did not follow the regulative principles for their birth. Such children are called demons, or Rākṣasas. There were only one or two Rākṣasas in the previous ages due to negligence of the disciplinary methods, but during the age of Kali there is no discipline in sex life. How, then, can one expect good children? Certainly unwanted children cannot be a source of happiness in society, but through the Kṛṣṇa consciousness movement they can be raised to the human standard by chanting the holy name of God. That is the unique contribution of Lord Caitanya to human society.

TEXT 39

भविष्यतस्तवाभद्रावभद्रे जाठराधमौ ।
लोकान् सपालांस्त्रींश्चण्डि मुहुराक्रन्दयिष्यतः ॥३९॥

bhaviṣyatas tavābhadrāv
abhadre jāṭharādhamau
lokān sa-pālāṁs trīṁś caṇḍi
muhur ākrandayiṣyataḥ

bhaviṣyataḥ—will take birth; *tava*—your; *abhadrau*—two contemptuous sons; *abhadre*—O unlucky one; *jāṭhara-adhamau*—born of a condemned womb; *lokān*—all planets; *sa-pālān*—with their rulers; *trīn*—three; *caṇḍi*—haughty one; *muhuḥ*—constantly; *ākrandayiṣyataḥ*—will cause lamentation.

TRANSLATION

O haughty one, you will have two contemptuous sons born of your condemned womb. Unlucky woman, they will cause constant lamentation to all the three worlds!

PURPORT

Contemptuous sons are born of the condemned womb of their mother. In *Bhagavad-gītā* (1.40) it is said, "When there is deliberate negligence of the regulative principles of religious life, the women as a class become polluted, and as a result there are unwanted children." This is especially true for boys; if the mother is not good, there cannot be good sons. The learned Kaśyapa could foresee the character of the sons who would be born of the condemned womb of Diti. The womb was condemned because of the mother's being too sexually inclined and thus transgressing all the laws and injunctions of the scriptures. In a society where such women are predominant, one should not expect good children.

TEXT 40

प्राणिनां हन्यमानानां दीनानामकृतागसाम् ।
स्त्रीणां निगृह्यमाणानां कोपितेषु महात्मसु ॥४०॥

prāṇināṁ hanyamānānāṁ
dīnānām akṛtāgasām
strīṇāṁ nigṛhyamāṇānāṁ
kopiteṣu mahātmasu

prāṇinām—when the living entities; *hanyamānānām*—being killed; *dīnānām*—of the poor; *akṛta-āgasām*—of the faultless; *strīṇām*—of the women; *nigṛhyamāṇānām*—being tortured; *kopiteṣu*—being enraged; *mahātmasu*—when the great souls.

TRANSLATION

They will kill poor, faultless living entities, torture women and enrage the great souls.

PURPORT

Demoniac activities are predominant when innocent, faultless living entities are killed, women are tortured, and the great souls engaged in Kṛṣṇa consciousness are enraged. In a demoniac society, innocent animals are killed to satisfy the tongue, and women are tortured by unnecessary sexual indulgence. Where there are women and meat, there must be liquor and sex indulgence. When these are prominent in society, by God's grace one can expect a change in the social order by the Lord Himself or by His bona fide representative.

TEXT 41

तदा विश्वेश्वरः क्रुद्धो भगवाल्लोकभावनः ।
हनिष्यत्यवतीर्यासौ यथाद्रीन् शतपर्वधृक् ॥४१॥

tadā viśveśvaraḥ kruddho
bhagavāl loka-bhāvanaḥ
haniṣyaty avatīryāsau
yathādrīn śataparva-dhṛk

tadā—at that time; *viśva-īśvaraḥ*—the Lord of the universe; *kruddhaḥ*—in great anger; *bhagavān*—the Supreme Personality of Godhead; *loka-bhāvanaḥ*—desiring the welfare of the people in general; *haniṣyati*—will kill; *avatīrya*—descending Himself; *asau*—He; *yathā*—as if; *adrīn*—the mountains; *śata-parva-dhṛk*—the controller of the thunderbolt (Indra).

TRANSLATION

At that time the Lord of the universe, the Supreme Personality of Godhead, who is the well-wisher of all living entities, will descend and kill them, just as Indra smashes the mountains with his thunderbolts.

PURPORT

As stated in *Bhagavad-gītā* (4.8), the Lord descends as an incarnation to deliver the devotees and kill the miscreants. The Lord of the universe and of everything would appear to kill the sons of Diti because of their offending the devotees of the Lord. There are many agents of the Lord, such as Indra, Candra, Varuṇa, goddess Durgā, and Kālī, who can chastise any formidable miscreants in the world. The example of mountains being smashed by a thunderbolt is very appropriate. The mountain is considered the most strongly built body within the universe, yet it can be easily smashed by the arrangement of the Supreme Lord. The Supreme Personality of Godhead does not need to descend in order to kill any strongly built body; He comes down just for the sake of His devotees. Everyone is subject to the miseries offered by material nature, but because the activities of miscreants, such as killing innocent people and animals or torturing women, are harmful to everyone and are therefore a source of pain for the devotees, the Lord comes down. He descends only to give relief to His ardent devotees. The killing of the miscreant by the Lord is also the mercy of the Lord towards the miscreant, although apparently the Lord takes the side of the devotee. Since the Lord is absolute, there is no difference between His activities of killing the miscreants and favoring the devotees.

TEXT 42

दितिरुवाच
वधं भगवता साक्षात्सुनाभोदारबाहुना ।
आशासे पुत्रयोर्मह्यं मा क्रुद्धाद्ब्राह्मणाद्प्रभो ॥४२॥

ditir uvāca
vadhaṁ bhagavatā sākṣāt
sunābhodāra-bāhunā
āśāse putrayor mahyaṁ
mā kruddhād brāhmaṇād prabho

ditiḥ uvāca—Diti said; *vadham*—the killing; *bhagavatā*—by the Supreme Personality of Godhead; *sākṣāt*—directly; *sunābha*—with His Sudarśana weapon; *udāra*—very magnanimous; *bāhunā*—by the arms; *āśāse*—I desire; *putrayoḥ*—of the sons; *mahyam*—of mine; *mā*—never be it so; *kruddhāt*—by the rage; *brāhmaṇāt*—of the *brāhmaṇas; prabho*—O my husband.

TRANSLATION

Diti said: It is very good that my sons will be magnanimously killed by the arms of the Personality of Godhead with His Sudarśana weapon. O my husband, may they never be killed by the wrath of the brāhmaṇa-devotees.

PURPORT

When Diti heard from her husband that the great souls would be angered by the activities of her sons, she was very anxious. She thought that her sons might be killed by the wrath of the *brāhmaṇas.* The Lord does not appear when the *brāhmaṇas* become angry at someone, because the wrath of a *brāhmaṇa* is sufficient in itself. He certainly appears, however, when His devotee simply becomes sorry. A devotee of the Lord never prays to the Lord to appear for the sake of the troubles the miscreants cause for him, and he never bothers Him by asking for protection. Rather, the Lord is anxious to give protection to the devotees. Diti knew well that the killing of her sons by the Lord would also be His mercy, and therefore she says that the wheel and arms of the Lord are magnanimous. If someone is killed by the wheel of the Lord and is thus fortunate enough to see the arms of the Lord, that is sufficient for his liberation. Such good fortune is not achieved even by the great sages.

TEXT 43

न ब्रह्मदण्डदग्धस्य न भूतभयदस्य च ।
नारकाश्चानुगृह्णन्ति यां यां योनिमसौ गतः ॥४३॥

na brahma-daṇḍa-dagdhasya
na bhūta-bhayadasya ca
nārakāś cānugṛhṇanti
yāṁ yāṁ yonim asau gataḥ

na—never; *brahma-daṇḍa*—punishment by a *brāhmaṇa; dagdhasya*—of one who is so punished; *na*—neither; *bhūta-bhaya-dasya*—of one who is always fearful to the living entities; *ca*—also; *nārakāḥ*—those condemned to hell; *ca*—also; *anugṛhṇanti*—do any favor; *yām*

yām—whichever; *yonim*—species of life; *asau*—the offender; *gataḥ*—goes.

TRANSLATION

A person who is condemned by a brāhmaṇa or is always fearful to other living entities is not favored either by those who are already in hell or by those in the species in which he is born.

PURPORT

A practical example of a condemned species of life is the dog. Dogs are so condemned that they never show any sympathy to their contemporaries.

TEXTS 44–45

कश्यप उवाच

कृतशोकानुतापेन सद्यः प्रत्यवमर्शनात् ।
भगवत्युरुमानाच्च भवे मय्यपि चादरात् ॥४४॥
पुत्रस्यैव च पुत्राणां भवितैकः सतां मतः ।
गास्यन्ति यद्यशः शुद्धं भगवद्यशसा समम् ॥४५॥

kaśyapa uvāca
kṛta-śokānutāpena
sadyaḥ pratyavamarśanāt
bhagavaty uru-mānāc ca
bhave mayy api cādarāt

putrasyaiva ca putrāṇāṁ
bhavitaikaḥ satāṁ mataḥ
gāsyanti yad-yaśaḥ śuddhaṁ
bhagavad-yaśasā samam

kaśyapaḥ uvāca—the learned Kaśyapa said; *kṛta-śoka*—having lamented; *anutāpena*—by penitence; *sadyaḥ*—immediately; *pratyavamarśanāt*—by proper deliberation; *bhagavati*—unto the Supreme Personality of Godhead; *uru*—great; *mānāt*—adoration; *ca*—and;

bhave—unto Lord Śiva; *mayi api*—unto me also; *ca*—and; *ādarāt*—by respect; *putrasya*—of the son; *eva*—certainly; *ca*—and; *putrāṇām*—of the sons; *bhavitā*—shall be born; *ekaḥ*—one; *satām*—of the devotees; *mataḥ*—approved; *gāsyanti*—will broadcast; *yat*—of whom; *yaśaḥ*—recognition; *śuddham*—transcendental; *bhagavat*—of the Personality of Godhead; *yaśasā*—with recognition; *samam*—equally.

TRANSLATION

The learned Kaśyapa said: Because of your lamentation, penitence and proper deliberation, and also because of your unflinching faith in the Supreme Personality of Godhead and your adoration for Lord Śiva and me, one of the sons [Prahlāda] of your son [Hiraṇyakaśipu] will be an approved devotee of the Lord, and his fame will be broadcast equally with that of the Personality of Godhead.

TEXT 46

योगैर्हेमेव दुर्वर्णं भावयिष्यन्ति साधवः ।
निर्वैरादिभिरात्मानं यच्छीलमनुवर्तितुम् ॥४६॥

yogair hemeva durvarṇaṁ
bhāvayiṣyanti sādhavaḥ
nirvairādibhir ātmānaṁ
yac-chīlam anuvartitum

yogaiḥ—by the rectifying processes; *hema*—gold; *iva*—like; *durvarṇam*—inferior quality; *bhāvayiṣyanti*—will purify; *sādhavaḥ*—saintly persons; *nirvaira-ādibhiḥ*—by practice of freedom from animosity, etc.; *ātmānam*—the self; *yat*—whose; *śīlam*—character; *anuvartitum*—to follow in the footsteps.

TRANSLATION

In order to follow in his footsteps, saintly persons will try to emulate his character by practicing freedom from animosity, just as the purifying processes rectify gold of inferior quality.

PURPORT

Yoga practice, the process of purifying one's existential identity, is based mainly on self-control. Without self-control one cannot practice freedom from animosity. In the conditional state, every living being is envious of another living being, but in the liberated state there is an absence of animosity. Prahlāda Mahārāja was tortured by his father in so many ways, yet after the death of his father he prayed for his father's liberation by the Supreme Personality of Godhead. He did not ask any benediction that he might have asked, but he prayed that his atheistic father might be liberated. He never cursed any of the persons who engaged in torturing him at the instigation of his father.

TEXT 47

यत्प्रसादादिदं विश्वं प्रसीदति यदात्मकम् ।
स स्वदृग्भगवान् यस्य तोष्यतेऽनन्यया दृशा ॥४७॥

yat-prasādād idaṁ viśvaṁ
prasīdati yad-ātmakam
sa sva-dṛg bhagavān yasya
toṣyate 'nanyayā dṛśā

yat—by whose; *prasādāt*—mercy of; *idam*—this; *viśvam*—universe; *prasīdati*—becomes happy; *yat*—whose; *ātmakam*—because of His omnipotence; *saḥ*—He; *sva-dṛk*—taking special care for His devotees; *bhagavān*—the Supreme Personality of Godhead; *yasya*—whose; *toṣyate*—becomes pleased; *ananyayā*—without deviation; *dṛśā*—by intelligence.

TRANSLATION

Everyone will be pleased with him because the Personality of Godhead, the supreme controller of the universe, is always satisfied with a devotee who does not wish for anything beyond Him.

PURPORT

The Supreme Personality of Godhead is situated everywhere as the Supersoul, and He can dictate to anyone and everyone as He likes. The would-be grandson of Diti, who was predicted to be a great devotee, would be liked by everyone, even by the enemies of his father, because he would have no other vision besides the Supreme Personality of Godhead. A pure devotee of the Lord sees the presence of his worshipable Lord everywhere. The Lord reciprocates in such a way that all living entities in whom the Lord is dwelling as the Supersoul also like a pure devotee because the Lord is present in their hearts and can dictate to them to be friendly to His devotee. There are many instances in history wherein even the most ferocious animal became friendly to a pure devotee of the Lord.

TEXT 48

स वै महाभागवतो महात्मा
महानुभावो महतां महिष्ठः ।
प्रवृद्धभक्त्या ह्यनुभाविताशये
निवेश्य वैकुण्ठमिमं विहास्यति ॥४८॥

sa vai mahā-bhāgavato mahātmā
mahānubhāvo mahatāṁ mahiṣṭhaḥ
pravṛddha-bhaktyā hy anubhāvitāśaye
niveśya vaikuṇṭham imaṁ vihāsyati

saḥ—he; *vai*—certainly; *mahā-bhāgavataḥ*—the topmost devotee; *mahā-ātmā*—expanded intelligence; *mahā-anubhāvaḥ*—expanded influence; *mahatām*—of the great souls; *mahiṣṭhaḥ*—the greatest; *pravṛddha*—well matured; *bhaktyā*—by devotional service; *hi*—certainly; *anubhāvita*—being situated in the *anubhāva* stage of ecstasy; *āśaye*—in the mind; *niveśya*—entering; *vaikuṇṭham*—in the spiritual sky; *imam*—this (material world); *vihāsyati*—will quit.

TRANSLATION

That topmost devotee of the Lord will have expanded intelligence and expanded influence and will be the greatest of the great souls. Due to matured devotional service, he will certainly be situated in transcendental ecstasy and will enter the spiritual sky after quitting this material world.

PURPORT

There are three stages of transcendental development in devotional service, which are technically called *sthāyi-bhāva*, *anubhāva* and *mahābhāva*. Continual perfect love of Godhead is called *sthāyi-bhāva*, and when it is performed in a particular type of transcendental relationship it is called *anubhāva*. But the stage of *mahābhāva* is visible amongst the personal pleasure potential energies of the Lord. It is understood that the grandson of Diti, namely Prahlāda Mahārāja, would constantly meditate on the Lord and reiterate His activities. Because he would constantly remain in meditation, he would easily transfer himself to the spiritual world after quitting his material body. Such meditation is still more conveniently performed by chanting and hearing the holy name of the Lord. This is especially recommended in this age of Kali.

TEXT 49

अलम्पटः शीलधरो गुणाकरो
हृष्टः परर्द्ध्या व्यथितो दुःखितेषु ।
अभूतशत्रुर्जगतः शोकहर्ता
नैदाघिकं तापमिवोडुराजः ॥४९॥

alampaṭaḥ śīla-dharo guṇākaro
hṛṣṭaḥ pararddhyā vyathito duḥkhiteṣu
abhūta-śatrur jagataḥ śoka-hartā
naidāghikaṁ tāpam ivoḍurājaḥ

alampaṭaḥ—virtuous; *śīla-dharaḥ*—qualified; *guṇa-ākaraḥ*—reservoir of all good qualities; *hṛṣṭaḥ*—jolly; *para-ṛddhyā*—by others' happiness; *vyathitaḥ*—distressed; *duḥkhiteṣu*—in others' unhappiness; *abhūta-śatruḥ*—without enemies; *jagataḥ*—of all the universe; *śoka-hartā*—destroyer of lamentation; *naidāghikam*—due to the summer sun; *tāpam*—distress; *iva*—likened; *uḍu-rājaḥ*—the moon.

TRANSLATION

He will be a virtuously qualified reservoir of all good qualities; he will be jolly and happy in others' happiness, distressed in

others' distress, and will have no enemies. He will be a destroyer of the lamentation of all the universes, like the pleasant moon after the summer sun.

PURPORT

Prahlāda Mahārāja, the exemplary devotee of the Lord, had all the good qualities humanly possible. Although he was the emperor of this world, he was not profligate. Beginning from his childhood he was the reservoir of all good qualities. Without enumerating those qualities, it is said here summarily that he was endowed with all good qualities. That is the sign of a pure devotee. The most important characteristic of a pure devotee is that he is not *lampaṭa*, or licentious, and another quality is that he is always eager to mitigate the miseries of suffering humanity. The most obnoxious misery of a living entity is his forgetfulness of Kṛṣṇa. A pure devotee, therefore, always tries to evoke everyone's Kṛṣṇa consciousness. This is the panacea for all miseries.

TEXT 50

अन्तर्बहिश्चामलमब्जनेत्रं
स्वपूरुषेच्छानुगृहीतरूपम् ।
पौत्रस्तव श्रीललनाललामं
द्रष्टा स्फुरत्कुण्डलमण्डिताननम् ॥५०॥

antar bahiś cāmalam abja-netraṁ
sva-pūruṣecchānugṛhīta-rūpam
pautras tava śrī-lalanā-lalāmaṁ
draṣṭā sphurat-kuṇḍala-maṇḍitānanam

antaḥ—within; *bahiḥ*—without; *ca*—also; *amalam*—spotless; *abja-netram*—lotus eyes; *sva-pūruṣa*—own devotee; *icchā-anugṛhīta-rūpam*—accepting form according to desire; *pautraḥ*—grandchild; *tava*—your; *śrī-lalanā*—beautiful goddess of fortune; *lalāmam*—decorated; *draṣṭā*—will see; *sphurat-kuṇḍala*—with brilliant earrings; *maṇḍita*—decorated; *ānanam*—face.

TRANSLATION

Your grandson will be able to see, inside and outside, the Supreme Personality of Godhead, whose wife is the beautiful goddess of fortune. The Lord can assume the form desired by the devotee, and His face is always beautifully decorated with earrings.

PURPORT

It is predicted herewith that the grandson of Diti, Prahlāda Mahārāja, would not only see the Personality of Godhead within himself by meditation but would also be able to see Him personally with his eyes. This direct vision is possible only for one who is highly elevated in Kṛṣṇa consciousness, for the Lord is not possible to see with material eyes. The Supreme Personality of Godhead has multifarious eternal forms such as Kṛṣṇa, Baladeva, Saṅkarṣaṇa, Aniruddha, Pradyumna, Vāsudeva, Nārāyaṇa, Rāma, Nṛsiṁha, Varāha and Vāmana, and the devotee of the Lord knows all those Viṣṇu forms. A pure devotee becomes attached to one of the eternal forms of the Lord, and the Lord is pleased to appear before him in the form desired. A devotee does not imagine something whimsical about the form of the Lord, nor does he ever think that the Lord is impersonal and can assume a form desired by the nondevotee. The nondevotee has no idea of the form of the Lord, and thus he cannot think of any one of the above-mentioned forms. But whenever a devotee sees the Lord, he sees Him in a most beautifully decorated form, accompanied by His constant companion the goddess of fortune, who is eternally beautiful.

TEXT 51

मैत्रेय उवाच

श्रुत्वा भागवतं पौत्रममोदत दितिर्भृशम् ।
पुत्रयोश्च वधं कृष्णाद्विदित्वासीन्महामनाः ॥५१॥

maitreya uvāca
śrutvā bhāgavataṁ pautram
amodata ditir bhṛśam
putrayoś ca vadhaṁ kṛṣṇād
viditvāsīn mahā-manāḥ

maitreyaḥ uvāca—the sage Maitreya said; *śrutvā*—by hearing; *bhāgavatam*—to be a great devotee of the Lord; *pautram*—grandson; *amodata*—took pleasure; *ditiḥ*—Diti; *bhṛśam*—very greatly; *putrayoḥ*—of two sons; *ca*—also; *vadham*—the killing; *kṛṣṇāt*—by Kṛṣṇa; *viditvā*—knowing this; *āsīt*—became; *mahā-manāḥ*—highly pleased in mind.

TRANSLATION

The sage Maitreya said: Hearing that her grandson would be a great devotee and that her sons would be killed by Kṛṣṇa, Diti was highly pleased in mind.

PURPORT

Diti was very aggrieved to learn that because of her untimely pregnancy her sons would be demons and would fight with the Lord. But when she heard that her grandson would be a great devotee and that her two sons would be killed by the Lord, she was very satisfied. As the wife of a great sage and the daughter of a great Prajāpati, Dakṣa, she knew that being killed by the Personality of Godhead is a great fortune. Since the Lord is absolute, His acts of violence and nonviolence are both on the absolute platform. There is no difference in such acts of the Lord. Mundane violence and nonviolence have nothing to do with the Lord's acts. A demon killed by Him attains the same result as one who attains liberation after many, many births of penance and austerity. The word *bhṛśam* is significant herein because it indicates that Diti was pleased beyond her expectations.

Thus end the Bhaktivedanta purports of the Third Canto, Fourteenth Chapter, of the Śrīmad-Bhāgavatam, *entitled "Pregnancy of Diti in the Evening."*

CHAPTER FIFTEEN

Description of the Kingdom of God

TEXT 1

मैत्रेय उवाच

प्राजापत्यं तु तत्तेजः परतेजोहनं दितिः ।
दधार वर्षाणि शतं शङ्कमाना सुरार्दनात् ॥ १ ॥

maitreya uvāca
prājāpatyaṁ tu tat tejaḥ
para-tejo-hanaṁ ditiḥ
dadhāra varṣāṇi śataṁ
śaṅkamānā surārdanāt

maitreyaḥ uvāca—the sage Maitreya said; *prājāpatyam*—of the great Prajāpati; *tu*—but; *tat tejaḥ*—his powerful semen; *para-tejaḥ*—others' prowess; *hanam*—troubling; *ditiḥ*—Diti (Kaśyapa's wife); *dadhāra*—bore; *varṣāṇi*—years; *śatam*—hundred; *śaṅkamānā*—being doubtful; *sura-ardanāt*—disturbing to the demigods.

TRANSLATION

Śrī Maitreya said: My dear Vidura, Diti, the wife of the sage Kaśyapa, could understand that the sons within her womb would be a cause of disturbance to the demigods. As such, she continuously bore the powerful semen of Kaśyapa Muni, which was meant to give trouble to others, for one hundred years.

PURPORT

The great sage Śrī Maitreya was explaining to Vidura the activities of the demigods, including Lord Brahmā. When Diti heard from her husband that the sons she bore within her abdomen would be causes of disturbances to the demigods, she was not very happy. There are two classes of men—devotees and nondevotees. Nondevotees are called demons, and devotees are called demigods. No sane man or woman can tolerate the nondevotees' giving trouble to devotees. Diti, therefore, was reluctant to give birth to her babies; she waited for one hundred years so that at least she could save the demigods from the disturbance for that period.

TEXT 2

लोके तेनाहतालोके लोकपाला हतौजसः ।
न्यवेदयन् विश्वसृजे ध्वान्तव्यतिकरं दिशाम् ॥ २ ॥

loke tenāhatāloke
loka-pālā hataujasaḥ
nyavedayan viśva-sṛje
dhvānta-vyatikaraṁ diśām

loke—within this universe; *tena*—by the force of the pregnancy of Diti; *āhata*—being devoid of; *āloke*—light; *loka-pālāḥ*—the demigods of various planets; *hata-ojasaḥ*—whose prowess was diminished; *nyavedayan*—asked; *viśva-sṛje*—Brahmā; *dhvānta-vyatikaram*—expansion of darkness; *diśām*—in all directions.

TRANSLATION

By the force of the pregnancy of Diti, the light of the sun and moon was impaired in all the planets, and the demigods of various planets, being disturbed by that force, asked the creator of the universe, Brahmā, "What is this expansion of darkness in all directions?"

PURPORT

It appears from this verse of *Śrīmad-Bhāgavatam* that the sun is the source of light for all the planets in the universe. The modern scientific theory which states that there are many suns in each universe is not supported by this verse. It is understood that in each universe there is only one sun, which supplies light to all the planets. In *Bhagavad-gītā* the moon is also stated to be one of the stars. There are many stars, and when we see them glittering at night we can understand that they are reflectors of light; just as moonlight is a reflection of sunlight, other planets also reflect sunlight, and there are many other planets which cannot be seen by our naked eyes. The demoniac influence of the sons in the womb of Diti expanded darkness throughout the universe.

TEXT 3

देवा ऊचुः
तम एतद्विभो वेत्थ संविग्ना यद्वयं भृशम् ।
न ह्यव्यक्तं भगवतः कालेनास्पृष्टवर्त्मनः ॥ ३ ॥

devā ūcuḥ
tama etad vibho vettha
saṁvignā yad vayaṁ bhṛśam
na hy avyaktaṁ bhagavataḥ
kālenāspṛṣṭa-vartmanaḥ

devāḥ ūcuḥ—the demigods said; *tamaḥ*—darkness; *etat*—this; *vibho*—O great one; *vettha*—you know; *saṁvignāḥ*—very anxious; *yat*—because; *vayam*—we; *bhṛśam*—very much; *na*—not; *hi*—because; *avyaktam*—unmanifest; *bhagavataḥ*—of You (the Supreme Personality of Godhead); *kālena*—by time; *aspṛṣṭa*—untouched; *vartmanaḥ*—whose way.

TRANSLATION

The fortunate demigods said: O great one, just see this darkness, which you know very well and which is causing us anxieties. Because the influence of time cannot touch you, there is nothing unmanifest before you.

PURPORT

Brahmā is addressed herein as Vibhu and as the Personality of Godhead. He is the Supreme Personality of Godhead's incarnation of the mode of passion in the material world. He is nondifferent, in the representative sense, from the Supreme Personality of Godhead, and therefore the influence of time cannot affect him. The influence of time, which manifests as past, present and future, cannot touch higher personalities like Brahmā and other demigods. Sometimes demigods and great sages who have attained such perfection are called *tri-kāla-jña.*

TEXT 4

देवदेव जगद्धातर्लोकनाथशिखामणे ।
परेषामपरेषां त्वं भूतानामसि भाववित् ॥ ४ ॥

deva-deva jagad-dhātar
lokanātha-śikhāmaṇe
pareṣām apareṣāṁ tvaṁ
bhūtānām asi bhāva-vit

deva-deva—O god of the demigods; *jagat-dhātaḥ*—O sustainer of the universe; *lokanātha-śikhāmaṇe*—O head jewel of all the demigods in other planets; *pareṣām*—of the spiritual world; *apareṣām*—of the material world; *tvam*—you; *bhūtānām*—of all living entities; *asi*—are; *bhāva-vit*—knowing the intentions.

TRANSLATION

O god of the demigods, sustainer of the universe, head jewel of all the demigods in other planets, you know the intentions of all living entities, in both the spiritual and material worlds.

PURPORT

Because Brahmā is almost on an equal footing with the Personality of Godhead, he is addressed here as the god of the demigods, and because he is the secondary creator of this universe, he is addressed as the sustainer of the universe. He is the head of all the demigods, and therefore he is addressed here as the head jewel of the demigods. It is not difficult for him to understand everything which is happening in both the spiritual and material worlds. He knows everyone's heart and everyone's intentions. Therefore he was requested to explain this incident. Why was the pregnancy of Diti causing such anxieties all over the universe?

TEXT 5

नमो विज्ञानवीर्याय माययेदमुपेयुषे ।
गृहीतगुणभेदाय नमस्तेऽव्यक्तयोनये ॥ ५ ॥

namo vijñāna-vīryāya
māyayedam upeyuṣe
gṛhīta-guṇa-bhedāya
namas te 'vyakta-yonaye

namaḥ—respectful obeisances; *vijñāna-vīryāya*—O original source of strength and scientific knowledge; *māyayā*—by the external energy; *idam*—this body of Brahmā; *upeyuṣe*—having obtained; *gṛhīta*—accepting; *guṇa-bhedāya*—the differentiated mode of passion; *namaḥ te*—offering obeisances unto you; *avyakta*—unmanifested; *yonaye*—source.

TRANSLATION

O original source of strength and scientific knowledge, all obeisances unto you! You have accepted the differentiated mode of passion from the Supreme Personality of Godhead. With the help of external energy you are born of the unmanifested source. All obeisances unto you!

PURPORT

The *Vedas* are the original scientific knowledge for all departments of understanding, and this knowledge of the *Vedas* was first impregnated into the heart of Brahmā by the Supreme Personality of Godhead. Therefore Brahmā is the original source of all scientific knowledge. He is born directly from the transcendental body of Garbhodakaśāyī Viṣṇu, who is never seen by any creature of this material universe and therefore always remains unmanifested. Brahmā is stated here to be born of the unmanifested. He is the incarnation of the mode of passion in material nature, which is the separated, external energy of the Supreme Lord.

TEXT 6

ये त्वानन्येन भावेन भावयन्त्यात्मभावनम् ।
आत्मनि प्रोतभुवनं परं सदसदात्मकम् ॥ ६ ॥

ye tvānanyena bhāvena
bhāvayanty ātma-bhāvanam
ātmani prota-bhuvanaṁ
paraṁ sad-asad-ātmakam

ye—those who; *tvā*—on you; *ananyena*—without deviation; *bhāvena*—with devotion; *bhāvayanti*—meditate; *ātma-bhāvanam*—who generates all living entities; *ātmani*—within your self; *prota*—linked; *bhuvanam*—all the planets; *param*—the supreme; *sat*—effect; *asat*—cause; *ātmakam*—generator.

TRANSLATION

O lord, all these planets exist within your self, and all the living entities are generated from you. Therefore you are the cause of this universe, and anyone who meditates upon you without deviation attains devotional service.

TEXT 7

तेषां सुपक्वयोगानां जितश्वासेन्द्रियात्मनाम् ।
लब्धयुष्मत्प्रसादानां न कुतश्चित्पराभवः ॥ ७ ॥

teṣāṁ supakva-yogānāṁ
jita-śvāsendriyātmanām
labdha-yuṣmat-prasādānāṁ
na kutaścit parābhavaḥ

teṣām—of them; *su-pakva-yogānām*—who are mature mystics; *jita*—controlled; *śvāsa*—breath; *indriya*—the senses; *ātmanām*—the mind; *labdha*—attained; *yuṣmat*—your; *prasādānām*—mercy; *na*—not; *kutaścit*—anywhere; *parābhavaḥ*—defeat.

TRANSLATION

There is no defeat in this material world for persons who control the mind and senses by controlling the breathing process and

who are therefore experienced, mature mystics. This is because by such perfection in yoga they have attained your mercy.

PURPORT

The purpose of yogic performances is explained here. It is said that an experienced mystic attains full control of the senses and the mind by controlling the breathing process. Therefore, controlling the breathing process is not the ultimate aim of *yoga*. The real purpose of yogic performances is to control the mind and the senses. Anyone who has such control is to be understood to be an experienced, mature mystic *yogī*. It is indicated herein that a *yogī* who has control over the mind and senses has the actual benediction of the Lord, and he has no fear. In other words, one cannot attain the mercy and benediction of the Supreme Lord until one is able to control the mind and the senses. This is actually possible when one fully engages in Kṛṣṇa consciousness. A person whose senses and mind are always engaged in the transcendental service of the Lord has no possibility of engaging in material activities. The devotees of the Lord are not defeated anywhere in the universe. It is stated, *nārāyaṇa-parāḥ sarve:* one who is *nārāyaṇa-para*, or a devotee of the Supreme Personality of Godhead, is not afraid anywhere, whether he is sent to hell or promoted to heaven (*Bhāg*. 6.17.28).

TEXT 8

यस्य वाचा प्रजाः सर्वा गावस्तन्त्येव यन्त्रिताः ।
हरन्ति बलिमायत्तास्तस्मै मुख्याय ते नमः ॥ ८ ॥

yasya vācā prajāḥ sarvā
gāvas tantyeva yantritāḥ
haranti balim āyattās
tasmai mukhyāya te namaḥ

yasya—of whom; *vācā*—by the Vedic directions; *prajāḥ*—living entities; *sarvāḥ*—all; *gāvaḥ*—bulls; *tantyā*—by a rope; *iva*—as; *yantritāḥ*—are directed; *haranti*—offer, take away; *balim*—presentation, ingredients for worship; *āyattāḥ*—under control; *tasmai*—unto him; *mukhyāya*—unto the chief person; *te*—unto you; *namaḥ*—respectful obeisances.

TRANSLATION

All the living entities within the universe are conducted by the Vedic directions, as a bull is directed by the rope attached to its nose. No one can violate the rules laid down in the Vedic literatures. To the chief person, who has contributed the Vedas, we offer our respect!

PURPORT

The Vedic literatures are the laws of the Supreme Personality of Godhead. One cannot violate the injunctions given in the Vedic literatures any more than one can violate the state laws. Any living creature who wants real benefit in life must act according to the direction of the Vedic literature. The conditioned souls who have come to this material world for material sense gratification are regulated by the injunctions of the Vedic literature. Sense gratification is just like salt. One cannot take too much or too little, but one must take some salt in order to make one's foodstuff palatable. Those conditioned souls who have come to this material world should utilize their senses according to the direction of the Vedic literature, otherwise they will be put into a more miserable condition of life. No human being or demigod can enact laws like those of the Vedic literature because the Vedic regulations are prescribed by the Supreme Lord.

TEXT 9

स त्वं विधत्स्व शं भूमंस्तमसा लुप्तकर्मणाम् ।
अदभ्रदयया दृष्ट्या आपन्नानर्हसीक्षितुम् ॥ ९ ॥

sa tvaṁ vidhatsva śaṁ bhūmaṁs
tamasā lupta-karmaṇām
adabhra-dayayā dṛṣṭyā
āpannān arhasīkṣitum

saḥ—he; *tvam*—you; *vidhatsva*—perform; *śam*—good fortune; *bhūman*—O great lord; *tamasā*—by the darkness; *lupta*—have been suspended; *karmaṇām*—of prescribed duties; *adabhra*—magnanimous, without reservation; *dayayā*—mercy; *dṛṣṭyā*—by your glance; *āpannān*—us, the surrendered; *arhasi*—are able; *īkṣitum*—to see.

TRANSLATION

The demigods prayed to Brahmā: Please look upon us mercifully, for we have fallen into a miserable condition; because of the darkness, all our work has been suspended.

PURPORT

Because of complete darkness throughout the universe, the regular activities and engagements of all the different planets were suspended. In the North and South Poles of this planet there are sometimes no divisions of day and night; similarly, when the sunlight does not approach the different planets within the universe, there is no distinction between day and night.

TEXT 10

एष देव दितेर्गर्भ ओजः काश्यपमर्पितम् ।
दिशस्तिमिरयन् सर्वा वर्धतेऽग्निरिवैधसि ॥१०॥

eṣa deva diter garbha
ojaḥ kāśyapam arpitam
diśas timirayan sarvā
vardhate 'gnir ivaidhasi

eṣaḥ—this; *deva*—O lord; *diteḥ*—of Diti; *garbhaḥ*—womb; *ojaḥ*—semen; *kāśyapam*—of Kaśyapa; *arpitam*—deposited; *diśaḥ*—directions; *timirayan*—causing complete darkness; *sarvāḥ*—all; *vardhate*—overloads; *agniḥ*—fire; *iva*—as; *edhasi*—fuel.

TRANSLATION

As fuel overloads a fire, so the embryo created by the semen of Kaśyapa in the womb of Diti has caused complete darkness throughout the universe.

PURPORT

The darkness throughout the universe is explained herewith as being caused by the embryo created in the womb of Diti by the semen of Kaśyapa.

TEXT 11

मैत्रेय उवाच
स प्रहस्य महाबाहो भगवान् शब्दगोचरः ।
प्रत्याचष्टात्मभूर्देवान् प्रीणन् रुचिरया गिरा ॥११॥

maitreya uvāca
sa prahasya mahā-bāho
bhagavān śabda-gocaraḥ
pratyācaṣṭātma-bhūr devān
prīṇan ruciraya girā

maitreyaḥ uvāca—Maitreya said; *saḥ*—he; *prahasya*—smiling; *mahā-bāho*—O mighty-armed (Vidura); *bhagavān*—the possessor of all opulences; *śabda-gocaraḥ*—who is understood by transcendental sound vibration; *pratyācaṣṭa*—replied; *ātma-bhūḥ*—Lord Brahmā; *devān*—the demigods; *prīṇan*—satisfying; *rucirayā*—with sweet; *girā*—words.

TRANSLATION

Śrī Maitreya said: Thus Lord Brahmā, who is understood by transcendental vibration, tried to satisfy the demigods, being pleased with their words of prayer.

PURPORT

Brahmā could understand the misdeeds of Diti, and therefore he smiled at the whole situation. He replied to the demigods present there in words they could understand.

TEXT 12

ब्रह्मोवाच
मानसा मे सुता युष्मत्पूर्वजाः सनकादयः ।
चेरुर्विहायसा लोकाल्लोकेषु विगतस्पृहाः ॥१२॥

brahmovāca
mānasā me sutā yuṣmat-
pūrvajāḥ sanakādayaḥ
cerur vihāyasā lokāl
lokeṣu vigata-spṛhāḥ

brahmā uvāca—Lord Brahmā said; *mānasāḥ*—born from the mind; *me*—my; *sutāḥ*—sons; *yuṣmat*—than you; *pūrva-jāḥ*—born previously; *sanaka-ādayaḥ*—headed by Sanaka; *ceruḥ*—traveled; *vihāyasā*—by traveling in outer space or flying in the sky; *lokān*—to the material and spiritual worlds; *lokeṣu*—among the people; *vigata-spṛhāḥ*—without any desire.

TRANSLATION

Lord Brahmā said: My four sons Sanaka, Sanātana, Sanandana and Sanat-kumāra, who were born from my mind, are your predecessors. Sometimes they travel throughout the material and spiritual skies without any definite desire.

PURPORT

When we speak of desire we refer to desire for material sense gratification. Saintly persons like Sanaka, Sanātana, Sanandana and Sanat-kumāra have no material desire, but sometimes they travel all over the universe, out of their own accord, to preach devotional service.

TEXT 13

त एकदा भगवतो वैकुण्ठस्यामलात्मनः ।
ययुर्वैकुण्ठनिलयं सर्वलोकनमस्कृतम् ॥१३॥

ta ekadā bhagavato
vaikuṇṭhasyāmalātmanaḥ
yayur vaikuṇṭha-nilayaṁ
sarva-loka-namaskṛtam

te—they; *ekadā*—once upon a time; *bhagavataḥ*—of the Supreme Personality of Godhead; *vaikuṇṭhasya*—of Lord Viṣṇu; *amala-ātmanaḥ*—being freed from all material contamination; *yayuḥ*—entered;

vaikuṇṭha-nilayam—the abode named Vaikuṇṭha; *sarva-loka*—by the residents of all the material planets; *namaskṛtam*—worshiped.

TRANSLATION

After thus traveling all over the universes, they also entered into the spiritual sky, for they were freed from all material contamination. In the spiritual sky there are spiritual planets known as Vaikuṇṭhas, which are the residence of the Supreme Personality of Godhead and His pure devotees and are worshiped by the residents of all the material planets.

PURPORT

The material world is full of cares and anxieties. In any one of the planets, beginning from the highest down to the lowest, Pātāla, every living creature must be full of cares and anxieties because in the material planets one cannot live eternally. The living entities, however, are actually eternal. They want an eternal home, an eternal residence, but because of accepting a temporal abode in the material world, they are naturally full of anxiety. In the spiritual sky the planets are called Vaikuṇṭha because the residents of these planets are free from all anxieties. For them there is no question of birth, death, old age and diseases, and therefore they are not anxious. On the other hand, the residents of the material planets are always afraid of birth, death, disease and old age, and therefore they are full of anxieties.

TEXT 14

वसन्ति यत्र पुरुषाः सर्वे वैकुण्ठमूर्तयः ।
येऽनिमित्तनिमित्तेन धर्मेणाराधयन् हरिम् ॥१४॥

vasanti yatra puruṣāḥ
sarve vaikuṇṭha-mūrtayaḥ
ye 'nimitta-nimittena
dharmeṇārādhayan harim

vasanti—they live; *yatra*—where; *puruṣāḥ*—persons; *sarve*—all; *vaikuṇṭha-mūrtayaḥ*—having a four-handed form similar to that of the

Supreme Lord, Viṣṇu; *ye*—those Vaikuṇṭha persons; *animitta*—without desire for sense gratification; *nimittena*—caused by; *dharmeṇa*—by devotional service; *ārādhayan*—continuously worshiping; *harim*—unto the Supreme Personality of Godhead.

TRANSLATION

In the Vaikuṇṭha planets all the residents are similar in form to the Supreme Personality of Godhead. They all engage in devotional service to the Lord without desires for sense gratification.

PURPORT

The residents and the form of living in Vaikuṇṭha are described in this verse. The residents are all like the Supreme Personality of Godhead Nārāyaṇa. In the Vaikuṇṭha planets Kṛṣṇa's plenary feature as four-handed Nārāyaṇa is the predominating Deity, and the residents of Vaikuṇṭhaloka are also four-handed, just contrary to our conception here in the material world. Nowhere in the material world do we find a human being with four hands. In Vaikuṇṭhaloka there is no occupation but the service of the Lord, and this service is not rendered with a purpose. Although every service has a particular result, the devotees never aspire for the fulfillment of their own desires; their desires are fulfilled by rendering transcendental loving service to the Lord.

TEXT 15

यत्र चाद्यः पुमानास्ते भगवान् शब्दगोचरः ।
सत्त्वं विष्टभ्य विरजं स्वानां नो मृडयन् वृषः ॥१५॥

yatra cādyaḥ pumān āste
bhagavān śabda-gocaraḥ
sattvaṁ viṣṭabhya virajaṁ
svānāṁ no mṛḍayan vṛṣaḥ

yatra—in the Vaikuṇṭha planets; *ca*—and; *ādyaḥ*—original; *pumān*—person; *āste*—is there; *bhagavān*—the Supreme Personality of Godhead; *śabda-gocaraḥ*—understood through the Vedic literature; *sattvam*—the mode of goodness; *viṣṭabhya*—accepting; *virajam*—

uncontaminated; *svānām*—of His own associates; *naḥ*—us; *mṛḍayan*—increasing happiness; *vṛṣaḥ*—the personification of religious principles.

TRANSLATION

In the Vaikuṇṭha planets is the Supreme Personality of Godhead, who is the original person and who can be understood through the Vedic literature. He is full of the uncontaminated mode of goodness, with no place for passion or ignorance. He contributes religious progress for the devotees.

PURPORT

The kingdom of the Supreme Personality of Godhead in the spiritual sky cannot be understood by any process other than hearing from the description of the *Vedas.* No one can go see it. In this material world also, one who is unable to pay to go to a far distant place by motorized conveyances can only understand about that place from authentic books. Similarly, the Vaikuṇṭha planets in the spiritual sky are beyond this material sky. The modern scientists who are trying to travel in space are having difficulty going even to the nearest planet, the moon, to say nothing of the highest planets within the universe. There is no possibility that they can go beyond the material sky, enter the spiritual sky and see for themselves the spiritual planets, Vaikuṇṭha. Therefore, the kingdom of God in the spiritual sky can be understood only through the authentic descriptions of the *Vedas* and *Purāṇas.*

In the material world there are three modes of material qualities—goodness, passion and ignorance—but in the spiritual world there is no trace of the modes of passion and ignorance; there is only the mode of goodness, which is uncontaminated by any tinge of ignorance or passion. In the material world, even if a person is completely in goodness, he is sometimes subject to be polluted by tinges of the modes of ignorance and passion. But in the Vaikuṇṭha world, the spiritual sky, only the mode of goodness in its pure form exists. The Lord and His devotees reside in the Vaikuṇṭha planets, and they are of the same transcendental quality, namely, *śuddha-sattva,* the mode of pure goodness. The Vaikuṇṭha planets are very dear to the Vaiṣṇavas, and for the progressive march of the

Vaiṣṇavas toward the kingdom of God, the Lord Himself helps His devotees.

TEXT 16

यत्र नैःश्रेयसं नाम वनं कामदुघैर्द्रुमैः ।
सर्वर्तुश्रीभिर्विभ्राजत्कैवल्यमिव मूर्तिमत् ॥१६॥

yatra naiḥśreyasaṁ nāma
vanaṁ kāma-dughair drumaiḥ
sarvartu-śrībhir vibhrājat
kaivalyam iva mūrtimat

yatra—in the Vaikuṇṭha planets; *naiḥśreyasam*—auspicious; *nāma*—named; *vanam*—forests; *kāma-dughaiḥ*—yielding desire; *drumaiḥ*—with trees; *sarva*—all; *ṛtu*—seasons; *śrībhiḥ*—with flowers and fruits; *vibhrājat*—splendid; *kaivalyam*—spiritual; *iva*—as; *mūrtimat*—personal.

TRANSLATION

In those Vaikuṇṭha planets there are many forests which are very auspicious. In those forests the trees are desire trees, and in all seasons they are filled with flowers and fruits because everything in the Vaikuṇṭha planets is spiritual and personal.

PURPORT

In the Vaikuṇṭha planets the land, the trees, the fruits and flowers and the cows—everything—is completely spiritual and personal. The trees are desire trees. On this material planet the trees can produce fruits and flowers according to the order of material energy, but in the Vaikuṇṭha planets the trees, the land, the residents and the animals are all spiritual. There is no difference between the tree and the animal or the animal and the man. Here the word *mūrtimat* indicates that everything has a spiritual form. Formlessness, as conceived by the impersonalists, is refuted in this verse; in the Vaikuṇṭha planets, although everything is spiritual, everything has a particular form. The trees and the men have form, and because all of them, although differently formed, are spiritual, there is no difference between them.

TEXT 17

वैमानिकाः सललनाश्चरितानि शश्वद्
गायन्ति यत्र शमलक्षपणानि भर्तुः ।
अन्तर्जलेऽनुविकसन्मधुमाधवीनां
गन्धेन खण्डितधियोऽप्यनिलं क्षिपन्तः ॥१७॥

vaimānikāḥ sa-lalanāś caritāni śaśvad
gāyanti yatra śamala-kṣapaṇāni bhartuḥ
antar-jale 'nuvikasan-madhu-mādhavīnāṁ
gandhena khaṇḍita-dhiyo 'py anilaṁ kṣipantaḥ

vaimānikāḥ—flying in their airplanes; *sa-lalanāḥ*—along with their wives; *caritāni*—activities; *śaśvat*—eternally; *gāyanti*—sing; *yatra*—in those Vaikuṇṭha planets; *śamala*—all inauspicious qualities; *kṣapa-ṇāni*—devoid of; *bhartuḥ*—of the Supreme Lord; *antaḥ-jale*—in the midst of the water; *anuvikasat*—blossoming; *madhu*—fragrant, laden with honey; *mādhavīnām*—of the *mādhavī* flowers; *gandhena*—by the fragrance; *khaṇḍita*—disturbed; *dhiyaḥ*—minds; *api*—even though; *anilam*—breeze; *kṣipantaḥ*—deriding.

TRANSLATION

In the Vaikuṇṭha planets the inhabitants fly in their airplanes, accompanied by their wives and consorts, and eternally sing of the character and activities of the Lord, which are always devoid of all inauspicious qualities. While singing the glories of the Lord, they deride even the presence of the blossoming mādhavī flowers, which are fragrant and laden with honey.

PURPORT

It appears from this verse that the Vaikuṇṭha planets are full of all opulences. There are airplanes in which the inhabitants travel in the spiritual sky with their sweethearts. There is a breeze carrying the fragrance of blossoming flowers, and this breeze is so nice that it also carries the honey of the flowers. The inhabitants of Vaikuṇṭha, however, are so interested in glorifying the Lord that they do not like the disturbance of such a nice breeze while they are chanting the Lord's glories. In other words, they are pure devotees. They consider glorification of the Lord more important than their own sense gratification. In the Vaikuṇṭha planets there is no question of sense gratification. To smell the fragrance of a blossoming flower is certainly very nice, but it is simply for sense gratification. The inhabitants of Vaikuṇṭha give first preference to the service of the Lord, not their own sense gratification. Serving the Lord in transcendental love yields such transcendental pleasure that, in comparison, sense gratification is counted as insignificant.

TEXT 18

पारावतान्यभृतसारसचक्रवाक-
दात्यूहहंसशुकतित्तिरिबर्हिणां यः ।
कोलाहलो विरमतेऽचिरमात्रमुच्चै-
र्भृङ्गाधिपे हरिकथामिव गायमाने ॥१८॥

pārāvatānyabhṛta-sārasa-cakravāka-
dātyūha-haṁsa-śuka-tittiri-barhiṇāṁ yaḥ
kolāhalo viramate 'cira-mātram uccair
bhṛṅgādhipe hari-kathām iva gāyamāne

pārāvata—pigeons; *anyabhṛta*—cuckoo; *sārasa*—crane; *cakravāka*—*cakravāka; dātyūha*—gallinule; *haṁsa*—swan; *śuka*—parrot; *tittiri*—partridge; *barhiṇām*—of the peacock; *yaḥ*—which; *kolāhalaḥ*—tumult; *viramate*—stops; *acira-mātram*—temporarily; *uccaiḥ*—loudly; *bhṛṅga-adhipe*—king of the bumblebees; *hari-kathām*—the glories of the Lord; *iva*—as; *gāyamāne*—while singing.

TRANSLATION

When the king of bees hums in a high pitch, singing the glories of the Lord, there is a temporary lull in the noise of the pigeon, the cuckoo, the crane, the cakravāka, the swan, the parrot, the partridge and the peacock. Such transcendental birds stop their own singing simply to hear the glories of the Lord.

PURPORT

This verse reveals the absolute nature of Vaikuṇṭha. There is no difference between the birds there and the human residents. The situation in the spiritual sky is that everything is spiritual and variegated. Spiritual variegatedness means that everything is animate. There is nothing inanimate. Even the trees, the ground, the plants, the flowers, the birds and the beasts are all on the level of Kṛṣṇa consciousness. The special feature of Vaikuṇṭhaloka is that there is no question of sense gratification. In the material world even an ass enjoys his sound vibration, but in the Vaikuṇṭhas such nice birds as the peacock, the *cakravāka* and the cuckoo prefer to hear the vibration of the glories of the Lord from the bees. The principles of devotional service, beginning with hearing and chanting, are very prominent in the Vaikuṇṭha world.

TEXT 19

मन्दारकुन्दकुरबोत्पलचम्पकार्ण-
पुन्नागनागबकुलाम्बुजपारिजाताः ।
गन्धेऽर्चिते तुलसिकाभरणेन तस्या
यस्मिंस्तपः सुमनसो बहु मानयन्ति ॥१९॥

mandāra-kunda-kurabotpala-campakārṇa-
punnāga-nāga-bakulāmbuja-pārijātāḥ
gandhe 'rcite tulasikābharaṇena tasyā
yasmiṁs tapaḥ sumanaso bahu mānayanti

mandāra—*mandāra;* *kunda*—*kunda;* *kuraba*—*kuraba;* *utpala*—*utpala;* *campaka*—*campaka;* *arṇa*—*arṇa* flower; *punnāga*—*punnāga;* *nāga*—*nāgakeśara;* *bakula*—*bakula;* *ambuja*—lily; *pārijātāḥ*—*pārijāta;* *gandhe*—fragrance; *arcite*—being worshiped; *tulasikā*—*tulasī;* *ābharaṇena*—with a garland; *tasyāḥ*—of her; *yasmin*—in which Vaikuṇṭha; *tapaḥ*—austerity; *su-manasaḥ*—good minded, Vaikuṇṭha minded; *bahu*—very much; *mānayanti*—glorify.

TRANSLATION

Although flowering plants like the mandāra, kunda, kurabaka, utpala, campaka, arṇa, punnāga, nāgakeśara, bakula, lily and pāri-

jāta are full of transcendental fragrance, they are still conscious of the austerities performed by tulasī, for tulasī is given special preference by the Lord, who garlands Himself with tulasī leaves.

PURPORT

The importance of *tulasī* leaves is very clearly mentioned here. *Tulasī* plants and their leaves are very important in devotional service. Devotees are recommended to water the *tulasī* tree every day and collect the leaves to worship the Lord. One time an atheistic *svāmī* remarked, "What is the use of watering the *tulasī* plant? It is better to water eggplant. By watering the eggplant one can get some fruits, but what is the use of watering the *tulasī*?" These foolish creatures, unacquainted with devotional service, sometimes play havoc with the education of people in general.

The most important thing about the spiritual world is that there is no envy among the devotees there. This is true even among the flowers, which are all conscious of the greatness of *tulasī*. In the Vaikuṇṭha world entered by the four Kumāras, even the birds and flowers are conscious of service to the Lord.

TEXT 20

यत्संकुलं हरिपदानतिमात्रदृष्टै-
वैंदूर्यमारकतहेममयैर्विमानैः ।
येषां बृहत्कटितटाः स्मितशोभिमुख्यः
कृष्णात्मनां न रज आदधुरुत्स्मयाद्यैः ॥२०॥

yat saṅkulaṁ hari-padānati-mātra-dṛṣṭair
vaidūrya-mārakata-hema-mayair vimānaiḥ
yeṣāṁ bṛhat-kaṭi-taṭāḥ smita-śobhi-mukhyaḥ
kṛṣṇātmanāṁ na raja ādadhur utsmayādyaiḥ

yat—that Vaikuṇṭha abode; *saṅkulam*—is pervaded; *hari-pada*—at the two lotus feet of Hari, the Supreme Personality of Godhead; *ānati*—by obeisances; *mātra*—simply; *dṛṣṭaiḥ*—are obtained; *vaidūrya*—lapis lazuli; *mārakata*—emeralds; *hema*—gold; *mayaiḥ*—made of; *vimānaiḥ*—with airplanes; *yeṣām*—of those passengers; *bṛhat*—large; *kaṭi-taṭāḥ*—hips; *smita*—smiling; *śobhi*—beautiful; *mukhyaḥ*—faces; *kṛṣṇa*—in Kṛṣṇa; *ātmanām*—whose minds are absorbed; *na*—not;

rajaḥ—sex desire; *ādadhuḥ*—stimulate; *utsmaya-ādyaiḥ*—by intimate friendly dealings, laughing and joking.

TRANSLATION

The inhabitants of Vaikuṇṭha travel in their airplanes made of lapis lazuli, emerald and gold. Although crowded by their consorts, who have large hips and beautiful smiling faces, they cannot be stimulated to passion by their mirth and beautiful charms.

PURPORT

In the material world, opulences are achieved by materialistic persons by dint of their labor. One cannot enjoy material prosperity unless he works very hard to achieve it. But the devotees of the Lord who are residents of Vaikuṇṭha have the opportunity to enjoy a transcendental situation of jewels and emeralds. Ornaments made of gold bedecked with jewels are achieved not by working hard but by the benediction of the Lord. In other words, devotees in the Vaikuṇṭha world, or even in this material world, cannot be poverty-stricken, as is sometimes supposed. They have ample opulences for enjoyment, but they need not labor to achieve them. It is also stated that in the Vaikuṇṭha world the consorts of the residents are many, many times more beautiful than we can find in this material world, even in the higher planets. It is specifically mentioned here that a woman's large hips are very attractive and they stimulate man's passion, but the wonderful feature of Vaikuṇṭha is that although the women have large hips and beautiful faces and are decorated with ornaments of emeralds and jewels, the men are so absorbed in Kṛṣṇa consciousness that the beautiful bodies of the women cannot attract them. In other words, there is enjoyment of the association of the opposite sex, but there is no sexual relationship. The residents of Vaikuṇṭha have a better standard of pleasure, so there is no need of sex pleasure.

TEXT 21

श्री रूपिणी क्वणयती चरणारविन्दं
लीलाम्बुजेन हरिसद्मनि मुक्तदोषा ।

संलक्ष्यते स्फटिककुड्य उपेतहेम्नि
सम्मार्जतीव यदनुग्रहणेऽन्ययत्नः ॥२१॥

śrī rūpiṇī kvaṇayatī caraṇāravindaṁ
līlāmbujena hari-sadmani mukta-doṣā
saṁlakṣyate sphaṭika-kuḍya upeta-hemni
sammārjatīva yad-anugrahaṇe 'nya-yatnaḥ

śrī—Lakṣmī, the goddess of fortune; *rūpiṇī*—assuming a beautiful form; *kvaṇayatī*—tinkling; *caraṇa-aravindam*—lotus feet; *līlā-ambujena*—playing with a lotus flower; *hari-sadmani*—the house of the Supreme Personality; *mukta-doṣā*—freed from all faults; *saṁlakṣyate*—becomes visible; *sphaṭika*—crystal; *kuḍye*—walls; *upeta*—mixed; *hemni*—gold; *sammārjatī iva*—appearing like a sweeper; *yat-anugrahaṇe*—to receive her favor; *anya*—others'; *yatnaḥ*—very much careful.

TRANSLATION

The ladies in the Vaikuṇṭha planets are as beautiful as the goddess of fortune herself. Such transcendentally beautiful ladies, their hands playing with lotuses and their leg bangles tinkling, are sometimes seen sweeping the marble walls, which are bedecked at intervals with golden borders, in order to receive the grace of the Supreme Personality of Godhead.

PURPORT

In the *Brahma-saṁhitā* it is stated that the Supreme Lord, Govinda, is always served in His abode by many, many millions of goddesses of fortune. *Lakṣmī-sahasra-śata-sambhrama-sevyamānam.* These millions and trillions of goddesses of fortune who reside in the Vaikuṇṭha planets are not exactly consorts of the Supreme Personality of Godhead, but are the wives of the devotees of the Lord and also engage in the service of the Supreme Personality of Godhead. It is stated here that in the Vaikuṇṭha planets the houses are made of marble. Similarly, in the *Brahma-saṁhitā* it is stated that the ground on the Vaikuṇṭha planets is made of touchstone. Thus there is no need to sweep the stone in Vaikuṇṭha, for there is hardly any dust on it, but still, in order to satisfy the Lord, the ladies there always engage in dusting the marble walls. Why? The reason is that they are eager to achieve the grace of the Lord by doing so.

It is also stated here that in the Vaikuṇṭha planets the goddesses of fortune are faultless. Generally the goddess of fortune does not remain steadily in one place. Her name is Cañcalā, which means "one who is not steady." We find, therefore, that a man who is very rich may become the poorest of the poor. Another example is Rāvaṇa. Rāvaṇa took away Lakṣmī, Sītājī, to his kingdom, and instead of being happy by the grace of Lakṣmī, his family and his kingdom were vanquished. Thus Lakṣmī in the house of Rāvaṇa is Cañcalā, or unsteady. Men of Rāvaṇa's class want Lakṣmī only, without her husband, Nārāyaṇa; therefore they become unsteady due to Lakṣmījī. Materialistic persons find fault on the part of Lakṣmī, but in Vaikuṇṭha Lakṣmījī is fixed in the service of the Lord. In spite of her being the goddess of fortune, she cannot be happy without the grace of the Lord. Even the goddess of fortune needs the Lord's grace in order to be happy, yet in the material world even Brahmā, the highest created being, seeks the favor of Lakṣmī for happiness.

TEXT 22

वापीषु विद्रुमतटास्वमलामृताप्सु
प्रेष्यान्विता निजवने तुलसीभिरीशम् ।
अभ्यर्चती स्वलकमुन्नसमीक्ष्य वक्त्र-
मुच्छेषितं भगवतेत्यमताङ्ग यच्छ्रीः ॥२२॥

vāpīṣu vidruma-taṭāsv amalāmṛtāpsu
preṣyānvitā nija-vane tulasībhir īśam
abhyarcatī svalakam unnasam īkṣya vaktram
uccheṣitaṁ bhagavatety amatāṅga yac-chrīḥ

vāpīṣu—in the ponds; *vidruma*—made of coral; *taṭāsu*—banks; *amala*—transparent; *amṛta*—nectarean; *apsu*—water; *preṣyā-anvitā*—surrounded by maidservants; *nija-vane*—in her own garden; *tulasībhiḥ*—with *tulasī; īśam*—the Supreme Lord; *abhyarcatī*—worship; *su-alakam*—with her face decorated with *tilaka; unnasam*—raised nose; *īkṣya*—by seeing; *vaktram*—face; *uccheṣitam*—being kissed;

bhagavatā—by the Supreme Lord; *iti*—thus; *amata*—thought; *aṅga*—O demigods; *yat-śrīḥ*—whose beauty.

TRANSLATION

The goddesses of fortune worship the Lord in their own gardens by offering tulasī leaves on the coral-paved banks of transcendental reservoirs of water. While offering worship to the Lord, they can see on the water the reflection of their beautiful faces with raised noses, and it appears that they have become more beautiful because of the Lord's kissing their faces.

PURPORT

Generally, when a woman is kissed by her husband, her face becomes more beautiful. In Vaikuṇṭha also, although the goddess of fortune is naturally as beautiful as can be imagined, she nevertheless awaits the kissing of the Lord to make her face more beautiful. The beautiful face of the goddess of fortune appears in ponds of transcendental crystal water when she worships the Lord with *tulasī* leaves in her garden.

TEXT 23

यन्न व्रजन्त्यघभिदो रचनानुवादा-
च्छृण्वन्ति येऽन्यविषयाः कुकथा मतिघ्नीः ।
यास्तु श्रुता हतभगैर्नृभिरात्तसारा-
स्तांस्तान् क्षिपन्त्यशरणेषु तमःसु हन्त ॥२३॥

yan na vrajanty agha-bhido racanānuvādāc
chṛṇvanti ye 'nya-viṣayāḥ kukathā mati-ghnīḥ
yās tu śrutā hata-bhagair nṛbhir ātta-sārās
tāṁs tān kṣipanty aśaraṇeṣu tamaḥsu hanta

yat—Vaikuṇṭha; *na*—never; *vrajanti*—approach; *agha-bhidaḥ*—of the vanquisher of all kinds of sins; *racanā*—of the creation; *anuvādāt*—than narrations; *śṛṇvanti*—hear; *ye*—those who; *anya*—other; *viṣayāḥ*—subject matter; *ku-kathāḥ*—bad words; *mati-ghnīḥ*—killing intelligence; *yāḥ*—which; *tu*—but; *śrutāḥ*—are heard; *hata-bhagaiḥ*—

unfortunate; *nṛbhiḥ*—by men; *ātta*—taken away; *sārāḥ*—values of life; *tān tān*—such persons; *kṣipanti*—are thrown; *aśaraṇeṣu*—devoid of all shelter; *tamaḥsu*—in the darkest part of material existence; *hanta*—alas.

TRANSLATION

It is very much regrettable that unfortunate people do not discuss the description of the Vaikuṇṭha planets but engage in topics which are unworthy to hear and which bewilder one's intelligence. Those who give up the topics of Vaikuṇṭha and take to talk of the material world are thrown into the darkest region of ignorance.

PURPORT

The most unfortunate persons are the impersonalists, who cannot understand the transcendental variegatedness of the spiritual world. They are afraid to talk about the beauty of the Vaikuṇṭha planets because they think that variegatedness must be material. Such impersonalists think that the spiritual world is completely void, or, in other words, that there is no variegatedness. This mentality is described here as *ku-kathā mati-ghnīḥ*, "intelligence bewildered by unworthy words." The philosophies of voidness and of the impersonal situation of the spiritual world are condemned here because they bewilder one's intelligence. How can the impersonalist and the void philosopher think of this material world, which is full of variegatedness, and then say that there is no variegatedness in the spiritual world? It is said that this material world is the perverted reflection of the spiritual world, so unless there is variegatedness in the spiritual world, how can there be temporary variegatedness in the material world? That one can transcend this material world does not imply that there is no transcendental variegatedness.

Here in the *Bhāgavatam*, in this verse particularly, it is stressed that people who try to discuss and understand the real spiritual nature of the spiritual sky and the Vaikuṇṭhas are fortunate. The variegatedness of the Vaikuṇṭha planets is described in relation to the transcendental pastimes of the Lord. But instead of trying to understand the spiritual abode and the spiritual activities of the Lord, people are more interested in politics and economic developments. They hold many conventions, meetings and discussions to solve the problems of this worldly situation, where they can remain for only a few years, but they are not interested in understanding the spiritual situation of the Vaikuṇṭha world. If they are at all fortunate, they become interested in going back home, back to Godhead, but unless they understand the spiritual world, they rot in this material darkness continuously.

TEXT 24

येऽभ्यर्थितामपि च नो नृगतिं प्रपन्ना
ज्ञानं च तत्त्वविषयं सहधर्म यत्र ।
नाराधनं भगवतो वितरन्त्यमुष्य
सम्मोहिता विततया बत मायया ते ॥२४॥

ye 'bhyarthitām api ca no nṛ-gatiṁ prapannā
jñānaṁ ca tattva-viṣayaṁ saha-dharmaṁ yatra
nārādhanaṁ bhagavato vitaranty amuṣya
sammohitā vitatayā bata māyayā te

ye—those persons; *abhyarthitām*—desired; *api*—certainly; *ca*—and; *naḥ*—by us (Brahmā and the other demigods); *nṛ-gatim*—the human form of life; *prapannāḥ*—have attained; *jñānam*—knowledge; *ca*—and; *tattva-viṣayam*—subject matter about the Absolute Truth; *saha-dharmam*—along with religious principles; *yatra*—where; *na*—not; *ārādhanam*—worship; *bhagavataḥ*—of the Supreme Personality of Godhead; *vitaranti*—perform; *amuṣya*—of the Supreme Lord; *sammohitāḥ*—being bewildered; *vitatayā*—all-pervading; *bata*—alas; *māyayā*—by the influence of the illusory energy; *te*—they.

TRANSLATION

Lord Brahmā said: My dear demigods, the human form of life is of such importance that we also desire to have such life, for in the human form one can attain perfect religious truth and knowledge. If one in this human form of life does not understand the Supreme Personality of Godhead and His abode, it is to be understood that he is very much affected by the influence of external nature.

PURPORT

Brahmājī condemns very vehemently the condition of the human being who does not take interest in the Personality of Godhead and His transcendental abode, Vaikuṇṭha. The human form of life is desired even by Brahmājī. Brahmā and other demigods have much better material bodies than human beings, yet the demigods, including Brahmā, nevertheless desire to attain the human form of life because it is specifically meant for the living entity who can attain transcendental knowledge and religious perfection. It is not possible to go back to Godhead in one life, but in the human form one should at least understand the goal of life and begin Kṛṣṇa consciousness. It is said that the human form is a great boon because it is the most suitable boat for crossing over the nescience ocean. The spiritual master is considered to be the most able captain in that boat, and the information from the scriptures is the favorable wind for floating over the ocean of nescience. The human being who does not take advantage of all these facilities in this life is committing suicide. Therefore one who does not begin Kṛṣṇa consciousness in the human form of life loses his life to the influence of the illusory energy. Brahmā regrets the situation of such a human being.

TEXT 25

यच्च व्रजन्त्यनिमिषामृषभानुवृत्त्या
दूरेयमा ह्युपरि नः स्पृहणीयशीलाः ।
भर्तुर्मिथः सुयशसः कथनानुराग-
वैक्लव्यबाष्पकलया पुलकीकृताङ्गाः ॥२५॥

yac ca vrajanty animiṣām ṛṣabhānuvṛttyā
dūre yamā hy upari naḥ spṛhaṇīya-śīlāḥ
bhartur mithaḥ suyaśasaḥ kathanānurāga-
vaiklavya-bāṣpa-kalayā pulakī-kṛtāṅgāḥ

yat—Vaikuṇṭha; *ca*—and; *vrajanti*—go; *animiṣām*—of the demigods; *ṛṣabha*—chief; *anuvṛttyā*—following in the footsteps; *dūre*—keeping at a distance; *yamāḥ*—regulative principles; *hi*—certainly; *upari*—above; *naḥ*—us; *spṛhaṇīya*—to be desired; *śīlāḥ*—good qualities; *bhartuḥ*—of the Supreme Lord; *mithaḥ*—for one another; *su-yaśasaḥ*—glories; *kathana*—by discussions, discourses; *anurāga*—attraction; *vaiklavya*—ecstasy; *bāṣpa-kalayā*—tears in the eyes; *pulakī-kṛta*—shivering; *aṅgāḥ*—bodies.

TRANSLATION

Persons whose bodily features change in ecstasy and who breathe heavily and perspire due to hearing the glories of the Lord are promoted to the kingdom of God, even though they do not care for meditation and other austerities. The kingdom of God is above the material universes, and it is desired by Brahmā and other demigods.

PURPORT

It is clearly stated herein that the kingdom of God is above the material universes. Just as there are many hundreds of thousands of higher planets above this earth, so there are many millions and billions of spiritual planets belonging to the spiritual sky. Brahmājī states herein that the spiritual kingdom is above the kingdom of the demigods. One can enter the kingdom of the Supreme Lord only when one is highly developed in desirable qualities. All good qualities develop in the person of a devotee. It is stated in *Śrīmad-Bhāgavatam,* Fifth Canto, Eighteenth Chapter, verse 12, that anyone who is Kṛṣṇa conscious is endowed with all the good qualities of the demigods. In the material world the qualities of the demigods are highly appreciated, just as, even in our experience, the qualities of a gentleman are more highly appreciated than the qualities of a man in ignorance or in a lower condition of life. The qualities of the demigods in the higher planets are far superior to the qualities of the inhabitants of this earth.

Brahmājī confirms herewith that only persons who have developed the desirable qualities can enter into the kingdom of God. In the *Caitanya-caritāmṛta,* the devotee's desirable qualities are described to be twenty-six in number. They are stated as follows: He is very kind; he does not quarrel with anyone; he accepts Kṛṣṇa consciousness as the highest goal of life; he is equal to everyone; no one can find fault in his character; he is magnanimous, mild and always clean, internally and externally; he does not profess to possess anything in this material world; he is a benefactor to all living entities; he is peaceful and is a soul completely surrendered to Kṛṣṇa; he has no material desire to fulfill; he is meek and humble, always steady, and has conquered the sensual activities; he does not eat more than required to maintain body and soul together; he is never mad after material identity; he is respectful to all others and does not demand respect for himself; he is very grave, very compassionate and very friendly; he is poetic; he is expert in all activities, and he is silent in nonsense. Similarly, in *Śrīmad-Bhāgavatam,* Third Canto, Twenty-fifth Chapter, verse 21, the qualifications of a saintly person are mentioned. It is said there that a saintly person eligible to enter into the kingdom of God is very tolerant and very kind to all living entities. He is not partial; he is kind both to human beings and to animals. He is not such a fool that he will kill a goat Nārāyaṇa to feed a human Nārāyaṇa, or *daridra-nārāyaṇa.* He is very kind to all living entities; therefore he has no enemy. He is very peaceful. These are the qualities of persons who are eligible to enter into the kingdom of God. That such a person gradually becomes liberated and enters the kingdom of God is confirmed in *Śrīmad-Bhāgavatam,* Fifth Canto, Fifth Chapter, verse 2. The *Śrīmad-Bhāgavatam,* Second Canto, Third Chapter, verse 24, also states that if a person does not cry or exhibit bodily changes after chanting the holy name of God without offense, it is to be understood that he is hardhearted and that therefore his heart does not change even after he chants the holy name of God, Hare Kṛṣṇa. These bodily changes can take place due to ecstasy when we offenselessly chant the holy names of God: Hare Kṛṣṇa, Hare Kṛṣṇa, Kṛṣṇa Kṛṣṇa, Hare Hare/ Hare Rāma, Hare Rāma, Rāma Rāma, Hare Hare.

It may be noted that there are ten offenses we should avoid. The first offense is to decry persons who try in their lives to broadcast the glories of the Lord. People must be educated in understanding the glories of the Supreme; therefore the devotees who engage in preaching the glories of the Lord are never to be decried. It is the greatest offense. Furthermore, the holy name of Viṣṇu is the most auspicious name, and His pastimes are also nondifferent from the holy name of the Lord. There are many foolish persons who say that one can chant Hare Kṛṣṇa or chant the name of Kālī or Durgā or Śiva because they are all the same. If one thinks that the holy name of the Supreme Personality of Godhead and the names and activities of the demigods are on the same level, or if one accepts the holy name of Viṣṇu to be a material sound vibration, that is also an offense. The third offense is to think of the spiritual master who spreads the glories of the Lord as an ordinary human being. The fourth offense is to consider the Vedic literatures, such as the *Purāṇas* or other transcendentally revealed scriptures, to be ordinary books of knowledge. The fifth offense is to think that devotees have given artificial importance to the holy name of God. The actual fact is that the Lord is nondifferent from His name. The highest realization of spiritual value is to chant the holy name of God, as prescribed for the age—Hare Kṛṣṇa, Hare Kṛṣṇa, Kṛṣṇa Kṛṣṇa, Hare Hare/ Hare Rāma, Hare Rāma, Rāma Rāma, Hare Hare. The sixth offense is to give some interpretation on the holy name of God. The seventh offense is to act sinfully on the strength of chanting the holy name of God. It is understood that one can be freed from all sinful reaction simply by chanting the holy name of God, but if one thinks that he is therefore at liberty to commit all kinds of sinful acts, that is a symptom of offense. The eighth offense is to equate the chanting of Hare Kṛṣṇa with other spiritual activities, such as meditation, austerity, penance or sacrifice. They cannot be equated at any level. The ninth offense is to specifically glorify the importance of the holy name before persons who have no interest. The tenth offense is to be attached to the misconception of possessing something, or to accept the body as one's self, while executing the process of spiritual cultivation.

When one is free from all ten of these offenses in chanting the holy name of God, he develops the ecstatic bodily features called *pulakāśru. Pulaka* means "symptoms of happiness," and *aśru* means "tears in the eyes." The symptoms of happiness and tears in the eyes must appear in a person who has chanted the holy name offenselessly. Here in this verse it is stated that those who have actually developed the symptoms of happiness and tears in the eyes by chanting the glories of the Lord are eligible to enter the kingdom of God. In the *Caitanya-caritāmṛta* it is said that if one does not develop these symptoms while chanting Hare Kṛṣṇa, it is to be understood that he is still offensive. *Caitanya-caritāmṛta* suggests a nice remedy in this connection. There it is said in verse 31, Chapter Eight, of *Ādi-līlā*, that if anyone takes shelter of Lord Caitanya and just chants the holy name of the Lord, Hare Kṛṣṇa, he becomes freed from all offenses.

TEXT 26

तद्विश्वगुर्वधिकृतं भुवनैकवन्द्यं
दिव्यं विचित्रविबुधाग्र्यविमानशोचिः ।
आपुः परां मुदमपूर्वमुपेत्य योग-
मायाबलेन मुनयस्तदथो विकुण्ठम् ॥२६॥

tad viśva-gurv-adhikṛtaṁ bhuvanaika-vandyaṁ
divyaṁ vicitra-vibudhāgrya-vimāna-śociḥ
āpuḥ parāṁ mudam apūrvam upetya yoga-
māyā-balena munayas tad atho vikuṇṭham

tat—then; *viśva-guru*—by the teacher of the universe, the Supreme Personality of Godhead; *adhikṛtam*—predominated; *bhuvana*—of the planets; *eka*—alone; *vandyam*—worthy to be worshiped; *divyam*—spiritual; *vicitra*—highly decorated; *vibudha-agrya*—of the devotees (who are the best of the learned); *vimāna*—of the airplanes; *śociḥ*—illuminated; *āpuḥ*—attained; *parām*—the highest; *mudam*—happiness; *apūrvam*—unprecedented; *upetya*—having attained; *yoga-māyā*—by spiritual potency; *balena*—by the influence; *munayaḥ*—the sages; *tat*—Vaikuṇṭha; *atho*—that; *vikuṇṭham*—Viṣṇu.

TRANSLATION

Thus the great sages, Sanaka, Sanātana, Sanandana and Sanatkumāra, upon reaching the above-mentioned Vaikuṇṭha in the spiritual world by dint of their mystic yoga performance, perceived unprecedented happiness. They found that the spiritual sky was illuminated by highly decorated airplanes piloted by the best devotees of Vaikuṇṭha and was predominated by the Supreme Personality of Godhead.

PURPORT

The Supreme Personality of Godhead is one without a second. He is above everyone. No one is equal to Him, nor is anyone greater than Him. Therefore He is described here as *viśva-guru.* He is the prime living entity of the entire material and spiritual creation and is *bhuvanaika-van-*

dyam, the only worshipable personality in the three worlds. The airplanes in the spiritual sky are self-illuminated and are piloted by great devotees of the Lord. In other words, in the Vaikuṇṭha planets there is no scarcity of the things which are available in the material world; they are available, but they are more valuable because they are spiritual and therefore eternal and blissful. The sages felt an unprecedented happiness because Vaikuṇṭha was not predominated by an ordinary man. The Vaikuṇṭha planets are predominated by expansions of Kṛṣṇa, who are differently named as Madhusūdana, Mādhava, Nārāyaṇa, Pradyumna, etc. These transcendental planets are worshipable because the Personality of Godhead personally rules them. It is said here that the sages reached the transcendental spiritual sky by dint of their mystic power. That is the perfection of the *yoga* system. The breathing exercises and disciplines to keep health in proper order are not the ultimate goals of *yoga* perfection. The *yoga* system as generally understood is *aṣṭāṅga-yoga*, or *siddhi*, eightfold perfection in *yoga*. By dint of perfection in *yoga* one can become lighter than the lightest and heavier than the heaviest; one can go wherever he likes and can achieve opulences as he likes. There are eight such perfections. The *ṛṣis*, the four Kumāras, reached Vaikuṇṭha by becoming lighter than the lightest and thus passing over the space of the material world. Modern mechanical space vehicles are unsuccessful because they cannot go to the highest region of this material creation, and they certainly cannot enter the spiritual sky. But by perfection of the *yoga* system one not only can travel through material space, but can surpass material space and enter the spiritual sky. We learn this fact also from an incident concerning Durvāsā Muni and Mahārāja Ambarīṣa. It is understood that in one year Durvāsā Muni traveled everywhere and went into the spiritual sky to meet the Supreme Personality of Godhead, Nārāyaṇa. By present standards, scientists calculate that if one could travel at the speed of light, it would take forty thousand years to reach the highest planet of this material world. But the *yoga* system can carry one without limitation or difficulty. The word *yogamāyā* is used in this verse. *Yoga-māyā-balena vikuṇṭham.* The transcendental happiness exhibited in the spiritual world and all other spiritual manifestations there are made possible by the influence of *yogamāyā*, the internal potency of the Supreme Personality of Godhead.

TEXT 27

तस्मिन्नतीत्य मुनयः षडसज्जमानाः
कक्षाः समानवयसावथ सप्तमायाम् ।
देवावचक्षत गृहीतगदौ परार्ध्य-
केयूरकुण्डलकिरीटविटङ्कवेषौ ॥२७॥

tasminn atītya munayaḥ ṣaḍ asajjamānāḥ
kakṣāḥ samāna-vayasāv atha saptamāyām
devāv acakṣata gṛhīta-gadau parārdhya-
keyūra-kuṇḍala-kirīṭa-viṭaṅka-veṣau

tasmin—in that Vaikuṇṭha; *atītya*—after passing through; *munayaḥ*—the great sages; *ṣaṭ*—six; *asajjamānāḥ*—without being much attracted; *kakṣāḥ*—walls; *samāna*—equal; *vayasau*—age; *atha*—thereafter; *saptamāyām*—at the seventh gate; *devau*—two Vaikuṇṭha doormen; *acakṣata*—saw; *gṛhīta*—carrying; *gadau*—maces; *para-ardhya*—most valuable; *keyūra*—bracelets; *kuṇḍala*—earrings; *kirīṭa*—helmets; *viṭaṅka*—beautiful; *veṣau*—garments.

TRANSLATION

After passing through the six entrances of Vaikuṇṭha-purī, the Lord's residence, without feeling astonishment at all the decorations, they saw at the seventh gate two shining beings of the same age, armed with maces and adorned with most valuable jewelry, earrings, diamonds, helmets, garments, etc.

PURPORT

The sages were so eager to see the Lord within Vaikuṇṭha-purī that they did not care to see the transcendental decorations of the six gates which they passed by one after another. But at the seventh door they found two doormen of the same age. The significance of the doormen's being of the same age is that in the Vaikuṇṭha planets there is no old age, so one cannot distinguish who is older than whom. The inhabitants of Vaikuṇṭha are decorated like the Supreme Personality of Godhead, Nārāyaṇa, with *śaṅkha*, *cakra*, *gadā* and *padma* (conch, wheel, club and lotus).

TEXT 28

मत्तद्विरेफवनमालिकया निवीतौ
विन्यस्तयासितचतुष्टयबाहुमध्ये ।
वक्त्रं भ्रुवा कुटिलया स्फुटनिर्गमाभ्यां
रक्तेक्षणेन च मनाग्रभसं दधानौ ॥२८॥

matta-dvirepha-vanamālikayā nivītau
vinyastayāsita-catuṣṭaya-bāhu-madhye
vaktraṁ bhruvā kuṭilayā sphuṭa-nirgamābhyām
rakteksaṇena ca manāg rabhasaṁ dadhānau

matta—intoxicated; *dvi-repha*—bees; *vana-mālikayā*—with a garland of fresh flowers; *nivītau*—hanging on the neck; *vinyastayā*—placed around; *asita*—blue; *catuṣṭaya*—four; *bāhu*—hands; *madhye*—between; *vaktram*—face; *bhruvā*—with their eyebrows; *kuṭilayā*—arched; *sphuṭa*—snorting; *nirgamābhyām*—breathing; *rakta*—reddish; *īkṣaṇena*—with eyes; *ca*—and; *manāk*—somewhat; *rabhasam*—agitated; *dadhānau*—glanced over.

TRANSLATION

The two doormen were garlanded with fresh flowers which attracted intoxicated bees and which were placed around their necks and between their four blue arms. From their arched eyebrows, discontented nostrils and reddish eyes, they appeared somewhat agitated.

PURPORT

Their garlands attracted swarms of bees because they were garlands of fresh flowers. In the Vaikuṇṭha world everything is fresh, new and transcendental. The inhabitants of Vaikuṇṭha have bodies of bluish color and four hands like Nārāyaṇa.

TEXT 29

द्वार्येतयोर्निविविशुर्मिषतोरपृष्ट्वा
पूर्वा यथा पुरटवज्रकपाटिका याः ।

सर्वत्र तेऽविषमया मुनयः स्वदृष्ट्या
ये सञ्चरन्त्यविहता विगताभिशङ्काः ॥२९॥

dvāry etayor nivivisur miṣator apṛṣṭvā
pūrvā yathā puraṭa-vajra-kapāṭikā yāḥ
sarvatra te 'viṣamayā munayaḥ sva-dṛṣṭyā
ye sañcaranty avihatā vigatābhiśaṅkāḥ

dvāri—in the door; *etayoḥ*—both doorkeepers; *nivivisuḥ*—entered; *miṣatoḥ*—while seeing; *apṛṣṭvā*—without asking; *pūrvāḥ*—as before; *yathā*—as; *puraṭa*—made of gold; *vajra*—and diamond; *kapāṭikāḥ*—the doors; *yāḥ*—which; *sarvatra*—everywhere; *te*—they; *aviṣamayā*—without any sense of discrimination; *munayaḥ*—the great sages; *sva-dṛṣṭyā*—out of their own will; *ye*—who; *sañcaranti*—move; *avihatāḥ*—without being checked; *vigata*—without; *abhiśaṅkāḥ*—doubt.

TRANSLATION

The great sages, headed by Sanaka, had opened doors everywhere. They had no idea of "ours" and "theirs." With open minds, they entered the seventh door out of their own will, just as they had passed through the six other doors, which were made of gold and diamonds.

PURPORT

The great sages—namely, Sanaka, Sanātana, Sanandana and Sanatkumāra—although very old in years, maintained themselves eternally as small children. They were not at all duplicitous, and they entered the doors exactly as little children enter places without any idea of what it is to trespass. That is a child's nature. A child can enter any place, and no one checks him. Indeed, a child is generally welcome in his attempts to go places, but if it so happens that a child is checked from entering a door, he naturally becomes very sorry and angry. That is the nature of a child. In this case, the same thing happened. The childlike saintly personalities entered all the six doors of the palace, and no one checked them; therefore when they attempted to enter the seventh door and were forbidden by the doormen, who checked them with their sticks, they naturally became very angry and sorrowful. An ordinary child would cry, but because these were not ordinary children, they immediately made preparations to punish the doormen, for the doormen had committed a great offense. Even to this day a saintly person is never checked from entering anyone's door in India.

TEXT 30

तान् वीक्ष्य वातरशनांश्चतुरः कुमारान्
वृद्धान्दशार्धवयसो विदितात्मतत्त्वान् ।
वेत्रेण चास्खलयतामतदर्हणांस्तौ
तेजो विहस्य भगवत्प्रतिकूलशीलौ ॥३०॥

tān vīkṣya vāta-raśanāṁś caturaḥ kumārān
vṛddhān daśārdha-vayaso viditātma-tattvān
vetreṇa cāskhalayatām atad-arhaṇāṁs tau
tejo vihasya bhagavat-pratikūla-śīlau

tān—them; *vīkṣya*—after seeing; *vāta-raśanān*—naked; *caturaḥ*—four; *kumārān*—boys; *vṛddhān*—aged; *daśa-ardha*—five years; *vayasaḥ*—appearing as of the age; *vidita*—had realized; *ātma-tattvān*—the truth of the self; *vetreṇa*—with their staffs; *ca*—also; *askhalayatām*—forbade; *a-tat-arhaṇān*—not deserving such from them; *tau*—those two porters; *tejaḥ*—glories; *vihasya*—disregarding the etiquette; *bhagavat-pratikūla-śīlau*—having a nature displeasing to the Lord.

TRANSLATION

The four boy-sages, who had nothing to cover their bodies but the atmosphere, looked only five years old, even though they were the oldest of all living creatures and had realized the truth of the self. But when the porters, who happened to possess a disposition quite unpalatable to the Lord, saw the sages, they blocked their way with their staffs, despising their glories, although the sages did not deserve such treatment at their hands.

PURPORT

The four sages were the first-born sons of Brahmā. Therefore all other living entities, including Lord Śiva, are born later and are therefore younger than the four Kumāras. Although they looked like five-year-old boys and traveled naked, the Kumāras were older than all other living creatures and had realized the truth of the self. Such saints were not to be forbidden to enter the kingdom of Vaikuṇṭha, but by chance the doormen objected to their entrance. This was not fitting. The Lord is always anxious to serve sages like the Kumāras, but in spite of knowing this fact, the doormen, astonishingly and outrageously, prohibited them from entering.

TEXT 31

ताभ्यां मिषत्स्वनिमिषेषु निषिध्यमानाः
स्वर्हत्तमा ह्यपि हरेः प्रतिहारपाभ्याम् ।
ऊचुः सुहृत्तमदिदृक्षितभङ्ग ईष-
त्कामानुजेन सहसा त उपप्लुताक्षाः ॥३१॥

tābhyāṁ miṣatsv animiṣeṣu niṣidhyamānāḥ
svarhattamā hy api hareḥ pratihāra-pābhyām
ūcuḥ suhṛttama-didṛkṣita-bhaṅga īṣat
kāmānujena sahasā ta upaplutākṣāḥ

tābhyām—by those two porters; *miṣatsu*—while looking on; *animiṣeṣu*—demigods living in Vaikuṇṭha; *niṣidhyamānāḥ*—being forbidden; *su-arhattamāḥ*—by far the fittest persons; *hi api*—although; *hareḥ*—of Hari, the Supreme Personality of Godhead; *pratihāra-pābhyām*—by the two doorkeepers; *ūcuḥ*—said; *suhṛt-tama*—most beloved; *didṛkṣita*—eagerness to see; *bhaṅge*—hindrance; *īṣat*—slight; *kāma-anujena*—by the younger brother of lust (anger); *sahasā*—suddenly; *te*—those great sages; *upapluta*—agitated; *akṣāḥ*—eyes.

TRANSLATION

When the Kumāras, although by far the fittest persons, were thus forbidden entrance by the two chief doorkeepers of Śrī Hari

while other divinities looked on, their eyes suddenly turned red because of anger due to their great eagerness to see their most beloved master, Śrī Hari, the Personality of Godhead.

PURPORT

According to the Vedic system, a *sannyāsī*, a person in the renounced order of life, is dressed in saffron-colored garments. This saffron dress is practically a passport for the mendicant and *sannyāsī* to go anywhere. The *sannyāsī's* duty is to enlighten people in Kṛṣṇa consciousness. Those in the renounced order of life have no other business but preaching the glories and supremacy of the Supreme Personality of Godhead. Therefore the Vedic sociological conception is that a *sannyāsī* should not be restricted; he is allowed to go anywhere and everywhere he wants, and he is not refused any gift he might demand from a householder. The four Kumāras came to see the Supreme Personality of Godhead Nārāyaṇa. The word *suhṛttama,* "best of all friends," is important. As Lord Kṛṣṇa states in the *Bhagavad-gītā,* He is the best friend of all living entities. *Suhṛdaṁ sarva-bhūtānām.* No one can be a greater well-wishing friend to any living entity than the Supreme Personality of Godhead. He is so kindly disposed towards everyone that in spite of our completely forgetting our relationship with the Supreme Lord, He comes Himself—sometimes personally, as Lord Kṛṣṇa appeared on this earth, and sometimes as His devotee, as did Lord Caitanya Mahāprabhu—and sometimes He sends His bona fide devotees to reclaim all the fallen souls. Therefore, He is the greatest well-wishing friend of everyone, and the Kumāras wanted to see Him. The doorkeepers should have known that the four sages had no other business, and therefore to restrict them from entering the palace was not apt.

In this verse it is figuratively stated that the younger brother of desire suddenly appeared in person when the sages were forbidden to see their most beloved Personality of Godhead. The younger brother of desire is anger. If one's desire is not fulfilled, the younger brother, anger, follows. Here we can mark that even great saintly persons like the Kumāras were also angry, but they were not angry for their personal interests. They were angry because they were forbidden to enter the palace to see the Personality of Godhead. Therefore the theory that in the perfectional stage one should not have anger is not supported in this verse. Anger will continue even in the liberated stage. These four mendicant brothers, the Kumāras, were considered liberated persons, but still they were angry because they were restricted in their service to the Lord. The difference between the anger of an ordinary person and that of a liberated person is that an ordinary person becomes angry because his sense desires are not being fulfilled, whereas a liberated person like the Kumāras becomes angry when restricted in the discharge of duties for serving the Supreme Personality of Godhead.

In the previous verse it has been clearly mentioned that the Kumāras were liberated persons. *Viditātma-tattva* means "one who understands the truth of self-realization." One who does not understand the truth of self-realization is called ignorant, but one who understands the self, the Superself, their interrelation, and activities in self-realization is called *viditātma-tattva.* Although the Kumāras were already liberated persons, they nevertheless became angry. This point is very important. Becoming liberated does not necessitate losing one's sensual activities. Sense activities continue even in the liberated stage. The difference is, however, that sense activities in liberation are accepted only in connection with Kṛṣṇa consciousness, whereas sense activities in the conditioned stage are enacted for personal sense gratification.

TEXT 32

मुनय ऊचुः
को वामिहैत्य भगवत्परिचर्ययोच्चै-
स्तद्धर्मिणां निवसतां विषमः स्वभावः ।
तस्मिन् प्रशान्तपुरुषे गतविग्रहे वां
को वात्मवत्कुहकयोः परिशङ्कनीयः ॥३२॥

munaya ūcuḥ
ko vām ihaitya bhagavat-paricaryayoccais
tad-dharmiṇām nivasatām viṣamaḥ svabhāvaḥ
tasmin praśānta-puruṣe gata-vigrahe vāṁ
ko vātmavat kuhakayoḥ pariśaṅkanīyaḥ

munayaḥ—the great sages; *ūcuḥ*—said; *kaḥ*—who; *vām*—you two; *iha*—in Vaikuṇṭha; *etya*—having attained; *bhagavat*—of the Supreme

Personality of Godhead; *paricaryayā*—by the service; *uccaiḥ*—having been developed by past pious actions; *tat-dharmiṇām*—of the devotees; *nivasatām*—dwelling in Vaikuṇṭha; *viṣamaḥ*—discordant; *sva-bhāvaḥ*—mentality; *tasmin*—in the Supreme Lord; *praśānta-puruṣe*—without anxieties; *gata-vigrahe*—without any enemy; *vām*—of you two; *kaḥ*—who; *vā*—or; *ātma-vat*—like yourselves; *kuhakayoḥ*—maintaining duplicity; *pariśaṅkanīyaḥ*—not becoming trustworthy.

TRANSLATION

The sages said: Who are these two persons who have developed such a discordant mentality even though they are posted in the service of the Lord in the highest position and are expected to have developed the same qualities as the Lord? How are these two persons living in Vaikuṇṭha? Where is the possibility of an enemy's coming into this kingdom of God? The Supreme Personality of Godhead has no enemy. Who could be envious of Him? Probably these two persons are imposters; therefore they suspect others to be like themselves.

PURPORT

The difference between the inhabitants of a Vaikuṇṭha planet and those of a material planet is that in Vaikuṇṭha all the residents engage in the service of the Lord Himself and are equipped with all His good qualities. It has been analyzed by great personalities that when a conditioned soul is liberated and becomes a devotee, about seventy-nine percent of all the good qualities of the Lord develop in his person. Therefore in the Vaikuṇṭha world there is no question of enmity between the Lord and the residents. Here in this material world the citizens may be inimical to the chief executives or heads of state, but in Vaikuṇṭha there is no such mentality. One is not allowed to enter Vaikuṇṭha unless he has completely developed the good qualities. The basic principle of goodness is to accept subordination to the Supreme Personality of Godhead. The sages, therefore, were surprised to see that the two doormen who checked them from entering the palace were not exactly like the residents of Vaikuṇṭhaloka. It may be said that a doorman's duty is to determine who should be allowed to enter the palace and who should not. But that is not relevant in this matter because no one is allowed to enter the Vaikuṇṭha planets unless he has developed one hundred percent his mentality of devotional service to the Supreme Lord. No enemy of the Lord can enter Vaikuṇṭhaloka. The Kumāras concluded that the only reason for the doormen's checking them was that the doormen themselves were imposters.

TEXT 33

न ह्यन्तरं भगवतीह समस्तकुक्षा-
वात्मानमात्मनि नभो नभसीव धीराः ।
पश्यन्ति यत्र युवयोः सुरलिङ्गिनोः किं
व्युत्पादितं ह्युदरभेदि भयं यतोऽस्य ॥३३॥

na hy antaraṁ bhagavatīha samasta-kukṣāv
ātmānam ātmani nabho nabhasīva dhīrāḥ
paśyanti yatra yuvayoḥ sura-liṅginoḥ kiṁ
vyutpāditaṁ hy udara-bhedi bhayaṁ yato 'sya

na—not; *hi*—because; *antaram*—distinction; *bhagavati*—in the Supreme Personality of Godhead; *iha*—here; *samasta-kukṣau*—everything is within the abdomen; *ātmānam*—the living entity; *ātmani*—in the Supersoul; *nabhaḥ*—the small quantity of air; *nabhasi*—within the whole air; *iva*—as; *dhīrāḥ*—the learned; *paśyanti*—see; *yatra*—in whom; *yuvayoḥ*—of you two; *sura-liṅginoḥ*—dressed like inhabitants of Vaikuṇṭha; *kim*—how; *vyutpāditam*—awakened, developed; *hi*—certainly; *udara-bhedi*—distinction between the body and the soul; *bhayam*—fearfulness; *yataḥ*—wherefrom; *asya*—of the Supreme Lord.

TRANSLATION

In the Vaikuṇṭha world there is complete harmony between the residents and the Supreme Personality of Godhead, just as there is complete harmony within space between the big and the small skies. Why then is there a seed of fear in this field of harmony? These two persons are dressed like inhabitants of Vaikuṇṭha, but wherefrom can their disharmony come into existence?

PURPORT

Just as there are different departments in each state in this material world—the civil department and the criminal department—so, in God's creation, there are two departments of existence. As in the material world we find that the criminal department is far, far smaller than the civil department, so this material world, which is considered the criminal department, is one fourth of the entire creation of the Lord. All living entities who are residents of the material universes are considered to be more or less criminals because they do not wish to abide by the order of the Lord or they are against the harmonious activities of God's will. The principle of creation is that the Supreme Lord, the Personality of Godhead, is by nature joyful, and He becomes many in order to enhance His transcendental joy. The living entities like ourselves, being part and parcel of the Supreme Lord, are meant to satisfy the senses of the Lord. Thus, whenever there is a discrepancy in that harmony, immediately the living entity is entrapped by *māyā*, or illusion.

The external energy of the Lord is called the material world, and the kingdom of the internal energy of the Lord is called Vaikuṇṭha, or the kingdom of God. In the Vaikuṇṭha world there is no disharmony between the Lord and the residents. Therefore God's creation in the Vaikuṇṭha world is perfect. There is no cause of fear. The entire kingdom of God is such a completely harmonious unit that there is no possibility of enmity. Everything there is absolute. Just as there are many physiological constructions within the body yet they work in one order for the satisfaction of the stomach, and just as in a machine there are hundreds and thousands of parts yet they run in harmony to fulfill the function of the machine, in the Vaikuṇṭha planets the Lord is perfect, and the inhabitants also perfectly engage in the service of the Lord.

The Māyāvādī philosophers, the impersonalists, interpret this verse of *Śrīmad-Bhāgavatam* to mean that the small sky and the big sky are one, but this idea cannot stand. The example of the big sky and the small skies is also applicable within a person's body. The big sky is the body itself, and the intestines and other parts of the body occupy the small sky. Each and every part of the body has individuality, even though occupying a small part of the total body. Similarly, the whole creation is the body of the Supreme Lord, and we created beings, or anything that is created, are but a small part of that body. The parts of the body are never equal to the whole. This is never possible. In *Bhagavad-gītā* it is said that the living entities, who are parts and parcels of the Supreme Lord, are eternally parts and parcels. According to the Māyāvādī philosophers, the living entity in illusion considers himself part and parcel although he is actually one and the same as the supreme whole. This theory is not valid. The oneness of the whole and the part is in their quality. The qualitative oneness of the small and large portions of the sky does not imply that the small sky becomes the big sky.

There is no cause for the politics of divide and rule in the Vaikuṇṭha planets; there is no fear, because of the united interests of the Lord and the residents. *Māyā* means disharmony between the living entities and the Supreme Lord, and Vaikuṇṭha means harmony between them. Actually all living entities are provided for and maintained by the Lord because He is the supreme living entity. But foolish creatures, although actually under the control of the supreme living entity, defy His existence, and that state is called *māyā*. Sometimes they deny that there is such a being as God. They say, "Everything is void." And sometimes they deny Him in a different way: "There may be a God, but He has no form." Both these conceptions arise from the rebellious condition of the living entity. As long as this rebellious condition prevails, the material world will continue in disharmony.

Harmony or disharmony is realized because of the law and order of a particular place. Religion is the law and order of the Supreme Lord. In the *Śrīmad Bhagavad-gītā* we find that religion means devotional service, or Kṛṣṇa consciousness. Kṛṣṇa says, "Give up all other religious principles and simply become a soul surrendered unto Me." This is religion. When one is fully conscious that Kṛṣṇa is the supreme enjoyer and Supreme Lord and one acts accordingly, that is real religion. Anything which goes against this principle is not religion. Kṛṣṇa therefore says: "Just give up all other religious principles." In the spiritual world this religious principle of Kṛṣṇa consciousness is maintained in harmony, and therefore that world is called Vaikuṇṭha. If the same principles can be adopted here, wholly or partially, then it is also Vaikuṇṭha. So it is with any society, such as the International Society for Krishna Consciousness: If the members of the International Society for Krishna Consciousness, putting faith in Kṛṣṇa as the center, live in harmony according to the order and principles of *Bhagavad-gītā*, then they are living in Vaikuṇṭha, not in this material world.

TEXT 34

तद्वाममुष्य परमस्य विकुण्ठभर्तुः
कर्तुं प्रकृष्टमिह धीमहि मन्दधीभ्याम् ।
लोकानितो व्रजतमन्तरभावदृष्ट्या
पापीयसस्त्रय इमे रिपवोऽस्य यत्र ॥३४॥

tad vām amuṣya paramasya vikuṇṭha-bhartuḥ
kartuṁ prakṛṣṭam iha dhīmahi manda-dhībhyām
lokān ito vrajatam antara-bhāva-dṛṣṭyā
pāpīyasas traya ime ripavo 'sya yatra

tat—therefore; *vām*—unto these two; *amuṣya*—of Him; *paramasya*—the Supreme; *vikuṇṭha-bhartuḥ*—the Lord of Vaikuṇṭha; *kartum*—to bestow; *prakṛṣṭam*—benefit; *iha*—in the matter of this offense; *dhīmahi*—let us consider; *manda-dhībhyām*—those whose intelligence is not very nice; *lokān*—to the material world; *itaḥ*—from this place (Vaikuṇṭha); *vrajatam*—go; *antara-bhāva*—duality; *dṛṣṭyā*—on account of seeing; *pāpīyasaḥ*—sinful; *trayaḥ*—three; *ime*—these; *ripavaḥ*—enemies; *asya*—of a living entity; *yatra*—where.

TRANSLATION

Therefore let us consider how these two contaminated persons should be punished. The punishment should be apt, for thus benefit can eventually be bestowed upon them. Since they find duality in the existence of Vaikuṇṭha life, they are contaminated and should be removed from this place to the material world, where the living entities have three kinds of enemies.

PURPORT

The reason why pure souls come into the existential circumstances of the material world, which is considered to be the criminal department of the Supreme Lord, is stated in *Bhagavad-gītā*, Seventh Chapter, verse 27. It is stated that as long as a living entity is pure, he is in complete harmony with the desires of the Supreme Lord, but as soon as he becomes impure he is in disharmony with the desires of the Lord. By contamination he is forced to transfer to this material world, where the living entities have three enemies, namely desire, anger and lust. These three enemies force the living entities to continue material existence, and when one is free from them he is eligible to enter the kingdom of God. One should not, therefore, be angry in the absence of an opportunity for sense gratification, and one should not be lusty to acquire more than necessary. In this verse it is clearly stated that the two doormen should be sent into the material world, where criminals are allowed to reside. Since the basic principles of criminality are sense gratification, anger and unnecessary lust, persons conducted by these three enemies of the living entity are never promoted to Vaikuṇṭhaloka. People should learn *Bhagavad-gītā* and accept the Supreme Personality of Godhead, Kṛṣṇa, as the Lord of everything; they should practice satisfying the senses of the Supreme Lord instead of trying to satisfy their own senses. Training in Kṛṣṇa consciousness will help one be promoted to Vaikuṇṭha.

TEXT 35

तेषामितीरितमुभाववधार्य घोरं
तं ब्रह्मदण्डमनिवारणमस्त्रपूगैः ।
सद्यो हरेरनुचरावुरु बिभ्यतस्तत्-
पादग्रहावपततामतिकातरेण ॥३५॥

teṣām itīritam ubhāv avadhārya ghoraṁ
taṁ brahma-daṇḍam anivāraṇam astra-pūgaiḥ
sadyo harer anucarāv uru bibhyatas tat-
pāda-grahāv apatatām atikātareṇa

teṣām—of the four Kumāras; *iti*—thus; *īritam*—uttered; *ubhau*—both doorkeepers; *avadhārya*—understanding; *ghoram*—terrible; *tam*—that; *brahma-daṇḍam*—curse of a *brāhmaṇa; anivāraṇam*—not able to be counteracted; *astra-pūgaiḥ*—by any kind of weapon; *sadyaḥ*—at once; *hareḥ*—of the Supreme Lord; *anucarau*—devotees; *uru*—very much; *bibhyataḥ*—became fearful; *tat-pāda-grahau*—

grasping their feet; *apatatām*—fell down; *ati-kātareṇa*—in great anxiety.

TRANSLATION

When the doormen of Vaikuṇṭhaloka, who were certainly devotees of the Lord, found that they were going to be cursed by the brāhmaṇas, they at once became very much afraid and fell down at the feet of the brāhmaṇas in great anxiety, for a brāhmaṇa's curse cannot be counteracted by any kind of weapon.

PURPORT

Although, by chance, the doormen committed a mistake by checking the *brāhmaṇas* from entering the gate of Vaikuṇṭha, they were at once aware of the gravity of the curse. There are many kinds of offenses, but the greatest offense is to offend a devotee of the Lord. Because the doormen were also devotees of the Lord, they were able to understand their mistake and were terrified when the four Kumāras were ready to curse them.

TEXT 36

भूयादघोनि भगवद्भिरकारि दण्डो
यो नौ हरेत सुरहेलनमप्यशेषम् ।
मा वोऽनुतापकलया भगवत्स्मृतिघ्नो
मोहो भवेदिह तु नौ व्रजतोरधोऽधः ॥३६॥

bhūyād aghoni bhagavadbhir akāri daṇḍo
yo nau hareta sura-helanam apy aśeṣam
mā vo 'nutāpa-kalayā bhagavat-smṛti-ghno
moho bhaved iha tu nau vrajator adho 'dhaḥ

bhūyāt—let it be; *aghoni*—for the sinful; *bhagavadbhiḥ*—by you; *akāri*—was done; *daṇḍaḥ*—punishment; *yaḥ*—that which; *nau*—in relation to us; *hareta*—should destroy; *sura-helanam*—disobeying great demigods; *api*—certainly; *aśeṣam*—unlimited; *mā*—not; *vaḥ*—of you; *anutāpa*—repentance; *kalayā*—by a little; *bhagavat*—of the Supreme Personality of Godhead; *smṛti-ghnaḥ*—destroying the memory of;

mohaḥ—illusion; *bhavet*—should be; *iha*—in the foolish species of life; *tu*—but; *nau*—of us; *vrajatoḥ*—who are going; *adhaḥ adhaḥ*—down to the material world.

TRANSLATION

After being cursed by the sages, the doormen said: It is quite apt that you have punished us for neglecting to respect sages like you. But we pray that due to your compassion at our repentance, the illusion of forgetting the Supreme Personality of Godhead will not come upon us as we go progressively downward.

PURPORT

To a devotee, any heavy punishment is tolerable but the one which effects forgetfulness of the Supreme Lord. The doormen, who were also devotees, could understand the punishment meted out to them, for they were conscious of the great offense they had committed by not allowing the sages to enter Vaikuṇṭhaloka. In the lowest species of life, including the animal species, forgetfulness of the Lord is very prominent. The doormen were aware that they were going to the criminal department of the material world, and they expected that they might go to the lowest species and forget the Supreme Lord. They prayed, therefore, that this might not happen in the lives they were going to accept because of the curse. In *Bhagavad-gītā*, Sixteenth Chapter, verses 19 and 20, it is said that those who are envious of the Lord and His devotees are thrown into the species of abominable life; life after life such fools are unable to remember the Supreme Personality of Godhead, and therefore they continue going down and down.

TEXT 37

एवं तदैव भगवानरविन्दनाभः
स्वानां विबुध्य सदतिक्रममार्यहृद्यः ।
तस्मिन् ययौ परमहंसमहामुनीना-
मन्वेषणीयचरणौ चलयन् सहश्रीः ॥३७॥

evaṁ tadaiva bhagavān aravinda-nābhaḥ
svānāṁ vibudhya sad-atikramam ārya-hṛdyaḥ

tasmin yayau paramahaṁsa-mahā-munīnām
anveṣaṇīya-caraṇau calayan saha-śrīḥ

evam—thus; *tadā eva*—at that very moment; *bhagavān*—the Supreme Personality of Godhead; *aravinda-nābhaḥ*—with a lotus growing from His navel; *svānām*—of His own servants; *vibudhya*—learned about; *sat*—to the great sages; *atikramam*—the insult; *ārya*—of the righteous; *hṛdyaḥ*—the delight; *tasmin*—there; *yayau*—went; *paramahaṁsa*—recluses; *mahā-munīnām*—by the great sages; *anveṣaṇīya*—which are worthy to be sought; *caraṇau*—the two lotus feet; *calayan*—walking; *saha-śrīḥ*—with the goddess of fortune.

TRANSLATION

At that very moment, the Lord, who is called Padmanābha because of the lotus grown from His navel and who is the delight of the righteous, learned about the insult offered by His own servants to the saints. Accompanied by His spouse, the goddess of fortune, He went to the spot on those very feet sought for by recluses and great sages.

PURPORT

In *Bhagavad-gītā* the Lord declares that His devotees cannot be vanquished at any time. The Lord could understand that the quarrel between the doormen and the sages was taking a different turn, and therefore He instantly came out of His place and went to the spot to stop further aggravation so that His devotees, the doormen, might not be vanquished for good.

TEXT 38

तं त्वागतं प्रतिहृतौपयिकं स्वपुम्भि-
स्तेऽचक्षताक्षविषयं स्वसमाधिभाग्यम् ।
हंसश्रियोर्व्यजनयोः शिववायुलोल-
च्छुभ्रातपत्रशशिकेसरशीकराम्बुम् ॥३८॥

taṁ tv āgataṁ pratihṛtaupayikaṁ sva-pumbhis
te 'cakṣatākṣa-viṣayaṁ sva-samādhi-bhāgyam

haṁsa-śriyor vyajanayoḥ śiva-vāyu-lolac-
chubhrātapatra-śaśi-kesara-śīkarāmbum

tam—Him; *tu*—but; *āgatam*—coming forward; *pratihṛta*—carried; *aupayikam*—the paraphernalia; *sva-pumbhiḥ*—by His own associates; *te*—the great sages (the Kumāras); *acakṣata*—saw; *akṣa-viṣayam*—now a subject matter for seeing; *sva-samādhi-bhāgyam*—visible simply by ecstatic trance; *haṁsa-śriyoḥ*—as beautiful as white swans; *vyajanayoḥ*—the *cāmaras* (bunches of white hair); *śiva-vāyu*—favorable winds; *lolat*—moving; *śubhra-ātapatra*—the white umbrella; *śaśi*—the moon; *kesara*—pearls; *śīkara*—drops; *ambum*—water.

TRANSLATION

The sages, headed by Sanaka Ṛṣi, saw that the Supreme Personality of Godhead, Viṣṇu, who was formerly visible only within their hearts in ecstatic trance, had now actually become visible to their eyes. As He came forward, accompanied by His own associates bearing all paraphernalia, such as an umbrella and a cāmara fan, the white bunches of hair moved very gently, like two swans, and due to their favorable breeze the pearls garlanding the umbrella also moved, like drops of nectar falling from the white full moon or ice melting due to a gust of wind.

PURPORT

In this verse we find the word *acakṣatākṣa-viṣayam.* The Supreme Lord cannot be seen by ordinary eyes, but He now became visible to the eyesight of the Kumāras. Another significant word is *samādhi-bhāgyam.* Meditators who are very fortunate can see the Viṣṇu form of the Lord within their hearts by following the yogic process. But to see Him face to face is a different matter. This is only possible for pure devotees. The Kumāras, therefore, upon seeing the Lord coming forward with His associates, who were holding an umbrella and a *cāmara* fan, were struck with wonder that they were seeing the Lord face to face. It is said in the *Brahma-saṁhitā* that devotees, being elevated in love of God, always see Śyāmasundara, the Supreme Personality of Godhead, within their hearts. But when they are mature, the same God is visible before them face to face. For ordinary persons the Lord is not visible; however, when one can understand the significance of His holy name and one engages himself in the devotional service of the Lord, beginning with the tongue, by chanting and tasting *prasāda*, then gradually the Lord reveals Himself. Thus the devotee constantly sees the Lord within his heart, and, in a more mature stage, one can see the same Lord directly, as we see everything else.

TEXT 39

कृत्स्नप्रसादसुमुखं स्पृहणीयधाम
स्नेहावलोककलया हृदि संस्पृशन्तम् ।
श्यामे पृथावुरसि शोभितया श्रिया स्व-
श्चूडामणिं सुभगयन्तमिवात्मधिष्ण्यम् ॥३९॥

kṛtsna-prasāda-sumukhaṁ spṛhaṇīya-dhāma
snehāvaloka-kalayā hṛdi saṁspṛśantam
śyāme pṛthāv urasi śobhitayā śriyā svaś-
cūḍāmaṇiṁ subhagayantam ivātma-dhiṣṇyam

kṛtsna-prasāda—blessing everyone; *su-mukham*—auspicious face; *spṛhaṇīya*—desirable; *dhāma*—shelter; *sneha*—affection; *avaloka*—looking upon; *kalayā*—by expansion; *hṛdi*—within the heart; *saṁspṛśantam*—touching; *śyāme*—unto the Lord with blackish color; *pṛthau*—broad; *urasi*—chest; *śobhitayā*—being decorated; *śriyā*—goddess of fortune; *svaḥ*—heavenly planets; *cūḍā-maṇim*—summit; *subhagayantam*—spreading good fortune; *iva*—like; *ātma*—the Supreme Personality of Godhead; *dhiṣṇyam*—abode.

TRANSLATION

The Lord is the reservoir of all pleasure. His auspicious presence is meant for everyone's benediction, and His affectionate smiling and glancing touch the core of the heart. The Lord's beautiful bodily color is blackish, and His broad chest is the resting place of the goddess of fortune, who glorifies the entire spiritual world, the summit of all heavenly planets. Thus it appeared that the Lord was personally spreading the beauty and good fortune of the spiritual world.

PURPORT

When the Lord came, He was pleased with everyone; therefore it is stated here, *kṛtsna-prasāda-sumukham.* The Lord knew that even the offensive doormen were His pure devotees, although by chance they committed an offense at the feet of other devotees. To commit an offense against a devotee is very dangerous in devotional service. Lord Caitanya therefore said that an offense to a devotee is just like a mad elephant run loose; when a mad elephant enters a garden, it tramples all the plants. Similarly, an offense unto the feet of a pure devotee murders one's position in devotional service. On the part of the Lord there was no offended mood because He does not accept any offense created by His sincere devotee. But a devotee should be very cautious of committing offenses at the feet of another devotee. The Lord, being equal to all, and being especially inclined to His devotee, looked as mercifully at the offenders as at the offended. This attitude of the Lord was due to His unlimited quantity of transcendental qualities. His cheerful attitude towards the devotees was so pleasing and heart-touching that His very smile was attractive for them. That attraction was glorious not only for all the higher planets of this material world, but beyond, for the spiritual world also. Generally a human being has no idea of what the constitutional position is in the higher material planets, which are far better constituted in regard to all paraphernalia, yet the Vaikuṇṭha planet is so pleasing and so celestial that it is compared to the middle jewel or locket in a necklace of jewels.

In this verse the words *spṛhaṇīya-dhāma* indicate that the Lord is the reservoir of all pleasure because He has all the transcendental qualities. Although only some of these are aspired for by persons who hanker after the pleasure of merging in the impersonal Brahman, there are other aspirants who want to associate with the Lord personally as His servants. The Lord is so kind that He gives shelter to everyone—both impersonalists and devotees. He gives shelter to the impersonalists in His impersonal Brahman effulgence, whereas He gives shelter to the devotees in His personal abodes known as the Vaikuṇṭhalokas. He is especially inclined to His devotee; He touches the core of the heart of the devotee simply by smiling and glancing over him. The Lord is always served in the Vaikuṇṭhaloka by many hundreds and thousands of goddesses of fortune, as stated by the *Brahma-saṁhitā* (*lakṣmī-sahasra-śata-sam-*

bhrama-sevyamānam). In this material world, one is glorified if he is favored even a pinch by the goddess of fortune, so we can simply imagine how glorified is the kingdom of God in the spiritual world, where many hundreds and thousands of goddesses of fortune engage in the direct service of the Lord. Another feature of this verse is that it openly declares where the Vaikuṇṭhalokas are situated. They are situated as the summit of all the heavenly planets, which are above the sun globe, at the upper limit of the universe, and are known as Satyaloka, or Brahmaloka. The spiritual world is situated beyond the universe. Therefore it is stated here that the spiritual world, Vaikuṇṭhaloka, is the summit of all planetary systems.

TEXT 40

पीतांशुके पृथुनितम्बिनि विस्फुरन्त्या
काञ्च्यालिभिर्विरुतया वनमालया च ।
वल्गुप्रकोष्ठवलयं विनतासुतांसे
विन्यस्तहस्तमितरेण धुनानमब्जम् ॥४०॥

pītāṁśuke pṛthu-nitambini visphurantyā
kāñcyālibhir virutayā vana-mālayā ca
valgu-prakoṣṭha-valayaṁ vinatā-sutāṁse
vinyasta-hastam itareṇa dhunānam abjam

pīta-aṁśuke—covered with a yellow cloth; *pṛthu-nitambini*—on His large hips; *visphurantyā*—shining brightly; *kāñcyā*—with a girdle; *alibhiḥ*—by the bees; *virutayā*—humming; *vana-mālayā*—with a garland of fresh flowers; *ca*—and; *valgu*—lovely; *prakoṣṭha*—wrists; *valayam*—bracelets; *vinatā-suta*—of Garuḍa, the son of Vinatā; *aṁse*—on the shoulder; *vinyasta*—rested; *hastam*—one hand; *itareṇa*—with another hand; *dhunānam*—being twirled; *abjam*—a lotus flower.

TRANSLATION

He was adorned with a girdle that shone brightly on the yellow cloth covering His large hips, and He wore a garland of fresh flowers which was distinguished by humming bees. His lovely

wrists were graced with bracelets, and He rested one of His hands on the shoulder of Garuḍa, His carrier, and twirled a lotus with another hand.

PURPORT

Here is a full description of the Personality of Godhead as personally experienced by the sages. The Lord's personal body was covered with yellow robes, and His waist was thin. In Vaikuṇṭha, whenever there is a flower garland on the chest of the Personality of Godhead or any one of His associates, it is described that the humming bees are there. All these features were very beautiful and attractive for the devotees. One of the Lord's hands rested on His carrier, Garuḍa, and in another hand He twirled a lotus flower. These are personal characteristics of the Personality of Godhead, Nārāyaṇa.

TEXT 41

विद्युत्क्षिपन्मकरकुण्डलमण्डनार्ह-
गण्डस्थलोन्नसमुखं मणिमत्किरीटम्।
दोर्दण्डषण्डविवरे हरता परार्घ्य-
हारेण कन्धरगतेन च कौस्तुभेन ॥४१॥

vidyut-kṣipan-makara-kuṇḍala-maṇḍanārha-
gaṇḍa-sthalonnasa-mukhaṁ maṇimat-kirīṭam
dor-daṇḍa-ṣaṇḍa-vivare haratā parārdhya-
hāreṇa kandhara-gatena ca kaustubhena

vidyut—lightning; *kṣipat*—outshining; *makara*—alligator-shaped; *kuṇḍala*—earrings; *maṇḍana*—decoration; *arha*—as it fits; *gaṇḍa-sthala*—cheeks; *unnasa*—prominent nose; *mukham*—countenance; *maṇi-mat*—gem-studded; *kirīṭam*—crown; *doḥ-daṇḍa*—of His four stout arms; *ṣaṇḍa*—group; *vivare*—between; *haratā*—charming; *para-ardhya*—by the most precious; *hāreṇa*—necklace; *kandhara-gatena*—adorning His neck; *ca*—and; *kaustubhena*—by the Kaustubha jewel.

TRANSLATION

His countenance was distinguished by cheeks that enhanced the beauty of His alligator-shaped pendants, which outshone light-

ning. His nose was prominent, and His head was covered with a gem-studded crown. A charming necklace hung between His stout arms, and His neck was adorned with the gem known by the name Kaustubha.

TEXT 42

अत्रोपसृष्टमिति चोत्स्मितमिन्दिरायाः
स्वानां धिया विरचितं बहुसौष्ठवाढ्यम् ।
मह्यं भवस्य भवतां च भजन्तमङ्गं
नेमुर्निरीक्ष्य नवितृप्तदृशो मुदा कैः ॥४२॥

atropasṛṣṭam iti cotsmitam indirāyāḥ
svānāṁ dhiyā viracitaṁ bahu-sauṣṭhavāḍhyam
mahyaṁ bhavasya bhavatāṁ ca bhajantam aṅgaṁ
nemur nirīkṣya na vitṛpta-dṛśo mudā kaiḥ

atra—here, in the matter of the beauty; *upasṛṣṭam*—curbed down; *iti*—thus; *ca*—and; *utsmitam*—the pride of her beauty; *indirāyāḥ*—of the goddess of fortune; *svānām*—of His own devotees; *dhiyā*—by intelligence; *viracitam*—meditated on; *bahu-sauṣṭhava-āḍhyam*—very beautifully decorated; *mahyam*—of me; *bhavasya*—of Lord Śiva; *bhavatām*—of all of you; *ca*—and; *bhajantam*—worshiped; *aṅgam*—the figure; *nemuḥ*—bowed down; *nirīkṣya*—after seeing; *na*—not; *vitṛpta*—satiated; *dṛśaḥ*—eyes; *mudā*—joyously; *kaiḥ*—by their heads.

TRANSLATION

The exquisite beauty of Nārāyaṇa, being many times magnified by the intelligence of His devotees, was so attractive that it defeated the pride of the goddess of fortune in being the most beautiful. My dear demigods, the Lord who thus manifested Himself is worshipable by me, by Lord Śiva and by all of you. The sages regarded Him with unsated eyes and joyously bowed their heads at His lotus feet.

PURPORT

The beauty of the Lord was so enchanting that it could not be sufficiently described. The goddess of fortune is supposed to be the most beautiful sight within the spiritual and material creations of the Lord; she has a sense of being the most beautiful, yet her beauty was defeated when the Lord appeared. In other words, the beauty of the goddess of fortune is secondary in the presence of the Lord. In the words of Vaiṣṇava poets, it is said that the Lord's beauty is so enchanting that it defeats hundreds of thousands of Cupids. He is therefore called Madana-mohana. It is also described that the Lord sometimes becomes mad after the beauty of Rādhārāṇī. Poets describe that under those circumstances, although Lord Kṛṣṇa is Madana-mohana, He becomes Madana-dāha, or enchanted by the beauty of Rādhārāṇī. Actually the Lord's beauty is superexcellent, surpassing even the beauty of Lakṣmī in Vaikuṇṭha. The devotees of the Lord in the Vaikuṇṭha planets want to see the Lord as the most beautiful, but the devotees in Gokula or Kṛṣṇaloka want to see Rādhārāṇī as more beautiful than Kṛṣṇa. The adjustment is that the Lord, being *bhakta-vatsala*, or one who wants to please His devotees, assumes such features so that devotees like Lord Brahmā, Lord Śiva and other demigods may be pleased. Here also, for the devotee-sages, the Kumāras, the Lord appeared in His most beautiful feature, and they continued to see Him without satiation and wanted to continue seeing Him more and more.

TEXT 43

तस्यारविन्दनयनस्य पदारविन्द-
किञ्जल्कमिश्रतुलसीमकरन्दवायुः ।
अन्तर्गतः स्वविवरेण चकार तेषां
सङ्क्षोभमक्षरजुषामपि चित्ततन्वोः ॥४३॥

tasyāravinda-nayanasya padāravinda-
kiñjalka-miśra-tulasī-makaranda-vāyuḥ
antar-gataḥ sva-vivareṇa cakāra teṣāṁ
saṅkṣobham akṣara-juṣām api citta-tanvoḥ

tasya—of Him; *aravinda-nayanasya*—of the lotus-eyed Lord; *pada-aravinda*—of the lotus feet; *kiñjalka*—with the toes; *miśra*—mixed; *tulasī*—the *tulasī* leaves; *makaranda*—fragrance; *vāyuḥ*—breeze; *an-*

taḥ-gataḥ—entered within; *sva-vivareṇa*—through their nostrils; *cakāra*—made; *teṣām*—of the Kumāras; *saṅkṣobham*—agitation for change; *akṣara-juṣām*—attached to impersonal Brahman realization; *api*—even though; *citta-tanvoḥ*—in both mind and body.

TRANSLATION

When the breeze carrying the aroma of tulasī leaves from the toes of the lotus feet of the Personality of Godhead entered the nostrils of those sages, they experienced a change both in body and in mind, even though they were attached to the impersonal Brahman understanding.

PURPORT

It appears from this verse that the four Kumāras were impersonalists or protagonists of the philosophy of monism, becoming one with the Lord. But as soon as they saw the Lord's features, their minds changed. In other words, the impersonalist who feels transcendental pleasure in striving to become one with the Lord is defeated when he sees the beautiful transcendental features of the Lord. Because of the fragrance of His lotus feet, carried by the air and mixed with the aroma of *tulasī*, their minds changed; instead of becoming one with the Supreme Lord, they thought it wise to be devotees. Becoming a servitor of the lotus feet of the Lord is better than becoming one with the Lord.

TEXT 44

ते वा अमुष्य वदनासितपद्मकोश-
मुद्वीक्ष्य सुन्दरतराधरकुन्दहासम् ।
लब्धाशिषः पुनरवेक्ष्य तदीयमङ्घ्रि-
द्वन्द्वं नखारुणमणिश्रयणं निदध्युः ॥४४॥

te vā amuṣya vadanāsita-padma-kośam
udvīkṣya sundaratarādhara-kunda-hāsam
labdhāśiṣaḥ punar avekṣya tadīyam aṅghri-
dvandvaṁ nakhāruṇa-maṇi-śrayaṇaṁ nidadhyuḥ

te—those sages; *vai*—certainly; *amuṣya*—of the Supreme Personality of Godhead; *vadana*—face; *asita*—blue; *padma*—lotus; *kośam*—inside; *udvīkṣya*—after looking up; *sundara-tara*—more beautiful; *adhara*—lips; *kunda*—jasmine flower; *hāsam*—smiling; *labdha*—achieved; *āśiṣaḥ*—aims of life; *punaḥ*—again; *avekṣya*—looking down; *tadīyam*—His; *aṅghri-dvandvam*—pair of lotus feet; *nakha*—nails; *aruṇa*—red; *maṇi*—rubies; *śrayaṇam*—shelter; *nidadhyuḥ*—meditated.

TRANSLATION

The Lord's beautiful face appeared to them like the inside of a blue lotus, and the Lord's smile appeared to be a blossoming jasmine flower. After seeing the face of the Lord, the sages were fully satisfied, and when they wanted to see Him further, they looked upon the nails of His lotus feet, which resembled rubies. Thus they viewed the Lord's transcendental body again and again, and so they finally achieved meditation on the Lord's personal feature.

TEXT 45

पुंसां गतिं मृगयतामिह योगमार्गै-
ध्यानास्पदं बहु मतं नयनाभिरामम् ।
पौंस्नं वपुर्दर्शयानमनन्यसिद्धै-
रौत्पत्तिकैः समगृणन् युतमष्टभोगैः ॥४५॥

puṁsāṁ gatiṁ mṛgayatām iha yoga-mārgair
dhyānāspadaṁ bahu-mataṁ nayanābhirāmam
pauṁsnaṁ vapur darśayānam ananya-siddhair
autpattikaiḥ samagṛṇan yutam aṣṭa-bhogaiḥ

puṁsām—of those persons; *gatim*—liberation; *mṛgayatām*—who are searching; *iha*—here in this world; *yoga-mārgaiḥ*—by the process of *aṣṭāṅga-yoga; dhyāna-āspadam*—object of meditation; *bahu*—by the great *yogīs; matam*—approved; *nayana*—eyes; *abhirāmam*—pleasing; *pauṁsnam*—human; *vapuḥ*—form; *darśayānam*—displaying; *ananya*—not by others; *siddhaiḥ*—perfected; *autpattikaiḥ*—eternally present; *samagṛṇan*—praised; *yutam*—the Supreme Personality of Godhead, who is endowed; *aṣṭa-bhogaiḥ*—with eight kinds of achievement.

TRANSLATION

This is the form of the Lord which is meditated upon by the followers of the yoga process, and it is pleasing to the yogīs in meditation. It is not imaginary but factual, as proved by great yogīs. The Lord is full in eight kinds of achievement, but for others these achievements are not possible in full perfection.

PURPORT

The success of the *yoga* process is very nicely described here. It is specifically mentioned that the form of the Lord as four-handed Nārāyaṇa is the object of meditation for the followers of *yoga-mārga.* In the modern age there are so many so-called *yogīs* who do not target their meditation on the four-handed Nārāyaṇa form. Some of them try to meditate on something impersonal or void, but that is not approved by the great *yogīs* who follow the standard method. The real *yoga-mārga* process is to control the senses, sit in a solitary and sanctified place and meditate on the four-handed form of Nārāyaṇa, decorated as described in this chapter as He appeared before the four sages. This Nārāyaṇa form is Kṛṣṇa's expansion; therefore the Kṛṣṇa consciousness movement which is now spreading is the real, topmost process of *yoga* practice.

Kṛṣṇa consciousness is the highest *yoga* performance by trained devotional *yogīs.* Despite all the allurement of *yoga* practice, the eight kinds of yogic perfections are hardly achievable by the common man. But here it is described that the Lord, who appeared before the four sages, is Himself full of all eight of those perfections. The highest *yoga-mārga* process is to concentrate the mind twenty-four hours a day on Kṛṣṇa. This is called Kṛṣṇa consciousness. The *yoga* system, as described in *Śrīmad-Bhāgavatam* and *Bhagavad-gītā* or as recommended in the Patañjali *yoga* process, is different from the nowadays-practiced *haṭha-yoga* as it is generally understood in the Western countries. Real *yoga* practice is to control the senses and, after such control is established, to concentrate the mind on the Nārāyaṇa form of the Supreme Personality of Godhead,

Śrī Kṛṣṇa. Lord Kṛṣṇa is the original Personality of Godhead, and all the other Viṣṇu forms—with four hands decorated with conch, lotus, club and wheel—are plenary expansions of Kṛṣṇa. In *Bhagavad-gītā* it is recommended that one meditate upon the form of the Lord. To practice concentration of the mind, one has to sit with the head and the back in a straight line, and one must practice in a secluded place, sanctified by a sacred atmosphere. The *yogī* should observe the rules and regulations of *brahmacarya*—to strictly live a life of self-restraint and celibacy. One cannot practice *yoga* in a congested city, living a life of extravagancy, including unrestricted sex indulgence and adultery of the tongue. *Yoga* practice necessitates controlling the senses, and the beginning of sense control is to control the tongue. One who can control the tongue can also have control over the other senses. One cannot allow the tongue to take all kinds of forbidden food and drink and at the same time advance in the practice of *yoga*. It is a very regrettable fact that many unauthorized so-called *yogīs* come to the Western countries and exploit people's inclination towards *yoga* practice. Such unauthorized *yogīs* even dare to say publicly that one can indulge in the habit of drinking and at the same time practice meditation.

Five thousand years ago Lord Kṛṣṇa recommended *yoga* practice to Arjuna, but Arjuna frankly expressed his inability to follow the stringent rules and regulations of the *yoga* system. One should be very practical in every field of activities and should not waste his valuable time in practicing useless gymnastic feats in the name of *yoga*. Real *yoga* is to search out the four-handed Supersoul within one's heart and see Him perpetually in meditation. Such continued meditation is called *samādhi*, and the object of this meditation is the four-handed Nārāyaṇa, with bodily decorations as described in this chapter of *Śrīmad-Bhāgavatam*. If, however, one wants to meditate upon something void or impersonal, it will take a very long time before he achieves success in *yoga* practice. We cannot concentrate our mind on something void or impersonal. Real *yoga* is to fix the mind on the form of the Lord, the four-handed Nārāyaṇa who is sitting in everyone's heart.

By meditation one can understand that God is seated within one's heart. Even if one does not know it, God is seated within the heart of everyone. Not only is He seated in the heart of the human being, but He is also within the hearts of cats and dogs. *Bhagavad-gītā* certifies this fact by the declaration of the Lord, *īśvaraḥ sarva-bhūtānāṁ hṛd-deśe.* The *īśvara,* the supreme controller of the world, is seated in the heart of everyone. Not only is He in everyone's heart, but He is also present within the atom. No place is vacant or devoid of the presence of the Lord. That is the statement of *Īśopaniṣad.* God is present everywhere, and His right of proprietorship applies to everything. The feature of the Lord by which He is present everywhere is called Paramātmā. *Ātmā* means the individual soul, and Paramātmā means the individual Supersoul; both *ātmā* and Paramātmā are individual persons. The difference between *ātmā* and Paramātmā is that the *ātmā,* or the soul, is present only in a particular body, whereas the Paramātmā is present everywhere. In this connection, the example of the sun is very nice. An individual person may be situated in one place, but the sun, even though a similar individual entity, is present on the head of every individual person. In *Bhagavad-gītā* this is explained. Therefore even though the qualities of all entities, including the Lord, are equal, the Supersoul is different from the individual soul by quantitative power of expansion. The Lord, or the Supersoul, can expand Himself into millions of different forms, whereas the individual soul cannot do so.

The Supersoul, being seated in everyone's heart, can witness everyone's activities—past, present and future. In the *Upaniṣads* the Supersoul is described as being seated with the individual soul as friend and witness. As a friend, the Lord is always anxious to get back His friend, the individual soul, and bring him back home, back to Godhead. As a witness He is the bestower of all benedictions, and He endows each individual with the result of his actions. The Supersoul gives the individual soul all facilities to achieve whatever he desires to enjoy in this material world. Suffering is a reaction to the living entity's propensity to try to lord it over the material world. But the Lord instructs His friend, the individual soul, who is also His son, to give up all other engagements and simply surrender unto Him for perpetual bliss and an eternal life full of knowledge. This is the last instruction of *Bhagavad-gītā,* the most authorized and widely read book on all varieties of *yoga.* Thus the last word of *Bhagavad-gītā* is the last word in the perfection of *yoga.*

It is stated in *Bhagavad-gītā* that a person who is always absorbed in Kṛṣṇa consciousness is the topmost *yogī.* What is Kṛṣṇa consciousness? As the individual soul is present by his consciousness throughout his entire body, so the Supersoul, or Paramātmā, is present throughout the whole creation by superconsciousness. This superconscious energy is imitated by the individual soul, who has limited consciousness. I can understand what is going on within my limited body, but I cannot feel what is going on in another's body. I am present throughout my body by my consciousness, but my consciousness is not present in another's body. The Supersoul, or Paramātmā, however, being present everywhere and within everyone, is also conscious of everyone's existence. The theory that the soul and the Supersoul are one is not acceptable because it is not confirmed by authoritative Vedic literature. The individual soul's consciousness cannot act in superconsciousness. This superconsciousness can be achieved, however, by dovetailing individual consciousness with the consciousness of the Supreme. This dovetailing process is called surrender, or Kṛṣṇa consciousness. From the teachings of *Bhagavad-gītā* we learn very clearly that Arjuna, in the beginning, did not want to fight with his brothers and relatives, but after understanding *Bhagavad-gītā* he dovetailed his consciousness with the superconsciousness of Kṛṣṇa. He was then in Kṛṣṇa consciousness.

A person in full Kṛṣṇa consciousness acts by the dictation of Kṛṣṇa. In the beginning of Kṛṣṇa consciousness, dictation is received through the transparent medium of the spiritual master. When one is sufficiently trained and acts in submissive faith and love for Kṛṣṇa under the direction of the bona fide spiritual master, the dovetailing process becomes more firm and accurate. This stage of devotional service by the devotee in Kṛṣṇa consciousness is the most perfect stage of the *yoga* system. At this stage, Kṛṣṇa, or the Supersoul, dictates from within, while from without the devotee is helped by the spiritual master, who is the bona fide representative of Kṛṣṇa. From within He helps the devotee as *caitya*, for He is seated within the heart of everyone. Understanding that God is seated within everyone's heart is not, however, sufficient. One has to be acquainted with God from both within and without, and one must take dictation from within and without to act in Kṛṣṇa consciousness. This is the highest perfectional stage of the human form of life and the topmost perfection of all *yoga*.

For a perfect *yogī*, there are eight kinds of superachievements: one can become lighter than air, one can become smaller than the atom, one can become bigger than a mountain, one can achieve whatever he desires, one can control like the Lord, and so on. But when one rises to the perfectional stage of receiving dictation from the Lord, that is greater than any stage of material achievements above mentioned. The breathing exercise of the *yoga* system which is generally practiced is just the beginning. Meditation on the Supersoul is just another step forward. But to obtain direct contact with the Supersoul and take dictation from Him is the highest perfectional stage. The breathing exercises of meditation practice were very difficult even five thousand years ago, otherwise Arjuna would not have rejected the proposal of Kṛṣṇa that he adopt this system. This age of Kali is called the fallen age. In this age, people in general are short-living and very slow to understand self-realization or spiritual life; they are mostly unfortunate, and therefore if someone is a little bit interested in self-realization he is likely to be misguided by so many frauds. The only way to realize the perfect stage of *yoga* is to follow the principles of *Bhagavad-gītā* as practiced by Lord Caitanya. This is the simplest and highest perfection of *yoga* practice. Lord Caitanya demonstrated this Kṛṣṇa consciousness *yoga* system in a practical manner simply by chanting the holy name of Kṛṣṇa, as prescribed in the *Vedānta*, *Śrīmad-Bhāgavatam*, *Bhagavad-gītā*, and many important *Purāṇas*.

The largest number of Indians follow this *yoga* process, and in the United States it is gradually spreading in many cities. It is very easy and practical for this age, especially for those who are serious about success in *yoga*. No other process of *yoga* can be successful in this age. The meditation process was possible in the golden age, Satya-yuga, because people in that age used to live for hundreds of thousands of years. If one wants success in practical *yoga* practice, it is advised that he take to the chanting of Hare Kṛṣṇa, Hare Kṛṣṇa, Kṛṣṇa Kṛṣṇa, Hare Hare/ Hare Rāma, Hare Rāma, Rāma Rāma, Hare Hare, and he will actually feel himself making progress. In *Bhagavad-gītā* this practice of Kṛṣṇa consciousness is prescribed as *rāja-vidyā*, or the king of all erudition.

Those who have taken to this most sublime *bhakti-yoga* system, who practice devotional service in transcendental love of Kṛṣṇa, can testify to its happy and easy execution. The four sages Sanaka, Sanātana, Sanandana and Sanat-kumāra also became attracted by the features of the Lord and the transcendental aroma of the dust of His lotus feet, as already described in verse 43.

Yoga necessitates controlling the senses, and *bhakti-yoga*, or Kṛṣṇa consciousness, is the process of purifying the senses. When the senses are purified, they are automatically controlled. One cannot stop the activities of the senses by artificial means, but if one purifies the senses by engaging in the service of the Lord, the senses not only can be controlled from rubbish engagement, but can be engaged in the Lord's transcendental service, as aspired to by the four sages Sanaka, Sanātana, Sanandana and Sanat-kumāra. Kṛṣṇa consciousness is not, therefore, a manufactured concoction of the speculative mind. It is the process enjoined in *Bhagavad-gītā* (9.34): *man-manā bhava mad-bhakto mad-yājī māṁ namaskuru.*

TEXT 46

कुमारा ऊचुः
योऽन्तर्हितो हृदि गतोऽपि दुरात्मनां त्वं
सोऽद्यैव नो नयनमूलमनन्त राद्धः ।
यर्ह्येव कर्णविवरेण गुहां गतो नः
पित्रानुवर्णितरहा भवदुद्भवेन ॥४६॥

kumārā ūcuḥ
yo 'ntarhito hṛdi gato 'pi durātmanāṁ tvaṁ
so 'dyaiva no nayana-mūlam ananta rāddhaḥ
yarhy eva karṇa-vivareṇa guhāṁ gato naḥ
pitrānuvarṇita-rahā bhavad-udbhavena

kumārāḥ ūcuḥ—the Kumāras said; *yaḥ*—He who; *antarhitaḥ*—not manifested; *hṛdi*—in the heart; *gataḥ*—is seated; *api*—even though; *durātmanām*—to the rascals; *tvam*—You; *saḥ*—He; *adya*—today; *eva*—certainly; *naḥ*—of us; *nayana-mūlam*—face to face; *ananta*—O unlimited one; *rāddhaḥ*—attained; *yarhi*—when; *eva*—certainly; *karṇa-vivareṇa*—through the ears; *guhām*—intelligence; *gataḥ*—have attained; *naḥ*—our; *pitrā*—by our father; *anuvarṇita*—described; *rahāḥ*—mysteries; *bhavat-udbhavena*—by Your appearance.

TRANSLATION

The Kumāras said: Our dear Lord, You are not manifested to rascals, even though You are seated within the heart of everyone.

But as far as we are concerned, we see You face to face, although You are unlimited. The statements we have heard about You from our father, Brahmā, through the ears have now been actually realized by Your kind appearance.

PURPORT

The so-called *yogīs* who concentrate their mind or meditate upon the impersonal or void are described here. This verse of *Śrīmad-Bhāgavatam* describes persons who are expected to be very expert *yogīs* engaged in meditation but who do not find the Supreme Personality of Godhead seated within the heart. These persons are described here as *durātmā*, which means a person who has a very crooked heart, or a less intelligent person, just opposite to a *mahātmā*, which means one who has a broad heart. Those so-called *yogīs* who, although engaged in meditation, are not broad-hearted cannot find the four-handed Nārāyaṇa form, even though He is seated within their heart. Although the first realization of the Supreme Absolute Truth is impersonal Brahman, one should not remain satisfied with experiencing the impersonal effulgence of the Supreme Lord. In the *Īśopaniṣad* also, the devotee prays that the glaring effulgence of Brahman may be removed from his eyes so that he can see the real, personal feature of the Lord and thus satisfy himself fully. Similarly, although the Lord is not visible in the beginning because of His glaring bodily effulgence, if a devotee sincerely wants to see Him, the Lord is revealed to him. It is said in *Bhagavad-gītā* that the Lord cannot be seen by our imperfect eyes, He cannot be heard by our imperfect ears, and He cannot be experienced by our imperfect senses; but if one engages in devotional service with faith and devotion, then God reveals Himself.

Here the four sages Sanat-kumāra, Sanātana, Sanandana and Sanaka are described as actually sincere devotees. Although they had heard from their father, Brahmā, about the personal feature of the Lord, only the impersonal feature—Brahman—was revealed to them. But because they were sincerely searching for the Lord, they finally saw His personal feature directly, which corresponded with the description given by their father. They thus became fully satisfied. Here they express their gratitude because although they were foolish impersonalists in the beginning, by the grace of the Lord they could now have the good fortune to see His personal feature. Another significant aspect of this verse is that the sages describe their experience of hearing from their father, Brahmā, who was born of the Lord directly. In other words, the disciplic succession from the Lord to Brahmā and from Brahmā to Nārada and from Nārada to Vyāsa, and so on, is accepted here. Because the Kumāras were sons of Brahmā, they had the opportunity to learn Vedic knowledge from the disciplic succession of Brahmā, and therefore, in spite of their impersonalist beginnings, they became, in the end, direct seers of the personal feature of the Lord.

TEXT 47

तं त्वां विदाम भगवन् परमात्मतत्त्वं
सत्त्वेन सम्प्रति रतिं रचयन्तमेषाम् ।
यत्तेऽनुतापविदितैर्दृढभक्तियोगै-
रुद्ग्रन्थयो हृदि विदुर्मुनयो विरागाः ॥४७॥

taṁ tvāṁ vidāma bhagavan param ātma-tattvaṁ
sattvena samprati ratiṁ racayantam eṣām
yat te 'nutāpa-viditair dṛḍha-bhakti-yogair
udgranthayo hṛdi vidur munayo virāgāḥ

tam—Him; *tvām*—You; *vidāma*—we know; *bhagavan*—O Supreme Personality of Godhead; *param*—the Supreme; *ātma-tattvam*—Absolute Truth; *sattvena*—by Your form of pure goodness; *samprati*—now; *ratim*—love of God; *racayantam*—creating; *eṣām*—of all of them; *yat*—which; *te*—Your; *anutāpa*—mercy; *viditaiḥ*—understood; *dṛḍha*—unflinching; *bhakti-yogaiḥ*—through devotional service; *udgranthayaḥ*—without attachment, free from material bondage; *hṛdi*—in the heart; *viduḥ*—understood; *munayaḥ*—great sages; *virāgāḥ*—not interested in material life.

TRANSLATION

We know that You are the Supreme Absolute Truth, the Personality of Godhead, who manifests His transcendental form in the uncontaminated mode of pure goodness. This transcendental, eternal form of Your personality can be understood only by Your

mercy, through unflinching devotional service, by great sages whose hearts have been purified in the devotional way.

PURPORT

The Absolute Truth can be understood in three features—impersonal Brahman, localized Paramātmā, and Bhagavān, the Supreme Personality of Godhead. Here it is admitted that the Supreme Personality of Godhead is the last word in understanding the Absolute Truth. Even though the four Kumāras were instructed by their great learned father, Brahmā, they could not actually understand the Absolute Truth. They could only understand the Supreme Absolute Truth when they personally saw the Personality of Godhead with their own eyes. In other words, if one sees or understands the Supreme Personality of Godhead, the other two features of the Absolute Truth—namely impersonal Brahman and localized Paramātmā—are also automatically understood. Therefore the Kumāras confirm: "You are the ultimate Absolute Truth." The impersonalist may argue that since the Supreme Personality of Godhead was so nicely decorated, He was therefore not the Absolute Truth. But here it is confirmed that all the variegatedness of the absolute platform is constituted of *śuddha-sattva,* pure goodness. In the material world, any quality—goodness, passion or ignorance—is contaminated. Even the quality of goodness here in the material world is not free from tinges of passion and ignorance. But in the transcendental world, only pure goodness, without any tinge of passion or ignorance, exists; therefore the form of the Supreme Personality of Godhead and His variegated pastimes and paraphernalia are all pure *sattva-guṇa.* Such variegatedness in pure goodness is exhibited eternally by the Lord for the satisfaction of the devotee. The devotee does not want to see the Supreme Personality of Absolute Truth in voidness or impersonalism. In one sense, absolute transcendental variegatedness is meant only for the devotees, not for others, because this distinct feature of transcendental variegatedness can be understood only by the mercy of the Supreme Lord and not by mental speculation or the ascending process. It is said that one can understand the Supreme Personality of Godhead when one is even slightly favored by Him; otherwise, without His mercy, a man may speculate for thousands of years and not understand what is actually the Absolute Truth.

This mercy can be perceived by the devotee when he is completely freed from contamination. It is stated, therefore, that only when all contamination is rooted out and the devotee is completely detached from material attractions can he receive this mercy of the Lord.

TEXT 48

नात्यन्तिकं विगणयन्त्यपि ते प्रसादं
किम्वन्यदर्पितभयं भ्रुव उन्नयैस्ते ।
येऽङ्ग त्वदङ्घ्रिशरणा भवतः कथायाः
कीर्तन्यतीर्थयशसः कुशला रसज्ञाः ॥४८॥

nātyantikaṁ vigaṇayanty api te prasādaṁ
kimv anyad arpita-bhayaṁ bhruva unnayais te
ye 'ṅga tvad-aṅghri-śaraṇā bhavataḥ kathāyāḥ
kīrtanya-tīrtha-yaśasaḥ kuśalā rasa-jñāḥ

na—not; *ātyantikam*—liberation; *vigaṇayanti*—care for; *api*—even; *te*—those; *prasādam*—benedictions; *kim u*—what to speak; *anyat*—other material happinesses; *arpita*—given; *bhayam*—fearfulness; *bhruvaḥ*—of the eyebrows; *unnayaiḥ*—by the raising; *te*—Your; *ye*—those devotees; *aṅga*—O Supreme Personality of Godhead; *tvat*—Your; *aṅghri*—lotus feet; *śaraṇāḥ*—who have taken shelter; *bhavataḥ*—Your; *kathāyāḥ*—narrations; *kīrtanya*—worth chanting; *tīrtha*—pure; *yaśasaḥ*—glories; *kuśalāḥ*—very expert; *rasa-jñāḥ*—knowers of the mellows or humors.

TRANSLATION

Persons who are very expert and most intelligent in understanding things as they are engage in hearing narrations of the auspicious activities and pastimes of the Lord, which are worth chanting and worth hearing. Such persons do not care even for the highest material benediction, namely liberation, to say nothing of other less important benedictions like the material happiness of the heavenly kingdom.

PURPORT

The transcendental bliss enjoyed by the devotees of the Lord is completely different from the material happiness enjoyed by less intelligent persons. The less intelligent persons in the material world are engaged by the four principles of benediction called *dharma, artha, kāma* and *mokṣa.* Generally they prefer to take to religious life to achieve some material benediction, the purpose of which is to satisfy the senses. When, by that process, they become confused or frustrated in fulfilling the maximum amount of sense enjoyment, they try to become one with the Supreme, which is, according to their conception, *mukti,* or liberation. There are five kinds of liberation, the least important of which is called *sāyujya,* to become one with the Supreme. Devotees don't care for such liberation because they are actually intelligent. Nor are they inclined to accept any of the other four kinds of liberation, namely to live on the same planet as the Lord, to live with Him side by side as an associate, to have the same opulence, and to attain the same bodily features. They are concerned only with glorifying the Supreme Lord and His auspicious activities. Pure devotional service is *śravaṇaṁ kīrtanam.* Pure devotees, who take transcendental pleasure in hearing and chanting the glories of the Lord, do not care for any kind of liberation; even if they are offered the five liberations, they refuse to accept them, as stated in the *Bhāgavatam* in the Third Canto. Materialistic persons aspire for the sense enjoyment of heavenly pleasure in the heavenly kingdom, but devotees reject such material pleasure at once. The devotee does not even care for the post of Indra. A devotee knows that any pleasurable material position is subject to be annihilated at a certain point. Even if one reaches the post of Indra, Candra, or any other demigod, he must be dissolved at a certain stage. A devotee is never interested in such temporary pleasure. From Vedic scriptures it is understood that sometimes even Brahmā and Indra fall down, but a devotee in the transcendental abode of the Lord never falls. This transcendental stage of life, in which one feels transcendental pleasure in hearing the Lord's pastimes, is also recommended by Lord Caitanya. When Lord Caitanya was talking with Rāmānanda Rāya, there were varieties of suggestions offered by Rāmānanda regarding spiritual realization, but Lord Caitanya rejected all but one—that one should hear the glories of the Lord in association with pure devotees.

That is acceptable for everyone, especially in this age. One should engage himself in hearing from pure devotees about the activities of the Lord. That is considered the supreme benediction for mankind.

TEXT 49

कामं भवः स्ववृजिनैर्निरयेषु नः स्ता-
च्चेतोऽलिवद्यदि नु ते पदयो रमेत ।
वाचश्च नस्तुलसिवद्यदि तेऽङ्घ्रिशोभाः
पूर्येत ते गुणगणैर्यदि कर्णरन्ध्रः ॥४९॥

kāmaṁ bhavaḥ sva-vṛjinair nirayeṣu naḥ stāc
ceto 'livad yadi nu te padayo rameta
vācaś ca nas tulasivad yadi te 'ṅghri-śobhāḥ
pūryeta te guṇa-gaṇair yadi karṇa-randhraḥ

kāmam—as much as deserved; *bhavaḥ*—birth; *sva-vṛjinaiḥ*—by our own sinful activities; *nirayeṣu*—in low births; *naḥ*—our; *stāt*—let it be; *cetaḥ*—minds; *ali-vat*—like bees; *yadi*—if; *nu*—may be; *te*—Your; *padayoḥ*—at Your lotus feet; *rameta*—are engaged; *vācaḥ*—words; *ca*—and; *naḥ*—our; *tulasi-vat*—like the *tulasī* leaves; *yadi*—if; *te*—Your; *aṅghri*—at Your lotus feet; *śobhāḥ*—beautified; *pūryeta*—are filled; *te*—Your; *guṇa-gaṇaiḥ*—by transcendental qualities; *yadi*—if; *karṇa-randhraḥ*—the holes of the ears.

TRANSLATION

O Lord, we pray that You let us be born in any hellish condition of life, just as long as our hearts and minds are always engaged in the service of Your lotus feet, our words are made beautiful [by speaking of Your activities] just as tulasī leaves are beautified when offered unto Your lotus feet, and as long as our ears are always filled with the chanting of Your transcendental qualities.

PURPORT

The four sages now offer their humility to the Personality of Godhead because of their having been haughty in cursing two other devotees of the Lord. Jaya and Vijaya, the two doorkeepers who checked them from entering the Vaikuṇṭha planet, were certainly offenders, but as Vaiṣṇavas, the four sages should not have cursed them in anger. After the incident, they became conscious that they had done wrong by cursing the devotees of the Lord, and they prayed to the Lord that even in the hellish condition of life their minds might not be distracted from the engagement of service to the lotus feet of Lord Nārāyaṇa. Those who are devotees of the Lord are not afraid of any condition of life, provided there is constant engagement in the service of the Lord. It is said of the *nārāyaṇa-para,* or those who are devotees of Nārāyaṇa, the Supreme Personality of Godhead, *na kutaścana bibhyati* (*Bhāg.* 6.17.28). They are not afraid of entering a hellish condition, for since they are engaged in the transcendental loving service of the Lord, heaven or hell is the same for them. In material life both heaven and hell are one and the same because they are material; in either place there is no engagement in the Lord's service. Therefore those who are engaged in the service of the Lord see no distinction between heaven and hell; it is only the materialists who prefer one to the other.

These four devotees prayed to the Lord that although they might go to hell because they had cursed devotees, they might not forget the service of the Lord. The transcendental loving service of the Lord is performed in three ways—with the body, with the mind and with words. Here the sages pray that their words may always be engaged in glorifying the Supreme Lord. One may speak very nicely with ornamental language or one may be expert at controlled grammatical presentation, but if one's words are not engaged in the service of the Lord, they have no flavor and no actual use. The example is given here of *tulasī* leaves. The *tulasī* leaf is very useful even from the medicinal or antiseptic point of view. It is considered sacred and is offered to the lotus feet of the Lord. The *tulasī* leaf has numerous good qualities, but if it were not offered to the lotus feet of the Lord, *tulasī* could not be of much value or importance. Similarly, one may speak very nicely from the rhetorical or grammatical point of view, which may be very much appreciated by a materialistic audience, but if one's words are not offered to the service of the Lord, they are useless. The holes of the ears are very small and can be filled with any insignificant sound, so how can they receive as great a vibration as the glorification of the Lord? The answer is that the holes of the ears are like the sky. As the sky can never be filled up, the quality of the ear is such that one may go on pouring in vibrations of various kinds, yet it is capable of receiving more and more vibrations. A devotee is not afraid of going to hell if he has the opportunity to hear the glories of the Lord constantly. This is the advantage of chanting Hare Kṛṣṇa, Hare Kṛṣṇa, Kṛṣṇa Kṛṣṇa, Hare Hare/ Hare Rāma, Hare Rāma, Rāma Rāma, Hare Hare. One may be put in any condition, but God gives him the prerogative to chant Hare Kṛṣṇa. In any condition of life, if one goes on chanting he will never be unhappy.

TEXT 50

प्रादुश्चकर्थ यदिदं पुरुहूत रूपं
तेनेश निर्वृतिमवापुरलं दृशो नः ।
तस्मा इदं भगवते नम इद्विधेम
योऽनात्मनां दुरुदयो भगवान् प्रतीतः ॥५०॥

prāduścakartha yad idaṁ puruhūta rūpaṁ
teneśa nirvṛtim avāpur alaṁ dṛśo naḥ
tasmā idaṁ bhagavate nama id vidhema
yo 'nātmanāṁ durudayo bhagavān pratītaḥ

prāduścakartha—You have manifested; *yat*—which; *idam*—this; *puruhūta*—O greatly worshiped; *rūpam*—eternal form; *tena*—by that form; *īśa*—O Lord; *nirvṛtim*—satisfaction; *avāpuḥ*—obtained; *alam*—so much; *dṛśaḥ*—vision; *naḥ*—our; *tasmai*—unto Him; *idam*—this; *bhagavate*—unto the Supreme Personality of Godhead; *namaḥ*—obeisances; *it*—only; *vidhema*—let us offer; *yaḥ*—who; *anātmanām*—of those who are less intelligent; *durudayaḥ*—cannot be seen; *bhagavān*—the Supreme Personality of Godhead; *pratītaḥ*—has been seen by us.

TRANSLATION

O Lord, we therefore offer our respectful obeisances unto Your eternal form as the Personality of Godhead, which You have so kindly manifested before us. Your supreme, eternal form cannot be seen by unfortunate, less intelligent persons, but we are so much satisfied in our mind and vision to see it.

PURPORT

The four sages were impersonalists in the beginning of their spiritual life, but afterwards, by the grace of their father and spiritual master, Brahmā, they understood the eternal, spiritual form of the Lord and felt completely satisfied. In other words, the transcendentalists who aspire to the impersonal Brahman or localized Paramātmā are not fully satisfied and still hanker for more. Even if they are satisfied in their minds, still, transcendentally, their eyes are not satisfied. But as soon as such persons come to realize the Supreme Personality of Godhead, they are satisfied in all respects. In other words, they become devotees and want to see the form of the Lord continually. It is confirmed in the *Brahma-saṁhitā* that one who has developed transcendental love of Kṛṣṇa by smearing his eyes with the ointment of love sees constantly the eternal form of the Lord. The particular word used in this connection, *anātmanām*, signifies those who have no control over the mind and senses and who therefore speculate and want to become one with the Lord. Such persons cannot have the pleasure of seeing the eternal form of the Lord. For the impersonalists and the so-called *yogīs*, the Lord is always hidden by the curtain of *yogamāyā*. *Bhagavad-gītā* says that even when Lord Kṛṣṇa was seen by everyone while He was present on the surface of the earth, the impersonalists and the so-called *yogīs* could not see Him because they were devoid of devotional eyesight. The theory of the impersonalists and so-called *yogīs* is that the Supreme Lord assumes a particular form when He comes in touch with *māyā*, although actually He has no form. This very conception of the impersonalists and so-called *yogīs* checks them from seeing the Supreme Personality of Godhead as He is. The Lord, therefore, is always beyond the sight of such nondevotees. The four sages felt so much obliged to the Lord that they offered their respectful obeisances unto Him again and again.

Thus end the Bhaktivedanta purports of the Third Canto, Fifteenth Chapter, of the Śrīmad-Bhāgavatam, *entitled "Description of the Kingdom of God."*

CHAPTER SIXTEEN

The Two Doorkeepers of Vaikuṇṭha, Jaya and Vijaya, Cursed by the Sages

TEXT 1

ब्रह्मोवाच

इति तद् गृणतां तेषां मुनीनां योगधर्मिणाम् ।
प्रतिनन्द्य जगादेदं विकुण्ठनिलयो विभुः ॥ १ ॥

brahmovāca
iti tad gṛṇatāṁ teṣāṁ
munīnāṁ yoga-dharmiṇām
pratinandya jagādedaṁ
vikuṇṭha-nilayo vibhuḥ

brahmā uvāca—Lord Brahmā said; *iti*—thus; *tat*—speech; *gṛṇatām*—praising; *teṣām*—of them; *munīnām*—those four sages; *yoga-dharmiṇām*—engaged in linking with the Supreme; *pratinandya*—after congratulating; *jagāda*—said; *idam*—these words; *vikuṇṭha-nilayaḥ*—whose abode is bereft of anxiety; *vibhuḥ*—the Supreme Personality of Godhead.

TRANSLATION

Lord Brahmā said: After thus congratulating the sages for their nice words, the Supreme Personality of Godhead, whose abode is in the kingdom of God, spoke as follows.

TEXT 2

श्रीभगवानुवाच

एतौ तौ पार्षदौ मह्यं जयो विजय एव च ।
कदर्थीकृत्य मां यद्वो बह्वक्रातामतिक्रमम् ॥ २ ॥

śrī-bhagavān uvāca
etau tau pārṣadau mahyaṁ
jayo vijaya eva ca
kadarthī-kṛtya māṁ yad vo
bahv akrātām atikramam

śrī-bhagavān uvāca—the Supreme Personality of Godhead said; *etau*—these two; *tau*—they; *pārṣadau*—attendants; *mahyam*—of Mine; *jayaḥ*—named Jaya; *vijayaḥ*—named Vijaya; *eva*—certainly; *ca*—and; *kadarthī-kṛtya*—by ignoring; *mām*—Me; *yat*—which; *vaḥ*—against you; *bahu*—great; *akrātām*—have committed; *atikramam*—offense.

TRANSLATION

The Personality of Godhead said: These attendants of Mine, Jaya and Vijaya by name, have committed a great offense against you because of ignoring Me.

PURPORT

To commit an offense at the feet of a devotee of the Lord is a great wrong. Even when a living entity is promoted to Vaikuṇṭha, there is still the chance that he may commit offenses, but the difference is that when one is in a Vaikuṇṭha planet, even if by chance one commits an offense, he is protected by the Lord. This is the remarkable fact in the dealings of the Lord and the servitor, as seen in the present incident concerning Jaya and Vijaya. The word *atikramam* used herein indicates that in offending a devotee one neglects the Supreme Lord Himself.

By mistake the doormen held the sages from entering Vaikuṇṭhaloka, but because they were engaged in the transcendental service of the Lord, their annihilation was not expected by advanced devotees. The Lord's presence on the spot was very pleasing to the hearts of the devotees. The Lord understood that the trouble was due to His lotus feet not being seen by the sages, and therefore He wanted to please them by personally going there. The Lord is so merciful that even if there is some impediment for the devotee, He Himself manages matters in such a way that the devotee is not bereft of having audience at His lotus feet. There is a very good example in the life of Haridāsa Ṭhākura. When Caitanya Mahāprabhu was residing at Jagannātha Purī, Haridāsa Ṭhākura, who happened to be Muhammadan by birth, was with Him. In Hindu temples, especially in those days, no one but a Hindu was allowed to enter. Although Haridāsa Ṭhākura was the greatest of all Hindus in his behavior, he considered himself a Muhammadan and did not enter the temple. Lord Caitanya could understand his humility, and since he did not go to see the temple, Lord Caitanya Himself, who is nondifferent from Jagannātha, used to come and sit with Haridāsa Ṭhākura daily. Here in *Śrīmad-Bhāgavatam* we also find this same behavior of the Lord. His devotees were prevented from seeing His lotus feet, but the Lord Himself came to see them on the same lotus feet for which they aspired. It is also significant that He was accompanied by the goddess of fortune. The goddess of fortune is not to be seen by ordinary persons, but the Lord was so kind that although the devotees did not aspire for such an honor, He appeared before them with the goddess of fortune.

TEXT 3

यस्त्वेतयोर्धृतो दण्डो भवद्भिर्मामनुव्रतैः ।
स एवानुमतोऽस्माभिर्मुनयो देवहेलनात् ॥ ३ ॥

yas tv etayor dhṛto daṇḍo
bhavadbhir mām anuvrataiḥ
sa evānumato 'smābhir
munayo deva-helanāt

yaḥ—which; *tu*—but; *etayoḥ*—regarding both Jaya and Vijaya; *dhṛtaḥ*—has been given; *daṇḍaḥ*—punishment; *bhavadbhiḥ*—by you; *mām*—Me; *anuvrataiḥ*—devoted to; *saḥ*—that; *eva*—certainly; *anumataḥ*—is approved; *asmābhiḥ*—by Me; *munayaḥ*—O great sages; *deva*—against you; *helanāt*—because of an offense.

TRANSLATION

O great sages, I approve of the punishment that you who are devoted to Me have meted out to them.

TEXT 4

तद्वः प्रसादयाम्यद्य ब्रह्म दैवं परं हि मे ।
तद्धीत्यात्मकृतं मन्ये यत्स्वपुम्भिरसत्कृताः ॥ ४ ॥

tad vaḥ prasādayāmy adya
brahma daivaṁ paraṁ hi me
tad dhīty ātma-kṛtaṁ manye
yat sva-pumbhir asat-kṛtāḥ

tat—therefore; *vaḥ*—you sages; *prasādayāmi*—I am seeking your forgiveness; *adya*—just now; *brahma*—the *brāhmaṇas; daivam*—most beloved personalities; *param*—highest; *hi*—because; *me*—My; *tat*—that offense; *hi*—because; *iti*—thus; *ātma-kṛtam*—done by Me; *manye*—I consider; *yat*—which; *sva-pumbhiḥ*—by My own attendants; *asat-kṛtāḥ*—having been disrespected.

TRANSLATION

To Me, the brāhmaṇa is the highest and most beloved personality. The disrespect shown by My attendants has actually been displayed by Me because the doormen are My servitors. I take this to be an offense by Myself; therefore I seek your forgiveness for the incident that has arisen.

PURPORT

The Lord is always in favor of the *brāhmaṇas* and the cows, and therefore it is said, *go-brāhmaṇa-hitāya ca.* Lord Kṛṣṇa, or Viṣṇu, the Supreme Personality of Godhead, is also the worshipable Deity of the *brāhmaṇas.* In the Vedic literature, in the *ṛg-mantra* hymns of the *Ṛg Veda,* it is stated that those who are actually *brāhmaṇas* always look to the lotus feet of Viṣṇu: *oṁ tad viṣṇoḥ paramaṁ padaṁ sadā paśyanti sūrayaḥ.* Those who are qualified *brāhmaṇas* worship only the Viṣṇu form of the Supreme Personality of Godhead, which means Kṛṣṇa, Rāma and all Viṣṇu expansions. A so-called *brāhmaṇa* who is born in the family of *brāhmaṇas* but performs activities aimed against the Vaiṣṇavas cannot be accepted as a *brāhmaṇa,* because *brāhmaṇa* means Vaiṣṇava and Vaiṣṇava means *brāhmaṇa.* One who has become a devotee of the

Lord is also a *brāhmaṇa.* The formula is *brahma jānātīti brāhmaṇaḥ.* A *brāhmaṇa* is one who has understood Brahman, and a Vaiṣṇava is one who has understood the Personality of Godhead. Brahman realization is the beginning of realization of the Personality of Godhead. One who understands the Personality of Godhead also knows the impersonal feature of the Supreme, which is Brahman. Therefore one who becomes a Vaiṣṇava is already a *brāhmaṇa.* It should be noted that the glories of the *brāhmaṇa* described in this chapter by the Lord Himself refer to His devotee-*brāhmaṇa,* or the Vaiṣṇava. It should never be misunderstood that the so-called *brāhmaṇas* who are born in *brāhmaṇa* families but have no brahminical qualifications are referred to in this connection.

TEXT 5

यन्नामानि च गृह्णाति लोको भृत्ये कृतागसि ।
सोऽसाधुवादस्तत्कीर्तिं हन्ति त्वचमिवामयः ॥ ५ ॥

yan-nāmāni ca gṛhṇāti
loko bhṛtye kṛtāgasi
so 'sādhu-vādas tat-kīrtiṁ
hanti tvacam ivāmayaḥ

yat—of whom; *nāmāni*—the names; *ca*—and; *gṛhṇāti*—take; *lokaḥ*—people in general; *bhṛtye*—when a servant; *kṛta-āgasi*—has committed something wrong; *saḥ*—that; *asādhu-vādaḥ*—blame; *tat*—of that person; *kīrtim*—the reputation; *hanti*—destroys; *tvacam*—the skin; *iva*—as; *āmayaḥ*—leprosy.

TRANSLATION

A wrong act committed by a servant leads people in general to blame his master, just as a spot of white leprosy on any part of the body pollutes all of the skin.

PURPORT

A Vaiṣṇava, therefore, should be fully qualified. As stated in the *Bhāgavatam,* anyone who has become a Vaiṣṇava has developed all the good qualities of the demigods. There are twenty-six qualifications mentioned in the *Caitanya-caritāmṛta.* A devotee should always see that his Vaiṣṇava qualities increase with the advancement of his Kṛṣṇa consciousness. A devotee should be blameless because any offense by the devotee is a scar on the Supreme Personality of Godhead. The devotee's duty is to be always conscious in his dealings with others, especially with another devotee of the Lord.

TEXT 6

यस्यामृतामलयशःश्रवणावगाहः
सद्यः पुनाति जगदाश्वपचाद्विकुण्ठः ।
सोऽहं भवद्भ्य उपलब्धसुतीर्थकीर्ति-
श्छिन्द्यां स्वबाहुमपि वः प्रतिकूलवृत्तिम् ॥ ६ ॥

yasyāmṛtāmala-yaśaḥ-śravaṇāvagāhaḥ
sadyaḥ punāti jagad āśvapacād vikuṇṭhaḥ
so 'haṁ bhavadbhya upalabdha-sutīrtha-kīrtiś
chindyāṁ sva-bāhum api vaḥ pratikūla-vṛttim

yasya—of whom; *amṛta*—nectar; *amala*—uncontaminated; *yaśaḥ*—glories; *śravaṇa*—hearing; *avagāhaḥ*—entering into; *sadyaḥ*—immediately; *punāti*—purifies; *jagat*—the universe; *āśva-pacāt*—including even the dog-eaters; *vikuṇṭhaḥ*—without anxiety; *saḥ*—that person; *aham*—I am; *bhavadbhyaḥ*—from you; *upalabdha*—obtained; *su-tīrtha*—the best place of pilgrimage; *kīrtiḥ*—the fame; *chindyām*—would cut off; *sva-bāhum*—My own arm; *api*—even; *vaḥ*—towards you; *pratikūla-vṛttim*—acting inimically.

TRANSLATION

Anyone in the entire world, even down to the caṇḍāla, who lives by cooking and eating the flesh of the dog, is immediately purified if he takes bath in hearing through the ear the glorification of My name, fame, etc. Now you have realized Me without doubt; therefore I will not hesitate to lop off My own arm if its conduct is found hostile to you.

PURPORT

Real purification can take place in human society if its members take to Kṛṣṇa consciousness. This is clearly stated in all Vedic literature. Anyone who takes to Kṛṣṇa consciousness in all sincerity, even if he is not very advanced in good behavior, is purified. A devotee can be recruited from any section of human society, although it is not expected that everyone in all segments of society is well behaved. As stated in this verse and in many places in *Bhagavad-gītā*, even if one is not born in a *brāhmaṇa* family, or even if he is born in a family of *caṇḍālas*, if he simply takes to Kṛṣṇa consciousness he is immediately purified. In *Bhagavad-gītā*, Ninth Chapter, verses 30–32, it is clearly stated that even though a man is not well behaved, if he simply takes to Kṛṣṇa consciousness he is understood to be a saintly person. As long as a person is in this material world he has two different relationships in his dealings with others—one relationship pertains to the body, and the other pertains to the spirit. As far as bodily affairs or social activities are concerned, although a person is purified on the spiritual platform, it is sometimes seen that he acts in terms of his bodily relationships. If a devotee born in the family of a *caṇḍāla* (the lowest caste) is sometimes found engaged in his habitual activities, he is not to be considered a *caṇḍāla.* In other words, a Vaiṣṇava should not be evaluated in terms of his body. The *śāstra* states that no one should think the Deity in the temple to be made of wood or stone, and no one should think that a person coming from a lower-caste family who has taken to Kṛṣṇa consciousness is still of the same low caste. These attitudes are forbidden because anyone who takes to Kṛṣṇa consciousness is understood to be fully purified. He is at least engaged in the process of purification, and if he sticks to the principle of Kṛṣṇa consciousness he will very soon be fully purified. The conclusion is that if one takes to Kṛṣṇa consciousness with all seriousness, he is to be understood as already purified, and Kṛṣṇa is ready to give him protection by all means. The Lord assures herein that He is ready to give protection to His devotee even if there is need to cut off part of His own body.

TEXT 7

यत्सेवया चरणपद्मपवित्ररेणुं
सद्यःक्षताखिलमलं प्रतिलब्धशीलम् ।

न श्रीर्विरक्तमपि मां विजहाति यस्याः
प्रेक्षालवार्थ इतरे नियमान् वहन्ति ॥ ७ ॥

yat-sevayā caraṇa-padma-pavitra-reṇuṁ
sadyaḥ kṣatākhila-malaṁ pratilabdha-śīlam
na śrīr viraktam api māṁ vijahāti yasyāḥ
prekṣā-lavārtha itare niyamān vahanti

yat—of whom; *sevayā*—by the service; *caraṇa*—feet; *padma*—lotus; *pavitra*—sacred; *reṇum*—the dust; *sadyaḥ*—immediately; *kṣata*—wiped out; *akhila*—all; *malam*—sins; *pratilabdha*—acquired; *śīlam*—disposition; *na*—not; *śrīḥ*—the goddess of fortune; *viraktam*—have no attachment; *api*—even though; *mām*—Me; *vijahāti*—leave; *yasyāḥ*—of the goddess of fortune; *prekṣā-lava-arthaḥ*—for obtaining a slight favor; *itare*—others, like Lord Brahmā; *niyamān*—sacred vows; *vahanti*—observe.

TRANSLATION

The Lord continued: Because I am the servitor of My devotees, My lotus feet have become so sacred that they immediately wipe out all sin, and I have acquired such a disposition that the goddess of fortune does not leave Me, even though I have no attachment for her and others praise her beauty and observe sacred vows to secure from her even a slight favor.

PURPORT

The relationship between the Lord and His devotee is transcendentally beautiful. As the devotee thinks that it is due to being a devotee of the Lord that he is elevated in all good qualities, so the Lord also thinks that it is because of His devotion to the servitor that all His transcendental glories have increased. In other words, as the devotee is always anxious to render service to the Lord, so the Lord is ever anxious to render service to the devotee. The Lord admits herein that although He certainly has the quality that anyone who receives a slight particle of the dust of His lotus feet becomes at once a great personality, this greatness is due to His affection for His devotee. It is because of this affection that the goddess of fortune does not leave Him and that not only one but many thousands of goddesses of fortune engage in His service. In the material world, simply to get a little favor from the goddess of fortune, people observe many rigid regulations of austerity and penance. The Lord cannot tolerate any inconvenience on the part of the devotee. He is therefore famous as *bhakta-vatsala.*

TEXT 8

नाहं तथाद्मि यजमानहविर्वितान
श्च्योतद्घृतप्लुतमदन् हुतभुङ्मुखेन ।
यद्ब्राह्मणस्य मुखतश्चरतोऽनुघासं
तुष्टस्य मय्यवहितैर्निजकर्मपाकैः ॥ ८ ॥

nāhaṁ tathādmi yajamāna-havir vitāne
ścyotad-ghṛta-plutam adan huta-bhuṅ-mukhena
yad brāhmaṇasya mukhataś carato 'nughāsaṁ
tuṣṭasya mayy avahitair nija-karma-pākaiḥ

na—not; *aham*—I; *tathā*—on the other hand; *admi*—I eat; *yajamāna*—by the sacrificer; *haviḥ*—the oblations; *vitāne*—in the sacrificial fire; *ścyotat*—pouring; *ghṛta*—ghee; *plutam*—mixed; *adan*—eating; *huta-bhuk*—the sacrificial fire; *mukhena*—by the mouth; *yat*—as; *brāhmaṇasya*—of the *brāhmaṇa; mukhataḥ*—from the mouth; *carataḥ*—acting; *anughāsam*—morsels; *tuṣṭasya*—satisfied; *mayi*—to Me; *avahitaiḥ*—offered; *nija*—own; *karma*—activities; *pākaiḥ*—by the results.

TRANSLATION

I do not enjoy the oblations offered by the sacrificers in the sacrificial fire, which is one of My own mouths, with the same relish as I do the delicacies overflowing with ghee which are offered to the mouths of the brāhmaṇas who have dedicated to Me the results of their activities and who are ever satisfied with My prasāda.

PURPORT

The devotee of the Lord, or the Vaiṣṇava, does not take anything without offering it to the Lord. Since a Vaiṣṇava dedicates all the results of his activities to the Lord, he does not taste anything eatable which is not first offered to Him. The Lord also relishes giving to the Vaiṣṇava's mouth all eatables offered to Him. It is clear from this verse that the Lord eats through the sacrificial fire and the *brāhmaṇa*'s mouth. So many articles—grains, ghee, etc.—are offered in sacrifice for the satisfaction of the Lord. The Lord accepts sacrificial offerings from the *brāhmaṇas* and devotees, and elsewhere it is stated that whatever is given for the *brāhmaṇas* and Vaiṣṇavas to eat is also accepted by the Lord. But here it is said that He accepts offerings to the mouths of *brāhmaṇas* and Vaiṣṇavas with even greater relish. The best example of this is found in the life of Advaita Prabhu in his dealings with Haridāsa Ṭhākura. Even though Haridāsa was born of a Muhammadan family, Advaita Prabhu offered him the first dish of *prasāda* after the performance of a sacred fire ceremony. Haridāsa Ṭhākura informed him that he was born of a Muhammadan family and asked why Advaita Prabhu was offering the first dish to a Muhammadan instead of an elevated *brāhmaṇa.* Out of his humbleness, Haridāsa condemned himself a Muhammadan, but Advaita Prabhu, being an experienced devotee, accepted him as a real *brāhmaṇa.* Advaita Prabhu asserted that by offering the first dish to Haridāsa Ṭhākura, he was getting the result of feeding one hundred thousand *brāhmaṇas.* The conclusion is that if one can feed a *brāhmaṇa* or Vaiṣṇava, it is better than performing hundreds of thousands of sacrifices. In this age, therefore, it is recommended that *harer nāma*—chanting the holy name of God—and pleasing the Vaiṣṇava are the only means to elevate oneself to spiritual life.

TEXT 9

येषां बिभर्म्यहमखण्डविकुण्ठयोग-
मायाविभूतिरमलाङ्घ्रिरजः किरीटैः ।
विप्रांस्तु को न विषहेत यदर्हणाम्भः
सद्यः पुनाति सहचन्द्रललामलोकान् ॥९॥

yeṣāṁ bibharmy aham akhaṇḍa-vikuṇṭha-yoga-
māyā-vibhūtir amalāṅghri-rajaḥ kirīṭaiḥ
viprāṁs tu ko na viṣaheta yad-arhaṇāmbhaḥ
sadyaḥ punāti saha-candra-lalāma-lokān

yeṣām—of the *brāhmaṇas; bibharmi*—I bear; *aham*—I; *akhaṇḍa*—unbroken; *vikuṇṭha*—unobstructed; *yoga-māyā*—internal energy; *vibhūtiḥ*—opulence; *amala*—pure; *aṅghri*—of the feet; *rajaḥ*—the dust; *kirīṭaiḥ*—on My helmet; *viprān*—the *brāhmaṇas; tu*—then; *kaḥ*—who; *na*—not; *viṣaheta*—carry; *yat*—of the Supreme Lord; *arhaṇa-ambhaḥ*—water which has washed the feet; *sadyaḥ*—at once; *punāti*—sanctifies; *saha*—along with; *candra-lalāma*—Lord Śiva; *lokān*—the three worlds.

TRANSLATION

I am the master of My unobstructed internal energy, and the water of the Ganges is the remnant left after My feet are washed. That water sanctifies the three worlds, along with Lord Śiva, who bears it on his head. If I can take the dust of the feet of the Vaiṣṇava on My head, who will refuse to do the same?

PURPORT

The difference between the internal and external energies of the Supreme Personality of Godhead is that in the internal energy, or in the spiritual world, all the opulences are undisturbed, whereas in the external or material energy, all the opulences are temporary manifestations. The Lord's supremacy is equal in both the spiritual and material worlds, but the spiritual world is called the kingdom of God, and the material world is called the kingdom of *māyā. Māyā* refers to that which is not actually fact. The opulence of the material world is a reflection. It is stated in *Bhagavad-gītā* that this material world is just like a tree whose roots are up and branches down. This means that the material world is the shadow of the spiritual world. Real opulence is in the spiritual world. In the spiritual world the predominating Deity is the Lord Himself, whereas in the material world there are many lords. That is the difference between the internal and external energies. The Lord says that although He is the predominating factor of the internal energy and although the material world is sanctified just by the water that has washed His feet, He has the greatest respect for the *brāhmaṇa* and the Vaiṣṇava. When the Lord Himself offers so much respect to the Vaiṣṇava and the *brāhmaṇa*, how can one deny such respect to such personalities?

TEXT 10

ये मे तनूर्द्विजवरान्दुहतीर्मदीया
भूतान्यलब्धशरणानि च भेदबुद्ध्या ।
द्रक्ष्यन्त्यघक्षतदृशो ह्यहिमन्यवस्तान्
गृध्रा रुषा मम कुषन्त्यधिदण्डनेतुः ॥१०॥

ye me tanūr dvija-varān duhatīr madīyā
bhūtāny alabdha-śaraṇāni ca bheda-buddhyā
drakṣyanty agha-kṣata-dṛśo hy ahi-manyavas tān
gṛdhrā ruṣā mama kuṣanty adhidaṇḍa-netuḥ

ye—which persons; *me*—My; *tanūḥ*—body; *dvija-varān*—the best of the *brāhmaṇas; duhatīḥ*—cows; *madīyāḥ*—relating to Me; *bhūtāni*—living entities; *alabdha-śaraṇāni*—defenseless; *ca*—and; *bheda-buddhyā*—considering as different; *drakṣyanti*—see; *agha*—by sin; *kṣata*—is impaired; *dṛśaḥ*—whose faculty of judgment; *hi*—because; *ahi*—like a snake; *manyavaḥ*—angry; *tān*—those same persons; *gṛdhrāḥ*—the vulturelike messengers; *ruṣā*—angrily; *mama*—My; *kuṣanti*—tear; *adhidaṇḍa-netuḥ*—of the superintendent of punishment, Yamarāja.

TRANSLATION

The brāhmaṇas, the cows and the defenseless creatures are My own body. Those whose faculty of judgment has been impaired by their own sin look upon these as distinct from Me. They are just like furious serpents, and they are angrily torn apart by the bills of the vulturelike messengers of Yamarāja, the superintendent of sinful persons.

PURPORT

The defenseless creatures, according to *Brahma-saṁhitā*, are the cows, *brāhmaṇas*, women, children and old men. Of these five, the *brāhmaṇas* and cows are especially mentioned in this verse because the Lord is always anxious about the benefit of the *brāhmaṇas* and the cows and is prayed to in this way. The Lord especially instructs, therefore, that no one should be envious of these five, especially the cows and *brāhmaṇas*. In some of the *Bhāgavatam* readings, the word *duhitṝḥ* is used instead of *duhatīḥ*. But in either case, the meaning is the same. *Duhatīḥ* means "cow," and *duhitṝḥ* can also be used to mean "cow" because the cow is supposed to be the daughter of the sun-god. Just as children are taken care of by the parents, women as a class should be taken care of by the father, husband or grown-up son. Those who are helpless must be taken care of by their respective guardians, otherwise the guardians will be subjected to the punishment of Yamarāja, who is appointed by the Lord to supervise the activities of sinful living creatures. The assistants, or messengers, of Yamarāja are likened here to vultures, and those who do not execute their respective duties in protecting their wards are compared to serpents. Vultures deal very seriously with serpents, and similarly the messengers will deal very seriously with neglectful guardians.

TEXT 11

ये ब्राह्मणान्मयि धिया क्षिपतोऽर्चयन्त-
स्तुष्यद्‍धृदः स्मितसुधोक्षितपद्मवक्त्राः।
वाण्यानुरागकलयात्मजवद् गृणन्तः
सम्बोधयन्त्यहमिवाहमुपाहृतस्तैः ॥११॥

ye brāhmaṇān mayi dhiyā kṣipato 'rcayantas
tuṣyad-dhṛdaḥ smita-sudhokṣita-padma-vaktrāḥ
vāṇyānurāga-kalayātmajavad gṛṇantaḥ
sambodhayanty aham ivāham upāhṛtas taiḥ

ye—which persons; *brāhmaṇān*—the *brāhmaṇas; mayi*—in Me; *dhiyā*—with intelligence; *kṣipataḥ*—uttering harsh words; *arcayantaḥ*—

respecting; *tuṣyat*—gladdened; *hṛdaḥ*—hearts; *smita*—smiling; *sudhā*—nectar; *ukṣita*—wet; *padma*—lotuslike; *vaktrāḥ*—faces; *vāṇyā*—with words; *anurāga-kalayā*—loving; *ātmaja-vat*—like a son; *gṛṇantaḥ*—praising; *sambodhayanti*—pacify; *aham*—I; *iva*—as; *aham*—I; *upāhṛtaḥ*—being controlled; *taiḥ*—by them.

TRANSLATION

On the other hand, they captivate My heart who are gladdened in heart and who, their lotus faces enlightened by nectarean smiles, respect the brāhmaṇas, even though the brāhmaṇas utter harsh words. They look upon the brāhmaṇas as My own Self and pacify them by praising them in loving words, even as a son would appease an angry father or as I am pacifying you.

PURPORT

It has been observed in many instances in the Vedic scriptures that when the *brāhmaṇas* or Vaiṣṇavas curse someone in an angry mood, the person who is cursed does not take it upon himself to treat the *brāhmaṇas* or Vaiṣṇavas in the same way. There are many examples of this. For instance, the sons of Kuvera, when cursed by the great sage Nārada, did not seek revenge in the same harsh way, but submitted. Here also, when Jaya and Vijaya were cursed by the four Kumāras, they did not become harsh towards them; rather, they submitted. That should be the way of treating *brāhmaṇas* and Vaiṣṇavas. One may sometimes be faced with a grievous situation created by a *brāhmaṇa*, but instead of meeting him with a similar mood, one should try to pacify him with a smiling face and mild treatment. *Brāhmaṇas* and Vaiṣṇavas should be accepted as earthly representatives of Nārāyaṇa. Nowadays some foolish persons have manufactured the term *daridra-nārāyaṇa*, indicating that the poor man should be accepted as the representative of Nārāyaṇa. But in Vedic literature we do not find that poor men should be treated as representatives of Nārāyaṇa. Of course, "those who are unprotected" are mentioned here, but the definition of this phrase is clear from the *śāstras.* The poor man should not be unprotected, but the *brāhmaṇa* should especially be treated as the representative of Nārāyaṇa and should be worshiped like Him. It is specifically said that to pacify the *brāhmaṇas,* one's face should be lotuslike. A lotuslike face is exhibited when one is adorned with love and affection. In this respect, the example of the father's being angry at the son and the son's trying to pacify the father with smiling and sweet words is very appropriate.

TEXT 12

तन्मे स्वभर्तुरवसायमलक्षमाणौ
युष्मद्व्यतिक्रमगतिं प्रतिपद्य सद्यः ।
भूयो ममान्तिकमितां तदनुग्रहो मे
यत्कल्पतामचिरतो भृतयोर्विवासः ॥ १२ ॥

tan me sva-bhartur avasāyam alakṣamāṇau
yuṣmad-vyatikrama-gatiṁ pratipadya sadyaḥ
bhūyo mamāntikam itāṁ tad anugraho me
yat kalpatām acirato bhṛtayor vivāsaḥ

tat—therefore; *me*—My; *sva-bhartuḥ*—of their master; *avasāyam*—the intention; *alakṣamāṇau*—not knowing; *yuṣmat*—against you; *vyatikrama*—offense; *gatim*—result; *pratipadya*—reaping; *sadyaḥ*—immediately; *bhūyaḥ*—again; *mama antikam*—near Me; *itām*—obtain; *tat*—that; *anugrahaḥ*—a favor; *me*—to Me; *yat*—which; *kalpatām*—let it be arranged; *aciratāḥ*—not long; *bhṛtayoḥ*—of these two servants; *vivāsaḥ*—exile.

TRANSLATION

These servants of Mine have transgressed against you, not knowing the mind of their master. I shall therefore deem it a favor done to Me if you order that, although reaping the fruit of their transgression, they may return to My presence soon and the time of their exile from My abode may expire before long.

PURPORT

From this statement we can understand how anxious the Lord is to get his servitor back into Vaikuṇṭha. This incident, therefore, proves that those who have once entered a Vaikuṇṭha planet can never fall down. The case of Jaya and Vijaya is not a falldown; it is just an accident. The Lord is always anxious to get such devotees back again to the Vaikuṇṭha planets as soon as possible. It is to be assumed that there is no possibility of a misunderstanding between the Lord and the devotees, but when there are discrepancies or disruptions between one devotee and another, one has to suffer the consequences, although that suffering is temporary. The Lord is so kind to His devotees that He took all the responsibility for the doormen's offense and requested the sages to give them facilities to return to Vaikuṇṭha as soon as possible.

TEXT 13

ब्रह्मोवाच
अथ तस्योशतीं देवीमृषिकुल्यां सरस्वतीम् ।
नास्वाद्य मन्युदष्टानां तेषामात्माप्यतृप्यत ॥१३॥

brahmovāca
atha tasyośatīṁ devīm
ṛṣi-kulyāṁ sarasvatīm
nāsvādya manyu-daṣṭānāṁ
teṣām ātmāpy atṛpyata

brahmā—Lord Brahmā; *uvāca*—said; *atha*—now; *tasya*—of the Supreme Lord; *uśatīm*—lovely; *devīm*—shining; *ṛṣi-kulyām*—like a series of Vedic hymns; *sarasvatīm*—speech; *na*—not; *āsvādya*—hearing; *manyu*—anger; *daṣṭānām*—bitten; *teṣām*—of those sages; *ātmā*—the mind; *api*—even though; *atṛpyata*—satiated.

TRANSLATION

Brahmā continued: Even though the sages had been bitten by the serpent of anger, their souls were not satiated with hearing the Lord's lovely and illuminating speech, which was like a series of Vedic hymns.

TEXT 14

सतीं व्यादाय शृण्वन्तो लघ्वीं गुर्वर्थगह्वराम् ।
विगाह्यागाधगम्भीरां न विदुस्तच्चिकीर्षितम् ॥१४॥

satīṁ vyādāya śṛṇvanto
laghvīṁ gurv-artha-gahvarām
vigāhyāgādha-gambhīrāṁ
na vidus tac-cikīrṣitam

satīm—excellent; *vyādāya*—with attentive aural reception; *śṛṇvantaḥ*—hearing; *laghvīm*—properly composed; *guru*—momentous; *artha*—import; *gahvarām*—difficult to understand; *vigāhya*—pondering; *agādha*—deep; *gambhīrām*—grave; *na*—not; *viduḥ*—understand; *tat*—of the Supreme Lord; *cikīrṣitam*—the intention.

TRANSLATION

The Lord's excellent speech was difficult to comprehend because of its momentous import and its most profound significance. The sages heard it with wide-open ears and pondered it as well. But although hearing, they could not understand what He intended to do.

PURPORT

It should be understood that no one can surpass the Supreme Personality of Godhead in speaking. There is no difference between the Supreme Person and His speeches, for He stands on the absolute platform. The sages tried with wide-open ears to understand the words from the lips of the Supreme Lord, but although His speech was very concise and meaningful, the sages could not completely comprehend what He was saying. They could not even comprehend the purport of the speech or what the Supreme Lord wanted to do. Nor could they understand whether the Lord was angry or pleased with them.

TEXT 15

ते योगमाययारब्धपारमेष्ठ्यमहोदयम् ।
प्रोचुः प्राञ्जलयो विप्राः प्रहृष्टाः क्षुभितत्वचः ॥१५॥

te yoga-māyayārabdha-
pārameṣṭhya-mahodayam
procuḥ prāñjalayo viprāḥ
prahṛṣṭāḥ kṣubhita-tvacaḥ

te—those; *yoga-māyayā*—through His internal potency; *ārabdha*—had been revealed; *pārameṣṭhya*—of the Supreme Personality of Godhead; *mahā-udayam*—multiglories; *procuḥ*—spoke; *prāñjalayaḥ*—with folded hands; *viprāḥ*—the four *brāhmaṇas; prahṛṣṭāḥ*—extremely delighted; *kṣubhita-tvacaḥ*—hair standing on end.

TRANSLATION

The four brāhmaṇa-sages were nevertheless extremely delighted to behold Him, and they experienced a thrill throughout their bodies. They then spoke as follows to the Lord, who had revealed the multiglories of the Supreme Personality through His internal potency, yogamāyā.

PURPORT

The sages were almost too puzzled to speak before the Supreme Personality of Godhead for the first time, and the hairs of their bodies stood erect due to their extreme joy. The highest opulence in the material world is called *pārameṣṭhya*, the opulence of Brahmā. But that material opulence of Brahmā, who lives on the topmost planet within this material world, cannot compare to the opulence of the Supreme Lord because the transcendental opulence in the spiritual world is caused by *yogamāyā*, whereas the opulence in the material world is caused by *mahāmāyā.*

TEXT 16

ऋषय ऊचुः
न वयं भगवन् विद्मस्तव देव चिकीर्षितम् ।
कृतो मेऽनुग्रहश्चेति यदध्यक्षः प्रभाषसे ॥१६॥

ṛṣaya ūcuḥ
na vayaṁ bhagavan vidmas
tava deva cikīrṣitam
kṛto me 'nugrahaś ceti
yad adhyakṣaḥ prabhāṣase

ṛṣayaḥ—the sages; *ūcuḥ*—said; *na*—not; *vayam*—we; *bhagavan*—O Supreme Personality of Godhead; *vidmaḥ*—did know; *tava*—Your; *deva*—O Lord; *cikīrṣitam*—wish for us to do; *kṛtaḥ*—has been done;

me—unto Me; *anugrahaḥ*—favor; *ca*—and; *iti*—thus; *yat*—which; *adhyakṣaḥ*—the supreme ruler; *prabhāṣase*—You say.

TRANSLATION

The sages said: O Supreme Personality of Godhead, we are unable to know what You intend for us to do, for even though You are the supreme ruler of all, You speak in our favor as if we had done something good for You.

PURPORT

The sages could understand that the Supreme Personality of Godhead, who is above everyone, was speaking as if He were in the wrong; therefore it was difficult for them to understand the words of the Lord. They could understand, however, that the Lord was speaking in such a humble way just to show them His all-merciful favor.

TEXT 17

ब्रह्मण्यस्य परं दैवं ब्राह्मणाः किल ते प्रभो ।
विप्राणां देवदेवानां भगवानात्मदैवतम् ॥१७॥

brahmaṇyasya paraṁ daivaṁ
brāhmaṇāḥ kila te prabho
viprāṇāṁ deva-devānāṁ
bhagavān ātma-daivatam

brahmaṇyasya—of the supreme director of the brahminical culture; *param*—the highest; *daivam*—position; *brāhmaṇāḥ*—the *brāhmaṇas; kila*—for the teaching of others; *te*—Your; *prabho*—O Lord; *viprāṇām*—of the *brāhmaṇas; deva-devānām*—to be worshiped by the demigods; *bhagavān*—the Supreme Personality of Godhead; *ātma*—the self; *daivatam*—worshipable Deity.

TRANSLATION

O Lord, You are the supreme director of the brahminical culture. Your considering the brāhmaṇas to be in the highest position is Your example for teaching others. Actually You are the

supreme worshipable Deity, not only for the gods but for the brāhmaṇas also.

PURPORT

In the *Brahma-saṁhitā* it is clearly stated that the Supreme Personality of Godhead is the cause of all causes. There are undoubtedly many demigods, the chiefs of whom are Brahmā and Śiva. Lord Viṣṇu is the Lord of Brahmā and Śiva, not to speak of the *brāhmaṇas* in this material world. As mentioned in *Bhagavad-gītā*, the Supreme Lord is very favorable towards all activities performed according to brahminical culture, or the qualities of control of the senses and mind, cleanliness, forbearance, faith in scripture, and practical and theoretical knowledge. The Lord is the Supersoul of everyone. In *Bhagavad-gītā* it is said that the Lord is the source of all emanations; thus He is also the source of Brahmā and Śiva.

TEXT 18

त्वत्तः सनातनो धर्मो रक्ष्यते तनुभिस्तव ।
धर्मस्य परमो गुह्यो निर्विकारो भवान्मतः ॥१८॥

tvattaḥ sanātano dharmo
rakṣyate tanubhis tava
dharmasya paramo guhyo
nirvikāro bhavān mataḥ

tvattaḥ—from You; *sanātanaḥ*—eternal; *dharmaḥ*—occupation; *rakṣyate*—is protected; *tanubhiḥ*—by multimanifestations; *tava*—Your; *dharmasya*—of religious principles; *paramaḥ*—the supreme; *guhyaḥ*—objective; *nirvikāraḥ*—unchangeable; *bhavān*—You; *mataḥ*—in our opinion.

TRANSLATION

You are the source of the eternal occupation of all living entities, and by Your multimanifestations of Personalities of Godhead, You have always protected religion. You are the supreme objective of religious principles, and in our opinion You are inexhaustible and unchangeable eternally.

PURPORT

The statement in this verse *dharmasya paramo guhyaḥ* refers to the most confidential part of all religious principles. This is confirmed in *Bhagavad-gītā.* The conclusion of Lord Kṛṣṇa in His advice to Arjuna is: "Give up all other religious engagement and just surrender unto Me." This is the most confidential knowledge in executing religious principles. In the *Bhāgavatam* also it is stated that if one does not become Kṛṣṇa conscious after very rigidly executing one's specified religious duties, all his labor in following so-called religious principles is simply a waste of time. Here also the sages confirm the statement that the Supreme Lord, not the demigods, is the ultimate goal of all religious principles. There are many foolish propagandists who say that worship of the demigods is also a way to reach the supreme goal, but in the authorized statements of *Śrīmad-Bhāgavatam* and *Bhagavad-gītā* this is not accepted. *Bhagavad-gītā* says that one who worships a particular demigod can reach the demigod's planet, but one who worships the Supreme Personality of Godhead can enter into Vaikuṇṭha. Some propagandists say that regardless of what one does he will ultimately reach the supreme abode of the Personality of Godhead, but this is not valid. The Lord is eternal, the Lord's servitor is eternal, and the Lord's abode is also eternal. They are all described here as *sanātana*, or eternal. The result of devotional service, therefore, is not temporary, as is the achievement of heavenly planets by worshiping the demigods. The sages wanted to stress that although the Lord, out of His causeless mercy, says that He worships the *brāhmaṇas* and Vaiṣṇavas, actually the Lord is worshipable not only by the *brāhmaṇas* and Vaiṣṇavas but also by the demigods.

TEXT 19

तरन्ति ह्यञ्जसा मृत्युं निवृत्ता यदनुग्रहात् ।
योगिनः स भवान् किंस्विदनुगृह्येत यत्परैः ॥१९॥

taranti hy añjasā mṛtyuṁ
nivṛttā yad-anugrahāt
yoginaḥ sa bhavān kiṁ svid
anugṛhyeta yat paraiḥ

taranti—cross over; *hi*—because; *añjasā*—easily; *mṛtyum*—birth and death; *nivṛttāḥ*—ceasing all material desires; *yat*—Your; *anugrahāt*—by mercy; *yoginaḥ*—transcendentalists; *saḥ*—the Supreme Lord; *bhavān*—You; *kim svit*—never possible; *anugṛhyeta*—may be favored; *yat*—which; *paraiḥ*—by others.

TRANSLATION

Mystics and transcendentalists, by the mercy of the Lord, cross beyond nescience by ceasing all material desires. It is not possible, therefore, that the Supreme Lord can be favored by others.

PURPORT

Unless one is favored by the Supreme Lord, one cannot cross over the ocean of the nescience of repeated birth and death. Here it is stated that *yogīs* or mystics cross beyond nescience by the mercy of the Supreme Personality of Godhead. There are many kinds of mystics, such as the *karma-yogī, jñāna-yogī, dhyāna-yogī* and *bhakti-yogī.* The *karmīs* particularly search after the favor of the demigods, the *jñānīs* want to become one with the Supreme Absolute Truth, and the *yogīs* are satisfied simply by partial vision of the Supreme Personality of Godhead, Paramātmā, and ultimately by oneness with Him. But the *bhaktas,* the devotees, want to associate with the Supreme Personality of Godhead eternally and serve Him. It has already been admitted that the Lord is eternal, and those who want the favor of the Supreme Lord perpetually are also eternal. Therefore *yogīs* here means devotees. By the mercy of the Lord, devotees can easily pass beyond the nescience of birth and death and attain the eternal abode of the Lord. The Lord is therefore not in need of another's favor because no one is equal to or greater than Him. Actually, everyone needs the favor of the Lord for successful understanding of his human mission.

TEXT 20

यं वै विभूतिरुपयात्यनुवेलमन्यै-
र्थार्थिभिः स्वशिरसा धृतपादरेणुः ।
धन्यार्पिताङ्घ्रितुलसीनवदामधाम्नो
लोकं मधुव्रतपतेरिव कामयाना ॥२०॥

yaṁ vai vibhūtir upayāty anuvelam anyair
arthārthibhiḥ sva-śirasā dhṛta-pāda-reṇuḥ
dhanyārpitāṅghri-tulasī-nava-dāma-dhāmno
lokaṁ madhuvrata-pater iva kāma-yānā

yam—whom; *vai*—certainly; *vibhūtiḥ*—Lakṣmī, the goddess of fortune; *upayāti*—waits upon; *anuvelam*—occasionally; *anyaiḥ*—by others; *artha*—material facility; *arthibhiḥ*—by those who desire; *sva-śirasā*—on their own heads; *dhṛta*—accepting; *pāda*—of the feet; *reṇuḥ*—the dust; *dhanya*—by the devotees; *arpita*—offered; *aṅghri*—at Your feet; *tulasī*—of *tulasī* leaves; *nava*—fresh; *dāma*—on the garland; *dhāmnaḥ*—having a place; *lokam*—the place; *madhu-vrata-pateḥ*—of the king of the bees; *iva*—like; *kāma-yānā*—is anxious to secure.

TRANSLATION

The goddess of fortune, Lakṣmī, the dust of whose feet is worn on the head by others, waits upon You, as appointed, for she is anxious to secure a place in the abode of the king of bees, who hovers on the fresh wreath of tulasī leaves offered at Your feet by some blessed devotee.

PURPORT

As previously described, *tulasī* has attained all superior qualities due to being placed at the lotus feet of the Lord. The comparison made here is very nice. As the king of bees hovers over the *tulasī* leaves offered to the lotus feet of the Lord, so Lakṣmī, the goddess who is sought by the demigods, *brāhmaṇas,* Vaiṣṇavas and everyone else, always engages in rendering service to the lotus feet of the Lord. The conclusion is that no one can be the benefactor of the Lord; everyone is actually the servant of the servant of the Lord.

TEXT 21

यस्तां विविक्तचरितैरनुवर्तमानां
नात्याद्रियत्परमभागवतप्रसङ्गः ।
स त्वं द्विजानुपथपुण्यरजःपुनीतः
श्रीवत्सलक्ष्म किमगा भगभाजनस्त्वम्॥२१॥

yas tāṁ vivikta-caritair anuvartamānāṁ
nātyādriyat parama-bhāgavata-prasaṅgaḥ
sa tvaṁ dvijānupatha-puṇya-rajaḥ-punītaḥ
śrīvatsa-lakṣma kim agā bhaga-bhājanas tvam

yaḥ—who; *tām*—Lakṣmī; *vivikta*—completely pure; *caritaiḥ*—devotional services; *anuvartamānām*—serving; *na*—not; *atyādriyat*—attached; *parama*—the highest; *bhāgavata*—devotees; *prasaṅgaḥ*—attached; *saḥ*—the Supreme Lord; *tvam*—You; *dvija*—of the *brāhmaṇas; anupatha*—on the path; *puṇya*—sanctified; *rajaḥ*—dust; *punītaḥ*—purified; *śrīvatsa*—of Śrīvatsa; *lakṣma*—the mark; *kim*—what; *agāḥ*—You obtained; *bhaga*—all opulences or all good qualities; *bhājanaḥ*—the reservoir; *tvam*—You.

TRANSLATION

O Lord, You are exceedingly attached to the activities of Your pure devotees, yet You are never attached to the goddesses of fortune who constantly engage in Your transcendental loving service. How can You be purified, therefore, by the dust of the path traversed by the brāhmaṇas, and how can You be glorified or made fortunate by the marks of Śrīvatsa on Your chest?

PURPORT

It is said in the *Brahma-saṁhitā* that the Lord is always served by many hundreds of thousands of goddesses of fortune in His Vaikuṇṭha planet, yet because of His attitude of renunciation of all opulences, He is not attached to any one of them. The Lord has six opulences—unlimited wealth, unlimited fame, unlimited strength, unlimited beauty, unlimited knowledge and unlimited renunciation. All the demigods and other living entities worship Lakṣmī, the goddess of fortune, just to get her favor, yet the Lord is never attached to her because He can create an unlimited number of such goddesses for His transcendental service. The goddess of fortune, Lakṣmī, is sometimes envious of the *tulasī* leaves which are placed at the lotus feet of the Lord, for they remain fixed there and do not move, whereas Lakṣmījī, although stationed by the chest of the Lord, sometimes has to please other devotees who pray for her favor. Lakṣmījī sometimes has to go to satisfy her numerous devotees, but *tulasī* leaves never forsake their position, and the Lord therefore appreciates the service of the *tulasī* more than the service of Lakṣmī. When the Lord says, therefore, that it is due to the causeless mercy of the *brāhmaṇas* that Lakṣmījī does not leave Him, we can understand that Lakṣmījī is attracted by the opulence of the Lord, not by the *brāhmaṇas'* benedictions upon Him. The Lord is not dependent on anyone's mercy for His opulence; He is always self-sufficient. The Lord's statement that His opulence is due to the benediction of the *brāhmaṇas* and Vaiṣṇavas is only to teach others that they should offer respect to the *brāhmaṇas* and Vaiṣṇavas, the devotees of the Lord.

TEXT 22

धर्मस्य ते भगवतस्त्रियुग त्रिभिः स्वैः
पद्भिश्चराचरमिदं द्विजदेवतार्थम् ।
नूनं भृतं तदभिघाति रजस्तमश्च
सत्त्वेन नो वरदया तनुवा निरस्य ॥२२॥

dharmasya te bhagavatas tri-yuga tribhiḥ svaiḥ
padbhiś carācaram idaṁ dvija-devatārtham
nūnaṁ bhṛtaṁ tad-abhighāti rajas tamaś ca
sattvena no varadayā tanuvā nirasya

dharmasya—of the personification of all religion; *te*—of You; *bhagavataḥ*—of the Supreme Personality of Godhead; *tri-yuga*—You who are manifest in all three millenniums; *tribhiḥ*—by three; *svaiḥ*—Your own; *padbhiḥ*—feet; *cara-acaram*—animate and inanimate; *idam*—this universe; *dvija*—the twice-born; *devatā*—the demigods; *artham*—for the sake of; *nūnam*—however; *bhṛtam*—protected; *tat*—those feet; *abhighāti*—destroying; *rajaḥ*—the mode of passion; *tamaḥ*—the mode of ignorance; *ca*—and; *sattvena*—of pure goodness; *naḥ*—unto us; *vara-dayā*—bestowing all blessings; *tanuvā*—by Your transcendental form; *nirasya*—driving away.

TRANSLATION

O Lord, You are the personification of all religion. Therefore You manifest Yourself in three millenniums, and thus You protect

this universe, which consists of animate and inanimate beings. By Your grace, which is of pure goodness and is the bestower of all blessings, kindly drive away the elements of rajas and tamas for the sake of the demigods and twice-born.

PURPORT

The Lord is addressed in this verse as *tri-yuga*, or one who appears in three millenniums—namely the Satya, Dvāpara and Tretā *yugas*. He is not mentioned as appearing in the fourth millennium, or Kali-yuga. It is described in Vedic literature that in Kali-yuga He comes as *channa-avatāra*, or an incarnation, but He does not appear as a manifest incarnation. In the other *yugas*, however, the Lord is a manifest incarnation, and therefore he is addressed as *tri-yuga*, or the Lord who appears in three *yugas*.

Śrīdhara Svāmī describes *tri-yuga* as follows: *yuga* means "couple," and *tri* means "three." The Lord is manifested as three couples by His six opulences, or three couples of opulences. In that way He can be addressed as *tri-yuga*. The Lord is the personality of religious principles. In three millenniums religious principles are protected by three kinds of spiritual culture, namely austerity, cleanliness and mercy. The Lord is called *tri-yuga* in that way also. In the age of Kali these three requisites to spiritual culture are almost absent, but the Lord is so kind that in spite of Kali-yuga's being devoid of these three spiritual qualities, He comes and protects the people of this age in His covered incarnation as Lord Caitanya. Lord Caitanya is called "covered" because although He is Kṛṣṇa Himself, He presents Himself as a devotee of Kṛṣṇa, not directly Kṛṣṇa. The devotees pray to Lord Caitanya, therefore, to eliminate their stock of passion and ignorance, the most conspicuous assets of this *yuga*. In the Kṛṣṇa consciousness movement one cleanses himself of the modes of passion and ignorance by chanting the holy name of the Lord, Hare Kṛṣṇa, Hare Kṛṣṇa, as introduced by Lord Caitanya.

The four Kumāras were cognizant of their situation in the modes of passion and ignorance because, although in Vaikuṇṭha, they wanted to curse devotees of the Lord. Since they were conscious of their own weakness, they prayed to the Lord to remove their still-existing passion and ignorance. The three transcendental qualifications—cleanliness, austerity and mercy—are the qualifications of the twice-born and the demigods. Those who are not situated in the quality of goodness cannot accept these three principles of spiritual culture. For the Kṛṣṇa consciousness movement, therefore, there are three sinful activities which are prohibited—namely illicit sex, intoxication, and eating food other than the *prasāda* offered to Kṛṣṇa. These three prohibitions are based on the principles of austerity, cleanliness and mercy. Devotees are merciful because they spare the poor animals, and they are clean because they are free of contamination from unwanted foodstuff and unwanted habits. Austerity is represented by restricted sex life. These principles, indicated by the prayers of the four Kumāras, should be followed by the devotees who are engaged in Kṛṣṇa consciousness.

TEXT 23

न त्वं द्विजोत्तमकुलं यदिहात्मगोपं
गोप्ता वृषः स्वर्हणेन ससूनृतेन ।
तर्ह्येव नङ्क्ष्यति शिवस्तव देव पन्था
लोकोऽग्रहीष्यदृषभस्य हि तत्प्रमाणम् ॥२३॥

na tvaṁ dvijottama-kulaṁ yadi hātma-gopaṁ
goptā vṛṣaḥ svarhaṇena sa-sūnṛtena
tarhy eva naṅkṣyati śivas tava deva panthā
loko 'grahīṣyad ṛṣabhasya hi tat pramāṇam

na—not; *tvam*—You; *dvija*—of the twice-born; *uttama-kulam*—the highest class; *yadi*—if; *ha*—indeed; *ātma-gopam*—worthy to be protected by You; *goptā*—the protector; *vṛṣaḥ*—the best; *su-arhaṇena*—by worship; *sa-sūnṛtena*—along with mild words; *tarhi*—then; *eva*—certainly; *naṅkṣyati*—will be lost; *śivaḥ*—auspicious; *tava*—Your; *deva*—O Lord; *panthāḥ*—the path; *lokaḥ*—the people in general; *agrahīṣyat*—would accept; *ṛṣabhasya*—of the best; *hi*—because; *tat*—that; *pramāṇam*—authority.

TRANSLATION

O Lord, You are the protector of the highest of the twice-born. If You do not protect them by offering worship and mild words,

then certainly the auspicious path of worship will be rejected by people in general, who act on the strength and authority of Your Lordship.

PURPORT

In *Bhagavad-gītā* it is stated by the Lord Himself that the acts and character of great authorities are followed by people in general. Leaders of ideal character are therefore needed in society. Kṛṣṇa, the Supreme Personality of Godhead, appeared in this material world just to show the example of perfect authority, and people have to follow His path. The Vedic injunction is that one cannot understand the Absolute Truth simply by mental speculation or logical argument. One has to follow the authorities. *Mahājano yena gataḥ sa panthāḥ.* Great authorities should be followed; otherwise, if we simply depend on the scriptures, we are sometimes misled by rascals, or else we cannot understand or follow the different spiritual injunctions. The best path is to follow the authorities. The four *brāhmaṇa*-sages stated that Kṛṣṇa is naturally the protector of the cows and *brāhmaṇas: go-brāhmaṇa-hitāya ca.* When Kṛṣṇa was on this planet, He set a practical example. He was a cowherd boy, and He was very respectful to the *brāhmaṇas* and devotees.

It is also affirmed herein that the *brāhmaṇas* are the best of the twice-born. *Brāhmaṇas, kṣatriyas* and *vaiśyas* are all twice-born, but the *brāhmaṇas* are the best. When there is a fight between two persons, each of them protects the upper part of his body—the head, the arms and the belly. Similarly, for the actual advancement of human civilization, the best part of the social body, namely the *brāhmaṇas*, the *kṣatriyas* and *vaiśyas* (the intelligent class of men, the military class and the mercantile men) should be given special protection. Protection of the laborers should not be neglected, but special protection should be given to the upper orders. Of all classes of men, the *brāhmaṇas* and the Vaiṣṇavas should be given special protection. They should be worshiped. When their protection is performed, it is just like worshiping God. That is not exactly protection; it is a duty. One should worship the *brāhmaṇas* and Vaiṣṇavas by offering them all kinds of endowments and sweet words, and if one has no means to offer anything, he must at least use sweet words to pacify them. The Lord personally exhibited this behavior towards the Kumāras.

If this system is not introduced by the leaders, then human civilization will be lost. When there is no protection and special treatment for persons who are devotees of the Lord, who are highly intelligent in spiritual life, then the whole society is lost. The word *naṅkṣyati* indicates that such a civilization becomes spoiled and is annihilated. The kind of civilization recommended is called *deva-patha*, which means the "royal road of the demigods." Demigods are supposed to be fully fixed in devotional service, or Kṛṣṇa consciousness; that is the auspicious path that should be protected. If the authorities or the leaders of society do not give special respect to the *brāhmaṇas* and Vaiṣṇavas and do not offer them not only sweet words but all facilities, then the path of progress will be lost to human civilization. The Lord personally wanted to teach this, and therefore He offered so much praise to the Kumāras.

TEXT 24

तच्चेऽनभीष्टमिव सत्त्वनिधेर्विधित्सोः
क्षेमं जनाय निजशक्तिभिरुद्धृतारेः ।
नैतावता त्र्यधिपतेर्बत विश्वभर्तु-
स्तेजः क्षतं त्ववनतस्य स ते विनोदः ॥२४॥

tat te 'nabhīṣṭam iva sattva-nidher vidhitsoḥ
kṣemaṁ janāya nija-śaktibhir uddhṛtāreḥ
naitāvatā try-adhipater bata viśva-bhartus
tejaḥ kṣataṁ tv avanatasya sa te vinodaḥ

tat—that destruction of the path of auspiciousness; *te*—by You; *anabhīṣṭam*—is not liked; *iva*—as; *sattva-nidheḥ*—the reservoir of all goodness; *vidhitsoḥ*—desiring to do; *kṣemam*—good; *janāya*—for the people in general; *nija-śaktibhiḥ*—by Your own potencies; *uddhṛta*—destroyed; *areḥ*—the opposite element; *na*—not; *etāvatā*—by this; *tri-adhipateḥ*—of the proprietor of the three kinds of creations; *bata*—O Lord; *viśva-bhartuḥ*—the maintainer of the universe; *tejaḥ*—potency; *kṣatam*—reduced; *tu*—but; *avanatasya*—submissive; *saḥ*—that; *te*—Your; *vinodaḥ*—pleasure.

TRANSLATION

Dear Lord, You never want the auspicious path to be destroyed, for You are the reservoir of all goodness. Just to benefit people in general, You destroy the evil element by Your mighty potency. You are the proprietor of the three creations and the maintainer of the entire universe. Therefore Your potency is not reduced by Your submissive behavior. Rather, by submission You exhibit Your transcendental pastimes.

PURPORT

Lord Kṛṣṇa was never reduced in His position by becoming a cowherd boy or by offering respect to Sudāmā Brāhmaṇa or His other devotees like Nanda Mahārāja, Vasudeva, Mahārāja Yudhiṣṭhira and the Pāṇḍavas' mother, Kuntī. Everyone knew that He was the Supreme Personality of Godhead, Kṛṣṇa, yet His behavior was exemplary. The Supreme Personality of Godhead is *sac-cid-ānanda-vigraha;* His form is completely spiritual, full of bliss and knowledge, and it is eternal. Because the living entities are His parts and parcels, originally they also belong to the same quality of eternal form as the Lord, but when they come in contact with *māyā,* the material potency, due to their forgetfulness their existential constitution is covered. We should try to understand the appearance of Lord Kṛṣṇa in this spirit, as the Kumāras pray to Him. He is eternally a cowherd boy at Vṛndāvana, He is eternally the leader of the Battle of Kurukṣetra, and He is eternally the opulent prince of Dvārakā and the lover of the damsels of Vṛndāvana; all His appearances are meaningful because they show His real characteristics to the conditioned souls, who have forgotten their relationship with the Supreme Lord. He does everything for their benefit. The force exhibited in the Battle of Kurukṣetra by the desire of Kṛṣṇa and through the agency of Arjuna was also necessary because when people become too irreligious, force is required. Nonviolence in this respect is rascaldom.

TEXT 25

यं वानयोर्दममधीश भवान् विधत्ते
वृत्तिं नु वा तदनुमन्महि निर्व्यलीकम् ।

असासु वा य उचितो ध्रियतां स दण्डो
येऽनागसौ वयमयुङ्क्ष्महि किल्बिषेण ॥२५॥

yaṁ vānayor damam adhīśa bhavān vidhatte
vṛttiṁ nu vā tad anumanmahi nirvyalīkam
asmāsu vā ya ucito dhriyatāṁ sa daṇḍo
ye 'nāgasau vayam ayuṅkṣmahi kilbiṣeṇa

yam—which; *vā*—or; *anayoḥ*—of both of them; *damam*—punishment; *adhīśa*—O Lord; *bhavān*—Your Lordship; *vidhatte*—awards; *vṛttim*—better existence; *nu*—certainly; *vā*—or; *tat*—that; *anumanmahi*—we accept; *nirvyalīkam*—without duplicity; *asmāsu*—to us; *vā*—or; *yaḥ*—whichever; *ucitaḥ*—is proper; *dhriyatām*—may be awarded; *saḥ*—that; *daṇḍaḥ*—punishment; *ye*—who; *anāgasau*—sinless; *vayam*—we; *ayuṅkṣmahi*—allotted; *kilbiṣeṇa*—with a curse.

TRANSLATION

O Lord, whatever punishment You wish to award to these two innocent persons or also to us we shall accept without duplicity. We understand that we have cursed two faultless persons.

PURPORT

The sages, the four Kumāras, now reject their cursing of the two doorkeepers, Jaya and Vijaya, because they are now conscious that persons who engage in the service of the Lord cannot be at fault at any stage. It is said that anyone who has implicit faith in the service of the Lord, or who actually engages in transcendental loving service, has all the good qualities of the demigods. Therefore, a devotee cannot be at fault. If sometimes it is found that he is in error by accident or by some temporary arrangement, that should not be taken very seriously. The cursing of Jaya and Vijaya is here repented. Now the Kumāras are thinking in terms of their position in the modes of passion and ignorance, and they are prepared to accept any kind of punishment from the Lord. In general, when dealing with devotees, we should not try to find faults. In *Bhagavad-gītā* also it is confirmed that the devotee who faithfully serves the Supreme Lord, even if found to commit a gross mistake, should be considered a *sādhu*, or saintly person. Due to former habits he may commit some wrong, but because he is engaged in the service of the Lord, that wrong should not be taken very seriously.

TEXT 26

श्रीभगवानुवाच
एतौ सुरेतरगतिं प्रतिपद्य सद्यः
संरम्भसम्भृतसमाध्यनुबद्धयोगौ ।
भूयः सकाशमुपयास्यत आशु यो वः
शापो मयैव निमितस्तदवेत विप्राः ॥२६॥

śrī-bhagavān uvāca
etau suretara-gatiṁ pratipadya sadyaḥ
saṁrambha-sambhṛta-samādhy-anubaddha-yogau
bhūyaḥ sakāśam upayāsyata āśu yo vaḥ
śāpo mayaiva nimitas tad aveta viprāḥ

śrī-bhagavān uvāca—the Supreme Personality of Godhead replied; *etau*—these two doorkeepers; *sura-itara*—demoniac; *gatim*—the womb; *pratipadya*—obtaining; *sadyaḥ*—quickly; *saṁrambha*—by anger; *sambhṛta*—intensified; *samādhi*—concentration of mind; *anubaddha*—firmly; *yogau*—united with Me; *bhūyaḥ*—again; *sakāśam*—to My presence; *upayāsyataḥ*—shall return; *āśu*—shortly; *yaḥ*—which; *vaḥ*—of you; *śāpaḥ*—curse; *mayā*—by Me; *eva*—alone; *nimitaḥ*—ordained; *tat*—that; *aveta*—know; *viprāḥ*—O *brāhmaṇas.*

TRANSLATION

The Lord replied: O brāhmaṇas, know that the punishment you inflicted on them was originally ordained by Me, and therefore they will fall to a birth in a demoniac family. But they will be firmly united with Me in thought through mental concentration intensified by anger, and they will return to My presence shortly.

PURPORT

The Lord stated that the punishment inflicted by the sages upon the doorkeepers Jaya and Vijaya was conceived by the Lord Himself. Without the Lord's sanction, nothing can happen. It is to be understood that there was a plan in the cursing of the Lord's devotees in Vaikuṇṭha, and His plan is explained by many stalwart authorities. The Lord sometimes desires to fight. The fighting spirit also exists in the Supreme Lord, otherwise how could fighting be manifested at all? Because the Lord is the source of everything, anger and fighting are also inherent in His personality. When He desires to fight with someone, He has to find an enemy, but in the Vaikuṇṭha world there is no enemy because everyone is engaged fully in His service. Therefore He sometimes comes to the material world as an incarnation in order to manifest His fighting spirit.

In *Bhagavad-gītā* (4.8) also it is said that the Lord appears just to give protection to the devotees and to annihilate the nondevotees. The nondevotees are found in the material world, not in the spiritual world; therefore, when the Lord wants to fight, He has to come to this world. But who will fight with the Supreme Lord? No one is able to fight with Him! Therefore, because the Lord's pastimes in the material world are always performed with His associates, not with others, He has to find some devotee who will play the part of an enemy. In *Bhagavad-gītā* the Lord says to Arjuna, "My dear Arjuna, both you and I have appeared many, many times in this material world, but you have forgotten, whereas I remember." Thus Jaya and Vijaya were selected by the Lord to fight with Him in the material world, and that was the reason the sages came to see Him and accidentally the doorkeepers were cursed. It was the Lord's desire to send them to the material world, not perpetually, but for some time. Therefore, just as on a theatrical stage someone takes the part of enemy to the proprietor of the stage, although the play is for a short time and there is no permanent enmity between the servant and the proprietor, so the *sura-janas* (devotees) were cursed by the sages to go to the *asura-jana*, or atheistic families. That a devotee should come into an atheistic family is surprising, but it is simply a show. After finishing their mock fighting, both the devotee and the Lord are again associated in the spiritual planets. That is very explicitly explained here. The conclusion is that no one falls from the spiritual world, or Vaikuṇṭha planet, for it is the eternal abode. But sometimes, as the Lord desires, devotees come into this material world as preachers or as atheists. In each case we must understand that there is a plan of the Lord. Lord Buddha, for example, was an incarnation, yet he preached atheism: "There is no God."

But actually there was a plan behind this, as explained in the *Bhāgavatam.*

TEXT 27

ब्रह्मोवाच
अथ ते मुनयो दृष्ट्वा नयनानन्दभाजनम् ।
वैकुण्ठं तदधिष्ठानं विकुण्ठं च स्वयंप्रभम् ॥२७॥

brahmovāca
atha te munayo dṛṣṭvā
nayanānanda-bhājanam
vaikuṇṭhaṁ tad-adhiṣṭhānaṁ
vikuṇṭhaṁ ca svayaṁ-prabham

brahmā uvāca—Lord Brahmā said; *atha*—now; *te*—those; *munayaḥ*—sages; *dṛṣṭvā*—after seeing; *nayana*—of the eyes; *ānanda*—pleasure; *bhājanam*—producing; *vaikuṇṭham*—the Vaikuṇṭha planet; *tat*—of Him; *adhiṣṭhānam*—the abode; *vikuṇṭham*—the Supreme Personality of Godhead; *ca*—and; *svayam-prabham*—self-illuminating.

TRANSLATION

Lord Brahmā said: After seeing the Lord of Vaikuṇṭha, the Supreme Personality of Godhead, in the self-illuminated Vaikuṇṭha planet, the sages left that transcendental abode.

PURPORT

The transcendental abode of the Supreme Personality of Godhead, as stated in *Bhagavad-gītā* and confirmed in this verse, is self-illuminated. In *Bhagavad-gītā* it is said that in the spiritual world there is no need of sun, moon or electricity. This indicates that all the planets there are self-illuminated, self-sufficient and independent; everything there is complete. Lord Kṛṣṇa says that once one goes to that Vaikuṇṭha planet, he never returns. The inhabitants of Vaikuṇṭha never return to the material world, but the incident of Jaya and Vijaya was a different case. They came to the material world for some time, and then they returned to Vaikuṇṭha.

TEXT 28

भगवन्तं परिक्रम्य प्रणिपत्यानुमान्य च ।
प्रतिजग्मुः प्रमुदिताः शंसन्तो वैष्णवीं श्रियम् ॥२८॥

bhagavantaṁ parikramya
praṇipatyānumānya ca
pratijagmuḥ pramuditāḥ
śaṁsanto vaiṣṇavīṁ śriyam

bhagavantam—the Supreme Personality of Godhead; *parikramya*—after circumambulating; *praṇipatya*—after offering obeisances; *anumānya*—after learning; *ca*—and; *pratijagmuḥ*—returned; *pramuditāḥ*—extremely delighted; *śaṁsantaḥ*—glorifying; *vaiṣṇavīm*—of the Vaiṣṇavas; *śriyam*—opulence.

TRANSLATION

The sages circumambulated the Supreme Lord, offered their obeisances and returned, extremely delighted at learning of the divine opulences of the Vaiṣṇava.

PURPORT

It is still a respectful practice to circumambulate the Lord in Hindu temples. Especially in Vaiṣṇava temples there is an arrangement for people to offer their respects to the Deity and circumambulate the temple at least three times.

TEXT 29

भगवाननुगावाह यातं मा भैष्टमस्तु शम् ।
ब्रह्मतेजः समर्थोऽपि हन्तुं नेच्छे मतं तु मे ॥२९॥

bhagavān anugāv āha
yātaṁ mā bhaiṣṭam astu śam
brahma-tejaḥ samartho 'pi
hantuṁ necche mataṁ tu me

bhagavān—the Supreme Personality of Godhead; *anugau*—to His two attendants; *āha*—said; *yātam*—depart from this place; *mā*—let there not be; *bhaiṣṭam*—fear; *astu*—let there be; *śam*—happiness; *brahma*—of a *brāhmaṇa; tejaḥ*—the curse; *samarthaḥ*—being able; *api*—even; *hantum*—to nullify; *na icche*—do not desire; *matam*—approved; *tu*—on the contrary; *me*—by Me.

TRANSLATION

The Lord then said to His attendants, Jaya and Vijaya: Depart this place, but fear not. All glories unto you. Though I am capable of nullifying the brāhmaṇas' curse, I would not do so. On the contrary, it has My approval.

PURPORT

As explained in connection with text 26, all the incidents that took place had the approval of the Lord. Ordinarily, there is no possibility that the four sages could be so angry with the doorkeepers, nor could the Supreme Lord neglect His two doorkeepers, nor can one come back from Vaikuṇṭha after once taking birth there. All these incidents, therefore, were designed by the Lord Himself for the sake of His pastimes in the material world. Thus He plainly says that it was done with His approval. Otherwise, it would have been impossible for inhabitants of Vaikuṇṭha to come back to this material world simply because of a brahminical curse. The Lord especially blesses the so-called culprits: "All glories unto you." A devotee, once accepted by the Lord, can never fall down. That is the conclusion of this incident.

TEXT 30

एतत्पुरैव निर्दिष्टं रमया क्रुद्धया यदा ।
पुरापवारिता द्वारि विशन्ती मय्युपारते ॥३०॥

etat puraiva nirdiṣṭaṁ
ramayā kruddhayā yadā
purāpavāritā dvāri
viśantī mayy upārate

etat—this departure; *purā*—formerly; *eva*—certainly; *nirdiṣṭam*—foretold; *ramayā*—by Lakṣmī; *kruddhayā*—furious; *yadā*—when; *purā*—previously; *apavāritā*—prevented; *dvāri*—at the gate; *viśantī*—entering; *mayi*—as I; *upārate*—was resting.

TRANSLATION

This departure from Vaikuṇṭha was foretold by Lakṣmī, the goddess of fortune. She was very angry because when she left My abode and then returned, you stopped her at the gate while I was sleeping.

TEXT 31

मयि संरम्भयोगेन निस्तीर्य ब्रह्महेलनम् ।
प्रत्येष्यतं निकाशं मे कालेनाल्पीयसा पुनः ॥३१॥

mayi saṁrambha-yogena
nistīrya brahma-helanam
pratyeṣyataṁ nikāśaṁ me
kālenālpīyasā punaḥ

mayi—unto Me; *saṁrambha-yogena*—by practice of mystic *yoga* in anger; *nistīrya*—being liberated from; *brahma-helanam*—the result of disobedience to the *brāhmaṇas; pratyeṣyatam*—will come back; *nikāśam*—near; *me*—Me; *kālena*—in due course of time; *alpīyasā*—very short; *punaḥ*—again.

TRANSLATION

The Lord assured the two Vaikuṇṭha inhabitants, Jaya and Vijaya: By practicing the mystic yoga system in anger, you will be cleansed of the sin of disobeying the brāhmaṇas and within a very short time return to Me.

PURPORT

The Supreme Personality of Godhead advised the two doorkeepers, Jaya and Vijaya, that by dint of *bhakti-yoga* in anger they would be delivered from the curses of the *brāhmaṇas*. Śrīla Madhva Muni remarks in this connection that by practicing *bhakti-yoga* one can become free from all sinful reactions. Even a *brahma-śāpa*, or curse by a *brāhmaṇa*, which cannot be overcome by any other means, can be overcome by *bhakti-yoga*.

One can practice *bhakti-yoga* in many *rasas*. There are twelve *rasas*, five primary and seven secondary. The five primary *rasas* constitute direct *bhakti-yoga*, but although the seven secondary *rasas* are indirect, they are also counted within *bhakti-yoga* if they are used in the service of the Lord. In other words, *bhakti-yoga* is all-inclusive. If one somehow or other becomes attached to the Supreme Personality of Godhead, he becomes engaged in *bhakti-yoga*, as described in *Śrīmad-Bhāgavatam* (10.29.15): *kāmaṁ krodhaṁ bhayam*. The *gopīs* were attracted to Kṛṣṇa by *bhakti-yoga* in a relationship of lusty desire (*kāma*). Similarly, Kaṁsa was attached to *bhakti-yoga* by dint of fear of his death. Thus *bhakti-yoga* is so powerful that even becoming an enemy of the Lord and always thinking of Him can deliver one very quickly. It is said, *viṣṇu-bhaktaḥ smṛto daiva āsuras tad-vipanyayaḥ:* "Devotees of Lord Viṣṇu are called demigods, whereas nondevotees are called *asuras*." But *bhakti-yoga* is so powerful that both demigods and *asuras* can derive its benefits if they always think of the Personality of Godhead. The basic principle of *bhakti-yoga* is to think of the Supreme Lord always. The Lord says in *Bhagavad-gītā* (18.65), *man-manā bhava mad-bhaktaḥ:* "Always think of Me." It doesn't matter which way one thinks; the very thought of the Personality of Godhead is the basic principle of *bhakti-yoga*.

In the material planets there are different grades of sinful activities, of which disrespecting a *brāhmaṇa* or a Vaiṣṇava is the most sinful. Here it is clearly stated that one can overcome even that grave sin simply by thinking of Viṣṇu, not even favorably but in anger. Thus even if those who are not devotees always think of Viṣṇu, they become free from all sinful activities. Kṛṣṇa consciousness is the highest form of thought. Lord Viṣṇu is thought of in this age by chanting Hare Kṛṣṇa, Hare Kṛṣṇa, Kṛṣṇa Kṛṣṇa, Hare Hare/ Hare Rāma, Hare Rāma, Rāma Rāma, Hare Hare. From the statements of the *Bhāgavatam* it appears that if one thinks of Kṛṣṇa, even as an enemy, that particular qualification—*thinking of Viṣṇu, or Kṛṣṇa*—cleanses one of all sins.

TEXT 32

द्वाःस्थावादिश्य भगवान् विमानश्रेणिभूषणम् ।
सर्वातिशयया लक्ष्म्या जुष्टं स्वं धिष्ण्यमाविशत् ॥३२॥

dvāḥsthāv ādiśya bhagavān
vimāna-śreṇi-bhūṣaṇam
sarvātiśayayā lakṣmyā
juṣṭaṁ svaṁ dhiṣṇyam āviśat

dvāḥ-sthau—to the doorkeepers; *ādiśya*—just directing them; *bhagavān*—the Supreme Personality of Godhead; *vimāna-śreṇi-bhūṣaṇam*—always decorated with first-class airplanes; *sarva-atiśayayā*—in every respect extensively opulent; *lakṣmyā*—opulences; *juṣṭam*—bedecked with; *svam*—His own; *dhiṣṇyam*—abode; *āviśat*—went back.

TRANSLATION

After thus speaking at the door of Vaikuṇṭha, the Lord returned to His abode, where there are many celestial airplanes and all-surpassing wealth and splendor.

PURPORT

It is clear from this verse that all the incidents took place at the entrance of Vaikuṇṭhaloka. In other words, the sages were not actually within Vaikuṇṭhaloka, but were at the gate. It could be asked, "How could they return to the material world if they entered Vaikuṇṭhaloka?" But factually they did not enter, and therefore they returned. There are many similar incidents where great *yogīs* and *brāhmaṇas*, by dint of their *yoga* practice, have gone from this material world to Vaikuṇṭhaloka—but they were not meant to stay there. They came back. It is also confirmed here that the Lord was surrounded by many Vaikuṇṭha airplanes. Vaikuṇṭhaloka is described here as having splendid opulence, far surpassing the splendor of this material world.

All other living creatures, including the demigods, are born of Brahmā, and Brahmā is born of Lord Viṣṇu. Kṛṣṇa states in *Bhagavad-gītā*, in the Tenth Chapter, *ahaṁ sarvasya prabhavaḥ:* Lord Viṣṇu is the origin of all manifestations in the material world. Those who know that Lord Viṣṇu is the origin of everything, who are conversant with the process of creation and who understand that Viṣṇu, or Kṛṣṇa, is the most worshipable object of all living entities, engage themselves in Viṣṇu worship as Vaiṣṇavas. The Vedic hymns also confirm this: *oṁ tad viṣṇoḥ paramaṁ padam.* The goal of life is to understand Viṣṇu. The *Bhāgavatam* also confirms this elsewhere. Foolish people, not knowing that Viṣṇu is the supreme worshipable object, create so many worshipable objects in this material world, and therefore they fall down.

TEXT 33

तौ तु गीर्वाणऋषभौ दुस्तराद्धरिलोकतः ।
हतश्रियौ ब्रह्मशापादभूतां विगतस्मयौ ॥३३॥

tau tu gīrvāṇa-ṛṣabhau
dustarād dhari-lokataḥ
hata-śriyau brahma-śāpād
abhūtāṁ vigata-smayau

tau—those two gatekeepers; *tu*—but; *gīrvāṇa-ṛṣabhau*—the best of the demigods; *dustarāt*—unable to be avoided; *hari-lokataḥ*—from Vaikuṇṭha, the abode of Lord Hari; *hata-śriyau*—diminished in beauty and luster; *brahma-śāpāt*—from the curse of a *brāhmaṇa; abhūtām*—became; *vigata-smayau*—morose.

TRANSLATION

But those two gatekeepers, the best of the demigods, their beauty and luster diminished by the curse of the brāhmaṇas, became morose and fell from Vaikuṇṭha, the abode of the Supreme Lord.

TEXT 34

तदा विकुण्ठधिषणात्तयोर्निपतमानयोः ।
हाहाकारो महानासीद्विमानाग्र्येषु पुत्रकाः ॥३४॥

tadā vikuṇṭha-dhiṣaṇāt
tayor nipatamānayoḥ
hāhā-kāro mahān āsīd
vimānāgryeṣu putrakāḥ

tadā—then; *vikuṇṭha*—of the Supreme Lord; *dhiṣaṇāt*—from the abode; *tayoḥ*—as both of them; *nipatamānayoḥ*—were falling; *hāhā-kāraḥ*—roaring in disappointment; *mahān*—great; *āsīt*—occurred; *vimāna-agryeṣu*—in the best of airplanes; *putrakāḥ*—O demigods.

TRANSLATION

Then, as Jaya and Vijaya fell from the Lord's abode, a great roar of disappointment arose from all the demigods, who were sitting in their splendid airplanes.

TEXT 35

तावेव ह्यधुना प्राप्तौ पार्षदप्रवरौ हरेः ।
दितेर्जठरनिर्विष्टं काश्यपं तेज उल्बणम् ॥३५॥

tāv eva hy adhunā prāptau
pārṣada-pravarau hareḥ
diter jaṭhara-nirviṣṭaṁ
kāśyapaṁ teja ulbaṇam

tau—those two doorkeepers; *eva*—certainly; *hi*—addressed; *adhunā*—now; *prāptau*—having gotten; *pārṣada-pravarau*—important associates; *hareḥ*—of the Supreme Personality of Godhead; *diteḥ*—of Diti; *jaṭhara*—womb; *nirviṣṭam*—entering; *kāśyapam*—of Kaśyapa Muni; *tejaḥ*—semen; *ulbaṇam*—very strong.

TRANSLATION

Lord Brahmā continued: Those two principal doorkeepers of the Personality of Godhead have now entered the womb of Diti, the powerful semen of Kaśyapa Muni having covered them.

PURPORT

Here is clear proof of how a living entity coming originally from Vaikuṇṭhaloka is encaged in material elements. The living entity takes shelter within the semen of a father, which is injected within the womb of a mother, and with the help of the mother's emulsified ovum the living entity grows a particular type of a body. In this connection it is to be remembered that the mind of Kaśyapa Muni was not in order when he conceived the two sons, Hiraṇyākṣa and Hiraṇyakaśipu. Therefore the semen he discharged was simultaneously extremely powerful and mixed with the quality of anger. It is to be concluded that while conceiving a child one's mind must be very sober and devotional. For this purpose the *Garbhādhāna-saṁskāra* is recommended in the Vedic scriptures. If the mind of the father is not sober, the semen discharged will not be very good. Thus the living entity, wrapped in the matter produced from the father and mother, will be demoniac like Hiraṇyākṣa and Hiraṇyakaśipu. The conditions of conception are to be carefully studied. This is a very great science.

TEXT 36

तयोरसुरयोरद्य तेजसा यमयोर्हि वः ।
आक्षिप्तं तेज एतर्हि भगवांस्तद्विधित्सति ॥३६॥

tayor asurayor adya
tejasā yamayor hi vaḥ
ākṣiptaṁ teja etarhi
bhagavāṁs tad vidhitsati

tayoḥ—of them; *asurayoḥ*—of the two *asuras; adya*—today; *tejasā*—by the prowess; *yamayoḥ*—of the twins; *hi*—certainly; *vaḥ*—of all you demigods; *ākṣiptam*—agitated; *tejaḥ*—power; *etarhi*—thus certainly; *bhagavān*—the Supreme Personality of Godhead; *tat*—that; *vidhitsati*—desires to do.

TRANSLATION

It is the prowess of these twin asuras [demons] that has disturbed you, for it has minimized your power. There is no remedy

within my power, however, for it is the Lord Himself who desires to do all this.

PURPORT

Although Hiraṇyakaśipu and Hiraṇyākṣa, formerly Jaya and Vijaya, became *asuras*, the demigods of this material world could not control them, and therefore Lord Brahmā said that neither he nor all the demigods could counteract the disturbance they created. They came within the material world by the order of the Supreme Personality of Godhead, and He alone could counteract such disturbances. In other words, although Jaya and Vijaya assumed the bodies of *asuras*, they remained more powerful than anyone, thus proving that the Supreme Personality of Godhead desired to fight because the fighting spirit is also within Him. He is the original in everything, but when He desires to fight He must fight with a devotee. Therefore by His desire only were Jaya and Vijaya cursed by the Kumāras. The Lord ordered the gatekeepers to go down to the material world to become His enemies so that He could fight with them and His fighting desires would be satisfied by the service of His personal devotees.

Brahmā showed the demigods that the situation created by the darkness, for which they were disturbed, was the desire of the Supreme Lord. He wanted to show that even though these two attendants were coming in the forms of demons, they were very powerful, greater than the demigods, who could not control them. No one can surpass the acts of the Supreme Lord. The demigods were also advised not to try to counteract this incident, because it was ordered by the Lord. Similarly, anyone who is ordered by the Lord to perform some action in this material world, especially preaching His glories, cannot be counteracted by anyone; the will of the Lord is executed under all circumstances.

TEXT 37

विश्वस्य यः स्थितिलयोद्भवहेतुराद्यो
योगेश्वरैरपि दुरत्यययोगमायः ।
क्षेमं विधास्यति स नो भगवांस्त्र्यधीश-
स्तत्रास्मदीयविमृशेन कियानिहार्थः ॥३७॥

viśvasya yaḥ sthiti-layodbhava-hetur ādyo
yogeśvarair api duratyaya-yogamāyaḥ
kṣemaṁ vidhāsyati sa no bhagavāṁs tryadhīśas
tatrāsmadīya-vimṛśena kiyān ihārthaḥ

viśvasya—of the universe; *yaḥ*—who; *sthiti*—maintenance; *laya*—destruction; *udbhava*—creation; *hetuḥ*—the cause; *ādyaḥ*—the most ancient person; *yoga-īśvaraiḥ*—by the masters of *yoga; api*—even; *duratyaya*—cannot be easily understood; *yoga-māyaḥ*—His *yogamāyā* potency; *kṣemam*—good; *vidhāsyati*—will do; *saḥ*—He; *naḥ*—of us; *bhagavān*—the Supreme Personality of Godhead; *tri-adhīśaḥ*—the controller of the three modes of material nature; *tatra*—there; *asmadīya*—by our; *vimṛśena*—deliberation; *kiyān*—what; *iha*—on this subject; *arthaḥ*—purpose.

TRANSLATION

My dear sons, the Lord is the controller of the three modes of nature and is responsible for the creation, preservation and dissolution of the universe. His wonderful creative power, yogamāyā, cannot be easily understood even by the masters of yoga. That most ancient person, the Personality of Godhead, will alone come to our rescue. What purpose can we serve on His behalf by deliberating on the subject?

PURPORT

When something is arranged by the Supreme Personality of Godhead, one should not be disturbed by it, even if it appears to be a reverse according to one's calculations. For example, sometimes we see that a powerful preacher is killed, or sometimes he is put into difficulty, just as Haridāsa Ṭhākura was. He was a great devotee who came into this material world to execute the will of the Lord by preaching the Lord's glories. But Haridāsa was punished at the hands of the Kazi by being beaten in twenty-two marketplaces. Similarly, Lord Jesus Christ was crucified, and Prahlāda Mahārāja was put through so many tribulations. The Pāṇḍavas, who were direct friends of Kṛṣṇa, lost their kingdom, their wife was insulted, and they had to undergo many severe tribulations. Seeing all these reverses affect devotees, one should not be disturbed; one should simply understand that in these matters there must be some plan of the Supreme Personality of Godhead. The *Bhāgavatam*'s conclusion is that a devotee is never disturbed by such reverses. He accepts even reverse conditions as the grace of the Lord. One who continues to serve the Lord even in reverse conditions is assured that he will go back to Godhead, back to the Vaikuṇṭha planets. Lord Brahmā assured the demigods that there was no use in talking about how the disturbing situation of darkness was taking place, since the actual fact was that it was ordered by the Supreme Lord. Brahmā knew this because he was a great devotee; it was possible for him to understand the plan of the Lord.

Thus end the Bhaktivedanta purports of the Third Canto, Sixteenth Chapter, of the Śrīmad-Bhāgavatam, *entitled "The Two Doorkeepers of Vaikuṇṭha, Jaya and Vijaya, Cursed by the Sages."*

Appendixes

About the Author

His Divine Grace A.C. Bhaktivedanta Swami Prabhupāda appeared in this world in 1896 in Calcutta, India. He first met his spiritual master, Śrīla Bhaktisiddhānta Sarasvatī Gosvāmī, in Calcutta in 1922. Bhaktisiddhānta Sarasvatī, a prominent religious scholar and the founder of sixty-four Gauḍīya Maṭhas (Vedic institutes), liked this educated young man and convinced him to dedicate his life to teaching Vedic knowledge. Śrīla Prabhupāda became his student, and eleven years later (1933) at Allahabad he became his formally initiated disciple.

At their first meeting, in 1922, Śrīla Bhaktisiddhānta Sarasvatī Ṭhākura requested Śrīla Prabhupāda to broadcast Vedic knowledge through the English language. In the years that followed, Śrīla Prabhupāda wrote a commentary on the *Bhagavad-gītā,* assisted the Gauḍīya Maṭha in its work and, in 1944, started *Back to Godhead,* an English fortnightly magazine. Maintaining the publication was a struggle. Singlehandedly, Śrīla Prabhupāda edited it, typed the manuscripts, checked the galley proofs, and even distributed the individual copies. Once begun, the magazine never stopped; it is now being continued by his disciples in the West and is published in over thirty languages.

Recognizing Śrīla Prabhupāda's philosophical learning and devotion, the Gauḍīya Vaiṣṇava Society honored him in 1947 with the title "Bhaktivedanta." In 1950, at the age of fifty-four, Śrīla Prabhupāda retired from married life, adopting the *vānaprastha* (retired) order to devote more time to his studies and writing. Śrīla Prabhupāda traveled to the holy city of Vṛndāvana, where he lived in very humble circumstances in the historic medieval temple of Rādhā-Dāmodara. There he engaged for several years in deep study and writing. He accepted the renounced order of life (*sannyāsa*) in 1959. At Rādhā-Dāmodara, Śrīla Prabhupāda began work on his life's masterpiece: a multivolume annotated translation of the eighteen-thousand-verse *Śrīmad-Bhāgavatam* (*Bhāgavata Purāṇa*). He also wrote *Easy Journey to Other Planets.*

After publishing three volumes of the *Bhāgavatam,* Śrīla Prabhupāda came to the United States, in September 1965, to fulfill the mission of his spiritual master. Subsequently, His Divine Grace wrote more than sixty volumes of authoritative annotated translations and summary studies of the philosophical and religious classics of India.

When he first arrived by freighter in New York City, Śrīla Prabhupāda was practically penniless. Only after almost a year of great difficulty did he establish the International Society for Krishna Consciousness, in July of 1966. Before his passing away on November 14, 1977, he guided the Society and saw it grow to a worldwide confederation of more than one hundred *āśramas*, schools, temples, institutes and farm communities.

In 1968, Śrīla Prabhupāda created New Vrindaban, an experimental Vedic community in the hills of West Virginia. Inspired by the success of New Vrindaban, now a thriving farm community of more than two thousand acres, his students have since founded several similar communities in the United States and abroad.

In 1972, His Divine Grace introduced the Vedic system of primary and secondary education in the West by founding the Gurukula school in Dallas, Texas. Since then, under his supervision, his disciples have established children's schools throughout the United States and the rest of the world, with the principal educational center now located in Vṛndāvana, India.

Śrīla Prabhupāda also inspired the construction of several large international cultural centers in India. The center at Śrīdhāma Māyāpur in West Bengal is the site for a planned spiritual city, an ambitious project for which construction will extend over many years to come. In Vṛndāvana, India, are the magnificent Kṛṣṇa-Balarāma Temple and International Guesthouse, and Śrīla Prabhupāda Memorial and Museum. There is also a major cultural and educational center in Bombay. Other centers are planned in a dozen important locations on the Indian subcontinent.

Śrīla Prabhupāda's most significant contribution, however, is his books. Highly respected by the academic community for their authority, depth and clarity, they are used as standard textbooks in numerous college courses. His writings have been translated into over fifty languages. The Bhaktivedanta Book Trust, established in 1972 to publish the works of His Divine Grace, has thus become the world's largest publisher of books in the field of Indian religion and philosophy.

In just twelve years, in spite of his advanced age, Śrīla Prabhupāda circled the globe fourteen times on lecture tours that took him to six continents. In spite of such a vigorous schedule, Śrīla Prabhupāda continued to write prolifically. His writings constitute a veritable library of Vedic philosophy, religion, literature and culture.

References

The purports of *Śrīmad-Bhāgavatam* are all confirmed by standard Vedic authorities. The following authentic scriptures are cited in this volume. For specific page references, consult the general index.

Amara-kośa

Bhagavad-gītā

Bhakti-rasāmṛta-sindhu

Brahma-saṁhitā

Bṛhan-nāradīya Purāṇa

Caitanya-caritāmṛta

Gopāla-tāpanī Upaniṣad

Īśopaniṣad

Kāśī-khaṇḍa

Kaṭha Upaniṣad

Ṛg Veda

Skanda Purāṇa

Śrīmad-Bhāgavatam

Vedānta-sūtra

Viṣṇu-dharma

Viṣṇu Purāṇa

GLOSSARY

A

Ācārya—an ideal teacher, who teaches by his personal example; a spiritual master.
Ārati—a ceremony for greeting the Lord with chanting and offerings of food, lamps, fans, flowers and incense.
Arcana—the devotional process of Deity worship.
Āśrama—one of four spiritual orders of life. *See also: Brahmacarya; Gṛhastha; Vānaprastha; Sannyāsa*
Asura—an atheistic demon; a gross materialist.
Avatāra—a descent, or incarnation, of the Supreme Lord.
Avidyā—ignorance; the illusory energy of the Supreme Lord.

B

Bhagavad-gītā—the discourse between the Supreme Lord, Kṛṣṇa, and His devotee Arjuna expounding devotional service as both the principal means and the ultimate end of spiritual perfection.
Bhakta—a devotee of the Supreme Lord.
Bhakti-yoga—linking with the Supreme Lord by devotional service.
Bhārata-varṣa—India, named after King Bharata.
Brahmacarya—celibate student life; the first order of Vedic spiritual life.
Brahman—the Absolute Truth; especially the impersonal aspect of the Absolute.
Brāhmaṇa—a member of the intellectual, priestly class; the first Vedic social order.
Brahmāstra—a nuclear weapon produced by chanting *mantras.*
Buddhi-yoga—the surrender of one's intelligence to the will of the Supreme Lord.

C

Cit-śakti—the knowledge potency of the Supreme Lord.

D

Dharma—religion; duty, especially everyone's eternal service nature.

E

Ekādaśī—a special day for increased remembrance of Kṛṣṇa, which comes on the eleventh day after both the full and new moon. Abstinence from grains and beans is prescribed.

G

Garbhādhāna-saṁskāra—the Vedic ceremony of purification to be performed by parents before conceiving a child.

Goloka Vṛndāvana (Kṛṣṇaloka)—the highest spiritual planet, Lord Kṛṣṇa's personal abode.

Gopīs—Kṛṣṇa's cowherd girl friends, who are His most surrendered and confidential devotees.

Gṛhastha—regulated householder life; the second order of Vedic spiritual life.

Guru—a spiritual master.

H

Hare Kṛṣṇa mantra—*See: Mahā-mantra*

J

Jīva-tattva—the living entities, atomic parts of the Supreme Lord.

K

Kali-yuga (Age of Kali)—the present age, characterized by quarrel; it is last in the cycle of four and began five thousand years ago.

Kalpa—Brahmā's daytime, 4,320,000,000 years.

Karatālas—hand cymbals used in *kīrtana.*

Karma—material, fruitive activity and its reactions.

Karmī—one engaged in *karma* (fruitive activity); a materialist.

Kīrtana—the devotional process of chanting the names and glories of the Supreme Lord.

Kṛṣṇa-kathā—discussions by or about the Supreme Lord, Kṛṣṇa.

Kṛṣṇaloka—*See:* Goloka Vṛndāvana

Kṣatriya—a warrior or administrator; the second Vedic social order.

M

Mahā-bhāva—the highest stage of love of God.

Mahā-mantra—the great chant for deliverance:
Hare Kṛṣṇa, Hare Kṛṣṇa, Kṛṣṇa Kṛṣṇa, Hare Hare
Hare Rāma, Hare Rāma, Rāma Rāma, Hare Hare.

Mahāmāyā—the illusory, material energy of the Supreme Lord.

Maṅgala-ārati—the daily predawn worship ceremony honoring the Deity of the Supreme Lord.

Mantra—a transcendental sound or Vedic hymn, which can deliver the mind from illusion.

Mathurā—Lord Kṛṣṇa's abode, surrounding Vṛndāvana, where He took birth and to which He later returned after performing His childhood Vṛndāvana pastimes.

Mauṣala-līlā—the pastime of the Yadu dynasty's departure from the earth.

Māyā—the inferior, illusory energy of the Supreme Lord, which rules over this material creation; forgetfulness of one's relationship with Kṛṣṇa.

Māyāvādī—an impersonalist philosopher who conceives of the Absolute as ultimately formless and the living entity as equal to God.

Mṛdaṅga—a clay drum used for congregational chanting.

Mukti—liberation from material bondage.

P

Pāñcarātrika-vidhi—the devotional process of Deity worship and *mantra* meditation as found in the *Pañcarātra* literature.

Paramparā—a disciplic succession of bona fide spiritual masters.

Prajāpatis—the demigods in charge of populating the universe.

Prasādam—the Lord's mercy; food or other items spiritualized by being first offered to the Supreme Lord.

Puruṣa—the enjoyer, or male; the living entity or the Supreme Lord.

S

Sac-cid-ānanda-vigraha—the Lord's transcendental form, which is eternal and full of knowledge and bliss.

Saguṇa—having only transcendental qualities.

Saṅkīrtana—congregational or public glorification of the Supreme Lord, Kṛṣṇa, especially through chanting of the Lord's holy names.

Sannyāsa—renounced life; the fourth order of Vedic spiritual life.
Sarga—the material creation.
Śāstra—revealed scripture, such as the Vedic literature.
Śravaṇaṁ kīrtanaṁ viṣṇoḥ—the devotional process of hearing and chanting about Lord Viṣṇu, or Kṛṣṇa.
Śūdra—a laborer; the fourth of the Vedic social orders.
Svāmī—a controller of the mind and senses; the title of one in the renounced, or *sannyāsa*, order.

T

Tapasya—austerity; accepting some voluntary inconvenience for a higher purpose.
Taṭastha-śakti—the living entities, the marginal potency of the Supreme Lord.
Tilaka—auspicious clay markings placed by devotees on the forehead and other parts of the body.

V

Vaikuṇṭha—the spiritual world, where there is no anxiety.
Vaiṣṇava—a devotee of Viṣṇu, or Kṛṣṇa, the Supreme Lord.
Vaiśyas—farmers and merchants; the third Vedic social order.
Vānaprastha—one who has retired from family life; the third order of Vedic spiritual life.
Varṇa—one of the four Vedic social-occupational divisions of society, distinguished by quality of work and situation with regard to the modes of nature (*guṇas*). *See also: Brāhmaṇa; Kṣatriya; Vaiśya; Śūdra*
Varṇāśrama-dharma—the Vedic social system of four social and four spiritual orders. *See also: Varṇa; Āśrama*
Vedas—the original revealed scriptures, first spoken by Lord Kṛṣṇa.
Viṣṇu—the Supreme Lord; Lord Kṛṣṇa's expansions in Vaikuṇṭha and for the creation and maintenance of the material universes.
Vṛndāvana—Kṛṣṇa's eternal abode, where He fully manifests His quality of sweetness; the village on earth in which He enacted His childhood pastimes five thousand years ago.
Vyāsadeva—the incarnation of Lord Kṛṣṇa who gave the *Vedas, Purāṇas, Vedānta-sūtra,* and *Mahābhārata* to mankind.

Y

Yajña—a Vedic sacrifice; also, the Supreme Lord, the goal and enjoyer of all sacrifices.

Yajña-puruṣa—the supreme enjoyer of all sacrifices.

Yogī—a transcendentalist who, in one way or another, is striving for union with the Supreme.

Yugas—ages in the life of a universe, occurring in a repeated cycle of four.

Sanskrit Pronunciation Guide

Throughout the centuries, the Sanskrit language has been written in a variety of alphabets. The mode of writing most widely used throughout India, however, is called *devanāgarī*, which means, literally, the writing used in "the cities of the demigods." The *devanāgarī* alphabet consists of forty-eight characters: thirteen vowels and thirty-five consonants. Ancient Sanskrit grammarians arranged this alphabet according to practical linguistic principles, and this order has been accepted by all Western scholars. The system of transliteration used in this book conforms to a system that scholars in the last fifty years have accepted to indicate the pronunciation of each Sanskrit sound.

Vowels

अ a आ ā इ i ई ī उ u ऊ ū ऋ ṛ
ॠ ṝ ऌ ḷ ए e ऐ ai ओ o औ au

Consonants

Gutturals:	क ka	ख kha	ग ga	घ gha	ङ ṅa
Palatals:	च ca	छ cha	ज ja	झ jha	ञ ña
Cerebrals:	ट ṭa	ठ ṭha	ड ḍa	ढ ḍha	ण ṇa
Dentals:	त ta	थ tha	द da	ध dha	न na
Labials:	प pa	फ pha	ब ba	भ bha	म ma
Semivowels:	य ya	र ra	ल la	व va	
Sibilants:		श śa	ष ṣa	स sa	
Aspirate:	ह ha	Anusvāra: ं ṁ		Visarga: ः ḥ	

Numerals

०-0 १-1 २-2 ३-3 ४-4 ५-5 ६-6 ७-7 ८-8 ९-9

The vowels are written as follows after a consonant:

ा ā ि i ी ī ु u ू ū ृ ṛ ॄ ṝ े e ै ai ो o ौ au

For example: क ka का kā कि ki की kī कु ku कू kū

कृ kṛ कॄ kṝ के ke कै kai को ko कौ kau

Generally two or more consonants in conjunction are written together in a special form, as for example: क्ष kṣa त्र tra

The vowel "**a**" is implied after a consonant with no vowel symbol.

The symbol virāma (्) indicates that there is no final vowel: क्

The vowels are pronounced as follows:

a — as in **but**
ā — as in **far** but held twice as long as **a**
ai — as in **aisle**
au — as in **how**
e — as in **they**
i — as in **pin**
ī — as in **pique** but held twice as long as **i**
ḷ — as in **lree**
o — as in **go**
ṛ — as in **rim**
ṝ — as in **reed** but held twice as long as **ṛ**
u — as in **push**
ū — as in **rule** but held twice as long as **u**

The consonants are pronounced as follows:

Gutturals
(pronounced from the throat)
k — as in **kite**
kh — as in **Eckhart**
g — as in **give**
gh — as in **dig-hard**
ṅ — as in **sing**

Labials
(pronounced with the lips)
p — as in **pine**
ph — as in **up-hill** (not **f**)
b — as in **bird**
bh — as in **rub-hard**
m — as in **mother**

Cerebrals
(pronounced with tip of tongue against roof of mouth)
ṭ — as in tub
ṭh — as in light-heart
ḍ — as in dove
ḍh — as in red-hot
ṇ — as in sing

Dentals
(pronounced as cerebrals but with tongue against teeth)
t — as in tub
th — as in light-heart
d — as in dove
dh — as in red-hot
n — as in nut

Aspirate
h — as in home

Anusvāra
ṁ — a resonant nasal sound like in the French word *bon*

Palatals
(pronounced with middle of tongue against palate)
c — as in chair
ch — as in staunch-heart
j — as in joy
jh — as in hedgehog
ñ — as in canyon

Semivowels
y — as in yes
r — as in run
l — as in light
v — as in vine, except when preceded in the same syllable by a consonant, then like in swan

Sibilants
ś — as in the German word *sprechen*
ṣ — as in shine
s — as in sun

Visarga
ḥ — a final **h**-sound: **aḥ** is pronounced like **aha**; **iḥ** like **ihi**

There is no strong accentuation of syllables in Sanskrit, or pausing between words in a line, only a flowing of short and long (twice as long as the short) syllables. A long syllable is one whose vowel is long (**ā, ai, au, e, ī, o, ṝ, ū**) or whose short vowel is followed by more than one consonant (including **ḥ** and **ṁ**). Aspirated consonants (consonants followed by an **h**) count as single consonants.

Index of Sanskrit Verses

This index constitutes a complete listing of the first and third lines of each of the Sanskrit poetry verses of this volume of *Śrīmad-Bhāgavatam*, arranged in English alphabetical order. The first column gives the Sanskrit transliteration; the second, the chapter-verse reference. Apostrophes are alphabetized as *a*'s.

P

T

Y

Index of Verses Quoted

This index lists the verses quoted in the purports and footnotes of this volume of *Śrīmad-Bhāgavatam*. Numerals in boldface type refer to the first or third lines of verses quoted in full; numerals in roman type refer to partially quoted verses.

General Index

Numerals in boldface type indicate references to translations of the verses of *Śrīmad-Bhāgavatam.*

A

Abhimanyu, **120**
Absolute Truth
  Lord as, 198-99
  Lord's mercy reveals, 703-4
  personal feature of, 173
  process for knowing, 738
  realization of, in stages, 701, 703
  See also: Kṛṣṇa; Supreme Lord
Ācāryas. See: Disciplic succession(s)
Acintya-bhedābheda-tattva (oneness & difference) philosophy, 2, 184
Activities
  energy source for, 259-60
  of lowborn devotees, 717
  material, relief from, 17
  origin of, 215
  pure & impure, 257, 287
  reactions to, good & bad, 192, 243
  symptomize consciousness, 286-87
  transcendental, 313
  See also: Duty; Fruitive activity; *Karma;* Pious activities; Sinful activities; Supreme Lord, pastimes of; Welfare activity
Acyuta-bhāva-siddha defined, 180
Adhokṣaja defined, 204
Ādhyātmika, ādhibhautika, & ādhidaivika, 228-29, 257, 264
Aditi, 108
Administrator(s)
  pride in, 416
  of universe, 234
    See also: Demigod(s)
  See also: Government, leader(s); King(s); *Kṣatriyas*
Advaita Prabhu & Haridāsa, 720
Advancement, spiritual. *See:* Knowledge, spiritual; Purification
Affection
  of *gopīs* for Kṛṣṇa, 76
  of Lord for His servitors, 718-19
  real object of, **429–**30
  See also: Attachment; Emotions; Love
Age, present. *See:* Kali-yuga
Agelessness in spiritual world, 670
Age of Kali. *See:* Kali-yuga
Agni-hotra, 574
Agriculture
  in society, **280**
  See also: Cow(s); *Vaiśya(s)*
Ahalyā, 244-45
Aham defined, 209, 293
Ahaṁ-mama defined, 235
Ahaṅkāra
  defined, 502
  See also: False ego
Airplanes, spiritual, 596, **668,** 669
Airs in body, 257, 259
Ajñāta-sukṛti defined, 142
Ākṛtim defined, 166, 167
Akrūra, **37**
Akuṇṭha-dhiṣṇya defined, 240
Ākūti, **538, 539**
Alcohol, 628
Alphabet, Sanskrit, 533
Amara-kośa dictionary quoted on *ākṛti,* 167
Analogies
  angry father & *brāhmaṇas,* **724–**25
  arrows & offenses, **16**
  bamboo fire & Yadus' destruction, **24, 136**

Goal of life (*continued*)
  creation facilitates, 211, 216, 217
  as freedom from "I and mine," 235
  via good marriage, 604-6
  human body facilitates, **663-64**
  spiritual blindness blocks, 6
  spiritual society oriented toward, 528, 605
God. *See:* Absolute Truth; Kṛṣṇa; Nārāyaṇa; Supersoul; Supreme Lord; Viṣṇu
God consciousness. *See:* Kṛṣṇa consciousness
Goddess of fortune (Lakṣmī), 290
  doorkeepers angered, **747**
  Lord's beauty surpasses, **691,** 692
  in Lord's service, 718-19, **733**
  as Ramā, **409**
  rarely seen, 713
  tulasī surpasses, 734-35
  unsteady, 660
  in Vaikuṇṭha, 659, 660
Goddess of learning, 514-15
Go defined, 67
"Gods." *See:* Demigod(s)
Gokula (Kṛṣṇaloka), Rādhā & Kṛṣṇa in, 692
Goloka Vṛndāvana, 85
  See also: Vṛndāvana
Goodness
  qualities of, 665-66
  in spiritual world, 652, 703
Goodness, mode of
  association with, 109
  foods in, 134
  heavenly planets in, **274,** 275
  impersonalists in, 195-96, 200, 217
  mind produced via, **218**
  symptoms of, 195-96
  transcending, 171
  Viṣṇu worship in, 233
  See also: Modes of material nature
Gopāla-tāpanī Upaniṣad
  cited on Lord's lotus feet, 366
  quoted on Kṛṣṇa & *gopīs,* 396
Gopīs
  as Lord's internal potencies, 125-26, 412
  as Lord's lovers, 76, **102,** 144
Gopīs (continued)
  lusty desires of, 748
  in *rāsa* dance, 396
Gosvāmī defined, 172
Govardhana Hill, Kṛṣṇa lifts, **102,** 398
Government(s)
  leader(s) of
    compared to blind men, 384
    duty of, 552
    enmity toward, 677
    Kṛṣṇa exemplary for, 738
    mundane interests of, 662-63
    See also: King(s); *Kṣatriyas*
  modern, 279
  monarchial, 41, 122
  worldwide, 23-24
  See also: King(s); *Kṣatriya(s)*
Government(s), leader(s) of
  food shortage due to, 186
  godless, 50
Grains
  as society's livelihood, **280**
  wealth based on, 97
  See also: Food
Gṛhastha(s)
  Kṛṣṇa's example for, **126**
  responsibility of, 528, 605-8
  in safest *āśrama,* 607, 608
  sannyāsīs honored by, 675
  See also: Children; Family life; Marriage; Sex life; *Varṇāśrama-dharma*
Guṇas. See: Modes of nature; *specific modes*
Guru. See: Spiritual master(s)

H

Happiness
  beyond material world, 71
  in devotional path, 238, 240
  formula for, 228-29
  good government brings, 122
  via internal energy, 124
  via *kṛṣṇa-kathā,* **198,** 199
  via Lord's grace, 31
  via Lord's narrations, 288, 290, 293
  via Lord's protection, 48

Knowledge
spiritual (*continued*)
bewilderment inspires, in pure devotees, 422-23
beyond erudition, 68
beyond goodness, 171
beyond material conceptions, **423,** 584, 585
beyond material qualifications, 425-26
beyond material senses, 424
blindness no hindrance to, 6
competent teacher for, 434
as complex, 315
defined, 123
via Deity, 170
devotees impart, 161-62
for devotees only, 418
via devotional service, 170, **183,** 184, 359, 361, 362, 377
as dictated from within & without, 413-14, 698
difficulties as favorable to, 2
via disciplic succession, 162
from effulgence to personal feature, 701, 703
via eyes tinged with love, 424-25
via faith & devotion, 701
via following authorities, 738
via hearing, 238, 267
via husband-wife team, 604
literature for reviving, 193, 197
via Lord's lotus feet, **231-32**
via Lord's mercy, 703-4
via love & devotion, 168
milk needed for, 189
via penance, 374
perfected by chanting holy names, 667
by pilgrimage, 22, 159
via pure devotees, 511-12
qualification for, 154-55, 181
via Sāṅkhya philosophy, 328
as seeing Lord everywhere, **419**
via sincerity, 391, 588
via speculative process, 83
via spiritual master, **332,** 335, 336
as spiritual society's goal, 605
via submissiveness, 219, 262

Knowledge
spiritual (*continued*)
three types of, 170
in *Vedas,* 526
via Vedic literature, 230
Vedic
brāhmaṇas inclined to, **276,** 277, 278
in Brahmā's succession, 547
by hearing, 267
perfection of, 277
See also: Knowledge, spiritual; *Vedas;* Vedic literature
See also: Absolute Truth
Krishna. *See:* Kṛṣṇa
Kṛkara air, 259
Krodha defined, 502
Kṛṣṇa, Lord
absolute nature of, 198-99
acted in exemplary way, 738
activities of. *See:* Kṛṣṇa, pastimes of
advent(s) of
compared to sunrise, 65-66
by devotee's request, **92**
eternal, 175
purpose of, 71, 740
superexcellence of, **72-**73
transcendental, 176
See also: Kṛṣṇa, incarnation(s) of; Supreme Lord, advent(s) of
in *arcā* (Deity) form, 21, 254
Arjuna &, **8,** 9
association with, 18-20
atheist's opinion of, 70
Balarāma expands from, 31
beauty of, 73, **74-**75, 85, 98, **124**
beyond reactions to work, 70
beyond Superself, 553
as blissful, 2, 12
Brahmā's realization of, 366
bulls subdued by, **107**
Caitanya as, 736
as *cakrī,* 27
as child, 89, 93, **95-**96
children of, **112**
compared to
covered flame, **92**
dramatic actor, 398

Kṛṣṇa
pastimes of (*continued*)
in two-handed form, 73
as Vasudeva's son, 80-81
as peace messenger, 9
playful, 79, 81
protecting cows & *brāhmaṇas,* 738
protecting surrendered souls, 717
prowess of, 12, **82, 98**–99
puruṣas accompany, 78
quoted on surrender to Himself, 731
Rādhārāṇī's beauty compared with, 692
as Ranchor, 113
in *rāsa* dance, 396
relationship with, as friend, 94
relationship with, as parent, 93, 96
remembrance of, 28
Rukmiṇī rescued by, **106**
as Sāndīpani Muni's student, **104–5,** 336
Śaṅkarācārya accepted, 156
search for, 28, 175
seeing, face to face, 28-29
senses of, 128
separation from, 67
service for satisfying, 553
as shelter, 89-90, **140**
Śiśupāla killed by, 83
Śiva worships, 616
as Soul of self, **40**
speeches by, **8,** 9
spiritual dictation from, 698
spiritual form of, **423**–24
spiritual master knows, 277-78
in submissive role, **740**
subordinate role of, 88
superexcellence of, 73, 74
as Supersoul, 68-69
surrender to, 87
as Śyāmasundara, 49
as teacher, 100
as tolerant, **49,** 50
topics about. *See: Kṛṣṇa-kathā*
Uddhava &, **29,** 30, **58–62**
Vasudeva &, 32, 93
Viṣṇu forms amalgamate in, 168, 169
Vṛndāvana &, 2, 40, 68, 93, 95

Kṛṣṇa (*continued*)
wheel symbol of, 27
wives of, **108, 110**
worshipable by all, **86,** 87
Yadus misunderstood, **66,** 67, **68**
See also: Supreme Lord
Kṛṣṇa consciousness
defined, 695, 697-98
of demigods & devotees, 242-43
as panacea, 636
perfection of, 619
See also: Devotional service; Knowledge, spiritual
Kṛṣṇa consciousness movement
harmony in, formula for, 680-81
invitation into, 196
prohibitions in, 737
society's progeny saved by, 626
Kṛṣṇa defined, 280
Kṛṣṇa-dvaipāyana Vyāsa. *See:* Vyāsadeva
Kṛṣṇa-kathā
as absolute & transcendental, 193, 198-99
as essential, **201**–2
"I and mine" concept dispelled by, 235
purifying power of, 194-96
See also: Hearing about Supreme Lord
Kṛṣṇaloka, Rādhā & Kṛṣṇa in, 692
Kṛṣṇa-sandarbha cited
on Cupid, 33
on Lord's disappearance, 168
Kṣatriya(s)
chivalry of, 12
defined, 528
marriage of, 15
quality & duty of, 8, **278,** 279, 280
as twice-born, 738
See also: Government(s), leader(s) of; King(s); *Varṇāśrama-dharma; specific* kṣatriyas
Kṣetrajña-śakti defined, 301
Kṣetrī defined, 280
Kṣīrodakaśāyī Viṣṇu. *See:* Supersoul
Kumāras (four), **347**
anger of, **674–75,** 676
Brahmā's narration about, **649, 650, 668–86**

Kumāras (*continued*)
childlike innocence of, **672**
converted to personalists, 701-2
disobedient, 550
as impersonalists, **693,** 701
Lord petitioning, **725**
Lord seen by, **686**
Lord's mercy on, 712, 713
Lord's speech bewildered, **727, 729**
mystic travel by, **668,** 669
as oldest beings, **673**-74
origin of, **496,** 497
rejected family life, **497**-98
repentance by, 706-7, 741
Sanat, **348**
at Vaikuṇṭha's entrance, 749
Kuntī, Queen (Pṛthā)
sons of, **11,** 44, **45,** 46
See also: Pāṇḍavas; *specific sons*
as Vasudeva's sister, 32
Kūrma air, 259
Kurukṣetra, Battle of, **7**-8, 41
cause of, 740
devotee as glorified by, 50-51, 113
history of, purpose of, 193
soldiers at, **84,** 85-86
spiritual effect of, 595
Kurus (Kauravas), 8, **18, 49,** 50
Kuryāt defined, 430

L

Lakṣmī. *See:* Goddess of fortune
Law(s)
of God, 115
harmony with, as religion, 680
living beings under, 385
unbreakable, **646**
of nature, 122, 181
See also: Fate; *Karma;* Supreme Lord, will of
Lawbook for human beings, 552
Leader(s), government. *See:* Government(s), leader(s) of; *Kṣatriyas*
Leprosy, **715**
Liberation
anger after, 675-76
Liberation (*continued*)
beyond modes of nature, 171-72
Brahman bliss follows, 36
chaste wife facilitates, 604
creation facilitates, 117, 122, 252
of demons killed by Lord, 85, 638
of devotees, 240
of devotees & demons compared, 90-91
by devotional service, 180, 240, 311, 421
for enemies of Kṛṣṇa, 84-86, 638
exclusive path toward, 389
from false ego, 219
five kinds of, 705
via hearing Lord's war pastimes, 595
of *jñānīs* & devotees compared, 421
via knowing Kṛṣṇa, 84-86, 291-92
via knowing soul & Supersoul, 259-60
via knowledge & devotion, 146, 311
via *kṛṣṇa-kathā,* 195, 196
Lord's grace needed for, 732
materialists desire, 705
via merging with Lord, 83
as parent's duty to children, 600
personal, compared with impersonal, 85, 149
qualification for, 666
via serving Lord, 217
via serving *mahātmās,* 320
son facilitates, 13
true & false, 227
via Vṛndāvana, 95
via *yoga,* 497
See also: Freedom; Independence
Life
airs of, 257, 259
animal compared with human, 123
duration of, **483-84**
early training in, 529
essence of, **201**
goal of. *See:* Goal of life
purpose of, 454, 600
See also: Goal of life
for spiritual life, 664
See also: Human being(s); Living entities; Soul(s)
Light
origin of, **221**

M

Q

R

Rādhārāṇī, Śrīmatī, 290
beauty of, 692
Rāga-bhakti defined, 184, 314
Rājasūya sacrifice, **74**, 83
Rāja-vidyā defined, 699
Rajo-guṇa. See: Passion, mode of
Rākṣasas defined, 626
Ramā, **409**
See also: Goddess of fortune
Rāma, Lord, 39
Rāmānanda Rāya, 705
Rameśvara, 159
Rāsa-līlā, 396, 412-13
as perfection of life, 211
in Vṛndāvana, 102
See also: Gopīs
Rāvaṇa, 626, 660
Reading, material, compared with spiritual, 189-90
Reality
compared with reflection, 400
See also: Absolute Truth; Spiritual world
Realization of God. *See:* Knowledge, spiritual; Kṛṣṇa consciousness
Reflection
in moon-on-water analogy, **309-**10
in theory about Supreme, 237
Regulative principles
in daily worship, 407
for human beings, 123
purpose of, 19, 184
See also: Religious principles; Vedic injunctions
Reincarnation. *See:* Transmigration of soul(s)
Relationships
bodily, compared with spiritual, 717
See also: Supreme Lord, relationships with
Religion
defined, 387, 388
devotional service essence of, 387-89
enforcement of, 740
goal of, 331
Religion (*continued*)
as harmony with Lord's laws, 680
for humans, 513
in Satya-yuga, 475
service attitude in, **281**
Yudhiṣṭhira established, 41
See also: Devotional service; Kṛṣṇa consciousness; Religious principles; Sacrifice; Worship
Religious principles
authorities on, 389
confidential conclusion of, 731
Deity form establishes, 20
good progeny by, 625-27
listed, **524, 528,** 736-37
Lord protects, **404**
purpose of, 58
See also: Regulative principles; Religion; Vedic injunction(s)
Remembering Supreme Lord
devotees saved via, 154
ecstasy from, 61
Lord identical with, 61
pilgrimage for, 54
tall temples for, 27
Uddhava enlivened via, **59-62**
Renunciants. *See: Sannyāsī(s)*
Renunciation
cause for, 17
via *kṛṣṇa-kathā,* **198-**99
by Lord, 734
on pilgrimage, 22
by Śiva, 617
See also: Detachment; *Sannyāsa*
Repentance
by Diti, **621-24**
See also: Austerity; Penance
Respect toward *brāhmaṇas,* **724**
Retirement
from mundane service, 60
value of, 331
in Vedic society, 528
See also: Renunciation; *Sannyāsī(s)*
Ṛg Veda
from Mahā-Viṣṇu, 40
quoted on *brāhmaṇas,* 714

Ritualistic ceremonies. *See:* Sacrifices; Vedic injunction(s)
Rituals, Vedic
seven listed, 574
See also: Sacrifice; Worship
Rivers, sacred, 231
See also: Ganges; Sarasvatī; Yamunā
Rohiṇī, 32
Ṛṣabhadeva cited on children, 600
Rudra, Lord, **272**
See also: Śiva
Rudra principle, effect of, 502
Rukmiṇī, **33, 106,** 127, 290
Rūpa Gosvāmī
as author, 62
quoted on devotional service, 366
teachings of, 337

S

Śabda-brahma defined, 533
Śacī, 108
Sacrifice(s)
by family men, 606
feeding *brāhmaṇas* vs., **719,** 720
food offered to Lord in, 133-34, 243, 313
to Indra, 100, 101
into fire, 598
to Lord, 395
by Parāśara, 350
plates in, 574
for present Age, 574
for protection of fallen father, 13
purpose of, 133
types of, **576**
Vedic *mantras* in, 581
by widows, 45-46
See also: Charity; Vedic rituals; Welfare activity; Worship
Sādhana-bhakti defined, 314
Sādhana-siddhas defined, 130
Sādhu defined, 742
Sādhus. See: Devotee(s); Sage(s); Saint(s); Transcendentalist(s)
Sage(s)
as *dvija-devas,* 26
See also: Devotee(s); Saint(s); Transcendentalist(s); *specific sages*
Sahadeva, 44
Saint(s)
mercy of, 25
qualities of, 666
See also: Brāhmaṇa(s); Devotee(s); Sage(s); Spiritual master(s); Transcendentalist(s)
Sakāma defined, 393
Śakti-tattvas defined, 246
Śaktyāveśa-avatāras defined, 208
Śakuni, **14**
Śālva, **113**
Salvation. *See:* Liberation
Samādhi
defined, 515, 696
See also: Trance
Samajāyata defined, 126
Samāna air, 259
Sāmba, 35
Śambara, **114**
Sampradāya defined, 497
Saṁsāra. See: Transmigration of soul(s)
Saṁvatsara defined, 468
Sanātana defined, 731
Sanat-kumāra, **348**
See also: Kumāras, four
Sāndīpani Muni, **104-5,** 336
Śaṅkara. *See:* Śiva
Śaṅkarācārya, Śrīpāda
avoided *Bhāgavatam,* 156
cited on Ganges, 231
Kṛṣṇa accepted by, 69
Śiva as, 611
Saṅkarṣaṇa, Lord, **348**
cosmic dissolution by, **481,** 482
Śaṅkha defined, 670
Sāṅkhya philosophy
Brahmā created, 496-97
purpose of, **123,** 328
subject of, 490
Sāṅkhyāyana Muni, **348, 349**
Saṅkīrtana
for Kali-yuga, 574
See also: Chanting holy names; Hare Kṛṣṇa *mantra;* Preachers; Glorification about Supreme Lord

W